Business Data Communications and Networking

SIXTH EDITION

Business Data Communications and Networking

Jerry FitzGerald

Jerry FitzGerald & Associates

Alan Dennis

The University of Georgia

JOHN WILEY & SONS, INC.

New York • Chichester • Weinheim • Brisbane • Singapore • Toronto

To Eileen and Alec

ACQUISITIONS EDITOR	Beth Lang Golub
MARKETING MANAGER	Carlise Paulson
PRODUCTION EDITOR	Kelly Tavares
ART DIRECTOR	Dawn L. Stanley
PHOTO EDITOR	Kim Khatchatourian
ILLUSTRATION COORDINATOR	Anna Melhorn
ART STUDIO	Radiant Illustration & Design
COVER PHOTO	©Mark Wagner/Tony Stone Images/New York, Inc.

This book was set in New Baskerville by UG and printed and bound by Donnelley/Crawfordsville. The cover was printed by Phoenix Color.

This book is printed on acid-free paper. ∞

Library of Congress Cataloging in Publication Data:
FitzGerald, Jerry.
   Business data communications and networking / Jerry FitzGerald.
Alan Dennis.—6th ed.
    p. cm.
   Includes Index.
   ISBN 0-471-23798-1 (alk. paper)
   1. Data transmission systems. 2. Computer networks. 3. Office practice—Automation. I. Dennis, Alan. II. Title.
TK5105.F577 1998
004.6—dc21   98-18875
                                     CIP

Printed in the United States of America

10 9 8 7

About the Authors

Dr. Jerry FitzGerald is the principal in Jerry FitzGerald & Associates, a firm he started in 1977. He has extensive experience in risk analysis, computer security, audit and control of computerized systems, data communications, networks, and systems analysis. He has been active in risk assessment studies, computer security, EDP audit reviews, designing controls into applications during the new system development process, data communication networks, bank wire transfer systems, and electronic data interchange (EDI) systems. He conducts training seminars on risk analysis, control and security, and data communication networks.

Dr. FitzGerald has a Ph.D. in business economics and a master's degree in business economics from the Claremont Graduate School, an MBA from the University of Santa Clara, and a bachelor's degree in industrial engineering from Michigan State University. He is a Certified Information Systems Auditor (CISA) and holds a Certificate in Data Processing (CDP). He belongs to the EDP Auditors Association (EDPAA), the Institute of Internal Auditors (IIA), and the Information Systems Security Association (ISSA). Dr. FitzGerald has been a faculty member at several California universities and a consultant at SRI International.

His publications and software include: *Business Data Communications: Basic Concepts, Security and Design,* 4th edition, 1993; *Designing Controls into Computerized Systems,* 2nd edition, 1990; RANK-IT A Risk Assessment Tool for Microcomputers; CONTROL-IT A Control Spreadsheet Methodology for Microcomputers; *Fundamentals of Systems Analysis: Using Structured Analysis and Design,* 3rd edition, 1987; *Online Auditing Using Microcomputers; Internal Controls for Computerized Systems;* and over sixty articles in various publications.

Dr. Alan Dennis is an Associate Professor of Management Information Systems in the Terry College of Business at The University of Georgia. In 1997, he won The University of Georgia's Richard B. Russell Award for Excellence in Undergraduate Teaching. Dr. Dennis has a bachelor's degree in computer science from Arcadia University in Nova Scotia, Canada and an MBA from Queen's University in Ontario, Canada. His Ph.D. in management information systems is from the University of Arizona. Prior to entering the Arizona doctoral program, he spent three years on the faculty of the Queen's School of Business.

Dr. Dennis has extensive experience in the development and application of groupware and Internet technologies, and developed a Web-based groupware package called Consensus @nyWARE,™ now owned by SoftBicycle Corporation. He has won seven awards for theoretical and applied research, and has published more than 80 business and research articles, including those in *Management Science, MIS Quarterly, Information Systems Research, Academy of Management Journal, Organizational Behavior and Human Decision Making, Journal of Applied Psychology, Communication of the ACM,* and *IEEE Transactions on Systems, Man, and Cybernetics*. His first book, co-authored with his wife Eileen, was *Getting Started with Microcomputers,* published in 1986. Dr. Dennis is the co-chair of the Internet Technologies Track of the Hawaii International Conference on System Sciences. He has served as a consultant to BellSouth, Boeing, IBM, Hughes Missile Systems, the U.S. Department of Defense, and the Australian Army.

Preface

Over the past years, many fundamental changes have occurred in data communications and networking that will shape the future for decades to come. Networking applications such as the Internet and World Wide Web have exploded into the business world. High speed modems providing 10 Mbps data rates over regular telephone lines are entering the market. New backbone network technologies such as ATM, gigabit ethernet, and switched ethernet will replace today's slower LANs. SONET, SMDS, and broadband ISDN that provide data rates up to 400 Gbps will replace current T-1 and T-3 WANs and MANs. Deregulation of the telecommunications industry will also have dramatic effects on how we communicate, obtain information, and access entertainment. Voice, data, and image communication will become integrated, and entrepreneurs will create new applications and entirely new technologies more rapidly than ever before.

Perhaps the most important change has been the recognition of the strategic importance of communications and networking in both the public and private sector. Today, most computers are networked; by the turn of the century, *all* will be. We will look back at the 1990s and realize that this was the decade in which the importance of the computer was surpassed by the importance of networks.

Purpose of This Book

Our goal is to combine the fundamental concepts of data communications and networking with practical applications. While technologies and applications change rapidly, the fundamental concepts evolve much more slowly; they provide the foundation from which new technologies and applications can be understood, evaluated, and compared.

This book has two intended audiences. First and foremost, it is a university textbook. Each chapter introduces, describes, and then summarizes fundamental concepts and applications. Management focus boxes highlight key issues and describe how networks are actually being used today. Technical focus boxes highlight key technical issues and provide additional detail. An ongoing case study at the end of each chapter provides the opportunity to apply these technical and management concepts. Moreover, the text is accompanied by a detailed *Instructor's Manual*, that provides additional background information, teaching tips, and sources of material for student exercises, assignments, and exams. Finally, our Web page will continue to update the book (www.wiley.com/college/dennis/datacomm6e).

Second, this book is intended for the professional who works in data communications and networking. The book has many detailed descriptions of the technical aspects of communications, along with illustrations where appropriate. Moreover, managerial, technical, and sales personnel can use this book to gain a better understanding of fundamental concepts and trade-offs not presented in technical books or product summaries.

What's New in this Edition

The sixth edition includes numerous new technologies, applications, and examples. There are two fundamental changes in this edition from the last. First, the fundamental four-layer network model that forms the educational foundation of the book is introduced sooner (Chapter 1) and used throughout to help students better understand the functions and importance of the layers. The OSI model is presented in an Appendix for those that prefer to use it. Second, we believe that TCP/IP will win the "protocol wars," so this edition focuses in more detail on TCP/IP. Chapter 6 provides a detailed example of how TCP/IP is used.

Part 1, *Introduction,* has two chapters. The first change from the fifth edition is the inclusion in Chapter 1 of the fundamental four-layer network model that forms the educational foundation of the book. Chapter 2 (applications) has been significantly revised to reflect the changing nature of the Internet and the increased importance of electronic commerce. Chapter 2 also contains more details on the need for and structure of packets used at the application layers. These packets are fairly straightforward in appearance and are useful in helping to explain what packets are and why different layers need different packets.

Part 2, *Fundamentals,* presents fundamental concepts and has had mostly minor revisions to reflect newer technologies, with a few exceptions. The old chapter on telephone communications has been eliminated, with its material moved into Chapter 1, Chapter 9, and an Appendix. Chapter 3 (physical layer hardware) now includes more detail on client-server technologies, while Chapter 4 (physical layer transmission) includes 56K modems. Chapter 5 (data link layer) has been expanded to include PPP and SLIP, while the OSI model has been moved to an Appendix. Chapter 6 (network layer) has had major revisions and now focuses on TCP/IP in much greater detail (SNA is now in an Appendix). Our objective in revising Chapter 6 was to help students *really* understand how TCP/IP actually works (and therefore the Internet, too). This focus also helps students understand the role of each layer and ties together much of the material in the first six chapters.

Part 3, *Networking,* covers specific technologies for LANs, backbones, and MANs/WANs. The chapters in this section have been reorganized so they flow from LANs, to backbones to WANs. Chapter 7 (LANs) has seen only minor updating. Chapter 8 (backbones) has been updated with gigabit Ethernet, Fibre Channel, and ATM LANE/MPOA. The section on collapsed backbone has been moved into the network design chapter (Chapter 10). Likewise, Chapter 9 (WANs) has been updated to reduce the discussion of the American telephone network and introduce DSL and cable modems.

Finally, Part 4 on *Network Management,* covers network design, network management, and network security. The Novell NetWare chapter has been omitted because of its rapid evolution over the past few years. Chapter 10 (network design) has been completely rewritten to focus on a *building-block* approach to network design and to present a few commonly used network designs for LANs, backbones, and WANs, including virtual LANs. Chapter 11 (network management) has been updated to reflect a new emphasis on cost reduction and Total Cost of Ownership. Chapter 12 (network security) has been updated to include new security statistics, biometric systems, smart cards, and proxy servers.

Acknowledgments

My thanks to the many people who contributed to the preparation of this sixth edition. I am indebted to the staff at John Wiley & Sons for their support, including: Beth Lang Golub, Information Systems editor; Kelly Tavares, senior production editor; Dawn Stanley, art director; Linda Muriello, senior production manager; Cheryl Ferguson, copy editor; Anna Melhorn, illustration coordinator; and Carlise Paulson, marketing manager.

I would also like to thank the reviewers for their assistance, often under short deadlines:

Myungha Bang, Kangnam University, South Korea

Mary B. Burns, Texas Tech University

Abhijit Gopal, University of Calgary, Canada

Rassule Hadidi, University of Illinois, Springfield

Susan Helms, Metropolitan State College of Denver

Qing Hu, Florida Atlantic University

Douglas J. Lavery, Sir Sandford Fleming College, Canada

Patricia A. McQuaid, California Polytechnic State University, San Luis Obispo

Barton J. Olesky, Northern Alberta Institute of Technology, Canada

Stephen Kiwin Palm, Rockwell Semiconductor Systems, Japan

Glenn G. Shephard, San Jose State University

Bernie Straub, Trident Technical College

Mike Whitman, Kennesaw State University

Alan Dennis
Athens, Georgia

Photo Credit List

Chapter 2

Figure 2–7: Group room photo of Ventana Corporation's Falls Church, Virginia offices. GroupSystems is a registered trademark of Ventana Corporation. Figure 2–8: Courtesy AT&T. Figure 2–9: Courtesy Intel. Figure 2–10a: Courtesy Dell Computer Corporation. Figure 2–10b: ©1998 CondéNet Inc. All rights reserved.

Chapter 3

Figure 3–10, 3–11 & 3–12: Courtesy South Hills Datacomm.

Chapter 7

Figure 7–3 & 7–5: Courtesy of International Business Machines Corporation. Figure 7–11a: Courtesy Digital Equipment Corporation. Figure 7–11b: Courtesy AMP Incorporated.

Summary
Table of Contents

Table of Contents

CHAPTER **11**   Network Management   **348**

CHAPTER 1

Introduction to Data Communications

The chapter introduces the basic concepts of data communications and shows how we have progressed from paper-based systems to modern computer networks. It begins by describing why it is important to study data communications and how the invention of the telephone and the computer have transformed the way we communicate. Next, the basic components of a data communication network and the importance of network standards are discussed. The chapter concludes with an overview of three key trends in the future of networking.

Objectives

* Become familiar with the history of communications and information systems
* Become familiar with the applications of data communication networks
* Become familiar with the major components of networks

* Understand the role of network layers
* Become familiar with the importance of standards
* Become familiar with three key trends in communications and networking

Chapter Outline

✳✳ WHY STUDY DATA COMMUNICATIONS

It all started around 3300 B.C. with Sumerian clay tablets. They were the ideal way to communicate—as long as you didn't drop them! Then came Greek messengers. Your scroll would always get there—if your runner didn't collapse first. Today you can send and receive vital business information—in writing, in seconds.

The reasons for studying data communications are embodied in the occupational history of the world. In the 1800s, most countries were agricultural societies dominated by farmers. By the 1900s, many countries had become industrial societies dominated by labor and management. Now, as we approach the twenty-first century, we have moved into an information society dominated by computers, data communications, and highly skilled individuals who use brain power instead of physical power. The industrial society has reached its zenith, and the communication/computer era, dubbed the *information age*, is advancing rapidly. In an industrial society, the strategic resource is *capital*. In an information age, the strategic resource is *information* that must flow on communication networks. At no other time has success (whether individual, corporate, or national) depended so heavily on intelligence and information.

The key technology of the information age is computer communications. The value of a high-speed data communication network is that it brings the message sender and receiver closer together in time. As a result, we have collapsed the *information lag*, which is the time it takes for information to be disseminated worldwide. In the 1800s it might have taken several weeks for a message to reach North America by ship from England. By the 1900s it could be transmitted within the

---

Management Focus: Fire at The University of Georgia

Knowledge of data communications is even more important when you realize that the Internet has transformed the earth into a "global village." On August 15, 1995, a fire broke out on the roof of Brooks Hall, home of the Terry College of Business at The University of Georgia. It took 100 firefighters more than eight hours and 1.5 million gallons of water to extinguish it. The top floor, which housed Ph.D. student offices and the telecommunications teaching lab, was completely destroyed. The rest of the building suffered extensive smoke and water damage.

During the fire, my colleagues and I sent messages describing the fire to the ISWorld listserv (an e-mail mailing list of about 2000 Information Systems faculty around the world). Before the fire was out, notes of condolence and offers of support began arriving from North America, Europe, Australia, and Asia. Web pages describing the fire and matching donations with needs were established at the University of Pittsburgh and the London School of Economics. Within ten days, more than $2000 had been raised worldwide, and many publishers had promised donations to replace the books and research journals lost in the fire. By the time classes started, several dozen faculty members from around the world had e-mailed or posted on the Web their lecture notes and course outlines to enable faculty to rebuild destroyed notes.

hour. Today, with modern data communication networks, it can be transmitted within seconds. Collapsing the information lag speeds the incorporation of new information into our daily lives. In fact, today's problem is that we cannot handle the quantities of information we receive.

Data communications and networking is a truly global area of study, both because the technology enables global communication and because new technologies and applications emerge from a variety of countries and spread rapidly around the world. The World Wide Web, for example, was born in a Swiss research lab, was nurtured through its first years primarily by European universities, and exploded into mainstream popular culture due to a development at a U.S. research lab.

One of the problems in studying a global phenomenon lies in explaining the different political and regulatory issues that have evolved and currently exist in different parts of the world. Rather than attempt to explain the different paths taken by different countries, we have chosen simplicity instead. Historically, the majority of readers of previous editions of this book have come from North America. Therefore, while we retain a global focus on technology and its business implications, we focus exclusively on North America in describing the political and regulatory issues surrounding communications and networking. We do, however, take care to discuss technological or business issues where fundamental differences exist between North America and the rest of the world (e.g., ISDN; see Chapter 9).

A Brief History of Communications in North America

Today we take data communications for granted, but pioneers like Samuel Morse, Alexander Graham Bell, and Thomas Edison developed the basic electrical and electronic systems that ultimately evolved into voice and data communication networks. Figure 1–1 provides a summary of the key points in the history of voice and data communications.

In 1837, Samuel Morse exhibited a working telegraph system; today we might consider it the first electronic data communication system. In 1841, a Scot named Alexander Bain used electromagnets to synchronize school clocks. Two years later, he patented a printing telegraph—the predecessor of today's fax machines. In

1837 Invention of the telegraph	1968 Carterfone court decision permits non-Bell telephone equipment to be used
1876 Invention of the telephone	
1892 Telephone system regulation begins in Canada	1970 Court permits MCI to provide long-distance services
1910 Telephone system regulation begins in the United States	1984 Breakup of AT&T
	1984 Cellular phones enter service
1951 Direct-dialed long-distance service begins	1996 Telecommunications Act of 1996 deregulates U.S. telephone system
1962 Satellites begin to transmit international telephone calls	

Figure 1–1 Some important events in the history of voice and data communications.

1874, Alexander Graham Bell developed the concept for the telephone at his father's home in Brantford, Ontario, Canada, but it would take him and his assistant, Tom Watson, another two years of work in Boston to develop the first telephone capable of transmitting understandable conversation. In 1876, Bell made the first long-distance call (about 10 miles) from Paris, Ontario, to his father in Brantford.

The telephone was greeted by both skepticism and adoration, but within five years it was clear to all that the world had changed. To meet the demand, Bell started a company in the United States, while his father started a company in Canada. In 1879, the first private manual telephone switchboard (private branch exchange, or PBX) was installed. By 1880, the first pay telephone was in use, making the telephone accessible to anyone. The certificate of incorporation for the American Telephone and Telegraph Company (AT&T) was registered in 1885. By 1889, AT&T had a recognized logo in the shape of the Liberty Bell with the words "Long Distance Telephone" written on it.

In 1892, the Canadian government began regulating telephone rates. By 1910, the U.S. Interstate Commerce Commission (ICC) had the authority to regulate interstate telephone businesses in the United States. In 1934, this was transferred to the Federal Communications Commission (FCC).

The first transcontinental telephone service and the first transatlantic voice connections were both established in 1915. The telephone system grew so rapidly that by the early 1920s there were serious concerns that even with the introduction of dial telephones (that eliminated the need for operators to make simple calls) there would not be enough trained operators to work the manual switchboards. Experts predicted that by 1980, every single woman in North America would have to work as a telephone operator if growth in telephone usage continued at the current rate (at the time, all telephone operators were women).

The first commercial microwave link for telephone transmission was established in Canada in 1948. In 1951, the first direct long-distance dialing without an operator began. The first international satellite telephone call was sent over the Telstar satellite in 1962. By 1965, there was widespread use of commercial international telephone service via satellite. Fax services were introduced in 1962. Touchtone telephones were first marketed in 1963. Picturefone service, which allows users to see as well as talk with one another, began operating in 1969. The first commercial packet-switched network for the transmission of computer data was introduced in 1976.

Until 1968, Bell Telephone/AT&T controlled the U.S. telephone system. No telephones or computer equipment other than those made by Bell Telephone could be connected to the phone system, and only AT&T could provide telephone services. In 1968, after a series of lawsuits, the Carterfone court decision allowed non-Bell equipment to be connected to the Bell System network. This important milestone permitted independent telephone and modem manufacturers to connect their equipment to the U.S. telephone networks for the first time.

Another key decision in 1970 permitted MCI to provide limited long-distance service in the United States in competition with AT&T. Throughout the 1970s,

AT&T's monopolistic position over U.S. communication service was the subject of debate and antitrust lawsuits. On January 1, 1984, AT&T was divided in two parts under a consent degree devised by a federal judge. The first part, AT&T, provided long-distance telephone services in competition with other *interexchange carriers (IXCs)* such as MCI and Sprint. The second part, a series of seven *regional Bell operating companies (RBOCs)* or *local exchange carriers (LECs)*, provided local telephone services to homes and businesses. AT&T was prohibited from providing local telephone services and the RBOCs were prohibited from providing long-distance services. Intense competition began in the long-distance market as MCI, Sprint, and a host of other companies began to offer services and dramatically cut prices under the watchful eye of the FCC. Competition was prohibited in the local telephone market, so the RBOCs remained a regulated monopoly under the control of a multitude of state laws. The Canadian long-distance market was opened to competition in 1992.

During 1983 and 1984 traditional radio telephone calls were supplanted by the newer cellular telephone networks. In the 1990s, cellular telephones became commonplace, and pocket-sized. Demand grew so much that in some cities (e.g., New York and Atlanta), it became difficult to get a dial tone at certain times of the day.

In February 1996, the U.S. Congress enacted the Telecommunications Competition and Deregulation Act of 1996. This act replaced all current laws, FCC regulations, and the 1984 consent degree and subsequent court rulings under which AT&T was broken up. It also overruled all existing state laws and prohibited states from introducing new laws. Practically overnight, the local telephone industry in the U.S. went from a highly regulated and legally restricted monopoly to open competition.

Local service in the United States is now open for competition. The RBOCs, IXCs, cable TV companies, and other LECs are permitted to build their own local telephone facilities and offer services to customers. To increase competition, the RBOCs must sell their telephone services to their competitors at wholesale prices, who can then resell them to consumers at retail prices. Most analysts expected the Big Three IXCs (AT&T, MCI, and Sprint) to quickly charge into the local telephone market, but they have been slow to move. Only MCI has begun building its own local telephone network, and then only in the largest urban centers. Meanwhile, the RBOCs have been aggressively fighting court battles to keep competitors out of their local telephone markets and have attempted to merge with each other and the IXCs, prompting many complaints from Congress and the FCC. At best, the RBOCs can only hope to delay competition, not prevent it, because it is clear that Congress and the FCC want competition.

There has been active competition in the long-distance telephone market for many years, but RBOCs have been prohibited from providing long-distance services. The Telecommunications Act now permits the RBOCs to provide long distance outside the regions in which they provide local telephone services. However, they are prohibited from providing long-distance services inside their region until at least one viable competitor exists for local telephone services. Several local telephone companies (e.g., GTE and SNET) have moved aggressively into the long-distance market, but have focused exclusively on out-of-region long distance by buying long-distance services from AT&T, MCI, and other IXCs and reselling them. Few RBOCs have moved into the in-region long-distance market because few face real local competition.

Management Focus: *Career Opportunities*

A 1997 survey of chief information officers found a shortage of experienced information systems staff in many technology areas, with the most critical shortage being in communications and networking. And the problem is getting worse (or better, if you are one of the people whose skills are in demand!). Annual starting salaries for our undergraduates at The University of Georgia often exceed $40,000. People with three or four years of experience can make $55,000 to $75,000. Networking is a stronger job market than general information systems.

The demand for networking expertise is growing for two reasons. First, the Internet and communication deregulation has significantly changed how businesses operate and has spawned thousands of small start-up companies. Second, new hardware and software innovations have significantly changed the way networking is done. Both trends will continue.

The Internet has been a different story. The Internet began in 1969 as a network of U.S. military and academic computers. Today the Internet connects computers in virtually every country of the world into one huge network. The Internet is described in more detail in Chapter 2.

Virtually all RBOCs, LECs, and IXCs have aggressively entered the Internet market. Today, there are more than 5000 Internet Service Providers (ISPs) who provide dial-in access to the Internet to millions of small business and home users. Most of these are small start-up companies that lease telecommunications circuits from the RBOCs, LECs, and IXCs and use them to provide Internet access to their customers. As these RBOCs, LECs, and IXCs move into the Internet market and provide the same services directly to consumers, the small ISPs are facing heavy competition. Most analysts expect the number of ISPs to drop to less than 1000 by the turn of the century, as many small ISPs close.

International competition should also be heightened by an international agreement signed in early 1997 by 68 countries to deregulate (or at least lessen regulation in) their telecommunications markets. The countries agreed to permit foreign firms to compete in their internal telephone markets. Major U.S. firms (e.g., AT&T, MCI, BellSouth) now offer telephone service in many of the industrialized and emerging countries in North America, South America, Europe, and Asia. Likewise, overseas telecommunications giants (e.g., British Telecom) are beginning to enter the United States market. This should increase competition in the United States, but the greatest effect is likely to be felt in emerging countries. For example, it costs almost 30 times more to use a telephone in India than it does in the United States.

A Brief History of Information Systems

The natural evolution of information systems in business, government and personal use has forced the widespread use of data communication networks to interconnect various computer systems. However, data communications have not always been considered important.

In the 1950s, computer systems used batch processing. Users prepared punched cards, which they took to the computer for processing. By the 1960s, data communication across telephone lines became more common. Users could type their own batches of data for processing using online terminals. Data communications involved the transmission of messages from these terminals to a large central mainframe computer and back to the user.

During the 1970s, online real-time systems were developed that moved the users from batch processing to single transaction-oriented processing. Database management systems replaced the older file systems. Integrated systems were developed, where the entry of an online transaction in one business system (e.g., order entry) might automatically trigger transactions in other business systems (e.g., accounting, purchasing). Computers entered the mainstream of business, and data communication networks became a necessity.

The 1980s witnessed the microcomputer revolution. At first, microcomputers were isolated from the major information systems applications, serving the needs of individual users (e.g., spreadsheets). As more people began to rely on microcomputers for essential applications, the need for networks to exchange data among microcomputers and between microcomputers and central mainframe computers became clear. By the early 1990s, more than 60 percent of all microcomputers in U.S. corporations were *networked*—connected to other computers.

Today, the microcomputer is a powerful, easy-to-use system, with a large amount of low-cost software. Today's microcomputers have more raw computing power than a mainframe of the 1980s. Perhaps more surprisingly, corporations today have far more total computing power sitting on desktops in the form of the microcomputers than they have in their large central mainframe computers.

As we move into the new century, the most important aspect of computers is *networking*. The Internet is everywhere, and virtually all corporate computers are networked. Most corporations are rapidly building distributed systems in which information system applications are divided among a network of computers. This form of computing, called client–server computing, will dramatically change the way information systems professionals and users interact with computers. The office of the future will put tremendous demands on data communication networks, interconnecting microcomputers, mainframe computers, fax machines, copiers, teleconferencing equipment, and other equipment.

These networks already have had a dramatic impact on the way business is conducted. Networking—among many other factors—played a key role in the growth of Wal-Mart into one of the largest retailers in North America, and in the process, it transformed the retailing industry. Wal-Mart has 34 mainframes, 5000 network file servers, 18,000 microcomputers, 90,000 handheld inventory computers, and 100,000 networked cash registers. (As an aside, it is interesting to note that every single microcomputer built by IBM in the United States during the third quarter of 1997 was purchased by Wal-Mart). At the other end of the spectrum, the lack of a sophisticated data communication network was one of the key factors in the bankruptcy of Macy's in the early 1990s.

In retail sales, it is critical to manage inventory. Macy's had a traditional 1970s inventory system. At the start of the season, buyers would order products in large lots to get volume discounts. Some products would be very popular and sell out quickly. When the sales clerks did a weekly inventory and noticed the shortage, they would order more. If the items were not available in the warehouse (and very popular products were often not available), it would take six to eight weeks to restock them. Customers would buy from other stores, and Macy's would lose the sales. Other products, also bought in large quantities, would be less popular and would have to be sold at deep discounts.

Management Focus: *Networks in the Gulf War*

The lack of a good network can cost more than money. During Operation Desert Shield/ Desert Storm, the U.S. Army, Navy, and Air Force lacked one integrated logistics communications network. Each service had its own series of networks, making communication and cooperation difficult. But communication among the systems was essential. Each day a Navy F-18 would fly into Saudi Arabia to exchange diskettes full of logistics information with the Army—an expensive form of "wireless" networking.

This lack of an integrated network also created problems transmitting information from the U.S. into the Gulf. More than 60 percent of the containers of supplies arrived without documentation. They had to be unloaded to see what was in them and then reloaded for shipment to combat units.

The logistics information systems and communication networks experienced such problems that some Air Force units were unable to quickly order and receive critical spare parts needed to keep planes flying. Officers telephoned the U.S.-based suppliers of these parts and instructed them to send the parts via Federal Express.

Fortunately, the war did not start until the United States and its allies were prepared. Had Iraq attacked, things might have turned out differently.

In contrast, Wal-Mart negotiates volume discounts with suppliers based on total purchases, but does not specify particular products. Buyers place initial orders in small quantities. Each time a product is sold, the sale is recorded. Every day or two, the complete list of purchases is transferred over the network (often via a satellite) to the head office, a distribution center, or the supplier. Replacements for the products sold are shipped almost immediately, and typically arrive within days. The result is that Wal-Mart seldom has a major problem with overstocking an unwanted product or running out of a popular product (unless, of course, the supplier is unable to produce it fast enough).

✳✳ DATA COMMUNICATION NETWORKS

Data communications is the movement of computer information from one point to another by means of electrical or optical transmission systems. Such systems often are called *data communication networks*. This is in contrast to the broader term *tele-communications*, which includes the transmission of voice and video (images and graphics) as well as data, and usually implies longer distances. In general, data communication networks collect data from microcomputers and other devices and transmit that data to a central point equipped with a more powerful microcomputer, minicomputer, or mainframe, or perform the reverse process, or some combination of the two. Data communication networks facilitate more efficient use of computers and improve the day-to-day control of a business by providing faster information flow. They also provide message-transfer services to allow computer users to talk to one another via electronic mail.

Components of a Network

There are three basic hardware components for a data communication network: a server or host computer (e.g., microcomputer, mainframe), a client (e.g., microcomputer, terminal), and a circuit (e.g., cable, modem) over which messages flow. The server and client also need special-purpose network software that enables them to communicate.

The *server* (or *host computer*) stores data or software that can be accessed by the clients. In client–server computing, several servers may work together over the network to support the business application.

The *client* is the input/output hardware device at the other end of a communication circuit. It typically provides users with access to the network and the data and software on the server.

The *circuit* is the pathway through which the messages travel. It is typically a copper wire, although fiber optic cable and wireless transmission are becoming more common. There are many devices in the circuit that perform special functions, such as hubs, switches, routers, and gateways.

Strictly speaking, a network does not need a server or host computer. Some networks are designed to connect a set of similar computers that share their data and software with each other. Such networks are called *peer-to-peer networks* because the computers function as equals, rather than relying on a central server or host computer to store the needed data and software.

Figure 1–2 shows a small network that has four microcomputers (clients) connected by a hub and cables (circuit). In this network, messages move through the hub to and from the computers. All computers share the same circuit and must take turns sending messages. The *router* is a special device that connects two or more networks. The router enables computers on this network to communicate with computers on other networks (e.g., the Internet).

This network has three servers. Although one server can perform many functions, networks are often designed so that a separate computer is used to provide different services. The *file server* stores data and software that can be used by com-

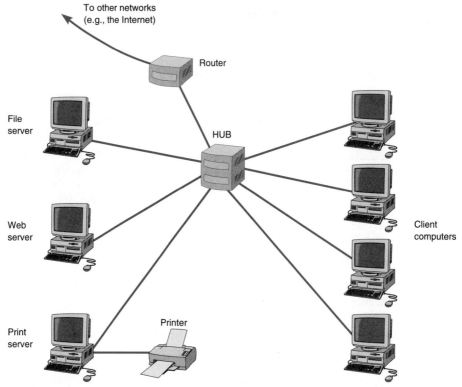

Figure 1-2 Example of a local area network (LAN).

puters on the network. The *print server*, which is connected to a printer, manages all printing requests from the clients on the network. The *Web server* stores documents and graphics that can be accessed with Netscape Navigator, Internet Explorer, or any other Web browser. The Web server can respond to requests from computers on this network or any computer on the Internet. Servers are usually microcomputers (often more powerful than the other microcomputers on the network), but they may be minicomputers or mainframes.

Types of Networks

There are many different ways to categorize networks. One of the most common ways is to look at the geographic scope of the network. Figure 1–3 illustrates four types of networks: local area networks, backbone networks, metropolitan area networks, and wide area networks. The distinctions between these are becoming blurry. Some network technologies now used in local area networks were originally developed for wide area networks, while some local area network technologies have influenced the development of metropolitan area network products. Any rigid classification of technologies is certain to have exceptions.

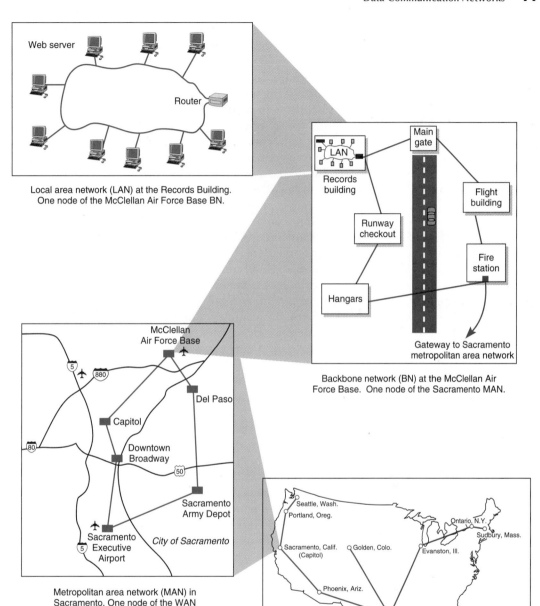

Local area network (LAN) at the Records Building.
One node of the McClellan Air Force Base BN.

Backbone network (BN) at the McClellan Air
Force Base. One node of the Sacramento MAN.

Metropolitan area network (MAN) in
Sacramento. One node of the WAN

Wide are network (WAN) showing Sacramento
connected to nine other cities throughout the U.S.

Figure 1–3 Shows the hierarchical relationship of a local area network (LAN) to a backbone network (BN) to a metropolitan area network (MAN) to a wide area network (WAN).

A *local area network* (LAN) is a group of microcomputers or other workstation devices located in the same general area and connected by a common circuit. A LAN covers a clearly defined small area, such as one floor or work area, a single building, or a group of buildings. In general, LANs use multipoint circuits, where all computers must take turns using the same shared circuit. The upper-left diagram in Figure 1–3 shows a small LAN located in the records building at McClellan Air Force Base in Sacramento. LANs support high-speed data transmission compared with standard telephone circuits, commonly operating at 10 to 100 million bits per second (Mbps). LANs are discussed in Chapter 7.

Most LANs are connected to a *backbone network (BN)*, a larger, central network connecting several LANs, other BNs, metropolitan area networks, and wide area networks. Backbone networks typically span up to several miles, and provide very high-speed data transmission, commonly 100 to 1000 Mbps. The second diagram in Figure 1–3 shows a backbone network that connects the LANs located in several buildings at McClellan Air Force Base. BNs are discussed in Chapter 8.

A *metropolitan area network (MAN)* connects LANs and BNs located in different areas to each other and to wide area networks. MANs typically span 3 to 30 miles. The third diagram in Figure 1–3 shows a MAN connecting the backbone networks at several military and government complexes in Sacramento. Some organizations develop their own MANs using similar technologies as BNs. These networks provide moderately fast transmission rates, but can prove costly to install and operate over long distances. Unless an organization has a continuing need to transfer large amounts of data, this type of MAN is too expensive. More commonly, organizations use public data networks provided by local carriers (e.g., the telephone company) as their MANs. With these MANs, data transmission rates typically range from 64,000 bits per second (Kbps) to 45 Mbps, although newer technologies promise data rates of more than 600 Mbps. MANs are discussed in Chapter 9.

Wide area networks (WANs) connect BNs and MANs (see Figure 1–3). Most organizations do not build their own WANs by laying cable, building microwave towers, or sending up satellites (unless they have unusually heavy data transmission needs or highly specialized requirements such as the Department of Defense). Instead, most organizations lease circuits from interexchange carriers (e.g., AT&T, MCI, Sprint), and use those to transmit data. WAN circuits provided by interexchange carriers come in all types and sizes, but typically span hundreds or thousands of miles and provide data transmission rates from 28.8 Kbps to 2 billion bits per second (Gbps). WANs are also discussed in Chapter 9.

❊❊ NETWORK MODEL

There are many ways to describe and analyze data communication networks. All networks provide the same basic functions to transfer a message from sender to receiver, but each network uses different network hardware and software to provide these functions. All of these hardware and software products have to work together to successfully transfer a message.

One way to accomplish this is to break the entire set of communications functions into a series of layers, each of which can be defined separately. In this way, vendors can develop software and hardware to provide the functions of each layer separately. The software or hardware can work in any manner and can be easily updated and improved, as long as the interface between that layer and the ones around it remain unchanged. Each piece of hardware and software can then work together in the overall network.

There are many different ways in which the network layers can be designed. One of the most important models for describing network layers is the open systems interconnection (OSI) model. The OSI model was developed in 1984, and it helped change the face of network computing. The OSI model is described in Appendix A. In recent years, other models (such as the TCP/IP model used by the Internet) have become more prominent in the design of networks and network technology. In this book, we use a simple four-layer model that closely follows the Internet model (see Figure 1–4).

The *application layer* (or layer 4) is the application software used by the network user. It is the user's access to the network. By using the application software, the user defines what messages are sent over the network. Chapter 2 discusses two types of network application software: Internet software (e.g., Web browsers, FTP) and groupware.

The *network layer* (or layer 3) takes the messages generated by the application layer and performs three functions before passing them to the data link layer. First, it translates the destination of the messages into an address understood by the network. Second, if there are several possible routes through the network that the messages could take to reach their destination, the network layer decides which route to take. Third, it may break long messages into several smaller messages to make them easier to transmit. Chapter 6 discusses the network layer.

The *data link layer* (or layer 2) takes the messages generated by the network layer and performs three functions before passing them to the physical layer. First, it controls the physical layer by deciding when to transmit messages over the media. Second, it formats the messages by indicating where they start and end, and which

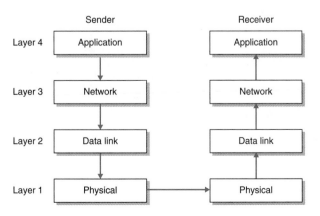

Figure 1–4 Four-layer model.

Technical Focus: Message Transmission Using Layers

All messages sent in a network pass through all layers. Figure 1–5 shows how a message requesting a Web page would be sent on the Internet. The user first creates the message with a Web browser (e.g., get the page at www.uga.edu). The browser formats the user's message by adding some information that conforms to a standard that the Web server will be able to understand (usually HTTP on the Web) and then passes the message (along with the HTTP information) to the network layer.

The network layer on the Internet is TCP/IP. It translates the address used by the browser (www.uga.edu) into an Internet numeric network address (e.g., 192.128.75.5) and selects the next stop on the message's route through the network. The network layer then passes the message (complete with address and next stop formatted using TCP/IP) to the data link layer.

If you are dialing into the Internet using a modem, your data link layer likely uses PPP. The data link layer formats the message with start and stop markers as defined by PPP, adds error checking information, and instructs the physical hardware to transmit it.

The physical layer in this case is your modem and telephone line. The modem will take the message (complete with the HTTP information, the TCP/IP information, and the PPP information) and send it as a series of sound waves through your telephone line to your ISP.

When the ISP gets the message, this process is performed in reverse. The physical hardware (modem) translates the sounds into computer data and passes the message to the data link layer. The data link layer uses the PPP start and stop markers to identify the message. The data link layer checks for errors; if it discovers one, it requests that the message be resent. If a message is received without error, the data link layer will then pass the message to the network layer. The network layer checks the TCP/IP address and, if it is destined for this computer, it passes it to the application layer for processing (e.g., the Web server). If the message is not destined for this computer (but simply has to pass through it on the way to its final destination), the network layer decides which computer to send it to next and passes the message back to the data link layer for retransmission to the next computer on the Internet.

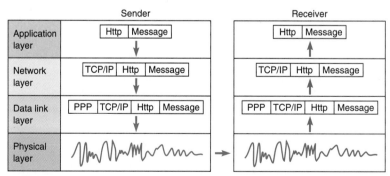

Figure 1–5 A Web example of message transmission using layers.

part is the address. Third, it detects and corrects any errors that have occurred during transmission. Chapter 5 discusses the data link layer.

The *physical layer* (or layer 1), as the name suggests, is the physical connection between the sender and receiver. Its role is to transfer a series of electrical, radio, or light signals through the circuit. The physical layer includes all the hardware devices (e.g., computers, modems, and hubs) and physical media (e.g., cables, and satellites). The physical layer specifies the type of connection and the electrical signals, radio waves, or light pulses that pass through it. Chapter 3 discusses the hardware devices in the physical layer, while Chapter 4 discusses how the physical layer actually transmits data.

It is important to note that for communication to be successful, each layer in one computer must be able to communicate with its matching layer in the other computer. This is accomplished by *standards*. For example, the physical layer connecting the server and client must use the same type of electrical signals to enable each to understand the other (or there must be a device to translate between the two). Likewise, the data link layer in both the server and client must use the same procedures for marking the start and end of messages, or they will not be able understand each other's messages. The same is true for the network layers; if the client network layer cannot understand the address and routing information provided by the server, the message will not be sent to the correct destination. Likewise, the two application layers must be compatible, or the message cannot be processed. Without standards, it would be impossible for computers to communicate.

✳✳ NETWORK STANDARDS

The Importance of Standards

Standards are necessary in almost every business and public service entity. For example, before 1904, firehose couplings in the United States were not standard, which meant a fire department in one community could not help in another community. The transmission of electric current was not standardized until the end of the nineteenth century, so customers had to choose between Thomas Edison's direct current (DC) and George Westinghouse's alternating current (AC).

The primary reason for standards is to ensure that hardware and software produced by different vendors can work together. Without networking standards, it would be difficult—if not impossible—to develop networks that easily share information. Standards also mean that customers are not locked into one vendor. They can buy hardware and software from any vendor whose equipment meets the standard. In this way, standards help to promote more competition and hold down prices.

The use of standards makes it much easier to develop software and hardware that link different networks because software and hardware can be developed one layer at a time. The software or hardware defined by the standard at one network layer can be easily updated, as long as the interface between that layer and the ones around it remains unchanged.

The Standards Making Process

There are two types of standards: *formal* and *de facto*. A formal standard is developed by an official industry or government body. For example, there are formal standards for applications such as Web browsers (e.g., HTML), for network layer software (e.g., TCP/IP), data link layer software (e.g., ethernet IEEE 802.3), and for physical hardware (e.g., V.34 modems). Formal standards typically take several years to develop, during which time technology changes, making them less useful. The current race between Netscape and Microsoft in Web browsers is a good example. Just as a new standard for HTML is developed, Netscape and Microsoft add new features to their browsers that do not conform to the standard, starting a new round of the standards process.

De facto standards are those that emerge in the marketplace and are supported by several vendors, but have no official standing. For example, Microsoft Windows is a product of one company and has not been formally recognized by any standards organization, yet it is a de facto standard. In the communications industry, de facto standards often become formal standards once they have been widely accepted.

The formal standardization process has three stages: specification, identification of choices, and acceptance. The *specification* stage consists of developing a nomenclature and identifying the problems to be addressed. In the *identification of choices* stage, those working on the standard identify various solutions and choose the optimum solution from among the alternatives. *Acceptance*, which is the most difficult stage, consists of defining the solution and getting recognized industry leaders to agree on a single, uniform solution. As with many other organizational processes that have the potential to influence the sales of hardware and software, standards-making processes are not immune to corporate politics and the influence of national governments.

International Organization for Standardization (ISO)

One of the most important standards-making bodies is the *International Organization for Standardization* (ISO), which makes technical recommendations about data communication interfaces. (The abbreviation ISO comes from its French name.) ISO is based in Geneva, Switzerland. The membership is comprised of the national standards organizations of each ISO member country. In turn, ISO is a member of the International Telecommunications Union (ITU), which makes technical recommendations about telephone, telegraph, and data communication interfaces on a worldwide basis. ISO and ITU usually cooperate on issues of telecommunication standards, but they are mutually independent standards-making bodies and they are not required to agree on the same standards.

International Telecommunications Union–Telecommunications Group (ITU–T)

The Telecommunications group (ITU–T) is the technical standards setting organization of the United Nations International Telecommunications Union (ITU). It was formerly called the *Consultative Committee on International Telegraph and Telephone (CCITT)*. It, too, is based in Geneva, Switzerland. It comprises representatives from more than 150 national Postal Telephone and Telegraphs (PTTs), private telecommunication agencies, and industrial and scientific organizations. ISO is a member of ITU–T. The PTTs are telephone companies outside of the United States. In the United States, these are the regional Bell operating companies (RBOCs, such as Bell South and PacBell), the inter-exchange carriers (IXCs, such as AT&T, Sprint and MCI), or other common carriers (such as GTE). ITU–T establishes recommendations for use by PTTs, other common carriers, and hardware and software vendors.

American National Standards Institute (ANSI)

The *American National Standards Institute* is the coordinating organization for the U.S. national system of standards. It comprises about 900 companies. ANSI is a standardization organization, not a standards-making body. It accepts standards developed by other organizations and publishes them as American standards. Its role is to coordinate the development of voluntary national standards and to interact with ISO to develop national standards that comply with ISO's international recommendations. ANSI is the United States' voting participant in ISO and ITU–T.

Institute of Electrical and Electronics Engineers (IEEE)

The *Institute of Electrical and Electronics Engineers (IEEE)* is a professional society in the United States. Its standards committees focus on local area network standards. Other countries have their own similar groups; for example, the British counterpart of IEEE is the Institution of Electrical Engineers.

Internet Engineering Task Force (IETF)

The *Internet Engineering Task Force (IETF)* sets the standards that govern how much of the Internet will operate. The IETF is described in more detail in the next focus box.

National Institute of Standards and Technology (NIST)

Formerly known as the National Bureau of Standards in Washington, D.C., the *National Institute of Standards and Technology (NIST)* is an agency of the U.S. Department of Commerce that develops information-processing standards for the federal government. Among its many test facilities is the Network Protocol Testing and Evaluation Facility, which has eight laboratories for research in the design, implementation, and testing of computer network protocols. This facility develops prototype implementations of protocols and then tests them in a variety of communication environments.

Management Focus: How Network Protocols Become Standards

There are many standards organizations around the world, but perhaps the best known is the Internet Engineering Task Force (IETF). IETF sets the standards that govern how much of the Internet will operate. Developing a standard usually takes one to two years.

IETF, like all standards organizations, tries to seek consensus among its members before issuing a standard. Usually, a standard begins as a protocol (i.e., a language or set of rules for operating) developed by a vendor (e.g., HTML). When a protocol is proposed for standardization, IETF forms a working group of technical experts to study it. The working group examines the protocol to identify potential problems and possible extensions and improvements, and then issues a report to IETF.

If the report is favorable, the IETF issues a request for comment (RFC) that describes the proposed standard and solicits comments from the entire world. Most large software companies likely to be affected by the proposed standard prepare detailed responses. Many "regular" Internet users also send their comments to the IETF.

The IETF reviews the comments, and possibly issues a new and improved RFC, which again is posted for more comments. Once no additional changes have been identified, it becomes a proposed standard.

Usually several vendors adopt the proposed standard and develop products based on it. Once at least two vendors have developed software based on it, and it has proven successful in operation, the proposed standard is changed to a draft standard. This is usually the final specification, although some protocols have been elevated to Internet standards, which usually signifies a mature standard not likely to change.

The process does not focus solely on technical issues; almost 90 percent of IETF's 3000 members work for manufacturers and vendors, so market forces and politics often complicate matters. One former IETF chair who worked for Cisco (a hardware manufacturer) has been accused of trying to delay the standards process until Cisco had a product ready, although he and other IETF members deny this. Likewise, former IETF directors have complained that members try to standardize every product their firms produce, leading to a proliferation of standards, only a few of which are truly useful.

Source: "How Networking Protocols Become Standards," *PC Week* (March 17, 1997); "Growing Pains," *Network World* (April 14, 1997).

Common Standards

There are many different standards used in networking today. Each standard usually covers one layer in a network. Figure 1–6 outlines some of the most commonly used standards. At this point, these models are probably just a maze of strange names and acronyms, but by the end of the book, you will have a good understanding of each of these. Figure 1–6 provides a brief roadmap for some of the important communication technologies we will discuss in this book.

For now, there is one important message you should understand from Figure 1–6: in order for a network to operate, many different standards must be used simultaneously. The sender of a message must use one standard at the application

Management Focus: Keeping Up with Technology

The data communications and networking area changes rapidly. Significant new technologies are introduced and new concepts are developed almost every year. It is therefore important for network managers to keep up with these changes.

There are at least three useful ways to keep up with change. First and foremost for users of this book is the Web site for this book (see the Preface).

It contains updates to the book, additional sections, teaching materials, and links to useful Web sites.

Second, there are literally hundreds of thousands of Web sites with data communications and networking-related information. The search engines described in Chapter 2 can help you find them.

Third, many useful magazines discuss computer technology in general and networking technology in particular. These include: *Network Computing, Communications Week, LAN Times, InfoWorld, InfoWeek,* and *Datamation.*

layer, another one at the network layer, another one at the data link layer, and another one at the physical layer. Each layer and standard is different, but each must work together in order to send and receive messages.

The sender and receiver of a message must use the same standards or, more likely, use devices that translate from one standard into another. Because different networks often use software and hardware designed for different standards, there is usually a lot of translation between different standards.

Layer	Common Standards
4. Application layer	HTTP, HTML (Web)
	H.323, MPEG (video conferencing)
	X.400, POP (e-mail)
3. Network layer	TCP/IP (Internet)
	IPX/SPX (Novell LANs)
2. Data link layer	802.3 Ethernet
	802.5 Token ring
	PPP, Slip SDLC, HDLC, LAP-B
	Kermit, X-modem, Z-modem
1. Physical layer	RS-232C Cable
	IEEE 802.3 Category 5 Cable
	V.34 modem

Figure 1–6 Some common data communications standards.

✹✹ FUTURE TRENDS IN COMMUNICATIONS AND NETWORKING

Between now and the year 2010, data communications will grow faster and become more important than computer processing itself. Both go hand in hand, but we have moved from the computer era to the communication era.

It was only about 15 years ago that we were first able to transmit at a speed of 9600 bits per second (bps) on a standard telephone circuit. Using various digital technologies, we can now transmit at 64,000 bits per second on the same telephone circuit, with transmission speeds of millions of bits per second available in some areas. With the use of fiber optics we can transmit at billions of bits per second. Three major trends are driving the future of communications and networking. All are interrelated, and it is difficult to consider one without the others.

Pervasive Networking

In the future, communication networks will be everywhere. This is due to technological advances and increasing competition, both of which drive down costs. Virtually all computers will be networked to other computers. Computers will be sold with network hardware and software as standard equipment, in much the same way as most microcomputers today are sold with an operating system software such as Microsoft Windows.

This pervasive networking means that virtually any computer will be able to communicate with any other computer in the world. This will increase *telecommuting*, in which employees perform some or all of their work at home instead of going to the office each day. If you were the telecommuter, some benefits might be less time wasted in driving to work, improved quality of life, optimized scheduling of both your work and personal life, monetary savings on both clothes and travel, less stress, greater time flexibility, and a higher level of concentration at home because of fewer distractions.

Cellular telephone networks will begin to compete directly with the current wired telephone network. With cellular telephones, radio transmission towers are placed in strategic locations throughout a city, enabling a user to place a telephone call from virtually anywhere. In Israel, the intense competition among cellular telephone companies has driven costs so low that using a cellular phone costs almost the same as using a traditional wired telephone. Once the cost of cellular service drops elsewhere in the world, more computer networks will begin to use it, making wireless networking commonplace.

Pervasive networking will also increase the use of *electronic data interchange (EDI)*, the paperless transmission between companies of orders, invoices, and other business documents. EDI enables companies to initiate transactions electronically and then transmit the transactions to another company, where they can be viewed on a microcomputer's video screen or printed if necessary. EDI improves efficiency and productivity, and reduces the number of times human operators have to handle and process documents.

The Internet, an international group of networks discussed in Chapter 2, has experienced such rapid growth over the past few years that it now connects millions of computers in virtually every country in the world. In this environment, the movement of communication, commerce, and data among people, groups, and organizations around the world will be unprecedented in human history. Economists have long talked about the globalization of world economies. Data communications has made it a reality.

The Integration of Voice, Video, and Data

A second key trend is the integration of voice, video, and data communication. In the past, the telecommunications systems used to transmit video signals (e.g., broadcast or cable TV), voice signals (e.g., telephone calls), and data (e.g., computer data or e-mail) were completely separate. One network was used for data, one for voice, and one for cable TV.

This is rapidly changing. The integration of voice and data is largely complete in wide area networks. The interexchange carriers such as AT&T, Sprint, and Worldcom/MCI all provide telecommunication services that support data and voice transmission over the same circuits, even intermixing voice and data on the same physical cable. The integration of voice and data has been much slower in local area networks and local telephone services. Some companies have successfully integrated both on the same network, but some still lay two separate cable networks into offices—one for voice and one for computer access. The biggest problem has been the lack of capacity on the traditional voice networks to support the high-volume transmissions generated by local area networks.

The integration of video into computer networks has been much slower, partly due to past legal restrictions and partly due to the immense communications needs of video. However, this integration is inevitable. CNN, in conjunction with Intel, now offers its CNN and Headline News broadcasts digitally. Subscribers to this service receive the regular TV broadcasts in a format that can be transmitted over local area networks. This way users can receive the same audio and video TV images in a window on their computer.

New Information Services

A third key trend is the provision of new information services on these rapidly expanding networks. In the same way that the construction of the U.S. interstate highway system spawned new businesses, so will the construction of worldwide integrated communications networks. One of the most important of these is World Wide Web, which is discussed in Chapter 2.

The Web has changed the nature of computing so that now almost anyone with a computer can be his or her own publisher. Millions of users provide information on their Web pages on countless topics. Thousands of companies use the Web to provide information on their services or products. One can find information on virtually anything. The problem becomes one of assessing the accuracy and value of information. In the future, we can expect information services to appear that help assure the quality of the information they contain.

Never before has so much information been available to ordinary citizens. The challenge we face as individuals and organizations is assimilating this information and using it effectively.

Summary

Why Study Data Communications   The information society—where information and intelligence are the key drivers of personal, business, and national success—has arrived. Data communications is the principal enabler of the rapid information exchange and will become more important than the use of computers themselves in the future. Successful users of data communications, such as Wal-Mart, can gain significant competitive advantage in the marketplace.

Communications in North America   Today, the North American local and long-distance telephone markets are open for competition. Although competition is fierce in the long-distance market, it has been slow to emerge for local telephone service. Competition among Internet access providers is also strong and will likely increase over the next few years.

Network Components   Communication networks are often broken into a series of layers, each of which can be defined separately, to enable vendors to develop software and hardware that can work together in the overall network. In this book, we use a four-layer model. The application layer is the application software used to create messages. The network layer takes a message and, if necessary, breaks it into several smaller messages. It then addresses the message(s) and determines their route through the network before passing it to the data link layer. The data link layer formats the message to indicate where it starts and ends, decides when to transmit it over the physical media, and detects and corrects any errors that occur in transmission. The physical layer is the physical connection between the sender and receiver, including the hardware devices (e.g., computers, terminals, and modems) and physical media (e.g., cables, and satellites).

Network Definitions   A local area network (LAN) is a group of microcomputers or terminals located in the same general area. A backbone network (BN) is a large, central network that connects almost everything on a single company site. A metropolitan area network (MAN) encompasses a city or county area. A wide area network (WAN) spans cities, states, or national boundaries.

Standards   Standards ensure that hardware and software produced by different vendors can work together. A formal standard is developed by an official industry or government body. De facto standards are those that emerge in the marketplace and are supported by several vendors, but have no official standing. Many different standards and standards-making organizations exist.

Future Trends   Pervasive networking will change how and where we work and with whom we do business. With virtually everyone able to connect to any other person or organization in the world, we will see a rise in telecommuting, EDI, and the globalization of industries. The integration of voice, video, and data onto the same networks will greatly simplify networks and enable anyone to access any media at any point. The rise in these pervasive, integrated networks will mean a significant increase in the availability of information and new information services.

Key Terms

American National Standards
   Institute (ANSI)

application layer

AT&T

backbone network (BN)

bps

circuit

client

Consultative Committee on
   International Telegraph and
   Telephone (CCITT)

data link layer

electronic data interchange
   (EDI)

Federal Communications
   Commission (FCC)

file server

Gbps

host computer

Institute of Electrical and
   Electronics Engineers (IEEE)

Interexchange carrier (IXC)

International
   Telecommunications Union–
   Telecommunications group
   (ITU–T)

Internet Engineering Task
   Force (IETF)

Internet Service Providers
   (ISPs)

Kbps

local area network (LAN)

local exchange carrier (LEC)

Mbps

MCI

metropolitan area network
   (MAN)

monopoly

National Institute of Standards
   and Technology (NIST)

network layer

peer-to-peer network

print server

physical layer

regional Bell operating
   company (RBOC)

Sprint

server

standards

Web server

wide area network (WAN)

Questions

1. How can data communication networks affect businesses?
2. Discuss three important applications of data communication networks in business and personal use.
3. Define information lag and discuss its importance.
4. Describe the progression of communications systems from the 1800s to the present.
5. Describe the progression of information systems from the 1950s to the present.
6. How do LANs differ from MANs, WANs, and BNs?
7. What is a circuit?
8. What is a client?
9. What is a host or server?
10. Why are network layers important?
11. Describe the four layers in the network model used in this book and what they do.
12. Explain how a message is transmitted from one computer to another using layers.
13. Describe the three stages of standardization.
14. How are Internet standards developed?
15. Describe two important data communications standards-making bodies. How do they differ?

16. What is the purpose of a data communication standard?

17. What are three of the largest interexchange carriers (IXCs) in North America?

18. Name two RBOCs. Which one(s) provide services in your area?

19. Discuss three trends in communications and networking.

Exercises

A. Investigate the long-distance carriers (IXCs) and local exchange carriers (LECs) in your area. What services do they provide, and what pricing plans do they have for residential users?

B. Discuss the issue of communications monopolies and open competition with an economics instructor. Relate the instructor's comments to your data communication class.

C. Find a college or university offering a degree in telecommunications or data communications and describe its program.

D. Describe a recent data communication development you have read about in a news paper or magazine and explain how it might affect businesses.

E. Investigate the networks in your school or organization. Describe the important LANs and backbone networks in use (but do not describe the specific clients, servers, or devices on them).

F. Use the Web to search the IETF Web site (www.ietf.org). Describe one standard that is in the request for comment stage.

G. Discuss how the revolution/evolution of communications and networking is likely to affect how you will work and live in the future.

NEXT DAY AIR SERVICE CASE STUDY

This is the beginning of a cumulative case study about a fictitious firm we call Next Day Air Service. The case study begins here in Chapter 1 and continues throughout the rest of the book. It requires you to complete tasks that are related to topics covered in each corresponding chapter of the text. The end of each chapter contains the case narrative, related figures, and a set of questions and problems. These do not have one unique solution. There are too many alternatives when dealing with LANs, WANs, MANs, BNs, and the Internet, so a real-life network design and development problem can have several workable answers.

As with any real-life problem with ambiguities or unresolved considerations, you must make your own assumptions. Feel free to read ahead or use the index to find related subjects that support your recommendations. Your instructor may provide additional guidelines regarding report formats, Web and library resources, key assumptions, and the like for the various questions and problems presented in this case study. Be sure to provide adequate justification for any recommendations you make.

The Next Day Air Service (NDAS) firm was founded in 1985 to compete in the expanding market for overnight package deliveries. Next Day Air Service provides local pickup and delivery of these parcels and other small freight items. The founders initially restricted their efforts to the rapidly growing central Florida region.

To support its operation, Next Day Air Service purchased a facility near the Tampa International Airport. This facility consisted of a main building and a secondary building for dispatch and fleet maintenance. Because Next Day Air Service intended to expand its services throughout the southeastern United States, this facility also served as NDAS's corporate headquarters.

From 1985 to 1992, Next Day Air Service experienced very rapid growth. As business volume increased and the company's reputation became firmly established, expansion of the facility became imperative. Consequently, NDAS purchased land adjacent to its corporate headquarters, so it would have room to relocate both the maintenance shop and the company's vehicle parking lot. In addition, NDAS tripled the size of its building to accommodate its growing business. Finally, in 1994 NDAS completed the expansion of the office building to house its corporate operations.

As its business volume increased, NDAS realized it had to develop branch offices throughout its service region in order to continue growing. In addition to the corporate offices in Tampa, NDAS also purchased or leased facilities in several other southeastern cities, including Orlando, Miami, Atlanta, New Orleans, Dallas, and Memphis. Figure 1–7 shows the Next Day Air Service map of operations.

Next Day Air Service contracted with the Chicago-based firm Overnight Delivery, Inc. (ODI), to provide overnight shipping service between Atlanta and the greater Chicago area. NDAS also entered into similar agreements with other air carriers. The purpose of these agreements was to enable NDAS to provide service throughout the United States.

As Figure 1–7 shows, connecting routes established with other carriers lead from Memphis to St. Louis and from Atlanta to Chicago and Washington, D.C. These routes allow NDAS to deliver parcels to the northeastern states and the Midwest. There are flight links out of Dallas to both Denver and Los Angeles. These two routes have been added recently to provide delivery service to the northwestern states and the West Coast, respectively. After extending its flight routes, NDAS added agents in the cities of Jacksonville, Montgomery, Jackson, and Houston. To date, this is the scope of NDAS's parcel delivery operation.

Initially, Next Day Air Service contracted a computing services company to handle billing. As the computing power of small computers increased, however, NDAS purchased a minicomputer and took responsibility for its own data processing. The Payroll Department now runs the payroll twice monthly on this computer. Employees submit their timecards and supporting documents on the first and third Mondays of the month. The Payroll Department then prepares the paychecks for both hourly and salaried employees. The paychecks are sent via overnight delivery on the following Thursdays.

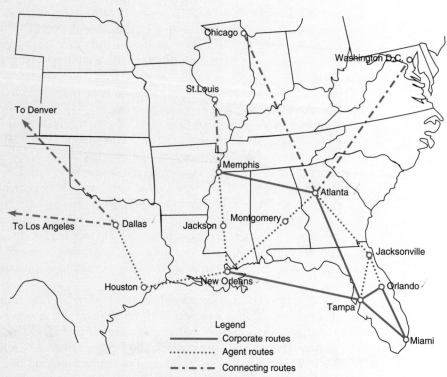

Figure 1–7 Next Day Air Service map of operations.

Although the Information Services/Data Processing Division, under Les Coone as acting manager, performs all data entry, processing, and check printing, John Lawson in Accounts Payable is the person who generates, reviews, and approves the reports and totals. Because so many new employees have been added at both the corporate and branch offices, a new full-time position has been added in Accounts Payable to handle the payroll and assist Mr. Lawson. The subject of paying employees weekly has been discussed as well. Figure 1–8 shows the Next Day Air Service organization chart.

The branch offices currently batch all billing data by order date and send it daily by overnight delivery to the corporate office, along with other interoffice correspondence. When Information Services/Data Processing receives the packages, it enters the batches and processes them daily. The billing processing normally takes place from 48 to 96 hours after freight and parcel delivery. Once this processing has been completed, the database supports the resolution of any questions or problems associated with the billings.

Because of an increasing volume of paperwork brought about by continued business expansion, the varying complexity of the billing process, and the preferred rates being given by competitors, Next Day Air Service's corporate management

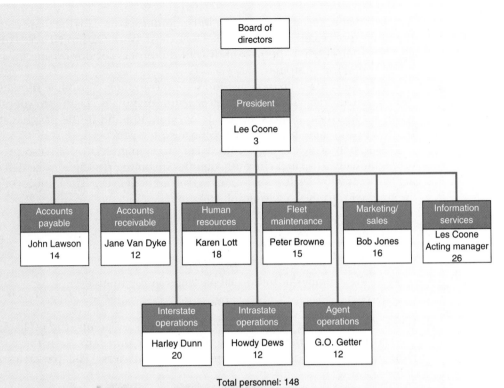

Total personnel: 148

Figure 1–8 Next Day Air Service organization chart showing key personnel and number of staff per area.

has decided to automate the billing process throughout its Florida offices. This is the first step in a series of strategic moves planned to provide online transaction processing and real-time customer information through the Internet. Management expects online transaction processing to speed the billing process and improve receivables collection time significantly. The online Query System will enable agents at remote offices to obtain information such as credit status, correct delivery address, and package delivery status. The Internet component will enable customers to obtain the delivery status of packages they have sent or are expecting to receive.

The status of automation varies greatly among the various departments. The Sales and Marketing Division, headed by Bob Jones, has a computer for each account representative. All of these computers are connected to a small local area network (LAN) that serves only Sales and Marketing.

The Accounts Receivable Division, headed by Jane Van Dyne, is responsible for all billing and collection activities. It recently replaced its aging minicomputer with a powerful microcomputer server. This new server provides databases for both customer billing and "bad debt" expenses.

The Accounts Payable Division, led by John Lawson, maintains its own vendor database that is stored on an older minicomputer server. This database also contains the other service carriers' billings, such as those from ODI to NDAS. This division also is responsible for the payroll. It is in the process of downsizing to a powerful modern desktop computer.

The Fleet Maintenance Division has no computer capability. Its management has chosen to trace all necessary information manually. Peter Browne, the maintenance supervisor, prefers this mode of operation and in the past has steadfastly refused to automate his division's recordkeeping processes.

Dispatch, which is part of the Fleet Maintenance Division, also processes its work manually. Dispatch currently bundles incoming packages twice daily, according to their major destination point, for overnight delivery. The bundles of packages are marked with the following information.

* DEST: City, State
* DATE: Current date
* TIME: Time package left dispatch
* NPKG: Number of individual packages in the bundle
* INIT: Initials of the person preparing the bundle

When the bundles arrive at their respective delivery points, the off-loaders mark the arrival time on the bundles' tags, write their own initials on the back of the tags, and return the tags to corporate headquarters. The packages are then delivered.

The various remote offices currently communicate with the corporate headquarters and with one another by voice mail, telephone, facsimile, mail, or interoffice mail, sent on company aircraft along with the daily batched transactions. There are desktop computers in each of the remote offices. However, some of the offices have Apple Macintosh computers, and others use Intel-based systems. A number of managers have laptop computers, which, again, come from various computer manufacturers.

NDAS corporate management realizes that these various stages of computer support are a far cry from an integrated system. It sees the necessity for standardizing and streamlining systems, equipment, and procedures before any serious networking can be accomplished. Moreover, corporate management has stated that Next Day Air Service must enter the international package delivery market to offer full service to its major customers. Any growth plans must be able to support international operations. Management also expects that electronic mail and automated package tracking will be part of the new system. In addition, management expects any system to allow for expansion into other information technology areas of networking, such as videoconferencing and the use of the Internet.

As its first step in this direction, NDAS has decided to hire a new systems analyst, who will work full-time to assess the current level of information system support, determine which functions should be automated, recommend the type of hardware and software systems to be installed, recommend appropriate organizational changes (if any), and, most important, determine the type of data communication support that will be required to meet the needs of NDAS's current operations and future growth.

You have been offered this position. Your experience is in information systems. Because you see the job as a remarkable opportunity to learn and grow, you accept the post. You report directly to Mr. Lee Coone, president of NDAS, and are expected to prepare your solution immediately.

Exercises

1. Briefly describe the current state of Next Day Air Service's office automation, system integration, and networking. Begin by explaining how each department uses information technology, what hardware it uses, and what functions currently are automated. Also assess which department is most in need of a network.

2. With the "types of networks" and future technologies discussed in this chapter, what kind of network would appear to be the most beneficial to Next Day Air Service? Justify your answer.

3. What are the current characteristics or practices that identify NDAS as a possible candidate for its proposed integrated data communication network?

4. Which two of the four networks (e.g., LAN) might be appropriate for NDAS?

5. When looking over the organization chart, you notice that the acting manager of the Information Services/Data Processing department is also named Coone (Les Coone). Inquiring, you learn that Les is President Coone's nephew. Les has just joined NDAS. This is his first job, and he has no background in information systems, data processing, or data communications. Will this be a problem for you? If so, why? How will you handle it?

CHAPTER 2

Network Applications

The widespread availability of data communications and networking has fostered the development and use of several software applications that have dramatically changed the way we communicate and do business. This chapter looks at the Internet and its primary software applications: the Web, e-mail, Telnet, and FTP. It also examines how two specific applications, electronic commerce and groupware, have the potential to change today's business world.

Objectives

* Become familiar with the Internet
* Understand how the Web and e-mail operate
* Become familiar with FTP and Telnet

* Become familiar with several different types of groupware
* Become familiar with electronic commerce

Chapter Outline

✳✳ INTRODUCTION

In the early days of information systems, most systems—such as payroll, order entry, and inventory—were designed to improve the productivity of entire departments or organizations. In the 1980s, microcomputers became affordable to individual users, enabling the widespread development and use of information systems such as spreadsheets. By the 1990s, the widespread availability of data communications and networking had begun to change our vision of the computer. Most people in organizations work as members of groups or teams: the creation of network application software allowed groups of people to work together more easily.

This chapter examines the Internet, the most important network in the history of computing, as important as the microcomputer revolution itself. We first discuss the nature and history of the Internet. Then we examine four Internet application software tools (the Web, e-mail, Telnet and FTP) and explain how they operate. Next we examine another set of applications that we believe are as fundamental as the Internet applications: groupware. In the final section, we focus on electronic commerce, another important set of business applications that are built on top of the Internet applications and groupware.

These sets of applications (Internet, groupware, and electronic commerce) are the future of information technology. We believe that these three will revolutionize the way we think about and use computers by making the computer a communications device. They have the potential to more greatly affect individuals, companies, and even countries than any computer application has before. The microcomputer revolutionized the way we thought about and used computers; it changed our understanding of computers from big storage and number-crunching machines to computers for individual work. These three applications have the same potential to transform society as the microcomputer or the telephone.

✳✳ THE INTERNET

The *Internet* or "information superhighway" is one of the most important developments in the history of information systems. It is also one of the most overhyped topics. From modest beginnings as a network of U.S. military and academic computers, the Internet now connects millions of computers around the world into one huge network. In the mid-1990s, the number of users on the Internet grew by an average of 15 percent per *month*, or more than 400 percent per year. Today growth has slowed slightly, but still continues at an astounding rate. No one knows how many people use the Internet, but estimates range from 25 to 45 million users worldwide. Most users are young (35 years old), male (67%), college educated (55%) and earn significantly more than average (in the United States, $50,000 versus $21,000 for the general population). As more and more users go online, these numbers will continue to drop and move closer to the underlying average in the population as a whole. For more up-to-date statistics on the Internet, see the Georgia Institute of Technology's semiannual Internet Survey (http://www.gatech.edu/gvu) and *Boardwatch* magazine's reports on Internet Service Providers (http://www.boardwatch.com).

Some people see the Internet and the World Wide Web as the same thing. They aren't. The Internet is a set of thousands of networks linked together around the world. The Internet enables any computer to communicate with any other computer. The Web is one application that uses the Internet as its network. The World Wide Web is arguably the most important application; although e-mail generates more traffic, the Web is the application that changed the Internet from a scientific network to everyone's network.

History of the Internet

The Internet was started by the U.S. Department of Defense in 1969 as a network of four computers called ARPANET. Its goal was to link a set of computers operated by several universities doing military research. The original network grew as more computers and more computer networks were linked to it. By 1974, 62 computers were attached. In 1983, the Internet split into two parts, one dedicated solely to military installations (called Milnet) and one dedicated to university research centers (called the Internet) that had just under 1000 host computers.

In 1985, the Canadian government completed its leg of BITNET to link all Canadian Universities from coast to coast and provided connections into the U.S. Internet (BITNET is a competing network to the Internet developed by the City University of New York and Yale University that uses different communications protocols). In 1986, U.S. National Science Foundation created NSFNET to connect leading U.S. universities. By the end of 1987, there were 10,000 host computers on the Internet and 1000 on BITNET.

Performance began to slow down due to increased network traffic, so in 1987, the National Science Foundation decided to improve performance by building a new high-speed backbone network for NSFNET. It leased high-speed circuits from several IXCs and in 1988 connected 13 regional Internet networks containing 170 LANs and 56,000 host computers. The Canadian National Research Council followed in 1989, replacing BITNET with a high-speed network called CA*net that used the Internet protocols. By the end of 1989 there were almost 200,000 host computers on the combined U.S. and Canadian Internet.

Similar initiatives were undertaken by other countries around world, so that by the early 1990s, most of the individual country networks were linked together into one worldwide network of networks. Each of these individual country networks was distinct (each had its own name, access rules, and fee structures), but all networks used the same standards as the U.S. Internet network so users could easily exchange messages with each other. Gradually, the distinctions among the networks in each of the countries began to disappear, and the U.S. name, the Internet, began to be used to mean the entire worldwide system of networks that used the Internet TCP/IP protocols. By the end of 1992, there were more than 1 million host computers on the Internet.

Originally, commercial traffic was forbidden on the Internet (and the other individual country networks), because the key portions of these networks were funded by the various national governments and research organizations. In the early 1990s, commercial networks began connecting into NSFNET, CA*net, and the other government-run networks in each country. New commercial online services began offering access to anyone willing to pay, and a connection into the worldwide Internet became an important marketing issue. The growth in the commercial portion of the Internet was so rapid that it quickly overshadowed university and research use. In 1994, with more than 4 million host computers on the Internet (most of which were commercial), the U.S. and Canadian governments stopped funding their few remaining circuits and turned them over to commercial firms. Most other national governments soon followed. The Internet was now commercial.

The Internet has continued to grow at a dramatic pace. For more recent statistics on the size of the Internet, see http://info.isoc.org/guest/zakon/Internet/History/hit.html.

Because it is a collection of networks, the Internet has no central administration. Each network has its own administrative structure, and most networks have their own *acceptable use policies* that define what behavior is permitted, although most policies are virtually identical from network to network. The Internet was intentionally designed to be very decentralized, and very amenable to new ideas because many of its creators and initial users openly distrusted any central authority. However, this decentralization has led to anarchy in many ways.

Internet Addresses

Anyone with access to the Internet can communicate with any computer on the Internet. Internet addresses are strictly regulated; otherwise, someone could add a computer to the Internet that had the same address as another computer. Each address has two parts, the computer name and its domain. The domain is the specific part of the Internet to which the computer is connected (e.g., Canada, Australia). The general format of an Internet address is therefore: *computer.domain.* Some computer names have several parts separated by periods, so some addresses have the format: *computer.computer.computer.domain.* For example, the main university Web server at The University of Georgia is called www.uga.edu, while the College of Business Administration's Web server is www.cba.uga.edu.

Each domain has an addressing board that assigns addresses for its domain. These boards generally do not make value judgments about names; they just ensure there are no duplicates. In one case, a company offering test-preparation courses (e.g., for the SAT and GMAT) registered two computer addresses: one was its own name, and the other was the name of its biggest competitor. By doing so, it hoped to prevent its competitor from gaining access to the Internet, and hoped to gain access to customers who thought they were sending e-mail to its competitor. When the competitor discovered this (by attempting to register its address with the board), it sued. A judge ruled that no company could use the name of a competitor as its Internet address. In 1996 this court case was heard in the United States, so it applies only to the United States, but it is reasonable to expect other jurisdictions to follow the U.S. precedent.

Technical Focus: Internet Domain Names

Since the Internet began in the United States, the U.S. address board was the first to assign domain names to indicate types of organization. Some common U.S. domain names are:

* edu   for an educational institution, usually a university
* com   for a commercial business
* gov   for a government department or agency
* mil   for a military unit
* org   for a nonprofit organization
* net   for an organization with ties to Internet administrative bodies

As networks in other countries were connected to the Internet, they were assigned their own domain names. Some international domain names are:

* ca   for Canada
* au   for Australia
* uk   for the United Kingdom
* de   for Germany

Many international domains structure their addresses in much the same way as the United States does. For example, Australia uses edu to indicate academic institutions, so an address such as xyz.edu.au would indicate an Australian university.

✷✷ INTERNET APPLICATION SOFTWARE

This section examines four important Internet application software tools and explains how they work: the Web, electronic mail (e-mail), file transfer protocol (FTP), and Telnet. There are several other Internet application software tools, such as gopher and WAIS, but these are not discussed in this book. We focus on the Web and e-mail in some depth because they are the two most commonly used applications. We discuss FTP and Telnet in less detail.

Electronic mail, Telnet, and FTP have been around almost as long as the Internet itself. The Web, however, was developed in the early 1990s. Each application (Web, e-mail, Telnet, and FTP) requires a special application layer software program running on the client computer and a similar application layer software program running on the server. Originally, we needed separate software packages for each application, but today more and more client applications incorporate one or more of these in one package (e.g., Netscape's software is a browser, as well as providing e-mail and groupware).

These applications were originally developed for the Internet, but many organizations are using them on their LANs or for private use on the Internet. An Internet application designed to support users inside one organization (often on a LAN) is called an *intranet*. Intranet applications are often combined with the organization's normal Web applications, but are hidden from those outside the organization. For example, several sections of our Web server (www.cba.uga.edu) are designed for internal use only; they appear only if you connect to the Web server from a computer located on The University of Georgia campus. *Extranets* work in much the same manner but provide information to selected users outside the organization. For example, the State of Georgia provides an Internet library of millions of articles (called Galileo), but it is available only to state employees and to faculty, staff, and students at colleges and universities in Georgia. To access the library, you must provide a password when you connect to the Internet site.

World Wide Web

One of the fastest-growing Internet software applications is the *World Wide Web.* The Web was first conceived in 1989 by Tim Berners-Lee at the European Laboratory for Particle Physics (*CERN*) in Geneva. His original idea was to develop a database of information on physics research, but he found it difficult to fit the information into a traditional database. Instead, he decided to use a *hypertext* network of information. With hypertext, any document can contain a link to any other document.

CERN's first Web browser was written in 1990, but it was 1991 before it was available on the Internet for other organizations to use. By the end of 1992, several browsers had been written for UNIX computers by CERN and several other European and American universities, and there were about 30 Web servers in the entire world. In 1993, Marc Andreessen, a student at the University of Illinois, led a team of students that wrote *Mosaic,* the first graphical Web browser, as part of a project for the university's National Center for Supercomputing Applications (*NCSA*). By the end of 1993, the Mosaic browser was available for UNIX, Windows, and Macintosh computers, and there were about 200 Web servers in the world. In 1994, Andreessen and some colleagues left NCSA to form *Netscape,* and a half a dozen other startup companies introduced commercial Web browsers. Within a year, it had become clear that the Web had changed the face of computing. NCSA stopped development of the Mosaic browser in 1996, as Netscape and Microsoft began to invest millions to improve their browsers.

How the Web Works

Figure 2–1 shows how the Web works. Each client computer needs an application layer software package called a *Web browser.* Netscape Navigator and Microsoft Internet Explorer are the most popular browsers. Each server on the network needs an application layer software package called a *Web server.* There are many different Web servers, such as those produced by Netscape, Microsoft, and Apache.

In order to get a page from the Web, users must type the Internet Uniform Resource Locator (*URL*) for the desired page, or must click on a link that provides the URL. The URL specifies the Internet address of the Web server, the directory, and name of the specific page wanted. If no directory or page is specified, the Web server will provide whatever page has been defined as its home page. If no server name is specified, the Web browser will presume the address is on the same server and directory as the last request.

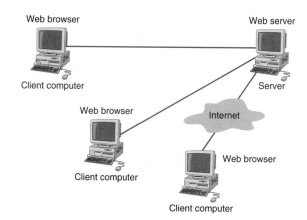

Figure 2–1 Web browsers and servers.

Management Focus: Ten Commandments for "Webifying" the Enterprise

1. Don't be too ambitious. Start with a non-critical internal project and learn the new technologies.

2. Focus on the business goals. Don't try to implement a "cool" new technology unless there is a business need.

3. Keep it simple. Deliver a small-scale system that works, and then grow it. Don't keep adding new requirements to the very first version.

4. Use good systems development and project management techniques. Don't "wing it."

5. Look at what others have done. Adopt ideas, graphics, and code from others who have given permission to use them.

6. Plan for change. Technology standards change quickly, so anticipate and manage for change.

7. Give yourself lots of time. Even "simple" things on the Web often take more time than you expect.

8. The Web is not an integrator yet. Many Web components (e.g., html and Java) are not yet seamlessly integrated.

9. Beware of betas, but try them. Don't use pre-release ("beta") versions of software because they contain bugs, but investigate them to be ready for the final product.

10. Manage customer expectations. Walk the fine line between ever-changing user needs and hard-to-update code.

Source: Enterprise Systems Journal (June 1997).

In order for the requests from the Web browser to be understood by the Web server, they must use the same standard protocol. If there was no standard and each Web browser used a different way to request pages, then it could be impossible for a Netscape Web browser to communicate with a Microsoft Web server, for example.

The standard protocol for communication between a Web browser and a Web server is Hypertext Transfer Protocol (*HTTP*). An HTTP request from a Web browser to a Web server has three parts. Only the first part is required; the other two are optional.

* The *request line*, which starts with a command (e.g., GET), provides the URL, and ends with the HTTP version number that the browser understands

* The *request header*, which contains a variety of optional information such as the Web browser being used (e.g., Internet Explorer), the date, and a user ID and password for use if the Web page is password-protected

* The *request body*, which contains information sent to the server, such as information from a form

Figure 2–2 shows an example of a request for a page on our Web server, formatted using version 1.1 of the HTTP standard. This request has only the request line and the request header, because no request body is needed for this request.

Many people believe that the Web is anonymous. No one can tell who they are when they request a Web page. Nothing could be further from the truth. Every Web access must provide the Internet address of the requester's computer; otherwise, the server would not know where to send the requested page. Some browsers also provide the requester's e-mail address as well. Most Web servers record the Internet addresses of all requests (and the e-mail addresses if provided by the browser). Some companies use this information to follow up with prospective customers.

The format of an HTTP response from the server to the browser is similar to the browser request. It has three parts, but only the last part is required; the first two are optional:

* The *response status*, which contains the HTTP version number the server has used, a status code (e.g., 200 means OK, 404 means page not found), and reason phrase (a text description of the status code)

* The *response header*, which contains a variety of optional information such as the Web server being used (e.g., Apache), the date, the exact URL of the page in the response body, and the format used for the body (e.g., HTML)

* The *response body*, which is the Web page itself

Figure 2–2 An example of a request from a Web browser to a Web server using the HTTP standard.

HTTP version Status code Reason phrase

```
HTTP/1.1 200 OK  ]- Response status

Date: Mon 03 Aug 1998 17:36:02 GMT ]- Date

Server: NCSA/1.3 ]- Web server                              ]- Response header

Location: http://tcbworks.cba.uga.edu/~adennis/res.htm ]- URL

Content-Type: text/html ]- Type of file


<html>

<head>

<title>Business Data Communications and Networking Web

Resources</title>

</head>

<body>

<H2>Resources on the Web </H2>                             ]- Response
                                                              body
<P>This section contains links to other resources on

the WEB that pertain to the field of data comunications

and networking. </P>
                          .
                          .
                          .

</body>

</html>
```

Figure 2–3 An example of a response from a Web server to a Web browser using the HTTP standard.

Figure 2–3 shows an example of a response from our Web server to the request in Figure 2–2. This example has all three parts. This example shows a Web page in Hypertext Markup Language (*HTML*). The response body can be in any format, such as text, Microsoft Word, Adobe PDF, or a host of other formats, but the most commonly used format is HTML. HTML was developed by CERN at the same time as the first Web browser and has evolved rapidly ever since. HTML is covered by a proposed standard produced by the IETF, but Microsoft and Netscape keep adding to the HTML standard with every release of their browsers, so the HTML standard keeps changing.

HTML is fairly easy to learn, so you can develop your own Web page. There are many Web sites with good tutorials on HTML; Yahoo lists more than a dozen. The easiest way to develop a page is to start with a page developed by someone else or to use an HTML editor.

The only certainty about the Web is that it will change. Some experts predict that within a year or two, Web browsers will be extinct. Web access will be integrated

Management Focus: *The Good, the Bad, and the Ugly of the Web*

The Good

✳ It is easy to create pages and publish information.

✳ It is relatively inexpensive to start and maintain a page.

✳ Navigating from page to page is simple.

✳ There is a browser for almost every type of computer and operating system.

The Bad

✳ Some browser and server software packages have bugs.

✳ Graphics take a long time to transfer over the Internet, particularly when there is a lot of traffic.

✳ Addresses change regularly, so you never really know what is out there.

✳ Weak server security means anyone can visit your site.

✳ Weak browser security permits Web servers to track and build lists from user IDs of everyone who visits.

The Ugly

✳ Not all browsers display HTML the same way, so what looks good with one browser may not with another.

✳ Graphics require a large amount of network capacity, so some users cannot view any graphics.

Source: "Internet Boomtown," *Datamation* (January 15, 1995).

into every application software package so that the Web will simply be an extension of your computer desktop.

Finding Information

The key problem with the Web is finding the information you need. There is no formal directory of all Web pages because almost anyone can develop and post a page on a Web server. There are three ways to discover interesting and useful Web pages.

First, someone could tell you about a page, or you could read an advertisement listing the Web address. Many businesses now include their Web address in their TV and print advertising. Web addresses often are easy to guess; many firms simply surround their name with www. in front and .com in back (e.g., www.microsoft.com, www.ibm.com, www.att.com).

Second, you could find a link from one page to another. Many industry organizations, magazines, and topic experts maintain pages that provide links from their pages to pages they think will be of interest to people visiting their page. For example, the home page for The University of Georgia provides links to tourist information and housing information for the town of Athens, in which it is located.

Third, and perhaps most useful, you could use a *search engine.* Search engines are Web sites that routinely use software *spiders* to explore the Web. These spiders methodically search all the pages on all the Web sites they can find and report back their discoveries. The search engine builds an index to these pages based on the words they contain. When you connect to a search engine, you type a few words describing what you want. The search engine will search its index for these keywords and provide you with a list of pages that contain them.

Management Focus: *How People Find Web Pages*

A 1997 survey conducted by Coopers & Lybrand asked people how they usually found sites on the Web (more than one answer was permitted):

✳ 44% said they heard about them from someone else

✳ 39% said they saw the URLs in a traditional medium (newspaper, magazine, TV)

✳ 32% said they followed links from other sites (not a directory/search engine)

✳ 10% said they used search engines or directories

Source: "Strategic Networks On . . ." *E-mail Newsletter* (June 1997).

There are literally dozens of search engines and directories on the Web. Three of the best are *Yahoo* (www.yahoo.com), *AltaVista* (www.altavista.digital.com), and *Excite* (www.excite.com). All three have good spiders to find Web sites. The major difference lies in how they organize information in response to your request.

Yahoo focuses on the largest and most important Web sites and organizes them in a directory format. Small or obscure Web sites are excluded. If you are looking for the address of a well-known company or product, or of a popular topic, Yahoo is probably the easiest way to find it.

AltaVista is the broadest of the three. It indexes absolutely everything it can find. AltaVista is probably the best choice if you are looking for an obscure topic or a very specific combination of topics or words (e.g., to find a famous quote). The downside is that you may have to look through dozens of sites before you find the ones you want, although AltaVista does provide some help in focusing your search.

Excite indexes almost as much as AltaVista. Its advantages lie in the use of advanced artificial intelligence techniques to help you focus your search on those pages that best match your interests. For example, after looking at the results of a search, you can tell Excite to find more pages that are similar to a specific page it has found. Excite will then search again and present those pages first. In this case, Excite is not using keywords to find pages, but rather, refining the search based on the characteristics of the page you have selected. Sometimes this works well; sometimes it does not.

Management Focus: *Finding Information With Search Engines*

Formatting searches is an art. Although each search engine is different, most follow the same basic rules.

Before you begin, you need to identify the best keywords to use. Search engines, like most computer software, are rather dumb. Usually, any letter you type must be matched exactly. If you are looking for cooking information and search on "cooking," you will miss anything that has the word "cookbook." The best idea is to use the shortest possible form of the keyword. Some searches are case-sensitive (i.e., an A is different from an a), so type carefully.

If you specify more than one word, most search engines look for each word separately. They list pages that contain any of the words you request, usually reporting the pages with the most occurrences of these words first. Some engines put more emphasis on the first word you enter, so you can sometimes change search results by changing the order of the terms.

If you only want to find pages that contain all the words you type, you can separate each word with a plus sign. For example, typing ap-ple pie will find all the pages that contain the word apple and all the pages that contain the word pie, but typing apple+pie will only find pages that contain both words.

Sometimes you need to find pages that contain words in a specific order. For example, typing air+force will find all the pages that contain both the words air and force, but not necessarily the two, one after the other, so you might end up with a lot of pages talking about air pressure forcing changes in the weather, and so on. If you want to find words that appear together, you can put quotes around them. For example, "air force" will only find pages where the two appear right after each other.

The biggest problem with search engines is that they find everything, good information and bad. Since almost anyone can put information on a Web page, there is no guarantee that the information is accurate. Before using information, you need to verify that it is accurate (e.g., comparing information from several different sources), or that the source (e.g., the company or person posting) is reliable.

Another useful site for finding information is a *metasearch engine* called MetaCrawler (www.metacrawler.com). MetaCrawler does not search the Web and index what it finds. Instead, whenever you enter a search request, it simultaneously sends the request to many search engines (including Yahoo and AltaVista) and then integrates and organizes the information it receives from all of them into one display. MetaCrawler has been rated by several magazines as the best way to search—but ratings do change.

Webcasting

Webcasting (or "push technology") is a special application of the Web that has the potential to dramatically change the way we use the Web. With Webcasting, the user signs up for a type of information on a set of *channels*. Every so often (minutes, hours, days), the user's browser will contact the Web server providing these channels to see if they have been updated. If so, the browser will load the new information and, if so desired by the user, will automatically display the information on the user's screen.

Webcasting changes the nature of the Web from one in which the user searches for information (a "pull" environment) into one in which the user accepts whatever information is on the Webcast server (a "push" environment). This is called *push* because the user does not request specific information, but rather, permits the Web server to "push" the information as it becomes available.

The Web has been likened to a library because users move from site to site and page to page in much the same way as they move from shelf to shelf and book to book in a library. Webcasting is more like TV, because the content and time of delivery is selected by the Webcaster; the user merely chooses the channels. Webcasting can be used for news (e.g., CNN) or financial reports (e.g., stock market quotes), corporate announcements, and as a replacement for broadcast e-mail. It even has the potential to provide automatic updates to software packages.

Electronic Mail

Electronic mail (or *e-mail*) was one of the earliest applications on the Internet and is still among the most heavily used today. With e-mail, users create and send messages to one user, several users, or all users on a *distribution list*. Most e-mail software

---

Management Focus: *Free Speech Reigns on the Internet . . . Or Does It?*

In a landmark decision in 1997, the U.S. Supreme Court ruled that the sections of the 1996 Telecommunications Act restricting the publication of indecent material on the Web and the sending of indecent e-mail were unconstitutional. This means that anyone can do anything on the Internet, right?

Well, not really. The court decision affects only Internet servers located in the United States. Each country in the world has different laws that govern what may and may not be placed on servers in their country. For example, British law restricts the publication of pornography, whether on paper or on Internet servers. The German courts have applied their pornography laws to companies providing Internet access, so several ISPs have been required to turn off access to pornographic material originating in other countries.

Many countries (e.g., Singapore, Saudi Arabia, and China) prohibit the publication of certain political information. Since much of this "subversive" information is published out-side of their countries, they actively restrict access to servers in other countries.

Other countries are very concerned about their individual cultures. In 1997, a French court convicted Georgia Institute of Technology of violating French language law. Georgia Tech operates a small campus in France that offers summer programs for American students. The information on the campus Web server was primarily in English because classes are conducted in English. This violated the law requiring French to be the predominant language on all Internet servers in France.

The most likely source of problems for North Americans lies in copyright law. Free speech does not give permission to copy from others. It is against the law to copy and republish on the Web any copyrighted material or any material produced by someone else without explicit permission. So don't copy graphics from someone else's Web site, or post your favorite cartoon on your Web site, unless you want to face a lawsuit.

enables users to send text messages and attach files from word processors, spreadsheets, or graphics programs.

Most e-mail packages allow you to do the same things you do with regular paper mail. You can file messages in electronic file cabinets, forward copies of messages to other users, send "carbon copies" of messages, request automatic confirmation of the delivery of the message, and so on. Many e-mail packages also permit you to filter or organize messages by priority. For example, all messages from a particular user (e.g., your boss) could be given top priority, so they always appear at the top of your list of messages.

E-mail has several major advantages over regular mail. First, it is fast: delivery of an e-mail message typically takes seconds or minutes, depending on the distance to the receiver. Even messages sent to other countries usually take only a few minutes or hours to deliver, compared to days for regular mail or courier services. E-mail users often call regular paper mail *snail mail* because it moves so slowly by comparison.

A second major benefit is cost. E-mail is cheaper because it costs virtually nothing to transmit the message over the network, compared to the cost of a stamp or a courier charge. E-mail is also cheaper in terms of the time invested in preparing the message. The expectations and culture of sending and receiving e-mail are different from that of sending regular letters. Regular business letters and inter-office memos are expected to be error-free and formatted according to certain standards. A recent analysis of office processes estimated that it costs between $3 to $10 to prepare and send a paper letter, including printing and supply costs, clerical time, and proofreading time. In contrast, most e-mail users accept less well-formatted messages, and slight typographical errors are often overlooked, so less time is spent on perfecting the appearance of the message.

E-mail can substitute for the telephone, thus allowing you to avoid *telephone tag* (the process of repeatedly exchanging voice mail messages because neither you nor the person you are trying to call is available when the other calls). A study of telephone tag in large organizations found that it took an average of three calls and messages before the parties actually spoke to each other. E-mail can often communicate enough of a message so that the entire "conversation" will take less time than a phone call. It is particularly effective for multinational organizations, which have people working in different time zones around the world.

E-mail Standards

Several standards have been developed to ensure compatibility between different e-mail software packages. Any software package that conforms to a certain standard can send messages that are formatted using its rules. Any other package that understands the standard can then relay the message to its correct destination. However, if an e-mail package receives a mail message in a different format, it may be unable to process it correctly. Many e-mail packages are designed to send using one standard but can understand messages received in several different standards. Three commonly used standards are SMTP, X.400, and CMC.

All three e-mail standards work in the same basic fashion. Figure 2–4 shows how an e-mail message can travel over a wide area network such as the Internet.

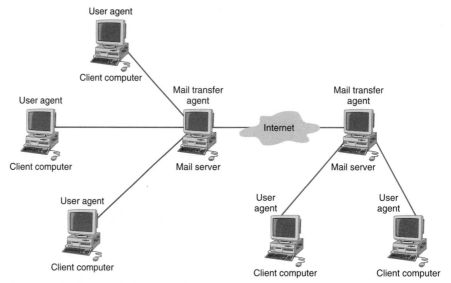

Figure 2–4 E-mail clients and servers.

Each client computer in the local area network runs an application layer software package called a *user agent*. Eudora, Lotus cc:mail, and Microsoft Mail are all e-mail software packages. The user writes the e-mail message using one of these user agents, which formats the message into two parts:

* The *header*, which lists source and destination e-mail addresses (possibly in text form (e.g., "Pat Smith") as well as the address itself (e.g., psmith@somewhere.com), date, subject, and so on
* The *body*, which is the message itself

The user agent sends the message (header and body) to a mail server that runs a special application layer software package called a *message transfer agent*. These agents read the envelope and then send the message through the network (possibly through dozens of message transfer agents) until the message arrives at the receiver's mail server. The message transfer agent on this server then stores the message in the receiver's mailbox on the server.

When the receiver next accesses his or her e-mail, the user agent on the receiver's client computer contacts the message transfer agent on the mail server and asks for the contents of the user's mailbox. The message transfer agent sends the e-mail message to the client computer, which the user reads with the user agent.

The Simple Mail Transfer Protocol (*SMTP*) is one of the most commonly used e-mail standards, simply because it is the e-mail standard used on the Internet. SMTP defines how message transfer agents operate and how they format messages sent to other message transfer agents. As the name suggests, SMTP is a simple standard that permits only the transfer of text messages; no nontext files such as graphics or word-processing documents are permitted. Several standards for non-

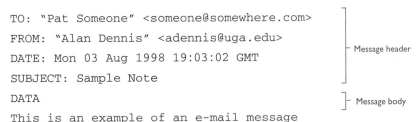

```
TO: "Pat Someone" <someone@somewhere.com>
FROM: "Alan Dennis" <adennis@uga.edu>
DATE: Mon 03 Aug 1998 19:03:02 GMT
SUBJECT: Sample Note
DATA
This is an example of an e-mail message
```
Message header

Message body

Figure 2–5 An example of an e-mail message using the SMTP standard.

text files have been developed that can operate together with SMTP, such as *Multipurpose Internet Mail Extension (MIME)*, uuencode, and binhex.

Figure 2–5 shows a simple e-mail message formatted using SMTP. The header of an SMTP message has a series of fields that provide specific information, such as the sender's e-mail address, the receiver's address, date, and so on. The information in quotes on the *to* and *from* lines is ignored by SMTP; only the information in the angle brackets is used as the e-mail address. The message body contains the actual text of the message itself, and must begin with the word DATA.

The SMTP standard covers message transmission between message transfer agents (i.e., mail server to mail server). A different standard called *Post Office Protocol (POP)* defines how user agents operate and how messages to and from mail transfer agents are formatted. POP is gradually being replaced by a newer standard called *Internet Mail Access Protocol (IMAP)*. Although there are several important technical differences between POP and IMAP, the most noticeable difference is that before a user can read a mail message with a POP user agent, the e-mail message must be copied to the client computer's hard disk and deleted from the mail server. With IMAP, e-mail messages can remain stored on the mail server after they are read. IMAP therefore offers considerable benefits to users who read their e-mail from many different computers (e.g., home, office, computer labs) because they no longer need to worry about having old e-mail messages scattered across several client computers; all e-mail is stored on the server until it is deleted.

Two other commonly used e-mail standards are X.400 and CMC. Both formats are different from SMTP, POP, and IMAP, so they cannot be used interchangeably. However, they are similar enough that it is straightforward to write *gateway* application software that can translate between the different standards. The *X.400* e-mail standard was developed by the CCITT in 1984. X.400 is a set of seven standards that define how e-mail is to be processed by user agents and mail transfer agents. The *Common Messaging Calls (CMC)* standard is a simpler version of the X.400 standard. CMC was developed by CCITT in conjunction with IBM, Lotus, and Microsoft in 1994. CMC is more popular than X.400 because of its simplicity and because of its support by a large number of leading vendors.

E-mail Directories

Before you can send an e-mail message, you must know the receiver's e-mail address (the same way you must know someone's telephone number before you call them).

Many organizations provide e-mail directories on their Web sites. Other e-mail addresses are well known. For example, the e-mail address of the president of the United States is president@whitehouse.gov (of course, the President doesn't actually read the e-mail; staff members do). In other cases, finding the e-mail address of someone on the Internet can be difficult because there is no central "phone book" for the Internet, although several commercial firms are trying to build Web sites to provide this information (e.g., www.four11.com). Nonetheless, there are still no universal e-mail directories in the same way that universal telephone directory assistance is available for every country and area code.

Several competing standards have been developed in an attempt to provide this universal directory service, but as yet little progress has been made to actually implement a worldwide system based on the standards. *X.500* is the directory service standard for X.400 mail users, but there are few standard application software packages that conform to X.500, making widespread use of X.500 problematic.

Management Focus: E-mail Saves a Life

On February 2, 1997, midway through her attempt to be the first American woman to sail solo around the world, Karen Thorndike sent the e-mail message that saved her life. Four days after leaving the Falkland Islands, she found herself seriously ill with the flu and in the middle of violent storm. Then the chest pains started.

She was too far out to sea for her radio to reach the Falklands, so she turned on her Emergency Distress beacon and sent an emergency e-mail message via satellite to John Oman at her home base in Seattle. The e-mail message was received by Oman, who immediately acknowledged it and attempted to telephone authorities in the Falklands. However, all telephone lines into the Falklands were out of order due to the storm. Oman contacted the U.S. Coast Guard, who passed the emergency request to the Argentine Coast Guard and the British Coast Guard in England.

The British Coast Guard sent a telex to Thorndike via satellite asking her to confirm the need for an emergency request. She could not respond using telex, so she e-mailed Oman, asking him to respond to the telephone number given in the telex, which he did.

The British Coast Guard then contacted the HMS Norfolk, a Royal Navy frigate sailing 200 miles away from Thorndike, and ordered it to begin a search and rescue operation. Thorndike could not communicate with the frigate because it, too, was out of radio range. Instead, every two hours she e-mailed her position to Oman in Seattle, who telephoned it to the Norfolk.

On the morning of February 3, the Norfolk located Thorndike on radar and rescued her. They treated her on board and she spent several days in hospital in the Falklands before returning to the United States for more treatment. Four Royal Navy sailors sailed Thorndike's boat to the Falklands and several months after the rescue, Thorndike returned to the Falklands to resume her solo voyage.

Source: HTTP://goals.com/amelia/karen.htm

Lightweight Directory Access Protocol (LDAP) is a subset of X.500. Several vendors (e.g., Netscape) have adopted LDAP for their mail software and are advocating its adoption as the primary Internet standard for e-mail directory services. The major advantage of LDAP is that it is simple and small. The major disadvantage is that it lacks some features that many users see as important, but this is likely to change as LDAP matures.

File Transfer Protocol (FTP)

File transfer protocol (FTP) enables you to send and receive files over the Internet. FTP requires an application layer program on the client computer and a FTP server application program on a server. Many software packages use the FTP standard (e.g., WS-FTP). Almost anyone can establish an FTP server, which permits anyone on Internet to log in and send and receive files.

There are two types of FTP sites: closed and anonymous. A closed site requires users to have permission before they can connect and gain access to the files. Access is granted by providing an account name with a secret password. For example, a network manager or webmaster would write a Web page using software on his or her client computer and then use FTP to send it to a specific account on the Web server.

The most common type is an *anonymous FTP* site, which permits any Internet user to login using the account name of *anonymous*. When using anonymous FTP, you will still be asked for a password. It is customary to enter your Internet e-mail address as the password (e.g., smith@allstate.edu).

Many files and documents available via FTP have been compressed to reduce the amount of disk space they require. Since there are many types of data compression programs, it is possible that a file you want has been compressed by a program you lack, so you won't be able to access the file until you find the decompression program it uses. That's one of the "advantages" of the decentralized, no-rules structure of the Internet.

Telnet

Telnet enables users on one computer to log in to other computers on the Internet. Telnet requires an application layer program on the client computer and an application layer program on the server or host computer. Many programs conform to the Telnet standard (e.g., EWAN). Once Telnet makes the connection from the client to the server, you can log in to the server or host computer in the same way as you would if you dialed in with a modem; you must know the account name and password of an authorized user. Telnet can be faster or slower than a modem, depending on the amount of traffic on the Internet. Modems are discussed in Chapter 3. In any event, Telnet enables you to connect to a remote computer without incurring long-distance telephone charges.

Telnet can be useful because it enables you to access your server or host computer without sitting at its keyboard. Most network managers use Telnet to work on servers, rather than physically sitting in front of them and using their keyboards. Telnet also poses a great security threat, because it means that anyone on the Internet can attempt to log in to your account and use it as they wish. One commonly used security precaution is to prohibit remote logins via Telnet unless a user specifically asks for his or her account to be authorized for it, or to permit remote logins only from a specific set of Internet addresses. For example, the Web server for this book will only accept Telnet logins from computers located on the College of Business network at The University of Georgia campus. Chapter 12 discusses network security.

✳✳ GROUPWARE

Groupware is software that helps groups of people to work together more productively. This is a very broad definition, but it is difficult to find a more specific one that includes all the different types of groupware applications. Groupware applications are often organized using a two-by-two grid (see Figure 2–6). Groupware permits people in different places to communicate either at the same time (as on a telephone) or at different times. Groupware also can be used to improve communication and decision making among those who work together in the same room, either at the same time or at different times.

Groupware allows people to exchange ideas, debate issues, make decisions, and write reports without actually having to meet face-to-face. Even when groups do meet in the same room at the same time, groupware can improve the meetings. There are many advantages of groupware, but the most important is its ability to help groups make decisions faster, particularly in situations where it is difficult for group members to meet in the same room at the same time.

This section examines four popular types of groupware: discussion groups, document-based groupware (e.g., Lotus Notes), group support systems, and video-conferencing. However, the lines between these different types of groupware are rapidly disappearing. Notes, for example, incorporates both discussion and video-conferencing capabilities.

	Same time	Different time
Same place	Group support systems	Group support systems
Different place	Video teleconferencing Desktop video teleconferencing	Electronic mail Discussion groups Document-based groupware

Figure 2–6 Different types of groupware.

Management Focus: Net Etiquette

Net etiquette (sometimes called *netiquette*) is the set of rules or generally accepted behaviors on the Internet, which includes:

* When you first join the net, listen and learn before contributing.
* Read the Frequently Asked Questions (FAQ) information.
* Always double check the address of your message. Even experts sometimes send private messages to public mailing lists by pressing the wrong key.
* Keep your messages brief.
* Don't make private messages public without permission.
* Don't send test messages.
* Don't include complete copies of other messages in your message if the recipients of the message have already seen them; small excerpts of other messages are fine.
* Don't waste others' time by sending "me too" or "I agree" messages.
* In general, spelling doesn't count.
* Don't send unsolicited advertisements. Brief announcements and instructions for interested people to request more information are acceptable.

* Don't flame (argue aggressively in an inflammatory style that often includes personal attacks on those individuals with whom you disagree).
* Don't type in ALL CAPITALS unless you want to SHOUT.
* Always include your name and address in messages; some systems delete them.
* Don't send messages where they don't belong (e.g., don't discuss the Brady Bunch in a Star Trek discussion group).
* Remember that the libel laws apply to the Internet.
* Copyright laws also apply. Don't send copyrighted material over the Internet without written permission from the copyright owner.
* You can use symbols to indicate the feelings you would normally communicate with your vocal tone. For example, to indicate you're joking, you could type :-)
* Don't believe everything you read. Not everyone knows what they are talking about, and people can put on fake personas (some celebrities do send messages, but most messages from famous people are fake).

Discussion Groups

Discussion groups are collections of users who have joined together to discuss some topic. Discussion groups are formed around just about every topic imaginable, including cooking, skydiving, politics, education, and British comedy. Some are short lived, while others continue indefinitely. Two are commonly used for business: usenet newsgroups, and listservs.

Usenet Newsgroups

Usenet newsgroups are the most formally organized of the discussion groups. Establishing a new one requires a vote of all interested people on the Internet. If enough people express interest, the new topic is established.

The usenet newsgroups are a set of huge bulletin boards on which anyone who wishes can read and post messages. The usenet "newsfeed" of the discussions within each of these groups is available to all computers on the Internet (about 70 megabytes of new messages each *day*). Some network managers choose not to provide access to all topics. For example, some universities do not provide access to the more sexually explicit newsgroups.

The exact commands to gain access to these newsgroups vary from computer to computer. The general process is to subscribe to a specific topic or set of topics. Once you have subscribed, each time you access the newsgroups, you are informed of any new messages added to the topics. You can then read these messages and respond to them by adding your own message.

Listservs

A listserver (or *listserv*) group is similar in concept to the usenet newsgroups, but is generally less formal. Anyone with the right e-mail server software can establish a listserv, which is simply a mailing list. The listserv processor processes commands such as requests to subscribe, unsubscribe, or to provide more information about the listserv. The listserv mailer routes messages to everyone on the mailing list. To use a listserv, you need to know the addresses of both the processor and the mailer.

To subscribe to a listserv, you send an e-mail message to the listserv *processor*, which adds your name to the list (see the technical focus box for the message format). It is important that you send this message to the processor, not the mailer,

---

Technical Focus: *Listserv Commands*

Many different commands can be sent to the listserv processor to perform a variety of functions. These commands are included as lines of text in the e-mail message sent to the processor. Each command must be placed on a separate line. Some useful commands include:

* SUBSCRIBE   listserv-mailer-name   your-name
   Subscribes you to a mailing list (e.g., *subscribe maps-l robin jones*)
* UNSUBSCRIBE   listserv-mailer-name   your-name
   Unsubscribes you from the mailing list (e.g., *unsubscribe maps-l robin jones*)

* HELP
   Requests the listserv to e-mail you a list of its commands
* LIST
   Requests the listserv to e-mail you a list of all listserv groups that are available on this listserv processor
* LIST DETAILED
   Requests the listserv to e-mail you a detailed description of all listserv groups that are available on this listserv processor
* LIST GLOBAL
   Requests e-mail list of all listserv groups known to this listserv processor (both locally and anywhere on the Internet)

otherwise your subscription message will be sent to everyone on the mailing list, and you may be embarrassed.

For example, you can join the listserv on group support systems. The processor address is listerv@uga.edu, and the mailer address is gss-l@uga.edu. To subscribe, you send an e-mail message to listerv@uga.edu containing the text *subscribe gss-l your name*. To send a message to everyone on this listserv, you would e-mail your message to gss-l@uga.edu.

Listservs generally are more focused than the usenet news groups and have fewer members. They are harder to find than the usenet newsgroups because literally anyone can create one. There is no centrally managed list of listservs, although many listservs keep track of some listservs on other listservs. To get a list of some of the most popular listservs, send an e-mail message to any listserv with the message *list global.*

Document-Based Groupware

One of the problems with e-mail is that it lacks a structured way to support an ongoing discussion. Each mail message is a separate item, unrelated to other messages. It is possible to group and file e-mail messages into separate file folders, but there is no overall way to integrate them.

Lotus Notes (also called Domino), a document database designed to store and manage large collections of text and graphics, was the first product to provide a solution. Documents can have different sections, and can be organized into a hierarchical structure of sections, documents, and folders. Lotus Notes can be used as a computer bulletin board to support ongoing discussions. Several topics and sub-topics can be created, and everyone in the organization (or selected individuals) can be given access. For example, a topic area about data communications could be created. Users could ask questions about problems they face, or they could contribute advice or post new company policies. These individuals can add messages to the different topics and read those contributed by others. Messages can be easily linked so that it is clear which messages are related to which others.

Lotus Notes can also be used to organize a discussion among certain people, such as a project team working to improve manufacturing quality. Notes might reduce the amount of time the team spent in face-to-face meetings, because many of the issues might be discussed before the meeting actually started. Notes also could be used to replace standard word processors in preparing the team's reports. Each team member could use Notes to write a portion of the report, which could then be passed to other team members for editing or comments.

Lotus Notes can also automate certain document-based processes (called *work-flow automation*). For example, insurance claims require people from several different parts of an insurance company to work together to process the claim. One person might handle the initial claim, which would then be passed to an insurance adjuster to finish a report. Another person would process the payment. All this paperwork could be replaced if Lotus Notes were used to prepare and pass the documents from one person to another.

Management Focus: CIA Spies Value in Lotus Notes

The Central Intelligence Agency has turned to Lotus Notes because of its strong security and flexible data access capabilities. Lotus Notes helped redefine the way the agency collects and distributes information, no small feat given that this is the agency's main task.

The goal of the CIA's use of Notes was to replace paper and automate as many processes as possible—in particular, the analysis and distribution of reports from overseas offices. Notes also allows the CIA to bring some order to an electronic mail network based on 18 different proprietary systems.

The agency especially liked what it saw in Lotus's security technology, including use of public-key encryption and access control lists for limiting who could see what (these are discussed in Chapter 12). It has also taken additional steps to make sure that Notes is secure: an audit trail logs each time a document is accessed and by whom.

Source: Network World (March 13, 1995).

One of Notes' greatest strengths is its *replication* abilities. Replication is the automatic sharing of information among servers when information changes. For example, Notes servers can be set to replicate the information they contain with any other Notes server on the network, so that a change to a document on one server will automatically be shared with all other servers that contain that same document.

More than 2 million people worldwide now use Lotus Notes, a fact that has not escaped the notice of other software vendors. Microsoft has introduced Microsoft Exchange and Netscape has introduced Communicator to compete with Notes. Currently, there are no standards for this type of groupware software, but more and more vendors are using Web browsers as their client software so that anyone with Web access can use their groupware server.

Group Support Systems

Both e-mail and document-based groupware are designed to support individuals and groups working in different places and different times. Neither is very suited to support the needs of groups working together at the same time in the same place. Likewise, both e-mail and document-based groupware provide support for the exchange of text, but neither provides more advanced tools for helping groups make decisions.

Group support systems (GSS) are software tools designed to improve group decision making. Most GSS are used in special-purpose meeting rooms that provide each group member with a networked computer, plus large-screen video projection systems that act as electronic blackboards (see Figure 2–7). These rooms are equipped with special-purpose GSS software that enables participants to communicate, propose ideas, analyze options, evaluate alternatives, and so on. Typically, a meeting facilitator assists the group.

Figure 2-7 A GSS room using laptop computers.

In the GSS meeting, group members can discuss issues verbally, as they could in any meeting room. However, they can also use the computers to type ideas and information, which are then shared with all other group members via the network. At first glance, it may seem strange to ask people who are sitting next to each other to type their ideas, because typing is slower than talking. For small groups, typing adds little value.

For large groups, however, typing ideas is faster than talking because only one person can speak at a time. Very few people get a chance to talk, so their ideas and opinions can be overlooked. For example, in a traditional meeting, if 10 people participate equally for one hour, each spends 6 minutes talking and 54 minutes listening (or at least not contributing). This is a very inefficient use of time. By typing ideas into a GSS, everyone has the same opportunity to contribute, and ideas can be collected much faster.

In addition, GSS enables users to make anonymous comments. Without anonymity, certain participants may withhold ideas because they fear their ideas may not be well received. Anonymity can help participants overcome pressure to conform to the views of the group majority or more senior participants, whether that pressure is or is not intended.

These systems also provide tools to support voting and ranking of alternatives, so that more structured decision-making processes can be used. Studies of GSS have shown that its use can reduce the amount of time taken to make decisions by 50 to 80 percent. There are no standards for GSS, so products from different vendors are not currently compatible. As with document groupware, more vendors are using

---

Management Focus: *The Department of Defense Saves Time and Money with Groupware*

The U.S. Department of Defense (DoD) logistics system experienced major problems during the Gulf War. One reason was that the information systems within each of the military services had evolved with little integrated planning; there were a total of 2000 separate logistics information systems in use in the DoD, which made sharing information and supplies very difficult.

The Army and Marine Corps, with support from the Office of the Secretary of Defense, decided to develop one set of standard logistics processes and supporting information systems for all Army and Marine ground units. They began by defining their current processes and systems, which required more than 26 weeks of meetings over a 15-month period at a cost of $3.3 million.

Given the difficulty in defining the current processes and system, the DoD decided to use a group support system to develop the specifications for the new integrated logistics processes and information systems. In 1993, 60 logistics experts from the Army and Marines spent three weeks in the groupware facility at Redstone Arsenal in Huntsville, Alabama, defining the new processes and systems. The total cost was $300,000, a savings of about 90 percent in both time and money.

The project was such a success that in 1994, the DoD conducted a follow-up project to integrate Navy and Air Force systems into the overall system. The results were similar. In three weeks, 80 logistics experts from the Army, Marines, Navy, and Air Force defined the new processes and systems for about $300,000, again a savings of about 90 percent in time and money.

---

the Web browser as their client software, so almost anyone can access a groupware server.

Videoconferencing

Discussion groups, document-based groupware, and GSS all focus on the transmission of text and graphical images. *Videoconferencing* provides real-time transmission of video and audio signals to enable people in two or more locations to have a meeting. In some cases, videoconferences are held in special-purpose meeting rooms with one or more cameras and several video display monitors to capture and display the video signals (see Figure 2–8). Special audio microphones and speakers are used to capture and play audio signals. The audio and video signals are combined into one signal that is transmitted though a metropolitan or wide area network to people at the other location. Most of this type of videoconferencing involves people in two meeting rooms, but some systems can support conferences of up to eight separate meeting rooms.

The fastest growing form of videoconferencing is *desktop videoconferencing.* Small cameras installed on top of each computer permit meetings to take place from individual offices (see Figure 2–9). Special application software (e.g., CUSeeMe) is installed on the client computer. It transmits the images across a

Figure 2–8 Room-based videoconferencing.

network to application software on a videoconferencing server. The server then sends the signals to the other client computers that are to participate in the video-conference. In some cases, the clients can communicate with each other without using the server. The cost of desktop videoconferencing ranges from less than $150 per computer for inexpensive systems to more than $4000 for high-quality systems. Some systems have integrated other types of groupware software with desktop vi-deoconferencing, enabling participants to communicate verbally—to attend the same "meeting" while they are sitting at the computers in their offices.

Figure 2–9 Desktop videoconferencing.

The key benefits of videoconferencing are the time and cost savings that result from reduced travel needs. Videoconferencing was slow to take hold in many organizations because of its high initial installation costs (between $20,000 to $100,000 per meeting room). Today, however, most large organizations with offices in different parts of the country or the world use it, and there is a growing demand for desktop systems. Desktop systems now outsell room-based systems three to one, but the growth has been slower than expected.

The transmission of video requires a lot of network capacity. Most videoconferencing uses data compression to reduce the amount of data transmitted. Surprisingly, the most common complaint is not the quality of the video image, but the quality of the voice transmissions. Special care needs to be taken in the design and placement of microphones and speakers to ensure quality sound and minimal feedback.

Like e-mail, most videoconferencing systems were originally developed by vendors using different formats, so many products were incompatible. The best solution was to ensure that all hardware and software used within an organization was supplied by the same vendor, and to hope that any other organizations with whom you wanted to communicate used the same equipment.

Management Focus: *Videoconferencing in the Real World*

Many businesses are just beginning to implement videoconferencing, but hospitals have been among the leading users for several years. Improving medical care is one application that can save more than dollars.

In the early morning hours of April 28, 1997, Dr. James Luecke was working his morning shift as a general practitioner at Big Bend Regional Medical Center in Alpine, Texas, when a 51-year-old man was brought in suffering from gunshot wounds. The man was a hostage who had been shot as he escaped from members of the Republic of Texas separatist group.

Luecke was able to remove some of the bullet fragments, but he needed a surgical consult to determine the danger from the remaining shrapnel. Rather than transport the victim to the nearest full-service hospital five hours away, Luecke used the TeleDoc videoconferencing system to talk with a surgeon at the University Medical Center in Lubbock. He completed his work based on the surgeon's advice.

Source: "Looking at the Big Picture," *PC Week* (June 16, 1997).

Four commonly used standards for videoconferencing promise to reduce many incompatibilities once they are widely adopted by vendors: H.320, H.323, MPEG-1, and MPEG-2. Each of these standards was developed by a different organization and is supported by different products. They are not compatible, although some application software packages understand more than one standard. H.320 is designed for room-to-room videoconferencing over high-speed telephone lines.

H.323 is designed for desktop videoconferencing over the Internet. MPEG-1 and MPEG-2 are designed for faster connections, such as a LAN or a specially designed, privately operated WAN.

Managing in a Groupware World

Groupware dramatically changes the way people interact. Communication is simpler and faster and anyone can communicate directly with anyone else, organizational rules permitting. Improved communication can provide large paybacks in increased productivity, especially when you consider that the primary task of most office workers (e.g., consultants, accountants, managers) is the processing and communication of information. A study of 65 Lotus Notes users conducted by International Data Corp. found an average three-year return on investment of 179 percent.

Nonetheless, groupware's ability to greatly improve communication can also create problems. Hewlett-Packard's 97,000 employees exchange about 20 million electronic mail messages each month—an average of about 10 messages per person per business day. At Sun Microsystems, the average is 120 messages per person per day. Managing in this glut of information can be difficult. Identifying priorities and not being distracted by less important issues are key to success; otherwise, you can drown in an endless sea of communication.

Social norms are one of the greatest limiting factors in the widespread use of groupware technologies, because the technology changes faster than the people who use it. Many organizations use groupware as a means to exchange information among their staff. The problem is, most organizations using groupware in this way do not reward people for contributing their expertise. Contributing information and helping others is important to help the organization achieve its goals, but it takes time from the person contributing the information and slows down their performance. This sets up conflicting goals for employees: Do I do my work or help others do theirs?

✳✳ ELECTRONIC COMMERCE

Almost all large and medium-sized companies use the Internet and many are actively using it for *electronic commerce*—doing business on the Internet. Making money, however, is still a risky proposition. While some businesses are making a profit, others have quickly failed. (This is also true for businesses in the "real" world; only about 20 percent of new businesses are still operating five years later.)

In the early days of the California gold rush, it wasn't the prospectors who got rich; it was the people selling the steamship tickets, blue jeans, and pick axes. Likewise, the fastest way to make money from the Internet may be to sell products and services to those trying to strike it rich. One of the most profitable niches today is providing consulting, tools, training, and services for electronic commerce, rather than actually doing it. For this reason, much business use of the Internet is not for making money per se. Rather, it is to find information, improve communications, and provide information—most of the same reasons that individuals use the Internet.

Figure 2–10 Two typical Web sites: Dell (electronic store) and Condé Nast Traveler (information provider).

Many people automatically focus on the retail aspects of electronic commerce; that is, selling products to individuals. However, that is just one small part of electronic commerce. The fastest growing and soon-to-be largest segment of electronic commerce is business-to-business selling.

In this section, we look at the types of sites on the Web that support electronic commerce and why companies and individuals want electronic commerce. There are many other ways to support electronic commerce, such as using FTP to share files. However, we believe that as Web browsers mature and include FTP and other functions, the Web will gradually become the most important.

There are four major ways in which the Web can be used to support electronic commerce: electronic store, electronic marketing, information/entertainment provider, and customer service. Figure 2–10 shows some examples. Most Web sites focus on just one approach, but it is possible to combine all four in one Web site. The most common type of Web site is electronic marketing. Today, less than 10 percent of corporate Web sites provide electronic stores, but this is expected to grow rapidly over the next few years.

Electronic Store

The most obvious approach to electronic commerce is an *electronic store.* With an electronic store, a company develops the Internet equivalent of a local store or a mail-order catalog. It develops a Web site that lists all of the products and services it wishes to sell and enables customers to purchase them by calling a toll-free number or by using the Internet itself. There is some concern about transmitting credit card information over the Internet, because this information can be copied by any computer through which the message flows, making it easy to "steal" information. Although this is possible, the risk of having credit card information stolen on the Internet is much less than having it stolen by a regular thief or unscrupulous store owner.

There are many examples of electronic stores. Many existing catalog companies (e.g., Land's End) have opened Web sites that operate in much the same manner as their traditional catalogs. Other entrepreneurs have opened electronic stores to compete with traditional stores. Dozens of online travel agents (such as Travelocity) and online bookstores (such as Amazon.Com) provide products and services in direct competition to local stores. Electronic stores have lower overhead costs than traditional stores because they do not have physical stores with lots of employees and because they usually carry little or no inventory; all orders are shipped directly from the manufacturer. Electronic stores do, however, have higher shipping costs because they ship purchases to each customer individually rather than in bulk to stores.

One of the more interesting electronic stores is that run by Boeing. Boeing sells millions of spare parts each year to the 700 or so airlines that use its airplanes. Boeing now operates an electronic store that enables these airlines to purchase spare parts through the Web. This has improved customer service, because now a customer anywhere in the world can order a needed part directly from Boeing, 24 hours a day. Surprisingly, this has also enabled Boeing to reduce costs and speed up delivery. The Boeing electronic store is a closed site (an extranet), which means that only Boeing customers can access it—so unless you own an airline, you won't be able to order a new engine for a 777.

Since there are few additional costs to providing more information on the Web (unlike a catalog, in which each page adds to the cost), electronic stores can provide much information. Electronic stores can also add value by providing dynamic information. Dell Computer, for example, sells computers that can be configured in many different ways (e.g., different-sized hard disks, more or less memory). A static catalog or magazine advertisement can only list a few configurations. The Dell electronic store enables customers to specify exactly what size of hard disk, how much memory, and so on, and get a price quote for the exact computer they want. It is simple for customers to price many different configurations, something that is not possible in a static paper medium. As an aside, Dell sells almost $1 billion of computers per year from its Web site alone—a staggering indication of the importance of the Web to Dell and to other computer companies.

One problem is verifying that the transaction is accurate and that the seller is what it claims to be. Suppose your electronic banker receives a message instructing the bank to transfer $10,000 into another account. The banker must ensure that the message actually came from your account (there are ways to mask a true address) and that you actually sent it (a hacker could have stolen your password). This is becoming possible with some new security tools discussed in Chapter 12, but will remain an issue for many years.

A variation on the electronic store is the *electronic mall*. An electronic mall is a collection of electronic stores. The mall usually provides all the computer infrastructure needed for electronic commerce, and advertises the mall to potential customers. In return, the stores pay the mall a monthly fee or some percentage of sales. One of the reasons for the success of real shopping malls is that location is extremely important for retail sales; if you are not near other stores, it is hard to attract customers. On the Web, location is unimportant. It is as simple to click to an electronic store in the United States or Canada as it is to one in England or Australia. Many electronic malls have closed because they cannot attract enough electronic stores to become profitable.

Electronic Marketing Site

A second common approach is the *electronic marketing site*. This type of site supports the sales process, but does not make actually sales. The goal is to attract and keep customers. The most common type of electronic commerce site is the electronic marketing site. The Web sites of the major automobile manufacturers in North America are good examples. These sites provide a wealth of information about their cars, complete with technical details and photographs. Customers can view these pages and obtain information without going to the dealer, but they cannot buy a car over the Web. The goal of these Web sites is to encourage the user to visit a local dealer, who will then make the sale. One Toyota dealer estimates that he sells two or three cars per month (that he would not otherwise have sold) due to Toyota's Web page. Although the numbers sound small, this translates into more than $150 million dollars per year in North America alone—a rather substantial payback for one Web site.

Many companies use electronic marketing sites to provide newsletters with information on the latest products and tips on how to use them. IBM and Microsoft, for example, use the Web to provide information on the latest versions of their software and on products that have been announced but not yet released. Other companies enable potential customers to sign up for notification of new product releases. Amazon.Com, for example, will notify you the next time your favorite author publishes a new book.

Electronic marketing is cheaper in many ways than traditional print, direct mail, TV, or radio marketing. Electronic marketing costs no more than other media to develop, but unlike print, direct mail, TV or radio there are no costs to sending the information to the consumer. It is also easier to customize the presentation of information to a potential customer, because the Web is interactive. In contrast, the other media are fixed once they are developed, and they provide the same marketing approach to all who see it.

Information/Entertainment Provider

As the name suggests, an *information/entertainment provider* supplies information or entertainment. The key difference between electronic stores and information/entertainment providers is the nature of the products. Electronic stores provide physical goods and services (e.g., flowers, airline tickets), while information/entertainment providers provide intangible things. The key difference between electronic marketing sites and information/entertainment providers is the nature of the information. Electronic marketing sites focus on the products and services of one company; their goal is to increase sales. Information/entertainment providers provide information from many sources; their goal is to help their user. Some of the most common information/entertainment providers are the search engines previously discussed.

Management Focus: 10 Net Marketing Mistakes

1. Don't spend all of your money on site construction. You will need money for special promotions and updates throughout the year.

2. Don't create a "mile-wide" and "half-inch deep" promotion. Focus on promotions that will add value for your key market segments.

3. Don't treat online promotion like off-line promotion. Keep your initial message short with links to more detail.

4. Don't let surfers get away without some closure. Get them to sign-up for e-mail updates or additional product information.

5. Don't think about sales as much as marketing. Focus on building relationships with customers, not on how many widgets were sold today.

6. Don't obsess over your domain name. It's likely that someone else already has your first choice, but their are many more good names.

7. Don't design for internal users. Design for the user surfing your net under the worst possible conditions.

8. Don't try to save money with a low-powered Web host. Get the best quality Web-hosting service you can; mistakes are too costly.

9. Don't separate the marketing people from the technical staff. The marketers have the skills to design the message; the techies know the current and emerging tools.

10. Don't load your site down with junk. Reuse existing material, but don't upload it in its current form.

Source: Net Guide (December 1996).

Information/entertainment providers can be very broad or very focused in topic coverage and can present information in a variety of media. For example, many national magazines and newspapers have gone on the Web. Most of these provide broad coverage of a wide range of topics. Other information/entertainment providers provide narrowly focused information and advice about specific topics (e.g., sports scores, movie reviews, used car prices).

Information/entertainment providers have typically offered information as text or graphics. Over the past year, however, several radio and TV stations have moved onto the Web, providing broadcasts of audio and video in much the same way as they do in their traditional media. The Web also offers new forms of entertainment. Virtual reality, for example, enables new multiplayer interactive games that are not available in any other media. Several studies have noticed a slight drop in TV viewing among longtime users of the Web, suggesting that for some people, the Web may replace some of their traditional sources of entertainment.

Most Web users expect information to be free, so most information/entertainment providers do not charge for access, although a few require subscriptions just like magazines before they will let you into their site. Many national newspapers initially tried to charge for subscriptions, but most dropped fees after failing to generate enough interest. Several narrowly focused information/entertainment providers have been very successful in charging fees, because the information they provide has a clear value to those who subscribe.

Management Focus: Electronic Commerce at Levi Straus

Levi Straus operates three primary Web sites: a corporate site (www.levistraus.com), a Levi's jeans site (www.levi.com), and a Dockers site (www.dockers.com). This set of Web sites evolved over several years and offers a full range of information. From the company's perspective, the last two sites, Levi's and Dockers, are the most important. These sites were developed first; the main corporate site came later. Levi's, after all, is one of the world's strongest brands.

Both brand sites provide information about their products, some product history, and a store finder. Both also provide lifestyle information designed to interest their primary buyers. The Levi's site provides media, image, and ad information designed for the teenagers and 20-year-olds. The Dockers site provides career, golf, and travel information designed for 30- and 40-year olds. Both sites provide the ability for customers to e-mail customer service staff, to obtain additional information, and to sign up for promotions. The Dockers site also provides specific cleaning and fashion advice.

The corporate site provides public relations information and press releases to the worldwide media. Two-line summaries are regularly e-mailed to the press, which provide links to the full press release on the corporate Web site. Last year, the corporate marketing department sent out more than 3000 information kits to students writing reports about Levi's. This information has been moved to the Web, saving the costs of printing and mailing.

The corporate site is also helping to build links to suppliers and potential employees. The complete guidelines for contractors and prospective contractors are on the site. It also contains job listings and enables individuals to submit resumes online. Not only does this make it easy to apply, but it saves Levi's from having to scan the resumes for internal circulation.

Source: "Levi Straus & Co: A Good Fit," *Corporate Online* (June 1997).

Like their print counterparts, information/entertainment providers generate revenue by selling advertising. Web advertising has been slow to build, but most experts believe that it will quickly grow as more businesses come to understand how to use the Web as one part of their marketing strategies. As one might expect, the largest advertisers on the Web are computer and telecommunications companies such as IBM, Microsoft, AT&T, and MCI, but many of the world's largest advertisers such as automobile manufacturers (e.g., General Motors) and packaged goods firms (e.g., Proctor & Gamble) have begun to advertise on the Web.

Customer Service Site

A *customer service site* provides a variety of information for customers after they have purchased a product or service. For example, Dell provides more than 30,000 Web pages of technical support information, service information, and frequently asked questions (FAQs) on its Web sites. Rather than telephoning the company during business hours—and possibly having to wait for a customer service representative—customers can now access the most commonly needed information 24 hours a day. Many software companies post updates to software on their Web sites so that customers can download the newest versions of software or updates that fix problems.

Federal Express has been one of the leading innovators in the use of the Web for customer service. Their Web site enables customers to track the packages they have sent. When a customer enters a package number, the Web site provides specific information about the current location of the package and when it was delivered (or when it is scheduled for delivery). Dell also provides an online order-tracking system, so customers can quickly find out the status of their order. This service receives about 15,000 requests per day, meaning 15,000 fewer telephone calls for the customer service staff.

Customer service sites benefit both the company and its customers. They enable the customer to more quickly access needed information and they provide support 24 hours a day. Customer service sites often reduce the number of staff needed by automating routine information requests that previously had to be handled by an employee. Many companies are now extending their customer service by targeting information to suppliers, partners, and employees. Many of the same concepts apply, and many of the same benefits are realized.

Summary

The Internet The Internet is a worldwide network of networks that is broken into a series of domains (e.g., edu, com). There is no central organization, but each domain has its own address board and policies. The Internet is growing very rapidly. Most organizations have access to the Internet. There are four commonly used applications on the Internet: the Web, e-mail, FTP, and Telnet. Each requires the user to have an application layer software package on his or her client computer and an application layer software package on the server.

World Wide Web (Web)   One of the fastest-growing Internet applications is the Web, which was first developed in 1990. The Web enables the display of rich graphical images, pictures, full-motion video, and sound. The Web is the most common way for businesses to establish a presence on the Internet. The Web has two application software packages, a Web browser on the client and a Web server on the server. Web browsers and servers communicate with each other using a standard called HTTP. Most Web pages are written in HTML, but many also use other formats. The Web contains information on just about every topic under the sun, but finding it and making sure the information is reliable are major problems.

Electronic Mail   With e-mail, users can create and send messages using an application layer software package on client computers called a user agent. The user agent sends the mail to a server running an application layer software package called a mail transfer agent, which then forwards the message through a series of mail transfer agents to the mail transfer agent on the receiver's server. E-mail is faster and cheaper than regular mail, and can substitute for telephone conversations in some cases. Several standards have been developed to ensure compatibility between different user agents and mail transfer agents. SMTP, POP and IMAP are used on the Internet. X.400 and CMC are other commonly used standards. LDAP and X.500 are standards for e-mail directories.

Discussion Groups   Discussion groups are Internet users who have joined together to discuss some topic. There are discussion groups on just about every topic imaginable, from cooking, skydiving, and politics, to education and British comedy. Usenet newsgroups are the most formally organized; they are a set of huge bulletin boards on which anyone on the Internet can read and post messages. A listserver (or listserv) is simply a mailing list. The listserv processor processes listserv commands such as requests to subscribe and unsubscribe, while the listserv mailer mails any message it receives to everyone on the mailing list.

Document-Based Groupware   Lotus Notes was the first document-based groupware product. It is a document database designed to store and manage large collections of text and graphics to support on-going discussions. Discussions can be organized into a hierarchical structure of sections, documents, and folders. Lotus Notes can also be used to automate certain document-based processes (called workflow automation).

Group Support Systems   Group support systems are software tools designed to improve group decision making in special-purpose meeting rooms that provide networked computers and large-screen video projection systems. These rooms are equiped with special-purpose GSS software that enables participants to communicate, propose ideas, analyze options, evaluate alternatives, and so on.

Videoconferencing   Videoconferencing provides real-time transmission of video and audio signals to help people at different locations to have a meeting. Videoconferencing can be done in special-purpose meeting rooms that have one or more cameras and several video display monitors to capture and display the video signals. The fastest growing form of videoconferencing is desktop videoconferencing, in which small cameras are installed on top of each user's computer so that participants can hold meetings from their offices. The key benefits of videoconferencing are the time and cost savings from reduced travel.

Electronic Store   An electronic store sells products and services over the Internet in much the same way as a catalog. Most people think of electronic stores that sell to individuals, but several large companies (e.g., Boeing) have opened electronic stores targeted at business-to-business sales. Electronic stores are often cheaper to operate than traditional stores because of their low overhead costs; however, like traditional stores, only a few actually make money.

Electronic Marketing Site   The electronic marketing site provides information and literature to potential customers. Its goal is to increase sales at traditional sales outlets and dealers. Electronic marketing is cheaper than traditional marketing (e.g., newspapers, magazines, direct mail, TV, radio) because there is no cost to distribute the information to the customer. The Web is also dynamic, meaning that the marketing message can be customized to each individual customer in a way not possible in the traditional media.

Information/Entertainment Provider   An information/entertainment provider supplies visitors with usually (but not always) free information. Sites can be very broad, such as newspapers and magazines, or very focused, such as restaurant reviews or used-car prices. Most sites make money by selling advertising.

Customer Service Site   Customer service sites support existing customers by providing answers to technical questions, order status information, and news about current and future products. Since the Web is open 24 hours a day, customers often enjoy better service. Companies save money because these sites reduce the number of telephone calls to customer service staff.

Key Terms

anonymous FTP

CA*net

CERN

Common Messaging Calls (CMC)

customer service site

desktop videoconferencing

discussion groups

distribution list

domain

electronic commerce

electronic mall

electronic marketing site

electronic store

e-mail

extranet

file transfer protocol (FTP)

group support system (GSS)

groupware

home page

Hypertext Markup Language (HTML)

Hypertext Transfer Protocol (HTTP)

H.320

H.323

information/entertainment provider

Internet

Internet Mail Access Protocol (IMAP)

intranet

Lightweight Directory Access Protocol (LDAP)

listserv

Lotus Notes

message transfer agent

metasearch engine

Multipurpose Internet Mail Extension (MIME)

NCSA

netiquette

Netscape

NSFNET

Post Office Protocol (POP)

replication

search engine

Simple Mail Transfer Protocol (SMTP)

snail mail

spider

telephone tag

Telnet

Universal Resource Locator (URL)

usenet newsgroups

user agent

videoconferencing

workflow automation

World Wide Web

Web browser

Web server

webcasting

X.400

X.500

Questions

1. What is the Internet?
2. Describe the history of the Internet and the Web.
3. Who are the primary users of the Internet?
4. Describe the address structure of computers on the Internet.
5. What do the following tools enable you to do: the Web, e-mail, FTP, Telnet?
6. What is the World Wide Web? How is it different from other Internet tools?
7. Use your Web browser to connect to the page for this textbook. What interesting information did you find?
8. What are some ways for finding information on the Internet?
9. How can the Internet be used for business?
10. Will the Internet become an essential business tool like the telephone, or will it go the way of the telegraph? Discuss.
11. For what is HTTP used? What are its major parts?
12. For what is HTML used? What are its major parts?
13. Describe how a Web browser and Web server work together to send a Web page to a user.
14. What is webcasting?

15. How is e-mail useful?
16. How can you find an e-mail address?
17. Describe how e-mail user agents and message transfer agents work together to transfer mail messages.
18. What roles do SMTP, POP, and IMAP play in sending and receiving e-mail on the Internet?
19. What are the major parts of an e-mail message?
20. What is X.400 and CMC?
21. What do the X.500 and LDAP standards do, and why are they important?
22. What is FTP, and why is it useful?
23. What is Telnet, and why is it useful?
24. What is groupware?
25. Describe four types of groupware. What are the benefits and limitations of each?
26. What are usenet newsgroups? How might they help you as a student?
27. What is a listserv, and how could you use it to get information?
28. What is Lotus Notes, and how can it be used to improve productivity?
29. How can GSS improve productivity?
30. Describe two types of videoconferencing. Which do you think will be more common in five years? Why?

31. How does groupware change the way you manage in an organization?
32. Will electronic commerce have a significant effect in North America?
33. Compare and contrast an electronic store, an electronic marketing site, an information/entertainment provider, and a customer service site. In what ways are they similar and different? How do each make money?
34. What type of electronic store would you open?

Exercises

A. Search the Internet and report how many host computers are connected to it today. No one knows the exact number, so be sure to identify your sources.
B. Investigate three Internet service providers in your area. What services do they provide, and what pricing plans do they have for residential users?
C. Find two electronic stores and compare how they operate.
D. Find one information provider and one entertainment provider. Compare what they provide and how they earn money.
E. Develop a prototype of an electronic commerce site for a local business.
F. Describe how you could use groupware in your class.
G. Do the following Internet scavenger hunt:
   1. What is the URL for the *official* home page of the Dilbert cartoon?
   2. What is the URL for the home page(s) of weather services giving the forecast for Honolulu, Hawaii, and White Horse, Yukon? What is the forecast for each city for the assignment due date?
   3. What is the URL for a travel service selling tickets over the Internet? What is the lowest fare for a seven-day return trip from Toronto to Los Angeles, departing exactly three weeks from the assignment due date (on what airline)?
   4. What is the URL for an electronic bookstore, and how much does this book cost at that bookstore (ignore shipping costs)?
   5. What is the URL for an electronic store selling CDs, and how much does the CD of Al Stewart's *Between the Wars* cost (ignore shipping costs)?
   6. What is the e-mail address of *The Late Show with David Letterman*?
   7. Who made the first trans-Atlantic flight, and in what year? *Hint:* It wasn't Charles Lindbergh and the flight ended near the town of Clifden, Ireland. Be sure to identify your source.

NEXT DAY AIR SERVICE CASE STUDY

Bob Jones, manager of Sales/Marketing, recently read an article about the Internet in *Business Week*. He has raised the issue of the Internet with President Coone. Bob Jones has asked you to help him understand the ways in which the Internet could help increase the NDAS presence in both the international and domestic markets. He is also interested in ways NDAS could make effective use of e-mail, groupware, and videoconferencing in achieving increased productivity.

The two most negative comments about Jones's ideas came from Peter Browne and Les Coone. Peter Browne stated that the Fleet Maintenance Division is doing just fine as it is, and that one should not "try to fix something that isn't broken." Les Coone commented that NDAS should not "jump the gun on videoconferencing; it is too early to invest in that new technology."

Exercises

President Coone has given you four tasks:

1. Review available groupware packages and Internet capabilities as they relate to NDAS and prepare a report on the ways e-mail and groupware can be integrated into the Fleet Maintenance Division. Convinced that the maintenance supervisor's support is required for a successful installation of data communications technology in the Fleet Maintenance Division, President Coone wants you to suggest how to involve Peter Browne. The president is sure that Peter Browne will be a valuable ally for a data communications system if you can show him that it will help him make his operation more productive and efficient.

2. Investigate the potential of software such as Lotus Notes for use in the Accounts Receivable Division. President Coone also wants you to determine how Jane Van Dyne and her staff could use Notes to reduce "bad debt" expenses. He wonders if Notes would be useful to John Lawson in the Accounts Payable Division and Bob Jones in Marketing and Sales, as well.

3. Prepare a brief management summary on the essential aspects of the Internet and the World Wide Web, how they work, what they will cost, and above all, how NDAS can use them to improve its competitive edge. President Coone is particularly intrigued with the potential of the Internet, but he and the other members of management are not exactly sure what the Internet is and how it works. He is confused about the relationship between the World Wide Web and the Internet. President Coone reminds you that NDAS expects to enlarge its scope in the international market. Plans call for first offerings to be services to Britain, France, and Germany, with later expansion to South America. President Coone has heard that a number of companies have "home pages." He is unclear about home pages and HTML and wants you to be sure to discuss them in your summary. He would also like some examples of home pages used by other companies that NDAS could examine. President Coone wants you to involve Bob Jones in your work on the Internet.

4. Prepare a brief discussion on the pros and cons of videoconferencing, as well as on the cost of using videoconferencing within the NDAS organization. Based on Les Coone's comments, President Coone is skeptical of videoconferencing and wonders if there are really any advantages to using it.

CHAPTER 3

Physical Layer: Architectures, Devices and Circuits

This chapter introduces three fundamental network architectures: host-based, client-based, and client–server. It then discusses the basic hardware used in data communications networks: servers, clients, circuits, and special-purpose communication devices. One commonly used data communication device is the modem, which is discussed in Chapter 4. Other devices commonly used for communications between networks (e.g., gateways, routers) are discussed in Chapter 8.

Objectives

* Understand the differences between host-based, client-based, and client-server networks
* Become familiar with different types of servers and clients
* Understand the different types of network circuits
* Become familiar with different media
* Become familiar with front-end processors
* Understand how multiplexing works

Chapter Outline

❋❋ INTRODUCTION

As mentioned in Chapter 1, there are three fundamental hardware components in a data communication network in addition to the network software: the servers or host computers, the client computers, and the network circuits that connect them. This chapter focuses on these three components. However, before we can discuss the various types of clients, servers, and circuits, we need to discuss fundamental network architectures—the way in which the application software is divided among the clients and servers.

❋❋ NETWORK ARCHITECTURES

There are three fundamental network architectures. In *host-based networks*, the host computer performs virtually all of the work. In *client-based networks*, the client computers perform most of the work. In *client–server networks*, the work is shared between the servers and clients. The client–server architecture is likely to become the dominant network architecture of the future.

The work done by any application program can be divided into four general functions. The first is *data storage*. Most application programs require data to be stored and retrieved, whether it is a small file (such as a memo produced by a word processor) or a large database (such as an organization's accounting records). The second function is *data access logic*, the processing required to access data, which often means database queries in SQL. The third function is the *application logic*, which also can be simple or complex, depending on the application. The fourth function is the *presentation logic*, the presentation of information to the user and the acceptance of the user's commands. These four functions are the basic building blocks of any application.

Host-Based Architectures

The very first data communications networks were host-based, with the host computer (usually a central mainframe computer) performing all four functions. The clients (usually terminals) enabled users to send and receive messages to and from the host computer. The clients merely captured key strokes and sent them to the host for processing, and accepted instructions from the host on what to display (see Figure 3–1).

This very simple architecture often works very well. Application software is developed and stored on one computer and all data are on the same computer. There is one point of control, because all messages flow through the one central host. In theory, there are economies of scale, because all computer resources are centralized. We will discuss costs later.

The fundamental problem with host-based networks is that the host must process all messages. As the demands for more and more network applications grow, many host computers become overloaded and cannot quickly process all the users' demands. Prioritizing users' access becomes difficult. Response time becomes

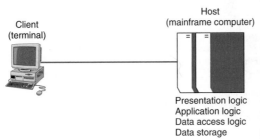

Client
(terminal)

Host
(mainframe computer)

Presentation logic
Application logic
Data access logic
Data storage

Figure 3-1 Host-based architecture.

slower, and network managers are required to spend increasingly more money to upgrade the host computer. Unfortunately, upgrades to host computers are "lumpy." That is, upgrades come in large increments and are expensive (e.g., $500,000); it is difficult to upgrade "a little."

In the late 1970s and early 1980s, intelligent terminals were developed that could perform some of the presentation function (intelligent terminals are discussed in more detail in the next section). This relieved only a little of the bottleneck, however, because the host still performed all of the processing and data storage. Hosts became somewhat less overloaded, but the network became more complex: developing applications was more difficult, and there were more points of failure.

Client-Based Architectures

In the late 1980s, there was an explosion in the use of microcomputers and microcomputer-based local area networks. Today, more than 80 percent of most organizations' total computer processing power resides on microcomputer-based LANs, not in centralized mainframe-based host computers. As this trend continues, many experts predict that by the end of the century, the host mainframe computer will contain 10 percent or less of an organization's total computing power.

Part of this expansion was fueled by a number of low-cost, highly popular applications such as word processors, spreadsheets, and presentation graphics programs. It was also fueled in part by managers' frustrations with application software on host mainframe computers. Most mainframe software is not as easy to use as microcomputer software, is far more expensive, and can take years to develop. In the late 1980s, many large organizations had application development backlogs of two to three years. That is, getting any new mainframe application program written would take years. New York City, for example, had a six-year backlog. In contrast, managers could buy microcomputer packages or develop microcomputer-based applications in a few months.

With client-based architectures, the clients are microcomputers on a local area network, and the host computer is a server on the same network. The application software on the client computers is responsible for the presentation logic, the application logic, and the data access logic; the server simply stores the data (see Figure 3-2).

Figure 3–2 Client-based architecture.

This simple architecture often works very well. However, as the demands for more and more network applications grow, the network circuits can become overloaded. The fundamental problem in client-based networks is that all data on the server must travel to the client for processing. For example, suppose the user wishes to display a list of all employees with company life insurance. All the data in the database (or all the indices) must travel from the server where the database is stored over the network circuit to the client, which then examines each record to see if it matches the data requested by the user. This can overload the network circuits, because far more data is transmitted from the server to the client than the client actually needs. If the files are very large, they may also overwhelm the power of the client computers.

Client–Server Architectures

Most organizations today are moving to client–server architectures. Client–server architectures attempt to balance the processing between the client and the server by having both do some of the logic. In these networks, the client is responsible for the presentation logic, while the server is responsible for the data access logic and data storage. The application logic may reside on the client or on the server, or it may be split between both.

Figure 3–3 shows the simplest case, with the presentation logic and application logic on the client and the data access logic and data storage on the server. In this case, the client software accepts user requests and performs the application logic that produces database requests that are transmitted to the server. The server software accepts the database requests, performs the data access logic, and transmits

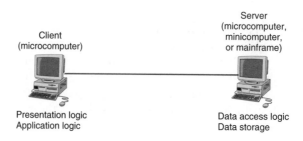

Figure 3–3 Two-tiered client–server architecture.

the results to the client. The client software accepts the results and presents them to the user.

For example, if the user requests a list of all employees with company life insurance, the client would accept the request, format it so that it could be understood by the server, and transmit it to the server. Upon receiving the request, the server searches the database for all requested records and then transmits only the matching records to the client, which would then present them to the user. The same would be true for database updates; the client accepts the request and sends it to the server. The server processes the update and responds (either accepting the update or explaining why not) to the client, which displays it to the user.

Costs and Benefits of Client–Server Architectures

Client–server architectures have some important benefits compared to host-based architectures. First and foremost, they are scalable. That means it is easy to increase or decrease the storage and processing capabilities of the servers. If one server becomes overloaded, you simply add another server and move some of the application logic or data storage to it. The cost to upgrade is much more gradual and you can upgrade in smaller steps (e.g., $3,000) rather than spending hundreds of thousands to upgrade a mainframe host.

Client–server architectures can support many different types of clients and servers. You are not locked into one vendor, as is often the case in host-based networks. Likewise, it is possible to connect computers that use different operating systems so that users can choose which type of computer they prefer (e.g., combining both IBM microcomputers and Apple Macintoshes on the same network). Some types of computers and operating systems are better suited to different tasks (e.g., transaction processing, real-time video, mathematical processing). Client–server architectures allow you to match the needs of individual applications to different types of computers to maximize performance.

Finally, because no single host computer supports all the applications, the network is generally more reliable. There is no central point of failure that will halt the entire network if it fails, as there is in a host-based network. If any one server fails in a client–server network, the network can continue to function using all the other servers (but, of course, any applications that require the failed server will not function).

Client–server networks also have some critical limitations, the most important of which is their complexity. All applications in a client–server network have two parts, the software on the client, and the software on the server. Writing this software is more complicated than writing the traditional all-in-one software used in host-based networks. Programmers often need to learn new programming languages and new programming techniques, which requires retraining.

Even updating the network with a new version of the software is more complicated. In a host-based network, there is one place in which application software is stored; to update the software, you simply replace it there. With client–server networks, you must update all clients and all servers. For example, suppose you want to add a new server and move some existing applications from the old server to the new one. All application software on all clients that send messages to the application on the old server must now be changed to send to the new server. Although this is not conceptually difficult, it can be an administrative nightmare.

Much of the debate between host-based and client–server networks has centered on cost. One of the great claims of host-based networks in the 1980s was that they provided economies of scale. Manufacturers of big mainframes claimed that it was cheaper to provide computer services on one big mainframe than on a set of smaller computers. The microcomputer revolution changed this. Over the past 20 years, the costs of microcomputers have continued to drop, while their performance has increased significantly. Today, microcomputer hardware is more than 1000 times cheaper than mainframe hardware for the same amount of computing power.

With cost differences like these, it is easy to see why there has been a sudden rush to microcomputer-based client–server networks. The problem with these cost comparisons is that they overlook the increased complexity associated with developing application software for client–server networks. Several surveys have attempted to discover the cost for software development and maintenance in client–server networks. The truth is, no one really knows, because we do not have enough long-term experience with them. Most experts believe that it costs four to five times more to develop and maintain application software for client–server networks than it does for host-based networks. As more companies gain experience with client–server applications, as new products are developed and refined, and as standards mature, these costs probably will decrease.

One of the strengths of client–server networks is that they enable software and hardware from different vendors to be used together. But this is also one of their disadvantages, because it can be difficult to get software from different vendors to work together. One solution to this problem is *middleware*, software that sits between the application software on the client and the application software on the

---

Management Focus: *Shutting Down a Mainframe*

I turned off my first mainframe at 1:11 P.M. on March 2, 1995. It was a small mainframe: an IBM 4381 Model 13. It had 16 megabytes of RAM and 7.5 gigabytes of disk space. Because it cost more than $250,000 per year to operate, it had reached the end of its cost-effective life. It was replaced by two microcomputers, one of which had more RAM and disk space than the 4381 had. It cost about as much to pay someone to haul the 4381 away as it did to buy one of the replacement microcomputers.

What made the moment of shutdown a sad one was that I was surrounded by people who had spent most of their careers caring for it—people who now needed to learn an entirely new set of computer and network systems and an entirely new approach to application development, people late in their careers, for whom the transition might prove as difficult as it had for the 4381.

Source: InfoWorld (April 17, 1995).

server. Middleware does two things. First, it provides a standard way of communicating that can translate between software from different vendors. Many middleware tools began as translation utilities that enabled messages sent from a specific client tool to be translated into a form understood by a specific server tool.

The second function of middleware is to manage the message transfer from clients to servers (and vice versa) so that clients need not know the specific server that contains the application's data. The application software on the client sends all messages to the middleware, which forwards them to the correct server. The application software on the client is therefore protected from any changes in the physical network. If the network layout changes (e.g., a new server is added), only the middleware must be updated.

There are literally dozens of standards for middleware, each of which is supported by different vendors, and each of which provides different functions. Two of the most important standards are Distributed Computing Environment (DCE) and Common Object Request Broker Architecture (CORBA). Both of these standards cover virtually all aspects of the client–server architecture, but are quite different. Any client or server software that conforms to one of these standards can communicate with any other software that conforms to the same standard. Another important standard is Open Database Connectivity (ODBC), which provides a standard for data access logic.

Two-Tier, Three-Tier, and N-Tier Architectures

There are many ways in which the application logic can be partitioned between the client and the server. The example in Figure 3–3 is one of the most common. In this case, the server is responsible for the data and the client is responsible for the application and presentation. This is called a *two-tiered architecture*, because it uses only two sets of computers, one client and one server.

A *three-tiered architecture* uses three sets of computers, as shown in Figure 3–4. In this case, the software on the client computer is responsible for presentation logic, an application server(s) is responsible for the application logic, and a separate database server(s) is responsible for the data access logic and data storage.

An *n-tiered architecture* uses more than three sets of computers. In this case, the client is responsible for presentation, a database server(s) is responsible for the data access logic and data storage, and the application logic is spread across two or more

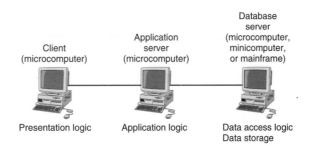

Figure 3–4 Three-tiered client–server architecture.

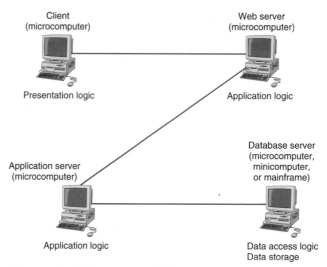

Figure 3–5 The *n*-tiered client–server architecture.

different sets of servers. Figure 3–5 shows an example of an *n*-tiered architecture of a groupware product called TCBWorks, developed at The University of Georgia (http://tcbworks.cba.uga.edu). TCBWorks has four major components. The first is the Web browser on the client computer that a user uses to access the system and enter commands (presentation logic). The second component is a Web server that responds to the user's requests, either by providing HTML pages and graphics (application logic), or by sending the request to the third component, a set of 28 C programs that perform various functions such as adding comments or voting (application logic). The fourth component is a database server that stores all the data (data access logic and data storage). Each of these four components is separate, making it easy to spread the different components on different servers, and to partition the application logic on two different servers.

The primary advantage of an *n*-tiered client–server architecture compared to a two-tiered architecture (or a three-tiered to a two-tiered) is that it separates out the processing that occurs to better balance the load on the different servers; it is more "scalable." In Figure 3–5, we have three separate servers, which provides more power than if we had used a two-tiered architecture with only one server. If we discover that the application server is too heavily loaded, we can simply replace it with a more powerful server, or even put in two application servers. Conversely, if we discover the database server is under-used, we could put data from another application on it.

There are two primary disadvantages to an *n*-tiered architecture compared to a two-tiered architecture (or a three-tiered to a two-tiered). First, it puts a greater load on the network. If you compare Figures 3–3, 3–4, and 3–5, you will see that the *n*-tiered model requires more communication among the servers; it generates more network traffic, so you need a higher capacity network. Second, it is much

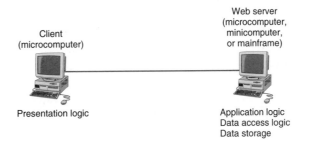

Figure 3–6 The typical two-tiered "thin client" architecture of the Web.

Client (microcomputer)

Presentation logic

Web server (microcomputer, minicomputer, or mainframe)

Application logic
Data access logic
Data storage

more difficult to program and test software in n-tiered architectures because more devices have to communicate to complete a user's transaction.

Thin Clients versus Fat Clients

Another way of classifying client–server architectures is by examining how much of the application logic is placed on the client computer. A *thin client* approach places little or no application logic on the client (e.g., Figure 3–5), while a *fat client* approach places all or almost all of the application logic on the client (e.g., Figure 3–3). There is no direct relationship between thin and fat clients and two-, three- and n-tiered architectures. For example, Figure 3–6 shows a typical Web architecture: a two-tiered architecture with a thin-client. One of the biggest forces favoring thin clients is the Web. More and more application systems are being written to use a Web browser as the client software.

Thin clients are much easier to manage. If an application changes, only the server with the application logic needs to be updated. With a fat client, the software on all of the clients would need to be updated. Conceptually, this is a simple task; one simply copies the new files to the hundreds of affected client computers. In practice, it can be a very difficult task.

✷ ✷ SERVERS

A computer's suitability to serve as the server or host for an online, real-time data communication network depends on both its own capabilities and the capabilities of its attached hardware. Many different types of computers can be used for this purpose, provided the ancillary hardware can handle the tasks for which the host computer is inefficient. The characteristics that make a computer good for "number crunching" may not make it suitable for data communications. Data communications requires fast responses to many short messages that arrive at virtually the same time. A computer whose hardware or software makes this kind of operation too clumsy does not perform well in the data communication environment. There are three typical types of hosts: mainframe computers, minicomputers, and microcomputers.

Management Focus: *Power Company Juices Up Its Customer Service*

The Washington Water Power Company (WWP) wanted to write new applications and modify its old ones to better reflect its business processes and to improve its efficiency. However, the organization relied on a host-based mainframe environment that made the goals either impossible or so difficult that the information systems (IS) department was years behind on implementing changes requested by managers.

WWP decided to scrap its old COBOL-based, mainframe customer service application in favor of client–server software that runs partly on the mainframe and partly on a new Novell LAN. The new system cost $16.5 million, but offers numerous benefits, including saving $500,000 per year in operating costs. The system is also portable, so WWP will be able to use it, should the utility decide to scrap the main-

frame altogether or move to different client hardware. It is also easy to program, so new applications can be written quickly or old ones easily modified.

The mainframe was kept because it better suited WWP's nightly large batch process than PC-based servers. Also, storing more than 20 gigabytes of data was impractical on anything other than the mainframe. Without a compelling reason to switch, WWP was eager to recoup its investment in mainframe storage arrays.

The new system solves many problems and inconveniences. When WWP and Electronic Data Systems Corp. (EDS) designed it, they made sure that all the applications fit together. The new system looks like one application to the user, and accesses one database.

Source: InfoWorld (February 6, 1995).

A *mainframe* is a very large, general-purpose computer usually costing millions of dollars. It is capable of performing many simultaneous functions. It is used for both data communications and application processing, but its emphasis is on the online, real-time data communication portion of the system.

A second type of server is a *minicomputer,* which is a large, general-purpose computer costing hundreds of thousands of dollars that is used both in data communications and application processing. Minicomputers are often used in manufacturing for process control and as database client–server networks.

A third type of server is a *microcomputer.* This type of server can range from a small microcomputer similar to a desktop one you might use, to a microcomputer costing $50,000 or more. Most microcomputer servers are dedicated to data communications and perform no other function.

✳✳ CLIENTS

The client, which is the input/output hardware device at the user's end of a communication circuit, probably is the one piece of equipment with which you are most familiar. There are four major categories of clients: terminals, microcomputers/ workstations, network computers, and special-purpose terminals.

When online transaction processing systems became common in the 1970s, so did the use of terminals. The very first terminals were *dumb terminals*, so named because they do not participate in the processing of the data they display. These terminals have the bare minimum required to operate as input and output devices, simply translating messages from the user to the communications circuit but doing nothing more. In most cases, when a character is typed, the terminal immediately transmits the character through the data communications circuit to the host. Every keystroke pressed on a dumb terminal has to be processed by the host computer, so simple activities—such as pressing the up arrow key or tab key to move the cursor around the screen—require processing time on the host computer. The primary problem with dumb terminals is that they place an immense burden on the host computer. But they are relatively cheap.

Intelligent terminals were developed to reduce these processing demands. An intelligent terminal has an internal memory and a built-in, programmable microprocessor chip. Many simple processing functions, such as moving the cursor or displaying certain words in different colors, are done by the terminal, thus saving processing time on the host. Intelligent terminals also typically send messages as entire blocks rather than one letter at a time, further saving processing time at the host. The downside, however, is that intelligent terminals are more expensive.

Microcomputers are the most common type of client today. Microcomputers are used for such functions as word processing, graphics, and spreadsheets, in addition to network access.

Management Focus: *Communications at Avis*

One major application for large national and international communication networks is the rental of automobiles. Avis Rent-A-Car was the first major company to develop an online real-time rental car network. This network interconnects the major locations where automobiles are rented, picked up, and returned.

A rental car network is quite similar to an airline network because it records rental agreements with people who rent the cars, calculates the cost and mileage used, keeps track of dates when cars must be returned, and performs other general accounting functions.

Avis uses handheld computer terminals that enable service representatives to check in returning cars almost before customers can unbuckle their seat belts. The Avis service, called Roving Rapid Return, allows customers to get a receipt at their car without having to enter the rental agency building, stand in line, and wait while someone processes the rental contract.

When a car enters the Avis lot a service representative enters the Avis registration number on the car's rear window into one of the handheld terminals. The terminal, which is linked locally to the Avis worldwide network by FM radio, retrieves the driver's name and rental information from a central mainframe database. It displays the customer's name so the service representative can use it while obtaining the car's odometer reading and gas tank level. Once that information has been entered, the mainframe totals the customer's bill and instructs the terminal's printer to produce a receipt. The customer can leave as soon as the receipt is printed.

Workstations are more powerful computers that are designed for use in more technical applications such as mathematical modeling, computer-assisted design (CAD), and intensive programming. As microcomputers begin to use more powerful microprocessor chips (Pentium, Power PC, and beyond), they may become as powerful as today's workstations.

A *network computer* is a new type of computer designed primarily as a thin client for use on the Internet (or an intranet or extranet). It is designed to communicate using Web-based standards (e.g., HTTP, HTML, Java) and videoconferencing standards (e.g., H.323). However, it has no hard disk, so it has only limited functionality.

Some terminals are designed for special purposes. One of the most common is a *transaction terminal*, designed to support certain business transactions. A familiar example is the automated teller machine (ATM) used by banking institutions for cash dispensing and related functions. Other transaction terminals are point-of-sale terminals in a supermarket; these enter charges directly from the supermarket to your credit card or bank account.

✳ ✳ CIRCUITS

Network Configuration

Network configuration is the basic physical layout of the network. There are two fundamental network configurations: point-to-point and multipoint. In practice, most complex computer networks have many circuits, some of which are point-to-point and some of which are multipoint.

Figure 3–7 illustrates a *point-to-point configuration*, which is so named because it goes from one point to another (e.g., one computer to another computer). These circuits sometimes are called *dedicated circuits* because they are dedicated to the use of these two computers. This type of configuration is used when the computers generate enough data to fill the capacity of the communication circuit. When an organization builds a network using point-to-point circuits, each computer has its own circuit running from itself to the other computers. This can get very expensive, particularly if there is some distance between the computers.

Figure 3–8 shows a *multipoint configuration* (also called a *shared circuit*). In this configuration, many computers are connected on the same circuit. This means that each must share the circuit with the others, much like a party line in telephone

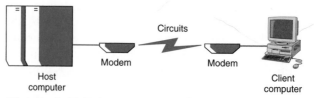

Figure 3–7 Point-to-point configuration.

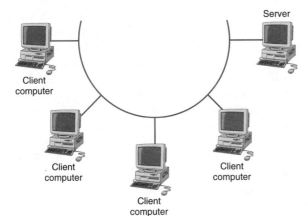

Figure 3–8 Multipoint configuration.

communications. The disadvantage is that only one computer can use the circuit at a time so when one computer is sending or receiving data, all others must wait. The advantage of multipoint circuits is that they reduce the amount of cable required and typically use the available communication circuit more efficiently. Imagine the amount of cable required if the network in Figure 3–8 was designed with separate point-to-point circuits. Multipoint configurations are cheaper than point-to-point configurations. Thus, multipoint configurations typically are used when each computer does not need to continuously use the entire capacity of the circuit, or when building point-to-point circuits is too expensive.

Data Flow

Circuits can be designed to permit data to flow in one direction or in both directions. Actually, there are three ways to transmit: simplex, half duplex, and full duplex (see Figure 3–9).

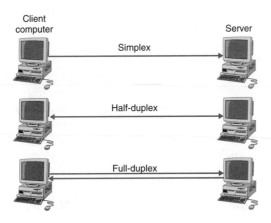

Figure 3–9 Simplex, half-duplex, and full-duplex transmissions.

Simplex is one-way transmission, such as that in radio or TV transmission.

Half duplex is two-way transmission, but you can transmit in only one direction at a time. A half-duplex communication link is similar to a walkie-talkie link; only one computer can transmit at a time. Computers use control signals to negotiate which will send and which will receive data. The amount of time half-duplex communication takes to switch between sending and receiving is called *turnaround time* (also called *retrain time* or *reclocking time*). The turnaround time for a specific circuit can be obtained from its technical specifications (often between 20 to 50 milliseconds). Europeans use the term *simplex circuit* to mean a half-duplex circuit.

With *full-duplex transmission*, you can transmit in both directions simultaneously, with no turnaround time.

How do you choose which data flow method to use? Obviously, one factor is the application. If data only ever need to flow in one direction (e.g., from a remote sensor to a host computer), then simplex is probably the best choice. In most cases, however, data must flow in both directions.

The initial temptation is to presume that a full-duplex channel is best; however, each circuit only has so much capacity to carry data. Creating a full-duplex circuit means that the available capacity in the circuit is divided—half in one direction and half in the other. In some cases, it makes more sense to build a set of simplex circuits in the same way a set of one-way streets can speed traffic. In other cases, a half-duplex circuit may work best. For example, terminals connected to mainframes often transmit data to the host, wait for a reply, transmit more data, and so on in a turn-taking process. Usually traffic does not need to flow in both directions simultaneously, so such a traffic pattern is ideally suited to half-duplex circuits.

Technical Focus: Circuit Terminology

Medium   The medium is the matter or substance that carries a message from one point to another. The medium might be copper wires, a thin strand of glass, or air for a satellite transmission.

Circuit   A circuit is simply the path over which data move. It can use a medium such as copper wire, satellite, or a combination of the two. Note the contrast between circuit, which is a path, and medium, which is the material over which the message travels.

Link   A link is the same as a circuit.

Line   This term frequently is used interchangeably with circuit, but a line implies a physical connection between two points, such as copper wire.

Channel   This term can be confusing because common usage allows for two definitions. In the first, *channel* is used interchangeably with *circuit*, such as when there is a communication channel or a communication circuit between two points. In the second, channel means the subdivision of a circuit. For example, a company that has a communication circuit between Los Angeles and New York subdivides it into four channels so four different messages can be transmitted simultaneously over a single circuit.

Communication Media

The *medium* (or media, if there is more than one) is the matter or substance that carries the voice or data transmission. Many different types of transmission media are currently in use, such as copper (wire), glass or plastic (fiber optic cable), or air (radio, infrared, microwave, or satellite). There are two basic types of media. *Guided media* are those in which the message flows through a physical media such as a twisted-pair wire, coaxial cable, or fiber optic cable; the media "guides" the signal. *Radiated media* are those in which the message is broadcast through the air, such as infrared, microwave, or satellite.

In many cases, the circuits used in wide area networks are provided by the various common carriers who sell usage of them to the public. We call the circuits sold by the common carriers *communication services.* Chapter 9 describes specific services available in North America. The following sections describe the medium and the basic characteristics of each circuit type, in the event you were establishing your own physical network. Chapter 9 describes how the circuits are packaged and marketed for purchase or lease from a common carrier. If your organization has leased a circuit from a common carrier, you are probably less interested in the media used, and more interested in whether the speed, cost, and reliability of the circuit meets your needs.

Guided Media

One of the most commonly used types of guided media is *twisted-pair cable*, insulated pairs of wires that can be packed quite close together (see Figure 3–10). Bundles of several thousand wire pairs are placed under city streets and in large buildings. Twisted-pair wires usually are twisted to minimize the electromagnetic interference between one pair and any other pair in the bundle. Your house or apartment probably has at least two sets of twisted-pair wires (i.e., four wires) from it to the telephone company network. One pair is used to connect your telephone; the other pair is a spare that can be used for a second telephone line. Wire cables are being replaced by more efficient transmission media, such as coaxial cable, micro-

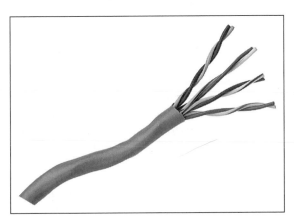

Figure 3–10 Twisted pair wire.

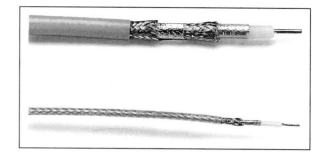

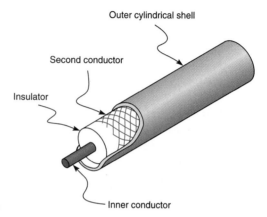

Figure 3-11 Coaxial cables. Thinnet and Thicknet Ethernet cables (top) and cross-sectional view (bottom).

wave, satellite, or optical fibers. Twisted-pair wires used in LANs are discussed in Chapter 7.

Coaxial cable is another type of commonly used guided media (see Figure 3-11). Coaxial cable has a copper core (the inner conductor) with an outer cylindrical shell for insulation. The outer shield, just under the shell, is the second conductor. Coaxial cables have very little distortion and are less prone to interference. They tend to have low error rates. Coaxial cables also are discussed Chapter 7.

Twisted-pair and coaxial cable are the most common types of guided media. However, a relatively new medium, fiber optics, is becoming much more widely used. Instead of carrying telecommunication signals in the traditional electrical form, this technology utilizes high-speed streams of light pulses from lasers or LEDs (light-emitting diodes) that carry information inside hair-thin strands of glass or plastic called optical fibers. Plastic is being used less, however, because glass can be made into a purer product, enabling the signal to be transmitted over a greater distance. Figure 3-12 shows a fiber optic cable and depicts the optical core, the cladding, and how light rays travel in optical fibers.

The earliest fiber optic systems were multimode, meaning that the light could

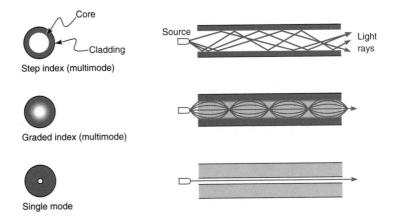

Figure 3-12 Fiber optic cable.

reflect inside the cable at many different angles. Multimode cables are plagued by excessive signal weakening (attenuation) and dispersion (spreading of the signal). *Single-mode* fiber optic cables transmit a single direct beam of light through a cable that ensures the light only reflects in one pattern, in part because the core diameter has been reduced from 50 microns to about 8 to 10 microns. This smaller diameter core allows the fiber to send a more concentrated light beam, resulting in faster data transmission speeds.

Management Focus: New Brunswick Turns on the Fiber

One of the most intensive per-capita users of fiber optic technologies is New Brunswick. New Brunswick occupies a land mass the size of Maine but has only about 750,000 people, most of whom (with the exception of the capital city of Fredericton) live close to the coast or the U.S. border.

Since 1986, New Brunswick Telephone and its primary competitor, Fundy Telecom, have invested hundreds of millions of dollars in fiber optic cable throughout their telephone and data communication networks (see Figure 3–13). Most of the fiber backbone networks operate at 2.5 Gbps (2.5 billion bits per second), with several new 10 Gbps circuits now being tested. More than 75 percent of residential and business customers are within two miles of a

fiber optic cable. Several test projects are underway to run fiber into homes.

This drive for fiber has been fueled by two factors. First, New Brunswick is the main east–west link for networks between central Canada and eastern Canada. Second, New Brunswick, Canada's only officially bilingual province, has been extremely successful in attracting call centers that provide 24-hour telephone support for customers of major computer and technology companies in Canada and the United States. These call centers require many telephone lines and usually a lot of data communication capacity.

Source: "Fiber Turns Provincial in New Brunswick," *Lightware* (June 1997).

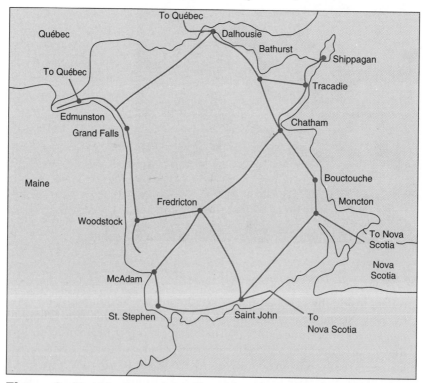

Figure 3–13 New Brunswick's fiber-optic backbone network.

Fiber optic technology is a revolutionary departure from the traditional message-carrying systems of copper wires. One of the main advantages of fiber optics is that it can carry huge amounts of information at extremely fast data rates which makes it ideal for the simultaneous transmission of voice, data, and image signals. In most cases, fiber optic cable works better under harsh environmental conditions than its metallic counterparts because it is not as fragile or brittle, and it is more resistant to corrosion than copper. Also, in case of fire, an optical fiber can withstand higher temperatures than copper wire. Even when the outside jacket surrounding the optical fiber has melted, a fiber optic system still can be used.

Radiated Media

One of the most commonly used forms of radiated media is *radio* (usually just called *wireless*). Radio data transmission uses the same basic principles as standard radio transmission. Each device or computer on the network has a radio receiver/transmitter on a specific frequency range that does not interfere with commercial radio stations. The transmitters are very low power, designed to transmit a signal up to 500 feet. They are often built into portable or handheld computers.

Infrared transmission uses low-frequency light waves (below the visible spectrum) to carry the data through the air on a direct line-of-sight path between two points. This technology is similar to the technology used in infrared TV remote controls. It is prone to interference, particularly from heavy rain, smoke, and fog that obscure the light transmission.

Infrared transmitters are quite small but are seldom used for regular communication among portable or handheld computers because of their line-of-sight transmission requirements. (However, a version of infrared has also been adopted by some portable microcomputer manufacturers to transfer data between portable computers and desktop computers at distances of less than three feet.) Infrared is not very common, but it is sometimes used to transmit data from building to building.

A *microwave* is an extremely high-frequency radio communication beam that is transmitted over a direct line-of-sight path between any two points. As its name implies, a microwave signal is an extremely short wavelength, thus the word *microwave*. Microwave radio transmissions perform the same functions as cables. For example, Point *A* communicates with Point *B* via a through-the-air microwave transmission path, instead of a copper wire cable. Because microwave signals approach the frequency of visible light waves, they exhibit the same characteristics as light waves, such as reflection, focusing, or refraction. As with visible light waves, microwave signals can be focused into narrow, powerful beams that can be projected over long distances. Just as a parabolic reflector focuses a searchlight into a beam, a parabolic reflector also focuses a high-frequency microwave into a narrow beam. As the distance between communication points increases, towers are used to elevate the radio antennas to account for the Earth's curvature and maintain a clear line-of-sight path between the two parabolic reflectors.

Technology Focus: *Wireless Communications at Yankee Stadium*

Food service operations at Yankee Stadium run more smoothly, thanks to a new wireless data communications system (see Figure 3–14).

Employees take orders from the seats using a handheld terminal. This terminal broadcasts a radio signal that is received by one of the three radio base stations located behind home plate, first base, and third base. These base stations are connected via twisted-pair cable to a wireless network controller that integrates the messages from the three base stations and directs them to the other network components.

The controller directs the orders to one of the three kitchens on twisted-pair cabling, where they are printed on one of twelve small receipt printers. The order is then prepared and sent to the customer.

A network server in the main office is connected to network controller via twisted pair. The server then records transactions for accounting purposes, and also provides access to a credit card authorization service via a modem and outside telephone line.

Source: "Food Service Without Missing the Game," *Network Computing* (October 1, 1996).

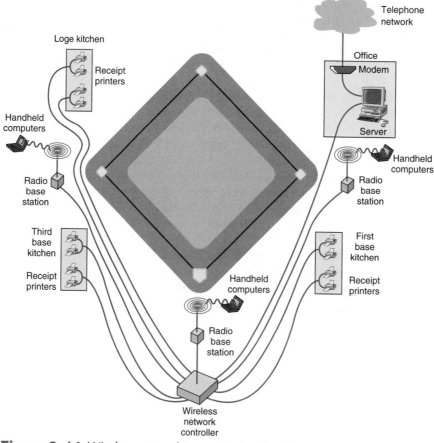

Figure 3–14 Wireless networking at Yankee Stadium.

This transmission medium is typically used for long-distance data or voice transmission. It does not require the laying of any cable, because long-distance antennas with microwave repeater stations can be placed approximately 25 to 50 miles apart. A typical long-distance antenna might be 10 feet wide, although over shorter distances in the inner cities, the dish antennas might be less than 2 feet in diameter. Larger cities are becoming congested. So many microwave dish antennas have been installed that they interfere with each other, and the air waves are saturated. This problem will force future users to seek alternative transmission media, such as satellite or optical fiber links.

Transmission via *satellite* is similar to transmission via microwave except, instead of transmitting to another nearby microwave dish antenna, it transmits to a satellite 500 to 22,300 miles in space. Figure 3–15 depicts a geosynchronous satellite—*geosynchronous* means that the satellite remains stationary over one point on the Earth.

One disadvantage of satellite transmission is the delay that occurs because the signal has to travel into space and back to Earth (*propagation delay*). For half-duplex transmission, the signal propagation delay is approximately 0.5 second for the round trip. This is because the message has to travel from the sending ground station to the satellite, and then from the satellite to the receiving ground station. In addition, the acknowledgment that the message was received without errors must do the reverse, going from receiving ground station to the satellite and from the satellite to the sending ground station. This covers four links of 22,300 miles each, and four times 22,300 divided by 186,000 equals 0.48 second. (Microwaves travel at

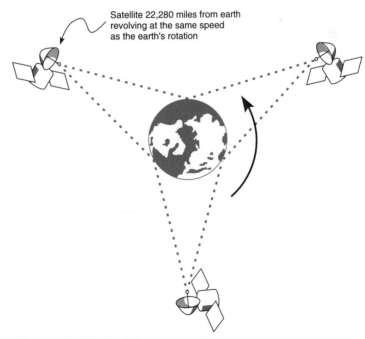

Satellite 22,280 miles from earth
revolving at the same speed
as the earth's rotation

Figure 3–15 Satellites in operation.

186,000 miles per second.) Moreover, there may be a further delay as the circuits from the ground station to the receiver go through ground-based circuits. The delay is controlled by common carriers to avoid disrupting voice telephone conversation. In data communications, however, this delay can prove difficult.

One of the problems associated with some types of satellite transmission is *raindrop attenuation*. This problem occurs because some satellite transmission waves at the high of the spectrum are so short that they can be absorbed by raindrops. It is not a major problem, but engineers need to work around it.

Management Focus: Satellite Communications Improve Performance

Boyle Transportation hauls hazardous materials nationwide for both commercial customers and the government, particularly the Department of Defense. The Department of Defense recently mandated that hazardous materials contractors use mobile communications systems with up-to-the-minute monitoring when hauling the department's hazardous cargoes.

After looking at the alternatives, Boyle realized that it would have to build its own system. Boyle needed a relational database at its operations center that contained information about customers, pickups, deliveries, truck location, and truck operating status. Data is distributed from this database via satellite to an antenna on each truck. Now, at any time, Boyle can notify the designated truck to make a new pickup via the bi-directional satellite link, and record the truck's acknowledgment.

Each truck contains a mobile data terminal connected to the satellite network. Each driver uses a keyboard to enter information, which transmits the location of the truck. This satellite data is received by the main offices via a leased line from the satellite Earth station.

This system increased productivity by an astounding 80 percent over two years, while administration costs only increased by 20 percent.

Ku-band satellites use waves that are so short they can be caught and concentrated in much smaller dish antennas, called *very small aperture terminals (VSATs)*, that can be installed on virtually any building (or vehicle). A typical Ku-band satellite network provides either one-way or full-duplex communications among VSATs installed at a large number of remote branch offices and a larger Earth dish or "hub" installed at a central site.

These large Earth dish hubs can cost as much as several hundred thousand dollars. Companies such as Tymnet and AT&T Communications offer shared services to customers. This means users only have to buy inexpensive VSATs instead of a significantly more expensive central hub dish. To put this cost in perspective, you can lease one-tenth of a satellite transponder for less than $10,000 per month. This portion of a transponder can support a 120-node full duplex network. (Transponders in the satellite receive the incoming signals and retransmit them back to Earth.)

In late 1994, RCA introduced a direct broadcast satellite (DBS) system that enables homeowners or businesses to install 18-inch Ku-band VSATs to receive satellite broadcasts for about $500. DBS lets owners receive more than 150 TV channels of higher-quality video and audio than traditional cable TV. The real potential for

DBS lies not only in the replacement of cable TV, but with the coming integration of video, voice, and data, as another high-speed circuit into the home and office.

Media Selection

Which media are best? It is hard to say, particularly when manufacturers continue to improve various media products. Several factors are important in selecting media, as Figure 3–16 summarizes.

* The *type of network* is one major consideration. Some media are only used for wide area networks (microwaves and satellite), while others typically are not (twisted pair, coaxial cable, radio, and infrared)—although we should note that some old WAN networks still use twisted pair. Fiber optic cable is unique in that it can be used for virtually any type of network.

* *Cost* is always a factor in any business decision. Costs are always changing as new technologies are developed and as competition among vendors drives prices down. Among the guided media, twisted-pair wire is generally the cheapest, coaxial cable is somewhat more expensive, and fiber optic cable is the most expensive. The costs of the radiated media are generally driven more by distance than any other factor. For very short distances (several hundred meters), radio and infrared are the cheapest; for moderate distances (several hundred miles), microwave is cheapest; and for long distances, satellite is cheapest.

* *Transmission distance* is a related factor. Twisted-pair wire, coaxial cable, infrared, and radio can only transmit data a short distance before the signal must be regenerated. Twisted pair and radio typically can transmit from 100 to 300 meters, and coaxial cable and infrared typically from 200 to 500 meters. Fiber optic cable can transmit up to 75 miles, with new types of fiber optic cable expected to reach more than 600 miles.

* *Security* is primarily determined by whether the media is guided or radiated. Radiated media (radio, infrared, microwave, and satellite) are the least secure because their signals are easily intercepted. Guided media (twisted pair, coaxial, and fiber optics) are more secure, with fiber optics being the most secure.

* *Error rates* are also important. Radiated media are most susceptible to interference and thus have the highest error rates. Among the guided media, fiber optic cable provides the lowest error rates, coaxial cable the next best, and twisted pair the worst—although twisted pair is generally better than the radiated media.

* *Transmission speeds* vary greatly among the different media. It is difficult to quote specific speeds for different media because transmission speeds are constantly improving, and because they vary within the same type of media depending on the specific type of cable and the vendor. In general, both twisted-pair and coaxial cable can provide data rates from 1 to 100 Mbps (one million bits per second), while fiber optic cable ranges from 100 Mbps to 10 Gbps (10 billion bits per second). Radio and infrared generally provide 1 to 4 Mbps, while microwave and satellite range from 20 to 50 Mbps.

Guided Media						
Media	Network Type	Cost	Transmission Distance	Security	Error Rates	Speed
Twisted Pair	LAN	Low	Short	Good	Low	Low–high
Coaxial Cable	LAN	Moderate	Short	Good	Low	Low–high
Fiber Optics	any	High	Moderate–long	Very Good	Very Low	High–very high

Radiated Media						
Media	Network Type	Cost	Transmission Distance	Security	Error Rates	Speed
Radio	LAN	Low	Short	Poor	Moderate	Low
Infrared	LAN, BN	Low	Short	Poor	Moderate	Low
Microwave	WAN	Moderate	Long	Poor	Low–moderate	Moderate
Satellite	WAN	Moderate	Long	Poor	Low–moderate	Moderate

Figure 3–16 Media summary

** SPECIAL PURPOSE COMMUNICATION DEVICES

In this section, we discuss two categories of communication devices that do specific things as part of the communication network. Front-end processors perform certain network functions for a host computer so that the host does not need to spend as much time managing the network. *Multiplexers* break one high-speed communication circuit into several lower-speed circuits so that many different devices can simultaneously use it. Multiplexers can also combine several low-speed circuits into one high-speed circuit. Many other devices such as gateways, routers, and switches perform special functions for backbone networks. These are discussed in Chapter 8.

Front-End Processors (FEP)

In general, most large mainframe computers that act as host computers for large networks are loaded with heavy application processing demands; they have very little spare processing capacity to perform data communications functions. Where these data communications functions place a heavy demand on the host computer, there is considerable pressure to move them onto special-purpose devices. This increases the efficiency of the network because each of these devices can be designed specifically to meet assigned tasks. Often, it is cheaper to buy several special-purpose devices than to upgrade the host computer. Figure 3–17 is an example of this.

One key device in this movement is the *front-end processor (FEP)*. An FEP can take two forms. The first is a nonprogrammable, hard-wired, communication control unit designed by the computer manufacturer to perform specific communi-

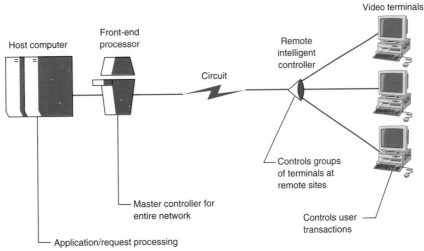

Figure 3–17 Downline network control.

cations services for one specific type of mainframe. The second form is a general-purpose minicomputer or microcomputer that can handle some or all the communication activities for many types of computers and can even perform some application layer processing, as well.

The primary application of the FEP is to serve as the interface between the host computer and the data communication network with its hundreds or even thousands of terminals or microcomputers. An FEP performs all the functions associated with the data link layer described in Chapter 5 (controlling access to the circuit, formatting messages to mark their beginning and end, and performing error control). Some FEPs also perform many of the functions associated with the network layer described in Chapter 6 (addressing, routing messages to the right computers, and breaking long messages into smaller packets). In some cases, FEPs translate between different communication protocols used by different devices.

Many of the more powerful front-end processors can do *message processing.* For example, the processor might receive inquiry messages from remote terminals, process the messages to determine the specific information required, retrieve the information from an attached disk, and send it back to the inquiring terminals without involving the host computer. In networks of this type, application-oriented processing is as important as message receipt and transmission.

Intelligent controllers are scaled-down FEPs. They perform the same function for the FEP that the FEP does for the host—they offload some of communications processing from the FEP, usually some of the data link layer functions. *Remote intelligent controllers* (also called *intelligent terminal controllers*) reside at the far end of a communication circuit and control 4 to 32 terminals. They are used because they reduce the transmission costs between the terminals and the host computer, and because they reduce the processing on the host or FEP. Figure 3–17 also shows a remote intelligent controller.

Multiplexers

A multiplexer puts two or more simultaneous transmissions on a single communication circuit. Multiplexing a voice telephone call means that two or more separate conversations are sent simultaneously over one communication circuit between two cities. Multiplexing a data communication network means that two or more messages are sent simultaneously over one communication circuit. In general, no person or device is aware of the multiplexer; it is "transparent." When the circuit is multiplexed at one end and demultiplexed at the other, each user's terminal or microcomputer thinks it has its own separate connection to the host computer.

Multiplexing usually is done in multiples of four (e.g., 4, 8, 16, and 32). Figure 3–18 shows a typical four-level multiplexed circuit. Note that two multiplexers are needed for each circuit; one to combine the four original circuits into the one multiplexed circuit and one to separate them back into the four separate circuits.

Generally speaking, the multiplexed circuit must have the same capacity as the sum of the circuits it combines. For example, if each of the four terminals in Figure 3–18 transmits at 9600 bits per second, then the multiplexed circuit must transmit at $4 \times 9600 = 38,400$ bits per second.

The primary benefit of multiplexing is to save money. Multiplexers reduce the amount of cable or the number of network circuits that must be installed. For example, if we did not use multiplexers in Figure 3–18, we would need to run four separate circuits from the terminals to the host computer. If the terminals were located close to the host, this would be inexpensive. However, if they were located several miles away, the extra costs could be substantial.

There are three major types of multiplexers: frequency division multiplexers (FDM), time division multiplexers (TDM), and statistical time division multiplexers (STDM). In general, TDM is preferred to FDM because it provides higher data transmission speeds and because TDM multiplexers are cheaper. STDM is also used fairly often because of its more efficient use of the available circuit capacity.

Frequency Division Multiplexing (FDM)

Frequency division multiplexing (FDM) can be described as dividing the circuit "horizontally" so that many signals can travel a single communication circuit simultaneously. The circuit is divided into a series of separate channels, each transmitting on a different frequency, much like a series of different radio or TV stations. All

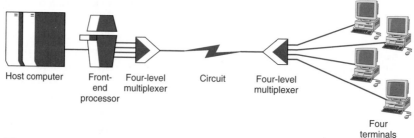

Figure 3–18 Multiplexed circuit.

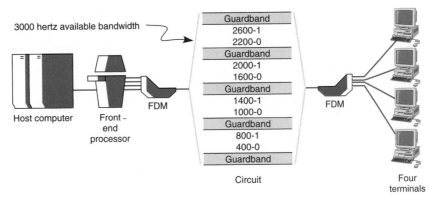

Figure 3–19 Frequency division multiplexed circuit (FDM).

signals exist in the media at the same time, but because they are on different frequencies, they do not interfere with each other.

Figure 3–19 illustrates the use of FDM to divide one circuit into four *channels*. Similar to the way radio stations must be assigned separate frequencies to prevent interference, so must the signals in a FDM circuit. The *guardbands* in Figure 3–19 are the unused portions of the circuit that separate these frequencies from each other.

Frequency division multiplexers are somewhat inflexible because once you determine how many channels are required, it may be difficult to add more channels without purchasing an entirely new multiplexer. In addition, maintenance costs are higher for frequency division multiplexing equipment than for time division multiplexing equipment.

Wavelength division multiplexing (WDM) is a version of FDM used in fiber optic cables. WDM works by using lasers to transmit different frequencies of light (i.e., colors) through the same fiber optic cable; each channel is assigned a different frequency so that the light generated by one laser does not interfere with the light produced by another. WDM permits up to 40 simultaneous circuits, each transmitting up to 10 Gbps, giving a total network capacity in one fiber optic cable of 400 Gbps (i.e., 400 billion bits per second). One WDM cable running at 400 Gbps could transmit almost the entire daily volume of telephone calls made in North America. Unfortunately, the reality is that telephone and Internet backbone networks are limited by the electronic switching equipment that they use. These devices require data to be converted from light to electronic data and back to light, which takes time and delays message transmission.

WDM is a relatively new technique, so it will continue to improve over the next few years. Experts predict that WDM transmission speeds should reach 25 terabits per second (i.e., 25 trillion bits) within five years—all without laying new fiber optic cable.

Time Division Multiplexing (TDM)

Time division multiplexing (TDM) shares a communication circuit among two or more terminals by having them take turns, dividing the circuit "vertically." Figure 3–20

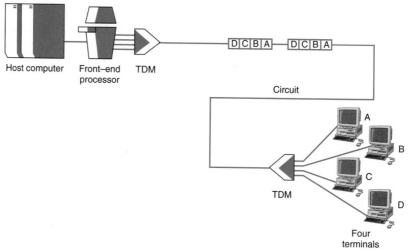

Figure 3–20 Time division multiplexed circuit (TDM).

shows the same four terminals connected using TDM. In this case, one character is taken from each terminal in turn, transmitted down the circuit, and delivered to the appropriate device at the far end (e.g., one character for terminal A then one from B, one from C, one from D, one from A, one from B, and so on). Time on the circuit is allocated even when data are not being transmitted, so that some capacity is wasted when terminals are idle.

Time division multiplexing generally is more efficient than frequency division multiplexing, because it does not need guardbands. Guardbands use "space" on the circuit that otherwise could be used to transmit data. It is not uncommon to have time division multiplexers that share a line among 32 different low-speed terminals. It is easy to change the number of channels in a time division multiplexer. All TDM channels usually originate at one location and all terminate at another location. Time division multiplexers generally are less costly to maintain.

Statistical Time Division Multiplexing (STDM)

Statistical time division multiplexing (STDM) is the exception to the rule that the capacity of the multiplexed circuit must equal the sum of the circuits it combines. STDM allows more terminals or computers to be connected to a circuit than FDM or TDM. If you have 12 terminals or microcomputers connected to a multiplexer and each can transmit at 9600 bits per second, then you should have a circuit capable of transmitting 112,000 bps (12 times 9600). However, not all terminals will be transmitting continuously at their maximum transmission speed. Users typically pause to read their screens or spend time typing at lower speeds. Therefore, you do not need to provide a speed of 112,000 bps on the multiplexed circuit. If only six terminals are transmitting at the same time, 64,000 bps might be enough, depending on how quickly the specific terminals and their users generate or request data. STDM is called *statistical* because selecting the transmission speed for the multiplexed circuit is based on a statistical analysis of the usage requirements of the circuits to be multiplexed.

The key benefit of STDM is that it provides more efficient use of the circuit and saves money. You can buy a lower-speed, less-expensive circuit than you could using FDM or TDM.

STDM introduces two additional complexities. First, STDM can cause time delays. If *all* devices start transmitting or receiving at the same time, the multiplexed circuit cannot transmit all the data it receives because it does not have sufficient capacity. Therefore, STDM must have internal memory to store the incoming data that it cannot immediately transmit. When traffic is particularly heavy, you may have a 1- to 30-second delay.

The second problem is that all data must be identified by an address that specifies the device to which it belongs. For example, assume an STDM multiplexes characters from 12 terminals. In this case, a terminal address is added to the characters and is inserted into the data stream. In Figure 3–21, notice that, in addition to the 8 bits for each individual character, we have added 5 bits of address space (Add). These 5 bits allow you to address 32 different terminals using binary arithmetic ($32 = 2^5$). Now the multiplexer takes a character from each terminal only when the terminal has a character to send. The technique used is to scan through

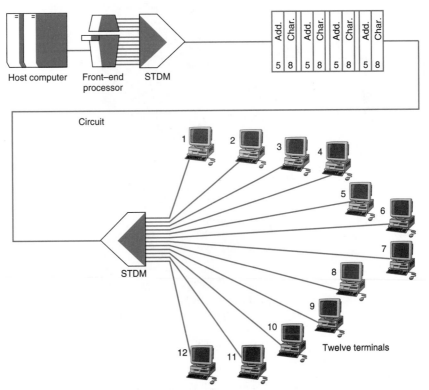

Figure 3–21 Statistical time division multiplexing (STDM).

NASA's communications network is extensive because its operations are spread out around the world and into space. The main Deep Space Network is controlled out of the Jet Propulsion Laboratory (JPL) in California. JPL is connected to the three main Deep Space Communications Centers (DSCC) that communicate with NASA spacecraft. The three DSCC are spread out equidistantly around the world, so that one will always be able to communicate with spacecraft no matter where they are in relation to the Earth: Canberra, Australia; Madrid, Spain; and Goldstone, California.

Figure 3–22 shows the JPL network. Each DSCC has four large dish antennas ranging in size from 85–230 feet (26–70 meters) that communicate with the spacecraft. These send and receive operational data such as telemetry, commands, tracking, and radio signals. Each DSCC also sends and receives administrative data such as e-mail, reports, and Web pages, as well as telephone calls and video.

The three DSCC and JPL use Ethernet local area networks connected to multiplexers that integrate the data, voice, and video signals for transmission. Satellite circuits are used between Canberra and JPL and Madrid and JPL. Fiber optic circuits are used between JPL and Goldstone.

Source: www.jpl.nasa.gov.

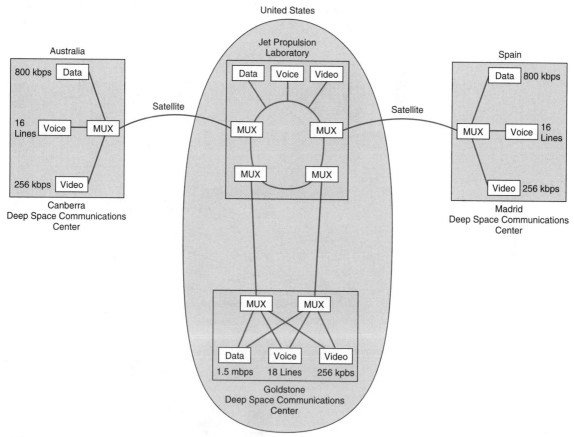

Figure 3–22 NASA's Deep Space Network ground communications network.

the 12 terminals and take characters from, say, terminals 1, 4, 5, and 12. These are sent immediately. Then all 12 are scanned again to determine which terminals need servicing. The process is repeated indefinitely. At the other end of the communication circuit, the character is given to the proper device because the 5-bit address included with each 8-bit character identifies the terminal. Remember, with regular time division multiplexing, there is no terminal addressing; each time position in the circuit is dedicated to a specific device. If only three terminals were transmitting, then one position would contain a blank (nothing) when transmitted.

In practice, most STDM multiplexers do not send one character at a time from each terminal, but instead send groups of characters at one time. For example, when terminal 1 has a message to send, the multiplexer sends up the entire message, after which the multiplexer immediately scans for the next terminal that has an entire message to send, and continues this process. This reduces the amount of addresses transferred, but can increase delays.

Inverse Multiplexing

Multiplexing uses one high-speed circuit to transmit a set of several lower-speed circuits. It can also be used to do the opposite. *Inverse multiplexing (IMUX)* combines several low-speed circuits to make them appear as one high-speed circuit to the user (see Figure 3–23).

One of the most common uses of inverse multiplexing is to provide *T-1* circuits for wide area networks. T-1 circuits provide data transmission rates of 1.544 Mbps (1,544,000 bits per second) by combining 24 slower speed circuits (64,000 bps). As far as the users are concerned, they have access to one high-speed circuit, even through their data actually travels across a set of slower circuits. T-1 and other circuits are discussed in Chapter 9.

Until recently, there were no standards for inverse multiplexing. If you wanted it, you had to ensure that you bought IMUXs from the same vendor so they could communicate. Several vendors have recently adopted the *BONDING* standard (Bandwidth ON Demand Interoperatibility Networking Group). Any IMUX that conforms to the BONDING standard can communicate with any other IMUX that conforms to the same standard. BONDING splits outgoing messages from one client or host across several low-speed telephone lines and combines incoming messages from several telephone lines into one circuit so that the client or host thinks it has a faster circuit.

The most common use for BONDING is for room-to-room videoconferencing. In this case, organizations usually have the telephone company install six telephone lines into their videoconferencing room that are connected to the IMUX (the tele-

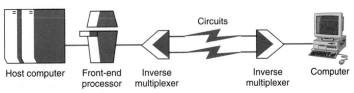

Figure 3–23 Inverse multiplexer.

Management Focus: Communications in Banking

One of the major users of data communications is the banking industry. Customers require around-the-clock service, multiple banking locations, and virtually instantaneous response to their transactions. To meet these demands, financial institutions have implemented massive data communication networks, automated teller machines (ATMs), and automated funds management systems not only for individuals, but also for business organizations and government agencies.

The four main applications in banking are checking accounts, savings accounts, loans, and credit cards. One customer may have several checking, savings, loan and credit card accounts scattered across several bank branches. All activities of this customer are cross-referenced and transmitted through the data communication network. This cross-referencing provides standardization of procedures and customer service across all branches, as well as the ability to extend banking services for easier customer access at any time. Such networks also

increase marketing opportunities for the bank to sell additional services to customers, such as stock sales, and to provide more timely and comprehensive customer information for management analysis.

Once a bank or group of banks develops a data communication network and interconnects it with one or more host computer processing locations, then any or all of these services can be offered. Some of these financial services include:

* Automated teller machines where users can deposit or withdraw money, make transfers between different bank accounts, and pay bills

* At-home banking and bill paying services via the Web

* Point-of-sale (POS) terminals tied directly to a customer's bank account from the retail store in which the POS terminal is located

* Automated clearing houses that facilitate the paperless dispensing and collection of

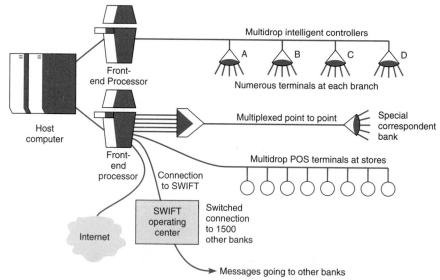

Figure 3–24 Bank networks—the terminals at bank branches A through D may be video terminals for tellers, ATMs for customers, or microcomputers.

thousands of financial transactions on a real-time basis

✳ National and international electronic funds transfer networks, check verification, check guarantees, credit authorizations, and the like

Many of the networks developed by banks are private networks that combine point-to-point circuits, multipoint circuits, and multiplexed circuits. Figure 3–24 shows a typical bank's retail network.

---

phone lines are usually 64Kbps ISDN telephone lines; see Chapter 9 for a description of ISDN). When they want to communicate with another videoconferencing room that has a similar six-telephone-line IMUX configuration, the IMUX uses one telephone line to call the other IMUX on one of its telephone lines. The two IMUX then exchange telephone numbers and call each other on the other five lines, until all six lines are connected. Once the connection has been established, the IMUX transmit data over the six lines simultaneously, thus giving a total data rate of 6×64 Kbps $= 384$ Kbps.

Summary

Network Architectures   There are three fundamental network architectures. In host-based networks, the host computer performs virtually all of the work. In client-based networks, the client computer does most of the work; the server is used only for data storage. In client–server networks, the work is shared between the servers and clients. The client performs all presentation logic, the server handles all data storage and data access logic, and one or both perform the application logic. Client–server networks can be cheaper to install and often better balance the network loads, but are far more complex and costly to develop and manage.

Basic Hardware   The basic hardware for any data communication network is a server or host computer (mainframe, minicomputer, or microcomputer), a client (dumb terminal, smart terminal, microcomputer, network computer, or special-purpose terminal), and the circuit through which the data flow. Microcomputers are becoming the most common client because, unlike dumb terminals, they can do some of the processing, thus reducing the load placed on the host computer.

Network Configuration   Networks can be configured so that there is a separate circuit from each client to the host (called a point-to-point configuration) or so that several clients share the same circuit (a multipoint configuration). Point-to-point configurations are simpler to operate, but they can be very expensive because of the amount of cable required to connect each client to the host, particularly if there is considerable distance between them. Multipoint connections are cheaper and more common, but require the clients to take turns sharing the circuit with all others on it.

Data Flow   Data can flow through the circuit in one direction only (simplex), in both directions simultaneously (full duplex), or by taking turns so that data sometimes flow in one direction and then in the other (half duplex). Half duplex is commonly used because many applications do not need data to flow in both directions simultaneously; for example, some applications require the client to send a message to the host and wait for a reply before transmitting new data. Simplex is also becoming common for the same reasons that cities sometimes use one-way streets to help traffic flows.

Media   Media are either guided, in that they travel through a physical cable (e.g., twisted-pair wires, coaxial cable, or fiber optic cable), or radiated, in that they are broadcast through the air (e.g., radio, infrared, microwave, or satellite). The choice is important if you are building your own network; it is less important if you are leasing a circuit from a carrier who guarantees the circuit's performance. Among the guided media, fiber optic cable can transmit data the fastest with the fewest errors and the greatest security, but it costs the most; twisted pair is the cheapest and most commonly used. The choice of radiated media depends more on distance than any other factor; infrared and radio are the cheapest for short distances, microwaves are cheapest for moderate distances, and satellites are cheapest for long distances.

Front-End Processor   A front-end processor is a special-purpose device that performs many network control functions so the host computer is free to do other tasks. The goal is to reduce the processing time the host spends to manage the network.

Multiplexer   A multiplexer is a device that combines several simultaneous low-speed circuits on one higher speed circuit so that each low-speed circuit believes it has a separate circuit. In general, the transmission capacity of the high-speed circuit must equal or exceed the sum of the low-speed circuits (e.g., one 57,600 bps circuit could multiplex a maximum of four 14,400 bps circuits). With frequency division multiplexing, each low-speed circuit is allocated a separate frequency on the high-speed circuit. Wavelength division multiplexing is a special form of frequency division multiplexing used in fiber optic circuits. With time division multiplexing (the most commonly used type of multiplexing), each low-speed circuit is allocated a separate time slice on the high-speed circuit. Relying on the fact that few terminals or microcomputers transmit continuously, statistical time division multiplexing combines more low-speed circuits than the high-speed circuit can support (e.g., six 14,000 bps circuits on one 64,000 bps circuit), although problems can occur if all low-speed circuits actually transmit at once. Inverse multiplexing enables several low-speed circuits to be treated as one high-speed circuit. BONDING is a commonly used inverse multiplexing standard.

Key Terms

application logic
BONDING
channel
client-based networks
client–server networks
coaxial cable
data access logic
data storage
dumb terminal
fat client
fiber optic cable
frequency division
  multiplexing (FDM)
front-end processor (FEP)
full-duplex transmission
guardband
guided media
half-duplex transmission
host-based networks

host computer
infrared transmission
intelligent controller
intelligent terminal
inverse multiplexing (IMUX)
mainframe computer
microcomputer
microwave transmission
middleware
minicomputer
multipoint circuit
multiplexers
n-tiered architecture
network computer
point-to-point circuit
presentation logic
radiated media
radio transmission
remote intelligent controller

satellite transmission
simplex
statistical time division
  multiplexing (STDM)
terminal
thin client
three-tiered architecture
time division multiplexing
  (TDM)
transaction terminal
turnaround time
twisted-pair cable
two-tiered architecture
very small aperture terminal
  (VSAT)
Video display unit (VDU)
wavelength division
  multiplexing (WDM)
workstation

Questions

1. What are the different types of network architectures?

2. Describe the four basic functions of an application software package.

3. What are the advantages and disadvantages of host-based networks versus client–server networks?

4. What is middleware, and what does it do?

5. Suppose your organization was contemplating switching from a host-based architecture to client–server. What problems would you foresee?

6. Which is less expensive: host-based networks or client–server networks? Explain.

7. Compare and contrast two-tiered, three-tiered, and *n*-tiered client–server architectures. What are the technical differences? What advantages and disadvantages do each offer?

8. How does a thin client differ from a fat client?

9. How do workstations differ from microcomputers?

10. What distinguishes a dumb terminal from other types of terminals?

11. What is a network computer?

12. How does a multipoint circuit differ from a point-to-point circuit?

13. Describe the three types of data flows.

14. Describe three types of guided media.

15. Describe four types of radiated media.

16. What is the term used to describe the placing of two or more signals on a single circuit?

17. What is the function of a front-end processor?

18. Explain the two forms a front-end processor can take.

19. What function do remote intelligent controllers serve?

20. What is the purpose of multiplexing?

21. In what multiple is multiplexing usually done?

22. Of the different types of multiplexing, what distinguishes:

    a. Frequency division multiplexing (FDM)?

    b. Time division multiplexing (TDM)?

    c. Statistical time division multiplexing (STDM)?

    d. Wavelength division multiplexing (WDM)?

23. What is the function of inverse multiplexing?

24. If you were buying a multiplexer, why would you choose either TDM or FDM?

Exercises

A. Investigate the use of the three major architectures by a local organization. Which architecture(s) do they use most often, and what do they see their organization doing in the future? Why?

B. What are the costs of client–server versus host-based architectures? Search the Web for at least two different studies and be sure to report your sources. What are the likely reasons for the differences between the two?

C. Investigate the costs of dumb terminals, intelligent terminals, network computers, minimally equipped microcomputers, and top-of-the-line microcomputers. Many equipment manufacturers and resellers are on the Web, so it's a good place to start looking.

D. Investigate the different types of cabling used in your organization and where they are used (e.g., LAN, backbone network).

E. Three terminals (T_1, T_2, T_3) are to be connected to three computers (C_1, C_2, C_3) so that T_1 is connected to C_1, T_2, to C_2, and T_3 to C_3. All are in different cities. T_1 and C_1 are 1,500 miles apart, as are T_2, C_2 and T_3, C_3. The points T_1, T_2, and T_3 are 25 miles apart, and the points C_1, C_2, and C_3 also are 25 miles apart. If telephone lines cost \$1 per mile, what is the line cost for three?

F. A few Internet service providers in some areas now have BONDING IMUXs and offer them to businesses wanting faster Internet access. Search the Web or call your local ISPs to see if they offer this service and if so, how much it costs.

NEXT DAY AIR SERVICE CASE STUDY

The Next Day Air Service managers discussed the Internet and the use of a wide area network at their last executive meeting. President Coone thinks that Next Day Air Service could benefit from an organization-wide multi-application network that would integrate word processing, electronic mail and voice mail, document and package tracking, billing, and payroll. The board of directors is also supportive of establishing a wide area network.

President Coone has asked you to start planning for that integrated corporate network. Ultimately, this network will link all the offices with Tampa and become the foundation on which to build a sophisticated data, voice, and image communication network that includes local area networks (LANs) at most NDAS sites. President Coone is still not completely convinced that NDAS needs image capabilities, but he wants you to include that potential in your plan.

As a first step, President Coone wants you to examine the current information flow within NDAS and to make recommendations on how to reduce circuit costs. You are considering the possibility of acquiring multiplexers.

President Coone reminds you that NDAS has downsized from minicomputers to microcomputers at a considerable saving. He does not want to "move backward" to a centralized host-based network. He also wants a state-of-the-art but cost-effective package tracking system, "like the big kids in the business." He believes that such a tracking system is imperative if NDAS is to remain competitive.

Exercises

1. What two cities appear to be the best locations for multiplexers in the NDAS communication network? Use the map in Figure 1–7.

2. What offices would you link to the multiplexers in the two cities identified in question 1? Justify your answer.

3. How would you link the cities if there were multiplexers located in Orlando, New Orleans, Dallas, and Atlanta?

4. Are there any special-purpose terminals that can be valuable to NDAS in improving productivity with package tracking and dispatching? Examine the way Dispatch processes its work (as presented in Chapter 1), and make suggestions based on your review.

5. President Coone wonders if it might be cost-effective to use a wireless connection from the company vehicle parking guardhouse to the main office building. Investigate the use and cost of wireless communication media, including infrared, microwave, and radio. Explain whether such a connection would be cost-effective in this application.

CHAPTER 4

Physical Layer: Data Transmission

This chapter discusses the basic technical concepts of how data are actually transmitted in the communication circuit. Four different types of transmission are described: digital transmission of digital data; analog transmission of digital data; digital transmission of analog voice data; and combined analog–digital transmission of digital data. You do not need an engineering-level understanding of the topics in order to effectively use and manage data communication applications. It is important, however, that you understand the basic concepts, so this chapter is somewhat technical.

Objectives

* **Understand digital transmission of digital data**
* **Understand analog transmission of digital data**
* **Be familiar with modems and several standard types of modems**
* **Understand digital transmission of analog data**
* **Understand how analog–digital modems work**

Chapter Outline

✳✳ INTRODUCTION

There are two fundamentally different types of data: *digital* and *analog*. Computers produce digital data that are binary—either on or off. In contrast, telephones produce analog data that are sent as electrical signals shaped like the sound waves they transfer.

Data can be transmitted through a circuit in the same form they are produced. Most computers, for example, transmit their data through digital circuits to printers and other attached devices. Likewise, analog voice data can be transmitted through telephone networks in analog form. In general, networks designed primarily to transmit digital computer data tend to use digital transmission. Networks designed primarily to transmit analog voice data tend to use analog transmission (at least for some parts of the transmission).

However, data can be converted from one form into the other for transmission over network circuits. For example, digital computer data can be transmitted over an analog telephone circuit by using a special device called a modem. A modem at the sender's computer translates the computer's digital data into analog data that can be transmitted through the voice communication circuits. A second modem at the receiver's end translates the analog transmission back into digital data for use by the receiver's computer.

Likewise, it is possible to translate analog voice data into digital form for transmission over digital computer circuits using a device called a codec. Once again there are two codecs, one at the sender's end and one at the receiver's end. Why bother to translate voice into digital? The answer is that digital transmission is "better" than analog transmission. Specifically, digital transmission offers five key benefits over analog transmission:

- ✳ Digital transmission produces fewer errors than analog transmission. Because the transmitted data is binary (only two distinct values), it is easier to detect and correct errors.

- ✳ Digital transmission is more efficient. In Chapter 3, we mentioned that time division multiplexing (TDM) is more efficient than frequency division multiplexing (FDM) because TDM requires no guardbands. TDM is commonly used for digital transmission, while FDM is used for analog transmission.

- ✳ Digital transmission permits higher maximum transmission rates. Fiber optic cable, for example, is designed for digital transmission.

- ✳ Digital transmission is more secure because it is easier to encrypt.

- ✳ Finally, and most importantly, integrating voice, video, and data on the same circuit is far simpler with digital transmission.

For these reasons, most long-distance telephone circuits built by the common carriers over the past decade use digital transmission. In the future, most transmissions (voice, data, and video) will be sent digitally.

In this chapter, we focus on how data is actually sent using analog and digital transmission. We also discuss how modems work, because analog transmission of digital data requires modems. Modems are commonly used from home over traditional telephone lines. There are many technologies that can be used instead of a modem to replace the traditional telephone lines—ISDN, ADSL, and cable modems are examples. Chapter 9 discusses these technologies, as well as the different metropolitan and wide area network services available to network managers. This chapter examines how the physical layer transmits data.

Technical Focus: *Digital versus Analog Data*

Analog data are signals that vary continuously within a range of values (e.g., temperature is analog). In an analog system, data are represented by measurements on a continuous scale, so the accuracy of the signal is determined by the accuracy of the scale (e.g., we can measure the temperature as 24 degrees or 24.2 or 24.23, and so on). The data produced by telephones usually are analog in nature because they represent the many different sounds that the human voice can produce. Analog is also called *broadband.*

In contrast, digital data can only take on specific discrete values (e.g., a typical traffic light is either red, green, or yellow). Digital data are either on or off like a light switch, whereas analog data vary like a dimmer switch, which allows you to vary the intensity of a light rather than just turn it on or off. The data produced by computers are digital in nature. Normally they are one of two discrete electrical voltages for binary 0s and 1s (e.g., five volts). A digital receiver must be capable of matching an electrical signal to a digital value (e.g., five volts means a binary 1). Digital is also called *baseband.*

✳✳ DIGITAL TRANSMISSION OF DIGITAL DATA

All computer systems produce binary data. For this data to be understood by both the sender and receiver, both must agree on a standard system for representing the letters, numbers, and symbols that compose messages.

✓ Coding

A *character* is a symbol that has a common, constant meaning. A character might be the letter A or B, or it might be a number such as 1 or 2. Characters also may be special symbols such as ? or &. Characters in data communications, as in computer systems, are represented by groups of *bits* that are binary zeros (0) and ones (1). The groups of bits representing the set of characters that are the "alphabet" of any given system are called a *coding scheme,* or simply a *code.*

A *byte* is a group of consecutive bits that is treated as a unit or character. One byte normally is comprised of 8 bits and usually represents one character; however, in data communications some codes use 5, 6, 7, 8, or 9 bits to represent a character.

Representation of the character A by a group of 7 bits (say, 1000001) is an example of coding. There are two predominant coding schemes in use today. United States of America Standard Code for Information Interchange (USASCII), or more commonly *ASCII* (pronounced *as'-key*), is the most popular code for data communications and is the standard code on most terminals and microcomputers. There are two types of ASCII; one is a 7-bit code that has 128 valid character combinations, and the other is an 8-bit code that has 256 combinations. The number of combinations can be determined by taking the number 2 and raising it to the power equal to the number of bits in the code. In this case, $2^7 = 128$ characters; $2^8 = 256$ characters. Extended Binary Coded Decimal Interchange Code, or (*EBCDIC*) (pronounced *eb'-si-dik*) is IBM's standard information code. This code has 8 bits, giving 256 valid character combinations.

Transmission Modes

Parallel Mode

Parallel mode is the way the internal transfer of binary data takes place inside a computer. If the internal structure of the computer is 8-bit, then all 8 bits of the data element are transferred between main memory and the central processing unit simultaneously on eight separate connections. The same is true of computers that use a 32-bit structure; all 32 bits are transferred simultaneously on 32 connections.

Figure 4–1 shows how all 8 bits of one character could travel down a parallel communication circuit. Parallel transfer is used rarely in data communications, but most printers use parallel communication. This is possible only when the printer is very close to the computer, because parallel cables require many wires (one for each bit) and may not work reliably in lengths of more than 25 feet.

Serial Mode

Serial mode is the predominant method of transferring information in data communications. Serial transmission means that a stream of data is sent over a communication circuit sequentially in a bit-by-bit fashion, as shown in Figure 4–2.

In general, with serial transmission, the transmitting device sends one bit, then a second bit, and so on, until all the bits are transmitted. It takes *n* iterations or

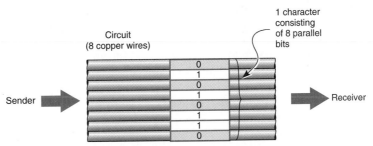

Figure 4–1 Parallel transmission of an 8-bit code.

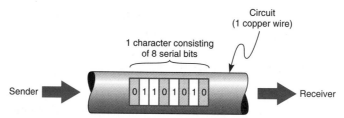

Figure 4-2 Serial transmission of an 8-bit code.

cycles to transmit *n* bits. Thus, serial transmission is considerably slower than parallel transmission—seven times slower in the case of ASCII (because there are 7 bits).

Baseband Transmission

Digital transmission is the transmission of electrical pulses. This digital information is binary in nature in that it only has two possible states, a 1 or a 0. The most commonly encountered voltage levels range from a low of $+3/-3$ to a high of $+24/-24$ volts. Digital signals are usually sent over wire of no more than a few thousand feet in length. Digital signals are commonly referred to as *baseband signals*.

Figure 4–3 shows three types of digital signaling techniques. With *unipolar signaling*, the voltage is always positive or negative (like a DC current). Figure 4–3 illustrates a unipolar technique in which a signal of 0 volts (no current) is used to transmit a zero, and a signal of $+5$ volts is used to transmit a 1.

An obvious question at this point is, if 0 volts means a zero, how do you send no data? This is discussed in detail in Chapter 5. For the moment, we will just say that there are ways to indicate when a message starts and stops, and when there are

---

Technical Focus: Basic Electricity

There are two general categories of electrical current: direct current and alternating current. *Current* is the movement or flow of electrons, normally from positive (+) to negative (−). The plus (+) or minus (−) measurements are known as *polarity*. *Direct current* (DC) travels in only one direction, whereas *alternating current* (AC) travels first in one direction and then in the other direction.

A copper wire transmitting electricity acts like a hose transferring water. We use three common terms when discussing electricity. *Voltage* is defined as electrical pressure—the amount of electrical force pushing electrons through a circuit. In principle, it is the same as pounds per square inch in a water pipe. *Amperes* (amps) are units of electrical flow, or volume. This measure is analogous to gallons per minute for water. The *watt* is the fundamental unit of electrical power. It is a rate unit, not a quantity. You obtain the wattage by multiplying the volts by the amperes.

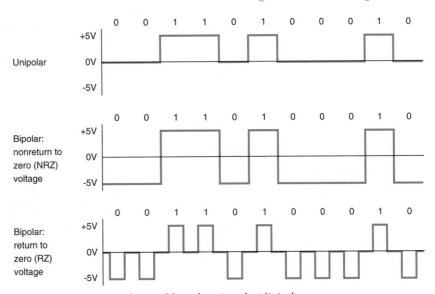

Figure 4–3 Unipolar and bipolar signals (digital).

no messages to send, the sender and receiver agree to ignore any electrical signal on the line.

In order to successfully send and receive a message, both the sender and receiver have to agree on how often the sender can transmit data—that is the *data rate.* For example, if the data rate on a circuit is 64 Kbps (64,000 bits per second), then the sender changes the voltage on the circuit once every 1/64,000 of a second and the receiver must examine the circuit once every 1/64,000 of a second to read the incoming data bits.

In *bipolar signaling,* the 1s and 0s vary from a plus voltage to a minus voltage (like an AC current). The first bipolar technique illustrated in Figure 4–3 is called nonreturn-to-zero (NRZ) because the voltage alternates from +5 volts (indicating a 1) and −5 volts (indicating a zero), without ever returning to zero volts. The second bipolar technique in this figure is called return-to-zero (RZ) because it always returns to zero volts after each bit before going to +5 volts (for a 1) or −5 volts (for a zero). In Europe, bipolar signaling sometimes is called *double current* signaling because you are moving between a positive and negative voltage potential.

In general, bipolar signaling experiences fewer errors than unipolar signaling, because the signals are more distinct. Noise or interference on the transmission circuit is less likely to cause the bipolar's +5 volts to be misread as a −5 volts than it is to cause the unipolar's 0 volts to be misread as a +5 volts. This is because changing the polarity of a current (from positive to negative, or vice versa) is more difficult than changing its magnitude.

Manchester encoding is a fourth type of signaling. Manchester encoding is a special type of unipolar signaling in which the signal is changed from high to low or from low to high in the middle of the signal. A change from high to low is used to represent a 1 (or a 0), while the opposite (a change from low to high) is used to represent a 0 (or a 1). Manchester encoding is less susceptible to having errors go undetected, because if there is no transition in mid-signal the receiver knows that an error must have occurred. Manchester encoding is commonly used in local area networks; Ethernet uses Manchester encoding, and token ring uses a variant on Manchester encoding.

✳✳ ANALOG TRANSMISSION OF DIGITAL DATA

Telephone networks were originally built for human speech rather than for data. They are designed to transmit the electrical representation of sound waves, rather than the binary data used by computers. There are many occasions when data need to be transmitted over a voice communications network. Many people use a microcomputer to dial up a server to transmit data, check their e-mail, or surf the Web.

Analog transmission occurs when the signal sent over the transmission media continuously varies from one state to another in a wavelike pattern. Modems trans-

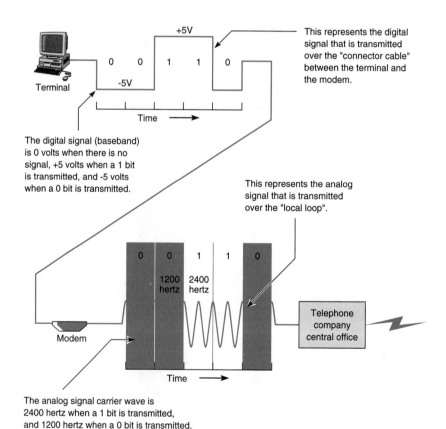

Figure 4–4 Operation of a modem.

late the digital binary data produced by computers into the analog signals required by voice transmission circuits (see Figure 4–4). One modem is used by the transmitter to produce the analog signals and a second by the receiver to translate the analog signals back into digital signals.

The North American Telephone System

The telephone system (commonly called *POTS* for plain old telephone service) enables voice communication between any two telephones within its network. The telephone converts the sound waves produced by the human voice at the sending end into electrical signals for the telephone network. These electric signals travel through the network until they reach the other telephone, where they are converted back into sound waves.

Figure 4–5 shows the basic organization of the telephone system in North America. Your house or office is connected to a telephone company *end office* (also called *central office class 5*) by a set of two twisted-pair wires (i.e., four wires). The wires from your house to the end office are called the *local loop*. The loop usually

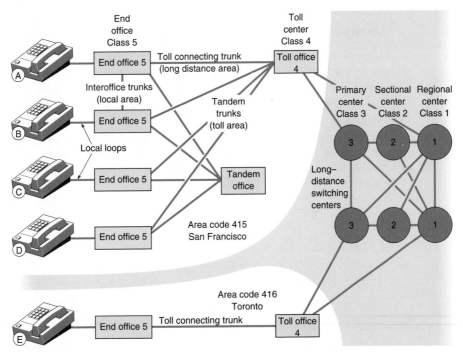

Figure 4–5 End office hierarchy. The end office (class 5), tandem office, and toll office (class 4) route calls throughout a city. Calls going outside a city use the class 3, 2, and 1 switching centers. Depending on the distance of the call and the traffic on the circuits, a call from Telephone A to Telephone E could be routed either by its most efficient route (5-4-3-3-4-5) or by its least efficient route (5-4-3-2-1-1-2-3-4-5).

runs two to five miles (three to eight kilometers). In most cases, telephones only use one set of twisted-pair wires, so it is easy to add a second telephone number to most homes by using this second, spare set of wires.

The end office is connected to a *central office class 4* by a *trunk line.* The central offices are arranged in a hierarchy: a class 4 office is connected to a class 3 office, which is connected to a class 2 office, which is connected to a class 1 office. Often several end offices are interconnected as well. Each end office and central office has a *switch* that routes your telephone call through the telephone system based on the number you dialed. Local calls stay within the same end office or go between end offices in the same geographic area. Long-distance calls go up the hierarchy to class 4 or higher offices.

The telephone system was originally designed as an analog system. Today in North America, the local loop remains almost entirely analog, but the trunk lines among the end offices and central offices are almost entirely digital. The end-office switches translate the analog voice signal from the local loop into a digital signal for transmission over the trunk lines to its destination. The end office at the receiver's end converts the digital signal back into an analog signal for transmission over the local loop to the receiver's telephone.

Bandwidth on a Voice Circuit

Figure 4–6 shows a typical sound wave. Every sound wave has two parts, half above the zero point (i.e., positive) and half below (i.e., negative). Both halves are the same distance away from zero. Sounds waves have three important characteristics. The first is the height of the wave, called *amplitude.* Our ears detect amplitude as the loudness or volume of sound. The second characteristic is the length of the wave, usually expressed as the number of waves per second, or *frequency.* Frequency is expressed in hertz (Hz).[1] Our ears detect frequency as the pitch of the sound. Human hearing ranges from about 20 hertz to about 14,000 hertz, although some people can hear up to 20,000 hertz. *Bandwidth* refers to a range of frequencies. It is the difference between the highest and the lowest frequencies in a band; thus,

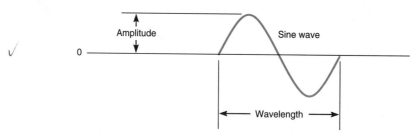

Figure 4–6 Sound wave.

---

[1]Hertz is the same as "cycles per second." One hertz (Hz) is the same as 1 cycle per second. One kilohertz (KHz) is 1000 cycles per second (kilocycles); 1 megahertz (MHz) is 1 million cycles per second (megacycles); and 1 gigahertz (GHz) is 1 billion cycles per second.

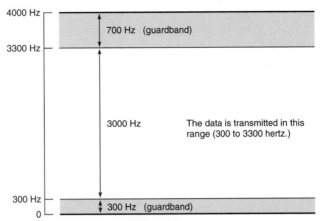

Figure 4–7 Voice grade circuit bandwidth (0 to 4000 hertz).

the bandwidth of human voice is from 20 Hz to 14,000 Hz or 13,880 Hz. The third characteristic is the *phase*. It refers to the direction in which the wave begins. The wave in Figure 4–6 starts up and to the right, which is called a 0° phase wave. Waves can also start down and to the right (a 180° phase wave), and in virtually any other part of the sound wave.

The bandwidth of a voice-grade telephone circuit is from 0 to 4000 Hz, or 4000 Hz; however, not all of this is available for use by telephone or data communications equipment. Figure 4–7 shows how this 4000 Hz bandwidth is allocated. To start, there is a 300 Hz *guardband* at the bottom of the bandwidth and a 700 Hz guardband at the top. These prevent data transmissions from interfering with other transmissions when these circuits are multiplexed using frequency division multiplexing. Figure 4–8 demonstrates how the guardbands provide 1000 Hz of empty space between adjacent communication circuits. This leaves the bandwidth from 300 to 3300 hertz, or a total of 3000 Hz for voice or data transmission. This is adequate for most speech, although it cannot convey the high notes in music.

It is important to note that this limit on bandwidth is imposed by the telephone and the switching equipment used in the telephone network. The actual capacity or bandwidth of the wires in the local loop running into your house depends on what exact type of wires were installed and the number of miles from your house to the telephone company's end office (the longer the distance, the lower the bandwidth[2]). About half of the homes and businesses in North America lie within two miles (or about three kilometers) of an end office, meaning the actual twisted-pair wire running into the home has a usable bandwidth of 1 MHz (i.e., 1 million hertz). Another 30 percent of homes lie between two and three miles

---

[2]As signals travel through the wire they gradually lose electrical strength and fade away, the same way that sound waves gradually lose strength and are harder to hear the farther you are away. The greater the distance, the more difficult it is to process the signal, and therefore, the less bandwidth before noise makes the signal unreadable.

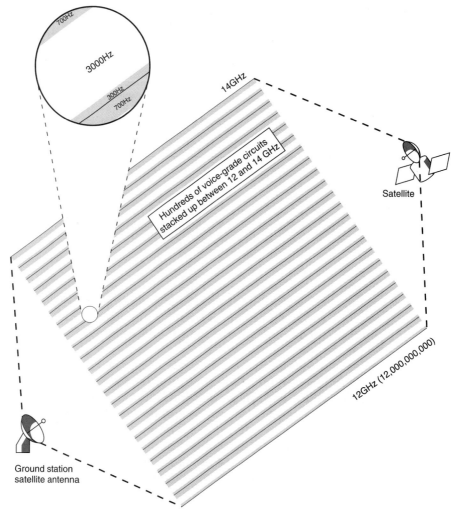

Figure 4–8 Guardbands.

from the end office (about three to five kilometers), at which point the usable bandwidth drops to about 300 KHz.

Modulation

Basic Modulation

Modulation is the technique that modifies the form of a electrical signal so the signal can carry information on a communication medium. The modulated signal often is referred to as an *analog signal.* The signal that does the carrying is the *carrier wave,* and modulation changes the shape of the carrier wave to transmit 0s and 1s. There are three fundamental methods: amplitude modulation, frequency modulation, and phase modulation.

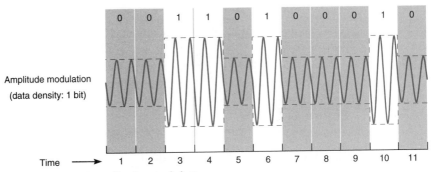

Figure 4–9 Amplitude modulation.

With *amplitude modulation (AM)* (also called amplitude shift keying, or ASK), the amplitude or height of the wave is changed. One amplitude is defined to be a 0, and another amplitude is defined to be a 1. In the amplitude modulation shown in Figure 4–9, the highest amplitude (tallest wave) represents a binary 1 and the lowest amplitude represents a binary 0. In this case, when the sending device wants to transmit a 1, it would send a high amplitude wave (i.e., a loud signal). Amplitude modulation is more susceptible to noise (errors) during transmission than frequency modulation or phase modulation.

Frequency modulation (FM) (also called frequency shift keying, or FSK), is a modulation technique whereby each 0 or 1 is represented by a number of waves per second (i.e., a different frequency). In this case, the amplitude does not vary. One frequency (i.e., a certain number of waves per second) is defined to be a 0, and a different frequency (a different number of waves per second) is defined to be a 1. In Figure 4–10, the higher frequency wave (more waves per time period) equals a binary 1, and the lower frequency wave equals a binary 0.

Phase modulation (PM) (also called phase shift keying, or PSK), is the most difficult to understand. Phase refers to the direction in which the wave begins. Until now, the waves we have shown start by moving up and to the right (this is called a 0° phase wave). Waves can also start down and to the right. This is called a phase of 180°. With phase modulation, one phase is defined to be a 0 and the other phase is defined to be a 1. Figure 4–11 shows the case where a phase of 0° is defined to be a binary 1 and a phase of 180° is defined to be a binary 0.

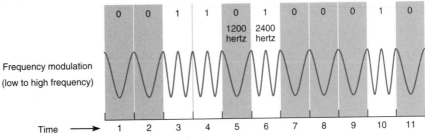

Figure 4–10 Frequency modulation.

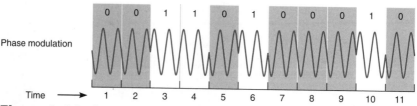

Figure 4–11 Phase modulation.

Sending Multiple Bits Simultaneously

Each of the three basic modulation techniques (AM, FM, and PM) can be refined to send more than one bit at one time. For example, basic amplitude modulation sends 1 bit per wave (or symbol) by defining two different amplitudes, one for a 1 and one for a 0. It is possible to send 2 bits on one wave or symbol by defining four different amplitudes. Figure 4–12 shows the case where the highest amplitude wave is defined to be 2 bits, both 1s. The next highest amplitude is defined to mean first a 1 and then a 0, and so on.

This technique could be further refined to send 3 bits at the same time by defining 8 different amplitude levels, or 4 bits by defining 16 amplitude levels, and so on. At some point, however, it becomes very difficult to differentiate between the different amplitudes. The differences are so small that even a small amount of noise could destroy the signal.

This same approach can be used for frequency modulation and phase modulation. Two bits could be sent on the same symbol by defining four different frequencies, one for 11, one for 10, and so on, or by defining four phases (0°, 90°, 180°, and 270°). Three bits could be sent by defining eight frequencies or by defining eight phases (0°, 45°, 90°, 135°, 180°, 225°, 270°, and 315°). These techniques are also subject to the same limitations as amplitude modulation; as the number of different frequencies or phases becomes larger, it becomes difficult to differentiate among them.

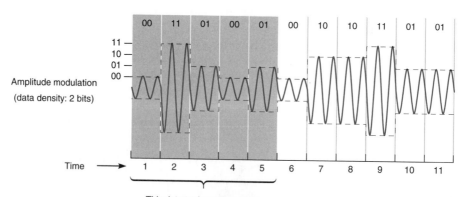

Figure 4–12 Two-bit amplitude modulation.

In practice, the maximum number of bits that can be sent with any *one* of these techniques is about 5 bits. When there are more than 32 different amplitudes, frequencies, or phases, it becomes extremely difficult to tell them apart.

The solution is to combine modulation techniques. It is possible to use amplitude modulation, frequency modulation, and phase modulation techniques on the same circuit. For example, we could combine amplitude modulation with four defined amplitudes (capable of sending 2 bits) with frequency modulation with four defined frequencies (capable of sending 2 bits) to enable us to send four bits on the same symbol.

One popular technique is *quadrature amplitude modulation (QAM)*. QAM involves splitting the symbol into eight different phases (3 bits) and two different amplitudes (1 bit), for a total of 16 possible values. Thus, one symbol in QAM can represent 4 bits.

Trellis-coded modulation (TCM) is an enhancement of QAM that combines phase modulation and amplitude modulation. TCM is unique in that it can transmit a different number of bits on each symbol (how TCM works is beyond the scope of this book). TCM can transmit 6, 7, 8, or 10 bits per symbol. The fastest version of TCM can average a maximum of 9.8 bits per symbol. The problem with high-speed modulation techniques that send many bits per symbol is that they are more sensitive to imperfections in the communication circuit.

Bits Rate versus Baud Rate versus Symbol Rate

The terms *bit rate* (i.e., the number bits per second transmitted) and *baud rate* are used incorrectly much of the time. They often are used interchangeably, but they are not the same. In reality, the network designer or network user is interested in bits per second, because it is the bits that are assembled into characters, and characters into words and, thus, business information.

A bit is a unit of information. A baud is a unit of signaling speed used to indicate the number of times per second the signal on the communication circuit changes. Because of the confusion over the term *baud rate* among the general public, ITU-T now recommends the term baud rate be replaced by the term *symbol rate*. The bit rate and the symbol rate (or baud rate) are the same only when 1 bit is sent on each symbol. For example, if we use amplitude modulation with two amplitudes, we send 1 bit on one symbol. Here the bit rate equals the symbol rate. However, if we use QAM, we can send 4 bits on every symbol; the bit rate would be four times the symbol rate. If we used an 8-bit TCM, the bit rate would be eight times the symbol rate. Virtually all of today's modems send multiple bits per symbol.

Capacity of a Voice Circuit

The capacity of a voice circuit (the maximum data rate) is the fastest rate at which you can send your data over the circuit. The data rate is calculated by multiplying the number of bits sent on each symbol by the maximum symbol rate. The number of bits per symbol depends on the modulation technique already discussed (e.g., QAM sends 4 bits per symbol).

The maximum symbol rate in any circuit depends on the bandwidth available and the signal-to-noise ratio (the strength of the signal compared to the amount of noise in the circuit). The maximum symbol rate is usually the same as the bandwidth as measured in hertz. If the circuit is very noisy, the maximum symbol rate may fall as low as 50 percent of the bandwidth. If the circuit has very little noise, it is possible to transmit at rates slightly higher than the bandwidth.

Voice-grade lines provide a bandwidth of 3000 Hz. Under "normal" circumstances, the maximum symbol rate is therefore 3000 symbols per second. If we were to use basic amplitude modulation (1 bit per symbol), the maximum data rate would be 3000 bits per second (bps). If we were to use QAM (4 bits per symbol) the maximum data rate would be 4 bits per symbol × 3000 symbols per second = 12,000 bps. Using TCM (with 6 bits per symbol), the maximum data rate would be 6 × 3000 = 18,000 bps. However, as you will see later in the chapter, it is possible to get very high data rates by changing the "normal" approach to data transmission.

✳✳ MODEMS

Modem is an acronym for *MOdulator/DEMOdulator*. A modem takes the digital electrical pulses received from a computer, terminal, or microcomputer and converts them into a continuous analog signal that is needed for transmission over an analog voice-grade circuit. Modems are either internal (i.e., inside the computer) or external (i.e., connected to the computer by a cable).

Most modems accept commands entered from a microcomputer keyboard. This command language controls their functions, such as changing speed and di-

Technical Focus: Modem Commands

The most popular modem command language was developed by Hayes for use in their modems. Many other modem manufacturers use this same language and therefore are "Hayes compatible." All commands begin with the letters AT. The letters that follow determine the command. Some useful commands include:

D#	Dial a telephone number (#)
DS	Dial stored telephone number (#)
D$	Display a list of ATD commands
L	Set the speaker volume
M0	Turn off the speaker
M1	Turn off the speaker after a connection is made
M2	Turn on the speaker
Z	Reset to default settings
$	Display a list of AT commands
&F	Reset to the factory settings
&N#	Set the maximum transmission speed (e.g., &n13 means 26,400 bps)
&Z=#	Store a phone number (#) for dialing using the ATDS command
&$	Display a list of AT& commands

aling calls. For example, if you use a Hayes modem or a Hayes-compatible modem that uses the same language, then you type the letters AT to enter a command. These letters instruct the modem to pay attention to the next set of letters because they constitute a command or parameter change. Therefore, typing the sequence ATD tells the modem to pay attention, and dial a number. The complete command might be ATD555-1212, which tells the modem to pay attention, and to dial 555-1212.

Modem Standards

There are many different types of modems available today (see Figure 4–13). Before data can be transmitted between two computers using modems, both need to use the same type of modem. Fortunately, several standards exist for modems. Any modem that conforms to a standard can communicate with any other modem that conforms to the same standard. When you buy a high-speed modem, remember that the computer at the other end of the telephone line also has to support the same standard.

Most modems support several standards (some high speed, some low speed) so that they can communicate with a variety of different modems. When these modems connect to another modem, they attempt to use the highest speed standard available and, if unsuccessful, keep trying lower speeds until they find one that works. Some modems can change data rates during transmission, so if a circuit is noisy, they can slow down to reduce the effects of errors. This changing of data rates during transmission is called *fast retrain*.

There are many modem standards. The *V.22* modem was used for many years, but is now obsolete in North America (still in use overseas). A V.22 can transmit at either 1200 symbols per second or 2400 symbols per second. V.22 uses frequency modulation (FM) to send one bit per symbol, resulting in a data rate of 1200 bps or 2400 bps.

V.32 modems transmit at 2400 symbols per second using QAM (4 bits per symbol) to achieve a 9600 bps data rate. *V.32bis* modems provide data rates of 14,400

Modem Standard	Maximum Symbol Rate	Maximum Bits per Symbol	Maximum Data Rate (bps)
V.22	1200	1	1200
	2400	1	2400
V.32	2400	4	9600
V.32bis	2400	6	14,000
V.34	3429	8.4	28,800
V.34+	3429	9.8	33,600

Figure 4–13 Modem standards.

bits per second by transmitting at 2400 symbols per second, using a form of TCM that provides 6 data bits per symbol.

V.34 modems were developed based on the assumption that the telephone network uses digital—not analog—transmission beyond the local loop. In other words, the analog signals produced by telephones are converted to digital signals at the telephone company's end office and transmitted digitally through the network to the last end office, where they are translated back into analog signals over the local loop to be received at the opposite end's telephone.

Such digital circuits are much more error free than older analog circuits. Building on this assumption, V.34 uses symbol rates above the 2400 symbols per second used by V.32 and V.32bis modems. The actual symbol rates depend on the quality of the circuit (e.g., 2400, 2800, 3000, and 3429). When V.34 modems first connect, they go through a "handshaking" sequence that tests the circuit and determines the optimum combination of symbol rate and modulation technique that will produce the highest throughput. The V.34 standard defines 59 combinations of symbol rate and modulation technique (the maximum is 28,800 bps at 3429 symbols per second using a form of TCM averaging 8.4 bits per symbol). During the transmission, this optimal combination can be changed if the modems encounter more errors or fewer errors than expected.

The maximum data rate is 28,800 bps, but even a short, poor-quality local loop can have sufficient noise to cause the V.34 to drop its symbol rate or use a

---

Management Focus: *Modem Pooling Saves Money*

Most modems are not in use at all times. In fact, even "heavily used" modems are often idle 50 percent of the time. Traditionally, companies have purchased one modem for every user who needs access to voice communication circuits. With *modem pooling*, several users share the same modem or set of modems. This is similar in concept to the use of a PBX to share a smaller set of telephone lines among a group of users.

Modem pooling saves money by reducing the number of modems that need to be purchased. It also reduces the number of connections to the common carrier's trunk lines. These costs can be significant, when you realize that annual cost of a business telephone connection can be three to five times the cost of a modem.

Pooling is typically done by a combination of hardware and software. For a local area network implementation, a special modem/communication server is used to manage the pool of modems. The users connect to the modems and dial out via the LAN. For a PBX implementation, the users connect to the PBX, which manages the modems.

Modem pooling is usually transparent; users do not notice that they do not have their own modem connected to their computer. If modems are heavily used, however, some users may have to wait for an available one. Such delays and the wasted management time and frustration that accompany it may outweigh savings. Modem pooling can be a wise decision, provided that you buy enough modems to prevent delays.

modulation technique with fewer bits per symbol, resulting in a much lower data rate. Nonetheless, tests of V.34 modems have shown that even in high-noise circuits, they produce higher data rates than V.32bis modems.

In 1996, ITU-T revised the V.34 standard to include a higher data rate of 33.6 Kbps. This revision is popularly known as *V.34+*. The faster data rate is accomplished by using a new form of TCM that averages 9.8 bits per symbol (symbol rate remains at 3429). It is unclear how many telephone lines are of sufficient quality to permit the use of 3429 symbols per second and TCM-9.8. Most experts believe that only 30 percent of North American telephone lines, mostly in urban areas, will be able to support so many bits per symbol and such high symbol rates. Most people using V.34+ will therefore not get 33.6 Kbps.

Data Compression

A modem's transmission rate is the primary factor that determines the throughput rate of data, but it is not the only factor. *Data compression* can increase throughput of data over a communication link literally by compressing the data.

The *MNP 5* standard uses *Huffman encoding*. Huffman encoding replaces the standard ASCII and EBCDIC code used for each letter. It uses coding tables that use a different number of bits to represent characters based on how often that character is used. Frequently used characters (e.g., the letter E) may be defined using only four bits, while seldomly used characters (e.g., X), may be defined using 11 bits. Different Huffman tables are built for each message. Even though the Huffman table must be sent along with the message, the size of the transmission can be reduced significantly. MNP 5 typically provides a compression ratio ranging between 1.3:1 and 2:1. A 2:1 compression ratio means that for every two characters in the original signal, only one is needed in the compressed signal (e.g., if the original signal contained 1000 bytes, only 500 would needed in the compressed signal).

V.42bis, the ISO standard for data compression, uses *Lempel–Ziv encoding*. As a message is being transmitted, Lempel–Ziv encoding builds a dictionary of two-, three-, and four-character combinations that occur in the message. Any time the same character pattern reoccurs in the message, the index to the dictionary entry is transmitted rather than sending the actual data. As with Huffman encoding, the reduction provided by V.42bis compression depends on the actual data sent, but usually ranges from 3.5:1 to 4:1 (i.e., almost four times as much data can be sent per second using V.42bis than without it).

V.42bis compression can be added to almost any modem standard; thus, a V.32 modem providing a data rate of 14,400 bps could provide a data rate of 57,600 bps when upgraded to use V.42bis. A V.34 modem providing a 28,800 bps data rate could provide 115,200 bps with V.42bis. V.34+ modems could provide 133.4 Kbps with V.42bis. Several tests of V34/42bis modems have found actual data rates of around 110 Kbps over a variety of North American telephone networks. Tests in Europe, where digital transmission is less common, have been less promising.

Remember, these data rates are provided using the standard voice-grade circuit that until recently was traditionally limited to 2400 bps. Once V.34+ modems using V.42bis data compression methods are more common, the use of the voice telephone network to transmit computer data will grow exponentially. Some manufacturers are even predicting that 8:1 data compression ratios will be available in the near future, theoretically boosting transmission rates on standard voice-grade telephone lines to more than 230 Kbps.

There are two drawbacks to the use of data compression. First, compressing already compressed data provides little gain. Many data files transferred over modems are compressed to begin with; bulletin boards and Internet FTP sites routinely compress files before they are posted for use. Therefore, 28,800 bps may be the effective data rate, not 115.2 Kbps.

The second problem is that data rates higher than 100 Kbps place considerable pressure on the traditional microcomputer serial port controller that controls the communication between the serial port and the modem (the UART chip (Universal Asynchronous Receiver/Transmitter)). Put simply, most UARTs rely on the microcomputer's CPU to transfer data. At these high data-transmission rates, when the CPU gets overloaded (as is common in Windows-based multitasking environments), data gets lost. The solution is to replace the UART chip with a newer version or to use a special board provided by the modem manufacturer.

Management Focus: Higher-Speed Modems Save Time and Money

High-speed modems save on line charges. Before transmitting data, you may want to calculate how long the process will take. File transfer time can be estimated easily by using the following formula:

File transfer time =

$$\frac{\text{Number of bytes} \times \text{Number of bits per byte}}{\text{Bits per second transmission speed}}$$

This formula will provide a close estimation, but it will not be accurate to the second, because it does not take into account control characters that may be transmitted to control the transmission flow, nor the need to retransmit data due to errors.

For example, a 50-page document or a good-sized spreadsheet might be a 150,000-byte file. With a V.32bis modem (14,400 bps) and 8 bits per byte, the transfer time would be:

(150,000 bytes × 8 bits per byte)/14,400 bits
per second = 83 seconds.

This gives an approximate time of 1½ minutes. As a rule of thumb, you might add 10 percent to this figure to account for transmission errors and the required control characters.

A V.34+ modem (33.6 Kbps) would require about 36 seconds. After adding V.42bis data compression to the V.34+ modem, this time drops to about 10 seconds. Although a few minutes of long-distance telephone time is not too costly, it can add up over the course of a year.

✳✳ DIGITAL TRANSMISSION OF ANALOG DATA

In the same way that digital computer data can be sent over analog telephone networks using analog transmission, analog voice data can be sent over digital networks using digital transmission. This process is somewhat similar to the analog transmission of digital data. A pair of special devices called *codecs* (*COde/DECode*) is used in the same way that a pair of modems is used to translate the data to send across the circuit. One codec is attached to the source of the signal (e.g., a telephone or the local loop at the end office) and translates the incoming analog voice signal into a digital signal for transmission across the digital circuit. A second codec at the receiver's end translates the digital data back into analog data.

Pulse Amplitude Modulation

Analog voice data must be translated into a series of binary digits before they can be transmitted. One means of doing this is called *pulse amplitude modulation (PAM)*. With PAM-based methods, the amplitude of the sound wave is sampled at regular intervals, and is translated into a binary number. Figure 4–14 shows an example where eight different amplitude levels are used (i.e., each amplitude level is represented by 3 bits). The top diagram shows the original signal and the bottom diagram shows the PAM signal.

A quick glance will show that the PAM signal is only a rough approximation of the original signal. The original signal had a smooth flow, but the PAM signal has jagged "steps." The difference between the two signals is called *quantizing error*. Voice transmissions using PAM-based methods that have a great deal of quantizing error sound metallic or machine-like to the ear.

There are two ways to reduce quantizing error and improve the quality of the PAM signal, but neither is without cost. The first method is to increase the number of amplitude levels which minimizes the difference between the levels (the "height" of the "steps") and results in a smoother signal. In Figure 4–14, we could define 16 amplitude levels instead of 8 levels. This would require 4 bits (rather than the current 3 bits) to represent the amplitude, thus increasing the amount of data needed to transmit the PAM signal.

No amount of levels or bits will ever result in perfect-quality sound reproduction, but in general, 7 bits ($2^7 = 128$ levels) reproduces human speech adequately. Music, on the other hand, usually requires 16 bits ($2^{16} = 65,536$ levels).

The second method is to sample more frequently which will reduce the "length" of each "step," also resulting in a smoother signal. To obtain a reasonable-quality voice signal, one must sample at least twice the highest possible frequency in the analog signal. You will recall that the highest frequency transmitted in telephone circuits is 3300 Hz. Thus PAM-based methods used to digitize telephone voice transmissions must sample the input voice signal at a minimum of 6600 times per second. Sampling more frequently than this (oversampling) will improve

The signal (original wave) is quantized into 128 pulse amplitudes (PAM). In this example we have used only eight pulse amplitudes for simplicity. These eight amplitudes can be depicted by using only a 3-bit code instead of the 8-bit code normally used to encode each pulse amplitude.

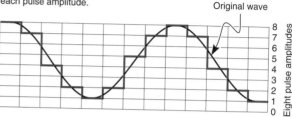

After quantizing, samples are taken at specific points to produce amplitude modulated pulses. These pulses are then coded. Because we used eight pulse levels, we only need three binary positions to code each pulse.[1] If we had used 128 pulse amplitudes, then a 7-bit code plus one parity bit would be required.

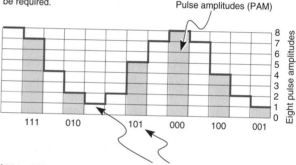

Figure 4–14 Pulse amplitude modulation (PAM).

[1] 001 = PAM level 1
010 = PAM level 2
011 = PAM level 3
100 = PAM level 4
101 = PAM level 5
110 = PAM level 6
111 = PAM level 7
000 = PAM level 8

For digitizing a voice signal, 8,000 samples per second are taken. These 8,000 samples are then transmitted as a serial stream of 0s and 1s. In our case 8,000 samples times 3 bits per sample would require a 24,000 bps transmission rate. In reality, 8 bits per sample times 8,000 samples requires a 64,000 bps transmission rate.

signal quality. For quality reproduction of music, for example, 32 times oversampling is common.

Pulse Code Modulation

PAM is a family of techniques that includes many different specific formats. For example, one type of PAM could sample 6600 times per second using 128 amplitude levels (i.e., 7 bits), while another type of PAM could sample at 13,200 times per second using 256 levels (i.e., 8 bits). The most commonly used type of PAM is *pulse code modulation (PCM)*. With PCM, the input voice signal is sampled 8000 times per second (slightly above the minimum of 6600 times per second just discussed). Each time the input voice signal is sampled, 8 bits are generated. Therefore, the transmission speed on the digital circuit must be 64,000 bits per second (8 bits per sample × 8,000 samples per second) in order to transmit a voice signal when it is in digital form.

✹✹ ANALOG–DIGITAL MODEMS (56K MODEMS)

The V.34+ modem is probably the fastest analog modem that will be developed. Its symbol rate and number of bits per symbol are almost the fastest that is possible with traditional telephone technology. A new type of "modem" has recently come into use that combines analog and digital transmission to overcome the limitations of the analog telephone system.

The basic idea behind 56K modems (*V.90*) is very simple. Most telephone companies today use PCM to convert analog voice telephone signals into digital signals for transmission. The data are then transmitted down a 64 Kbps digital circuit to another codec at the receiver's end that translates it back into voice data.

56K modems take the basic concepts of PCM and turn them backward. If PCM needs a codec that samples 8000 times per second and produces 8 bits in each sample to accurately digitize human voice on a telephone circuit, it makes sense that the same telephone circuit can accurately transmit (and enable the receiver to recognize) up to 8 bits transmitted 8000 times per second.

The new 56K modems are designed to recognize an 8-bit digital symbol (one of 256 possible amplitudes or voltages) 8000 times per second. This gives a theoretical transmission speed of 64 Kbps. However, one of the bits in the PCM symbol is used by some telephone services in North America for control purposes, so in practice the user can use only 7 bits. This means the maximum data rate becomes 56 Kbps (8000 symbols × 7 bits per symbol).

Noise is a critical issue. Distinguishing among 128 different possible symbols (i.e., 7 bits means 128 symbols while 8 bits means 256 symbols) is difficult unless the telephone line is very clear. In noisy conditions, the modem can accurately recognize fewer bits per symbol, so the number of bits per symbol must be reduced, thus reducing the data rate. It is estimated that about 20 percent of the telephone lines in North America (mostly the older rural exchanges) are too noisy to use 56K modems. Recent tests in Atlanta (which has a very modern telephone network) found 56K modems to connect at less than 40 Kbps 18 percent of the time, at 40–50 Kbps 80 percent of the time, and above 50 Kbps 2 percent of the time.

For technical reasons beyond the scope of this discussion, it is easier to control noise in the channel transmitting from the server to the client than in the opposite direction. Therefore, the 56K transmission rates are available only in the "downstream" channel from server to client. "Upstream" communication from client to server uses traditional analog transmission, which means a maximum of 33.6 Kbps using V.34+. Several companies are working on new approaches to overcome this limitation.

Because the current 56K technology is based on the PCM standard, it cannot be used on services that do not use this standard. AT&T's TrueVoice service, for example, is not compatible with current 56K technology, so V.90 modems will use V.34+ in both directions.

Summary

Digital Transmission of Digital Data   Digital transmission (also called baseband transmission) is done by sending a series of electrical (or light) pulses through the media. Digital transmission is preferred to analog transmission because it produces fewer errors, is more efficient, permits higher maximum transmission rates, is more secure, and simplifies the integration of voice, video, and data on the same circuit. With unipolar digital transmission, the voltage changes between zero volts to represent a binary 0 and some positive value (e.g., +15 volts) to represent a binary 1. With bipolar digital transmission, the voltage changes polarity (i.e., positive or negative) to represent a 1 or a 0. Bipolar is less susceptible to errors.

Analog Transmission of Digital Data   Modems are used to translate the digital data produced by computers into the analog signals for transmission in today's voice communication circuits. Both the sender and receiver need to have a modem. Data is transmitted by changing (or modulating) a carrier sound wave's amplitude (height), frequency (length), or phase (shape) to indicate a binary 1 or 0. For example, in amplitude modulation, one amplitude is defined to be a 1 and another amplitude is defined to be a 0.

Bit Rate versus Baud Rate versus Symbol Rate   The symbol rate (or baud rate) is the number of symbols sent per second. It is possible to send more than 1 bit on every symbol (or wave). For example, with amplitude modulation, you could send 2 bits on each wave by defining four amplitude levels. You can combine techniques to send even more bits. Two popular techniques are QAM, which sends 4 bits per symbol, and TCM which averages 6 to 9.8 bits per symbol; both use a combination of amplitude and phase modulation.

Bandwidth and the Capacity of a Voice Circuit   The range of frequencies available in a circuit is called bandwidth. Voice telephone lines can transmit sound waves with frequencies from 300 Hz to 3300 Hz, so their bandwidth is 3000 Hz (3300 − 300). The capacity or maximum data rate that a circuit can provide is determined by multiplying the symbol rate (symbols per second) by the number of bits per symbol. Generally (but not always), the symbol rate is the same as the bandwidth, so bandwidth is often used as a measure of capacity. The maximum data rate of a voice telephone circuit is the symbol rate times the number of bits per symbol. At 2400 symbols per second with QAM (4 bits per symbol), the maximum data rate would be 2400 $\times$ 4 = 9600 bits per second. Using 6-bit TCM at 2400 symbols per second would produce a data rate of 14,400 bps.

Modems Many categories of modems are currently available, including:

* V.22, which sends at 1200 or 2400 bps
* V.32, which sends at 9600 bps
* V.32bis, which sends at 14,400 bps
* V.34, which sends at 28,800 bps
* V.34+, which sends at 33,600 bps

V.42bis is a data compression standard that can be combined with any of the foregoing types of modems to reduce the amount of data in the transmitted signal by a factor of four. Thus, a V.34 modem using V.42bis could provide an effective data rate of 28,800 $\times$ 4 = 115,200 bps.

Digital Transmission of Analog Data Because digital transmission is better, analog voice data is sometimes converted to digital transmission. Pulse code modulation (PCM) is the most commonly used technique. PCM samples the amplitude of the incoming voice signal 8000 times per second and uses 8 bits to represent the signal. PCM produces a reasonable approximation of the human voice, but more sophisticated techniques are needed to adequately reproduce more complex sounds such as music.

Analog–Digital Modems Analog–digital modems are newer modems that combine analog and digital transmission to overcome the limitations of the traditional telephone network. 56K modems (V.90) use analog transmission (V.34+) to transmit from the client to the server (upstream), but use digital techniques based on reversing PCM to transmit at up to 56 Kbps from the server to the client (downstream).

Key Terms

56K modem	carrier wave	frequency
amplitude	central office	frequency modulation (FM)
amplitude modulation (AM)	codec	guardband
analog transmission	coding	Hertz (Hz)
ASCII	cycles per second	Huffman encoding
bandwidth	data compression	Lempel–Ziv encoding
baseband signals	data rate	Manchester encoding
baud rate	Digital transmission	MNP 5
bipolar signaling	EBCDIC	modem
bit rate	end office	modem pooling
broadband	fast retrain	parallel transmission

phase	quantizing error	V.22
phase modulation (PM)	serial transmissions	V.32
polarity	switch	V.32bis
pulse amplitude modulation (PAM)	symbol rate	V.34
	trellis-coded modulation (TCM)	V.34+
pulse code modulation (PCM)		V.42bis
quadrature amplitude modulation (QAM)	trunk line	V.90
	unipolar signaling	

Questions

1. How do analog data differ from digital data?
2. Clearly explain the differences between analog data, analog transmission, digital data, and digital transmission.
3. Explain why most telephone company trunk lines are now digital.
4. How does baseband differ from broadband?
5. What is coding?
6. Briefly describe the two most important coding schemes.
7. How are data transmitted in parallel?
8. What feature distinguishes serial mode from parallel mode?
9. How does bipolar signaling differ from unipolar signaling? Why is Manchester encoding more popular than either of these?
10. Describe how the North American telephone network is organized.
11. What are three important characteristics of a sound wave?
12. What is bandwidth? What is the bandwidth in a traditional North American telephone circuit?
13. Describe how data could be transmitted using amplitude modulation.
14. Describe how data could be transmitted using frequency modulation.
15. Describe how data could be transmitted using phase modulation.
16. Describe how data could be transmitted using a combination of modulation techniques.
17. Is the bit rate the same as the symbol rate? Explain.
18. What is a modem?
19. What is QAM?
20. Explain the importance of trellis-coded modulation.
21. What factors affect transmission speed?
22. How are modems classified?
23. Define retrain time.
24. Describe four common modem standards.
25. Why is data compression so useful?
26. What data compression standard uses Huffman encoding? Describe how it works.
27. What data compression standard uses Lempel–Ziv encoding? Describe how it works.
28. Explain how PCM works.
29. How does PCM differ from PAM?
30. Explain how V.90 modems work.

Exercises

A. Find the current prices for V.34+ modems and V.90 modems.
B. Study the actual data rates you get with your V.34, V.34+, or V.90 modem. Calculate the average speed you get over a one-week period.

C. Draw how the bit pattern 01101100 would be sent using:
1. Single-bit AM
2. Single-bit FM
3. Single-bit PM
4. Two-bit AM (i.e., four amplitude levels)
5. Two-bit FM (i.e., four frequencies)
6. Two-bit PM (i.e., four different phases)
7. Single-bit AM combined with single-bit FM
8. Single-bit AM combined with single-bit PM
9. Two-bit AM combined with two-bit PM

D. If you had to download a 20-page paper of 40,000 bytes from your professor, approximately how long would it take to transfer it over the following modems? Assume that control characters add an extra 10 percent to the message.
1. V.32bis modem
2. V.34+ modem (assume it can transfer at its maximum speed)
3. V.90 modem (assume it can transfer at its maximum speed)
4. If the modem includes V.42bis with a 4 to 1 data compression ratio, what is the data rate in bits per second you actually see in part 2 above?

NEXT DAY AIR SERVICE CASE STUDY

President Coone has asked you to continue planning for an integrated corporate NDAS network. Ultimately, this network will link all the offices with the Tampa head office and become the foundation on which to build a sophisticated data, voice, and image communication network that includes local area networks (LANs) at most NDAS sites. President Coone is still not completely convinced that NDAS needs image capabilities, but he wants you to include that in your plan.

As a first step, President Coone wants you to examine the current information flow within NDAS. Figure 4–15 shows the movement of invoice information. In reality, it shows the number of packages that are transferred between offices, but each package also requires an invoice. These averages were compiled from a two-week survey of each office. The average length of each invoice is 750 characters. Use this statistic as the basis for your computations.

Every number in the figure represents the number of packages (each of which requires an invoice) that move from the city of origin to a destination city for delivery in the latter city's delivery zone. Local deliveries are indicated in situations in which the origins and destinations are the same. For example, the intersection of the Atlanta column and the Atlanta row shows 500 local deliveries.

Invoice information is transmitted from the origin to the destination. In addition, a copy of all invoice information is transmitted to the home office in Tampa for billing. For example, every day Los Angeles ships 150 packages to Memphis, and each one requires an invoice. This means that Los Angeles will transmit fifteen 750-character invoices to both Memphis and Tampa, every day.

Origin \ Destination	Atlanta	Chicago	Dallas	Denver	Houston	Jackson	Jacksonville	Los Angeles	Memphis	Miami	Montgomery	New Orleans	Orlando	St. Louis	Tampa	Washington	Avg total pakgs/Day
Atlanta	500	400	350	15	320	100	250	100	200	300	120	250	200	120	450	400	4075
Chicago	300	N/A	400	N/A	100	50	100	N/A	200	400	70	250	300	N/A	350	N/A	2520
Dallas	250	300	800	350	450	50	150	700	300	250	50	300	150	250	300	250	4900
Denver	200	N/A	300	N/A	150	30	20	N/A	30	150	20	130	40	N/A	80	N/A	1150
Houston	150	70	450	70	N/A	20	80	70	130	120	20	230	170	120	300	10	2010
Jackson	110	N/A	120	60	120	N/A	30	N/A	220	40	30	340	110	70	210	N/A	1460
Jacksonville	130	70	130	10	80	20	N/A	30	70	200	30	50	200	10	350	30	1410
Los Angeles	150	N/A	70	N/A	80	N/A	20	N/A	150	150	N/A	30	10	N/A	110	N/A	770
Memphis	160	40	130	20	70	90	30	80	700	110	40	90	20	210	60	20	1870
Miami	330	50	70	20	30	10	160	20	40	1100	20	210	260	10	450	30	2810
Montgomery	80	10	60	N/A	40	30	20	N/A	20	30	N/A	90	20	10	30	10	450
New Orleans	120	70	160	10	120	60	30	20	70	30	60	1000	80	20	250	20	2120
Orlando	270	70	120	30	60	20	230	10	30	310	40	110	950	20	450	30	2750
St. Louis	140	N/A	70	N/A	60	20	20	N/A	310	40	20	210	40	N/A	60	N/A	990
Tampa	550	110	130	40	80	30	220	30	70	310	30	170	430	60	900	30	3190
Washington	210	N/A	20	N/A	30	N/A	70	N/A	20	40	10	30	20	N/A	40	N/A	490

Inbound (columns) / Outbound (rows)

Total 33100

Figure 4–15 Daily invoice (package) traffic for Next Day Air Service.

Exercises

1. President Coone is baffled about how digital information from a computer can be sent over a telephone line. Prepare a brief position paper for management, explaining the way information is transferred from one computer to another over telephone lines. Keep it simple. Be sure to describe the types of modems used in data transmission over telephone circuits. Include comments on the role of data compression in increasing transmission rates. Justify the observation that as a general rule, it is best to purchase the fastest modem your communications lines can support.

2. Compute each office's number of bits sent per day (origin to destination) based on the data provided in Figure 4–15. Use 10 bits per character to keep computations simple, and assume all transmissions are error free. (*Hint:* Bits per day = Packages $\times$ 750 $\times$ 10 $\times$ 2.)

3. How many minutes will it take for each city's modem to transmit its invoices? Use the bits per day calculated in question 2, and assume that the V.34 modems transmit at an average rate of 28,800 bits per second.

4. In question 3, you calculated the transmission time in minutes per day, based on a 28,800 bps modem and 10 bits per character. Now calculate the "file transfer time" for Atlanta to transmit all of its invoices to Tampa at the end of the workday. Why is this answer different from the time calculated for Atlanta in question 3?

5. Could all the NDAS offices transmit their invoices to Tampa between 5:00 P.M. and 6:00 P.M. each evening? How can NDAS achieve this goal?

CHAPTER 5

Data Link Layer

The data link layer (also called layer 2) controls the way messages are sent on the physical media. Both the sender and receiver have to agree on the rules or *protocols* that govern how they will communicate with each other. A data link protocol determines who can transmit at what time, where a message begins and ends, and how a receiver recognizes and corrects a transmission error. In this chapter we discuss these processes, as well as several important sources of errors.

Objectives

* Understand the role of the data link layer
* Become familiar with two basic approaches to controlling access to the media
* Become familiar with common sources of error and its prevention
* Understand three common error detection and correction methods
* Become familiar with several commonly used data link protocols

Chapter Outline

✴✴ INTRODUCTION

In Chapter 1, we introduced the concept of layers in data communications. The data link layers sit between the physical layer (hardware such as the circuits, computers, and special-purpose devices described in Chapters 3 and 4) and the network layer (that performs addressing and routing as described in Chapter 6).

The data link layer accepts messages from the network layer and controls the hardware that actually transmits them. The data link layer is responsible for getting a message from one computer to another without errors. The data link layer also accepts streams of bits from the physical layer and organizes them into coherent messages that it passes to the network layer.

Both the sender and receiver have to agree on the rules that govern how their data link layers will communicate with each other. A *data link protocol* provides three functions:

* Controls when computers transmit (*media access control*)
* Detects and corrects transmission errors (*error control*)
* Identifies the start and end of a message (*message delineation*)

✴✴ MEDIA ACCESS CONTROL

Media access control refers to the need to control when computers transmit. With point-to-point full-duplex configurations, media access control is unnecessary because there are only two computers on the circuit, and full duplex permits either computer to transmit at anytime. There is no media access control.

Media access control becomes important when several computers share the same communication circuit, such as a point-to-point configuration with a half-duplex line that requires computers to take turns, or a multipoint configuration in which several computers share the same circuit. Here, it is critical to ensure that no two computers attempt to transmit data at the same time—or if they do, there must be a way to recover from the problem. Media access control is critical in local area networks and will be discussed in more detail in Chapter 7. There are two fundamental approaches to media access control: controlled access and contention.

Controlled Access

Most computer networks managed by a host mainframe computer use *controlled access*. In this case, the mainframe or its front-end processor controls the circuit and determines which clients can access media at what time. Controlled access is also common in one type of local area network.

X-ON/X-OFF

X-ON/X-OFF is one of the oldest media access control protocols, dating back to the days of the teletype. It was not really designed for computer networks, but is still used today. X-ON/X-OFF is only used for the transmission of text messages (not binary files such as .EXE files), often on half-duplex, point-to-point circuits, or between a computer and a printer.

The basic concept is simple. Computer A sends something to computer B, and computer B acknowledges that it is ready to receive it by sending an X-ON signal, which tells A to begin transmitting. Computer A periodically pauses its transmission to let computer B send a message. If B is receiving without problems, it does nothing, and A continues to transmit. If B becomes busy, it sends the X-OFF signal and A stops transmitting until B sends an X-ON signal.

Because the X-ON and X-OFF signals can be easily lost during transmission, this simple scheme can lead to confusion. More sophisticated approaches have been developed, so its use is rapidly fading.

Polling

Polling is the process of sending a signal to a client (a computer or terminal) that gives it permission to transmit or asks it to receive. With polling, the client terminals and computers store all messages that need to be transmitted. Periodically, the host or front-end processor (FEP) polls the client to see if it has data to send. If the client has data to send, it sends the data. If the client has no data to send, it responds negatively, and the host or FEP asks another client if it has data to send.

In other words, polling is analogous to a classroom situation in which the instructor calls on the students who raise their hands. The instructor acts like the FEP or host. To gain access to the media, students raise their hands and the instructor recognizes them so they can contribute. When they have finished, the instructor again takes charge, and allows someone else to comment.

There are several types of polling. With *roll call polling*, the front-end processor works consecutively through a list of clients, first polling terminal 1, then terminal 2, and so on, until all are polled. Roll call polling can be modified to select clients in priority so that some get polled more often than others. For example, one could increase the priority of terminal 1 by using a polling sequence such as 1, 2, 3, 1, 4, 5, 1, 6, 7, 1, 8, 9.

Typically, roll call polling involves some waiting because the front-end processor has to poll a terminal and then wait for a response. The response might be an incoming message that was waiting to be sent or a negative response indicating nothing is to be sent. Alternately, the full "time-out period" may expire because the terminal is temporarily out of service (e.g., the terminal is malfunctioning or the user has turned it off). Usually, a timer "times out" the terminal after waiting several seconds without getting a response. If some sort of fail-safe time-out is not used, the system poll might lock up indefinitely on an out-of-service terminal.

Hub polling (often called token passing) is often used in LAN multipoint configurations (i.e., token ring) that do not have a central host computer. One computer starts the poll and passes it to the next computer on the multipoint circuit, which sends its message and passes the poll to the next computer. That computer then passes the poll to the next, and so on, until it reaches the first computer, which restarts the process again.

Contention

Contention is the opposite of controlled access. Computers wait until the circuit is free (i.e., no other computers are transmitting), and then transmit whenever they have data to send. Contention is commonly used in Ethernet local area networks.

As an analogy, suppose that you are talking with some friends. Each person tries to "get the floor" when the previous speaker finishes. Usually, the others yield to the first person who jumps in at the precise moment the previous speaker stops. Sometimes two people attempt to talk at the same time, so there must be some technique to continue the conversation after such a verbal "collision" occurs.

Relative Performance

Which media access control approach is best: controlled access or contention? There is no simple answer. The key consideration is *throughput*—which approach will permit the greatest amount of user data to be transmitted through the network.

In general, contention approaches work better than controlled approaches for small networks that have low usage. In this case, each computer can transmit when necessary, without waiting for permission. In high-volume networks, many computers want to transmit at the same time, and a well-controlled circuit prevents collisions. We will discuss media access control LANs in more detail in Chapter 7.

✳✳ ERROR CONTROL IN NETWORKS

Before describing the control mechanisms that can be implemented to protect a network from errors, you should realize that there are human errors and network errors. Human errors, such as a mistake in typing a number, usually are controlled through the application program. Network errors, such as those that occur during transmission, are controlled by the network hardware and software.

There are two categories of network errors: *corrupted data* (data that have been changed) and *lost data*. Networks should be designed to prevent, detect, and correct both corrupted data and lost data. We begin by examining the sources of errors and how to prevent them, and then turn to error detection and correction.

What Are Network Errors?

Depending on the type of circuit and the amount of noise on the lines, network errors occur every few hours, minutes, or seconds. No network can eliminate all errors, but most errors can be prevented, detected, and corrected by proper design. Interexchange carriers that provide data transmission circuits provide statistical measures specifying typical *error rates* and the pattern of errors that can be expected on the circuits they lease. For example, the error rate might be stated as 1 in 500,000, meaning there is 1 bit in error for every 500,000 bits transmitted.

Normally, errors appear in bursts. In a *burst error*, more than one data bit is changed by the error-causing condition. In other words, errors are not uniformly distributed in time. Although an error rate might be stated as 1 in 500,000, errors are more likely to occur as 100 bits every 50 million bits. The fact that errors tend to be clustered in bursts rather than evenly dispersed is both good and bad. If the errors were not clustered, an error rate of 1 bit in 500,000 would make it rare for two erroneous bits to occur in the same character. Consequently, simple character-checking schemes would be effective at detecting errors. When errors are #ore or less evenly distrib#ted, it is not di#ficult to gras# the me#ning even when the error #ate is high, as it is in this #entence (1 charac#er in 20). But bursts errors are the rule rather than the exception, often obliterating a hundred or more bits at a time. This makes it more difficult to recover the meaning, so more reliance must be placed on knowledge of the message #######[1] or on special logical or numerical error detection and correction methods. The positive side is that there are long periods of error-free transmission, meaning that only a very few messages encounter errors.

The error rate in transmissions sent over the dial-up network (i.e., telephone company circuits) varies from one circuit to another. Dial-up lines are more prone to errors than private dedicated lines because they have less stable transmission parameters. In some cases, users must transmit the data at a slower speed because higher transmission speeds are more error prone. Because different calls use different circuits, they usually experience different transmission conditions. A bad line is not necessarily a serious problem because a new call might use a better line.

What Causes Errors?

Line noise and distortion can cause data communication errors. The focus in this section is on electrical media such as twisted-pair and coaxial cable, because they are more likely to suffer from noise than optical media such as fiber optic cable. In this case, noise is undesirable electrical signals (for fiber optic cable, it is undesirable light). Noise is introduced by equipment or natural disturbances, and it degrades the performance of a communication circuit. Noise manifests itself as extra bits, missing bits, or bits that have been "flipped" (i.e., changed from 1 to 0 or vice versa). Figure 5–1 summarizes the major sources of error and ways to prevent them. The first six in Figure 5–1 are the most important; the last three are more common in analog rather that digital circuits.

Line outages are a catastrophic cause of errors and incomplete transmission. Occasionally, a communication circuit fails for a brief period. This type of failure may be caused by faulty telephone end office equipment, storms, loss of the carrier signal, or any other failure that causes a short circuit.

White noise or *gaussian noise* (the familiar background hiss or static on radios and telephones) is caused by the thermal agitation of electrons and therefore is inescapable. Even if the equipment were perfect and the wires were perfectly insulated from any and all external interference, there still would be some white noise.

---

[1]In case you could not guess, the word is "context."

Source of Error	What Causes It	How to Prevent It
Line Outages	Storms, accidents	
White Noise	Movement of electrons	Increase signal strength
Impulse Noise	Sudden increases in electricity (e.g., lightning)	Shield or move the wires
Cross-talk	Multiplexer guardbands too small, or wires too close together	Increase the guardbands, or move or shield the wires
Echo	Poor connections	Fix the connections, or tune equipment
Attenuation	Gradual decrease in signal over distance	Use repeaters or amplifiers
Intermodulation Noise	Signals from several circuits combine	Move or shield the wires
Jitter	Analog signals change phase	Tune equipment
Harmonic Distortion	Amplifier changes phase	Tune equipment

Figure 5–1 Sources of errors and ways to minimize them.

White noise usually is not a problem unless it becomes so strong that it obliterates the transmission. In this case, the strength of the electrical signal is increased so it overpowers the white noise. In technical terms, we increase the signal-to-noise ratio.

Impulse noise (sometimes called spikes) is the primary source of errors in data communications. Impulse noise is heard as a click or a crackling noise and can last as long as 1/100 of a second. Such a click does not really affect voice communications, but it can obliterate a group of data, causing a burst error. At 300 bps, 3 bits would be changed by a spike of 1/100 of a second, whereas at 33,600 bps, 336 bits would be changed. Some of the sources of impulse noise are voltage changes in adjacent lines, lightning flashes during thunderstorms, fluorescent lights, and poor connections in circuits.

Cross-talk occurs when one circuit picks up signals in another. You experience cross-talk during telephone calls when you hear other conversations in the background. It occurs between pairs of wires that are carrying separate signals, in multiplexed links carrying many discrete signals, or in microwave links in which one antenna picks up a minute reflection from another antenna. Cross-talk between lines increases with greater communication distance, increased proximity of the two wires, stronger signals, and higher frequency signals. Wet or damp weather can also increase cross-talk. Like white noise, cross-talk has such a low signal strength that it normally is not bothersome.

Echoes can cause errors. Echoes are caused by poor connections that cause the signal to reflect back to the transmitting equipment. If the strength of the echo is strong enough to be detected, it causes errors. Echoes, like cross-talk and white noise, have such a low signal strength that they normally are not bothersome. Echoes can also occur in fiber optic cables when connections between cables are not properly aligned.

Attenuation is the loss of power a signal suffers as it travels from the transmitting computer to the receiving computer. Some power is absorbed by the medium or is lost before it reaches the receiver. As the medium absorbs power, the signal becomes weaker, and the receiving equipment has less and less chance of correctly interpreting the data. This power loss is a function of the transmission method and circuit medium. High frequencies lose power more rapidly than low frequencies during transmission, so the received signal can be distorted by unequal loss of its component frequencies. Attenuation increases as frequency increases or as the diameter of the wire decreases.

Intermodulation noise is a special type of cross-talk. The signals from two circuits combine to form a new signal that falls into a frequency band reserved for another signal. This type of noise is similar to harmonics in music. On a multiplexed line, many different signals are amplified together, and slight variations in the adjustment of the equipment can cause intermodulation noise. A maladjusted modem may transmit a strong frequency tone when not transmitting data, thus producing this type of noise.

Jitter may affect the accuracy of the data being transmitted because minute variations in amplitude, phase, and frequency always occur. The generation of a pure carrier signal in an analog circuit is impossible. The signal may be impaired by continuous and rapid gain and/or phase changes. This jitter may be random or periodic. Phase jitter during a telephone call causes the voice to fluctuate in volume.

Harmonic distortion usually is caused by an amplifier on a circuit that does not correctly represent its output with what was delivered to it on the input side. Phase hits are short-term shifts "out of phase," with the possibility of a shift back into phase.

Error Prevention

There are many techniques to prevent errors (or at least reduce them), depending on the situation. *Shielding* (protecting wires by covering them with an insulating coating) is one of the best ways to prevent impulse noise, cross-talk and intermodulation noise. Many different types of wires and cables are available with different amounts of shielding. In general, the greater the shielding, the more expensive the cable, and the more difficult it is to install.

Moving cables away from sources of noise (especially power sources) can also reduce impulse noise cross-talk and intermodulation noise. For impulse noise, this means avoiding lights and heavy machinery. Locating communication cables away from power cables is always a good idea. For cross-talk, this means physically separating the cables from other communication cables.

Cross-talk and intermodulation noise are often caused by improper multiplexing. Changing multiplexing techniques (e.g., from FDM to TDM), or changing the frequencies or size of the guardbands in frequency division multiplexing can help.

Many types of noise (e.g., echoes, white noise, jitter, harmonic distortion) can be caused by poorly maintained equipment or poor connections and splices among cables. This is particularly true for echo in fiber optic cables, which is almost always caused by poor connections. The solution here is obvious: tune the transmission equipment and redo the connections.

To avoid attenuation, telephone circuits have *repeaters* or *amplifiers* spaced throughout their length. The distance between them depends on the amount of power lost per unit length of the transmission line. An amplifier takes the incoming signal, increases its strength, and retransmits it on the next section of the circuit. They are typically used on analog circuits such as the telephone company's voice circuits. The distance between the amplifiers depends on the amount of attenuation, although one- to ten-mile intervals are common. On analog circuits, it is important to recognize that the noise and distortion are *also* amplified, along with the signal. This means some noise from a previous circuit is regenerated and amplified each time the signal is amplified.

Repeaters are commonly used on digital circuits. A repeater receives the incoming signal, translates it into a digital message, and retransmits the message. Because the message is recreated at each repeater, noise and distortion from the previous circuit are not amplified which provides a much cleaner signal and results in a lower error rate for digital circuits.

If the circuit is provided by a common carrier such as the telephone company, you can lease a more expensive *conditioned* circuit. A conditioned circuit is one that has been certified by the carrier to experience fewer errors. Several levels of conditioning provide increasingly fewer errors at increasingly higher cost. Conditioned circuits employ a variety of the techniques described previously (e.g., shielding) to provide less noise.

Error Detection

It is possible to develop data transmission methodologies that give very high *error detection and correction* performance. The only way to do error detection and correction is to send extra data with each message. These error detection data are added to each message by the data link layer of the sender based on some mathematical calculations performed on the message (in some cases, error detection methods are built into the hardware itself). The receiver performs the same mathematical calculations on the message it receives and matches its results against the error detection data that were transmitted with the message. If the two match, the message is assumed to be correct. If they don't match, an error has occurred.

In general, the larger the amount of error detection data sent, the greater the ability to detect an error. However, as the amount of error detection data is increased, the throughput of useful data is reduced, because more of the available capacity is used to transmit these error detection data and less is used to transmit the actual message itself. Therefore, the efficiency of data throughput varies inversely as the desired amount of error detection is increased.

Three common error detection methods are parity checking, longitudinal redundancy checking, and polynomial checking (particularly checksum and cyclic redundancy checking).

Parity Checking

One of the oldest and simplest error detection methods is *parity*. With this technique, one additional bit is added to each byte in the message. The value of this additional *parity bit* is based on the number of 1s in each byte transmitted. This

Assume we are using even parity with 7-bit ASCII.
The letter V in 7-bit ASCII is encoded as 0110101.
Because there are four 1s (an even number), parity is set to zero.
This would be transmitted as: 01101010.

Assume we are using even parity with 7-bit ASCII.
The letter W in 7-bit ASCII is encoded as 0001101.
Because there are three 1s (an odd number), parity is set to one.
This would be transmitted as: 00011011.

Figure 5–2 Using parity for error detection.

parity bit is set to make the total number of 1s in the byte (including the parity bit) either an even number or an odd number. Figure 5–2 gives an example.

A little thought will convince you that any single error (a switch of a 1 to a 0 or vice versa) will be detected by parity, but it cannot determine which bit was in error. You will know an error occurred, but not what the error was. But, if 2 bits are switched, the parity check will not detect any error. It is easy to see that parity can detect errors only when an odd number of bits have been switched; any even number of errors cancel each other out. Therefore, the probability of detecting an error, given that one has occurred, is only about 50 percent. Many networks today do not use parity because of its low error detection rate. When parity is used, protocols are described as having *odd parity* or *even parity*.

Longitudinal Redundancy Checking (LRC)

The longitudinal redundancy checking (LRC) method was developed to overcome the problems with parity's low probability of detection. LRC adds one additional character, called the block check character (BCC), to the end of the entire message or packet of data. The value of the BCC is determined in the same manner as the parity bit, but by counting longitudinally through the message, rather than by counting vertically through each character. The first bit of the LRC is determined by counting the number of 1s in the first bits of all characters in the message, and setting the first bit of the LRC to a 1 or a 0, depending upon whether the sum is

For example, suppose we were to send the message "DATA" using odd parity and LRC with 7-bit ASCII:

Letter	ASCII	Parity bit
D	1000100	1
A	1000001	1
T	1010100	0
A	1000001	1
BCC	1101111	1

(Note that the parity bit in the BCC is determined by parity, not LRC.)

Figure 5–3 Using LRC for error detection.

odd or even. The second bit of the BCC is determined by counting the number of 1s in the second bits of characters in the message, and so on for all bits in the BCC. LRC is usually used in conjunction with parity, producing an error detection rate above 98 percent for typical burst errors of 10 bits or more. LRC is less capable of detecting single bit errors, but is still much better than parity—and fortunately, single bit errors are rare. Figure 5–3 provides an example.

Polynomial Checking

A 98 percent error detection rate is reasonably good, but it is still not perfect. Like LRC, *polynomial checking* adds a character or series of characters to the end of the message based on a mathematical algorithm.

With the *checksum* technique, a checksum (typically 1 byte) is added to the end of the message. The checksum is calculated by adding the decimal value of each character in the message, dividing the sum by 255, and using the remainder as the checksum. The receiver calculates its own checksum in the same way and compares it with the transmitted checksum. If the two values are equal, the message is presumed to contain no errors. Use of checksum detects close to 95 percent of the errors for multiple-bit burst errors.

The most popular polynomial error checking scheme is cyclical redundancy check (CRC). It adds 8, 16, 24, or 32 bits to the message. With CRC, a message is treated as one long binary number, P. Before transmission, the data link layer (or hardware device) divides P by a fixed binary number, G, resulting in a whole number, Q, and a remainder, R/G. So, $P/G = Q + R/G$. For example, if $P = 58$ and $G = 8$, then $Q = 7$ and $R = 2$. G is chosen so that the remainder R will be either 8 bits, 16 bits, 24 bits, or 32 bits.

The remainder, R, is appended to the message as the error checking characters before transmission. The receiving hardware divides the received message by the same G, which generates an R. The receiving hardware checks to ascertain whether the received R agrees with the locally generated R. If it does not, the message is assumed to be in error.

CRC performs quite well. The most commonly used CRC codes are CRC-16 (a 16-bit version), CRC-CCITT (another 16-bit version), and CRC-32 (a 32-bit version). The probability of detecting an error is 100 percent for all errors of the same length as the CRC or less. For example, CRC-16 is guaranteed to detect errors if 16 or fewer bits are affected. If the burst error is longer than the CRC, then CRC is not perfect but is close to it. CRC-16 will detect about 99.998 percent of all burst errors longer than 16 bits, while CRC-32 will detect about 99.99999998 percent of all burst errors longer than 32 bits.

Error Correction via Retransmission

Once an error has been detected, it must be corrected. The simplest, most effective, least expensive, and most commonly used method for error correction is *retransmission*. With retransmission, a receiver that detects an error simply asks the sender to retransmit the message until it is received without error. This is often called

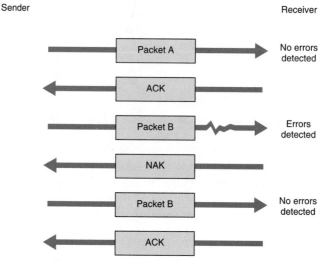

Figure 5–4 Stop and wait ARQ.

Automatic Repeat reQuest (ARQ). There are two types of ARQ: stop-and-wait and continuous.

Stop-and-wait ARQ

With *stop-and-wait ARQ*, the sender stops and waits for a response from the receiver after each message or data packet. After receiving a packet, the receiver sends either an acknowledgment (*ACK*) if the message was received without error, or a negative acknowledgment (*NAK*) if the message contained an error. If it is a NAK, the sender resends the previous message. If it is an ACK, the sender continues with the next message. Stop-and-wait ARQ is, by definition, a half-duplex transmission technique (see Figure 5–4).

Continuous ARQ

With *continuous ARQ*, the sender does not wait for an acknowledgment after sending a message; it immediately sends the next one. While the messages are being transmitted, the sender examines the stream of returning acknowledgments. If it receives a NAK, the sender retransmits the needed messages. The packets that are retransmitted may be only those containing an error (called *Link Access Protocol for Modems (LAP–M)*), or may be the first packet with an error and all those that followed it (called *Go-Back-N ARQ*). LAP–M is better because it is more efficient.

Continuous ARQ is, by definition, a full-duplex transmission technique, because both the sender and the receiver are transmitting simultaneously (the sender is sending messages, and the receiver is sending ACKs and NAKs). Continuous ARQ is sometimes called *sliding window*. Figure 5–5 illustrates the flow of messages on a communication circuit using continuous ARQ.

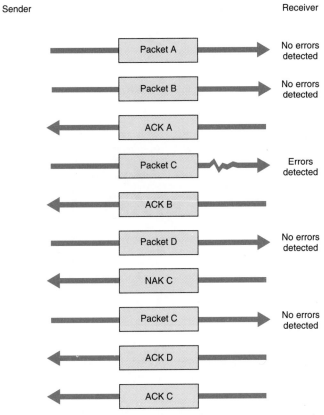

Figure 5–5 Continuous ARQ.

Forward Error Correction

Forward error correction uses codes containing sufficient redundancy to prevent errors by detecting and correcting them at the receiving end *without* retransmission of the original message. The redundancy, or extra bits required, varies with different schemes. It ranges from a small percentage of extra bits to 100 percent redundancy, with the number of error detecting bits roughly equaling the number of data bits. One characteristic of many error-correcting codes is that there must be a minimum number of error-free bits between bursts of errors.

To show how such a code works, consider the example of a forward error checking code in Figure 5–6, called a *Hamming code*, after its inventor, R. W. Hamming. This code is very simple, capable of correcting 1-bit errors. More sophisticated techniques (e.g., Reed–Solomon) are commonly used today, but this will give you a sense of how they work.

The Hamming code associates even parity bits with unique combinations of data bits. Using a 4-data-bit code as an example, a character might be represented

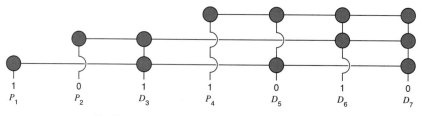

Checking relations between parity bits (P) and data bits (D)

0 = Corresponding parity check is correct 1 = Corresponding parity check fails				Determines in which bit the error occured
P_4	P_2	P_1		
0	0	0	⟶	no error
0	0	1	⟶	P_1
0	1	0	⟶	P_2
0	1	1	⟶	D_3
1	0	0	⟶	P_4
1	0	1	⟶	D_5
1	1	0	⟶	D_6
1	1	1	⟶	D_7

Interpreting parity bit patterns

Figure 5–6 Hamming code for forward error correction.

by the data bit configuration 1010. Three parity bits P_1, P_2, and P_4 are added, resulting in a 7-bit code, shown in the upper half of Figure 5–6. Notice that the data bits (D_3, D_5, D_6, D_7) are 1010, and the parity bits (P_1, P_2, P_4) are 101.

As depicted in the upper half of Figure 5–6, parity bit P_1 applies to data bits D_3, D_5, and D_7. Parity bit P_2 applies to data bits D_3, D_6, and D_7. Parity bit P_4 applies to data bits D_5, D_6, and D_7. For the example, in which D_3, D_5, D_6, D_7 = 1010, P_1 must equal 1 because there is only a single 1 among D_3, D_5, and D_7, and parity must be even. Similarly, P_2 must be 0 because D_3 and D_6 are 1s. P_4 is a 1 because D_6 is the only 1 among D_5, D_6, and D_7.

Now, assume that during the transmission, data bit D_7 is changed from a 0 to a 1 by line noise. Because this data bit is being checked by P_1, P_2, and P_4, all three parity bits now show odd parity instead of the correct even parity. (D_7 is the only data bit that is monitored by all three parity bits; therefore, when D_7 is in error, all three parity bits show an incorrect parity.) In this way, the receiving equipment can determine which bit was in error and reverse its state, thus correcting the error without retransmission.

The lower half of Figure 5–6 is a table that determines the location of the bit in error. A 1 in the table means that the corresponding parity bit indicates a parity error. Conversely, a 0 means the parity check is correct. These 0s and 1s form a binary number that indicates the numerical location of the erroneous bit. In the previous example, P_1, P_2, and P_4 checks all failed, yielding 111, or a decimal 7, the subscript of the erroneous bit.

Forward error correction is commonly used in satellite transmission. A round trip from the Earth station to the satellite and back includes a significant delay. Error rates can fluctuate, depending on the condition of equipment, sun spots, or the weather. Indeed, some weather conditions make it impossible to transmit without some errors, making forward error correction essential. Compared to satellite equipment costs, the additional cost of forward error correction is insignificant.

The use of forward error correction in broader markets such as modem-based communications is limited today but is becoming more common as chip implementations of forward error correction come on the market. The V.34 modem standard, for example, includes forward error checking.

✳✳ DATA LINK PROTOCOLS

In this section, we outline several commonly used data link layer protocols, which are summarized in Figure 5–7. Here we focus on message delineation—which indicates where a message starts and stops—and the various parts, or fields, within the message. For example, you must clearly indicate which part of a message or packet of data is the error-control portion. Otherwise, the receiver cannot use it properly to determine if an error has occurred.

Protocol	Size	Error Detection	Retransmission	Media Access
Asynchronous Transmission	1	Parity	Continuous ARQ	Full Duplex
File Transfer Protocols				
XMODEM	132	8-bit checksum	Stop-and-wait ARQ	Controlled Access
XMODEM-CRC	132	8-bit CRC	Stop-and-wait ARQ	Controlled Access
XMODEM-1K	1028	8-bit CRC	Stop-and-wait ARQ	Controlled Access
YMODEM	1029	16-bit CRC	Stop-and-wait ARQ	Controlled Access
ZMODEM	*	32-bit CRC	Continuous ARQ	Controlled Access
KERMIT	*	24-bit CRC	Continuous ARQ	Controlled Access
Synchronous Protocols				
SDLC	*	16-bit CRC	Continuous ARQ	Controlled Access
HDLC	*	16-bit CRC	Continuous ARQ	Controlled Access
Token ring	*	32-bit CRC	Stop-and-wait ARQ	Controlled Access
Ethernet	*	32-bit CRC	Stop-and-wait ARQ	Contention
SLIP	*	None	None	Full Duplex
PPP	*	16-bit CRC	Continuous ARQ	Full Duplex

Varies, depending on the message length.

Figure 5–7 Protocol summary.

Asynchronous Transmission

Asynchronous transmission is often referred to as start–stop transmission because the transmitting computer can transmit a character whenever it is convenient, and the receiving computer will accept that character. It is typically used on point-to-point full-duplex circuits (i.e., circuits that have only two computers on them), so media access control is not a concern.

With *asynchronous transmission*, each character is transmitted independent of all other characters. In order to separate the characters and synchronize transmission, a *start bit* and a *stop bit* are put on the front and back of *each* individual character. For example, if we are using 7-bit ASCII with even parity, the total transmission is 10 bits for each character (1 start bit, 7 bits for the letter, 1 parity bit, 1 stop bit).

The start bit and stop bit are the opposite of each other. Typically, the start bit is a 0 and the stop bit is a 1. There is no fixed distance between characters, because the terminal transmits the character as soon as it is typed, which varies with the speed of the typist. The recognition of the start and stop of each message (called *synchronization*) takes place for an individual character because the *start bit* is a signal that tells the receiver to start sampling the incoming bits of a character so the data bits can be interpreted into their proper character structure. A *stop bit* informs the receiver that the character has been received and resets it for recognition of the next start bit.

When the sender is waiting for the user to type the next character, no data is sent; the communication circuit is idle. This idle time really is artificial—some signal must always be sent down the circuit. For example, suppose we are using a unipolar digital signaling technique where +5 volts indicates a 1 and 0 volts indicates a 0 (see Chapter 4). Even if we send 0 volts, we are still sending a signal, a 0 in this case. Asynchronous transmission defines the idle signal (the signal that is sent down the circuit when no data are being transmitted) as the same as the stop bit. When the sender finishes transmitting a letter and is waiting for more data to send, it sends a continuous series of stop bits. Figure 5–8 shows an example of asynchronous transmission.

Some older protocols have two stop bits instead of the traditional single stop bit. The use of both a start bit and a stop bit is changing; some protocols have eliminated the stop bit altogether.

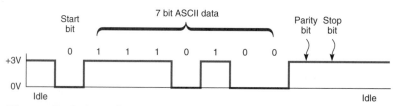

Figure 5–8 Asynchronous transmission.

Asynchronous File Transfer Protocols

Today, data transmission by microcomputers often means the transfer of data files. In general, microcomputer file transfer protocols are used on asynchronous point-to-point circuits, typically across telephone lines via a modem. All file transfer protocols have two characteristics in common. First, these protocols are designed to transmit error-free data from one computer to another. Second, since there is a large amount of data to be transmitted, it makes more sense to group the data together into blocks of data that are transmitted at the same time, rather than sending each character individually via standard asynchronous transmission. This section discusses the structure of the data blocks (also called packets or frames) used by several common protocols.

XMODEM

The *XMODEM* protocol takes the data being transmitted and divides it into blocks (see Figure 5–9). Each block has a start-of-header character (SOH), a 1-byte block number, 128 bytes of data, and a 1-byte checksum for error checking. Even though this protocol was developed for microcomputer-to-microcomputer communications, it often is used for microcomputer-to-mainframe communications. XMODEM uses stop-and-wait ARQ.

XMODEM-CRC improves error detection accuracy of the XMODEM protocol. It replaces the checksum with a more rigorous one-byte cyclical redundancy check (CRC-8). XMODEM-1K increases the efficiency of XMODEM-CRC by using data blocks of 1024 bytes instead of the 128-character blocks of the original XMODEM. Efficiency and throughput is discussed in more detail later in this chapter.

YMODEM

The primary benefit of the *YMODEM* protocol is CRC-16 error checking. YMODEM is the XMODEM-1K protocol with CRC-16 error checking and multiple file transfer capability, although there are several other minor differences as well.

ZMODEM

ZMODEM is a newer protocol written to overcome some of the problems in packet switching networks like SprintNet or Tymnet. It is not a subset of XMODEM, but instead incorporates features of several protocols. It uses a more powerful error

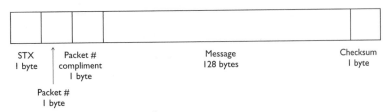

Figure 5–9 XMODEM format.

detection method (CRC-32) with continuous ARQ. ZMODEM also dynamically adjusts its packet size according to communication circuit conditions to increase efficiency. Usually ZMODEM is preferred to XMODEM or YMODEM.

KERMIT

KERMIT is a very popular protocol (and yes, it is named after Kermit the Frog of *Sesame Street* fame). The KERMIT protocol was developed by Columbia University, which also developed a software communication package that uses the same protocol.

KERMIT is an extremely flexible protocol that can be adjusted to support a variety of different packet sizes and error detection methods. Kermit typically uses 1000 byte packets with CRC-24, but these are adjusted during transmission to optimize performance. It uses either stop-and-wait ARQ or continuous ARQ. It is especially suited to microcomputer-to-mainframe connections, but it works equally well with microcomputer-to-microcomputer or mainframe-to-mainframe connections. KERMIT-based programs provide error-checked transfer of text and binary files using both 7- and 8-bit codes.

Synchronous Transmission

With *synchronous transmission,* all the letters or data in one group of data are transmitted at one time as a block of data. This block of data is called a *frame* or *packet,* depending on the protocol, but the meaning is the same. For example, a terminal or microcomputer will save all the keystrokes typed by the user and only transmit them when the user presses a special "transmit" key. In this case, the start and end of the entire packet must be marked, not the start and end of each letter. Synchronous transmission is often used on both point-to-point and multipoint circuits. Use on multipoint circuits means that each packet must include a destination address and a source address, and that media access control is important.

The start and end of each packet (synchronization) sometimes is marked by adding synchronization characters (SYN) to the start of the packet. Depending on the protocol, there might be anywhere from one to eight SYN characters. After the SYN characters, the transmitting computer sends a long stream of data that may contain thousands of bits. Knowing what code is being used, the receiving computer counts off the appropriate number of bits for the first character, assumes this is the first character, and passes it to the computer. It then counts off the bits for the second character, and so on.

In summary, asynchronous data transmission means that each character is transmitted as a totally independent entity with its own start and stop bits to inform the receiving computer that the character is beginning and ending. Synchronous transmission means that whole blocks of data are transmitted as packets after the sender and the receiver have been synchronized.

There are many protocols for synchronous transmission. These protocols fall into three broad categories: byte-oriented protocols, bit-oriented protocols, and byte-count protocols. In this next section, we discuss six common synchronous data link protocols.

Synchronous Data Link Control (SDLC)

Synchronous Data Link Control (SDLC) is a mainframe protocol developed by IBM in 1972 that is still in use today. SDLC is a *bit-oriented protocol*, because the data contained in the packet do not have to be in 8-bit bytes. SDLC is therefore more flexible than byte-oriented protocols. It uses a controlled-access media access protocol.

Figure 5–10 shows a typical SDLC packet (or *frame*, as it is called). Each SDLC frame begins and ends with a special bit pattern (01111110), known as the flag. The address field identifies the destination. The length of the address field is usually 8 bits but can be set at 16 bits; all computers on the same network must use the same length. The control field identifies the kind of frame that is being transmitted, either information or supervisory. An information frame is used for the transfer and reception of messages, frame numbering of contiguous frames, and the like. A supervisory frame is used to transmit acknowledgments (ACKs and NAKs). The message field is of variable length and is the user's message. The frame check sequence field is a 16-bit or 32-bit cyclical redundancy checking (CRC) code.

SDLC and other bit-oriented protocols suffer from a *transparency problem*; that is, the protocol is not "transparent" because it cannot automatically send all types of data with any bit patterns. It is possible that the user's data to be transmitted contains the same bit pattern as the flag (01111110). If this is not prevented, the receiver will mistakenly believe that these data mark the end of the frame and will ignore all the data that follow it. The solution is called bit stuffing. Anytime the sender encounters five 1s in a row in the user's data to be transmitted, the sender "stuffs" one extra bit, a 0, into the message and continues to transmit. Anytime the receiver encounters five 1s followed by a 0 (i.e., 111110), the receiver automatically deletes the 0 and continues to process the data stream. Conversely, if the receiver encounters five 1s followed by a 1 (i.e., 111111), it knows to expect another zero as part of the flag. This technique works, but increases the complexity of the protocol.

High-level Data Link Control (HDLC)

High-level Data Link Control (HDLC) is a formal standard developed by the International Organization for Standardization (ISO). HDLC is essentially the same as SDLC, except that the address and control fields can be longer. HDLC also has several additional benefits that are beyond the scope of this book, such as a larger

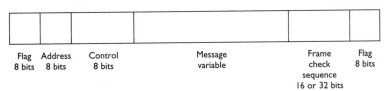

Flag 8 bits | Address 8 bits | Control 8 bits | Message variable | Frame check sequence 16 or 32 bits | Flag 8 bits

Figure 5–10 SDLC format.

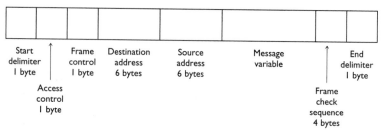

Figure 5–11 Token ring format.

sliding window. It uses a controlled-access media access protocol. One variant, *Link Access Procedure–Balanced (LAP–B)*, uses the same structure as HDLC, but is a scaled down version of HDLC (i.e., provides fewer of those benefits mentioned that are "beyond the scope of this book").

Token Ring (IEEE 802.5)

One very popular local area network protocol is *token ring*. Token ring was developed by IBM (by a team under the direction of Olaf Soderblum) in the early 1980s, and later became a formal standard of the Institute of Electrical and Electronics Engineers (IEEE) called IEEE 802.5. It uses a controlled-access media access protocol.

Figure 5–11 shows a typical token ring frame. Token ring is a byte-oriented protocol that does not suffer the same transparency problems as SDLC. Each token ring frame starts and ends with a special delimiter that is a special electrical signal produced in a manner different from any other pattern of bits,[2] and thus cannot be confused with a data bit. The next two fields, access control and frame control, are control fields used by its media access control protocol. The destination address specifies the receiver, while the source address specifies the sender. The size of the message field is variable, but in general is limited to 4500 bytes. The frame check sequence is a 32-bit CRC code.

Ethernet (IEEE 802.3)

Ethernet is another very popular LAN protocol, conceived by Bob Metcalfe in 1973 and developed jointly by Digital, Intel, and Xerox in the 1970s. Since then, Ethernet has been further refined and developed into a formal standard called IEEE 802.3.[3] Ethernet is a *byte-count protocol* because instead of using special characters or bit patterns to mark the end of a packet, it includes a field that specifies the length of the message portion of the packet. Unlike SDLC and HDLC, Ethernet has no trans-

---

[2]Token ring uses differential Manchester encoding, which is a special form of bipolar signaling. The delimiter violates the rules of this signaling technique, so that the data link layer can distinguish it from data.

[3]A competing version of Ethernet called Ethernet II is also available. Ethernet II and IEEE 802.3 Ethernet are similar, but differ enough to be incompatible. In this book, we discuss only IEEE 802.3 Ethernet.

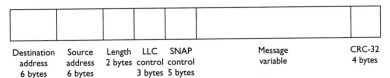

Figure 5-12 Ethernet packet layout.

parency problems. Any bit pattern can be transmitted, because Ethernet uses the number of bytes, not control characters, to delineate the message. Ethernet uses a contention media access protocol.

Figure 5–12 shows a typical ethernet packet. The destination address specifies the receiver, while the source address specifies the sender. The length indicates the length in 8-bit bytes of the message portion of the packet. The LLC control and SNAP control are used to pass control information between the sender and receiver and often indicate the type of network layer protocol the packet contains (e.g., TCP/IP or IPX/SPX, as described in Chapter 6). The maximum length of the message is 1492 bytes. The packet ends with a CRC-32 frame check sequence used for error detection.

Serial Line Internet Protocol (SLIP)

Serial Line Internet Protocol (SLIP) is a byte-oriented protocol developed in the mid-1980s. It was designed as an extremely simple protocol for connecting two computers using Internet protocols (TCP/IP, which is described in Chapter 6) over a point-to-point telephone line. It was intended to be temporary and not widely used, because it has some serious limitations as we shall see. However, it has become one of two standard protocols for connecting from a client computer to an Internet service provider. The other protocol, PPP (discussed in the next section), will gradually replace SLIP in the coming years. SLIP uses full duplex, so media access protocols are unimportant.

Figure 5–13 shows a typical SLIP packet. SLIP simply adds an ''END'' character (11000000) to the front and back of the data packet produced by the network layer. There is no addressing, because SLIP was designed for use over a telephone line connecting only two computers. There is no error control, which is a serious problem because errors go undetected unless the network layer protocol performs error checking (which is possible, but seldom done).

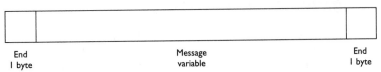

Figure 5-13 SLIP packet layout.

Figure 5–14 PPP packet layout.

SLIP suffers from the same transparency problems as SDLC. It is possible that the user's message contains the same bit pattern as the END character, which, if transmitted, would cause a premature end of the packet. Therefore, the sender scans the message. If it discovers a bit pattern in the user's message that matches the END character, it replaces it with two bytes for transmission: an ESC character (11011001) and an END replacement character (11011100). Any time a receiver sees these two bytes together, it knows that the user's message contained the END character. It replaces the two bytes with the END character before sending the message to the network layer for processing.

Likewise, the ESC character could also be present in the user's message. The sender uses the same process to translate any ESC characters in the user's message into another two-byte code—ESC and an ESC replacement character (11011101)—and the receiver uses the same process to reverse it.

Compressed SLIP (CSLIP) was developed in 1990, and is sometimes called van Jacobson compression after the person who created it. As the name suggests, CSLIP uses data compression to reduce the amount of data transmitted.

Point-to-Point Protocol (PPP)

Point-to-Point Protocol (PPP) is a byte-oriented protocol developed in the early 1990s as a replacement for SLIP. It too is designed to transfer data over a point-to-point telephone line, but it provides two important advantages over SLIP or CSLIP. First, it includes error control. Second, it will support network layer protocols other than just the Internet protocols. It also suffers from the same transparency problems. PPP uses full duplex, so media access protocols are unimportant.

Figure 5–14 shows a PPP packet. The packet begins and ends with a flag (01111110). The next two fields (address and control) are generally fixed for the duration of any one connection (i.e., telephone call). The protocol field specifies the network layer protocol (e.g., TCP/IP, IPX/SPX). The message may be up to 1500 bytes in length. PPP uses CRC-16 for error control.

✸✸ TRANSMISSION EFFICIENCY

One objective of a data communication network is to move the highest possible volume of accurate information through the network. The higher the volume, the greater the resulting network's efficiency and the lower the cost. Network efficiency is affected by characteristics of the circuits such as error rates and maximum transmission speed, as well as by the speed of transmitting and receiving equipment, the error detection and control methodology, and the protocol used by the data link layer.

Each protocol we discussed uses some bits or bytes to delineate the start and end of each message and for error control. These bits and bytes are necessary for the transmission to occur, but they are not part of the message. They add no value to the user, but they count against the total number of bits that can be transmitted.

Each communication protocol has both information bits and overhead bits. *Information bits* are those used to convey the user's meaning. *Overhead bits* are used for purposes such as error checking, and marking the start and end of characters and packets. A parity bit used for error checking is an overhead bit because it is not used to send the user's data; if you did not care about errors, the overhead error checking bit could be omitted and the users could still understand the message.

Transmission efficiency is defined as the total number of information bits (i.e., bits in the message sent by the user) divided by the total bits in transmission (i.e., information bits plus overhead bits).

For example, let's calculate the transmission efficiency of asynchronous transmission. Assume we are using 7-bit ASCII. We have 1 bit for parity, plus 1 start bit and 1 stop bit. Therefore, there are 7 bits of information in each letter, but the total bits per letter is 10 (7 + 3). The efficiency of the asynchronous transmission system is 7 bits of information divided by 10 total bits, for an efficiency of 70 percent.

In other words, with asynchronous transmission, only 70 percent of the data rate is available for the user; 30 percent is used by the transmission protocol. If we have a communication circuit using a V.34+ modem transmitting 33,600 bps, the user sees an effective data rate (or throughput) of 23,520 bps. This is very inefficient.

We can improve efficiency by reducing the number of overhead bits in each message or by increasing the number of information bits. For example, if we remove the stop bits from asynchronous transmission, efficiency increases to 7/9, or 77.8 percent. The throughput of a V.34+ modem would increase from 23,520 bps to 26,133 bps, which is not great, but at least is a little better.

The same basic formula can be used to calculate the efficiency of asynchronous file transfer or synchronous transmission. For example, suppose we are using SDLC. The number of information bits are calculated by determining how many information characters are in the message. If the message portion of the frame contains 100 information characters and we are using an 8-bit code, then there are $100 \times 8 = 800$ bits of information. The total number of bits is the 800 information bits plus the overhead bits that are inserted for delineation and error control. Figure 5–10 shows that SDLC has a beginning flag (8 bits), an address (8 bits), a control field (8 bits), a frame check sequence (assume we use a CRC-32 with 32 bits), and an ending flag (8 bits). This is a total of $8 + 8 + 8 + 32 + 8 = 64$ overhead bits; thus, efficiency is $800/(800 + 64) = 92.6$ percent. If the circuit provides a data rate of 33,600 bps, then the effective data rate available to the user is about 31,114 bps.

This example shows that synchronous networks usually are more efficient than asynchronous networks and some protocols are more efficient than others. The longer the message (1000 characters as opposed to 100), the more efficient the

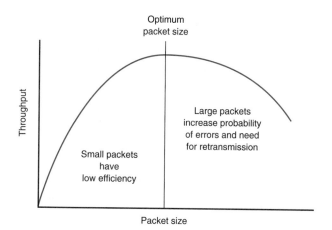

Figure 5–15 Packet size effects on throughput.

protocol. For example, suppose the message in the SDLC example was 1000 bytes. The efficiency here is 99.2 percent $(8000/(8000 + 64))$, giving an effective data rate of about 33,331 bps.

This example should also show why YMODEM (with a message length of 1024 bytes) is more efficient than XMODEM (with a message length of 128 bytes). The general rule is that the larger the message field, the more efficient the protocol.

So why not have 10K or even 100K packets to really increase efficiency? The answer is that anytime a packet is received containing an error, the entire packet must be retransmitted. Thus, if an entire file were sent as one large packet (e.g., 100K) and one bit was received in error, the entire 100K would have to be sent again. Clearly this is a waste of capacity. Furthermore, the probability that a packet contains an error increases with the size of the packet; larger packets are more likely to contain errors than smaller ones, simply due to the laws of probability.

Thus, in designing a protocol, there is a trade-off between large and small packets. Small packets are less efficient, but are less likely to contain errors. Thus, they "cost" less (in terms of circuit capacity) to retransmit if there is an error. See Figure 5–15.

Throughput is the total number of information bits received per second, after taking into account the overhead bits and the need to retransmit packets containing errors. Generally speaking, small packets provide better throughput for circuits with more errors, while larger packets provide better throughput in less error-prone networks. Packet sizes vary greatly among different networks, but most packet sizes tend to be from 50 bytes to 5,000 bytes.

Throughput (TRIB)

Calculating the actual throughput of a data communication network is complex. The maximum data rate in the circuit is clearly the most important, but as we have

Management Focus: Sleuthing for the Right Packet Size

Optimizing performance in a network, particularly a client–server network, can be difficult because few network managers realize the importance of the packet size. Selecting the right—or the wrong—packet size can have greater effects on performance than anything you might do to the server.

Standard Commercial, a multinational tobacco and agricultural company, noticed a decrease in network performance when it upgraded to a new server. They tested the effects of using packet sizes from 500 bytes to 32,000 bytes. In their tests, a packet size of 512 bytes required a total of 455K bytes transmitted over their network to transfer the test messages. In contrast, the 32K packet sizes were far more

efficient, cutting the total data by 44 percent to 257K bytes.

However, the problem with 32K byte packets was a noticeable response time delay, because messages were saved until the 32K byte packets were full.

The ideal packet size depends on the specific application and the pattern of messages it generates. For Standard Commercial, the ideal packet size appeared to be between 4K and 8K. Unfortunately, not all network software packages enable network managers to fine-tune packet sizes in this way.

Source: Infoworld, January 16, 1995.

shown, the efficiency of the data link protocol (and the network layer and application layer protocols) can significantly affect the throughput.

The use of a shared multipoint circuit, rather than a dedicated point-to-point circuit, will affect throughput, because the total capacity in the circuit must now be shared among several computers. Likewise, the use of a half-duplex circuit that must be shared between two computers (and that experiences turnaround delays) can reduce throughput. Propagation time (the time it takes the message to travel through the circuit from sender to receiver), especially on satellite circuits, affects throughput. Error rates on the communication circuit affect throughput, because errors require retransmissions of the same message. The ability of the server or host to handle multiple communication circuits is also important. If the server becomes overwhelmed at the number of simultaneous messages, the capacity of the network as a whole is reduced.

The term *transmission rate of information bits (TRIB)* describes the effective rate of data transfer. It is a measure of the effective quantity of information that is transmitted over a communication circuit per unit of time. The American National Standards Institute (ANSI) provides definitions for calculating the transfer rate of information bits. TRIB calculations may vary with the type of protocol used because of different numbers of control characters required and different time between blocks. The basic TRIB equation is shown in Figure 5–16, along with an example.

FORMULA FOR CALCULATING TRIB

$$\text{TRIB} = \frac{\text{Number of information bits accepted}}{\text{Total time required to get the bits accepted}}$$

$$\text{TRIB} = \frac{K(M - C)(1 - P)}{(M/R) + T}$$

where K = information bits per character
M = block length in characters
R = modem transmission rate in characters per second
C = average number of noninformation characters per block (control characters)
P = probability that a block will require retransmission because of error
T = time between blocks in seconds, such as modem delay/turnaround time on half duplex, echo suppressor delay on dial-up, and propagation delay on satellite transmission. This is the time required to reverse the direction of transmission from send to receive or recieve to send on a half-duplex (HDX) circuit. It can be obtained from the modem specification book and may be referred to as *reclocking time*.

The following TRIB example shows the calculation of throughput assuming a 4800 bits per second half-duplex circuit.

$$\text{TRIB} = \frac{7(400 - 10)(1 - 0.01)}{(400/600) + 0.025} = 3908 \text{ bits per second}$$

where K = 7 bits per character (information)
M = 400 characters per block
R = 600 characters per second (derived from 4800 bits per second divided by 8 bits/character)
C = 10 control characters per block
P = 0.01 (10^{-2}) or one retransmission out of 100 blocks transmitted—1%
T = 25 milliseconds (0.025) turnaround time

If all factors in the calculation remain constant except for the circuit, which is changed to full duplex (no turnaround time delays, $T = 0$), then the TRIB increases to 4054 bits per second.

Look at the equation where the turnaround value (T) is 0.025. If there is a further propagation delay time of 475 milliseconds (0.475), this figure changes to 0.500. For demonstrating how a satellite channel affects TRIB, the total delay time is now 500 milliseconds. Still using the figures above (except for the new 0.500 delay time), we reduce the TRIB for our half-duplex, satellite link to 2317 bits per second, which is almost one-half of the full-duplex (no turnaround time) 4054 bits per second.

Figure 5–16 Calculating TRIB.

Summary

Media Access Control   Media access control refers to controlling when computers transmit. There are three basic approaches. With roll call polling, a host mainframe or front-end processor polls client computers to see if they have data to send; computers can transmit only when they have been polled. With hub polling or token passing, the computers themselves manage when they can transmit by passing a token to each other; no computer can transmit unless it has the token. With contention, computers listen and transmit only when no others are transmitting. In general, contention approaches work better for small networks that have low levels of usage, while polling approaches work better for networks with high usage.

Sources and Prevention of Error   Errors occur in all networks, usually in groups (or bursts) rather than one bit at a time. The primary sources of errors are impulse noise (e.g., lightning), cross-talk, echo, and attenuation. Errors can be prevented (or at least reduced) by shielding the cables, moving cables away from sources of noise and power sources, using repeaters (and to a lesser extent amplifiers), and improving the quality of the equipment, media, and their connections.

Error Detection and Correction   All error detection schemes attach additional error detection data to the user's message based on a mathematical calculation. The receiver performs the same calculation on incoming messages and if the results of this calculation do not match the error detection data on the incoming message, an error has occurred. Parity, LRC, and CRC are the most common error detection schemes. The most common error correction technique is simply to ask the sender to retransmit the message until it is received without error. A different approach, forward error correction, includes sufficient information to allow the receiver to correct the error in most cases without asking for a retransmission.

Message Delineation   Message delineation means to indicate the start and end of message. Asynchronous transmission uses start and stop bits on each letter to mark where they begin and end. Synchronous techniques (e.g., SDLC, HDLC, token ring, Ethernet, SLIP, PPP) or file transfer protocols (e.g., XMODEM, YMODEM, ZMODEM, KERMIT) group blocks of data together into packets or frames that use special characters or bit patterns to mark the start and end of entire messages.

Transmission Efficiency and Throughput   Every protocol adds additional bits to the user's message before sending it (e.g., for error detection). These bits are called overhead bits because they add no value to the user; they simply ensure correct data transfer. The efficiency of a transmission protocol is the number of information bits sent by the user divided by the total number of bits transferred (information bits plus overhead bits). Synchronous transmission provides greater efficiency than asynchronous transmission. In general, protocols with larger packet sizes provide greater efficiency than those with small packet sizes. The drawback to large packet sizes is that they are more likely to be affected by errors and thus require more retransmission. Small packet sizes are therefore better suited to error-prone circuits and large packets to error-free circuits.

Key Terms

ACK
amplifier
asynchronous transmission
attenuation
Automatic Repeat reQuest
  (ARQ)
bit-oriented protocol
burst error
byte-count protocol
checksum
Compressed SLIP (CSLIP)
contention
continuous ARQ (sliding
  window)
controlled access
corrupted data
cross-talk
data link protocol
echoes
efficiency
error control
error detection and correction
error rate
Ethernet (IEEE 802.3)
even parity
forward error correction
frame

gaussian noise
Go-Back-N ARQ
Hamming code
harmonic distortion
High-level Data Link Control
  (HDLC)
hub polling
impulse noise
intermodulation noise
jitter
KERMIT
Link Access Procedure–
  Balanced (LAP–B)
Link Access Procedure for
  Modems (LAP–M)
line noise
line outage
lost data
media access control
message delineation
NAK
odd parity
packet
parity
parity bit
Point-to-Point Protocol (PPP)

polling
polynomial checking
repeater
retransmission
roll call polling
Serial Line Internet Protocol
  (SLIP)
shielding
start bit
stop-and-wait ARQ
stop bit
synchronization
Synchronous Data Link
  Control (SDLC)
synchronous transmission
throughput
token ring (IEEE 802.5)
transmission efficiency
transmission rate of
  information bits (TRIB)
transparency problem
white noise
X-ON/X-OFF
XMODEM
YMODEM
ZMODEM

Questions

1. What does the data link layer do?
2. What is media access control, and why is it important?
3. Under what conditions is media access control unimportant?
4. Compare and contrast roll call polling, hub polling (or token passing), and contention.
5. Which is better, hub polling or contention? Explain.
6. Define two fundamental types of errors.

7. Errors normally appear in _____, which is when more than one data bit is changed by the error-causing condition.
8. Is there any difference in the error rates of lower speed lines and of higher speed lines?
9. Briefly define noise.
10. Describe five types of noise. Which is likely to pose the greatest problem to network managers?
11. How do amplifiers differ from repeaters?

12. What are three ways of reducing errors and the types of noise they affect?

13. Describe three approaches to *detecting* errors, including how they work, the probability of detecting an error, and any other benefits or limitations.

14. Briefly describe how even parity and odd parity work.

15. Briefly describe how polynomial checking works.

16. How does cyclical redundancy checking work?

17. How does forward error correction work? How is it different from other error correction methods?

18. Under what circumstances is forward error correction desirable?

19. Compare and contrast stop-and-wait ARQ and continuous ARQ.

20. Which is the simplest (least sophisticated) protocol described in this chapter?

21. How do the various types of XMODEM differ from YMODEM and ZMODEM?

22. Describe the packet layout for SDLC, Ethernet, token ring, SLIP, and PPP.

23. What is transparency, and why is this a problem with SDLC?

24. How do SDLC and SLIP overcome their transparency problems?

25. Explain why Ethernet and token ring do not suffer from transparency problems.

26. What are the major problems with SLIP?

27. How does SLIP differ from CSLIP?

28. Why do SDLC packets need an address and SLIP packets do not?

29. What is transmission efficiency?

30. How do information bits differ from overhead bits?

Exercises

A. Are stop bits necessary in asynchronous transmission? Explain using a diagram.

B. How efficient would a 6-bit code be in asynchronous transmission if it had one parity bit, one start bit, and two stop bits? (Some old equipment uses two stop bits.)

C. What is the transmission rate of information bits if you use EBCDIC (8 bits plus 1 parity bit), a 1000-character block, 28,800 bps modem transmission speed, 20 control characters per block, an error rate of 1 percent, and a 30-millisecond turnaround time? What is the TRIB if you add a half-second delay to the turnaround time because of satellite delay?

D. Search the Web to find a software vendor that sells a package that supports each of the following protocols: KERMIT, ZMODEM, SDLC, HDLC, Ethernet, token ring, SLIP, and PPP (i.e., one package that supports KERMIT, another (or the same) for ZMODEM, and so on).

E. Investigate the network at your organization (or a service offered by an interexchange carrier) to find out the average error rates.

NEXT DAY AIR SERVICE CASE STUDY

The Next Day Air Service board of directors has decided that NDAS will centralize communications along two major data links (Atlanta to Tampa and New Orleans to Tampa), as shown in Figure 5–17. Both Atlanta and New Orleans have multiplexers. Although you recommended a different approach and the purchase of

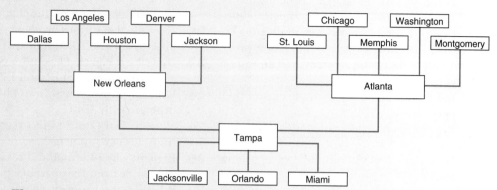

Figure 5–17 Next Day Air Service's communication network circuit configuration. Both of the circuits from New Orleans and Atlanta to Tampa are 64,000 bps leased circuits. All other circuits from the branch offices to the New Orleans, Atlanta, and Tampa hubs are considered capable of supporting 28,800 bps V.34 modems.

additional multiplexers, the board of directors would not approve further outlays at this time. You hear a rumor that Les Coone suggested to several board members that developments in data communication, such as Integrated Services Digital Network (ISDN), might make added multiplexers obsolete before they could pay for themselves and that these conservative board members vetoed the funding for the additional circuits and multiplexers.

As you continue to work on the network plan, you perceive that you are becoming much more involved with the firm's strategic planning initiatives and survival. You realize that NDAS will become dependent on its communication facilities for its very existence. In other words, the communication systems at NDAS are the foundation for the firm's mission-critical applications.

You are burdened with all sorts of thoughts about potential problems and possible errors that can threaten Next Day Air Service's communication capabilities. For example, you worry about recent major circuit and switch outages experienced by some of the leading common carriers. You recognize the fact that even though your operations were affected only slightly by these outages, someday NDAS could undergo a costly disruption of its communication network.

You do not view such a situation as a major competitive threat, because Next Day Air Service's principal competitors have similar networks, and all the parcel delivery services would be paralyzed in the event of a disastrous outage. You do, however, want to examine sources of errors in networks and find reasonable error control mechanisms that will provide NDAS with a competitive edge. For example, are there specialized techniques that can be used for error detection and correction in NDAS communication networks? You decide to research these possibilities further and add this project to your ever-growing list of "things to do."

For now, you have been asked to explore the feasibility of integrating both data and voice traffic onto a single transmission circuit. You must determine whether this is a viable option. In order to make this decision, you want to examine the current transmission circuits and assess their ability to handle the anticipated workload.

Exercises

1. Calculate the TRIB for the 28,800 bps circuits in the Next Day Air Service network shown in Figure 5–15. Assume an average of 1600 characters per message, with a 1 percent probability of an erroneous transmission. The modems transmit with a 0.2 second turnaround delay. The transmissions use an 8-bit ASCII code. The transmission using 28,800 bps modems uses one start bit and one stop bit, and each message block has ten control characters, for further error checking. Assume that the data is sent synchronously over the 28,800 bps circuits, using a 1600-character block, but that each block has 55 control characters. Consider the transmission load data for NDAS provided in the case study for Chapter 4. Are these TRIB ratings adequate?

2. What file transfer protocols would you recommend? Be prepared to support your recommendations.

3. Prepare a brief position paper on the types of errors you can expect in the NDAS network and the steps you believe NDAS can take to prevent, detect, and correct these errors.

CHAPTER 6

Network Layer

The network layer (also called Layer 3) performs three important functions: addressing, routing, and breaking long messages into smaller packets for transmission by the data link layer. There are several standard network layer protocols that specify how network layer packets are to be organized, in the same way that there are standards for data link layer packets. In this chapter, we look at four commonly used protocols: TCP/IP, IPX/SPX, X.25, and SNA. TCP/IP, the protocol used on the Internet, is probably the most important, so this chapter takes a detailed look at how it works.

Objectives

* **Become familiar with four standard network protocols**
* **Become familiar with network addressing**
* **Become familiar with different types of routing**
* **Understand how TCP/IP works**

Chapter Outline

✳✳ INTRODUCTION

The network layer sits between the application layer and the data link layer. The network layer accepts messages from the application layer (e.g., the Web, e-mail, and so on as described in Chapter 2) and formats and addresses them for transmission by the data link layer (which is responsible for error-free delivery to the destination). The network layer also accepts individual messages from the data link layer and organizes them into coherent messages that it passes to the application layer. For example, a large Web page might require several data link layer packets to transmit. The network layer at the sender would break the page into several smaller packets and give the packets to the data link layer to transmit. The network layer at the receiver would receive the individual packets from the data link layer and reassemble them into the one Web page, and give the page to the application layer.

Both the sender and receiver have to agree on the rules or protocols that govern how their network layers will communicate with each other. A network protocol provides three functions:

* Breaks large messages into packets for transmission and reassembles them at the receiver's end (*packetizing*)

* Determines the correct network layer and data link layer addresses (*addressing*)

* Determines where the message should be sent next on its way to its final destination (*routing*)

Some network layer protocols (e.g., TCP/IP, IPX/SPX) are compatible with a variety of different data link layer protocols (e.g., Ethernet, token ring) and can be used interchangeably in the same network. In other cases, network layer protocols are tightly coupled with data link layer protocols and applications and cannot easily be used with other protocols (e.g., X.25, SNA). These differences reflect the philosophy of the protocol's developers. SNA, for example, was originally developed as a complete networking architecture, designed to provide an end-to-end solution for IBM customers using entirely IBM or IBM-compatible hardware and software. TCP/IP, in contrast, was designed to be used by a variety of organizations, each of whom might be using very different hardware and software, and therefore had to combine easily with many different types of data link layer protocols.

✳✳ NETWORK PROTOCOLS

There are many different network layer protocols. Each protocol performs essentially the same functions, but each is incompatible with others unless there is a special device to translate between them. Several venders have recently announced software with *multiprotocol stacks*, which means that the software supports several different network protocols. The software recognizes which protocol an incoming message uses and automatically uses that protocol to process the message.

Source ID	Destination ID	Sequence number	ACK number	Header length	Unused	Flags	Flow control	CRC 16	Urgent pointer	Options	User data
16 bits	16 bits	32 bits	32 bits	4 bits	6 bits	6 bits	16 bits	16 bits	16 bits	32 bits	Varies

Figure 6–1 TCP packet.

This section discusses the four most commonly used network protocols: TCP/IP, IPX/SPX, X.25, and SNA. We believe that within five years, TCP/IP will become the dominant protocol, so the subsequent sections in this chapter discuss addressing and routing using TCP/IP as the primary example.

Transmission Control Protocol/Internet Protocol (TCP/IP)

The *Transmission Control Protocol/Internet Protocol (TCP/IP)* was developed for the U.S. Department of Defense's Advanced Research Project Agency NETwork (ARPANET) by Vinton Cerf and Bob Kahn in 1974. TCP/IP is the network layer protocol now used on the Internet. It is also the world's most popular network layer protocol, used by almost 70 percent of all backbone, metropolitan, and wide area networks. In 1998, TCP/IP moved past IPX/SPX as the most common protocol used on LANs.

TCP/IP allows reasonably efficient and error-free transmission. Because it performs error checking, it can send large files across sometimes unreliable networks with great assurance that the data will arrive uncorrupted. TCP/IP is compatible with a variety of data link protocols, which is one reason for its popularity. In a 1995 survey, 98 percent of mainframe network managers said that TCP/IP was important to their future plans.

As the name implies, TCP/IP has two parts. TCP performs packetizing: breaking the data into smaller packets, numbering them, ensuring each packet is reliably delivered, and putting them in the proper order at the destination. IP performs routing and addressing. IP software is used at each of the intervening computers through which the message passes; it is IP that routes the message to the final destination. The TCP software only needs to be active at the sender and the receiver, because TCP is only involved when data comes from or goes to the application layer.

A typical TCP packet has 192-bit header (24 bytes) of control information (see Figure 6–1). Among other fields, it contains the source and destination port identifier at the application layer (see the Technical Focus box later in this chapter),

Version number	Header length	Type of service	Total length	Identifiers	Flags	Packet offset	Hop limit	Protocol	CRC 16	Source address	Destination address	Options	User data
4 bits	4 bits	8 bits	16 bits	16 bits	3 bits	13 bits	8 bits	8 bits	16 bits	32 bits	32 bits	32 bits	Varies

Figure 6–2 IP packet (version 4).

Version number	Priority	Flow name	Total length	Next header	Hop limit	Source address	Destination address	User data
4 bits	4 bits	24 bits	16 bits	8 bits	8 bits	128 bits	128 bits	Varies

Figure 6–3 IP packet (version 6).

packet sequence number, and error checking information. TCP routinely performs error checking, which duplicates this function of the data link layer.

Two forms of IP are currently defined. The older form is IP version 4 (IPv4), which also has a 192-bit header (see Figure 6–2). This header contains source and destination addresses, packet length, and packet number. IPv4 is being replaced by IPv6, which has a 320-bit header (40 bytes) (see Figure 6–3). The primary reason for the increase in the packet size is an increase in the address size from 32 bits to 128 bits. Simply put, the dramatic growth in the usage of the Internet meant that unless the addressing format was changed, no more addresses would be available by the turn of the century. IPv6's simpler packet structure makes it easier to perform routing and supports a variety of new approaches to addressing and routing. The changes included in IPv6 also suggested ways to improve TCP, so a new version of TCP is currently under development.

The size of the message field depends on the data link layer protocol used. TCP/IP is commonly combined with Ethernet. Ethernet has a maximum packet size of 1492 bytes, so the maximum size of a TCP message field if IPv4 is used is

$$1492 - 24 \text{ (the size of the TCP header)} - 24 \text{ (the size of the IPv4 header)} = 1444.$$

Internetwork Packet Exchange/Sequenced Packet Exchange (IPX/SPX)

Internetwork Packet Exchange/Sequenced Packet Exchange (IPX/SPX) is based on a routing protocol developed by Xerox in the 1970s. IPX/SPX is the primary network protocol used by Novell Netware, but Novell intends to replace IPX/SPX with TCP/IP. About 35 percent of all local area networks currently use IPX/SPX.

As the name implies, IPX/SPX has two parts. IPX/SPX is similar to TCP/IP in concept, but different in structure. SPX performs the same packetizing functions of TCP: breaking the data into smaller packets, numbering them, ensuring each packet is reliably delivered, and putting them in the proper order at the destination. IPX performs the same routing and addressing functions as IP.

A typical SPX packet has 12-byte header of control information (see Figure 6–4). It contains, among other fields, the source and destination, and packet se-

Control	Type	Source ID	Destination ID	Sequence number	ACK number	Allocation number	User data
1 byte	1 byte	2 bytes	2 bytes	2 bytes	2 bytes	2 bytes	Varies

Figure 6–4 SPX packet.

Checksum	Lensill	Control	Type	Destination address	Destination network address	Destination socket	Source address	Source network address	Source socket	User data
2 bytes	2 bytes	1 byte	1 byte	6 bytes	4 bytes	2 bytes	6 bytes	4 bytes	2 bytes	Varies

Figure 6–5 IPX packet.

quence number. A typical IPX packet has a 30-byte header, as Figure 6–5 shows. This header contains source and destination addresses, as well as packet length.

The size of the message field depends on the data link layer protocol used. IPX/SPX is often combined with Ethernet. Ethernet has a maximum packet size of 1492 bytes, so the maximum size of a SPX message field is

$1492 - 12$ (the size of the SPX header) $- 30$ (the size of the IPX header) $= 1450.$

Management Focus: IP-Only Spoken Here

A small but growing number of companies are living the fantasy of ridding all protocols except TCP/IP from their backbone network. Single-protocol backbones require less complex network architectures, are simpler to manage, and enable the use of standardized software.

"The protocol battle is over and TCP/IP has won," says Phil Elmer, Assistant Director for Network Technology at North Carolina State University. NCSU has a new policy requiring all backbone traffic to be TCP/IP. Users are free to use any network protocol inside their LANs, but no traffic is allowed on the backbone unless it is TCP/IP.

The Oregon Department of Corrections is in the middle of a project to migrate from SNA on two IBM AS/400 computers to an entirely TCP/IP network based on Windows NT servers. The AS/400s will likely remain, but only if they can easily fit into the new TCP/IP environment.

Source: Network World, March 24, 1997.

X.25

X.25 is a standard developed by ITU-T for use in wide area networks. It is a mature, global standard used by many international organizations. It is seldom used in North America, except by organizations with WANs that have extensive non–North-American sections. X.25 also has two parts. *Packet Layer Protocol (PLP)* is the routing protocol that performs the routing and addressing functions similar to IP. *X.3* performs the packetizing functions of TCP.

There are several types of PLP packets. A typical PLP packet used to transmit data (as opposed to transmitting network control information) has a 3-byte header. PLP is typically combined with LAP–B at the data link layer. ITU-T recommends that packets contain 128 bytes of application data, but can support packets containing up to 1024 bytes.

Systems Network Architecture (SNA)

Systems Network Architecture (SNA) is an approach to networking developed by IBM in 1974. SNA is used only on IBM and IBM-compatible mainframes (e.g., Amdahl). The major problem with SNA is that it uses proprietary nonstandard protocols, which makes it difficult to integrate SNA networks with other networks that use industry standard protocols. Routing messages between SNA networks and other networks, and even between IBM SNA networks and IBM LANs (which use industry standard protocols), requires special equipment. In a 1995 survey of mainframe network managers currently using SNA, 68 percent said that SNA was *not* important to their future plans.

In response to these problems, IBM developed a new version of SNA called Advanced Peer-to-Peer Networking (APPN) that supports TCP/IP in addition to SNA protocols. Most experts expect that SNA will disappear in time, either because current SNA users will switch to other products that use TCP/IP, or because IBM will replace the use of the proprietary SNA protocols with an approach based on TCP/IP.

As with the other network layer protocols, SNA has two parts. The *transmission control* layer performs functions similar to TCP, and the *path control* layer performs functions similar to IP. SNA typically uses SDLC as its data link layer protocol. SNA is described in more detail in Appendix E.

✳✳ ADDRESSING

Before you can send a message, you must know the destination address. It is extremely important to understand that each computer has several addresses, each used by a different layer. One address is used by the data link layer, another by the network layer, and still another by the application layer.

When the users work with application software, they typically use the application layer address. For example, in Chapter 2, we discussed application software that used Internet addresses (e.g., www.cba.uga.edu). This is an *application layer address* (or a *server name*). When a user types an Internet address into a Web browser, the request is passed to the network layer as part of an application layer packet formatted using the HTTP standard (see Chapter 2). See Figure 6–6.

The network layer software translates this application layer address into a *network layer address*. The network layer protocol used on the Internet is TCP/IP, so

Address	Example Software	Example Address
Application Layer	Web browser	www.cba.uga.edu
Network Layer	TCP/IP	128.192.98.5
Data Link Layer	Ethernet	00-0C-00-F5-03-5A

Figure 6–6 Types of addresses.

this Web address (www.cba.uga.edu) is translated into a TCP/IP address (usually just called an IP address for short), which is four bytes long when using IPv4 (e.g., 128.192.78.5); see Figure 6–6. This process is similar to using a phone book to go from someone's name to their phone number.

The network layer then determines the best route through the network to the final destination. Based on this routing, the network layer identifies the *data link layer address* of the next computer to which the message should be sent. If the data link layer is running Ethernet, then the network layer IP address would be translated into an Ethernet address. Chapter 5 shows that Ethernet addresses are six bytes in length, so a possible address might be 00-0F-00-81-14-00 (Ethernet addresses are usually expressed in hexadecimal); see Figure 6–6. The network layer adds network layer packets to the application layer packet and then gives the message and the data link layer address of the destination to the data link layer to transmit.

Assigning Addresses

In general, the data link layer address is permanently encoded in each network card. This address is part of the hardware (e.g., Ethernet or token ring card) and can never be changed. Hardware manufacturers have an agreement that assigns each manufacturer a unique set of permitted addresses, so even if you buy hardware from different companies, they will never have the same address. Whenever you install a network card into a computer, it immediately has its own data link layer address that uniquely identifies it from every other computer in the world.

Network layer addresses are generally assigned by software. A network layer software package usually has a configuration file that specifies the network layer address for that computer. Network managers can assign any network layer addresses they want. It is important to ensure that every computer on the same network has a unique network layer address so every network has a standards group that defines what network layer addresses can be used by each organization.

Application layer addresses (or server names) are also assigned by a software configuration file. Virtually all servers have an application layer address, but most client computers do not. This is because it is important for users to easily access servers and the information they contain, but there is usually little need for someone to access someone else's client computer. As with network layer addresses, network managers can assign any application layer address they want, but a network standards group must approve application layer addresses to ensure that no two computers have the same application layer address. Network layer addresses and application layer addresses go hand in hand, so the same standards group usually assigns both (e.g., www.uga.edu at the application layer means 192.128.98.53 at the network layer). It is possible to have several application layer addresses for the same computer. For example, one of the Web servers in the College of Business at the University of Georgia is called both www.cba.uga.edu and blaze.cba.uga.edu.

Internet Addresses

On the Internet, InterNIC is responsible for network layer addresses (i.e., IP addresses) and application layer addresses or *domain names* (e.g., www.uga.edu). Users are not permitted to connect a computer to the Internet unless they use approved addresses. Application layer addresses and network layer addresses are usually assigned at the same time. IP addresses are usually assigned in groups or classes, so that one organization receives a set of numerically similar addresses for use on its computers.

Technical Focus: *TCP/IP Application Layer Port Addresses*

Most computers have many application layer software packages running at the same time. Users often have Web browsers, e-mail programs, word processors, and so on in use at the same time on their client computers. Likewise, many servers act as Web servers, mail servers, FTP servers, and so on. When the network layer receives a message, it needs to know which application layer software package should receive the message. It makes no sense to send a Web page request to e-mail server software.

With TCP/IP protocols, each application layer software package must have a unique port address. Any message sent to the computer must tell TCP/IP the application layer port address that is to receive the message. The first two fields in the TCP packet give the sender's port address and the destination port address (see Figure 6–1).

Every standard application layer software on the Internet has a predefined port number. Web servers, for example, typically use port 80, while FTP servers typically use port 21, Telnet 23, SMTP 25, and so on. Network managers are free to use whatever port addresses they want, but if they use a nonstandard port number, then the application layer software on the client must specify the correct port number.

For example, when a user asks for a Web page using a Web browser, the browser assumes port 80 and gives this number to the TCP/IP software. If the Web server is using a different port number for the Web server software, the user must explicitly provide the port number as part of the Web address. For example, when we were developing our Web groupware, we tested several different Web server software packages on the same server. The NCSA Web software was configured to run on port 8080, while the Apache Web server software was configured to run on port 80. Connecting to our server using an address of *tcbworks.cba.uga.edu* would use the default port of 80 and connect to the Apache server. Using an address of *tcbworks.cba.uga.edu:8080* would use the 8080 port and connect to the NCSA server.

There are five classes of Internet addresses. See Figure 6–7. With a Class A address, an organization is assigned an IP address whose first byte is fixed (e.g., 50.x.x.x). (These are sometimes called */8* addresses because the first 8 bits are fixed.) The organization is then free to assign the last three bytes to any computer under its control. Any IP address whose first digit is between 1 and 127 is a Class A address. Class A addresses provide over 16 million possible addresses. Class A ad-

Class	Number of Addresses Available to User	Address Structure	Example
Class A	16 million	First byte fixed Organization assigns last three bytes	50.x.x.x
Class B	65,000	First two bytes fixed Organization assigns last two bytes	128.192.x.x
Class C	254	First three bytes fixed Organization assigns last byte	192.12.56.x

Figure 6-7 Internet address classes.

dresses are no longer assigned because all 127 possible addresses are in use or have been reserved (0.x.x.x is not used as an address).

With a Class B address (also called a *16* address), an organization is assigned an IP address whose first two bytes are fixed (e.g., 128.192.x.x). The organization is then free to assign the last two bytes to its computers. Any IP address whose first digit is between 128 and 191 is a Class B address. Class B addresses provide more than 65,000 possible addresses. There are just over 16,000 possible Class B addresses that can be assigned, and nearly 80 percent are now assigned to organizations.

With a Class C address (also called a *24* address), an organization is assigned an IP address whose first three bytes are fixed (e.g., 192.12.56.x). The organization is then free to assign the last byte to any computer under its control. Any IP address whose first digit is between 192 and 223 is a Class C address. Class C addresses provide 254 addresses (IP addresses cannot end in 0 or 255). There are a little more than 2 million possible Class C addresses that can be assigned and almost 30 percent are now in use.

The remaining two types of addresses, Class D and Class E addresses, are reserved for special purposes and are not assigned to organizations. All addresses starting with 240 and higher are Class D or E addresses.

One of the problems with the current address class system is that the Internet is quickly running out of addresses. Although the four-byte address of IPv4 provides more than 1 billion possible addresses, the fact that they are assigned in sets significantly limits the number of usable addresses. For example, not every organization with a Class B address will actually use all 65,000 possible addresses; many will go unused. There are only about 2 million possible sets of IP addresses that can be assigned, so once the first 2 million organizations in the world apply for addresses, the Internet will be full; no new computers can be added unless they connect from one of the existing addresses that have been registered. Clearly, this cannot be permitted to occur.

The IP address shortage was one of the reasons behind the development of IPv6 discussed previously (see Figure 6–3). IPv6 has 16-byte addresses, meaning there are in theory about 3.2×10^{38} possible addresses—more than we can dream about. Once IPv6 is in wide use, the current Internet address class system will be replaced by a totally new system based on 16-byte addresses.

Subnets

Each organization must assign the IP addresses it has received to specific computers on its networks. In general, IP addresses are assigned so that all computers on the same local area network have similar addresses. For example, suppose a university has just received a set of Class B addresses starting with 128.184.x.x. It is customary to assign all the computers in the same LAN numbers that start with the same first three digits, so the Business School LAN might be assigned 128.184.56.x while the Computer Science LAN might be assigned 128.184.55.x (see Figure 6–8). Likewise, all the other LANs at the university and the backbone network that connects them would have a different set of numbers. Each of these LANs is called a TCP/IP *subnet* because they are logically grouped together by IP number.

While it is customary to use the last byte of the IP address to indicate different subnets, it is not required. Any portion of the IP address can be designated as a subnet by using a *subnet mask*. Every computer in a TCP/IP network is given a subnet mask to enable it to determine which computers are on the same subnet (i.e., LAN) as it is, and which computers are outside of its subnet. Knowing whether a computer is on your subnet is very important for message routing, as we shall see later in this chapter.

For example, a network could be configured so that the first two bytes indicated a subnet (e.g., 128.184.x.x) so all computers would be given a subnet mask giving the first two bytes as the subnet indicator. This would mean that a computer with an IP address of 128.184.22.33 would be on the same subnet as 128.184.78.90.

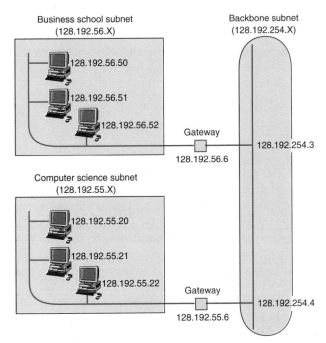

Figure 6–8 Address subnets.

IP addresses are binary numbers, so partial bytes can also be used as subnets. For example, we could create a subnet that has IP addresses from 128.184.55.1 to 128.184.55.127, and another subnet with addresses from 128.184.55.128 to 128.184.55.254.

Dynamic Addressing

To this point, we have said that every computer knows its network layer address from a configuration file that is installed when the computer is first attached to the network. However, this leads to a major network management problem. Any time a computer is moved or its network is assigned a new address, the software on each individual computer must be updated. This is not difficult, but is very time-consuming, because someone must go from office to office editing files on each individual computer.

Technical Focus: Subnet Masks

Subnet masks tell computers what part of an IP address is to be used to determine whether a destination is the same subnet or in a different subnet. A subnet mask is a four-byte binary number that has the same format as an IP address. A 1 in the subnet mask indicates that that position is part of the subnet address. A 0 indicates that it is not.

A subnet mask of 255.255.255.0 means that the first three bytes indicate the subnet; all computers with the same first three bytes in their IP addresses are on the same subnet. This is because 255 expressed in binary is 11111111.

In contrast a subnet mask of 255.255.0.0 indicates that the first two bytes indicate the same subnet.

Things get more complicated when we use partial-byte subnet masks. For example, 255.255.255.128 means the first three bytes and the next bit indicate the same subnet, because 128 in binary is 10000000. Likewise 255.255.254.000 would indicate the first two bytes and seven bits, because 254 in binary is 11111110.

The easiest way around this is *dynamic addressing*. With this approach, a server is designated to supply a network layer address to a computer each time the computer connects to the network. This is commonly done for client computers, but usually not done for servers.

Two standards for dynamic addressing are commonly used in TCP/IP networks: *Bootstrap Protocol (bootp)*, developed in 1985, and *Dynamic Host Control Protocol (DHCP)*, developed in 1993. The two approaches are different, but work in the same fundamental way. Instead of providing a network layer address in a configuration file, a special software package is installed on the client that instructs it to contact bootp or DHCP servers using data link layer addresses. This message asks the servers to assign the requesting computer a unique network layer address. The server runs a corresponding bootp or DHCP software package that responds to these requests and sends a message back to the client giving it its network layer address (and its subnet mask).

The bootp or DHCP server can be configured to assign the same network layer address to the computer each time it requests an address (based on its data link layer address), or it can lease the address to the computer by picking the "next available" network layer address from a list of authorized addresses. Addresses can be leased for as long as the computer is connected to the network or for a specified time limit (e.g., two hours). When the lease expires, the client computer must contact the bootp or DHCP server to get a new address. Address leasing is commonly used by Internet service providers (ISPs) for dial-up users. ISPs have many more authorized users than they have authorized network layer addresses, because not all users can log in at the same time. When a user logs in, the user is assigned a temporary TCP/IP address that is reassigned to the next user when he or she hangs up.

Dynamic addressing greatly simplifies network management in non–dial-up networks, too. With dynamic addressing, address changes need to be done only to the bootp or DHCP server, not each individual computer. The next time each computer connects to the network or whenever the address lease expires, it automatically gets the new address.

Address Resolution

In order to send a message, the sender must be able to translate the application layer address (or server name) of the destination into a network layer address and, in turn, translate that into a data link layer address. This process is called *address resolution*. There are many different approaches to address resolution, ranging from completely decentralized (each computer is responsible for knowing all addresses) to completely centralized (there is one computer that knows all addresses). TCP/IP uses two different approaches, one for resolving application layer addresses into IP addresses and a different one for resolving IP addresses into data link layer addresses.

Server Name Resolution

Server name resolution is the translation of application layer addresses into network layer addresses (e.g., translating an Internet address such as www.cba.uga.edu into an IP address such as 128.192.98.3). This is done using the *Domain Name Service (DNS)*. Throughout the Internet there are a series of computers called *name servers* that provide DNS services. These name servers run special address databases that store thousands of Internet addresses and their corresponding IP addresses. These name servers are in effect the "directory assistance" computers for the Internet. Any time a computer does not know the IP number for a computer, it sends a message to the name server requesting the IP number. There are about a dozen high-level name servers that provide IP addresses for most of the Internet, with thousands of others that provide IP addresses for specific domains.

Whenever you receive a set of Internet addresses (e.g., Class A, B, or C), you must inform InterNIC of the name and IP address of the name server that will provide DNS information for all addresses in that class. Almost every organization with a Class B Internet address also has its own DNS server. Organizations with Class C addresses sometimes have their own DNS servers, but often rely on a DNS server provided by an Internet service provider. DNS servers are maintained by network managers, who update their address information as the network changes. Name servers can also exchange information about new and changed addresses among themselves (replication).

When TCP/IP needs to translate an application layer address into an IP address, it sends a special TCP-level packet to the nearest DNS server. This packet asks the DNS server to send the requesting computer the IP address that matches the Internet address provided. If the DNS server has a matching name in its database, it sends back a special TCP packet with the correct IP address. If that DNS server does not have that Internet address in its database, it will issue the same request to another DNS server elsewhere on the Internet.

For example, if someone at the University of Toronto asked for a Web page on our server at the University of Georgia, the TCP/IP software on their computer will issue a DNS request to the University of Toronto DNS server. This DNS server probably does not know the IP address of our server, so it will forward the request to a DNS server that it knows stores addresses for the *.edu* domain. This server probably does not know our server's IP address either, but it knows that the DNS server, on our campus can supply the address. So it forwards the request to the University of Georgia DNS server, which responds with the correct IP address.

This is why it sometimes takes a long time to access certain sites. Most name servers only know the names and IP addresses for the computers in their part of the network although some name servers store frequently used addresses (e.g., www.yahoo.com). If you try to access a computer that is far away, it may take a while before your computer receives a response from a DNS server that knows the IP address.

Once your computer receives an IP address, it is stored in a server address table so that if you ever need to access the same computer again, your computer

---

Management Focus: *Operator Error Makes Net Go Nuts*

At 2:30 A.M. on July 17, 1997, the Internet was thrown into chaos. A computer operator at Network Solutions Inc., the company that maintains the master DNS server for the Internet, ignored alarms on the computer, which then sent incorrect DNS information for the *.com* and *.net* domains to the ten primary Internet DNS servers around the world.

The problem was corrected by 6:30 A.M.,

but it took several more hours before the corrected information was replicated around the world to other, lower-level, DNS servers. By then several million requests for Web pages and e-mail messages sent to the *.com* and *.net* domains were returned as undeliverable because of the bad DNS information.

Source: Atlanta Journal-Constitution, July 18, 1997.

does not need to contact a DNS server. Most server address tables are routinely deleted whenever you turn off your computer.

Data Link Layer Address Resolution

In order to actually send a message, the network layer software must know the data link layer address of the destination computer. The final destination may be far away (e.g., sending from Toronto to Georgia). In this case, the network layer would *route* the message by selecting a path through the network that would ultimately lead to the destination (routing is discussed in the next section). The first step would be to send the message to a computer in its network that is the first step on this route.

To send a message to a computer in its network, a computer must know the correct data link layer address. In this case, the TCP/IP software sends a *broadcast message* to all computers in its subnet. A broadcast message, as the name suggests, is received and processed by all computers in the same LAN (which is usually designed to match the IP subnet). The message is a specially formatted TCP-level request using *Address Resolution Protocol (ARP)* that says "Whoever is IP address xxx.xxx.xxx.xxx, please send me your data link layer address." The TCP software in the computer with that IP address then responds with its data link layer address. The sender transmits its message using that data link layer address. The sender also stores the data link layer address in its address table for future use.

✳ ✳ ROUTING

In many networks, there are many possible routes or paths a message can take to get from one computer to another. For example, in Figure 6–9, a message sent from computer A to computer F could travel first to computer B, then to computer

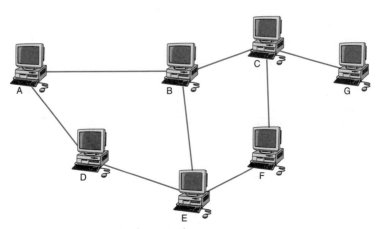

Figure 6–9 A typical network.

Destination	Route
A	A
C	C
D	A
E	E
F	E
G	C

Figure 6–10 Routing table.

C to get to computer F—or it could go to computer D first and then to computer E to get to computer F.

Routing is the process of determining the route or path through the network that a message will travel from the sending computer to the receiving computer. Every computer that performs routing has a *routing table* developed by the network manager that specifies how messages will travel through the network. In its simplest form, the routing table is a two-column table. The first column lists every computer in the network, while the second column lists the computer to which this computer should send messages if they are destined for the computer in the first column. Figure 6–10 shows a routing table that might be used by computer B in Figure 6–9.

There are two fundamental approaches to routing: centralized and decentralized. With centralized routing, all routing decisions are made by one central host computer. Centralized routing is used typically only in host-based networks (see Chapter 3), and in this case, routing decisions are rather simple. All computers are connected to the central computer by individual point-to-point circuits, so any message received is simply retransmitted on the point-to-point circuit connected to the destination.

Decentralized routing allows all computers in the network to make their own routing decisions following a formal routing protocol. In MANs and WANs, the routing table for each computer is developed by its individual network manager (although network managers often share information). In local area networks or backbone networks, the routing tables used by all computers on the network are usually developed by one individual or a committee. Most decentralized routing protocols are self-adjusting, meaning that they can automatically adapt to changes in the network configuration (e.g., adding and deleting computers and circuits). There are two types of decentralized routing.

Static Routing

With *static routing*, the routing table is developed by the network manager, and changes only when computers are added to or removed from the network. For example, if the computer recognizes that a circuit is broken or unusable (e.g., after the data link layer retry limit has been exceeded without receiving an acknowledgment), the computer will update the routing table to indicate the failed circuit. If an alternate route is available, it will be used for all subsequent messages. Otherwise, messages will be stored until the circuit is repaired. When new computers are added to the network, they announce their presence to the other computers, which automatically add them into their routing tables.

Static routing is commonly used in networks that have few routing options. For example, most LANs are connected to the backbone network in only one place. There is only one route from the LAN to the backbone, so static routing is used. All computers in the LAN (or TCP/IP subnet) are told which computer is the connection or *gateway* from the LAN to the outside world (i.e., all computers outside the subnet).

Dynamic Routing

Dynamic routing (or adaptive routing) is used when there are multiple routes through a network and it is important to select the best route. Dynamic routing attempts to improve network performance by routing messages over the fastest possible route, away from busy circuits and busy computers. An initial routing table is developed by the network manager, but is continuously updated by the computers themselves to reflect changing network conditions, such as network traffic. This updating can be done by monitoring outgoing messages to see how long they take to transmit and how long it takes for the receiving computer to acknowledge them. A more common approach is to have each computer that performs routing periodically send messages to others that report how busy it is, so that all the computers connected to it can assess the traffic on each route and update their tables to avoid trouble spots.

Routing Information Protocol (RIP) is a commonly used dynamic routing protocol. The network manager uses RIP to develop the routing table. When new computers are added, RIP simply counts the number of computers in the possible routes to the destination and selects the route with the least number. Computers using RIP send broadcast messages every minute or so (the timing is set by the network manager), announcing their routing status to all other computers. RIP is used by both TCP/IP and IPX/SPX.

Internet Control Message Protocol (ICMP), as the name suggests, is used on the Internet with TCP/IP. Computers using ICMP use a combination of broadcast messages (usually sent only when a new computer joins a network) and messages to specific computers to exchange routing information.

Open Shortest Path First (OSPF) is another commonly used dynamic routing protocol that uses the number of computers in a route, as well as network traffic and error rates, to select the best route. OSPF is more efficient than RIP, because it normally doesn't use broadcast messages. Instead, it selectively sends status update messages directly to selected computers. OSPF is used by TCP/IP.

There are two drawbacks to dynamic routing. First, it requires more processing by each computer in the network than centralized routing or static routing. Computing resources are devoted to adjusting routing tables rather than sending messages, which can slow down the network. Second, the transmission of status information "wastes" network capacity. Some dynamic routing protocols transmit status information every minute, which can significantly reduce performance.

Connectionless versus Connection-Oriented Routing

Some messages or blocks of application data are small enough that they can be transmitted in one packet or frame at the data link layer (e.g., DNS requests). However, in other cases, the application data in one "message" is too large and must be broken into several packets (e.g., Web pages, graphic images). As far as the application layer is concerned, the message should be transmitted and received as one large block of data. However, the data link layer can only transmit messages of certain lengths. It is therefore up to the sender's network layer to break the data into several smaller packets that can be sent by the data link layer across the circuit. At the other end, the receiver's network layer must receive all these separate packets from its data link layer and recombine them into one large block of data that is passed to the receiver's application layer as though it were received intact. There are two fundamental ways that these sets of packets can be routed through a network.

Connectionless routing means that each packet is treated separately and makes its own way through the network. It is possible that different packets will take different routes through the network, depending on the type of routing used and the amount of traffic. Because packets following different routes may travel at different speeds, they may arrive out of sequence at their destination. The sender's network layer therefore puts a sequence number on each packet, in addition to information about the message stream to which the packet belongs. The network layer must reassemble them in the correct order before passing the message to the application layer.

Connection-oriented routing sets up a *virtual circuit* between the sender and receiver. A virtual circuit is one that *appears* to the application software to use a point-to-point circuit, even though it actually does not. In this case, a temporary virtual circuit is defined between the sender and receiver. The network layer makes one routing decision when the connection is established, and all packets follow the same route. All packets in the same message arrive at the destination in the same order in which they were sent. In this case, packets only need to contain information about the stream to which it belongs; sequence numbers are not needed, although many connection-oriented protocols include a sequence number to ensure that all packets are actually received.

Connection-oriented routing has greater overhead than connectionless routing, because the sender must first "open" the circuit by sending a control packet that instructs all the intervening devices to establish the circuit routing. Likewise, when the transmission is complete, the sender must "close" the circuit. Connection-oriented protocols also tend to have more overhead bits in each packet.

TCP/IP can operate either as connection-oriented or connectionless routing. When connection-oriented routing is desired, both TCP and IP are used. TCP establishes the virtual circuit with the destination and informs IP to route all messages along this virtual circuit. When connectionless routing is desired, only IP is needed and the TCP packet is replaced with a User Datagram Protocol (UDP) packet. However, since TCP is bypassed, the application layer must perform the functions of TCP (e.g., ensuring that all packets are received and putting them in the correct order). Connectionless routing is commonly used when the application data or message can fit into one packet, such as control messages.

IPX/SPX can operate either as connection-oriented or connectionless routing. Both SPX and IPX are used when connection-oriented routing is desired. SPX is responsible for establishing the virtual circuit and instructing IPX to route all messages along the circuit. When connectionless routing is desired, only IPX is used; SPX is bypassed. However, since SPX is bypassed, the application layer must ensure that all packets are received. Connectionless routing is usually used when the application data or message can fit into one packet.

Quality of service (QoS) routing is a special type of connection-oriented dynamic routing in which different messages or packets are assigned different priorities. For example, videoconferencing requires fast delivery of packets to ensure that the images and voices appear smooth and continuous; they are very time-dependent, because delays in routing will seriously affect the quality of the service provided. E-mail packets, on the other hand, have no such requirements. Although everyone would like to receive e-mail as fast as possible, a 10-second delay in transmitting an e-mail message will not have the same consequences as a 10-second delay in a videoconferencing packet.

With QoS routing, different classes of service are defined, each with different priorities. For example, a packet of videoconferencing images would likely get higher priority than an SMTP packet with an e-mail message, and would thus be routed first. When network layer software attempts to establish a connection (i.e., a virtual circuit), it specifies the class of service that connection requires. Each path through the network is designed to support a different number and mix of service classes. When a connection is established, the network ensures that no connections are established that exceed the maximum number of that class on a given circuit.

QoS routing is common in certain types of networks (e.g., ATM, as discussed in Chapter 8). A new version of OSPF is now under development (called QOSPF) that will provide QoS routing in TCP/IP networks, but this is still early in its development.

Multicasting

The most common type of message in a network is the usual transmission between two computers. One computer sends a message to another computer (e.g., a client requesting a Web page). This is called a *unicast message.* Earlier in the chapter, we introduced the concept of a *broadcast message* that is sent to all computers on a specific LAN or subnet. A third type of message, called a *multicast message,* is used to send the same message to a group of computers.

Consider a videoconferencing situation in which four people want to participate in the same conference. Each computer could send the same voice and video data from its camera to the computers of each of the other three participants using unicasts. In this case, each computer would send three identical messages, each addressed to the three different computers. This would work, but would require a lot of network capacity. Alternately, each computer could send one broadcast message. This would reduce network traffic (since each computer would send only one message) but every computer on the network would process it, distracting them from other tasks. Broadcast messages usually are transmitted only within the same LAN or subnet, so this would not work if one of the computers was outside the subnet.

The solution is multicast messaging. Computers wishing to participate in a multicast send a message to the sending computer or some other computer performing routing along the way using a special type of TCP-level packet called *Internet Group Management Protocol (IGMP)*. Each multicast group is assigned a special Class D IP address (see the previous section) to identify the group. Any computer performing routing knows to route all multicast messages with this Class D IP address onto the subnet that contains the requesting computer. The routing computer sets the data link layer address on multicast messages to a matching multicast data link layer address. Each requesting computer must inform its data link layer software to process incoming messages with this multicast data link layer address. When the multicast session ends (e.g., the videoconference is over), the client computer sends another IGMP message to the organizing computer or the computer performing routing to remove it from the multicast group.

✳✳ TCP/IP EXAMPLE

This chapter has discussed the functions of the network layer: packetizing, addressing, and routing. In this section, we tie all of these concepts together to take a closer look at how these functions actually work using TCP/IP.

Management Focus: Toy Story

You don't have to be a math major to figure out that it's more efficient to send one file once to 200 locations than to send the 200 copies of the same file, one at a time, to each of those locations. But that's what Toys "R" Us did for 10 years before multicasting.

Toys "R" Us used to send software updates to its 865 stores over its VSAT satellite network one file at a time, using unicast messages. This took so much network capacity that it could only be done at night when the stores were closed. It also took so much time that not all stores could be updated on the same night. Transferring a 1-megabyte file to 250 stores took just over six hours.

With IP multicasting, transferring the same 1-megabyte file now takes less than four minutes.

Source: PC Week, October 21, 1996.

When a computer is installed on a TCP/IP network (or dials into a TCP/IP network), it must be given four pieces of network layer addressing and routing information before it can operate. This information can be provided by a configuration file, or via a bootp or DHCP server. The information is:

1. Its IP address

2. A subnet mask, so it can determine what addresses are part of its subnet

3. The IP address of a DNS server, so it can translate application layer addresses into IP addresses

4. The IP address of a gateway[1] computer leading outside of its subnet, so it can route messages addressed to computers outside of its subnet (This presumes the computer is using static routing and there is only one connection from it to the outside world through which all messages must flow; if it used dynamic routing, some routing software would be needed instead.)

These four pieces of information are the minimum required. A server would also need to know its application layer address.

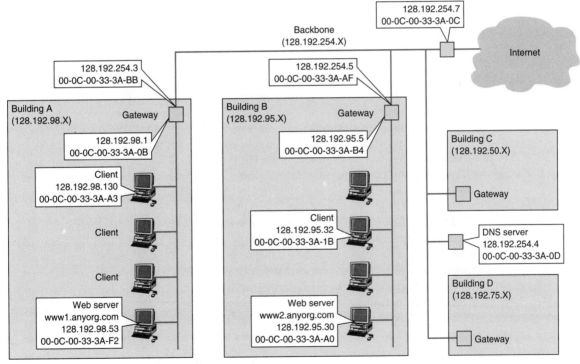

Figure 6–11 Example TCP/IP network.

---

[1]For the moment, we will call this computer that connects to other networks a gateway computer. As we shall see in Chapter 8, it could be a gateway, router, or a switch.

In this section, we will use the simple network shown in Figure 6–11 to illustrate how TCP/IP works. This figure shows an organization that has four LANs connected by a backbone network. The backbone network also has a connection to the Internet. Each building is configured as a separate subnet. For example, Building A has the 128.192.98.x subnet, while Building B has the 128.192.95.x subnet. The backbone is its own subnet 128.192.254.x. Each building is connected to the backbone via a gateway that has two IP addresses and two data link layer addresses, one for the connection into the building and one for the connection onto the backbone. The organization has several Web servers spread throughout the four buildings. The DNS server and the gateway onto the Internet are located directly on the backbone itself. For simplicity, we will assume that all networks use Ethernet as the data link layer, and will only focus on Web requests at the application layer.

Known Addresses, Same Subnet

Let's start with the simplest case. Suppose that a user on a client computer in Building A (128.192.98.130) requests a Web page from the Web server in the same building (www1.anyorg.com). We will assume that this computer knows the network layer and data link layer address of the Web server (e.g., it has previously requested pages from this server and the addresses are in its address tables).

In this case, the application layer software (i.e., Web browser) passes an HTTP packet containing the user request to the TCP/IP software requesting a page from www1.anyorg.com. The network layer software will search its network layer address table and find the IP address for this server (128.192.98.53). This address will be compared to the subnet mask (255.255.255.0), indicating that this computer is on the same subnet. The network layer software will then search its data link layer address table and find the matching data link layer address (00-0C-00-33-3A-F2). The network layer would then take the HTTP packet and attach a TCP packet and an IP packet, and pass it to the data link layer, along with the destination Ethernet address. The data link layer would surround the packet with an Ethernet packet (see Figure 6–12) and transmit it to the Web server.

The data link layer on the Web server would perform error checking and send an acknowledgment back, before passing the HTTP packet with the TCP and IP packet attached to its network layer software. The network layer software would then process the IP packet, see that it was destined to this computer, and process the TCP packet, see that there was only one packet, and pass the HTTP packet to the Web server software.

The Web server software would find the page requested, and would pass it to its network layer software. The network layer software would break the Web page

Ethernet packet header	IP packet	TCP packet	HTTP packet	User data	Ethernet packet trailer

Figure 6–12 Data transmission using TCP/IP and Ethernet.

into several smaller packets, each less than 1500 bytes in length, and attach a TCP packet (with a packet number to indicate the order) to each. Each would then get an IP packet attached that specified the IP address of the requesting client (128.192.98.130) and be given to the data link layer with the client's Ethernet address (00-0C-00-33-3A-A3) for transmission. The data link layer on the server would transmit the packets in the order in which the network layer passed them to it.

The client's data link layer software would receive the packets, perform error checking and issue an acknowledgment on each packet, and pass each to the network layer. The network layer software (IP, to be specific) would check to see that the packets were destined for this computer. Then the network layer software (TCP, to be specific) would assemble the separate data link layer packets back into the Web page, and pass it to the Web browser to display on the screen.

Known Addresses, Different Subnet

Suppose this time that the same client computer wanted to get a Web page from a Web server located somewhere in Building B (say www2.anyorg.com). Again assume that all addresses are known and are in the address tables of all computers. In this case, the application layer software would pass an HTTP packet to the network layer software with an Internet address of www2.anyorg.com. The network software (TCP) would make sure that the request fit in one packet. The network layer software (IP) would then check its network layer address table and see that its IP address was 128.192.95.30. The network layer software (IP), using its subnet mask, would recognize that the Web server is located outside of its subnet. Any messages going outside the subnet must be sent to the gateway (128.192.98.1), whose job it is to process the message and send the message on its way into the outside network. The network layer software would check its address table and find the Ethernet address for the gateway. It would therefore set the data link layer address the gateway's Ethernet address on this subnet (00-0C-00-33-3A-0B) and pass it to the data link layer for transmission.

The gateway would receive the message and its data link layer would perform error checking and send an acknowledgement before passing the message to the network layer software. The network layer software (IP) would read the IP address to determine the final destination. The gateway would recognize that this address (128.192.95.30) needed to be sent to the 128.192.95.x subnet. It knows the gateway for this subnet is 128.192.254.5. It would pass the packet back to its data link layer, giving the Ethernet address of this gateway (00-0C-00-33-3A-AF).

This gateway would receive the message (do error checking, etc.) and read the IP address to determine the final destination. The gateway would recognize that this address (128.192.95.30) was inside its 128.192.95.x subnet, and search its data link layer address table for this computer. It would then pass the packet the data link layer, along with the Ethernet address of (00-0C-00-33-3A-A0), for transmission.

The www2.anyorg.com Web server would receive the message and process it. This would result in a series of TCP/IP packets addressed to the requesting client (128.192.98.130). These would make their way through the network in reverse order. The Web server would recognize that this IP address is outside its subnet, and send the message to the 128.192.95.5 gateway using its Ethernet address (00-0C-00-33-3A-B4). This gateway would then send the message to the gateway for the 128.192.98.x subnet (128.192.254.3) using its Ethernet address (00-0C-00-33-3A-BB). This gateway would, in turn, send the message back to the client (128.192.98.130) using its Ethernet address (00-0C-00-33-3A-A3).

This process would work in the same way for Web servers located outside the organization on the Internet. In this case, the message would go from the client to the 128.192.98.x gateway, which would send it to the Internet gateway (128.192.254.7), which would send it to its Internet connection. The message would be routed through the Internet from gateway to gateway until it reached its destination. Then the process would work in reverse to return the requested page.

Unknown Addresses

Let's return to the simplest case (requesting a Web page from a Web server on the same subnet), only this time we will assume that the client computer does not know the network layer or data link layer address of the Web server. For simplicity, we will assume that the client knows the data link layer address of its subnet gateway, but after you read through this example, you will realize that obtaining the data link layer address of the subnet gateway is straightforward (it is done the same way as the client obtains the data link layer address of the Web server).

Suppose the client computer in Building A (128.192.98.130) wants to retrieve a Web page from the www1.anyorg.com Web server, but does not know its addresses. The network layer software will realize it lacks the IP address after searching its network layer address table and not finding a matching entry. In this case, it will issue a DNS request to its name server (128.192.254.4). Using its subnet mask, it will recognize that the name server is outside of its subnet. It will create a TCP/IP DNS request packet and set the data link layer address to its gateway's address.

The gateway would process the message, and would recognize that the 128.192.254.4 IP address is on the backbone. It would transmit the packet using the DNS server's Ethernet address.

The name server would process the DNS request, and send the matching IP address back to the client via the 128.198.98.x subnet gateway.

Once the client received the IP address for the Web server (128.192.98.53) and stored it in its network layer address table, it would use its subnet mask and recognize that this computer is on its subnet. However, it does not know the Web server's Ethernet address. Therefore, TCP would broadcast an ARP request to all computers on its subnet, requesting the computer with the IP address of 128.192.98.53 to respond with its Ethernet address.

This request would be processed by all computers on the subnet, but only the Web server would respond with an ARP packet giving its Ethernet address. The network layer software on the client would store this address in its data link layer address table and would send the original Web request to the Web server using its Ethernet address.

This process works the same for a Web server outside the subnet, whether in the same organization or anyway in the Internet. If the Web server is far away (e.g.,

Australia), it will likely involve searching more than one name server, but the process is the same.

Summary

Network Protocols   Many different standard network protocols exist to perform addressing (finding destination addresses), routing (finding the "best" route through the network), and packetizing (breaking large messages into smaller packets for transmission and reassembling them at the destination). All provide formal definitions for how addressing and routing are to be executed, and specify packet structures to transfer this information between computers. TCP/IP, IPX/SPX, X.25, and SNA are the four most commonly used network layer protocols. TCP/IP is likely to be the most common in the future.

Addressing   Computers can have three different addresses: application layer address, network layer address, and data link layer address. Data link layer addresses are usually part of the hardware, while network layer and application layer addresses are set by software. Network layer and application layer addresses for the Internet are assigned by InterNIC and are either Class A, Class B, or Class C addresses. Addresses are usually assigned so that computers in the same LAN or subnet have similar addresses, usually with the first two or three bytes the same. Subnet masks are used to indicate whether the first two or three bytes (or partial bytes) indicate the same subnet. Some networks assign network layer addresses in a configuration file on the client computer, while others use dynamic addressing in which a bootp or DHCP server assigns addresses when a computer first joins the network.

Address Resolution   Address resolution is the process of translating an application layer address into a network layer address, or translating a network layer address into a data link layer address. On the Internet, network layer resolution is done by sending a special message to a DNS server (also called a name server) that asks for the IP address (e.g., 128.192.98.5) for a given Internet address (e.g., www.cba.uga.edu). If a DNS server does not have an entry for the requested Internet address, it will forward the request to another DNS server that it thinks is likely to have the address, which will either respond or forward it to another DNS server and so on, until the address is found or it becomes clear that the address is unknown. Resolving data link layer addresses is done by sending an ARP request in a broadcast message to all computers on the same subnet that asks the computer with the requested IP address to respond with its data link layer address.

Routing   Routing is the process of selecting the route or path through the network that a message will travel from the sending computer to the receiving computer. There are two major types of decentralized routing. With static routing, the routing table is developed by the network manager, and remains unchanged until the network manager updates it. With dynamic routing, the goal is to improve network performance by routing messages over the fastest possible route; an initial routing table is developed by the network manager, but is continuously updated to reflect changing network conditions, such as message traffic. RIP, ICMP, and OSPF are examples of dynamic routing protocols.

Some messages or blocks of application data are small enough that they can be transmitted in one packet or frame at the data link layer. However, in other cases (e.g., file transfer), the application data in one "message" is too large and must be broken into several packets. Connectionless routing means that each packet is treated separately and makes its own way through the network. With connection-oriented routing, the network layer makes one routing decision for all the packets and all packets for that message take the same route. Quality of Service (QoS) routing assigns routes and priorities on those routes based on the type of packet. For example, voice or video packets would likely get higher priority because delays will have a greater effect on users than will delays of pure data packets. Multicasting is a special type of connection-oriented routing in which each packet is routed to a group of computers that have requested to be part of a multicast group.

TCP/IP Example   In TCP/IP, it is important to remember that the TCP/IP packet is created by the sending computer. It contains the sending computer's IP address and the IP address of the final destination of the message. The TCP/IP packet never changes until the message reaches its final destination. The sending computer also creates a data link layer packet (e.g., Ethernet) for each message. This packet contains the data link layer address of the sending computer and the data link layer address of the next computer in the route through the network. The data link layer packet is removed and replaced with a new packet at each computer at which the message stops as it works its way through the network. Thus the source and destination data link layer addresses change at each step along the route, whereas the TCP/IP source and destination addresses never change.

Key Terms

address resolution

Address Resolution Protocol (ARP)

addressing

application layer address

Bootstrap Protocol (bootp)

broadcast message

connectionless routing

connection-oriented routing

data link layer address

domain name

Domain Name Service (DNS)

dynamic addressing

Dynamic Host Control Protocol (DHCP)

dynamic routing

gateway

Internet address classes

Internet Control Message Protocol (ICMP)

Internet Group Management Protocol (IGMP)

Internetwork Packet Exchange/ Sequenced Packet Exchange (IPX/SPX)

multicast message

multiprotocol stacks

name server

network layer address

Open Shortest Path First (OSPF)

Packet Layer Protocol (PLP)

packetizing

path control

Quality of Service (QoS)

routing

Routing Information Protocol (RIP)

routing table

static routing

subnet

subnet mask

System Network Architecture
(SNA)

transmission control

Transmission Control
Protocol/Internet Protocol
(TCP/IP)

unicast message

virtual circuit

X.25

X.3

Questions

1. What does the network layer do?

2. What are the parts of TCP/IP, and what do they do? Who is the primary user of TCP/IP?

3. What are the parts of IPX/SPX, and what do they do? Who is the primary user of IPX/SPX?

4. What are the parts of X.25, and what do they do? Who is the primary user of X.25?

5. What are the parts of SNA, and what do they do? Who is the primary user of SNA?

6. Compare and contrast the three types of addresses used in a network.

7. What are the different classes of Internet addresses, and how are they different?

8. What is a subnet? Why do networks need them?

9. What is a subnet mask?

10. How does dynamic addressing work?

11. What benefits and problems do dynamic addressing provide?

12. What is address resolution?

13. How does TCP/IP perform address resolution for network layer addresses?

14. How does TCP/IP perform address resolution for data link layer addresses?

15. What is routing?

16. How does decentralized routing differ from centralized routing?

17. How does static routing differ from dynamic routing? When would you use static routing? When would you use dynamic routing?

18. What are three types of dynamic routing?

19. What are the differences between connectionless and connection-oriented routing?

20. What is a virtual circuit?

21. What is Quality of Service routing, and why is it useful?

22. Compare and contrast unicast, broadcast, and multicast messages.

23. Explain how multicasting works.

24. Explain how the client computer in Figure 6–11 (128.192.98.130) would obtain the data link layer address of its subnet gateway.

Exercises

A. What network layer protocol(s) are used your organization's backbone network? Why?

B. Would you recommend dynamic addressing for your organization? Why?

C. Use the Web to explore the differences between bootp and DHCP. Which is likely to become more popular? Why?

D. Look at your network layer software (either on a LAN or dial-in) and see what options are set—but don't change them! How do these match the fundamental addressing and routing concepts discussed in this chapter? What class of Internet addresses does your organization (or Internet service provider) have?

E. Suppose a client computer (128.192.95.32) in Building B in Figure 6–11 requests a large Web page on the server in Building A (www1.anyorg.com). Assume that the client computer has just been turned on and does not know any addresses other than those in its configuration tables. Assume that all gateways and Web servers know all network layer and data link layer addresses.

1. Explain what messages would be sent and how they would flow through the network to deliver the Web page request to the server.

2. Explain what messages would be sent and how they would flow through the network as the Web server sent the requested page to the client.

3. Describe, but do not explain in detail, what would happen if the Web page contained several graphic images (e.g., GIF or JPEG files).

NEXT DAY AIR SERVICE CASE STUDY

As you continue to work on the data communications network plans for NDAS, you realize that it is imperative for you to gain a broader base of management and staff support for the new network and for the additional investment in information technology.

Many of the board members and staff at NDAS have little or no understanding of data communications and are therefore unwilling to support or fund developments in this area. You discuss this matter with Bob Jones, who has become one of your major backers since you helped him with the Internet and the World Wide Web. NDAS's home page and inquiry/response system on the Internet is now considered an industry model. Bob Jones suggests a training session on data communications basics for management and staff. The training should not be too technical, but should be detailed enough so that management and staff can understand and appreciate just what occurs, what equipment is needed, what is important, how much it will cost, and how to be sure it is working properly. He is also confused about the TCP/IP protocol used on the Internet and hopes you will clarify that for him in the training session. He reminds you that your position paper on how computer data are transferred over telephone lines was well received by President Coone and NDAS top management. "Use that approach," he suggests.

You bring the idea of a training session up with President Coone. He is very interested, but he wants you to consider a series rather than a single session. The initial training topic will be network concepts. President Coone confesses that the concept of a network is a mystery to him. He schedules the first session for next Tuesday, just before the monthly management meeting. You will have thirty minutes.

It is clear that you have a great deal riding on this session. It will be your first contact with several key top and middle managers. If the session is a success, it will be much easier for you to get their support. You call Bob Jones to thank him for suggesting a training session. Bob recommends that you use a presentation software package like Microsoft's PowerPoint to prepare bullet charts as the basis for the presentation. You must start work on your preparations immediately.

Exercises

1. Review the topics in this chapter. Prepare an agenda for your training session. The agenda should be an outline, showing topics and subtopics with enough detail to allow the reader to follow. Remember Bob Jones's advice on what the management and staff will want and expect from your session.

2. Bob Jones calls to warn you that the new manager of International Services, Sally Wong, will be present at the training session. She wants to be sure any new data communications system will be able to handle international messaging. Bob suggests that you include material in the session on how adherence to standards can ensure smooth integration of the NDAS data communication with overseas systems. You agree. Present a review of standards and standardizing groups for data communications. Which standards do you consider most important for NDAS? Be prepared to defend your view.

3. Bob Jones also reminds you that he needs a straightforward, simple, and understandable explanation of the Internet TCP/IP protocol. Prepare a bullet chart that describes the key concepts of TCP/IP.

4. You have just finished your preparations when President Coone's secretary calls to tell you that IBM sales representatives have asked President Coone for an appointment to discuss SNA and how it can be used at NDAS. Because IBM is a valued customer of NDAS, President Coone thinks he must pay attention to their request. However, he wants you to send him a brief memo covering the differences between SNA and TCP/IP before he responds to IBM. Prepare the memo, and include your observations of SNA's importance in the development of a data communication system at NDAS.

CHAPTER 7

Local Area Networks

The preceding chapters provided the fundamental understanding of the four layers in a typical network. This chapter draws together these concepts to describe a basic local area network (LAN). We first summarize the three major components of a LAN, and then describe the two most commonly used LANs (Ethernet and token ring), as well as several other types of LANs. The chapter ends with a discussion of how to improve LAN performance and how to select a LAN. In this chapter we focus only on the basics of LANs; the next chapter describes some newer technologies used in higher speed LANs and backbone networks.

Objectives

* Become familiar with the roles of LANs in organizations
* Understand the three major components of LANs
* Understand how Ethernet LANs operate
* Understand how Token Ring LANs operate
* Become familiar with other types of LANs (e.g., wireless LANs)
* Understand how to improve LAN performance
* Become familiar with the issues involved in selecting a LAN

Chapter Outline

✳✳ INTRODUCTION

Most large organizations have numerous local area networks (LANs) connected by backbone networks. In many cases, these LANs also provide access to the organization's mainframe computer. In this chapter, we discuss the fundamental components of a LAN, and discuss two commonly used types of LANs—Ethernet and token ring. Both of these LAN standards are supported by many vendors and together account for almost 95 percent of all LANs installed today.

Why Use a LAN?

There are two basic reasons for developing a LAN: information sharing and resource sharing. *Information sharing* refers to having users who access the same data files, exchange information via electronic mail, or search the Internet for information. For example, a single purchase-order database might be maintained so all users can access its contents over the LAN. (Many information sharing applications were described in Chapter 2.) The main benefit of information sharing is improved decision making, which makes it generally more important than resource sharing.

Resource sharing refers to one computer sharing a hardware device (e.g., printer) or software package with other computers on the network, in order to save costs. For example, suppose we have 30 computers on a LAN, each of which needs access to a word-processing package. One option is to purchase 30 copies of the software and install 1 copy on each computer. This would use disk space on each computer and require a significant amount of staff time to perform the installation and maintain the software, particularly if the package were updated regularly.

An alternative is to install the software on the network for all to use. This would eliminate the need to keep a copy on every computer and free up disk space. It would also simplify software maintenance, because any software upgrades would be installed once on the *network server*, staff would no longer have to upgrade all computers.

In most cases, not all users would need to access the word-processing package simultaneously. Therefore, rather than purchasing a license for each computer in the network, you could instead purchase 10 licenses, presuming that only 10 users would simultaneously use the software. Of course, the temptation is to purchase only one copy of the software, and permit everyone to use it simultaneously. The cost savings would be significant, but this is illegal. Virtually all software licenses require one copy to be purchased for each simultaneous user. Most companies and all government agencies have policies forbidding the violation of software licenses, and many terminate employees who knowingly violate them.

One approach to controlling the number of copies of a particular software package is to use *LAN metering software* that prohibits using more copies of a package than there are installed licenses. Many software packages now sell LAN versions that do this automatically, and a number of third-party packages are also available.

Nonetheless, the Software Publishers Association (SPA) in Washington, D.C., estimates that about 40 percent of all the software in the world is used illegally—an annual total of more than $13 billion. North America has the lowest rate of software piracy (28 percent). Although piracy has been on the decline, it still exceeds 75 percent in many parts of the world, with the exception of Western Europe (43 percent), Australia (32 percent), New Zealand (35 percent) and Japan (41 percent).

SPA has recently undertaken an aggressive *software audit* program to check the number of illegal software copies on LANs. Whistle-blowers receive rewards from SPA, while the violating organizations and employees are brought to court. SPA will work with companies that voluntarily submit to an audit. It offers an audit kit that scrutinizes networks in search of software sold by SPA members (see www.spa.org).

Dedicated Server versus Peer-to-Peer LANs

One common way to categorize LANs is by whether they have a dedicated server or whether they operate as a peer-to-peer LAN without a dedicated server. This chapter focuses primarily on dedicated server LANs because they account for more than 90 percent of all installed LANs, although many of the issues are also common in peer-to-peer networks.

Management Focus: LANs at Hallmark

Hallmark has turned the need to greet others into a $3 billion empire with operations in 100 countries. But while the company's cards make it easier for others to keep in touch, Hallmark's financial managers had less luck communicating. Management was struggling under time-consuming and unwieldy financial reporting process, because since 1992, Hallmark acquired 22 international subsidiaries, each with different financial information systems. Integrating their information with the rest of Hallmark proved challenging.

To unify and streamline financial reporting, the greeting card giant undertook a massive re-engineering of its standard operating practices. In conjunction with its new information system, Hallmark implemented a client–server solution to bridge the gulf between the mainframe-based U.S. corporate offices and the PC-based international offices.

Client–server LANs were installed at both the U.S. corporate headquarters and the international headquarters. The LANs use Compaq computer servers running Microsoft LAN Manager, and connect a total of 120 Compaq PC clients. Comshare Commander consolidates data from multiple general ledgers, enables simpler financial analysis, and serves as a front end to Hallmark's old mainframe-based financial system.

The re-engineering has paid off in numerous ways: Hallmark has redesigned its financial statement, reduced the monthly book-closing time by 40 percent, and cleared the way for more timely and relevant information to be delivered to senior management worldwide.

Source: InfoWorld, December 19, 1994.

Dedicated Server Networks

As the name suggests, a *dedicated server LAN* has one or more computers that are permanently assigned to being the network server(s). These servers enable users to share files and often are also used to share printers. A dedicated server LAN can connect with almost any other network, can handle very large files and databases, and uses sophisticated LAN software. Moreover, high-end dedicated server LANs can be easily interconnected to form enterprise-wide networks or, in some cases, can replace a host mainframe computer. Generally speaking, the dedicated servers are powerful microcomputers or minicomputers.

In a dedicated server LAN, the server's usual operating system (e.g., Windows) is replaced by a network operating system (e.g., Novell NetWare, Windows NT). Special-purpose network communication software is also installed on each client computer, and is the link between the client computer's operating system and the network operating system on the server. This set of communication software provides the data link layer and network layer protocols that allow data transmissions to take place. Three software components must work together and in conjunction with the network hardware to enable communications: the network operating system in the dedicated server, the network communication software on the client, and the application software that runs on the server and client computers.

A LAN can have many different types of dedicated servers. Four common types are file servers, database servers, print servers, and communication servers (see Figure 7–1).

File servers allow many users to share the same set of files on a common, shared disk drive. The size of hard disk volume can be of any size, limited only by the size of the disk storage itself. Files on the shared disk drive can be made freely available to all network users, shared only among authorized users, or restricted to only one user.

A *database server* usually is more powerful than a file server. It not only provides shared access to the files on the server, but also can perform database processing on those files associated with client–server computing. For example, database servers can receive requests for information contained in a database (e.g., find all customers in New York) and search through the database to find the requested information, which is then sent back to the client requesting the information. In contrast, file servers can only send entire files, requiring any processing to be done by the client. The key benefit of database servers is that they reduce the amount of data moved between the server and the client workstation. They can also minimize data loss and prevent widespread data inconsistencies if the system fails.

Print servers handle print requests on the LAN. By offloading the management of printing from the main LAN file server or database server, print servers help reduce the load on them and increase network efficiency in much the same way that front-end processors improve the efficiency of mainframe computers. Print servers have traditionally been separate computers, but many vendors now sell "black boxes" that perform all the functions of a print server at a much less than the cost of a stand-alone computer.

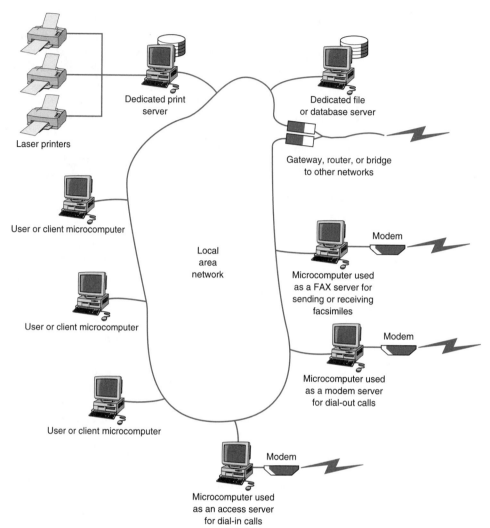

Figure 7-1 A typical LAN.

Communications servers are dedicated to performing communication processing. There are three fundamental types: fax servers, modem servers, and access servers. As the name suggests, *fax servers* manage a pool of fax-boards that enable LAN users to send or receive faxes.

Access servers and *modem servers* allow users to dial into and out of the LAN by telephone. Dialing into the LAN is accomplished with an access server, whereas dialing out is accomplished with a modem server. An access server connects to the LAN and retrieves applications from the network server's hard disk to run on its own CPU or to transfer files to the computer that dialed into the LAN. Callers dialing into an access server can check their e-mail, transfer files, print files, run

Management Focus: *Fax System Cuts Costs of Daily Reports*

Litle & Co. is one of the behind-the-scenes players that allows companies like Lands' End and other mail-order catalog businesses to flourish. Litle provides credit card authorizations and transaction processing services. Litle owns close to one-quarter of this market, which is mainly populated by banks.

A key component of Litle's services is a daily report of sales transactions, which used to be faxed to its 750 customers. This tied up fax machines for 12 to 16 hours per day and drove up telephone costs.

With the implementation of a more efficient LAN fax server, payback has come in two areas—less time is spent dialing out, which in turn has greatly reduced long distance phone costs. Litle now only spends 4 to 5 hours per day faxing, with much of it occurring during off hours. Phone charges have dropped by almost $50,000 per year.

Source: InfoWorld, December 26, 1994.

application programs, or send faxes via the fax server. Access servers are ideal for database applications in which the amount of information moved is small and does not require high speed beyond the limited capabilities of regular voice-grade telephone lines. (LANs typically provide data transmission rates of 1 to 100 Mbps, while telephone lines typically provide only 28.8 Kbps to 128 Kbps).

Peer-to-Peer Networks

Peer-to-peer networks do not require a dedicated server. All computers run special network software that enables them to function both as a client and as a server. Authorized users can connect to any computer in the LAN that permits access and can use their hard drive(s) and printer as though they were physically attached to their own computers. Peer-to-peer networks often are slower than dedicated server networks because if you access a computer that is also being used by its owner, it slows down both the owner and the network.

In general, peer-to-peer LANs have less capability, support a more limited number of computers, provide less sophisticated software, and can prove more difficult to manage than dedicated server LANs. However, they are cheaper both in hardware and software. Peer-to-peer LANs are most appropriate for sharing resources in small LANs. Examples of peer-to-peer LANs include Artisoft's LANtastic, Novell's NetWare Lite, and Windows.

✳✳ LAN COMPONENTS

There are five basic components to a LAN (see Figure 7–2). The first two are the client computer and the server (but see the section on peer-to-peer networks). Clients and servers have been discussed in Chapter 3 and earlier in this chapter,

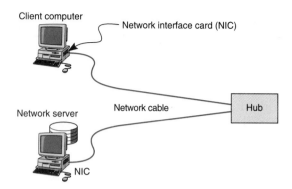

Figure 7–2 LAN components.

and will not be discussed further. The other three components are network interface cards, network cables and hubs, and the network operating system.

Network Interface Cards

Most computers are not yet manufactured with a built-in network interface. As a result, one of the first steps when installing a LAN is to install a special *network interface card (NIC)*. The NIC allows the computer to be physically connected to the network cable, which provides the physical layer connection among the computers in the network. (See Figure 7–3).

Most NICs are installed inside the computer. The computer must be physically opened and the NIC inserted into a slot on the computer's bus. A few computers, particularly laptops, have an NIC already installed, or a special port that enables network cards to be installed without physically opening them (i.e., *PCMCIA slots*). Both trends reflect the growing importance of networking.

Figure 7–3 10/100 Ethernet network interface card.

Network Cables and Hubs

Each computer must be physically connected by network cable to the other computers in the network. Just as highways carry all kinds of traffic, the perfect cabling system also should be able to carry all kinds of electronic transmissions within the building. But in practice, it isn't that simple. The selection of a LAN can be influenced greatly by the type of cable that already exists in the building where the LAN is to be installed.

Network Cable

Most LANs are built with *unshielded twisted-pair (UTP) wires, shielded twisted-pair (STP) wires,* coaxial cable, or fiber optic cable (although fiber optic cable is far more commonly used in backbone networks, discussed in Chapter 8). You even can obtain wireless LANs that run on infrared or radio frequencies, eliminating the installation of cables. (Common cable standards are discussed in the technology focus box. We should add that these cable standards specify the minimum quality cable required; it is possible, for example, to use category 4 UTP for a 10Base-T Ethernet.)

Many LANs use a combination of shielded and unshielded twisted pair. Although initially it appeared that twisted pair would not be able to meet long-term capacity and distance requirements, today this is one of the leading LAN cabling technologies. Its low cost and the availability of shielded wiring that can handle higher transmission make it very useful.

Technology Focus: Commonly Used Network Cable Standards

Name	Type	Maximum Data Rate (Mbps)	Maximum Distance (Meters)	Often Used by	Cost* ($/foot)
Category 1**	UTP	1	90	Modem	.04
Category 2	UTP	4	90	Token Ring-4	.05
Category 3	UTP	10	100	10Base-T Ethernet	.06
Category 4	STP	16	100	Token Ring-16	.27
Category 5	UTP	100	200	100Base-T Ethernet***	.15
Category 5	STP	100	200	100Base-T Ethernet***	.27
RG-58	Coax	10	185	10Base-2 Ethernet	.17
RG-8	Coax	10	500	10Base-5 Ethernet	.60
X3T9.5	Fiber	100	2000	FDDI***	1.00

*These costs are approximate and often change, but will give you a sense of the relative differences in costs among the different options.

**Category 1 is standard voice-grade twisted pair, but can also be used to support low-speed analog data transmission.

***100Base-T and FDDI are discussed in Chapter 8.

Coaxial cable used to be the most common type of LAN cable, but today it is less commonly used than UTP or STP. By definition, coaxial cable is shielded because its outer conductor is also a shield. Coax is physically larger than twisted pair, weighing anywhere from 20 to 90 pounds per 1000 feet, which can be detrimental in an overhead ceiling—especially if it collapses because of the cable's weight! Coax is also not as flexible as twisted pair, so it is sometimes harder to install in older buildings not designed for computer cabling.

Fiber optic cable is even thinner than unshielded twisted pair and therefore takes far less space when cabled throughout a building. It also is much lighter, weighing less than 10 pounds per 1000 feet. Because of its high capacity, fiber optic cabling is perfect for backbone networks, although it is beginning to be used in LANs.

Although most LANs use only one type of cable, it is possible to buy devices that permit different types of cable to be connected together. A *BALUN* (*BAL*anced *UN*balanced) is a small device about ½ inch in diameter and 3 inches long that connects twisted-pair cabling with coaxial cable. One end has a standard twisted-pair connection and the other has a standard screw-in coaxial connector lead. Similar devices are available to connect fiber optic cable to twisted pair and coax, but are significantly larger and more expensive, because they must convert between electricity and light.

Network Hubs

Network *hubs* go by many names, depending upon the type of network and the specific vendor, such as multistation access unit (MAU) or *transceiver*. Network hubs

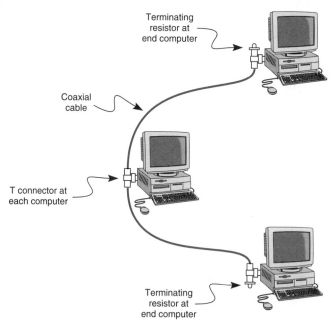

Figure 7–4 A three-station Ethernet LAN using coaxial cable and T-connectors.

Figure 7–5 Network hub.

serve two purposes. First, they provide an easy way to connect network cables. In general, network cables can be directly connected by splicing two cables together. For example, T-connectors are often used to connect coaxial cable but they leave little room for expansion; a technician must cut the cable and install a new connector to add a new connection (see Figure 7–4).

A better approach is to use a hub in any area in which the network might expand. A hub can be thought of as a junction box, permitting new computers to be connected to the network as easily as plugging a power cord into an electrical socket (see Figure 7–5). Simple hubs are commonly available in 4-, 8-, and 16-port sizes, meaning that they provide anywhere from 4 to 16 ports into which network

---

Management Focus: *Cable Problems at The University of Georgia*

Like many organizations, the Terry College of Business at The University of Georgia is headquartered in a building built before the computer age. When LAN cabling was first installed in the early 1980s, no one foresaw the rapid expansion that was to come. Cables and hubs were installed piecemeal to support the needs of the handful of early users.

The network eventually grew far beyond the number of users it was designed to support. The network cable plan gradually became a complex, confusing, and inefficient mess of cables. There was no logical pattern for the cables, and there was no network cable plan. Worse still, no one knew where all the cables and hubs were physically located. Before a new user was added, a network technician had to open up a ceiling and crawl around to find a hub. If the hub did not have an unused port to connect the new user, the technician would have to find another hub with an empty port.

To complicate matters even more, asbestos was discovered. Now network technicians could not open the ceiling and work on the cable unless asbestos precautions were taken. This meant calling in the university's asbestos team, and sealing off nearby offices. Installing a new user to the network (or fixing a network cable problem) now took two days and cost $2000.

The solution was obvious. In 1994, the university spent $400,000 to install new twisted-pair cable to every office, and to install a new high-speed fiber optic backbone network between network segments.

cables can be plugged. When no cables are plugged in, the signal bypasses the unused port. When a cable is plugged into a port, the signal travels down the cable as though it were directly connected to the cables attached to the hub. Some hubs also enable different types of cables to be connected and perform the necessary conversions (e.g., twisted pair to coaxial cable, coaxial cable to fiber optic).

Second, many hubs act as repeaters or amplifiers. Signals can travel only so far in a network cable before they attenuate and can no longer be recognized (attenuation was discussed in Chapter 5). All LAN cables are rated for the maximum distance they can be used (see the technology focus box). Any LAN that spans more than these distances—and most LANs do—must use hubs with repeaters or amplifiers.

Some hubs are "smart" because they can detect and respond to network problems. For example, a "smart" hub could detect faulty transmissions from a failing network card, and disable the incoming port so that the card could not send any more messages that would disrupt the network. Many "smart" hubs go one step farther and alert the network manager about the problem and the action taken. With "smart" hubs, finding and fixing faults is much easier. We will discuss smart hubs in more detail in Chapter 11.

Network Cable Plans

In the early days of LANs, it was common practice to install network cable wherever it was convenient. Little long-term planning was done. Hubs were placed at random intervals to meet the needs of the few users, and cable was laid where it was convenient. The exact placement of the cables and hubs was often not documented, making future expansion more difficult—you had to find the cable and a hub before you could add a new user.

With today's explosion in LAN use, it is critical to plan for the effective installation and use of LAN cabling. The cheapest time to install network is during the construction of the building; adding cable to an existing building costs significantly more. Indeed, the costs to install cable (i.e., paying those doing the installation and additional construction) are usually substantially more than the cost of the cable itself, making it expensive to re-install the cable if the cable plan does not meet the organization's needs.

Most buildings under construction today have a separate LAN *cable plan*, as they do for telephone cables and electrical cables. The same is true for older buildings in which new LAN cabling is being installed. Most cable plans are similar in style to electrical and telephone plans. Each floor has a telecommunications wiring closet that contains one or more network hubs, with cables run from each room on the floor to this wiring closet. It is common to install 20 to 50 percent more cables than you actually need to make future expansion simple. Any reconfiguration or expansion can be done easily by adding a network hub and connecting the unused cables in the wiring closet, which saves the difficulty and expense of attempting to locate network hubs and installing new cables.

Management Focus: Managing Network Cabling

You must consider a number of items when installing cables or when performing cable maintenance:

* Perform a physical inventory of any existing cabling systems and document those findings in the network cable plan.
* Properly maintain the network cable plan. Always update cable documentation immediately upon installing or removing cable or hub. Insist that any cabling contractor provide "as-built" plans that document where the cabling was actually placed, in case of minor differences from the construction plan.
* Establish a long-term plan for the evolution

of the current cabling system to whatever cabling system will be in place in the future.

* Obtain a copy of the local city fire codes and follow them. For example, cables used in airways without conduit need to be plenum-certified (i.e., covered with a fire-retardant jacket).
* Conceal all cables as much as possible to protect them from damage and for security reasons.
* Properly number and mark both ends of all cable installations as you install them. If a contractor installs cabling, always make a complete inspection to ensure that all cables are labeled.

Network Operating System

The *network operating system (NOS)* is the software that controls the network. Every NOS provides two sets of software: one that runs on the network server(s), and one that runs on the network client(s). The server version of the NOS provides the software that performs the functions associated with the data link, network, and application layers and usually the computer's own operating system. The client version of the NOS provides the software that performs the functions associated with the data link and the network layers, and must interact with the application software and the computer's own operating system. Most NOS provide different versions of their client software that run on different types of computers, so that Windows computers, for example, can function on the same network as Apples. In some cases (e.g., Windows, UNIX), the client NOS software is included with the operating system itself.

NOS Server Software

The NOS server software enables the file server, print server, or database server to operate. In addition to handling all the required network functions, it acts as the application software by executing the requests sent to it by the clients (e.g., copying a file from its hard disk and transferring it to the client, printing a file on the printer, executing a database request, and sending the result to the client).

NOS server software typically replaces the normal operating system on the server. By replacing the existing operating system, NOS provide better performance and faster response time because NOS are optimized for their limited range of operations. The following focus box introduces several common NOS.

NOS Client Software

The NOS software running at the client computers provides the data link layer and network layer. To work effectively with the application software, the NOS must also work together with the client's own operating system. Most operating systems today are designed with networking in mind. For example, Windows provides built-in software that will enable it to act as a client computer with a Novell NetWare server or a Windows NT server.

Management Focus: Popular Network Operating Systems

The most popular network operating system is Novell NetWare, holding almost a 50 percent market share worldwide. Novell supports a wide variety of topologies, protocols, types of computers, and languages (e.g., English, French, and Japanese). It was one of the first NOS, and has consistently been the market leader in performance, but over the past few years, new NetWare versions have not been as innovative as earlier ones. Novell supports the Ethernet, token ring protocols (described later in this chapter), and a host of others.

The second most popular NOS is Microsoft's Windows NT. NT holds a 30 percent worldwide market share and is rapidly growing. Novell still appears to have the edge in performance over NT, but given Microsoft's past track record and strength in application software, some analysts expect NT to become more popular than Novell by 2000. NT supports Ethernet and token ring, among others.

The third most popular NOS is Artisoft's LANtastic (a peer-to-peer NOS) with just under a 10 percent market share. LANtastic has long been the market leader in peer-to-peer NOS, providing many features commonly found in server-based NOS at a much lower cost. Several newer companies now offer competing peer-to-peer NOS, but LANtastic continues to prosper. LANtastic supports Ethernet, and its own proprietary protocol.

There are many other NOS available, but these three together account for about 90 percent of all NOS sold in the world. If you're in a large organization (or even a small one), chances are you'll be using one of them.

Network Profiles

A *network profile* specifies what resources on each server are available on the network for use by other computers and which devices or people are allowed what access to the network. The network profile normally is configured when the network is established, and remains in place until someone makes a change. In a LAN, the server hard disk may have various resources that can or cannot be accessed by a specific network user (e.g., data files, printers). Furthermore, a password may be required to grant network access to the resources.

If a device such as a hard disk on one of the network's con
included on the network profile, it cannot be used by another con
network. For example, if you have a hard disk (C) on your compi
computer is connected to this LAN but the hard disk is not included o
profile assignment list, then no other computer can access it.

In addition to profiling disks and printers, you must build a *user profile* for
each person who uses the LAN in order to add some of security. Each device and
each user is assigned various access codes. Only those users who login with the
correct code can use a specific device. Most LANs keep audit files to track who uses
which resource. Security is discussed in Chapter 12.

✳ ✳ ETHERNET (IEEE 802.3)

Almost 70 percent of all LANs in the world use *Ethernet*. Ethernet LAN was originally
developed by DEC, Xerox, and Intel, but it has since become a standard formalized
by the Institute of Electrical and Electronics Engineers (IEEE) as *IEEE 802.3*. The
IEEE 802.3 version of Ethernet is slightly different than the original version, but
the differences are minor. Likewise, another version of Ethernet has also been
developed that differs slightly from the 802.3 standard.

Topology

Topology is the basic geometric layout of the network—the way in which the computers on the network are interconnected. Ethernet uses a *bus topology*. All computers are connected to one circuit running the length of the network that is called
the bus (see Figure 7–6). The top part of this figure shows the *logical topology*. All
messages from any computer flow onto the central cable (or bus) and through it
to all computers on the LAN. Data *may* pass directly from one computer to another,
or it may be routed through a head end controller, which sends it back down the
cable in the opposite direction to the terminator. Every computer on the bus receives *all* messages sent on the bus, even those intended for other computers. Before
processing an incoming message, the Ethernet software checks the data link layer
address and only processes those addressed to that computer.

The term *bus* implies a high-speed circuit and a limited distance between the
computers, such as within one building. These distances can be increased by using
a hub, which is a repeater. The bottom part of Figure 7–6 shows the *physical topology*
of an Ethernet LAN when a hub is used. From the outside, an ethernet LAN *appears*
to be a star topology, because all cables connect to the central hub. Nonetheless,
it is really a bus.

Most Ethernet LANs span sufficient distance to require several hubs. In this
case, the hubs are connected via cable in the same manner as any other connection
in the network (see Figure 7–7).

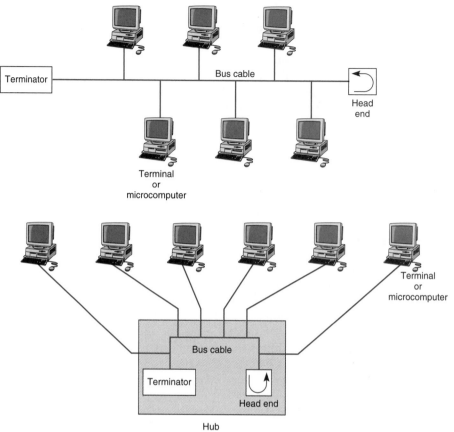

Figure 7–6 Ethernet topology.

Some Ethernet LANs are built without the use of hubs. In this case, the physical topology matches the logical topology. The computers are simply attached to one central cable by the use of T-connectors, as discussed previously.

Media Access Control

When several computers share the same communication circuit, it is important to control their access to the media. If two computers on the same circuit transmit at the same time, their transmissions will become garbled. These "collisions" must be prevented, or if they are permitted to occur, there must be a way to recover from them. This is called media access control.

Ethernet uses a contention-based media access control technique called *carrier sense multiple access with collision detection* (CSMA/CD). *CSMA/CD*, like all contention-

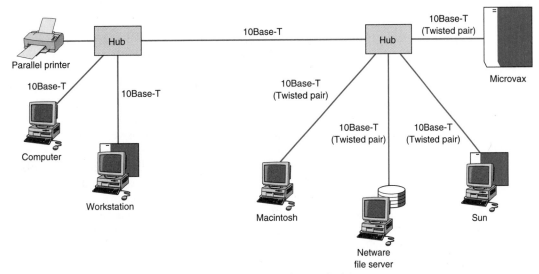

Figure 7–7 An example of an Ethernet LAN with two hubs.

based techniques, is very simple in concept: wait until the bus is free and then transmit. Computers wait until no other devices are transmitting, and then transmit their data. As an analogy, suppose you are talking with a small group of friends (four or five people). As the discussion progresses, each person tries to "grab the floor" when the previous speaker finishes. Usually, the other members of the group yield to the first person who jumps in after the previous speaker.

Ethernet's CSMA/CD protocol can be termed "ordered chaos." As long as no other computer attempts to transmit at the same time, everything is fine. However, it is possible that two computers located some distance from one another can both listen to the circuit, find it empty, and begin to transmit simultaneously. This simultaneous transmission is called a *collision.* The two messages collide and destroy each other.

The solution to this is to listen while transmitting, better known as *collision detection (CD).* If the NIC detects any signal other than its own, it presumes that a collision has occurred, and sends a jamming signal. All computers stop transmitting and wait for the circuit to become free before trying to retransmit. The problem is that the computers that caused the collision could attempt to retransmit at the same time. To prevent this, each computer waits a random amount of time after the colliding message disappears before attempting to retransmit. Chances are that both computers will choose a different random amount of time and one will begin to transmit before the other, thus preventing a second collision. However, if another collision occurs, the computers wait a random amount of time before trying again. This does not eliminate collisions completely, but it reduces them to manageable proportions.

Types of Ethernet

There are many different types of Ethernet, but all are classified as either baseband or broadband. *Baseband* uses digital signaling. It treats the cable as one single channel, so it can carry only a single transmission at any one moment. *Broadband* uses analog signaling and splits the cable into many different channels (using frequency division multiplexing) so more than one transmission can occupy the LAN cable at the same time; thus, we can intermix voice, data, and image signals on the same network. Baseband is less complex, and usually is less expensive because it does not need modulation devices (i.e., modems) built in the NICs.

The original Ethernet specification was a 10 Mbps data rate using baseband signaling on thick coaxial cable, called *10Base-5* (or *Thicknet*), capable of running 500 meters between hubs. Today, thin coaxial cable (*10Base-2*) is rapidly replacing the original thick coax because it is considerably cheaper and easier to work with, although it is limited to 185 meters between hubs. The 10Base-2 standard is often called *Thinnet* or *Cheapnet*.

10Base-T is the most commonly used type of Ethernet. The name means 10 Mbps, baseband, and the "T" means it uses *twisted-pair wiring* (actually unshielded twisted pair). It was the 10Base-T standard that revolutionized Ethernet, and made it the most popular type of LAN in the world. The extremely low cost of 10Base-T made it very inexpensive compared to its foremost competitor, IEEE 802.5 token ring, which is discussed next.

Technical Focus: *Installing a LAN*

Buying a LAN usually is easier than getting it to work. Before you buy, recognize that the LAN implementation includes cabling the building, installing hardware and software, testing the LAN, training the users, establishing network security, managing the system, supervising the ongoing maintenance of the LAN, and planning future enhancements.

During the LAN's implementation you must either install the cabling yourself or contract for someone to pull the wires through the building to each computer location. Do not be surprised if the installation of the cabling costs far more than the cable itself.

Hardware installation means setting up each computer or workstation, along with any centralized items such as the server. Software installation means installing the NOS onto the server (if you have one) and onto all client computers.

By the end of software installation, you should have the cabling in place, the user computers connected, and the software up and running. Testing can begin. Testing is the process that verifies all the LAN features and equipment are working properly.

At this point, you must establish general operating policies, and the levels of security to be provided. This includes what files and directories are public (accessible to everyone), who is authorized to put files on the server, and how to prevent the spread of viruses.

Training begins simultaneously with testing. Users must be trained in how to use the new LAN software commands so they can send files to a shared printer and transfer or modify files on a file server.

Broadband Ethernet is also available as a *10Broad-36* network. Again, 10Broad-36 means 10 Mbps, broadband, with a maximum distance of 3600 meters. The 10Broad-36 standard is most commonly used in backbone networks (discussed in the next chapter). Several new types of Ethernet that transmit at 100 Mbps have been developed, and are discussed in the next chapter.

✳ ✳ TOKEN RING (IEEE 802.5)

The second most popular type of LAN is the *token-ring network*. Almost 25 percent of all LANs worldwide are token ring LANs. Token ring was originally developed by IBM, and has since been standardized by IEEE as *IEEE 802.5*. As with Ethernet, the 803.5 version is slightly different than the original version developed by IBM. Use of token ring is declining as Ethernet becomes more popular.

Topology

As the name suggests, token ring uses a *ring topology*. A ring topology connects all computers on the LAN in one closed loop circuit with each computer linked to the next. The top half of Figure 7–8 shows the logical topology. Messages pass around

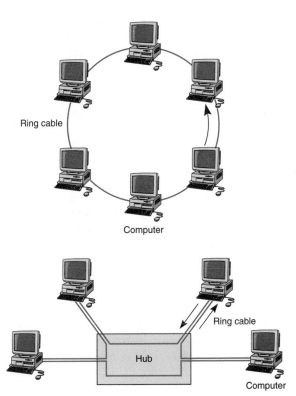

Figure 7–8 Token ring topology.

the ring in one direction only to each computer in turn. Each computer receives messages intended for all computers, but only processes those addressed to itself; it transmits other messages to the next computer in the ring.

The bottom part of Figure 7–8 shows the *physical topology* of a token ring LAN when a hub is used. From the outside, a token ring LAN *appears* to be a star—because all cables flow into the central hub—but it is truly a ring, with messages passing from one computer to the next. Most token ring LANs span sufficient distance to require several hubs. In this case, the hubs are connected via two cables like any other connection in the network.

Now compare the bottom of Figure 7–6 with the bottom of Figure 7–8. From the outside, token ring and Ethernet LANs look almost identical. They have the same physical topology (a star), but really use very different topology internally.

Media Access Control

All computers in a token ring LAN share the same common circuit, so it is essential that access to the media be controlled by the data link layer. Token ring uses a controlled-access technique called token passing.

The *token passing* access method can be compared to a relay race in which the track belongs to you as long as you have the baton. When your run is finished, you hand the baton to the next runner. In a token-passing network, the baton is the *token*, a short electronic message that is generated when the network is started.

The token moves between the computers on the network in a predetermined sequence (much like hub polling). A computer with a message to transmit waits until it receives what is called a *free token*; that is, one available for use. The computer then changes the free token into a *busy token* and attaches its message to it. The computer retransmits the token and the message on the circuit to the next computer in the sequence. Should that computer want to transmit a message, it must wait, because the token is busy. It simply forwards the message with the busy token to the next computer in sequence. When the token and message arrive at the destination computer, it copies the data in the message, sets the acknowledgment (ACK) bit (or NAK, if there was an error in transmission), and the message continues around the ring, making a complete round trip back to the transmitting computer. The transmitting computer then removes the message and inserts a new free token on the ring (see Figure 7–9). Most token passing methods restrict the maximum number of messages that a computer can transmit before it must issue a free token and permit other computers to send messages. This ensures that no one computer monopolizes the circuit.

One problem with token-passing protocols is dealing with "lost" tokens. Suppose the computer that has the token crashes before it can retransmit it, or suppose a computer that has just transmitted a message (and marked the token as busy) crashes before it can receive an acknowledgment and create a free token. In this case, the token is "lost" because no other computer on the network can use the token. Unless some action is taken, the entire network will cease to function.

The solution is to designate one computer in the network to be the *token monitor*. If no token circulates through the network for a certain length of time or

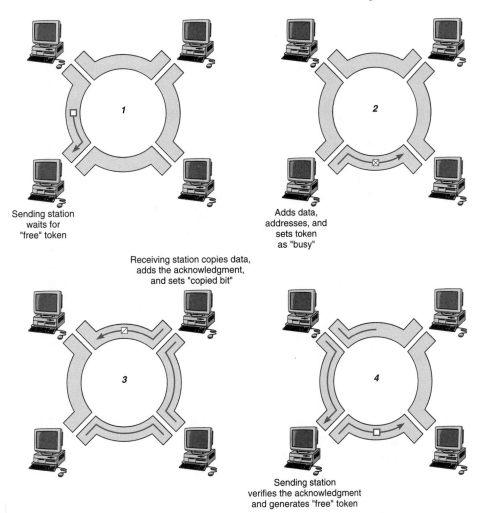

Figure 7–9 Message transfer with token ring.

if a busy token circulates too often, the token monitor will create a new free token (and destroy the busy token, if necessary). Unfortunately, the problem is not that simple, because the computer that crashed (causing the lost token) could be the token monitor itself. Therefore, there is a backup token monitor to ensure that the first token monitor is operating and steps in if the primary token monitor malfunctions.

Types of Token Ring

There are two common types of token ring. The original token ring was Token-ring-4, operating at 4 Mbps over unshielded twisted pair (UTP). The newer token ring is Token-ring-16, which operates at 16 Mbps over higher-quality twisted-pair cable.

❋ ❋ OTHER TYPES OF LANs

Although Ethernet and token ring are the two most popular types of LANs in use today, there are several other types. In this section, we discuss two older protocols that are fading from use (Arcnet and AppleTalk) and one emerging new protocol (wireless LANs IEEE 802.11).

ARCNET

Arcnet (Attached Resource Computing Network) is another popular peer-to-peer LAN. Arcnet was developed by Datapoint Corporation in 1977 in response to the need for a low-cost PC LAN. Arcnet is a baseband token-passing bus or star architecture. Its topology is a bus-like Ethernet, but it uses a token-passing media access control-like token ring. All computers on the bus receive each message, they only process messages addressed to themselves. The network maintains a table of addresses for all computers in the order in which each computer should receive the token. A computer requiring the token is frequently listed several times in the table so it can receive the token more often. Before a computer can transmit, it must have the token. Once the computer is finished transmitting, it sends a message containing the token to the next computer that should receive it.

Its low cost has made Arcnet very popular—so much so that the ANSI is expected to designate Arcnet as ANSI standard 878.1. The Arcnet Trade Association (ATA), which is accredited by ANSI to set standards, plans to seek approval of the International Organization for Standardization to make Arcnet a worldwide standard after ANSI approves it.

Arcnet originally transmitted over a coaxial cable at 2.5 Mbps. Transmission over twisted wire pairs or fiber optic cable was added later. The newer Arcnet Plus transmits at 20 Mbps over coaxial cable. When Arcnet has a bus configuration, the maximum distance between computers is 1000 feet.

AppleTalk

Macintosh computers have a built-in network hardware and software called *AppleTalk*, which is a nonstandard set of protocols similar to Ethernet that works with the Apple *LocalTalk* cabling system. LocalTalk transmits at 230 Kbps, has a 1000-foot cable length, and supports up to 32 computers. AppleTalk was a major innovation when it was first introduced because it automatically provided networking, and did so very simply.

Like Ethernet, LocalTalk uses a carrier sense multiple access (CSMA) scheme to put packets on the network. It does not rely on collision detection, but instead reserves space on the media as a *collision avoidance* procedure (*CSMA/CA*). LocalTalk link access protocol (LLAP) sends out a small, 3-byte packet to signal its intent to put data on the network. This packet tells the other Macintoshes to wait until the data from the first Macintosh has been sent before attempting to send their data. If collisions occur, they happen between these preliminary 3-byte packets instead of between the data packets.

Technical Focus: IEEE LAN Standards

IEEE has established many committees that examine and publish standards for different parts of the LAN environment and different types of LANs. Not all 802 committees have produced formal standards that have been incorporated into products. For example, the 802.1 committee has produced definitions and procedures for the network layer and network management, but none has been widely adopted into products. Today, the most commonly used IEEE 802 standards are:

* 802.2: IEEE divides the data link layer into two parts. The logical link control layer (LLC) is covered by the 802.2 standard, which specifies how lower-level data-link layer protocols (e.g., 802.3, 802.5) will communicate with the network layer.
* 802.3: Ethernet CSMA/CD protocol.
* 802.4: Token bus (also called Manufacturing Automated Protocol (MAP)). An old protocol that uses controlled access via tokens on a bus topology. Used (rarely) in the automobile industry.
* 802.5: Token ring protocol.
* 802.6: Distributed queue dual bus (DQDB) protocol. A protocol similar to FDDI (see Chapter 8) that was last updated in 1995. Rarely used today.
* 802.9: Integrated voice and data networking, including Iso-ethernet (discussed in Chapter 8) and Integrated Services Digital Network (ISDN) (discussed in Chapter 9).
* 802.11: Wireless LAN protocol.
* 802.12: 100Base-VG Ethernet protocol discussed in Chapter 8.
* 802.13: 100Base-X Ethernet protocol discussed in Chapter 8.

The major problems with AppleTalk are its very slow data transmission rate and its use of nonstandard protocols. Most networked Apple computers now use Ethernet.

Wireless LANS (IEEE 802.11)

Wireless LANs form a very small percentage of LANs in operation today, but their use is growing rapidly. Wireless LANs transmit data through the air using radio or infrared transmission rather than through coaxial cable, twisted pair, or fiber optic cable. The *IEEE 802.11* standard uses a version of the carrier sense multiple access with collision avoidance (CSMA/CA) protocol that is very similar to Ethernet's CSMA/CD protocol and AppleTalk's CSMA/CA protocol. Many vendors sell wireless hubs that can be connected directly into existing Ethernet LANs. Although the protocols are slightly different between the wired Ethernet portion and the wireless 802.11 portion, they are similar enough so that the hub can easily translate between the two. There are three commonly used types of wireless LANs covered by the 802.11 standard: infrared, direct-sequence spread-spectrum radio, and frequency-hopping spread-spectrum radio.

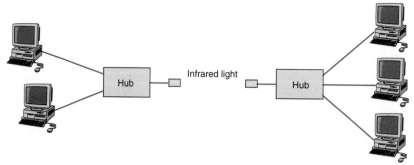

Figure 7-10 Infrared transmission between network hubs.

Infrared Wireless LANs

In general, infrared LANs are the least flexible because most require a direct line of sight between the transmitters and receivers, which are usually mounted in fixed positions. Therefore, most direct-line-of-sight infrared LANs are wireless only between the hubs. The NICs inside the computers are connected via traditional wires to a network hub that contains the transmitter (see Figure 7–10). The hubs use wireless transmission to communicate from hub to hub.

The primary advantage of a wireless LAN is the reduction in wiring. Infrared-based LANs are sometimes used for communication between buildings where installing underground cable would be expensive. In an old building where wiring is difficult and costs are extremely high, wireless LANs offer a low-cost alternative by enabling communication without the installation of cables. The primary disadvantage is the low speed, only 1–4 Mbps.

A new version of infrared, called diffuse infrared, operates without a direct line of sight by bouncing infrared light around a room. Most diffuse infrared systems have extremely short ranges (usually only 50–75 feet) and will only operate in the same room because the light cannot travel through walls.

Radio Wireless LANs

Radio waves travel in all directions and through nonmetal objects and thus are more flexible than infrared systems. Most radio LANs have a NIC inside the computer that is connected to an external transmitter (see Figure 7–11). The external transmitter transmits radio signals to a receiver that acts like a network hub and enables wireless computers to communicate with each other and with traditional wired networks. Most radio LANs have a range of 100–500 feet and may even reach 1000 feet in open areas without obstructions or sources of interference.

Wireless LANs are also being used increasingly with laptop computers, permitting new capabilities for mobile computing. When configured with a wireless network, a set of laptops becomes an effective way to provide a portable groupware configuration or to enable workers to walk through a facility and have constant network access at any point (e.g., warehouse, factory).

Figure 7–11a Radio hub.

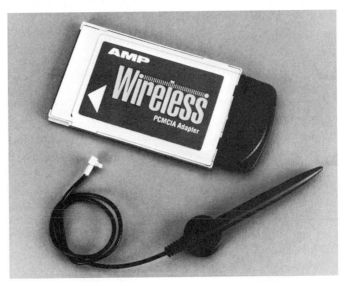

Figure 7–11b Radio PCMCIA NIC for portable computers.

Direct-sequence spread-spectrum (DSSS) systems transmit signals through a wide spectrum of radio frequencies simultaneously (in either the 900 MHz or 2.4 GHz bands). The signal is divided into many different parts and is sent on different frequencies simultaneously. Because several radio devices could be operating in these same frequency bands (not just wireless LANs, but also cordless phones), devices add a special code to each bit transmitted that uniquely identifies the signal and enables the intended receiver to identify it.

Frequency-hopping spread-spectrum (FHSS) systems transmit signals through the same wide spectrum of radio frequencies, but use each frequency in turn. A short burst of data is sent on one frequency (usually less than half a second) and then the sender changes to another pseudorandom frequency and broadcasts another burst of data before changing to another frequency, and so on. The transmitter and receiver are synchronized so that they both know which frequencies will be used at which point. This approach minimizes jamming and eavesdropping because it is difficult for an outside listener to know what frequencies will be used next.

Radio LANs (both DSSS and FHSS) have two disadvantages compared to traditional wired LANs. The first is the increased opportunity for noise to disrupt transmissions. Microwave ovens, cordless phones, and baby monitors can cause interference making radio LANs problematic to use. The second—and most important—disadvantage is that wireless LANs have much slower data transmission rates than "wired" networks. Although the 802.11 standard specifies data rates of 1–2 Mbps, a 1997 test by Canterbury University found data rates to vary greatly. Data rates ranged from a low of 100 Kbps to a high of 1.5 Mbps, depending on the location of the system and the manufacturer (Lucent Technology's WaveLAN outperformed all other products).

Management Focus: WaveLAN Lets Wireless Users Roam

Lucent Technology's WaveLAN is one of the most versatile and most commonly used radio LANs. The WaveLAN NIC plugs into a PCMCIA slot on laptop computers and provides a wireless radio connection up to 75 meters to a network hub.

WaveLAN also permits users to "roam," move from one hub to another, while still maintaining a continuous network connection. This dramatically improves the potential applications for wireless networks.

Grandview Hospital in Dayton, Ohio, for example, has created a wireless network where medical workers carry laptop computers with WaveLAN. The hospital is totally covered by a series of WaveLAN hubs, so workers can be anywhere in the hospital and have access to medical information.

Source: "AT&T Lets Wireless Users Roam," LAN Times, October 17, 1994.

✳✳ IMPROVING LAN PERFORMANCE

When LANs had only a few users, performance was usually very good. Today, however, when most computers in an organization are on LANs, performance can be a problem. Performance is usually expressed in terms of throughput (the total amount of user data transmitted in a given time period). In this section, we discuss how to improve throughput. We focus on dedicated server networks, because they are the most commonly used type of LANs, but many of these concepts also apply to peer-to-peer networks.

In order to improve performance, you must locate the *bottleneck*, the part of the network that is restricting the data flow. Generally speaking, the bottleneck will lie in one of two places. The first is the network server. In this case, the client computers have no difficulty sending requests to the network server, but the server lacks sufficient capacity to process all the requests it receives in a timely manner. The second location is the network circuit. The network server can easily process all the client requests it receives, but the network circuit lacks enough capacity to transmit all the requests to the server. It is also possible that the bottleneck could lie in the client computers themselves (e.g., they are receiving data too fast for them to process it), but this is extremely unlikely—unless, of course, you are still using some old 486 computers!

The first step in improving performance, therefore, is to identify whether the bottleneck lies in the circuit or the server. To do so, you simply watch the utilization of the server during periods of poor performance. If the server utilization is high (e.g., 60 to 100 percent), then the bottleneck is the server; it cannot process all the requests it receives in a timely manner. If the server utilization is low during periods of poor performance (e.g., 10–40 percent), then the problem lies with the network circuit; the circuit cannot transmit requests to the server as quickly as necessary. Things become more difficult if utilization is in the mid-range (e.g., 40–60 percent). This suggests that the bottleneck may shift between the server and the circuit depending on the type of request, and suggests that both should be upgraded to provide the best performance.

Now, we will focus attention on ways to improve the server and the circuit to remove bottlenecks. These actions address only the supply side of the equation; that is, increasing the capacity of the LAN as a whole. The other way to reduce performance problems is to attack the demand side: reduce the amount of network use by the clients, which we also discuss. See Figure 7–12 for a performance checklist.

Improving Server Performance

Improving server performance can be approached from two directions simultaneously: software and hardware.

Software

The NOS is the primary software-based approach to improving network performance. Some NOS are faster than others, so replacing the NOS with a faster one will improve performance.

Performance Checklist

Increase Server Performance

* Software
  * Upgrade to a faster network operating system
  * Fine-tune the network operating system settings
* Hardware
  * Add more servers and spread the network applications across the servers to balance the load
  * Upgrade to a faster computer
  * Increase the server's memory
  * Increase the number and speed of the server's hard disk(s)
  * Upgrade to a faster NIC

Increase Circuit Capacity

* Upgrade to a faster circuit
* Change protocols
* Segment the network

Reduce Network Demand

* Move files from the server to the client computers
* Increase the use of disk caching on client computers
* Change user behavior

Figure 7-12 Improving LAN performance.

Because a network server primarily reads and writes information to and from disk, the best NOS are highly tuned to improve the disk access speed on the server. Two commonly used techniques are disk caching and disk elevatoring. *Disk caching* stores commonly used data in memory. Because memory is much faster than disk, performance is greatly improved. The problem, of course, is that there is never enough memory to store all the data on the disk, but even if only 20 to 30 percent of the data needed are present in memory, disk caching can improve performance significantly.

Disk elevatoring refers to the order in which data are accessed on the hard disk. Hard disks are designed with a read/write head that must physically move to sections of the disk. Requests from clients to read or write information can be processed in the order they are received, but this is very inefficient. A hard disk is much like an office building with the read/write head like an elevator that moves between floors (i.e., sections on the disk). Processing read/write requests in the order received may mean the read/write head goes to floor 30 (i.e., section 30), then floor 55, then floor 40, then floor 60, and so on. Elevators never move to floors in the order in which the buttons are pressed because they would have to travel past floors and go back to them. Instead, they arrange a group of requests to minimize the distance they must travel. Disk elevatoring works the same way. Requests are constantly grouped and processed so that the read/write head travels the minimum distance, thus significantly improving server speed.

Each NOS provides a number of software settings to fine-tune network performance. Depending on the number, size, and type of messages and requests in your LAN, different settings can significantly affect performance. The specific settings differ by NOS, but often include things such as the amount of memory used for disk caches, the number of simultaneously open files, the amount of buffer space, and so on.

Hardware

One obvious solution if your network server is overloaded is to buy a second server (or more). Each server is then dedicated to supporting one set of application software (e.g., one handles e-mail, another handles the financial database, and another stores customer records). The bottleneck can be broken by carefully identifying the demands each major application software package places on the server, and then allocating them to different servers.

Sometimes, however, most of the demand on the server is produced by one application that cannot be split across several servers. In this case, the server itself must be upgraded. The first place to start is with the server's CPU. Faster CPUs mean better performance. If you are still using an old computer as a LAN server, this may be the answer; you probably need to upgrade to the latest and greatest. Clock speed also matters; the faster the better. Most computers today also come with CPU-cache (a very fast memory module directly connected to the CPU). Increasing the cache will increase CPU performance.

A second bottleneck is the amount of memory in the server. Increasing the amount of memory increases the probability that disk caching will work, thus increasing performance.

A third bottleneck is the number and speed of the hard disks in the server. The primary function of the LAN server is to process requests for information on its disks. Slow hard disk(s) give slow network performance. The obvious solution is to buy the fastest disk drive possible. Even more importantly, however, is the number of hard disks. Each computer hard disk has only one read/write head, meaning that all requests must go through this one device. By using several smaller disks rather than one larger disk (e.g., four 2-gigabyte disks rather than one 8-gigabyte disk), you now have four read/write heads, each of which can be used simultaneously, dramatically improving throughput. A special type of disk drive called *redundant array of inexpensive disks (RAID)* builds on this concept, and is typically used in applications requiring very fast processing of large volumes of data, such as multimedia. Of course, RAID is more expensive than traditional disk drives, but costs have been shrinking. RAID can also provide fault tolerance, which is discussed in Chapter 12.

A fourth bottleneck is the network interface card itself. Simply put, some network interface cards (NICs) are faster than others. Some NICs provide built-in CPUs to perform some of the network functions usually handled by the server (much like front-end processors in mainframe networks). Others provide memory and cache to improve the access time to and from the network.

Several vendors sell special-purpose network servers that are optimized to provide extremely fast performance. Many of these provide RAID and use *symmetric multiprocessing (SMP)* that enables one server to use up to 16 CPUs. Each of these CPUs may be an Intel chip such as Pentium, or may be RISC-based. Such servers provide excellent performance, but cost more than a standard microcomputer (often $20,000 to $50,000).

Improving Circuit Capacity

Improving the capacity of the circuit means increasing the volume of simultaneous messages the circuit can transmit from network clients to the server(s). One obvious approach is simply to buy a bigger circuit. For example, if you are now using 4 Mbps token ring, upgrading to 16 Mbps will improve capacity. Two other basic approaches are to re-examine the LAN protocol used (i.e., Ethernet versus token ring), and to segment the network.

Ethernet versus Token Ring

Token ring performance should be about 60 percent better than Ethernet, because token ring provides a 16 Mbps data transmission rate compared to Ethernet's 10 Mbps. Unfortunately, it is more complicated than this. The question of whether token ring or Ethernet provides the best performance really comes down to how the two manage the available transmission rates—in other words, the media access control approaches they use: token passing versus CSMA/CD.

In general, contention approaches such as CSMA/CD work better than controlled approaches such as token passing for small networks that have low usage. In this case, each computer can transmit when necessary without waiting for permission. Since usage is low, there is little chance of a collision.

The opposite is true for large networks with high usage: token passing works better. In high-volume networks, many computers want to transmit, and the probability of a collision using CSMA/CD is high. Collisions are very costly in terms of throughput because they waste circuit capacity during the collision and require both computers to retransmit later. Controlled access prevents collisions and makes more efficient use of the circuit. Tests of various Ethernet LANs show that when they are heavily used, the actual data throughput drops by almost 50 percent to about 5 Mbps, due to collisions. In contrast, tests of token ring networks show that even when they are heavily used, the actual throughput is almost the entire 16 Mbps. So, when throughput performance matters, token ring is about three times as fast as Ethernet.

A second performance consideration is response time. Generally speaking, response time in token ring networks is more consistent than that in Ethernet networks. As already noted, response time for token passing may be worse when the circuit is little used (because the token is passed to all computers in turn). However, response time generally does not increase as rapidly in token ring net-

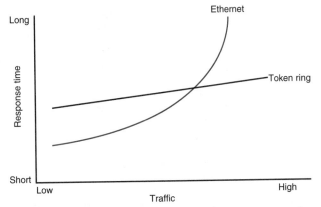

Figure 7–13 Response times in Ethernet versus token ring.

works as traffic increases (see Figure 7–13). The key to selecting the fastest protocol is to find the cross-over point between token ring and Ethernet.

There are limits on how long a computer can transmit, in token ring networks, so that no one monopolizes the network. In Ethernet networks, there is a greater chance that one computer could monopolize the network. Response time in token ring networks is therefore more consistent and predictable.

So why is Ethernet so popular? Cost is always a factor. In general, 10Base-T Ethernet cables, NICs, and hubs cost much less than their token ring counterparts. Also, Ethernet networks that are overloaded can easily be segmented (see below).

Network Segmentation

If there is more traffic on a LAN than the network circuit and media access protocol can handle, the solution is to divide the LAN into several smaller segments. Breaking a network into smaller parts is called *network segmentation.* By carefully identifying how much each computer contributes to the demand on the server, and carefully spreading those computers to different network segments, the network bottleneck can often be broken.

Figure 7–14 presents an example in which each network segment is connected into the same server. Most servers can support up to 16 separate networks or network segments, simply by adding one NIC into the server for each network. As the number of NICs in the server increases, however, the server spends more of its processing capacity monitoring and managing the NICs, and has less capacity left to process client requests. Most experts recommend no more than three or four NICs per server. There are two ways to create more network segments: one is to use more servers, each dedicated to one or more segments; and the other is to use a backbone network to connect different segments. Backbone networks are discussed in the next chapter.

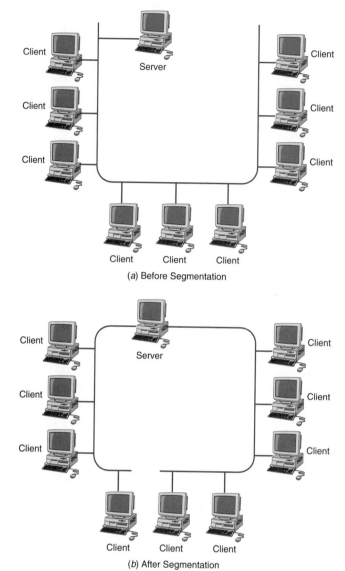

(a) Before Segmentation

(b) After Segmentation

Figure 7-14 Network segmentation.

Reducing Network Demand

Upgrading the server hardware and software, choosing a different LAN protocol, or segmenting the LAN are all strategies to increase network capacity. Performance also can be improved by attempting to reduce the demand on the network.

One way to reduce network demand is to move files to client computers. Heavily used software packages that continually access and load modules from the network can place unusually heavy demands on the network. While user data and messages are often only a few kilobytes in size, today's software packages can be many megabytes in size. Placing even one or two such applications on client computers can greatly improve network performance (although this can create other problems, such as increasing the difficulty in upgrading to new versions of the software).

Another way is to increase the use of disk caching software on the client machines in order to reduce the client's need to access disk files stored on the server. For example, most Web browsers store Web pages in their cache so that they can access previously used pages from their hard disks, without accessing the network.

Because the demand on most LANs is uneven, network performance can be improved by attempting to move user demands from peak times to off-peak times. For example, early morning and after lunch are often busy times when people check their e-mail. Telling network users about the peak times and encouraging them to change their habits may help. In practice, however, it is often difficult to get users to change. Nonetheless, finding one application that places a large demand on the network and moving it can have a significant impact (e.g., printing several thousand customer records after midnight).

✳✳ SELECTING A LAN

Selecting a LAN for your organization is not easy. The marketplace is crowded with vendors, all claiming their products are the best. To complicate matters, the small, simple LAN you start with today may turn into a large multifloor, multibuilding, or enterprise-wide network in the future. You should start by asking some basic questions: how many users are expected, how much data will be stored and transmitted, how easy it will be to add workstations, what cabling is needed, whose software should be selected, and how much security is needed. The design steps in Chapter 10 will help in designing and selecting a LAN, as will the issues discussed in this section. These issues are summarized in Figure 7–15. One cautionary note before we proceed: Many high-speed network technologies developed for backbone networks (discussed in the next chapter) are finding their way into LANs, replacing traditional Ethernet and token ring. In selecting a LAN, you should also consider these new technologies.

Network Needs

The first place to begin is with the specific needs of your network. The maximum number of client computers probably will be an issue in the future, and you must plan for it now. Today, you may develop a LAN with only a dozen computers, but will the LAN be able to grow to meet the demand five years from now? Many companies install more cable and hubs with more ports than they need to simplify future growth.

LAN Selection Cheklist

Network Needs

* Number of client computers
* Number of dedicated severs
* Distance between computers
* Internetworking requirements
* Specific application needs
* User training, documentation, and network policies
* Future growth

Technology

* Protocol
* Cabling/Wireless
* Network Operating System
  * Reliability
  * Ease of use
  * Performance
* LAN management software
* LAN backup software and hardware

Vendor

* Experience with network hardware and software
* Experience with your network application
* Vendor service and support

Figure 7–15 LAN selection checklist.

Another critical decision is the server. You must decide whether you are going to use dedicated file server(s) and, if so, how many. The servers may be standard computers, or ones designed specifically as network servers. You must also decide whether to have print servers, access/modem servers, fax servers, network servers, or database servers.

The distance between computers is important. In general, LAN segments are limited to 100 to 1000 feet between each computer, 3000 feet from the network server to the computer, and up to 7000 feet in end-to-end length. (This is not absolute, because you always can add repeaters or amplifiers to extend the medium for several thousand more feet; however, there are often limits on the number of repeaters or amplifiers in one LAN circuit.)

You must determine whether the LAN is going to internetwork with another corporate LAN or backbone network, the organization's host mainframe, or some of the public dial-up networks outside of the organization. The question to ask is, what devices are needed to connect our network with other networks within the organization? These are discussed in more detail in the next two chapters.

Management Focus: The Hidden Costs of LANs

Over the last few years, the costs of LANs have steadily decreased. Today Ethernet NICs can be purchased for between $50 and $75. Network cable is less than 20 cents a foot and hubs cost less than $20 per connected computer. On the surface, building a LAN appears cheap, about $100 per computer.

This is misleading, because there are many hidden costs that surface only after you begin installing and operating the LAN. Experienced LAN managers plan on at least $1000 per computer for a LAN installation. The cost of installing cabling alone in an existing multifloor building, for example, can range from $200 to $2000 per computer. An even greater hidden cost is that for network management (which is discussed in Chapter 11). The average *annual* network management cost is often several thousand dollars per computer—more than the cost of the computer and initial network installation combined!

The amount of energy and money devoted to LAN operations depends on the complexity of the LAN. A part-time network supervisor probably can manage a small network used for simple applications. A large network with 100 users dispersed throughout a multistory building requires a full-time LAN manager with top-notch technical and programming skills. As a rule of thumb, it requires half of a full-time-equivalent (FTE) person to administer a LAN with 15 computers, one and a half FTEs for 50 stations, and two FTEs for 100 stations.

Operating costs include:

* Network administration: cost of the network administrator and staff who add and delete users, answer questions, set priorities, and so on

* Maintenance: installation of upgrades, fixing cables or hardware "glitches," and correcting incompatibilities between network software and application programs

* Training: specialized training for the network administrator and all network users

* Security: costs related to network security, such as changing passwords regularly or installing specialized security hardware and software

* Backup: backing up the network server daily (also may include purchase of specialized backup hardware and software)

* Future growth: planning for and purchasing additional LAN resources

Future growth will be a major point. You must determine whether the LAN can grow to meet the changing needs of the organization's application systems, geographic locations, interconnectivity, users, and hardware requirements. Is there enough built-in flexibility and modularity for the LAN to survive if or when LAN standards change?

There may also be some specific needs for the initial applications you intend to use. The ideal network for use as an intranet or to provide Internet access may be very different than one designed to support file sharing.

Proper written documentation should be provided for all the hardware, software, users, and so forth. Training must be considered. You must examine both the cost of the training and the time required for each user to attend these training sessions. Legal issues, such as purchasing the proper software licenses and formulating policies on employee copying of software, must be addressed. Employee policies should prohibit the use of personal diskettes and software on the organization's LANs. Such policies help prevent the spread of computer viruses and the theft of privileged information. These policies should also address the connection of employee-owned hardware to the organization's LANs.

Technology Issues

One of the first technology issues that must be addressed is the protocol—Ethernet or token ring. These considerations are critical in determining the LAN's growth potential. Token ring offers some benefits, but new backbone technologies discussed in the next chapter suggest that Ethernet may have some additional benefits. Ethernet is becoming the dominant technology, because Ethernet components cost 30–40 percent less than token ring components.

Then you must decide which cabling to use: unshielded twisted pair, shielded twisted pair, coaxial cable, or fiber optics. Remember, the cost of installing the cables through the building may be greater than the cost of the cable itself, so many companies choose high-speed twisted-pair cable. Although it is more expensive than the lower-speed cable they need now, it provides an easy upgrade path when they decide to use higher-speed LANs. Conversely, a wireless LAN may be more cost-effective.

The network operating system is another critical consideration because it must work together with the various computer operating systems, computers, and other LAN hardware, and must interface with application programs and host mainframe.

Management Focus: What You Should Expect from a NOS

NOS provides seven fundamental network functions:

* Network directory: an integrated database that provides access to all users, information, and resources located anywhere in the network
* Messaging: automatic transfer of data and messages using a variety of industry standard applications and APIs (e.g., e-mail)
* Network management: a single point of control for all network resources that provides easy-to-use graphical tools
* Security: a variety of network security features including auditing and encryption

* Routing support: the ability to use a variety of network layer routing protocols such as TCP/IP and SPX/IPX to simplify interconnecting different networks
* File services: data compression and the ability to store files from many different types of computers (e.g., Windows, Macintosh, UNIX)
* Print services: ability for users to simply direct their print requests to any authorized printer anywhere in the network

Source: Novell, *Guide to Networking,* 1995.

Perhaps the most important aspect of the NOS is how easy it is to manage (network management is discussed in Chapter 12). Novell NetWare and Windows NT are the two most popular NOS. It is difficult to argue which is "best"—NT or NetWare—because both products are changing. Before selecting one or the other, you should consider their reliability, ease of use, and performance.

Determine whether it is possible to actively manage the LAN and all of the related network elements with LAN management software. For example, you must decide if third-party software, such as menu support, memory management, word processing, and spreadsheets, work with the LAN's operating system. Chapter 12 discusses network management.

Proper backup and recovery hardware, software, and procedures must be provided. The server disk certainly must be backed up, and recovery features for each user's disk files must be provided. Backup electrical power or surge/sag protection may be required on both the electric utility power lines and any connecting telephone lines.

Vendor Issues

At this point, you also must take the vendor into account. You should evaluate the vendor's experience with the specific network hardware and software you intend to install and with the specific application software you intend to use. Does the vendor have experience with the application? What level of service and support does the vendor provide (e.g., 8 hours a day, Monday through Friday, or 24 hours a day, 7 days a week)? In general, it is safer to purchase all network components from one vendor. This way, blame cannot be shifted to someone else if something goes wrong.

Summary

Why Use a LAN?   The two basic reasons for developing a LAN are information sharing and resource sharing. Information sharing refers to business needs that require users to access the same data files, exchange information via e-mail, or search the Internet for information, as discussed in Chapter 2. Resource sharing refers to one computer sharing a hardware device (e.g., printer) or software package with other computers on the network. The main benefit of resource sharing is cost savings, while the main benefit of information sharing is improved decision making.

Dedicated Server versus Peer-to-Peer Networks   A dedicated server LAN has one computer that acts as the network server. It can connect with almost any other network, handle very large databases, and use sophisticated LAN software. Moreover, high-end dedicated server LANs can be interconnected easily to form enterprise-wide networks or, in some cases, replace the host mainframe central computer. Four common types of dedicated server LANs are file servers, database servers, print servers, and communication servers. All computers on a peer-to-peer LAN run special-network software that enables them to function both as a client and as a server.

LAN Components   The Network Interface Card (NIC) enables the computer to be physically connected to the network cable, which provides the physical layer connection among the computers in the network. Most LANs are formed with unshielded twisted-pair (UTP) wires, shielded twisted-pair (STP) wires, coaxial cable, and/or fiber optic cable. Network hubs provide an easy way to connect network cables and act as repeaters or amplifiers. Most buildings built today have a separate LAN cable plan, as they do for telephone cables and electrical cables. Wireless LANs use similar protocols (Ethernet, for example) as other LANs, but they transmit data through the air rather than by cable. The network operating system (NOS) is the software that performs the functions associated with the data link and the network layers, and interacts with the application software and the computer's own operating system. Every NOS provides two sets of software: one that runs on the network server(s), and one that runs on the network client(s). A network profile specifies what resources on each server are available for network use by other computers and which devices or people are allowed what access to the network.

Ethernet (IEEE 802.3)   Ethernet is the most commonly used LAN in the world, accounting for almost 70 percent of all LANs. Ethernet uses a bus topology and a contention-based media access technique called carrier sense multiple access with collision detection (CSMA/CD). Many different types of Ethernet use different network cabling (e.g., 10Base-2, 10Base-5, 10Base-T, and 10Broad-36).

Token Ring (IEEE 802.5)   Token ring is the second most popular type of LAN, with almost 25 percent of the worldwide market. Token ring uses a ring topology with a controlled-access technique called token passing.

Other LANs   Arcnet and AppleTalk are two older protocols not commonly used today. Wireless LANs (IEEE 802.11) are a rapidly growing type of LAN and can use infrared, or more commonly, radio transmission (either direct-sequence spread-spectrum or frequency-hopping spread-spectrum). Although wireless LANs enable communication with wires, they suffer from interference and low transmission rates (usually less than 2 Mbps).

Improving LAN Performance   Every LAN has a bottleneck, a narrow point in the network that limits the number of messages that can be processed. Generally speaking, the bottleneck will lie either in the network server or the network circuit. Server performance can be improved with a faster NOS that provides better disk caching and disk elevatoring, by buying more servers and spreading applications among them, or by upgrading the server's CPU, memory, NIC, and the speed and number of its hard disks. Circuit capacity can be improved by using token ring rather than Ethernet, and by segmenting the network into several separate LANs. Overall LAN performance also can be improved by reducing the demand for the LAN by moving files off the LAN, using disk caching on the client computers, and by shifting the user's routines.

Selecting a LAN   There are a host of issues to be considered in selecting a LAN including: protocol (Ethernet vs. token ring), configuration/topology, network operating system, vendor service and support, application systems, number and type of servers, client computers and users, and network interface cards.

Key Terms

access server

AppleTalk

Arcnet

backup and recovery

BALUN

baseband

bottleneck

broadband

bus topology

busy token

cable plan

Cheapnet

coaxial cable

collision

collision avoidance (CA)

collision detection (CD)

communications server

CSMA/CA

CSMA/CD

database server

dedicated server LAN

direct-sequence spread-
   spectrum (DSSS)

disk caching

disk elevatoring

Ethernet

fiber optic cable

file server

free token

frequency-hopping spread-
   spectrum (FHSS)

hub

IEEE 802.3

IEEE 802.5

IEEE 802.11

information sharing

LAN management software

LAN metering software

LocalTalk

logical topology

modem server

network interface card (NIC)

network operating system
   (NOS)

network profile

network segmentation

network server

PCMCIA slots

peer-to-peer networks

physical topology

print server

redundant array of inexpensive
   disks (RAID)

resource sharing

ring topology

shielded twisted-pair (STP)
   wires

software audit

software piracy

Software Publishers
   Association (SPA)

star topology

symmetric multiprocessing
   (SMP)

Thicknet

Thinnet

token

token monitor

token passing

token-ring network

topology

transceiver

twisted-pair wiring

unshielded twisted-pair (UTP)
   wires

user profile

wireless LAN

10Base-T

10Base-2

10Base-5

10Broad-36

Questions

1. Define local area network.

2. What are the distinguishing features of a LAN?

3. What are two reasons for developing LANs?

4. What is the function of LAN metering software?

5. Discuss the legal issue of using single-computer license software on networks.

6. Discuss why it is important for organizations to enforce policies restricting use of employee-owned hardware and software and unauthorized copies of software.

7. In some LANs, most of the computers talk with the server, but others use no server. What are these two approaches called?

8. Describe at least three types of servers.

9. What is a NIC? What is a hub?

10. What media do LANs normally use?

11. What is the purpose of a BALUN? (See Balanced and Unbalanced in the Glossary.)

12. Compare and contrast category 3 UTP, category 5 UTP, and category 5 STP.

13. What is a cable plan, and why would you want one?

14. Discuss the primary advantages and disadvantage of a wireless LAN. Why would you want or not want one?

15. What does a NOS do? What are the major software parts of a NOS?

16. What is the most important characteristic of a NOS?

17. What is a network profile?

18. What is Ethernet? How does it work?

19. What is the difference between Thicknet and Cheapnet?

20. What are the commonly used LAN topologies? How are they the same? How are they different?

21. How does baseband differ from broadband?

22. Compare and contrast Ethernet and token ring in terms of media access control.

23. Briefly describe CSMA, CD, and CA.

24. Why should CSMA/CD networks be built so that no more than 50 percent of their capacity is dedicated to actual network traffic?

25. Explain the terms 10Base-2, 10Base-5, 10Broad-36, and 10Base-T.

26. What is token ring? How does it work?

27. How does a token passing network operate?

28. What are the primary advantages and disadvantages of infrared wireless LANs?

29. What are the primary advantages and disadvantages of radio wireless LANs?

30. How do direct-sequence spread-spectrum (DSSS) radio LANs differ from frequency-hopping spread-spectrum (FHSS) radio LANs?

31. Describe four important issues when installing a LAN.

32. What is a bottleneck, and how can you locate one?

33. Describe four ways to improve network performance on the server.

34. Describe four ways to improve network performance on the circuit.

35. What are disk caching and disk elevatoring and why are they useful?

36. Why does network segmentation improve LAN performance?

37. Should you select a network because of its protocol or its performance characteristics? Explain.

38. Discuss what makes LAN selection so difficult.

39. It is said that hooking some computers together with a cable does not make a network. Why?

40. Assume you want to install a LAN but are concerned about its cost. Realizing there are both inexpensive and expensive LANs, what features should you compare to help in the decision?

41. This chapter discusses a number of key issues that must be considered when selecting a LAN. Explain six of them.

Exercises

A. Survey the LANs used in your organization. Are they Ethernet, token ring, or some other standard? Why?

B. Document one LAN (or LAN segment) in detail. What devices are attached, what cabling is used, and what is the topology? What does the cable plan look like?

C. You have been hired by a small company to install a simple LAN for their 18 Windows computers. Develop a simple LAN and determine the total cost—i.e., select the NOS and price it, select the cabling and price it, select the NIC and hubs and price them, and so on.

NEXT DAY AIR SERVICE CASE STUDY

Sally Wong is excited about including a LAN as a key element of her new International Service department. She wants you to assist her in developing a plan and proposal for a departmental LAN. You see this as an opportunity to build a model LAN within NDAS. You can start from the beginning with new equipment and procedures. Sally Wong is very well respected in the company. NDAS is committed to moving strongly into the international arena. A successful LAN (or for that matter, an unsuccessful one) in her department will get a great deal of attention at NDAS.

Now you need to revisit the issue of LAN protocols and configurations so that you can make a final recommendation. You also need to consider the operational and managerial procedures that will have to be adopted to ensure successful operation of the department LAN.

The type of LAN should be analyzed carefully in view of its scope, configuration, and protocols and in terms of the methods by which users will access the data. You realize that connecting with other LANs and the Internet will become more important as the LAN grows and its utilization increases.

Sally Wong is even more interested in learning how to manage the LAN. Investigate what should be managed and how such management should be enacted. For example, who should be responsible for the creation and maintenance of the various corporate files that will be stored on the server? Will it be necessary to hire a separate database administrator, or should this responsibility be integrated with other work duties? How will the procurement or development of new software applications be handled? Should there be one central office that controls and standardizes all acquisitions for LAN use, or should each user assume such responsibility? Then there is the area of network and equipment maintenance to consider. In a multivendor environment, such as the one at NDAS, this can be touchy. Finally, you are aware that the topic of end-user application development has been receiving quite a bit of attention. Because LAN management is so closely related to the kinds of applications users want to execute on a network, it seems worthwhile to consider incorporating end-user application development efforts within the framework of LAN management.

Other issues that need to be considered at this time include the LAN's cabling, installation, security, and anticipated growth. You should also consider access: who or which remote offices can access the LAN. And, of course, there are cost considerations.

Sally is excited about starting off with a LAN in her department. She has told you that her group will be using specialized software and creating a departmental database of customers and vendors. The group will initially consist of eight people but is expected to grow rapidly to twice that number. Sally is already interviewing people, and most of them have experience using LANs. The best candidates expect that there will be data communications support at their new job.

However, Sally is concerned that President Coone may take a wait-and-see attitude about a department LAN. She wants a well-thought-out LAN proposal for President Coone.

Exercises

1. Which is best for the International Service department: a high-end full network, a low-end peer-to-peer LAN? Explain your choice.

2. Draw a configuration for a bus, and for a ring topology for the LAN. Now you must decide which LAN would be best for NDAS: Ethernet (e.g., 10Base-2, 10Base-T) or token ring. Which do you recommend? Justify your recommendation with three to five reasons.

3. Which do you think would be the most costly items in the LAN?

4. Sally Wong has heard "horror stories" about LAN bottlenecks. Prepare a brief discussion of LAN bottlenecks and what can be done to improve LAN performance.

5. What safeguards do you recommend for NDAS to control illegal copies of software on the LANs?

CHAPTER 8

High-Speed LAN and Backbone Networks

This chapter examines high-speed networks developed primarily for backbone networks (BNs), many of which are now used in local area networks (LANs). We begin with the various types of devices used in backbone networks, then discuss two fundamental types of these networks. The first are extensions of traditional LANs that use shared multipoint circuits (fast Ethernet, fast token ring, and FDDI). The second are switched networks that use point-to-point circuits (switched Ethernet, switched token ring, ATM, and fibre channel). The chapter ends with a discussion of how to improve BN performance and how to select a BN.

Objectives

* Understand the internetworking devices used in backbone networks
* Understand several types of fast Ethernet and fast token ring
* Become familiar with FDDI
* Understand several types of switched Ethernet and switched token ring
* Become familiar with ATM and fibre channel
* Become familiar with ways to improve backbone network performance
* Become familiar with key factors in selecting backbone networks

Chapter Outline

❋❋ INTRODUCTION

The driving force behind enterprise networking is the shift toward an information-based business economy and the Internet. Most business organizations realize that information must be stored, retrieved, analyzed, acted upon, and shared with others at a moment's notice. Without an enterprise-wide network or an Internet connection, moving information from one department LAN to another or to customers is difficult, and often relies on "sneakernet," diskettes carried from one computer to another.

Interconnecting the organization's diverse networks is one way to meet this challenge. A *backbone network* is a high-speed network that connects many networks on a single company or government site. Backbone networks typically use higher-speed circuits to interconnect a series of LANs and provide connections to other BNs, MANs, WANs, and the Internet. A backbone network also may be called an *enterprise network* if it connects all networks within a company, regardless of whether it crosses state, national, or international boundaries.

In this chapter, we will focus on the high-speed network technologies typically used in backbone networks. Many of these higher-speed technologies are now beginning to be used in local area networks in place of the traditional LAN technologies described in the previous chapter.

There are two fundamentally different approaches to providing high-speed networking. The simplest and most straightforward is to simply "speed up" the technologies currently used in local area networks. "Fast Ethernet" and "fast token ring" (and related technologies such as FDDI) use the same basic approach to networking as discussed in Chapter 7: they provide one very fast shared multipoint circuit and the attached computers and devices take turns using it. These shared media approaches are simple but suffer from the same media-sharing problems inherent in LANs.

The second approach is to develop new high-speed technologies that provide a set of dedicated point-to-point communication circuits between computers. Technologies that use this approach, called *switched networks*, are quite different from their shared media counterparts, and offer distinct advantages and disadvantages.

A 1997 survey of 1000 network managers by Business Research Group found that although 90 percent of those surveyed used traditional shared multipoint LANs (e.g., Ethernet and token ring), less than 10 percent planned to implement new LANs and BNs using those same traditional technologies. Instead, most planned to implement faster shared media or switched media technologies discussed in this chapter.

❋❋ BACKBONE NETWORK COMPONENTS

There are two basic components to a backbone network: the network cable and the hardware devices that connect other networks to the backbone. The cable is essentially the same as that used in LANs, except that it is usually higher quality to provide

Device	Operates at	Messages	Physical Layer	Data Link Layer	Network Layer
Hub	Physical layer	All messages transferred	Same or different	Same	Same
Bridge	Data link layer	Filtered using data link layer addresses	Same or different	Same	Same
Switch	Data link layer	Switched using data link layer addresses	Same or different	Same	Same
Router	Network layer	Routed using network layer addresses	Same or different	Same or different	Same
Brouter	Data link layer and Network layer	Filtered and routed	Same or different	Same or different	Same
Gateway	Network layer	Routed using network layer addresses	Same or different	Same or different	Same or different

Figure 8–1 Backbone network devices.

higher data rates (e.g., fiber optic or category 5 twisted pair). The hardware devices can be computers or special-purpose devices that just transfer messages from one network to another. These include hubs, bridges, routers, brouters, gateways, and switches (see Figure 8–1).

Hubs

Operating at the physical layer, *hubs* are simple devices that pass all traffic in both directions between the LAN sections they link. Hubs forward *every* message they receive to the other sections of the LAN, even those that do not need to go there. They may connect *different* types of cable, but use the *same* data link and network protocol (see Figure 8–2).

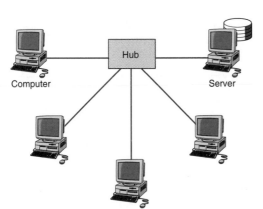

Figure 8–2 Use of hubs to connect computers in a LAN.

Strictly speaking, hubs are not usually considered part of a backbone network. They are usually repeaters or amplifiers that increase the strength of the signal in the circuit to enable the circuit to run longer distances than cable alone. For example, hubs allow you to create an Ethernet network several thousand meters in length, which is much more than the typical limit of less than 200 meters for 10Base-2. Repeaters can also be used to extend the distance, but typically only connect two LAN segments.

Bridges

Bridges operate at the data link layer. They connect two or more network segments that use the same data link and network protocol. They understand only data link layer protocols and addresses. They may connect the *same or different* types of cable. Bridges are more sophisticated than hubs because they only forward those messages that need to go to other network segments (see Figure 8–3). Bridges are commonly used to segment local area networks to improve performance (see Chapter 7).

Bridges "learn" whether to forward packets from one network segment to another. When a bridge receives a packet, it reads the packet's data link layer source address and compares this address to its own internal *address table.* If the source address is not in the address table, the bridge adds it, along with the network segment on which it is located. Thus, the bridge is said to learn the data link layer addresses of the devices on the network.

If a bridge receives a packet with a destination address that is not in the address table, the bridge forwards the packet to all networks or network segments except the one on which it was received. If the destination address is in the address

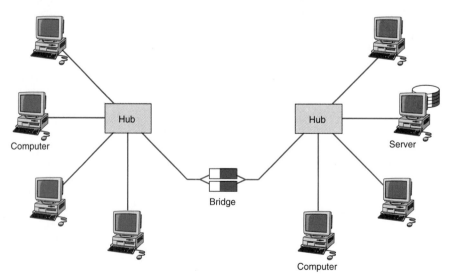

Figure 8–3 Use of bridges to connect LAN segments.

table and is on a different network segment from the one sending the packet, the bridge forwards the packet to the destination network. If the destination address is on the same network segment from which the packet arrived, the bridge discards the packet, which is a process known as *filtering*. The bridge can discard the packet because the computer to which it is addressed will already have received it.

Bridges are a combination of both hardware and software. A typical bridge is an inexpensive "black box" that sits between the two networks and has its own processor, memory, and software; its operations are transparent to the network user. A bridge can also be a regular computer with two or more NICs and special bridging software.

Switches

Like bridges, *switches* operate at the data link layer (again understanding only data link layer protocols and addresses). Switches connect two or more computers or network segments that use the *same* data link and network protocol. They may connect the *same or different* types of cable. Switches typically provide ports for 4, 8, 16, or 32 separate network segments. See Figure 8–4.

Switches operate at the same layers as bridges but differ from them in two ways. First, most switches enable *all* ports to be in use simultaneously. Since all ports can be active at once, switches usually are faster than bridges. Second, unlike bridges, switches don't learn addresses; switches need to have addresses defined explicitly.

There are two types of switches. *Cut-through switches* examine the destination of the incoming packet and immediately connect the port with the incoming message to the correct outgoing port. This decision is made in hardware, so cut-though switches are very fast. *Store-and-forward switches* copy the incoming packet into

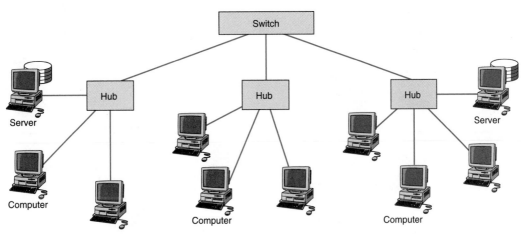

Figure 8–4 Use of switches to connect LANs.

memory before processing the destination address. If the outgoing circuit is available, the packet is immediately forwarded to it. If the outgoing circuit is in use, the packet is held in memory until later. Many store-and-forward switches also do error checking and can discard bad packets. Store-and-forward switches tend to be more expensive and slower than cut-through switches, but rapid changes in cost and speed are eliminating these differences.

Routers

Routers operate at the network layer. Routers connect two or more networks that use the *same or different* data link protocols, but the *same* network protocol. They may connect the *same or different* types of cable. They strip off the data link layer packet and process the network layer packet. Routers forward only those messages that need to go to other networks, based on their network layer address (see Figure 8–5). Routers allow the logical separation of a network into many smaller networks or subnets by using the network layer address, rather than the data link layer address.

Routers may be "black boxes," computers with several NICs, or special network modules in computers or other devices. In general, they perform more processing on each message than bridges, and therefore operate more slowly.

One major feature of a router is that it can choose the "best" route between networks when there are several possible routes between them. Because a router knows its own location, as well as the packet's final destination, it looks in a routing table to identify the best route or *path.*

One other important difference between a router and a bridge is that the router only processes messages that are specifically addressed to it. Bridges process

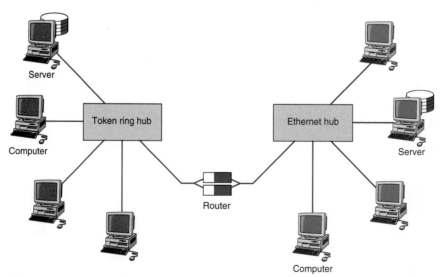

Figure 8–5 Use of routers to connect LANs.

all messages that appear on the network and forward them to the appropriate network based on their data link layer address. Bridges simply forward the message unchanged onto the other network. In contrast, because routers operate at the network layer, the router's data link layer must first recognize that the incoming message is specifically addressed to the router at the data link layer level, before the message it is passed to the network layer for processing. The router will then process the message by building an entirely new data link layer packet, and will then transmit it on the other network.

The router attempts to make no changes to the network layer packet and user data it receives (as noted previously, it creates a new data link layer packet). Sometimes, however, changes are needed, such as when the maximum data link layer packet size on one network is different from another, which forces the router to split a message into several smaller messages for transmission.

Brouter

Brouters (see Figure 8–6) are devices that combine the functions of both bridges and routers. These operate at both the data link and network layers. A brouter

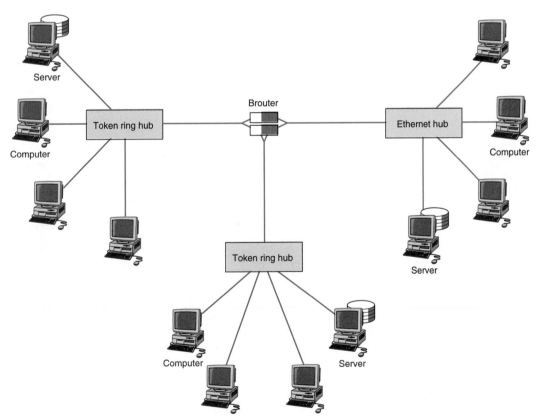

Figure 8–6 Use of brouters to connect LANs.

connects both the same data link type network segments and different data link ones. Like a bridge, it examines the data link layer addresses of all messages on the network (not just those addressed to it) and forwards them as needed to other networks. At the same time, any messages explicitly addressed to it using its data link layer address are routed. The advantage of brouters is that they are as fast as bridges for same data link type networks, but can also connect different data link type networks.

Gateways

Gateways operate at the network layer and use network layer addresses in processing messages. Gateways are more complex than bridges or routers because they are the interface between two or more dissimilar networks. Gateways connect two or more networks that use the *same or different* (usually different) data link and network protocols. They may connect the *same or different* types of cable. Some gateways operate at the application layer as well. Gateways process only those messages explicitly addressed to them (i.e., using their data link layer address) and route those messages that need to go to other networks. See Figure 8–7.

Gateways translate one network layer protocol into another, translate data link layer protocols, and open sessions between application programs, thus overcoming both hardware and software incompatibilities. More complex gateways even take

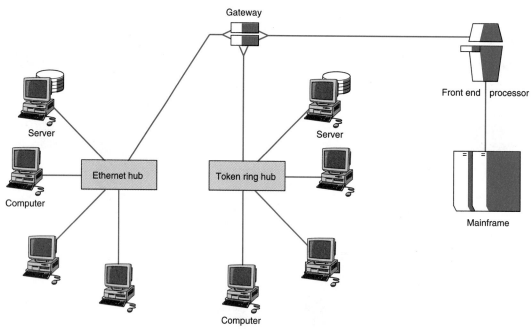

Figure 8–7 Use of gateways to connect LANs and a mainframe.

care of such tasks as code conversion (e.g., converting from ASCII into EBCDIC). A gateway may be a stand-alone computer with several NICs and special software or a front-end processor connected to a mainframe computer.

One of the most common uses of gateways is to enable LANs that use TCP/IP and Ethernet to communicate with IBM mainframes that use SNA. In this case, the gateway converts the microcomputer LAN transmissions into a transmission that looks like it came from a smart terminal.

The gateway provides both the basic system interconnection and the necessary translation between the protocols in both directions. Without this SNA gateway on their local area network, each microcomputer would have to have its own SNA hardware and software in addition to the TCP/IP and Ethernet hardware and software (e.g., software to make the microcomputer act like an IBM 3270 terminal, 3270 hardware emulation card, coaxial cable, and mainframe controller port). The SNA gateway eliminates the need for additional hardware for the microcomputer, and it requires only one connection to the client computer because all data are sent through the local area network.

A Caveat

One warning is in order. The terminology used in the marketplace may differ substantially from the preceding discussion. Many new types of bridges, switches, and routers are being developed, so that one vendor's "bridge" may actually provide the functions of a "router."

Multiprotocol bridges translate between different data link layer protocols. They receive data from one network using one data link protocol (e.g., Ethernet), and translate it into another protocol (e.g., token ring) for use on another network. The most common type of multiprotocol bridge translates between Ethernet and token ring.

Multiprotocol routers can understand several different network layer protocols. If they receive a message in one protocol, they process it and send it out using the same protocol. The most common multiprotocol routers understand both TCP/IP and IPX/SPX and are commonly used in Novell LANs connected through the backbone to the Internet. They enable the LAN to use IPX/SPX internally or for communications to other Novell LANs inside the organization, and simultaneously to use TCP/IP for Internet access. Some vendors' "multiprotocol routers" translate between different network layer protocols (usually TCP/IP and IPX/SPX) so, technically, they are gateways.

Protocol filtering bridges are multiprotocol bridges that forward only packets of a certain type. For example, they may understand both Ethernet and token ring, but only forward Ethernet packets.

Encapsulating bridges connect networks with different data link protocols. They simply surround a packet using one protocol with a packet of a different protocol for transmission over a backbone network, which uses a different protocol. When the message is received at the destination LAN, the encapsulating bridge at the other end removes the encapsulating packet and transmits the original packet.

Layer-3 switches (also called IP switches, swouters, or britches) function in the same way as switches discussed previously, but can also switch messages based on their network layer address (usually TCP/IP address, but some also support IPX/SPX). These switches provide the best of both switches and routers (or brouters). They operate as routers, but provide the benefits of traditional layer-2 switches: much faster transmission and more simultaneously active ports than routers. GartnerGroup, a market research firm, predicts that layer-3 switches will replace about 60 percent of the currently installed routers by the end of 1999.

Many layer-3 switches work in the same manner as their router cousins. They support industry-standard routing protocols (e.g., RIP, OSPF) and integrate well with existing routers. These switches, for example, can translate between Ethernet and token ring at the data link layer and routinely trade RIP or OSPF route information with other layer-3 switches and routers. In contrast, layer-3 switches that use proprietary routing protocols are not as easy to integrate into existing networks. They require a network manager to maintain a proprietary "route server" to supply their address and route information (much like a DNS server for TCP/IP), rather than exchanging information with other devices.

Management Focus: *Country Music Network Kicks Up Its Heels*

Gaylord Entertainment in Nashville runs the grand Ole Opry, Opryland Hotel, Opryland Theme Park, and several TV and radio stations. Singers like Shania Twain, Reba McEntire, and Garth Brooks bring down the house every time. But when you manage the networks at Gaylord, you want to make sure that that's all they bring down.

Workers at all the retail outlets, from hotel to theme park, use the same point-of-sale application that runs on Gaylord's IBM ES/9000 mainframe. Other sales and marketing applications run on their three AS/400 minicomputers. Staffers use Notes for project management and Novell NetWare on their LANs. The Web also plays an important role, both providing information (www.country.com) and enabling employees to gather information.

The resulting network is rather complex, both in terms of size and the number of different applications that must be supported (see Figure 8–8). Gaylord has standardized on token ring at the data link layer, because it supports their IBM LANs, minicomputers, and mainframes. There are two exceptions to this: fast Ethernet is used between the Internet router and the communication group LAN, and the connections to remote locations (the Music Group, River Side) use T1 circuits (T1 circuits are wide area network connections, discussed in Chapter 9). Because both Novell and the Web are widely used, the network uses both TCP/IP and IPX/SPX.

Source: Network Computing, March 1, 1997.

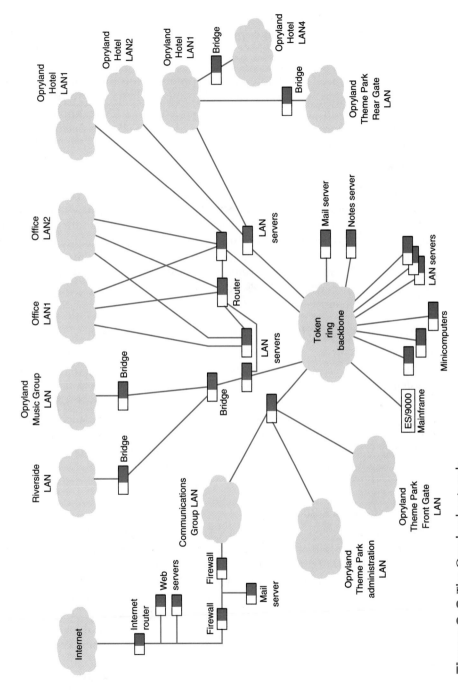

Figure 8-8 The Opryland network.

✳✳ SHARED MEDIA TECHNOLOGIES

One approach to providing high-speed networks is to develop faster versions of the same technologies used in LANs. These technologies operate by providing a high-speed circuit that is shared among all computers on the LAN or backbone network. As discussed in Chapter 7, the computers on these networks must take turns when using the network, because no two computers can transmit at the same time. In this section, we discuss faster versions of two LAN technologies (fast Ethernet and fast token ring), as well as a technology developed specifically for MANs and backbone networks that operates in the same basic manner (FDDI).

Fast Ethernet

The concept behind fast Ethernet is simple: take an Ethernet LAN and make it run faster. Unfortunately, this is easier to say than do. Different vendors have proposed several different types of fast Ethernet. There are several fundamentally different approaches in the marketplace, each of which has been standardized. In general, the term *fast Ethernet* is used to refer to the various types of Ethernet that run at 100 Mbps. In this section, we also discuss two other types of "faster" Ethernet: gigabit Ethernet and Iso-ENET.

100Base-X Ethernet (IEEE 802.13)

100Base-X (sometimes called *100Base-T*) is virtually identical to 10Base-T Ethernet (IEEE 802.3). It provides a 100 Mbps data rate using the standard Ethernet bus topology, Ethernet data link layer packets, and Ethernet CSMA/CD media access protocol. Three versions of 100Base-X are in common use, and they differ only at the physical layer—they use different media. *100Base-TX* uses category 5 unshielded twisted-pair cable. *100Base-FX* uses fiber optic cable. *100Base-T4* uses four sets of category 3 unshielded twisted-pair cable; the signal is inverse multiplexed so that each of the four sets of cable is actually running at 25 Mbps, which, when combined, provide a 100 Mbps rate.

100Base-VG (IEEE 802.12)

100Base-VG (also called *100VG-AnyLAN*) is considered part of the fast Ethernet family, but in fact it really is not Ethernet. There are two major differences between 100Base-VG and 100Base-X. First, 100Base-VG can send and receive both Ethernet and token ring packets. Second, 100Base-VG does not use Ethernet's standard CSMA/CD media access control. Instead, 100Base-VG uses *demand priority access method (DPAM)*, which is similar to roll call polling (discussed in Chapter 5). The network hub polls each connected computer in turn to see if it has data to send. If it does, the computer transmits; if not, the hub moves to the next computer. DPAM also permits computers to issue high-priority requests to the hub without being polled so that these requests are processed more quickly. Like 100Base-T4, 100Base-VG uses four sets of category 3 twisted pair, each running at 25 Mbps (it can also use inverse multiplexing to combine four sets of category 4 or 5 twisted pair into one high-speed circuit).

In theory, 100Base-VG should be faster than 100Base-T when network traffic becomes heavy because controlled media access techniques such as DPAM perform better than contention-based approaches like CSMA/CD. In Chapter 7, we explained that the throughput of Ethernet drops to about 50 percent because of the collisions that occur when traffic is heavy. This suggests that 100Base-T has a maximum throughput of about 50 Mbps. This is true for larger packets; however, for small packets, the extremely fast transmission rate of 100Base-T minimizes the probability of a collision. Tests have shown that for small packet sizes (i.e., about 1K), 100Base-T has almost a 100 Mbps throughput; for larger packets (i.e., 4K or larger), throughput falls to about 50 Mbps. Tests have shown 100Base-VG's throughput to be close to 100 Mbps regardless of packet size.

Gigabit Ethernet (IEEE 802.3z)

Similar to 100Base-X, *1000Base-X* is a set of standards that provide 1 Gbps (i.e., 1000 Mbps). One problem with 1000Base-X is that using the standard Ethernet CSMA/CD media access protocol on a shared network may cause problems. Because of the high speed of transmission, collisions may occur but go undetected. Two computers at the opposite ends of a shared circuit could transmit at the same time, but if they have short messages, it is possible that each could finish transmitting before the other's signal reached them. Neither would realize there was a collision, although the stations in between would receive a jumbled signal and know a collision occurred. The result would be that both computers would time-out and attempt to retransmit (see Chapter 5), likely having another undetected collision.

For this reason, gigabit Ethernet may remain primarily a backbone technology for use only in point-to-point full-duplex communication links. Further complicating the issue is the fact that the PCs used as today's client computers simply cannot generate (or receive) data at 1 Gbps. The fastest PC today can generate data at a maximum speed of about 100 Mbps. Although these data rates will increase, it is hard to conceive of desktop applications that will require 1 Gbps. For the near future, gigabit Ethernet will likely remain in the backbone, not the LAN.

Four versions of 100Base-X are now in use, and they differ only at the physical layer by using different media. 1000Base-LX and 1000Base-SX both use fiber optic cable, running up to 440 meters and 260 meters respectively. 1000Base-T will run on four pairs of category 5 twisted pair cable, but only up to 100 meters. 1000Base-CX is a specialized form that will run up to 24 meters on one category 5 cable.

Iso-ENET (IEEE 802.9A)

Iso-ENET (isochronous Ethernet,) is standard 10Base-T Ethernet with an additional 6.144 Mbps circuit placed on top. The two circuits are carried in the same physical twisted-pair cable but are completely separate so that traffic in one circuit does not interfere with traffic in the other. This extra 6.144 Mbps circuit supports the transmission of voice and video using ISDN, which is discussed in the next chapter. Several vendors have developed desktop videoconferencing application software that uses iso-ENET, with several more multimedia products under development.

Management Focus: GMAC Growing into Fast Ethernet

Sometimes building a network is like buying new clothes for kids: you always try to buy one size bigger than they need so they can grow into them. GMAC has grown from managing $2.5 billion in loans in 1993 to $22 billion today, and this growth is expected to continue.

When GMAC moved into its new building, it scrapped its existing token ring and mainframe SNA network in favor of a fast Ethernet network (see Figure 8–9). Today, the 200 users use only about 4 percent of the network capacity, but this will change quickly.

GMAC is planning to install three network-intensive video applications. The first is the broadcast of CNN TV news over the network so its portfolio managers can have immediate access to breaking news. The second is the provision of training videos over the network from its internal Web server. The third is a document imaging system to store customer loan information, which will be housed on 25 Windows NT servers.

Source: CommunicationsWeek, March 3, 1997.

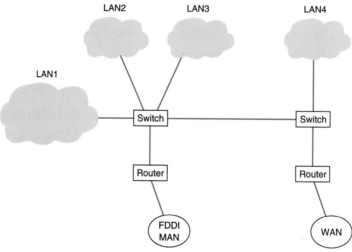

Figure 8–9 Fast Ethernet at GMAC.

Fast Token Ring

Fast token ring (also called high-speed token ring (HSTR)) is similar in concept to fast Ethernet. Fast token ring uses the standard token ring topology, protocols, and media access control, but runs at 100 Mbps, rather than 16 Mbps. Fast token ring will run on category 5 cable or fiber optic cable. IBM has also announced plans to develop gigabit token ring that will run at 1 Gbps.

Sales of token ring have declined in recent years as more and more networks have switched to Ethernet, which remains much cheaper. Although some network managers are excited about the prospects for fast token ring, most experts believe that it will do little to slow the decline in sales.

Fiber Distributed Data Interface (FDDI)

The *fiber distributed data interface (FDDI)* is a set of standards originally designed in the late 1980s for use in MANs (ANSI X3T9.5). FDDI has since made its way into backbone networks, and in some limited cases, into the LAN itself. FDDI was once seen as the logical replacement for token ring, but its future is probably limited to specialized applications as fast Ethernet and ATM (discussed in the next section) become more popular.

Topology

FDDI is a token-passing ring network (similar in many respects to token ring) that operates at 100 Mbps over a fiber optic cable. The FDDI standard assumes a maximum of 1000 stations (nodes) and a 200-kilometer (120 miles) path that requires a repeater every 2 kilometers. FDDI uses two counter-rotating rings called the *primary ring* and the *secondary ring*. Data traffic normally travels on the primary ring. The secondary ring mainly serves as a backup circuit.

All computers on an FDDI network are connected to the primary ring. Some computers are also connected to the secondary ring. Thus, there are two types of FDDI computers: the *dual-attachment station (DAS)* on both rings and the *single-attachment station* (SAS) on just the primary ring (see Figure 8–10).

If the cable in the FDDI ring is broken, the ring can still operate in a limited fashion. The DAS nearest to the break reroutes traffic from the primary ring onto the secondary ring. Since the secondary ring is running in the opposite direction, the data travels back around the ring. The DAS nearest the break on the opposite

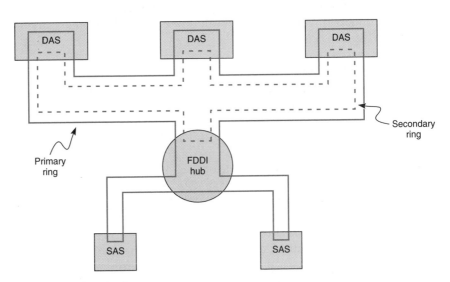

DAS: Dual-attachment station
SAS: Single-attachment station

Figure 8–10 Optical cable topology for an FDDI LAN. The FDDI has two rings. Data traffic normally travels on the primary ring.

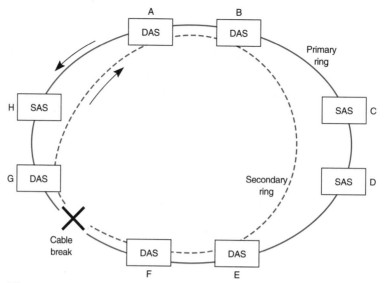

Figure 8–11 Managing a broken circuit.

side of the break receives the data on the secondary ring and reroutes it back onto the primary ring. In Figure 8–11, for example, there is a break in the ring between computers F and G. Since both are DAS, G can reroute traffic from H on the primary ring back to A on the secondary ring. The data will travel along the secondary ring from A to B to E to F. F will then reroute the traffic back to E on the primary ring, from where it will flow back on the primary ring to G (F to E to D to C to B to A to H to G).

Media Access Control

The FDDI media access control scheme uses a variation of the IEEE 802.5 token-passing standard used for token ring networks. IEEE 802.5 token ring networks use two types of tokens—free tokens and busy tokens. When a computer receives a free token, it transmits its message and marks the token as busy. No other computer can transmit a message until the message acknowledgment sent by the recipient is received by the message sender, which then changes the busy token to a free token. Under this approach, only one message can be attached to the token at one time.

When a computer on an FDDI network receives the token with a message attached, it first removes the token from the ring, and then transmits all messages that were attached to it. The computer then transmits whatever messages it wants before transmitting the token. As long as the computer holds onto the token, no other computer can transmit, so collisions are avoided. This way, many messages (or data packets) can be on the network at one time, which significantly increases the amount of data that FDDI can transmit compared to the one-packet-at-a-time approach of IEEE 802.5 token ring.

Types of FDDI

There are two types of FDDI in addition to the basic FDDI described above. *FDDI on Copper (FDDI-C)*, sometimes called *copper distributed data interface (CDDI)*, uses the same topology and media access protocol as FDDI, but uses two pairs of either shielded or unshielded category 5 twisted-pair cable instead of fiber optic cable. It is identical to FDDI in every other way.

FDDI-II permits the transmission of voice and video over the same cable as the normal FDDI token-passing data. FDDI-II functions like FDDI, but adds the ability to divide the 100 Mbps circuit between the standard FDDI token passing data circuit and one or more circuits for voice and/or video.

FDDI-II uses time division multiplexing to break up the available 100 Mbps into 17 separate channels, one channel of 768 Kbps and 16 *wide band channels* of 6.144 Mbps each. The 768 Kbps channel is permanently dedicated to the token-passing data circuit. The 16 wide-band channels can be allocated either to the token-passing data circuit or to separate circuits used for the transmission of voice and/or video (or alternately, more data).

✳✳ SWITCHED MEDIA TECHNOLOGIES

Over the past few years, there has been a major change in the way we think about LANs and backbone networks. LANs have traditionally used shared multipoint circuits in which all computers take turns sharing the same circuit. In contrast, WANs have traditionally used point-to-point circuits, where each computer has a dedicated direct connection to one or more computers in the same network. As the shared circuits in LANs and BNs have become overloaded with message traffic, networks are starting to use switched point-to-point circuits rather than shared multipoint circuits. Although many of these technologies were originally designed for use in the backbone, many are now moving into the LAN. In fact, many experts are predicting the "death" of the traditional shared media LANs as the use of switched LANs becomes more common. In this section, we examine four switched technologies: switched Ethernet, switched token ring, ATM, and fibre channel.

Switched Ethernet

The concept behind *switched Ethernet*—and all switched media technologies—is simple: replace the hub with a switch (see Figure 8–12). In traditional Ethernet, all devices share the same multipoint circuit, and must take turns. The hub is a simple physical connection between the different computers, much like a splice. All computers share one 10 Mbps circuit.

With switched Ethernet, a switch replaces the hub. Each computer now has its own dedicated point-to-point circuit to the switch. The switch manages the connections between the computers so that many computers can be transmitting simul-

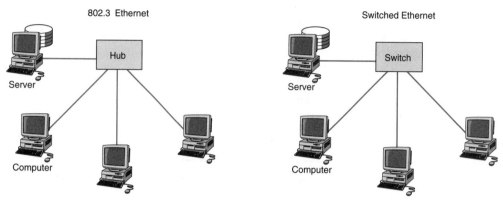

Figure 8–12 802.3 Ethernet versus switched Ethernet.

taneously. If they are transmitting to different computers, the switch connects them immediately. If some are trying to transmit to the same computers, the switch stores and forwards the data later to avoid collisions. Each computer has its own 10 Mbps connection instead of sharing one 10 Mbps with several other computers.

Switched Ethernet dramatically improves network performance because each computer has its own circuit. However, since much of the network traffic is to and from the server, the circuit to the server is often the network bottleneck. Each computer is transmitting at 10 Mbps, but if the circuit to the server is also 10 Mbps, there is often a traffic jam on the server's circuit.

One obvious solution is to increase the number of connections from the server to the switch so that traffic can reach the server on several circuits. Of course, adding more connections increases server overhead and can slow it down. Most experts recommend no more than three or four connections. Other solutions include full-duplex Ethernet and 10/100 switched Ethernet.

Full-Duplex Ethernet

Full-duplex Ethernet uses the same 10Base-T cables as regular Ethernet or switched Ethernet, but as the name suggests, it provides a full-duplex connection. Full-duplex Ethernet assigns one cable for incoming messages and the other for outgoing messages, enabling the same computer to be transmitting and receiving at the same time. Full-duplex Ethernet nominally doubles the speed of the connection to 20 Mbps; however, this is only true if the same computer is both sending and receiving simultaneously, because it still provides only 10 Mbps in each direction. The need for simultaneous sending and receiving is usually common only in network servers, so full-duplex Ethernet primarily is used for connections from the switch to the server. In high-traffic switched networks, two or three full-duplex Ethernet connections may be used from the switch to the server (see Figure 8–13). Even so, full-duplex Ethernet only adds value if the server needs to send and receive data simultaneously, an event that occurs less often than its vendors might admit.

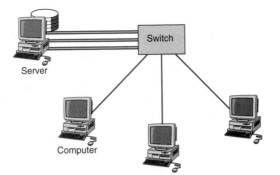

Server

Computer

Figure 8–13 Full-duplex
Ethernet.

10/100 Switched Ethernet

Sometimes a LAN needs more capacity to the server than full-duplex Ethernet can
provide, so the next step up is *10/100 switched Ethernet*, which combines 10Base-T
Ethernet and 100Base-T Ethernet. Each switch in the network has ports that can
support either 10Base-T or 100Base-T. Some switches provide ports that support
both; they sense the incoming signal and adjust accordingly.

10/100 switched Ethernet is often used to provide traditional 10 Mbps Ethernet connections to client computers utilizing traditional 10Base-T, with 100Base-T
used to connect to the server or to other switches. This version of switched Ethernet
will become very popular in the future, because it provides several advantages over
other types of Ethernet LANs and BNs. Compared to 10 Mbps switched Ethernet,
10/100 switched Ethernet greatly reduces congestion at the network server, thereby
providing better network performance. It is cheaper to install than 100Base-T because it does not require new cable to the client computers; you simply replace the
existing hub with a 10/100 switch. Depending on the application and the number
of computers in the network, 10/100 may be as fast as fast Ethernet.

Switched Token Ring

Switched token ring is similar to switched Ethernet. A token ring switch replaces the
token ring hub, providing a series of point-to-point connections from the computers
to the switch instead of the traditional shared multipoint circuit. The network has
a star topology instead of a ring. The token is no longer needed because all computers can transmit and receive at will. It is called "token ring" because it uses the
802.5 token ring packet format and is fully compatible with 802.5 hardware.

Dedicated token ring (DTR) (or *full-duplex token ring*) is a version of switched
token ring that is similar to full-duplex Ethernet. Each computer has a full-duplex
connection to the switch, providing a 32 Mbps data rate (16 Mbps in each direction). Sometimes new software or a new chip for each token ring network interface
card is needed. DTR can operate seamlessly with 802.5 token rings, so that both
DTR and 802.5 token ring networks can be connected to the same DTR switch.

Switched FDDI

Switched FDDI is similar to switched Ethernet. A FDDI switch replaces the FDDI hub, providing a series of point-to-point connections from the computers to the switch instead of the traditional shared multipoint circuit. The network has a star topology instead of a ring. The token is no longer needed because all computers can transmit and receive at will. It is called "switched FDDI" because it uses the same packet format and is fully compatible with other FDDI hardware.

Asynchronous Transfer Mode (ATM)

Asynchronous Transfer Mode (ATM) is a technology originally designed for use in wide area networks that is now often used in backbone networks. ATM is sometimes called cell relay.

ATM backbone switches typically provide point-to-point full duplex circuits at 155 Mbps (for a total of 310 Mbps). Although ATM was originally designed to run on fiber optic cable, some versions can run on category 5 twisted pair cables (although the cables cannot be run as far as they would for 100Base-T).

ATM is a switched network, but differs from switched Ethernet and switched token ring in four important ways. First, ATM uses fixed-length packets (or "cells") of 53 bytes (a 5-byte header containing addressing and quality of service information, and 48 bytes of user data). The small fixed-length packets make switching much faster because it is so simple it can be done in hardware—and hardware switching is substantially faster than using software.

Management Focus: Switched Ethernet and the Law

For many attorneys and judges, reading a brief with a legal citation to a previous case means finding and dragging out a 20-pound law book and looking it up. But for the intellectual property lawyers at Fish & Richardson, checking such a reference means clicking on a hyperlink. While electronic documents are used extensively internally, the firm must convert them to paper for use in court, because legal guidelines do not yet permit the submission of electronic documents.

Two years ago, the Fish & Richardson network was entirely token ring. However, with the move to electronic materials, they needed a much faster network capable of transmitting network-intensive graphical images. The move to switched Ethernet has proved very successful. The backbone is a 100Base-T Ethernet network that connects several servers to the two primary 100 Mbps Ethernet switches (see Figure 8–14). These two switches, in turn, each connect at 100 Mbps to a set of three switches that provide switched 10Base-T to users. A few of the more than 200 users who have a need for greater network performance are connected directly to the 100 Mbps switches using switched 100Base-T.

Source: PC Week, June 16, 1997.

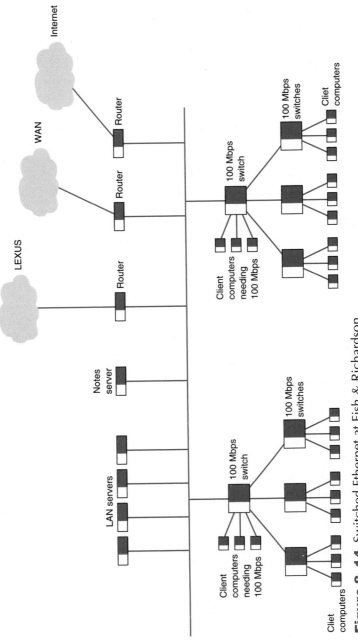

Figure 8–14 Switched Ethernet at Fish & Richardson.

Second, ATM provides no error correction on the user data (error checking is provided on the 5-byte header and if an unrecoverable error is detected, the packet is discarded). All other types of data link layer protocols we have discussed in this book perform error checking at each computer in the network. Any errors in transmission are corrected immediately, so that the network layer and application software can assume error-free transmission. However, this error control is one of the most time-consuming processes at the data link layer. By not checking for errors, ATM devices can run significantly faster. However, it is up to the network layer or application layer software at the source and destination to perform error correction and to control for lost messages.

Third, ATM uses a very different type of addressing from traditional data link layer protocols such as Ethernet or token ring. Ethernet and token ring assign a permanent address to each computer so that all messages sent to the same computer use the same address. ATM does not use permanent addresses. Instead, ATM defines a *virtual circuit* between each sender and receiver, and all packets use the virtual circuit identifier as the address. Each virtual circuit identifier has two parts, a path number and a circuit number within that path. Each ATM switch contains a circuit table that lists all virtual circuits known to that switch (analogous to a routing table in TCP/IP). Because there are potentially thousands of virtual circuits and because each switch knows only those virtual circuits in its circuit table, a given virtual circuit identifier is used only between one switch and the next.

When an ATM packet arrives at a switch, the switch looks up the packet's virtual circuit identifier in its circuit table to determine where to send it and what virtual circuit identifier should be used when the packet is transmitted on the outgoing circuit. Figure 8–15, for example, shows two switches each with four ports (or physical circuits). When an incoming packet arrives, the switch looks up its virtual circuit identifier in the circuit table, switches the packet to the outgoing

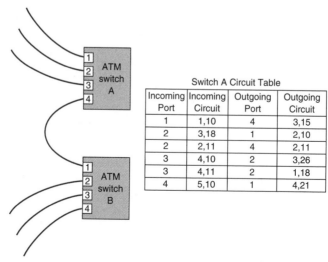

Switch A Circuit Table

Incoming Port	Incoming Circuit	Outgoing Port	Outgoing Circuit
1	1,10	4	3,15
2	3,18	1	2,10
2	2,11	4	2,11
3	4,10	2	3,26
3	4,11	2	1,18
4	5,10	1	4,21

Figure 8–15 Addressing and forwarding with ATM virtual circuits.

port, and changes the virtual circuit identifier it had when it arrived to a new virtual circuit identifier used by the switch at its destination. For example, a packet arriving at Switch A via port 1 with a virtual circuit identifier of 1,10 would be transmitted out on port 4 to Switch B and would be given a new virtual circuit identifier of 3,15.

ATM is connection-oriented, so all packets travel in order through the virtual circuit. A virtual circuit can be either a *permanent virtual circuit (PVC)* (i.e., defined when the network is established or modified) or a *switched virtual circuit (SVC)* (i.e., defined temporarily for one transmission and deleted when the transmission is completed). ATM provides a separate control circuit that is used for non-data communication between devices, such as the setup and takedown of an SVC.

The final major difference between ATM and other switched backbone technologies such as switched Ethernet is that ATM prioritizes transmissions based on quality of service (QoS). You may recall that Chapter 6 briefly discussed QoS routing. With QoS routing or QoS switching, different *classes of service* are defined, each with different priorities. Each virtual circuit is assigned a specific class of service when it is first established. ATM defines five service classes (see the technology focus box) that enable the network to prioritize transmissions. For example, circuits containing voice transmissions receive higher priority than circuits containing e-mail transmissions, because delays in voice transmissions can seriously affect transmission quality, while delays in e-mail transmission are less important. If an ATM switch becomes overloaded and it receives traffic on a low-priority circuit, it may simply refuse the request until it has sufficient capacity.

ATM and Traditional LANs

ATM uses a very different type of protocol than traditional LANs. It has a small 53-byte fixed-length packet and is connection-oriented (meaning that devices establish a virtual circuit before transmitting). Ethernet and token ring use larger variable-length packets and are typically connectionless. In order to use ATM in a backbone network that connects traditional Ethernet or token ring LANs, some translation must be done to enable the LAN packets to flow over the ATM backbone. There are two approaches to this, LANE and MPOA.

With *LAN encapsulation* (LANE), the data link layer packets from the LAN are left intact; they are broken into 48-byte blocks and surrounded by ATM packets. This process is called *encapsulation* and is done by an *edge switch*. The packets flow through the ATM network and are reassembled at an edge switch at the other end before being transmitted into the destination LAN (see Figure 8–16). The use of ATM is transparent to users because LANE leaves the original data link layer packets intact and uses the packet's data link layer address to forward the message through the ATM network.

Translating from Ethernet or token ring into ATM (and vice-versa) is not simple. First, the Ethernet (or token ring) address must be translated into an ATM virtual circuit identifier for the circuit that leads from the edge switch to the edge switch nearest the destination. This is done through a process similar to that of using a broadcast message on a subnet to locate a data link layer address (see Chapter 6). ATM is a switched point-to-point network, so it lacks a simple built-in

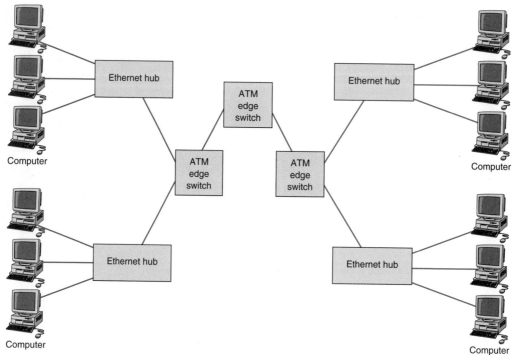

Figure 8–16 ATM encapsulation.

ability to issue broadcast messages. LANE enables the transmission of broadcast messages, but to date, it has been problematic.

Once the virtual circuit address for the destination data link layer address has been found, it can be used to transmit the packet through the ATM backbone. However, if no virtual circuit is currently defined from the edge switch to the destination edge switch, then the edge switch must establish a new virtual circuit.

Once the virtual circuit is ready, the LAN packet is broken into the series of ATM cells, and is transmitted over the ATM backbone using the ATM virtual circuit identifier. The destination edge switch then reassembles the ATM cells into the LAN packet and forwards it to the appropriate device.

This process is not without cost. The resolution of the Ethernet (or token ring) address into an ATM virtual circuit identifier, the setup of the virtual circuit, the packetization, and reassembly of the LAN packets to and from ATM cells can impose quite a delay. Recent tests of ATM edge switches suggest that even though they are capable of transmitting at 155 Mbps, the encapsulation delays can reduce performance by 40 to 50 percent. Most edge switches provided less than 100 Mbps into the ATM backbone.

Multiprotocol over ATM (MPOA) is an extension to LANE that uses the network layer address (i.e., IP or IPX address) in addition to the data link layer address. If the packet destination is in the same subnet, MPOA will use data link layer ad

Technology Focus: *ATM Classes of Service*

ATM provides five classes of service. Each receives different priorities in traveling though the network:

* **Constant Bit Rate (CBR)** means that the circuit must provide a constant, pre-defined data rate at all times, much like having a point-to-point physical circuit between the devices. Whenever a CBR circuit is established, ATM guarantees that the switch can provide the circuit; the sum of all CBR circuits at one switch cannot exceed its capacity, even if they are not all active simultaneously. In some ways, CBR is like time-division multiplexing, discussed in Chapter 3. CBR was originally designed to support voice transmissions.

* **Variable Bit Rate–Real Time (VBR-RT)** means that the data transmission rate in the circuit will vary, but that all cells received must be switched immediately upon arrival because the devices (or people) on the opposite ends of the circuit are waiting for the transmission and expect to receive it in a timely fashion. Each VBR-RT circuit is as-

signed a standard transmission rate but can exceed it. If the cells in a VBR-RT circuit arrive too fast to transmit, they are lost. In some ways, CBR is like statistical time-division multiplexing, discussed in Chapter 3. Most voice traffic today uses VBR-RT rather CBR.

* **Variable Bit Rate–Non-Real Time (VBR-NRT)** means that the data transmission rate in the circuit will vary and that the application is tolerant of delays.

* **Available Bit Rate (ABR)** means that the circuit can tolerate wide variation in transmission speeds and many delays. AVR circuits have lower priority than VBR-NRT circuits. They receive the lowest amount of guaranteed capacity but can use whatever capacity is available (i.e., not in use by CBR, VBR-RT, and VBR-NRT circuits).

* **Unspecified Bit Rate (UBR)** means that the circuit has no guaranteed data rate, but are transported when capacity is available. When the network is busy, UBR packets are the first to be discarded. UBR is a bit like flying standby on an airline.

---

dresses in the same manner as LANE. If the packet is addressed to a different subnet, MPOA will use the network layer address to forward the packet. In this case, the ATM backbone is operating somewhat similar to a network of brouters. In an ATM MPOA network, a series of *route servers* (also called MPOA servers or MPS) are provided that perform somewhat the same function as DNS servers in TCP/IP networks (see Chapter 6): route servers translate network layer addresses (e.g., IP addresses) into ATM virtual circuit identifiers.

ATM to the Desktop

In early 1995, the ATM Forum, the standards body for ATM, accepted a proposal from a consortium of vendors led by IBM for a ''low-speed'' version of ATM to compete with traditional Ethernet and token ring LANs. *ATM-25* is designed for use in LANs and provides point-to-point full-duplex circuits at 25.6 Mbps in each direction (51.2 Mbps total) from computers to the switch. ATM-25 is an adaptation

Carnival Cruise Lines is one of the leading cruise ship operators in the world. When its Miami headquarters network, a series of 10Base-T LANs connected via a FDDI backbone, began to falter under rapidly growing network traffic, Carnival looked for a radically new approach to networking.

Carnival needed to support a Unisys

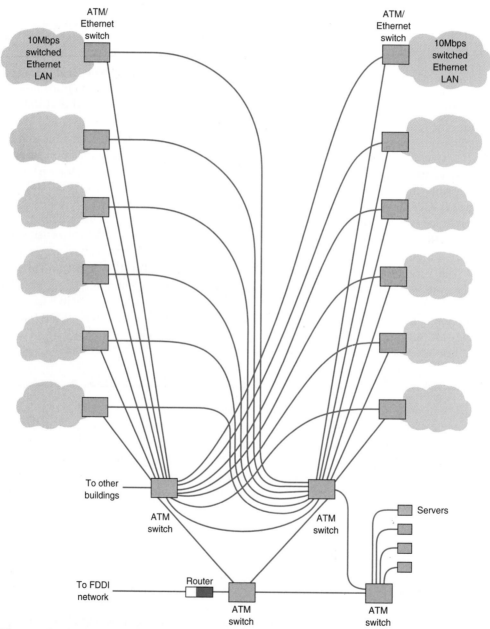

Figure 8–17 ATM at Carnival Cruise Lines headquarters.

mainframe and a series of Unisys minicomputers, in addition to more than 2500 desktop PCs. It also wanted to have the ability to move voice and video traffic over the network. Carnival was unique in that it wanted to use the same networking technology on its newer cruise ships.

The solution was an ATM/Ethernet combination (see Figure 8–17). There are 12 main LANs, two on each floor, that use switched 10Base-T. The switches in these LANs are connected using ATM (155 Mbps full duplex) to two main ATM backbone switches in the data center; two switches are used to provide redundancy in case one switch fails. These ATM switches, in turn, are connected to other ATM switches that provide access to the servers, to other buildings on the ATM backbone, and to the remaining part of the old FDDI backbone.

Source: Net Age, May 1997.

---

of token ring that runs over category 3 cable and will even use token ring hardware with a chip upgrade.

Another version of ATM designed for the desktop is *ATM-51*, which provides point-to-point full duplex circuits at 51.84 Mbps (103.68 Mbps total) from computers to the switch. Although ATM-51 was developed before ATM-25, it has received far less vendor support. Today, ATM-25 is far more common than ATM-51.

Both of these ATMs appear to be good choices for desktop connections when ATM backbone networks are used. The packet sizes are the same; the protocols are the same; and no translation or encapsulation is required so the switches are simpler and cheaper than edge switches needed for LAN to ATM translation. They also offer the promise of almost seamless connection to ATM MANs and WANs. However, industry has been very slow to accept ATM-25 or ATM-51. Most organizations that need high-speed LAN circuits have instead moved to fast Ethernet, which is both cheaper and faster than ATM-25. Most experts see ATM-25 as no more than a niche application that will be used by only a few organizations that have very specialized network needs.

Fibre Channel

Fibre channel is relatively new networking technology, although it has been used inside computers and disk storage devices for several years (ANSI X3T11). Fibre channel is designed to provide the best elements of a high-speed hardware channel (such as a computer's internal bus) with a multi-protocol network. Fibre channel consists of a set of full-duplex point-to-point switched circuits between devices. Networks can be designed using a traditional switch topology or a ring topology (called an arbitrated loop topology in fibre channel terminology); see Figure 8–18.

As the name implies, fibre channel was originally designed to provide high-speed transmission over fiber optic cable. The maximum data rate today is 1.062 Gbps over fiber optic cable up to 10 kilometers, with data rates of 2.13 Gbps and 4.26 Gbps currently under development. Slower speed versions are also available: 133 Mbps, 266 Mbps, and 533 Mbps. Several versions have also been defined for use on category 5 twisted-pair cable: 1.062 Gbps up to 24 meters or 266 Mbps up to 47 meters.

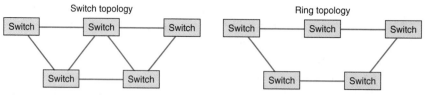

Figure 8–18 Fibre channel topologies.

Fibre channel is a switched technology like ATM, and like ATM, all circuits are full duplex and provide several classes of service (see the technology focus box). Fibre channel also has much in common with Ethernet. Fibre channel uses variable length data link layer packets with a maximum of 2048 bytes of user data in each, and performs routine error control using CRC-32. Like Ethernet, all fibre channel network interface cards are assigned a permanent worldwide data link layer address (which is 8 bytes in length, compared to Ethernet's 6 bytes). Data link layer address resolution is done using essentially the same ARP broadcast approach used by TCP/IP (see Chapter 6).

✳✳ IMPROVING BACKBONE PERFORMANCE

Improving the performance of backbone networks is similar to improving LAN performance. First, find the bottleneck, and then solve it (or more accurately, move the bottleneck somewhere else). You can improve the performance of the network by improving the computers and other devices in the network, by upgrading the

---

Technology Focus: *Fibre Channel Classes of Service*

Fibre channel provides four classes of service.

✳ **Class 1** (also called Circuit Switched Service) is similar to ATM's CBR service. With class 1 service, a virtual circuit is established that is guaranteed to provide the requested data transmission rate. All packets arrive in the order in which they were transmitted.

✳ **Class 2** (also called Connectionless Service) is similar to ATM's VBR-NRT service. All packets are guaranteed to be transmitted error-free to the destination, although they

may suffer traffic delays and may arrive out of order.

✳ **Class 3** (also called Unacknowledged Connectionless Service) is similar to ATM's ABR service. Packets are transmitted when possible, but error-free delivery is not guaranteed; no acknowledgments are sent. This is commonly used for broadcast messages.

✳ **Intermix service** is an extension of class 1 service in which class 1 traffic is guaranteed its requested data transmission rate, but class 2 and 3 traffic is permitted to use some of the capacity when it would otherwise go unused.

Performance Checklist

Increase Computer and Device Performance

* Change to a more appropriate routing protocol (either static or dynamic)
* Buy devices and software from one vendor
* Reduce translation between different protocols
* Increase the devices' memory

Increase Circuit Capacity

* Upgrade to a faster circuit
* Add circuits

Reduce Network Demand

* Change user behavior
* Reduce broadcast messages

Figure 8–19 Improving backbone performance.

circuits between computers, and by changing the demand placed on the network. See Figure 8–19.

Improving Computer and Device Performance

The primary functions of computers and devices in backbone networks are routing and protocol translations. If the devices and computers are the bottleneck, routing can be improved with faster devices or a faster routing protocol. Static routing is accomplished faster than dynamic routing, but it obviously can impair circuit performance in high traffic situations. Dynamic routing is usually used in WANs and MANs because there are many possible routes through the network. Backbone networks often have only a few routes through the network. In this case, dynamic routing may not be too helpful, because it will delay processing and increase the network traffic due to the status reports sent through the network. Static routing will simplify processing and improve performance.

Many of the newer backbone technologies (ATM, gigabit Ethernet) have standards that are not fully developed. Routing packets between switches from different vendors sometimes decrease network performance because of translations that must be performed. In this case, performance can be improved by using one vendor's equipment.

FDDI and ATM require the translation or encapsulation of Ethernet and token ring packets before they can flow through the backbone. This slows processing at the devices connecting the backbone network to the attached LANs. One obvious solution is to use the same protocols in the backbone and the LANs. If you have Ethernet LANs, fast Ethernet backbones can reduce processing at the connecting devices. If you have ATM backbones, ATM to the desktop will reduce device processing.

Translating protocols typically requires more processing than encapsulation, so encapsulation can improve performance if the backbone devices are the bottleneck. With translation, the LAN data link layer packet is removed and a new backbone data link layer packet is added in its place (e.g., the Ethernet packet is removed and an FDDI packet added). This process is reversed at the end of the backbone network. With encapsulation, the existing LAN data link layer packet is left intact, and a new backbone data link layer packet is wrapped around it. The backbone data link layer is stripped off at the destination.

Most backbone devices are store-and-forward devices. One simple way to improve performance is to ensure that they have sufficient memory. If they don't, the devices will lose packets, requiring them to be retransmitted.

Improving Circuit Capacity

If network circuits are the bottlenecks, there are several options. One is to increase overall circuit capacity; for example, by going from 10 Mbps Ethernet to fast Ethernet or gigabit Ethernet. Another option is to add additional circuits alongside heavily used ones. Circuit capacity can also be improved by replacing a shared circuit backbone with a switched circuit backbone; for example, by replacing Ethernet with switched Ethernet.

In many cases, the bottleneck on the circuit is only in one place—the circuit to the server. A switched network that provides the usual 10 Mbps to the client computers but a faster circuit to the server (e.g., full duplex at 20 Mbps or fast Ethernet at 100 Mbps) can improve performance at very little cost. All one needs to do is replace the Ethernet hub with a switch and change one network interface card in the server.

Reducing Network Demand

One way to reduce network demand is to restrict applications that use a lot of network capacity, such as desktop videoconferencing, medical imaging, or multimedia. In practice, it is often difficult to restrict users. Nonetheless, finding one application that places a large demand on the network and moving it can have a significant effect.

Much network demand is caused by broadcast messages, such as those used to find data link layer addresses (see Chapter 6). Some application software packages and network operating system modules written for use on LANs also use broadcast messages to send status information to all computers on the LAN. For example, broadcast messages inform users when printers are out of paper, or when the network manager is about to shut down the server. When used in a LAN, such messages place little extra demand on the network because every computer on the LAN gets every message.

This is not the case for switched LANs or LANs connected to backbone networks because messages do not normally flow to all computers. Broadcast messages can consume a fair amount of network capacity. In many cases, broadcast messages have little value outside their individual LAN. Therefore, some switches, bridges, and routers can be set to filter broadcast messages so that they do not go to other networks. This reduces network traffic and improves performance.

✳✳ SELECTING A BACKBONE NETWORK

Selecting a backbone network for your organization is not easy. New backbone network products are being introduced monthly, and at least one entirely new technology is introduced each year. Most new products and technologies are not standardized, which further complicates matters. There are five important factors to consider in selecting a backbone network (see Figure 8–20).

Throughput is the amount of user data the network can transmit from one device to another. In this chapter, we have discussed two fundamentally different approaches to backbone networks: shared multipoint circuits (fast Ethernet, fast token ring, FDDI), and switched networks (switched Ethernet, switched token ring, ATM, and fibre channel).

Among the multipoint circuit backbone networks, one would expect the controlled media access networks (e.g., 100Base-VG and FDDI) to outperform contention-based ones (e.g., 100Base-T) when network traffic was heavy, and the reverse to be true when network traffic was light (see Chapter 7). However, tests of specific 100 Mbps backbone network products have not found this to be completely true. Tests show all three approaches (100Base-VG, 100Base-T, and FDDI) produce almost the same throughput under light network traffic. Under heavy traffic conditions, there were still no differences for small-sized packets (1 Kbyte or less), but for larger sized packets (4 Kbytes and above), the throughput of 100Base-T was significantly below that of 100Base-VG and FDDI. Therefore, if your network uses small packet sizes, there is no clear winner. If your network uses larger-sized packets, 100Base-T will not perform as well under heavy network traffic conditions.

There have been fewer tests of the newer switched networks. All switched networks maintain dedicated point-to-point circuits between switches and computers, so the medium access methodology is irrelevant to throughput. The key determinant of throughput is simply the data rate possible in the point-to-point circuits (e.g., 10 Mbps for switched Ethernet versus 25 Mbps for desktop ATM, or 1000 Mbps for gigabit Ethernet versus 155 Mbps for ATM). The use of full duplex has the potential to improve throughput even more, because data can travel in both directions simultaneously. However, full duplex is only useful in situations where the same device is simultaneously sending and receiving; this is more likely to be a server or a heavily used backbone circuit than client computers.

Comparing the throughput of high-speed multipoint backbone technologies (e.g., fast Ethernet) against lower-speed switched networks is difficult. With switched networks, each computer (or device to a connected LAN) has a guaranteed data

Backbone Selection Checklist

✳ Throughput

✳ Cost

✳ Type of application

✳ Ease of network management

✳ Compatibility with current and future technologies

Figure 8–20 Backbone selection checklist.

transmission rate of 10, 16, 25 or 100 Mbps. With multipoint networks, the total capacity (100 Mbps) is shared among all the computers (or LANs) on the network. If there are only a few computers (or LANs) on the backbone, the multipoint networks should perform as well as the switched networks. However, if there are many connected computers (or LANs), the available capacity must be shared, resulting in less than the 100 Mbps available to any one computer.

In theory, the entire switched connection capacity is available in the switched network, but this is not always the case. If every computer in the switched network has a 100 Mbps connection and several attempt to transmit to the same computer (e.g., a server or highly used LAN), there will still be a need to share the connection(s) to it. Switched networks should provide better throughput than equivalent-speed shared networks, but will do so only if the traffic on highly used circuits is well managed.

Network *cost* is always a critical issue. Costs change rapidly in the marketplace, based on competition and demand. The management focus box provides a comparison of the relative costs of different shared and switched technologies. By the time you read it, the prices will have changed, but the relative costs should be somewhat the same.

The *type of application* may also influence the choice of backbone networks. In general, all backbone networks are equally appropriate for most data applications. Suitability for voice and video is a different matter. ATM's small fixed-length packet and built-in quality of service (QoS) capability makes it more suitable for voice and video transmission; small fixed-length packets make routing and packetizing easier and minimize the effects of lost packets, while QoS enables the network to give higher priority to time-sensitive voice and video transmissions. This advantage may change, however, once QoS routing is implemented in TCP/IP. Several vendors have also announced plans to provide QoS support in gigabit Ethernet products as well, although no standards currently exist. Most experts expect that the QoS routing in TCP/IP and gigabit Ethernet will prove as good as ATM's QoS, thus reducing one of the major advantages that ATM has enjoyed.

Management Focus: *The Relative Costs of Commonly Used Technologies*

The costs of network technologies change rapidly, so the numbers in the following table should be used with caution; all costs are approximate. However, the table should give you some sense of the relative costs of different technologies. All costs are the approximate cost of one port or circuit on a hub or switch (network interface cards tend to be a bit cheaper).

Technology	Cost
Fast Ethernet	$150
Switched Ethernet	200
ATM-25 Mbps	300
Switched Fast Ethernet	500
FDDI	700
Fibre Channel-266 Mbps	800
Gigabit Ethernet	1000
Switched FDDI	1500
ATM-155 Mbps	1500
Fibre Channel-1062 Mbps	2500

The *management* of backbone networks can be extremely costly and challenging, and therefore, the quality of the network management tools available in each type of network is very important (network management is discussed in more detail in Chapter 11). In general, newer technologies such as switched Ethernet and ATM are harder to manage than older, more established ones such as Ethernet or FDDI. Vendors tend to develop technologies first, and provide management support for them later. Newer technologies are also developed before they become standardized, making it more difficult to manage a multivendor network. For example, there are no formal standardized management protocols for backbone ATM switches.

Compatibility with current and future technologies is also important in the management of networks. Most network managers strive to have similar technologies throughout their networks to reduce management costs. Backbone networks link LANs and WANs. ATM is a dominant technology in the WAN, and versions of ATM are available to the desktop (ATM-25). One group of industry experts therefore predicts that ATM will become common in the backbone because it enables a complete end-to-end solution (LAN to BN to WAN). However, the response to ATM-25 has been rather poor; the dominant LAN technology is Ethernet. Therefore, another group of industry experts predicts that fast Ethernet and gigabit Ethernet will dominate the backbone.

The network managers in the corporate world are equally divided. A 1997 survey of Fortune 1000 firms found that about half plan to install ATM in their backbone, while the other half plan to install some form of Ethernet. See Figure 8–21.

Although it is difficult to predict the future, we believe that a major revolution in LANs and BNs has begun. By the turn of the century, very few low-speed shared multipoint circuit LANs such as 16 Mbps token ring or 10 Mbps Ethernet will exist. We believe that most LANs will instead use fast Ethernet or switched Ethernet. Likewise, we believe that most backbone networks will use some form of Ethernet, most likely fast Ethernet or gigabit Ethernet—however, we should note that only half of the industry experts agree with us; the other half favors ATM.

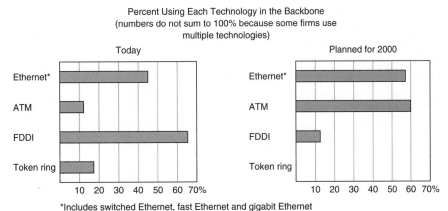

Figure 8–21 Survey of Fortune 1000 network managers. *Source:* "Ethernet Ends Network Nightmare," *PC Week*, March 12, 1997.

Summary

Network Components   There are two basic components to a backbone network: the network cable and the hardware devices that connect other networks to the backbone. The cable is essentially the same as that used in LANs, except that it is usually higher quality to provide higher data rates. The hardware devices include hubs, bridges, switches, routers, brouters, and gateways. Hubs are very simple devices that pass all traffic in both directions between the LAN sections they link. Bridges connect two LAN segments that use the same data link and network protocol, and only forward those messages that need to go to other network segments. Switches are similar to bridges but connect more than two LAN segments. Routers connect two or more LANs that use the same or different data link protocols but employ the same network protocol. Brouters are devices that combine the functions of both bridges and routers; they bridge same data link layer LANs and route different data link layer LANs. Gateways connect two or more LANs that use the same or different data link and network protocols (usually different). However, the terminology used in the marketplace may differ substantially from this discussion because different vendors use different names in order to gain market advantage. Multiprotocol bridges, multiprotocol routers, and layer-3 switches will increase in importance.

Fast Ethernet   The concept behind fast Ethernet is simple: take an Ethernet LAN and make it run faster. 100Base-T is a set of three data link layer protocols (100Base-TX, 100Base-FX, 100Base-T4) that provide a 100 Mbps data rate using the standard Ethernet bus topology, Ethernet data link packets, and Ethernet CSMA/CD media access protocol; they differ only in the type of cabling they use. 100Base-VG supports both Ethernet and token ring packets, and uses demand priority access method instead of CSMA/CD. Gigabit Ethernet (1000Base-X) provides 1000 Mbps. Iso-ENET is standard 10Base-T Ethernet with an additional 6.144 Mbps circuit for voice and video transmission.

FDDI   FDDI is a token-passing ring network that operates at 100 Mbps over a fiber optic cable arranged in two rings. Unlike 802.3 token ring, FDDI permits any number of messages to be on the ring at one time. FDDI on copper (FDDI-C) is FDDI operating on twisted-pair cable instead of fiber optic cable. FDDI-II functions the same way as FDDI, but adds the ability to divide the 100 Mbps circuit between the standard FDDI token-passing data circuit and one or more circuit-switched circuits for voice and/or video. There is also a switched version of FDDI.

Switched Ethernet   Switched Ethernet simply replaces the network hub with a switch. In traditional Ethernet, all devices share the same multipoint circuit, and must take turns. With switched Ethernet, each computer has its own dedicated point-to-point circuit to the switch. The switch manages the connection between the computers so that collisions are avoided even when several are transmitting simultaneously. Each computer has its own 10 Mbps connection instead of sharing one 10 Mbps with several other computers. Full-duplex Ethernet provides a full-duplex connection between the computer and the switch. 10/100 switched Ethernet combines 10Base-T Ethernet and 100Base-T Ethernet. Each switch in the network has ports that can support either 10Base-T or 100Base-T.

Switched Token Ring   Switched token ring is similar to switched Ethernet. A token ring switch replaces the token ring hub, providing a series of point-to-point connections from the computers to the switch instead of the traditional shared multipoint circuit. Dedicated token ring (or full-duplex token ring) is similar to full-duplex Ethernet. Each computer has a full-duplex connection from it to the switch.

ATM   ATM (asynchronous transfer mode) is a packet-switched technology originally designed for use in wide area networks. ATM uses 53-byte fixed-length packets with no error control on full-duplex 155 Mbps point-to-point circuits. ATM enables QoS, and uses virtual circuits rather than permanently assigning addresses to devices. In order to use ATM in a backbone network that connects LANs, some conversion must be done on the LAN packets to enable them to flow over the ATM backbone. With LANE, an ATM edge switch encapsulates the Ethernet (or token ring) packet, leaving the existing data link layer packet intact, and transmits it based on data link layer addresses. MPOA is an alternative that can use network layer addresses for transmission. ATM-25 and ATM-51 are versions of ATM intended for use in the LAN, but neither is very popular.

Fibre Channel   Fibre channel uses a set of full duplex point-to-point switched circuits between devices running at 133 Mbps, 266 Mbps, and 533 Mbps, and 1.062 Gbps over fiber optic cable and category 5 twisted pair. Like ATM, fibre channel provides several classes of service. Like Ethernet, fibre channel uses variable-length data link layer packets, performs error control, and assigns network interface cards a permanent worldwide data link layer address.

Improving Backbone Performance   Network performance can be improved by upgrading the computers and other devices in the network, by using static rather than dynamic routing if there are few routes through the network, by reducing switch-to-switch traffic in networks without standard protocols, by using the same protocols in the backbone network as in the attached LANs, by encapsulating rather than translating between different protocols, and by increasing the memory in backbone devices. Performance can also be improved by adding additional circuits to increase capacity, by changing to controlled access rather than contention protocols, by going to a switched network, and by increasing the circuits on high-traffic circuits. In addition, performance can be enhanced by reducing demand or by restricting applications that use lots of network capacity, and by using switches that filter broadcast messages.

Selecting a Backbone   Selecting a backbone network for your organization is difficult because new products and completely new technologies are constantly being introduced. There are several factors to consider. Throughput is the amount of user data the network can transmit. In general, switched networks are faster than shared networks. There have been few throughput differences found among the high-speed multipoint technologies, although for heavy traffic networks with large packet sizes, FDDI and 100Base-VG outperformed 100Base-T. Among switched networks, the best determinant of throughput is the data transmission rate, although full duplex may help on heavily used circuits or circuits to servers. New technologies (e.g., switched networks) are often harder to manage, but switched networks often are more flexible. It appears that switched networks are the way of the future. The type of application may also influence the choice of network: ATM is well suited to voice and video, although new QoS capabilities in TCP/IP and gigabit Ethernet may reduce ATM's advantage.

Key Terms

address table	FDDI on copper (FDDI-C)	protocol filtering bridges
Asynchronous Transfer Mode (ATM)	fiber distributed data interface (FDDI)	routers
ATM-25	fiber distributed data interface-II (FDDI-II)	route servers
ATM-51	Fibre channel	shared media networks
backbone network	filtering	single-attachment station (SAS)
bridges	full-duplex Ethernet	store-and-forward switches
brouters	full-duplex token ring	switches
classes of service	gateways	switched Ethernet
copper distribution data interface (CDDI)	gigabit Ethernet	switched FDDI
cut-through switches	hubs	switched networks
dedicated token ring (DTR)	Iso-ENET	switched token ring
demand priority access method (DPAM)	LAN Emulation (LANE)	switched virtual circuit (SVC)
dual-attachment station (DAS)	layer-3 switches	virtual circuit
edge switch	multiprotocol over ATM (MPOA)	10/100 switched Ethernet
encapsulation	multiprotocol bridges	100Base-FX
enterprise network	multiprotocol routers	100Base-T
fast Ethernet	permanent virtual circuit (PVC)	100Base-VG
fast token ring		100Base-X
		1000Base-X

Questions

1. What is a hub?
2. How does a bridge differ from a switch?
3. What is different between a bridge, a router, and a gateway?
4. What is a brouter?

5. Under what circumstances would you want to replace a router with a brouter?
6. What happens when you replace a hub with a switch?
7. What is an enterprise network?

8. Explain the differences between a store-and-forward switch and a cut-through switch.

9. What is a multiprotocol bridge? multiprotocol router?

10. How does a layer-3 switch differ from a "normal" switch?

11. What are the three types of 100Base-T, and how are they different?

12. How does 100Base-VG differ from other types of Ethernet?

13. How can fast Ethernet such as 100Base-T and 100Base-VG provide 100 Mbps data rates using the same cable used for 10Base-T?

14. How can gigabit Ethernet use category 5 cables to provide 1000 Mbps?

15. What is Iso-ENET? Why would you want to use it?

16. How does FDDI differ from 803.5 token ring?

17. How does FDDI differ from 100Base-FX?

18. What is the difference between a DAS and an SAS?

19. What is FDDI-C? FDDI-II?

20. How does switched FDDI differ from shared FDDI?

21. What is switched Ethernet? What advantages does it provide?

22. Where would you want to use full-duplex Ethernet?

23. Is full-duplex token ring really token ring? Explain.

24. Some people argue that full-duplex Ethernet does not really provide 20 Mbps. Why?

25. What is 10/100 switched Ethernet? How would you use it to design a LAN or BN?

26. If you currently have an 803.3 Ethernet LAN, is fast Ethernet or switched Ethernet cheaper to install? Why?

27. Discuss four important characteristics of ATM.

28. How does ATM perform addressing?

29. How can ATM be used to link Ethernet LANs?

30. What is ATM-25? ATM-51?

31. What is encapsulation? How does it differ from translation?

32. How does fibre channel work?

33. How can you improve the performance of a backbone network?

34. What are broadcast messages?

35. What are five factors in selecting a backbone network?

36. Which has greatest throughput: 100Base-T, 100Base-VG, or FDDI?

37. Which has greater throughput: FDDI or switched Ethernet?

38. How does an FDDI LAN carry an Ethernet packet?

39. How does ATM LANE carry an Ethernet packet?

Exercises

A. Survey the backbone networks used in your organization. Are they Ethernet, ATM, or some other standard? Why?

B. Document one backbone network in detail. What devices are attached, what cabling is used, and what is the topology? What networks does the backbone connect?

C. You have been hired by a small company to install a backbone to connect four 10Base-T Ethernet LANs and to provide a connection to the Internet. Develop a simple backbone and determine the total cost—i.e., select the backbone technology and price it, select the cabling and price it, select the devices and price them, and so on.

NEXT DAY AIR SERVICE CASE STUDY

There are now four functioning LANs at NDAS Tampa headquarters and President Coone says he is getting requests for LANs "from all over the place, even from Peter Browne, of the Fleet Maintenance Division!" You notice that he seems to be a bit upset over this situation. He says that Les Coone, now manager of the Information Service department (no longer "acting" manager), has complained that things are "getting out of control." Instead of a planned, orderly movement to an integrated NDAS data communications network, everyone wants to move their departments

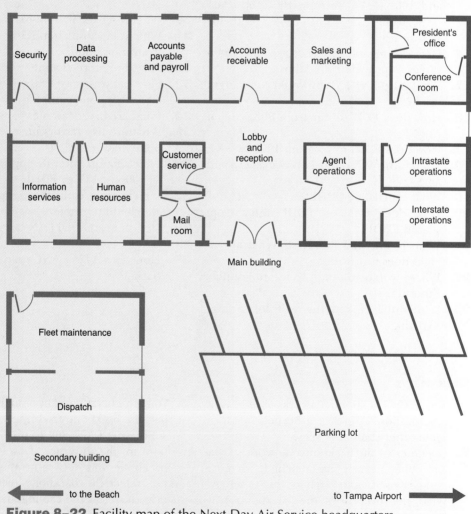

Figure 8–22 Facility map of the Next Day Air Service headquarters.

to their own LANs, all at once. President Coone did meet with the IBM representatives to talk about SNA. They stressed that SNA would "ensure interoperability of NDAS internal networks." He wants to be sure that all the current LANs will "interoperate." You point out to President Coone that the NDAS Backbone Network is designed to allow all the company's LANs to share information and data. President Coone does not seem to be listening.

It is clear that President Coone is worried. Although he did not say it, he implied that things are getting out of control in your area—data communications. And it was, in a way, your fault for encouraging many departments to ask President Coone for their own LANs.

You talk to Bob Jones about the problem. He says that you don't want to get President Coone upset with you. He suggests that the best thing to do is to show President Coone that the system will "talk together" and you have everything under control. You resolve to do this immediately, and you set up an appointment with President Coone.

Exercises

1. Figure 8–22 shows a facility map of the NDAS headquarters. Assume that there are LANs in four department offices (Data Processing, Accounts Payable, Information Services, and Agent Operations) and at Fleet Maintenance and Dispatch in the Secondary Building. What type of backbone network do you recommend for NDAS headquarters? Be prepared to justify your recommendation. Remember to consider the expected growth of the company.

2. Indicate to President Coone how you will monitor the NDAS headquarters Backbone Network and what steps can be taken if NDAS needs to improve its performance.

CHAPTER 9

Metropolitan and Wide Area Networks

Most organizations do not build their own metropolitan or long-distance communication circuits, preferring instead to rent or lease them from common carriers. Therefore, this chapter focuses on the telecommunications services offered by common carriers for use in MANs and WANs, not the underlying technology that the carriers use to provide them, because network managers purchase services, not technologies. We discuss the four principal types of MAN and WAN services that are available from these carriers: dialed circuits, dedicated circuits, switched circuits, and packet-switched services. We conclude by discussing how to improve MAN and WAN performance, and how to select services.

Objectives

* Become familiar with the common carriers and the nature of competition
* Understand the role of common carriers in organizational MANs and WANs
* Understand the four basic categories of MAN and WAN circuits
* Understand dialed circuit services

* Understand dedicated circuit services
* Understand circuit switched services
* Understand packet switched services
* Become familiar with how to improve MAN and WAN performance
* Become familiar with several factors in selecting MAN and WAN services

Chapter Outline

✳✳ INTRODUCTION

Metropolitan area networks (MANs) typically span from 3 to 30 miles and connect backbone networks (BNs) and LANs. MANs also provide dial-in and dial-out capability to LANs, BNs, and mainframes. *Wide area networks (WANs)* connect BNs and MANs across longer distances, often hundreds or thousands of miles.

The communication media used in MANs and WANs were described in Chapter 3 (e.g., twisted pair, coaxial cable, fiber optics, microwave, satellite, infrared). Although some organizations build their own metropolitan and wide area networks using these media, most do not. Most organizations cannot afford to lay long stretches of cable, build microwave towers, or lease satellites. Instead, most rent or lease circuits from *common carriers* such as AT&T, Bell Canada, MCI, BellSouth, PACTEL, or NYNEX. As a customer, you do not actually lease cables per se; you simply lease circuits that provide certain transmission characteristics. The carrier decides whether it will use twisted pair, coaxial, fiber optics, or something else for your circuits.

In this chapter, we examine the MAN and WAN technologies from the viewpoint of a network manager, rather than that of a common carrier. We focus less on internal operations and how the specific technologies work, and more on how these services are offered to network managers and how they can be used to build networks.

The Telephone Network

Although there are many similarities in the way data communication networks and services have evolved in different countries, there also are many differences. Most countries have a federal government agency that regulates data and voice communications. In the United States, the agency is the *Federal Communications Commission (FCC)*; in Canada it is the *Canadian Radio–Television and Telecommunications Commission (CRTC)*. Each state or province also has its own *public utilities commission (PUC)* to regulate communications within its borders.

The communications industry in North America operates as a series of private companies that are regulated by the government. In many other countries, government-owned PTTs (postal telephone and telegraph services) own, control, and sell all voice and data communication services, although many countries are gradually moving to privatize their PTTs.

A common carrier is a private company that sells or leases communication services and facilities to the public. Common carriers are profit-oriented, and their primary products are services for voice and data transmissions, both over traditional wired circuits as well as cellular services. Common carriers often supply a broad range of computer-based services, such as the manufacturing and marketing of specialized communication hardware and software. A common carrier that provides local telephone services (e.g., BellSouth) is commonly called a *local exchange carrier (LEC)*, while one that provides long-distance services (e.g., MCI) is commonly called an *interexchange carrier (IXC)*. As the LECs move into the long-distance market and IXCs move into the local telephone market, this distinction may disappear.

In the United States, 90 percent of the telephone system used to be run by one common carrier, AT&T. Today, there are more than 1200 common carriers in the United States and Canada, with the largest being AT&T, Bell Canada, the U.S. *regional Bell operating companies* (*RBOC*s such as BellSouth or NYNEX), MCI, WorldCom, Sprint, and General Telephone and Electronics (GTE). Most other common carriers are much smaller and offer communication facilities to a very small segment of the population.

✸✸ DIALED CIRCUIT SERVICES

Dialed circuit services are the simplest and one of the most common types of MAN and WAN connections. As the name suggests, this type of connection uses the normal voice telephone network. To use dialed circuit services, the users simply lease connection points (i.e., telephone lines) into the common carrier's network (see Figure 9–1). A person (or computer) then dials the telephone number of the destination computer and transfers data using a modem (analog transmission). Dialed services often are called public switched telephone network (PSTN) or *plain old telephone service (POTS)*.

Dialed circuit services may use different circuit paths between the two computers each time a number is dialed. Some circuits have more noise and distortion than others, so the quality and maximum data transmission rate can vary. In this section, we discuss two types of dialed circuit services: direct dialing and WATS.

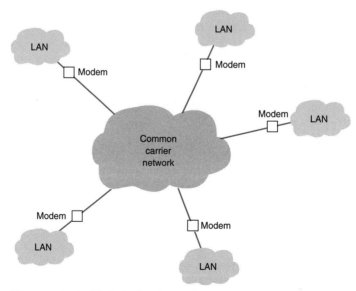

Figure 9–1 Dialed circuit services.

Direct Dialing (DD)

Direct dialing (DD) (also called *dial-up*) is the most commonly used dialed circuit service. Every time you call your Internet service provider from your home phone, you are using direct dialing.

Charges for direct dialing are based on the distance between the two telephones (in miles) and the number of minutes the connection is used. Data communication users pay the same rate as voice communication users. In general, most local calls are free, but this depends on the type of local telephone service you have purchased. Long-distance calls are charged at the rate agreed with your long-distance carrier.

Wide Area Telephone Services (WATS)

Wide area telephone services (WATS) are special-rate services that allow dialed circuit calls for both voice communications and data transmission to be purchased in large quantities. For example, you might purchase 100 hours of usage per month for one fixed rate, and be charged so many dollars per hour thereafter.

WATS service is limited to one direction only; it is either outward dialing or inward dialing. In general, inward WATS uses the toll-free 800 and 888 area code series in North America, and similar numbers in other countries (e.g., 1800 in Australia, 0800 in the UK).

The United States and Canada are divided into more than 60 different WATS service areas. (Some states and provinces have more than one service area.) The geographical coverage of WATS from any one of these areas is determined by the band of service to which the customer subscribes. For example, American interstate WATS service from California uses six bands:

* **Band 1:** Arizona, Idaho, Nevada, Oregon, Utah, and Washington
* **Band 2:** Colorado, Montana, Nebraska, New Mexico, and Wyoming
* **Band 3:** Iowa, Kansas, Minnesota, Missouri, North Dakota, Oklahoma, South Dakota, and Texas
* **Band 4:** Alabama, Arkansas, Illinois, Indiana, Kentucky, Louisiana, Michigan, Mississippi, Tennessee, and Wisconsin
* **Band 5:** Connecticut, Delaware, Florida, Georgia, Maine, Maryland, Massachusetts, New Hampshire, New Jersey, New York, North Carolina, Ohio, Pennsylvania, Rhode Island, South Carolina, Vermont, Virginia, Washington, D.C., West Virginia, Hawaii, Puerto Rico, and the U.S. Virgin Islands
* **Band 6:** Alaska

✸✸ DEDICATED CIRCUIT SERVICES

There are two main problems with dialed circuits. First, each connection goes through the regular telephone network on a different circuit. These circuits may

Management Focus: Legend of a Computer Network for Motown Cafe

Motown Cafe operates a series of music theme restaurants, similar to the Hard Rock Cafe. Motown has corporate offices in New York and operates restaurants in New York and Las Vegas, with new restaurants planned for London, Mexico, South America, and the Pacific Rim.

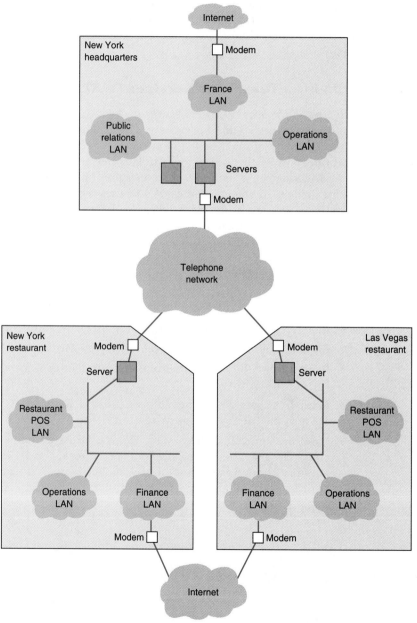

Figure 9–2 Motown Cafe network.

Each restaurant has an IBM restaurant management system that enables servers to record orders and print bills using touch screens through the restaurant. This system, and Novell LANs for Operations and Finance, use 10Base-T Ethernet connected via a 10Base-2 backbone (see Figure 9–2). All inventory and accounting information from each restaurant is transferred daily to the corporate head offices in New York over standard dial-up voice telephone lines using V.34 modems. Motown considered other network services that provided greater capacity, but in the end, the small amount of data could not justify more expensive, complex WAN services.

Source: Network Computing, December 1, 1996.

---

vary in quality, meaning that while one connection will be fairly clear, the next call may be noisy. Second, the data transmission rates on these dialed circuits are usually low. Generally speaking, transmission rates for dialed circuits range from 28.8 Kbps to 56 Kbps (which can be increased if data compression is used).

One alternative is to establish a private *dedicated circuit*, which the user leases from the common carrier for their exclusive use 24 hours a day, 7 days a week. All connections are point to point, from one building in one city to another building in the same or a different city. The carrier installs the circuit connections at the two end points of the circuit and makes the connection between them. See Figure 9–3.

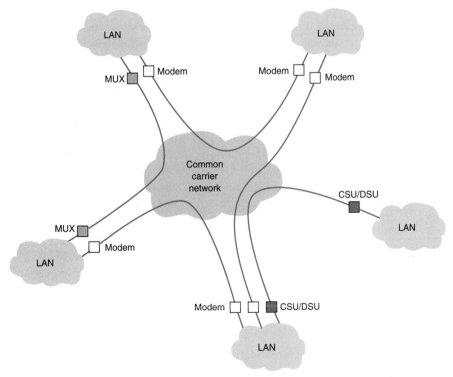

Figure 9–3 Dedicated circuit services.

Technology Focus: How 800 and 888 Area Code Numbers Work

To see how a toll-free 800 call is handled, let us follow a call as it moves through the network. Assume that the number is 800-999-5676 and that you have New York Telephone as your local telephone company.

When you begin dialing, New York Telephone sees this call as a 1+ number, a long-distance call that should be assigned to AT&T, MCI, US Sprint, or the like. The local telephone switching equipment then checks the first six digits of the number, which is 800-999. The local telephone company immediately knows it is an 800 call and one that should be switched to MCI because the 999 identifies it as an MCI call. If the first six digits were 800-542, the call would be switched to AT&T because 542 designates AT&T.

The local telephone company now routes the call to the MCI point of presence (POP) switching office. The *point of presence* is the switching office to which the local telephone terminates subscribers' circuits for long-distance dial-up or leased line communications. At this point, whether the call is destined for MCI, US Sprint, or AT&T, it enters a large network database switch. The MCI switch receives all the information about the call, including the 800 number dialed and the telephone number from which the call originated. The MCI network database switch knows it has a call coming from, let's say, 212-591-6500 and going to 800-999-5676. The database switching computer might look at the time of day, the day of the week, or even a specific day

of the year. After looking at these parameters, it sends a message through the network to indicate a call coming from New York City, and the call starts moving through the network to the destination number in less than a second.

In actuality, the destination number might not be the 800 number. Depending on the time of day, day of week, or specific day of the year, the switch knows from its database to translate the 800 number to another number. For example, if the call is made after noon on any day, it might convert the number dialed (800-999-5676) to 415-291-0616. Before noon, the calls might be routed to another number in either the same city or some other city. Another option is for it to translate the 800 number to one that connects to a dedicated access line going directly to a corporate headquarters where the calls are answered. The concept of switching calls to different numbers based on the time of day means calls can be answered by people in Philadelphia in the morning and by people in San Francisco or even Honolulu later in the day.

In summary, the database switching computer receives the telephone number of the caller and the 800 number being dialed. It then establishes the time of day, the day of the week, or the day of the year so it can determine the telephone number or dedicated access line to which the call will be switched. As you can see, 800 numbers often switch their calls to some other area code and telephone number in a manner that is transparent to the caller.

Dedicated circuits are billed at a flat fee per month and the user has unlimited use of the circuit. Once you sign a contract, making changes can be expensive because it means rewiring the buildings and signing a new contract with the carrier.

Dedicated circuits therefore require more care in network design than using dialed circuits. Rather than simply leasing a telephone line for each computer, you

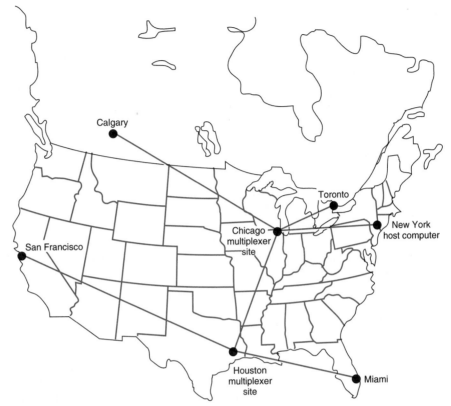

Figure 9–4 WAN using dedicated circuits.

must know which locations will need what speed circuit connections to what other locations.

Figure 9–4 shows how a WAN can be built in this manner. In this case, each location is connected to one or more other locations. For example, Calgary is connected only to Chicago, but Chicago is connected to three other locations besides Calgary. Any messages that Calgary wants to send to locations other than Chicago must go via Chicago. If Calgary is transmitting and receiving data from many other locations, the Chicago computer may spend much of its time routing messages to Calgary. So it may make more sense to connect Calgary directly to these other computers instead.

In this section, we discuss five types of dedicated circuits: voice-grade circuits, wideband analog services, T-carrier circuits, SONET circuits, and digital subscriber line circuits.

Voice-Grade Circuits

Voice-grade circuits are analog circuits that work in exactly the same manner as traditional telephone lines, except that you do not dial them. They are permanently connected from one end to the other. Since they are analog, the computers connected to them must use modems to enable data transmission.

Dedicated voice-grade channels often have *conditioning* (sometimes called equalization) done on them. Conditioning improves data transmission qualities by reducing noise and distortion. There are several different types of conditioning. C type conditioning limits attenuation distortion and envelope delay distortion. D type conditioning limits noise and harmonic distortion.

Wideband Analog Services

Wideband analog services are similar to voice-grade circuits but they provide much greater bandwidth. Typically, wideband analog services provide one 48,000 hertz bandwidth channel for use with frequency division multiplexing (FDM), or as 12 individual voice-grade channels (48,000 hertz ÷ 12 = 4000 hertz per channel). Since they are analog, the user must use an FDM multiplexer or modem to connect them to internal computer networks. Although many common carriers still provide wideband analog services, digital services are rapidly replacing them.

T-Carrier Circuits

T-carrier circuits are dedicated digital circuits. They are the most commonly used form of dedicated circuit services in North America today. As with all dedicated circuit services, you lease a dedicated circuit from one building in one city to another building in the same or different city. In this case, however, the circuit uses digital transmission. Instead of a modem, a *channel service unit (CSU)* and/or a *data service unit (DSU)* are used to connect the circuit into your computer network. The CSU/DSU is the WAN equivalent of a sophisticated network interface card (NIC) in a LAN. It performs several functions, such as signal generation and equalization, circuit testing, and synchronization between the devices on opposite ends of the circuit. There are several types of T-carrier circuits (see Figure 9–5).

A *T-1 circuit* (sometimes called a DS-1 circuit) provides a data rate of 1.544 Mbps. T-1 circuits can be used to transmit data, but often are used to transmit both data and voice. In this case, a time division multiplexer (TDM) provides 24 64 Kbps

T-Carrier Designation	DS Designation	Speed
	DS-0	64 Kbps
T-1	DS-1	1.544 Mbps
T-2	DS-2	6.312 Mbps
T-3	DS-3	44.375 Mbps
T-4	DS-4	274.176 Mbps

Figure 9–5 T-carrier circuits.

circuits.[1] Digitized voice using pulse code modulation (PCM) requires a 64 Kbps circuit (see Chapter 5) so a T-1 circuit enables 24 simultaneous voice channels. Most common carriers make extensive use of PCM internally and transmit most of their voice telephone calls in digital format using PCM, so you will see most digital services offering combinations of the standard PCM 64 Kbps circuit.

A *T-2 circuit* transmits data at a rate of 6.312 Mbps. Basically, it is a multiplexed bundle of four T-1 circuits. A *T-3 circuit* allows transmission at a rate of 44.376 Mbps, although most articles refer to this rate as 45 megabits per second. This is equal to the capacity of 28 T-1 circuits. T-3 circuits are becoming popular as the transmission medium for corporate MANs and WANs because of their higher data rates. At low speed, these T-3 circuits can be used as 672 different 64 Kbps channels or voice channels. A *T-4 circuit* transmits at 274.176 Mbps, which is equal to the capacity of 178 T-1 circuits. Obviously, an organization using either T-3 or T-4 circuits must have a tremendous need to transmit very large quantities of data.

Fractional T-1, sometimes called FT-1, offers portions of a 1.544 Mbps T-1 circuit for a fraction of its full cost. Many (but not all) common carriers offer to lease sets of 64 Kbps DS-0 channels on T-1 circuits. The most common FT-1 services provide 128 Kbps, 256 Kbps, 384 Kbps, 512 Kbps, and 768 Kbps.

Synchronous Optical Network (SONET)

The *synchronous optical network (SONET)* has recently been accepted by the U.S. standards agency (ANSI) as a standard for optical transmission at gigabit-per-second speeds. The international telecommunications standards agency (ITU-T) also recently standardized a version of SONET under the name of *synchronous digital hierarchy (SDH)*. SONET and SDH are very similar and can be easily interconnected, although the SONET standard includes more data rates than the SDH standard. As with T-carrier services, a CSU/DSU is needed to connect the user's network into the SONET/SDH circuit.

SONET transmission speeds begin at the OC-1 level (optical carrier level 1) of 51.84 Mbps. Each succeeding rate in the SONET fiber hierarchy is defined as a multiple of OC-1, with SONET data rates defined as high as OC-192, or about 10 Gbps. Figure 9–6 presents the other major SONET and SDH services. Each level above OC-1 is created by multiplexing. Notice that the slowest SONET transmission rate (OC-1) of 51.84 Mbps is slightly faster than the T-3 rate of 44.376 Mbps. Although not yet available in all locations, SONET/SDH is available in most large cities worldwide.

Several common carriers (e.g., MCI) now use OC-12 circuits at 622.08 Mbps to carry digitized voice traffic. With these speeds, it is easy to see why the telephone companies in most cities are installing optical fiber cable MANs and long-distance circuits. Even new undersea cables are optical fiber instead of copper.

---

[1]If you multiply 24 circuits by 64 Kbps per circuit you will get 1.536 Mbps, not 1.544 Mbps. This is because some of the 1.544 Mbps circuit capacity is used by the common carrier for control signals used to "frame" the data (i.e., mark the start and stop of packets).

SONET Designation	SDH Designation	Speed
OC-1		51.84 Mbps
OC-3	STM-1	155.52 Mbps
OC-9	STM-3	466.56 Mbps
OC-12	STM-4	622.08 Mbps
OC-18	STM-6	933.12 Mbps
OC-24	STM-8	1.244 Gbps
OC-36	STM-12	1.866 Gbps
OC-48	STM-16	2.488 Gbps
OC-192		9.952 Gbps

Figure 9–6 SONET and SDH circuits.

Digital Subscriber Line (DSL)

The ITU-T standards committee is considering several proposals to significantly increase the data rates over traditional telephone lines. One of the most promising is the *digital subscriber line (DSL)*.

The reason for the limited capacity on voice telephone circuits lies with the telephone and the switching equipment at the end offices. The actual cable in the local loop is capable of providing much higher data transmission rates. Unlike all the other services discussed in this section that operate through the telephone network end-to-end from the sender to the receiver, DSL only operates in the local loop from the carrier's end office to the customer's telephone. DSL uses the existing local loop cable, but places one DSL network interface device (called customer premises equipment, or CPE) in the home or business and another one in the common carrier's end office. The end office DSL device is then connected to a high-speed digital line from the end office to elsewhere in the carrier's network (often an Internet service provider) using some other service (e.g., T-carrier, SMDS).

Two general categories of DSL services have emerged in the market. *Symmetric DSL (SDSL)* provides two same speed digital circuits (one to the end office, one from the end office) in addition to the normal analog voice circuit. The maximum transmission rate depends on the distance from the carrier's end office to the customer's CPE; the shorter the distance, the higher the speed, because the line suffers less attenuation. The minimum data rate is 128 Kbps, with rates up to 1.024 Mbps possible if the distance is less than two miles (three kilometers).

Asymmetric DSL (ADSL) works in the same way as SDSL, but provides different data transmission rates to and from the carrier's end office, as well as an analog channel for voice transmissions. ADSL uses frequency division multiplexing to create three channels over the local loop from the end office to the CPE. The first channel is the usual 4000-Hz voice telephone circuit; the other two are digital— one upstream from the CPE to the end office, and one downstream from the end office to the CPE. As with SDSL, the size of the two digital channels depends on

Management Focus: New York Information Technology Center

The New York Information Technology Center (NYITC) rents out office space linked to a vast array of network services. The main office complex is located on Broad Street in Manhattan, with connections to two other locations (see Figure 9–7). Current tenants include a host of Web site developers, electronic commerce companies, and Internet technology companies.

NYITC provides high-speed T-3, OC-3, and OC-48 connections into the networks of a variety of common carriers, each linked into a 100Base-F backbone. Individual companies can lease 100Base-F connections from their office suites into the backbone, or can opt for T-1, T-3, or FT-1 connections.

Source: "For Rent: Prime Office Space Linked to Network," *Network Computing*, September 1, 1996.

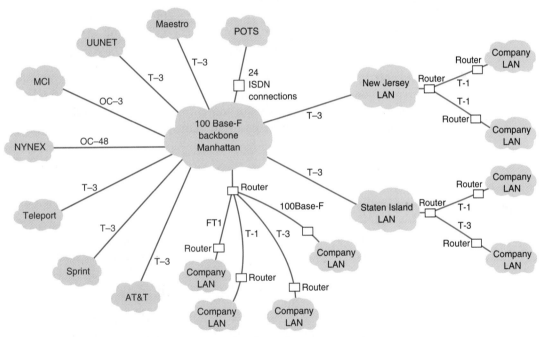

Figure 9–7 New York Information Technology Center network.

the distance from the CPE to the end office. The most common configuration for distances of two miles or less (three kilometers) provides an upstream digital channel of 640 Kbps and a downstream digital channel of 6.144 Mbps. The most common configuration for distances of two to three miles (three to five kilometers) provides an upstream digital channel of 64 Kbps and a downstream digital channel of 1.544 Mbps. A few telephone companies have installed other versions of ADSL that provide upstream data rates of up to 1 Mbps and downstream data rates of up to 9.1 Mbps.

A new version of ADSL, called *very high rate digital subscriber line (VDSL)*, has been designed for use over local loops of 1000 feet or less (300 meters). It also uses FDM to provide three channels: the normal analog voice channel, an upstream digital channel of 1.6 Mbps, and a downstream digital channel of 51.84 Mbps. VDSL has not yet been standardized, so these channels are likely to change as manufacturers, telephone companies, and ITU-T gain more experience.

One potential competitor to DSL is the so-called *cable modem*, a digital service offered by cable television companies. At present, very few cable companies offer cable modem services, and there are virtually no standards. As with DSL services, cable modems will only connect from the customer's home or office into the main switch office of the cable television company. An additional service is needed to carry the data from there to the final destination. Unlike DSL, cable services offer *shared* multipoint circuits. As with LANs, each user must compete with other users for the available capacity. Furthermore, since the cable circuit is a multipoint circuit, all messages on the circuit go to all computers on the circuit. If your neighbors were hackers they could modify their computer to read all messages that travel over the cable.

Most cable services today offer asymmetric data rates. Upstream rates of 1.5 to 10 Mbps with downstream rates of 2 to 30 Mbps are typical. A few cable companies offer downstream only, with all upstream communications using regular telephone lines. Although cable modems have had little impact thus far, they have immense potential.

✳ ✳ CIRCUIT-SWITCHED SERVICES

The major problem with dedicated circuit services is that you must carefully plan all the circuits you need. To be successful, you must understand the data transmission patterns in your network *and* these patterns must be relatively stable. Both can be a challenge, especially if you are adding new applications to the network or building new network connections.

In contrast, *circuit-switched services* work much like dialed services. You buy a connection into the common carrier's network from the end points of the WAN, without specifying all the interconnecting circuits you will need (see Figure 9–8). When you want to transfer data, you request a circuit from your connection point to the destination connection point and the common carrier's network establishes a temporary circuit between the two connections (in much the same way as a dialed telephone call). You send data, in digital form, through this temporary circuit, and when you are done, you request that the circuit be disconnected.

The primary differences from dialed services are that the circuits are entirely digital (and thus less susceptible to noise) and that they offer higher data transmission rates. As with dialed services, you must pay a fixed fee per month, plus additional charges based on the amount of time the circuits are used. The most common switched service is narrowband ISDN, with broadband ISDN not yet widely available.

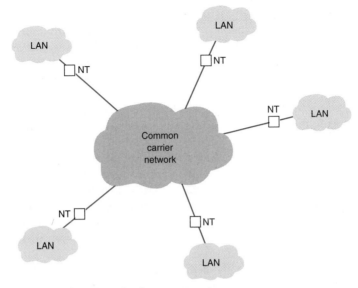

Figure 9–8 Switched circuit services.

Narrowband Integrated Services Digital Network (ISDN)

The first generation of *integrated services digital network (ISDN)*, commonly called *narrowband ISDN*, combines voice, video, and data over the same digital circuit. Narrowband ISDN is widely available from a number of common carriers in North America. Users need an ISDN *network terminator* (*NT-1* or *NT-2*) that functions much like a hub, and a network interface card (called a terminal adapter, TA, or even an "ISDN modem") in all computers attached to the NT-1/NT-2. In most cases, the ISDN service appears identical to the regular dialed telephone service, with the exception that usually (but not always), each device attached to the NT-1/NT-2 needs a unique *service profile identifier (SPID)* to identify it. To connect to another computer using ISDN, you dial that computer's telephone number(s) using the ISDN NIC in much the same way as you would with a modem on a regular telephone line.

ISDN has long been more of a concept than a reliable service in North America. It has been available since the late 1970s, although it has not been widely adopted. Its largest problems are a lack of standards and a lack of interest from common carriers. For example, ISDN is more popular in California than New York because PACTEL has actively marketed it while NYNEX has not.

Acceptance of ISDN has also been slowed because equipment vendors and common carriers have conflicting interpretations of the ISDN standards. Equipment from different vendors that conforms to the ISDN standard won't necessarily work together or with a specific common carrier's ISDN line. Even switching ISDN transmissions between common carriers can be problematic. Vendors and common carriers in North America have worked for years to develop common interpretations of the standards, called National ISDN-1 (NI-1), National ISDN-2 (NI-2), and National ISDN-3 (NI-3) to specify exactly how ISDN services will be provided. Many experts believe that as NI-1, NI-2, and NI-3 are implemented, many of the current standardization problems will disappear. However, in the past, just as the industry appeared to have resolved its differences, more incompatibilities arose. Skeptics claim that ISDN actually stands for "*I Still Don't Know*," "*I Still Don't Need it*" or "*It Still Does Nothing*."

Narrowband ISDN offers two types of service. The first is *basic rate interface (BRI)* (sometimes called basic access service or *2B+D*), which provides a communication circuit with two 64 Kbps digital transmission channels (called B channels) and one 16 Kbps control signaling channel (called a D channel). The two B channels handle digitized voice, data, and image transmissions, providing a total of 128 Kbps. The D channel is used for control messages such as acknowledgments, call setup and termination, and other functions such as automatic number identification.

One advantage of BRI is that it can be installed in many existing telephone locations without adding any new cable. If the connection from the customer's telephone to the common carrier's end office is less than 3.5 miles, the ISDN line can use the existing two pairs of twisted-pair wires. The only changes are the end connections at the customer's location and at the carrier's end office. If the connection is longer than 3.5 miles, then new cable will have to be laid.

Management Focus: *Trials and Tribulations at General [ISDN] Hospital*

The experience of Brigham and Women's Hospital in Boston demonstrates the numerous problems with ISDN. Trouble began immediately after NYNEX (the Boston area RBOC) installed the ISDN line. After testing several newly installed lines, the network manager could not find the ISDN line. NYNEX identified the problem as a missing NT-1 connector, which links the ISDN line to the telephone network. The installation was delayed while the missing part was ordered.

After the NT-1 arrived and was installed, the motherboard in the network server melted. No one knew how or why, but installation was again delayed while a new motherboard was ordered and installed. The line still did not work.

The hospital then contacted NYNEX for "provisioning information," which describes how the ISDN line and connection is configured. After three different experts were consulted, it was determined that the wrong configuration was being used in the server. Finally, the server was up and running.

But this was only half the job. A second server remained to be set up. It seemed simple enough; just copy the settings from the first server. Not really. NYNEX used a different type of telephone switch to provide the ISDN service to this server, and did not have the provisioning information for it. Once again, the manufacturer, Northern Telecom, provided the information. And again the server experienced a meltdown (this time destroying only the NT-1 connector).

When this was replaced, the second server was able to use the ISDN line, but could not establish a connection to the first server. The problem was an incompatibility between the second server's ISDN network interface card and the Northern Telecom switch. After the new ISDN card was installed, the system finally worked.

Source: "Trials and Tribulations at General Hospital," *InfoWorld*, February, 6, 1995.

Primary rate interface (PRI) (also called primary access service, or *23B+D*) is typically offered to commercial customers. It consists of 23 64 Kbps B channels plus one 64 Kbps D channel, so PRI has almost the same capacity as a T-1 circuit (1.544 Mbps). In Europe, PRI is defined as 30 B channels plus one D channel, making interconnection between North America and Europe difficult.

Broadband Integrated Services Digital Network (ISDN)

The second generation of ISDN is called *broadband ISDN (B-ISDN)*. Although not yet widely available, it has the potential to change the future of high-speed networking. B-ISDN is very different than narrowband ISDN—so different in fact, that it really is not ISDN.

On the surface, B-ISDN is an enhancement of narrowband ISDN. It is a circuit-switched service, which means that the user purchases connections into the common carrier's network and places calls requesting a circuit to be established from one location to another. Once connected, the user is guaranteed to have a circuit providing a given data rate between the two end points. However, B-ISDN actually uses ATM to move data from one end point to the other. Unlike narrowband ISDN, which simply provides a digital circuit through which users send their own packets, B-ISDN encapsulates the users' existing data link layer packets with ATM cells and moves them through an ATM network to the destination, where the ATM cells are removed and the users' packets are rebuilt. This process is transparent to the users, so they are unaware that ATM was ever used; to them, it appears as though they have a traditional ISDN circuit switched.

B-ISDN is backward-compatible with narrowband ISDN, which means it can accept narrowband BRI and PRI transmissions. B-ISDN currently defines three additional services. The first is a full-duplex channel that operates at 155.52 Mbps; the second provides a full-duplex channel that operates at 622.08 Mbps; and the third is an asymmetrical service with two simplex channels—one from the subscriber at 155.52 Mbps, and one from the host to the subscriber at 622.08 Mbps. The first two services are intended for normal bi-directional information exchange. The third, asymmetrical, service is intended to be used for information distribution services such as digital broadcast television.

✳✳ PACKET-SWITCHED SERVICES

Packet-switched services are quite different from the three types of network services discussed previously. For each of these three—dialed circuit services, dedicated circuit services, and circuit-switched services—a physical circuit was established between the two communicating computers. This circuit provided a guaranteed data transmission capability that was available for use by only those two computers. For example, for Computer A to transmit data on a narrowband BRI ISDN B channel to Computer B, a channel at both A and B must be available. Once in use for this transmission, it is assigned solely to that transmission. No other transmission is

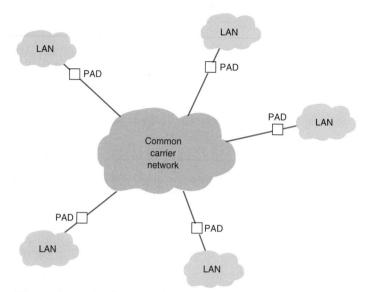

Figure 9–9 Packet-switched services.

possible until the circuit is closed. So, for example, if Computer C attempted to reach Computer B, it would have to wait until the circuit was closed.

In contrast, packet-switched services enable multiple connections to exist simultaneously between computers. With packet-switched services, the user again buys a connection into the common carrier network (see Figure 9–9). The user pays a fixed fee for the connection into the network and is charged for the number of packets transmitted. The user's connection into the network is a *packet assembly/disassembly device (PAD)*, which can be owned and operated by the customer or by the common carrier. The PAD converts the sender's data into the network layer and data link layer packets used by the packet network and sends them through the packet-switched network. At the other end, another PAD reassembles the packets back into the network layer and data link layer protocols expected by the destination and delivers it to the appropriate computer. This *packetizing* and reassembly is almost instantaneous, and data are transmitted continuously. The PAD can translate between different data link layer protocols between the sender and the destination (e.g., Ethernet at the sender and token ring at the receiver). It may also provide conversion from one code to another (i.e., ASCII to EBCDIC). The PAD also compensates for differences in transmission speed between sender and receiver.

Figure 9–10 shows a packet-switching connection between six different cities. The little boat-shaped figures (shown on the communication circuits) represent individual packets of separate messages. Notice how packets from separate messages are *interleaved* with other packets for transmission. Packet switching is popular because most data communications consist of short bursts of data with intervening spaces that usually last longer than the actual burst of data. Packet switching takes

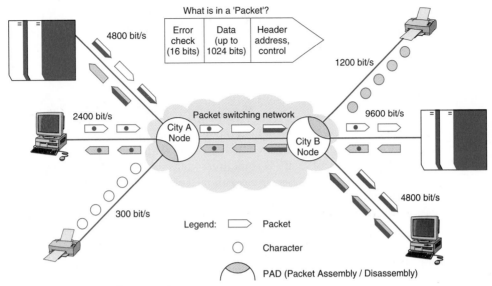

Figure 9–10 Packet-switching concepts.

advantage of this characteristic by interleaving bursts of data from many users to maximize use of the shared communication network.

Although the packets in one data stream may mix with several other data streams during their journey, it is unlikely that packets from two different data streams will travel together during the entire length of their transmission. The two communicating computers do not need to know through which intermediate nodes their data are routed, because the packet network takes care of it by either of two methods.

The first method, called *datagram,* is a connectionless service. It adds a destination address and sequence number to each packet, in addition to information about the data stream to which the packet belongs. In this case, a route is chosen for each packet as it is accepted into the packet network. Each packet may follow a different route through the network. At the destination address the sequence number tells the network how to reassemble the packets into a continuous message. The sequence number is necessary because different routes may deliver packets at different speeds, so data packets often arrive out of sequence.

The second routing method is a connection-oriented approach called a *virtual circuit.* In this case, the packet-switched network establishes what appears to be one end-to-end circuit between the sender and receiver. *All* packets for that transmission take the same route over the virtual circuit that has been set up for that particular transmission. The two computers believe they have a dedicated point-to-point circuit (but in fact, they do not).

Packet-switched services are often provided by different common carriers than the one from which organizations get their usual telephone and data services. Therefore, organizations often lease a dedicated circuit (e.g., T-1) from their offices to the packet-switched network point of presence (POP). The POP is the location at which the packet-switched network (or any common carrier network, for that matter) connects into the local telephone exchange.

X.25

The oldest packet-switched service is *X.25*, a standard developed by ITU-T. X.25 offers datagram, switched virtual circuit, and permanent virtual circuit services. As discussed in Chapter 6, X.25 uses the LAPB data link layer protocol and the PLP network layer protocol. X.25 is sometimes called a *reliable packet service* because it provides complete error checking on all packets transmitted.

Although widely used in Europe, X.25 is not widespread in North America, because of its transmission speed. For many years, the maximum speed into North American X.25 networks was 64 Kbps, but this was recently increased to 2.048 Mbps, which is the European standard for narrowband ISDN. But for many users, 2.048 Mbps is still not fast enough.

Frame Relay

Frame relay is a newer packet-switching technology that transmits data faster than X.25. In many ways, frame relay networks work the same as X.25 networks. Users connect to them by *frame relay access devices (FRADs)* that perform the same function as the PADs. Both datagram and virtual circuit services are available. Frame relay networks tend to offer faster data rates than X.25 networks.

Frame relay differs from X.25 and traditional networks in three important ways. First, frame relay operates only at the data link layer (layer 2). Frame relay, like other packet-switched networks, takes the incoming packets from the user network and converts them to its own packet structure for internal transmission. However, unlike X.25, frame relay does not replace the user's network layer or data link layer packets with its own. Instead, it encapsulates the entire incoming packet with its own data link layer packet, leaving the user's network and data link layer packets intact. Frame relay uses variable-length packets that adapt to the size of the incoming packet (up to 8K), unlike X.25 which uses fixed-length packets.

Second, frame relay networks do not perform error control. X.25 networks (and virtually all other types of networks) perform error checking at each computer in the network. Any errors in transmission are corrected immediately, so that the network layer and application software can assume error-free transmission. However, error control is one of the most time-consuming processes in a network. Most networks today are relatively error-free, so frame relay networks do not ensure error-free delivery of the packets (they do perform error checking, but simply discard packets with errors; they do not generate NAKs and ask for retransmission). It is up to the software at the source and destination to perform error correction and to control for lost messages. Since the user's data link packet remains intact, it is simple for the devices at the edge of the frame relay network to check the error control information in the user's data link layer packet to ensure that no errors

Management Focus: *Solid Foundation for the Home Depot Network*

The Home Depot network connects the retailer's Atlanta head office complex with its more than 500 stores, distribution centers, and divisional offices across North America. The head office complex uses a high-speed ATM backbone to connect 2,500 employees to its two mainframes, three minicomputers, and dozens of Ethernet LANs. The ATM backbone also provides connections to the WAN (see Figure 9–11).

Communications between the head office and the divisional offices is intensive and fairly constant, so Home Depot has a dedicated T-1 line to each of the divisional offices. Communications with the stores and distribution centers is less intensive, so Home Depot uses a frame relay network. The head office complex has a set of six 1.544 Mbps connections into the frame relay network, while each store and distribution center has one 1.544 Mbps connection. Although most of the communications are data, Home Depot also regularly uses video conferencing to communicate with the stores and divisional offices.

Source: Network Computing, January 15, 1997.

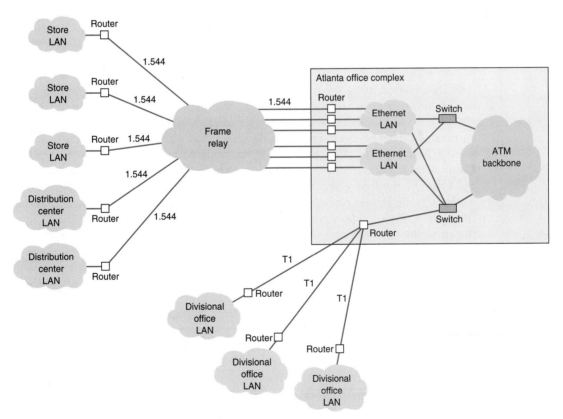

Figure 9–11 Home Depot network.

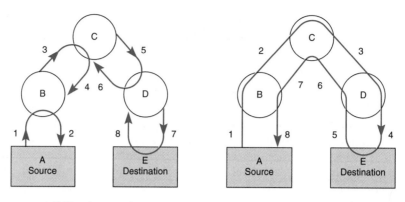

X.25 packet network Frame relay packet network

Figure 9–12 Frame relay compared to X.25 packet switching. With X.25, each node sends an acknowledgment immediately on receiving a packet. With frame relay, the final destination sends an acknowledgment, making this technique faster than the X.25 technique.

have occurred and to request transmission of damaged or lost packets. For this reason, frame relay networks are called *unreliable packet services*. Some common carriers have started using the term *fast packet services* instead to refer to these services that do not provide error control because it sounds better for marketing!

Figure 9–12 illustrates the difference in error control between X.25 networks and frame relay networks. The left side shows that when an X.25 packet leaves its Source A and moves through Node B, to Node C, to Node D, and finally to its Destination E, each intermediate node acknowledges the packet as it passes. The right side of the figure shows how a frame relay packet moves through Node B, Node C, Node D, and on to Destination E. When Destination E receives the frame correctly, a single acknowledgment is sent back through the nodes to Source A, as shown by the numbers 5, 6, 7, and 8. This acknowledgment may or may not follow the same route as the packet.

A third major difference is that frame relay defines two connection data rates that are negotiated per connection and for each virtual circuit as it is established. The *committed information rate (CIR)* is the data rate the circuit must guarantee to transmit. If the network accepts the connection, it guarantees to provide that level of service. Most connections also specify a *maximum allowable rate (MAR)*, which is the maximum rate that the frame relay network will attempt to provide, over and above the CIR. The circuit will attempt to transmit all packets up to the MAR, but all packets that exceed the CIR are marked as *discard eligible (DE)*. If the network becomes overloaded, DE packets are discarded. So while devices can transmit faster than the CIR, they do so at a risk of lost packets.

Different common carriers offer frame relay networks with different transmission speeds. Most offer a range of CIR speeds that include 56 Kbps, 128 Kbps, 256 Kbps, 384 Kbps, 1.544 Mbps, 2.048 Mbps, and 45 Mbps.

At present, frame relay suffers from some of the same problems as ISDN—a lack of standards. Not all common carriers provide frame relay in the same way, so some frame relay networks cannot communicate with others. The frame relay standards group has recently developed a set of standards called Network-to-Network

---

Management Focus: *Nortel's ATM WAN Backbone*

Nortel, the giant Canadian manufacturer of network switches, recently implemented a wide area ATM backbone using its own equipment. Prior to implementing the ATM network, Nortel had used a set of more than 100 T-1 dedicated circuits that was proving to be more and more expensive and unwieldy to manage.

Nortel started by identifying the 20 percent of its sites that accounted for 80 percent of the network traffic. These were the first to move to the ATM network. By the time the

switchover is complete, more than 100 sites will be connected.

There are two primary parts to the network (see Figure 9–13). The largest part uses a public ATM network provided by WorldCom. Nortel also operates a private ATM network over its own circuits in Ontario. Both parts of the network use T-3 ATM, but Nortel is planning to move to OC-3 when costs drop.

Source: "A Case for ATM," *Network World,* June 2, 1997.

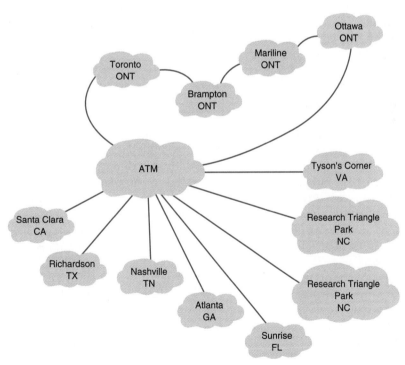

Figure 9–13 Nortel's ATM WAN backbone network.

Interface (NNI) that will eliminate this problem, but for the moment, the best advice is to stick with one vendor for all frame relay services.

Asynchronous Transfer Mode (ATM)

Asynchronous Transfer Mode (ATM), is one of the fastest growing new technologies. ATM was discussed in Chapter 8. We present a summary of ATM in this section.

ATM is similar to frame relay. All data are packet-switched, and there is no error control at the intermediate computers within the network; error control is the responsibility of the source and destination (ATM is considered an unreliable packet service). CIR and MAR (which ATM calls *available bit rate,* or *ABR*) can be negotiated when circuits are established.

ATM has three important differences from frame relay. First, ATM uses fixed-length packets of 53 bytes (5 bytes of overhead and 48 bytes of user data), which is more suitable for voice transmissions. Second, ATM provides extensive QoS information that enables the setting of very precise priorities among different types of transmissions: high priority for voice and video, lower priority for e-mail. Quality of service is now being implemented in many frame relay and SMDS services, so this difference may disappear. Third, ATM is scalable; it is easy to multiplex basic ATM circuits into much faster ATM circuits. Most common carriers offer ATM circuits that provide the same data transmission rates as SONET: 51.84 Mbps, 466.56 Mbps, 622.08 Mbps, and so on. New versions, called T-1 ATM (1.544 Mbps) and T-3 ATM (45 Mbps), are also available.

Switched Multimegabit Data Service (SMDS)

Switched multimegabit data service (SMDS) is an unreliable packet service, like ATM and frame relay. SMDS encapsulates incoming packets from the user's network with ATM-like 53-byte cells, although the address is different than an ATM address. The user's data link layer address is mapped to the SMDS address, which is used for transmission through the SMDS network. The SMDS cell is stripped off at the destination and the user's data link layer packet is reassembled.

Like ATM and frame relay, SMDS does not perform error checking; the user is responsible for error checking. SMDS provides only a connectionless datagram service.

SMDS is not yet a widely accepted standard. Most (but not all) RBOCs and a few interexchange carriers offer it (e.g., MCI, but not AT&T). SMDS was originally aimed at the metropolitan area networks, particularly the interconnection of local area networks. Recently, it has also made its way into the wide area network environment via MCI. RBOCs offer SMDS at a variety of transmission rates, ranging from 56 Kbps to 44.376 Mbps. There are no widely accepted standards, so transmissions rates vary by carrier. The future of SMDS is uncertain because not all common carriers support it.

Management Focus: Grumman Embraces SMDS Nationwide

Northrop Grumman is a leading manufacturer of aircraft and aircraft parts to a variety of manufacturers, including the U.S. defense industry. Grumman instituted a series of integrated project teams that bring together skilled engineers from each of the geographically separate divisions in different parts of the United States. The teams work together, exchanging complex engineering drawings and using videoconferencing.

Grumman used to use a series of T-1 and T-3 circuits between the different offices, but the network could not keep up with the changing demands and growing number of offices. Grumman now has 40 offices across the U.S. and plans to grow to 100 offices within two

years, so building a network using dedicated lines was virtually impossible.

Grumman examined a number of alternatives, including ATM and frame relay, before selecting SMDS from MCI (see Figure 9–14). SMDS offered the fastest, most flexible data service for the least cost. Grumman executives were initially concerned with the lack of standards and the limited number of carriers offering SMDS, but MCI's assurance of continued support for SMDS and guaranteed performance (99.7 percent availability with no more than a 70 millisecond delay) overcame objections.

Source: Communications Week, June 2, 1997.

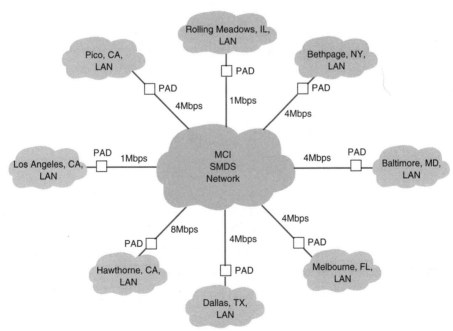

Figure 9–14 Northrop Grumman network.

✳✳ IMPROVING MAN/WAN PERFORMANCE

Improving the performance of MANs and WANs is handled in the same way as improving LAN performance. You begin by checking the devices in the network, by upgrading the circuits between the computers, and by changing the demand placed on the network. See Figure 9–15.

Improving Device Performance

In many cases, the key bottleneck in the network is not the circuits; it is the devices that provide access to the circuits (e.g., routers). One way to improve network performance is to upgrade the devices and computers that connect backbones to the WAN. Most devices are rated for their speed in converting input packets to output packets (called latency). Not all devices are created equal; some vendors produce devices with lower latencies than others.

Another strategy is to examine the routing protocol, either static or dynamic. Dynamic routing will increase performance in networks that have many possible routes from one computer to another, and in which message traffic is "bursty;" that is, occurs in spurts, with many messages at one time and few at others. But dynamic routing imposes an overhead cost by increasing network traffic. In some cases, the traffic and status information sent between computers accounts for more than 50 percent of all WAN message traffic. This is clearly a problem, because it drastically reduces the amount of network capacity available for users' messages. Dynamic routing should use no more than 10 to 20 percent of the total networks' capacity.

Performance Checklist

Increase Computer and Device Performance
- ✳ Upgrade devices
- ✳ Change to a more appropriate routing protocol (either static or dynamic)

Increase Circuit Capacity
- ✳ Analyze message traffic and upgrade to faster circuits where needed
- ✳ Check error rates

Reduce Network Demand
- ✳ Change user behavior
- ✳ Analyze network needs of all new systems
- ✳ Move data closer to users

Figure 9–15 Improving MAN and WAN performance.

Improving Circuit Capacity

The first step is to analyze the message traffic in the network to find which circuits are approaching capacity. These circuits then can be upgraded to provide more capacity. Less-used circuits can be downgraded to save costs. A more sophisticated analysis involves examining *why* circuits are heavily used. For example in Figure 9–4, the circuit from Chicago to Houston may be heavily used, but much traffic on this circuit may not originate in Chicago or be destined for Houston. It may, for example, be going from Calgary to San Francisco, suggesting that adding a circuit here would improve performance to a greater extent than upgrading the Chicago to Houston circuit.

The capacity may be adequate for most traffic, but not for meeting peak demand. One solution may be to add a circuit-switched or packet-switched service that is only used when demand exceeds circuit capacity. The use of a service as a backup for heavy traffic provides the best of both worlds because the lower-cost dedicated circuit is used constantly, and the higher-cost backup service is used only when necessary to avoid poor response times.

Sometimes a shortage of capacity may be caused by a faulty circuit. As circuits deteriorate, the number of errors increases and as the error rate increases, throughput falls because more messages have to be retransmitted. Before installing new circuits, monitor the existing ones to ensure that they are operating properly, or ask the common carrier to do it.

Reducing Network Demand

There are many ways to reduce network demand. One simple step is to require a network impact statement for all new application software developed or purchased by the organization. This focuses attention on the network effects at any early stage in application development. Another simple approach is to use data compression techniques for all data in the network.

Another, sometimes more difficult, approach is to shift network usage from peak or high cost times to lower demand or lower cost times. For example, the transmission of detailed sales and inventory reports from a retail store to headquarters could be done after the store closes. This takes advantage of off-peak-rate charges and avoids interfering with transmissions requiring higher priority, such as customer credit card authorizations.

The network can be redesigned to move data closer to the applications and people who use them, which will reduce the amount of traffic in the network. Distributed database applications enable databases to be spread across several different computers. For example, instead of storing customer records in one central location, you could store them according to region.

Management Focus: *Hacienda School District Network Makes the Grade*

Los Angeles' Hacienda La Puente Unified School District is one of the most highly networked school districts in North America. Their network connects the district offices with dozens of elementary, middle, and high schools, and even five correctional facility schools.

More than 33,000 students have accounts on the network and have access to e-mail, the Internet, videoconferencing, instructional videos, and educational software. Inmates in the correctional facilities have much more limited access to the network. Desktop videoconferencing is also available for use by teachers and administrators for staff development and planning.

The district administrative offices have a series of 10/100 Ethernet networks, connected via an FDDI backbone (see Figure 9–16). There are three T-1 lines into the Internet. Connections from the administrative offices to the schools depends upon the type of school. Connections to the correctional facilities have the slowest connections: a frame relay network with 1.544 Mbps from the administrative offices but only 56 Kbps from the correctional facilities. The Los Angeles County Office of Education is also on this same frame relay network. The middle schools and most elementary schools are on a higher-capacity ISDN network: PRI from the administrative offices (1.544 Mbps) and BRI from the schools (128 Kbps). Each of the schools and correctional facilities have their own 10Base-T Ethernet LAN.

The high schools, and a few select elementary schools, have more intensive network requirements because they use the TCI cable network in the classroom. They write, direct, produce, and anchor a morning news program that is broadcast on TCI's local community cable channel. These schools have both 10 Mbps SMDS connections and ATM OC-3 connections (155 Mbps).

Source: Network Computing, November 1, 1996.

✳✳ SELECTING MAN/WAN SERVICES

A 1995 survey of network managers found that on average, 45 percent of WAN costs were for network management, especially support staff salaries. On average, 35 percent was spent on services, primarily the cost of leasing circuits from common carriers. Only 20 percent was spent on equipment.

Two important points here are: (1) the most expensive part of your WAN will be the people required to plan, install, and operate it, so pick the one that is easy to manage; (2) it costs more to lease services from common carriers than to buy hardware, so selection decisions should be driven more by the services than the hardware.

Key Issues

There are so many services available that identifying the ideal service is difficult. Figure 9–17 summarizes the current services, but new common carriers and new services are added almost monthly. Prices change rapidly due to intense competi-

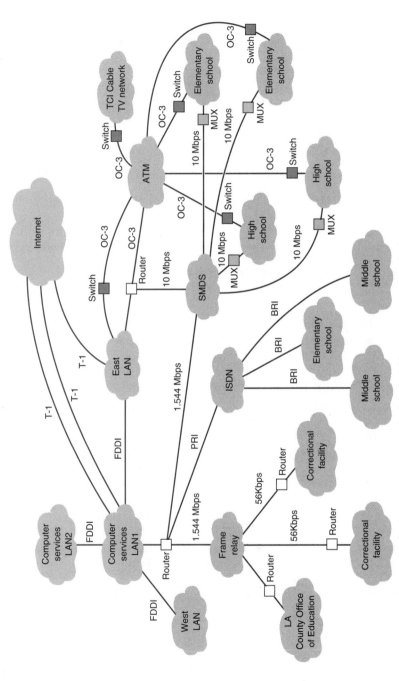

Figure 9–16 Hacienda La Puente Unified School District network.

Type of Service	Approximate Data Rates
Dialed Circuit Services	
Voice-grade	28.8 Kbps to 56 Kbps
WATS	28.8 Kbps to 56 Kbps
Dedicated Circuit Services	
Voice-grade	28.8 Kbps to 56 Kbps
Wideband analog	288 Kbps to 336 Kbps
T-carrier	64 Kbps to 274 Mbps
SONET	52 Mbps to 622 Mbps
Circuit-Switched Sercices	
Narrowband ISDN	128 Kbps to 1.5 Mbps
Broadband ISDN	155 Mbps to 622 Mbps
Packet-Switched Services	
X.25	56 Kbps to 2 Mbps
Frame relay	56 Kbps to 45 Mbps
ATM	1.5 Mbps to 622 Mbps
SMDS	56 Kbps to 45 Mbps

Figure 9–17 Commonly available services.

tion and the fact that many services are essentially commodities; a T-1 line from one vendor is the same as a T-1 line from another. Nonetheless, selecting a MAN/WAN service requires answering some basic questions. The design steps in Chapter 10 will help in MAN/WAN service selection, as will the key issues examined in the following discussion. These issues are summarized in Figure 9–18.

The first issue is the *vendor*. The best ones provide high-quality service, quickly respond to network problems, adapt to changing customer needs, and provide useful network management services along with the data transmission services.

A second consideration is the network *capacity* you need. A variety of services are available at many different data transmission rates. Try to estimate the general capacity you need at each network site, and be aware that users' needs change.

Flexibility is important. In general, dedicated circuits are much less flexible than switched services. A common strategy is to build new networks with switched services, and monitor the traffic flows. Once the network traffic is somewhat stable, dedicated circuits often replace switched services on high-use circuits, because dedicated circuits are often cheaper when the volume of traffic between two points is

* Vendor capabilities
* Capacity
* Flexibility
* Control
* Reliability

Figure 9–18 Key issues in selecting MAN/WAN services.

fairly constant. Circuit-switched services are then used as a secondary service in case demand exceeds the capacity of the dedicated circuits.

Control is another important issue. With dedicated circuits, you have more control over how your messages get routed in the network because your computers do the routing. With switched services, the service provider is responsible for the routing, and your messages get intermixed with those of other network users.

The *reliability* of a network service—both in terms of average error rates and any circuit failures—is also important. In general, switched networks generally are more reliable than dedicated circuits because they have redundant circuits between various cities. This means that if part of a common carrier's network fails, an entirely different path might be utilized, producing little effect on network users.

Value Added Networks (VAN) and Virtual Private Networks (VPN)

Several companies offer *value added networks (VANs)* that are alternatives to building networks by leasing circuits from common carriers. VANs provide additional services over and above those provided by common carriers, such as network management, e-mail, electronic data interchange (EDI) standardization, and security features. VANs tend to be more expensive than leasing common carrier circuits, but can reduce management and personnel costs. VANs often integrate services that you would otherwise have to purchase from a variety of common carriers, greatly simplifying network management.

A new type of VAN, called a *virtual private network (VPN)* (or sometimes software defined network) has recently emerged. VPNs provide circuits that run over the Internet but appear to the user to be private networks. Different VPNs provide different services, but most offer packet-switching hardware that will communicate via the Internet, or VPN services that you lease from the VPN in much the same way as leasing a service from a common carrier. These VPN hardware (or services) take your data, encrypt it, and send it through the Internet through a series of "tunnels"—a virtual circuit through the Internet that constrains the source and destination to only those within the VPN.

The primary advantage of the VPN is low cost. Internet access is inexpensive compared to the cost of leasing dedicated circuits, circuit-switched services, or packet-switched services from a common carrier.

There are two important disadvantages. First, traffic on the Internet is unpredictable. Sometimes packets travel quickly, while at other times, they take a long time to reach their destination. Second, at present, there are several competing standards for Internet-based VPNs, so not all vendors' equipment and services are compatible. The best advice is to buy from only one VPN provider.

Summary

Types of Communication Services   Communication services come in four basic groups. A dialed circuit is a regular dialed telephone call from one point to another through the telephone network. A dedicated circuit is a point-to-point circuit available for the exclusive use of the leasing organization that connects two offices. A circuit-switched service is one in which the organization establishes network connection points at a variety of locations and uses the carrier's network to make temporary (switched) connections between locations. A packet-switched service works very much like a circuit-switched service, except that the user breaks data transmissions into predefined packets that conform to network protocols. With a dedicated circuit, the organization pays a fixed monthly fee, while with the other three, the organization pays on a per-use basis.

Dialed Circuit Services Dialed circuits are usually slow and noisy. With direct dialing, the normal voice telephone network is used for data transmission; the user dials the host computer telephone number through a modem. WATS is a special bulk rate service for direct-dial calls.

Dedicated Circuit Services A dedicated circuit is leased from the common carrier for exclusive use twenty-four hours per day, seven days per week. Faster and more noise-free transmissions are possible, but you must carefully plan the circuits you need because changes can be expensive. Voice-grade channels are analog circuits that are less noisy than dialed circuits. Wideband analog services are used for either data or voice transmission at higher speeds. T-carrier circuits are leased digital circuits with a range of digital services ranging from FT-1 (64 Kbps) to T-1 (1.544 Mbps) to T-4 (274 Mbps). The Synchronous Optical Network (SONET) uses fiber optics to provide services ranging from OC-1 (51 Mbps) to OC-12 (622 Mbps). Digital Subscriber Line service (DSL) and cable modems provide connections only from the subscriber's network to the common carrier's end office at a range of speeds from 64 Kbps to 30 Mbps, but suffer from a lack of standards.

Circuit-Switched Services Circuit-switched services enable you to define the end points of the wide area network, without specifying all the interconnecting circuits you will need, and still get the high data rates possible with dedicated circuit services. Narrowband Integrated Services Digital Network (ISDN) has been available since the late 1970s, but has not been widely adopted, due in part to conflicting interpretations of the ISDN standards by different vendors and common carriers. Basic rate interface ISDN provides a communication circuit with two 64 Kbps digital transmission channels and one 16 Kbps control channel. Primary rate interface ISDN consists of 23 64 Kbps data channels and one 64 Kbps control channel. Broadband ISDN, not yet widely available, offers much faster data speeds, ranging up to 622 Mbps.

Packet-Switched Services Packet switching is a technique in which messages are split into small segments. X.25 is an older, traditional service that provides slower service (up to 2 Mbps), but guarantees error-free delivery. Frame relay is a newer packet-switching service with higher data rates (up to 45 Mbps) but no error control. Asynchronous transfer mode (ATM) is one of the fastest-growing new technologies. ATM is similar to frame relay, in that it also does not perform error control and offers data rates up to 622 Mbps. Switched multimegabit data service (SMDS) is offered by many but not all common carriers. It offers data rates up to 45 Mbps.

Improving MAN/WAN Performance   One can improve network performance by utilizing front-end processors, by improving the speed of the devices themselves, and by using a better routing protocol. Analyzing network usage can show what circuits need to be increased or decreased in capacity, what new circuits need to be leased, and when additional switched circuits may be needed to meet peak demand. Performance may also be improved by reducing network demand by including a network usage analysis in all new application software, using data compression, shifting usage to off-peak times, establishing priorities for some applications, or redesigning the network to move data closer to those who use it.

Selecting MAN/WAN Services   The first issue is the quality of the vendor, because the largest cost in operating a MAN/WAN is network management. A second consideration is the network capacity you need. Flexibility is important because it is often hard to predict network usage. Dedicated circuits are less flexible than switched circuits, but can be cheaper if used constantly. Dedicated circuits also provide more control over message routing because your computers handle it. With switched services, the service provider performs the routing. The reliability of a network service—both in terms of average error rates and any circuit failures—is also important. In general, switched networks are more reliable because they have redundant circuits between various cities. VANs and VPNs are alternatives to service provided by common carriers.

Key Terms

2B+D

23B+D

available bit rate (ABR)

asynchronous transfer mode (ATM)

asymmetric digital subscriber line (ADSL)

basic rate interface (BRI)

broadband ISDN (B-ISDN)

cable modem

Canadian Radio–Television and Telecommunications Commission (CRTC)

channel service unit/data service unit (CSU/DSU)

circuit-switched services

committed information rate (CIR)

common carrier

conditioning

datagram

dedicated circuit services

dialed circuit services

digital service

digital subscriber line (DSL)

direct dialing (DD) service

discard eligible (DE)

fast packet services

Federal Communications Commission (FCC)

Fractional T-1

frame relay

frame relay access device (FRAD)

integrated services digital network (ISDN)

interexchange carrier (IXC)

local exchange carrier (LEC)

maximum allowable rate (MAR)

metropolitan area network (MAN)

narrowband ISDN

network terminator (NT-1, NT-2)

packet assembly/disassembly device (PAD)

packet-switched services

packetizing

permanent virtual circuit (PVC)

plain old telephone service (POTS)

point of presence (POP)

primary rate interface (PRI)

public utilities commission (PUC)

regional Bell operating company (RBOC)

reliable packet service

service profile identifier (SPID)

switched multimegabit data service (SMDS)

switched virtual circuit (SVC)

symmetric digital subscriber line (SDSL)

synchronous digital hierarchy (SDH)

synchronous optical network (SONET)

T-carrier circuit

T-1/T-2/T-3/T-4 circuits

unreliable packet services

value added network (VAN)

very high rate digital subscriber line (VDSL)

virtual circuit

virtual private network (VPN)

voice-grade circuit

wide area network (WAN)

wide area telephone service (WATS)

wideband analog service

X.25

Questions

1. Other than geographic differences, how do wide area networks differ from small local area networks?
2. What are a common carrier, local exchange carrier, and interexchange carrier?
3. Name three of the largest common carriers in North America.
4. Who regulates common carriers, and how is it done?
5. What is the difference between the FCC/CRTC and a PUC?
6. Describe how direct dialing services work.
7. What is WATS service?
8. How do dedicated circuits differ from dial-up circuits?
9. Is a WAN that uses dedicated circuits easier or harder to design than one that uses dialed circuits? Explain.
10. Are voice-grade circuits digital or analog?
11. How do wideband services differ from voice-grade services?
12. Why is conditioning performed?
13. Can the telephone company condition dial-up circuits? Why or why not?
14. What are the most commonly used T-carrier services? What data rates do they provide?
15. What are the two factors that distinguish T-1 circuits from voice-grade circuits?
16. Distinguish between T-1, T-2, T-3, and T-4 circuits.

17. Describe SONET. How does it differ from SDH?
18. What is DSL?
19. How does SDSL differ from ADSL?
20. What is a cable modem?
21. What distinguishes ISDN from other services?
22. How do basic rate interface and primary rate interface differ?
23. What is a 2B+D? Define it.
24. How does broadband ISDN differ from narrowband ISDN?
25. What are the problems with ISDN in North America today?
26. How do packet-switching services differ from other wide area networks services?
27. How is a virtual circuit distinguished from other circuits?
28. Where does packetizing take place?
29. What does a packet contain?
30. How does a reliable packet service differ from an unreliable packet service?
31. How do datagram services differ from virtual circuit services?
32. How does a switched virtual circuit differ from a permanent virtual circuit?
33. How does frame relay differ from ATM?
34. How does ATM differ from frame relay?
35. How does SMDS differ from ATM?
36. Which is likely to be the longer-term winner, X.25, frame relay, ATM, or SMDS?

37. Explain the differences between CIR and MAR.

38. How can you improve WAN performance?

39. Describe five important factors in selecting WAN services.

40. What is a VAN?

41. How do VPN services differ from common carrier services?

Exercises

A. Find out the data rates and costs of T-carrier and ISDN services in your area.

B. Find out the data rates and costs of packet-switched services in your area.

C. Find out the data rates and costs of DSL and cable modem services in your area.

D. Find a new type of service in the DSL family (e.g., Rate Adaptive DSL: RADSL) and describe how it works and the data rates it provides.

E. Examine Figure 9–11. What other options did Home Depot likely consider? Explain the trade-offs among the different services available to Home Depot. What services would you have selected?

F. Examine Figure 9–14. What other options did Northrop Grumman likely consider? Explain the trade-offs among the different services available to Grumman. What services would you have selected?

G. Examine Figure 9–15. The school district chose to use a wide variety of network services. What other options did they likely consider? Explain the trade-offs among the different services available. What services would you have selected?

NEXT DAY AIR SERVICE CASE STUDY

President Coone and the board of directors are focusing on the kinds of communication facilities NDAS will need over the next several years. The current WAN uses dial-up circuits to connect the remote offices to Atlanta and New Orleans and private leased circuits to connect these two hubs to Tampa. Figure 1–6 shows the current NDAS offices.

President Coone meets with you to discuss the future of communications for Next Day Air Service. He believes that NDAS needs a network that can be expanded readily without having a major effect on the way the company conducts its routine business. He assumes that NDAS will continue its rapid growth pattern, and he wants a recommendation on what steps may be necessary to enable NDAS to meet the competition. Next Day Air Service considers the Mississippi River as the East/West dividing line for the continental United States. The projected growth trends are as follows:

* **Western United States:** Traffic volumes will increase by 400 percent over the next three years, and one additional office will be opened every four months.

* **Eastern United States:** Traffic volumes will increase by 300 percent over the next three years, and one additional office will be opened every six months.

* **International Market:** Traffic volumes will increase by 100 percent each year over the next three years, and additional offices will be opened in London, Paris, Rome, Berlin, Madrid, Bogota, and Caracas.

Exercises

1. With your knowledge of NDAS's network, what service would you recommend for the future to connect the remote offices to the hubs at Atlanta and New Orleans and the hubs to the corporate office in Tampa? Will the current facilities be adequate?

2. President Coone has just informed you that NDAS is considering placing several new offices in Chicago and Los Angeles. Each office would have its own LAN. What factors would determine the use of a metropolitan area network (MAN) to connect NDAS offices in a single city together?

CHAPTER 10

Network Design

Network managers perform two key tasks: (1) designing new networks and network upgrades; and (2) managing the day-to-day operation of existing networks. This chapter examines network design. One problem when designing data communication networks is how best to adapt new technology to meet the changing and challenging networking needs of organizations. This chapter presents one approach to designing networks and then discusses several commonly used MAN/WAN, backbone, and LAN designs.

Objectives

* Become familiar with the overall process of designing and implementing a network
* Become familiar with commonly used MAN and WAN designs
* Understand commonly used backbone designs
* Understand commonly used LAN designs

Chapter Outline

❋❋ INTRODUCTION

Most organizations today have LANs, BNs, and WANs. Therefore, most network design projects involve the design of upgrades or extensions to existing networks, rather than the construction of entirely new networks. Even the network for an entirely new building is likely to be integrated with the organization's existing BN or WAN, so even new projects can be seen as extensions to existing networks. Nonetheless, network design is very challenging.

The *traditional network design approach* follows a structured systems analysis and design process similar to that used to build application systems. First, the network analyst meets with users to identify user needs and the application systems planned for the network. Second, the analyst develops a precise estimate of the amount of data that each user will send and receive and uses this to estimate the total amount of traffic on each part of the network. Third, the analyst designs circuits needed to support this traffic plus a modest increase in traffic and obtains costs estimates from vendors. Finally, a year or two later the network is built and implemented.

This traditional approach, although expensive and time-consuming, works well for static or slowly evolving networks. Unfortunately, networking today is significantly different than it was when the traditional approach was developed. Three forces are making the traditional design approach less appropriate for many of today's networks.

First, the underlying technology of the client and server computers, networking devices, and the circuits themselves is rapidly changing. Ten years ago, mainframes dominated networks, the typical client computer was an 8 MHz 386 with 1 Mb of RAM and 40 Mb of hard disk space, and a typical circuit was a 9600 bps mainframe connection or (rarely) an amazingly fast 1 Mbps LAN connection. Five years ago, the typical client was a 33 MHz 486 with 4 Mb of RAM and a 120-Mb hard disk, and the typical circuit was a 2400 or 9600 bps modem connection or an amazingly fast 4 Mbps LAN connection.

Second, the growth in network traffic is immense. The challenge is not in estimating today's user demand, but in estimating its rate of growth. Ten years ago, electronic mail and the Internet were novelties primarily used by university professors and scientists. Five years ago, virtually no one had heard of the Web. In the past, network demand essentially was driven by predictable business systems such as order processing. Today, much network demand is driven by less predictable user behavior, such as e-mail and Web searches. Many experts expect the rapid increase in network demand to continue, especially as video, voice and multimedia applications become commonplace on networks. At a 10 percent growth rate, user demand on a given network will increase by one-third in three years. At 20 percent, it will increase by about 75 percent in three years. At 30 percent, it will double in less than three years. A minor mistake in estimating the growth rate can lead to major problems. With such rapid growth, it is no longer possible to accurately predict network needs. In the past, it was not uncommon for networks to be designed to last for five to ten years. Today, most network designers use at most a three-year planning horizon.

Finally, the balance of costs has changed dramatically over the past ten years. Ten years ago, the most expensive item in any network was the hardware (circuits, devices, and servers). Today, the most expensive part of the network is the staff who design, operate, and maintain it. As the costs have shifted, the emphasis in network design is no longer on minimizing hardware cost (although it is important); the emphasis today is on designing networks to reduce the time taken to operate them. One way of reducing costs is to standardize network components by using as many of the same circuits, devices, and servers as possible.

Management Focus: *The End of Architecture*

All good things must end. After a century of predictability, the telephone network as we know it is fading into oblivion. Lulled to sleep by relatively predictable voice and data traffic forecasts, interexchange carriers (IXCs) set a timetable for a gradual replacement of existing networks with faster all-ATM network architectures. Their leisurely replacement timetable ran smack into a brick wall.

Huge increases in data traffic, primarily due to the booming growth of the Internet, have caused IXCs to throw out the nicely planned replacements of their core telephone networks. Rather than investing in all-ATM architectures whose main benefit is the ability to handle voice, data and video on the same circuits, IXCs have started building "overlay networks." Overlay networks co-exist with the primary core voice networks and support

separate services in an attempt to keep up with the demand. One set of overlay networks, for example, is designed to support Internet traffic, another carries frame relay WAN traffic, another carries SMDS services, and so on.

The core telephone network is gradually changing from a centrally designed and managed hierarchical network to a decentralized set of networks, much the same changes that have been seen in the office environment as decentralized client-server LANs have replaced the centralized host-based mainframe systems. The key challenges now facing IXCs are how to manage this huge—and rapidly growing—collection of distinct networks and how to route traffic from one network to another.

Source: tele.com, September 1996.

Some organizations still use the traditional approach to network design, particularly for those applications requiring unusually expensive hardware or network circuits (e.g., WANs that cover long distances through many different countries). However, many other organizations now use a simpler approach to network design that we call the *building block approach*. Rather than attempting to accurately predict user traffic on the network, and building networks to meet those demands, the building block approach starts by classifying users (or sets of users at one location) as "typical" or "high volume." The network is then planned by adding circuits using a few standard network designs. These circuits are again classified as "typical" or "high volume." In some cases, the designer uses several categories of high-volume users or circuits, but the goal is to keep the design simple, rather than to be very precise.

Once the network is designed in these terms, the designer estimates the network needs of each category of user and circuit in terms of current technology (e.g., 10Base-T, 100Base-T). In this way, the network design is general and can easily be changed as needs and technologies change. The difficulty, of course, lies in predicting user demand so one can define the technologies needed. Most organizations solve this by building far more capacity than they expect to need, and by designing networks that can easily grow and then closely monitoring growth. Thus, they expand the network ahead of the growth pattern.

This chapter focuses on the building block approach to network design. In the following section, we describe the basic process used to design networks following the building block approach. We then examine several commonly used designs for WANs/MANs, backbone networks, and LANs.

✳✳ THE NETWORK DESIGN PROCESS

The network design process discussed in this section is a simple, straightforward approach that we call the building block approach. The building block approach attempts to build the network using a series of simple, predefined building com-

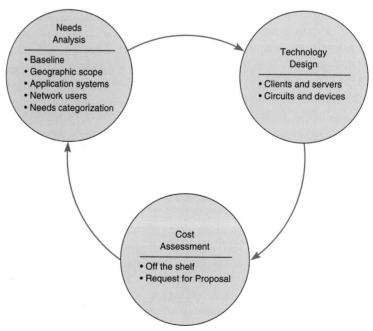

Figure 10–1 Network design.

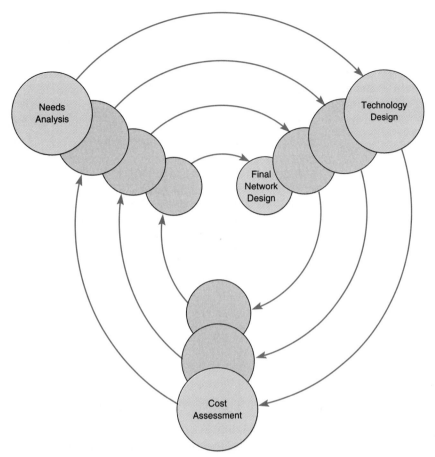

Figure 10–2 The cyclical nature of network design.

ponents, rather than attempting to develop precise estimates of a network for each network user or network segment. The result is a simpler design process and a more easily managed network built with a smaller range of components.

The basic process involves three steps that are performed repeatedly: *needs analysis*, *technology design*, and *cost assessment* (see Figure 10–1). During needs analysis, the designer attempts to understand the current and future network needs of the various users, departments, and applications. This is likely to be an educated guess, at best. Next the designer examines the available technologies and begins to assess which options will meet the users' needs. Then, the relative costs of the technologies are considered. The process then cycles back to the needs analysis, which is refined using the technology and cost information to produce a new assessment of users' needs. This, in turn, triggers changes in the technology design and cost assessment, and so on. By cycling through these three processes, the network design process settles on the final network design (see Figure 10–2).

One key element of network design is the analysis and design of network security. Network security is discussed in the next chapter.

Needs Analysis

The goal of needs analysis is to understand why the network is being built and what users and applications it will support. In many cases, the network is being designed to improve poor performance or enable new applications to be used. In other cases, the network is upgraded to replace unreliable or aging equipment, or to standardize equipment so that only one type of equipment, one protocol (e.g., TCP/IP, Ethernet), or one vendor's equipment is used everywhere in the network.

The first point that must be made about a needs analysis is that much of the work may already have been done. Most network design projects today are network upgrades, rather than the design of entirely new networks so there is already a fairly good understanding of the existing traffic in the network, and most importantly, of the rate of growth of network traffic. In this case, it is important to understand the current operations (application systems and messages). This step provides a *baseline* against which future design requirements can be gauged. It should provide a clear picture of the current sequence of operations, processing times, work volumes, current communication network (if one exists), existing costs, and user/management needs. Whether the network is a new network or a network upgrade, the primary objective of this stage is to define the geographic scope of the network and the users and applications that will use it.

Geographic Scope

The first step is to define the geographic scope of the network. A data communication network can have four basic levels of *geographic scope.*

* Wide area network (within several states, provinces, or countries)
* Metropolitan area network (within a city)
* Campus area network (within a series of buildings located in the same general area)
* Local area network (within one building)

It is easiest to start with the highest level, so most designers begin by drawing a network map with all the international or country-wide locations that must be connected. A map that shows lines going between the countries/cities is sufficient. Details such as the type of circuit and other considerations will be added later. Next, the designer prepares a map for each city and maps for the campus-area networks. Finally, the designer prepares the local facility "maps" (really pictorial diagrams, because designers generally use blueprints or drawings of the buildings).

At this point, the designers gather general information and characteristics of the environment in which the network must operate. For example, they determine whether there are any legal requirements, such as local, state/provincial, federal, or international laws, regulations, or building codes, that might affect the network.

Application Systems

The designers must review the list of applications that currently use the network and identify the location of each one so that all of them will be interconnected by the planned network. This information should be added to the preliminary geographic maps. This process is called *baselining*. Next those applications that are expected to use the network in the future are added.

In many cases, the applications will be relatively well defined. Specific internal applications (e.g., payroll), and external applications (e.g., Web servers) may already be part of the "old" network. However, it is important to review the organization's long-range and short-range plans concerning changes in company goals, strategic plans, development plans for new products or services, projections of sales, research and development projects, major capital expenditures, possible changes in product mix, new offices that must be served by the communication network, security issues, and future commitments to technology. For example, a major expansion in the number of offices or a major electronic commerce initiative will significantly affect network requirements.

It also is helpful to identify the hardware and software requirements of each application that will use the network, and, if possible, the message type each application uses. This knowledge helps now, and will be particularly useful later when developing technological solutions. For example, if the main financial application payroll runs on an IBM mainframe, the network will need to support SNA traffic, or provide a gateway to translate it into more standard protocols.

Network Users

In the past, application systems accounted for the majority of network traffic. Today, much network traffic is produced by the discretionary use of the Internet. Applications such electronic mail and the Web are generating significant traffic. This is likely to continue in the future as network-hungry applications such as desktop videoconferencing become more common. Therefore, in addition to understanding the applications, you must also assess the number and type of users that will generate and receive network traffic. The network manager is no longer in control of the network traffic generated on his or her networks.

Categorizing Network Needs

At this point, the network has been designed in terms of geographic scope, application systems and users. The next step is to assess the relative amount of traffic generated in each segment of the network. With the traditional design approach, this involves considerable detailed analysis. With the building block approach, the goal is to provide some rough assessment of the relative magnitude of network needs. Each application system is assessed in general terms to determine the amount of network traffic it can be expected to generate today and in the future, compared to other applications. Likewise, each user is categorized as a "typical" user or a "high traffic" user. These assessments will be refined in the next stage of the design process.

This assessment can be problematic, but the goal is some relative understanding of the network needs. Some simple rules of thumb can help. For example, applications that require large amounts of multimedia data or those that load executables over the network are likely to be high-traffic applications. Applications

---

Management Focus: Why Projects Fail

CIMI Corporation surveyed almost 300 organizations about the key success factors in network design. These 300 organizations reported on 1370 network design projects. Of these, 475 (35 percent) were considered complete successes and 125 (9 percent) were considered complete failures. The rest were partial successes.

Network managers reported that the key problems leading to failure in the 125 failed projects were (multiple answers were permitted):

* Technology design problems
  * 99 percent bought the wrong equipment or services; often the right technology but the wrong products or features
  * 38 percent encountered vendor misrepresentation; the products and/or services did not work as promised

* Needs analysis problems
  * 64 percent had incomplete or inaccurate requirements
  * 30 percent encountered a significant change in business requirements as the network was installed.
* Overall problems with the design process
  * 34 percent lacked network design skills internally and did not use external consultants or systems integrators
  * 32 percent used external network consultants or systems integrators who bungled the project

Source: Network World, July 7, 1997.

---

that are time sensitive or need constant updates (e.g., financial information systems, order processing) are likely to be high-traffic applications.

Once the network requirements have been identified, they also should be organized into *mandatory requirements, desirable requirements,* and *wish list requirements.* This information enables you to develop a minimum level of mandatory requirements and a negotiable list of desirable requirements that are dependent on cost and availability. For example, desktop videoconferencing may be a wish list item, but will be omitted if it increases the cost of the network beyond the desired cost.

Deliverables

The key deliverables for the needs assessment stage are a set of network maps, showing the applications and the circuits, clients, and servers in the proposed network. These will be categorized as "typical" or "high traffic."

For example, Figure 10–3 shows the results of a needs assessment for a simple network in one building. This shows a series of six LANs connected by one backbone network, that is in turn connected onto a campus area backbone network. One of the six LANs is highlighted as a high-traffic LAN, while the others are typical. Three mandatory applications are identified that will be used by all network users: e-mail, Web, and file sharing. One wish list requirement (desktop videoconferencing) is also identified for a portion of the network.

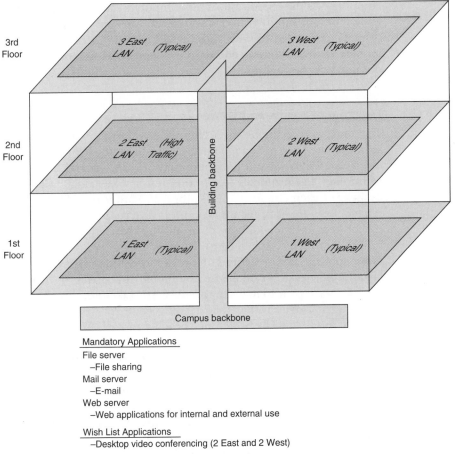

Figure 10–3 Example needs assessment.

Technology Design

Once the needs have been defined, the next step is to develop a *technology design* (or set of possible designs) for the network. The network design starts with the application systems, the users and the client and server computers needed to support them. If the network is a new network, new computers will need to be purchased. If the network is an existing network, the servers may need to be upgraded to the newest technology. Once these are designed, then the circuits connecting them are designed.

Designing Clients and Servers

The idea behind the building block approach is to specify the computers needed in terms of some standard units. "Typical" users are allocated the "base level" client computers, as are servers supporting "typical" applications. Users and servers for applications needing more powerful computers are assigned some "advanced" computer. As the specifications for computers rapidly improve and costs drop (usually every four months), today's "typical" user may receive the type of computer originally intended for the "advanced" user when the network is actually implemented (and the "advanced" users may end up with a computer not available when the network was designed).

Designing Circuits and Devices

The same is true for network circuits and devices (e.g., hubs, routers, switches), although the pace of change is slower for these than for computers. There are two interrelated decisions in designing network circuits and devices: the fundamental technology and protocols (e.g., Ethernet or token ring, TCP/IP or SNA) and the capacity of each circuit (e.g., 10 Mbps, 100 Mbps or 1000 Mbps). These are interrelated, because each technology offers different circuit capacities. In some cases, certain technologies look more promising than others (e.g., most experts expect Ethernet to replace token ring). In other cases, certain technologies are obviously more appropriate for existing network environments (e.g., it makes little sense to install Ethernet in an otherwise completely token ring environment, unless there is a long-term plan to migrate to Ethernet). Likewise, it is always safer to use established technologies rather than leading edge (or "bleeding edge") technologies that are unstable or for which no formal standards exist.

Designing the circuit capacity means *capacity planning*, estimating the size and type of the "standard" and "advanced" network circuits for each type of network (LAN, BN, WAN). For example, should the standard LAN circuit be 10Base-T, 100Base-X, or 10/100 switched Ethernet? Likewise, should the standard backbone circuit be 100Base-X or ATM-155?

This requires some assessment of the current and future *circuit loading* (the amount of data transmitted on a circuit). This analysis can focus on either the *average* circuit traffic or the *peak* circuit traffic. For example, in an online banking network, traffic volume peaks usually are in the midmorning (bank opening) and just prior to closing. Airline and rental car reservations network designers look for peak message volumes during holidays or other vacation periods, and telephone companies normally have their highest peak volumes on Mother's Day. Designing for peak circuit traffic is the ideal.

The designer usually starts with the total characters transmitted per day on each circuit or, if possible, the maximum number of characters transmitted per two-second interval if peaks must be met. You can calculate message volumes by counting messages in a current network and applying some estimated growth rate. If an existing network is in place, network monitors/analyzers may be able to provide an actual circuit character count of the volume transmitted per minute or per day.

A good rule of thumb is that 80 percent of this circuit loading information is easy to gather. The last 20 percent needed for very precise estimates is extremely difficult and expensive to find. However, precision is not a major concern because of the stairstep nature of communication circuits and the need to project future needs. For example, the difference between 10Base-T and 100-Base-X is quite large, and assessing which level is needed for "typical" traffic does not require a lot of precision. Forecasts are inherently less precise than understanding current network traffic. The *turnpike effect* results when the network is used to a greater extent than was anticipated because it is available, is very efficient, and provides new services. The growth factor for network use varies from 5 to 50 percent and, in some cases, can exceed 100 percent for high-growth organizations.

Although no organization wants to overbuild its network and pay for more capacity than it needs, in most cases, going back and upgrading a network significantly increases costs. Few organizations complain about having too much network capacity, but being under capacity can cause significant problems. Given the rapid growth in network demand and the difficulty in accurately predicting it, most organizations intentionally overbuild (build more capacity into their network than they plan to use), and most end up using this supposedly unneeded capacity within a few years.

Network Design Tools

Network modeling and design tools can perform a number of functions to help in the technology design process. With most tools, the first step is to enter a map or model of the existing network or proposed network design. Some modeling tools require the user to create the network map from scratch. That is, the user must enter all of the network components by hand, placing each server, client computer, and circuit on the map and defining what each is (e.g., 10base-T, frame relay circuit with a 1 Mbps committed information rate).

Other tools can "discover" the existing network. In this case, the user provides some starting point, and the modeling software explores the network and automatically draws the map itself. Once the map is complete, the user can then change

---

Management Focus: *Capacity Planning at Airborne Express*

The 1997 strike at United Parcel Service (UPS) caused many problems for other parcel delivery companies and their customers. Airborne Express emerged from the strike with few problems.

Airborne has two teams dedicated to capacity planning. One eight-person team tracks usage of Airborne's mainframes and servers. A second two-person team tracks circuit usage. Both teams use capacity planning tools from Computer Associates to help monitor and design Airborne's networks.

These teams had tracked Airborne's growth in network usage for many years prior to the strike and had predicted a major surge in network usage (unrelated to the UPS strike). As a result, Airborne increased its circuit capacities by 40 percent and replaced one of its mainframes with a 30 percent faster one early in 1997.

When the UPS strike occurred, Airborne experienced a 40 percent increase in shipments over the same period in 1996. The network performed flawlessly.

Source: "Delivered on Time," *PC Week*, September 8, 1997.

it to reflect the new network design. Obviously, a tool that can perform network discovery by itself is most helpful when the network being designed is an upgrade to an existing network, and when the network is very complex.

Once the map is complete, the next step is to add information about the expected network traffic to see if the network can support the level of traffic that is expected. *Simulation* is used to model the behavior of the communication network. Simulation is a mathematical technique in which the network comes to life and behaves as it would under "real" conditions; applications and users generate and respond to messages and the simulator tracks the number of packets in the network, and the delays encountered at each point in the network.

Simulation models may be tailored to the user's needs by entering parameter values specific to the network at hand (e.g., this computer will generate an average of three 100-byte packets per minute). Alternatively, the user may prefer to rely primarily on the set of average values provided by the network.

Technology Focus: Network Design Tools

There are many network design tools currently available to assist in capacity planning. Some of the most commonly used tools include:

* Comnet by CACI International Inc. (www.caci.com)
* Block Oriented Network Simulator by Cadence Design Systems Inc. (www.cadence.com)
* CA-MICS by Computer Associates International Inc. (www.cai.com)

* NetArchitect by Zitel Corp. (www.zitel.com)
* NetMaker Solution by Make Systems Inc. (www.make.com)
* Optimal Solution by Optimal Networks Inc. (www.optimal.com)

Source: "Cool Tools," *PC Week*, September 8, 1997, and "Predicting the Future," *Infoworld*, May 5, 1997.

Once the simulation is complete, the user can examine the results to see the estimated response times and throughput. It is important to note that these network design tools only provide estimates, which may vary from the actual results. At this point the user can change the network design in an attempt to eliminate bottlenecks and re-run the simulation. Good modeling tools not only produce simulation results, but also highlight potential trouble spots (e.g., servers, circuits, or devices that experienced long response times). The very best tools offer suggestions on how to overcome the problems that the simulation identified (e.g., network segmentation, increasing from T1 to T3).

Deliverables

The key deliverables at this point are a revised set of network maps that include general specifications for the hardware and software required. In most cases, the

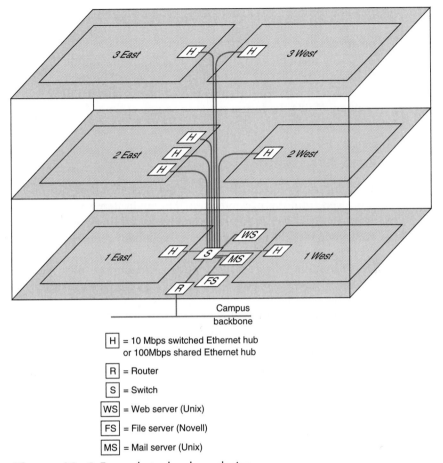

Figure 10–4 Example technology design.

critical part is the design of the network circuits. In the case of a new network designed from scratch, it is also very important to define the client computers with care, because these will form a large portion of the total cost of the network. Usually, however, the network will replace an existing network and only a few of the client computers in the existing network will be upgraded.

Figure 10–4 shows the results of the technology design for the simple network in Figure 10–3. In this case, 10/100 Ethernet has been chosen as the standard network. Typical users initially will be allocated 10Base-T Ethernet, while the high-traffic users will be allocated either switched 10 Mbps Ethernet or 100Base-T shared Ethernet, depending on cost. The high-traffic LAN on 2 East has been segmented into three LAN segments to improve performance. All LAN cabling will be category 5 cable so that all users can easily move to 100 Mbps in the future.

The building backbone will be connected directly into the campus backbone using a router. The building backbone will use fiber optic cable to enable the possible future addition of desktop videoconferencing. The backbone will be either switched 10 Mbps Ethernet (as shown) or 100Base-F shared Ethernet, depending on cost.

The main file server will be a high-power computer running Novell NetWare to provide file sharing. Two separate severs will be used as a mail server and a Web server, both Unix. All three servers will be connected directly to the building backbone to enable the fastest possible response time.

Cost Assessment

The purpose of *cost assessment* is to assess the costs of various network alternatives produced from the previous step. The main items are the costs of software, hardware, and circuits. These three factors are all interconnected and must be considered along with the performance and reliability required. All factors are interrelated with regard to cost.

Estimating the cost of a network is quite complex because many factors are not immediately obvious. Some of the costs to consider are:

* Circuit costs, including costs of circuits provided by common carriers or the cost of purchasing and installing your own cable

* Internetworking devices such as bridges, switches, routers, or gateways

* Hardware costs including server computers, network interface cards, hubs, memory, printers, uninterruptible power supplies, and backup tape drives

* Software costs for network operating system, application software, and middleware

* Network management costs including special hardware, software, and training needed to develop a network management system for ongoing redesign, monitoring, and diagnosing of problems

* Test and maintenance costs for special monitoring equipment and software, plus the cost of on-site spare parts

Request for Proposal (RFP)

Although some network components can be purchased "off-the-shelf," most organizations develop a *request for proposal (RFP)* before making large network purchases. RFPs specify what equipment, software, and services are desired and ask vendors to provide their best prices. Some RFPs are very specific about what items are to be provided in what time frame. In other cases, items are defined as mandatory, important, or desirable, or several scenarios are provided and the vendor is asked to propose the best solution. In a few cases, RFPs specify generally what is required and the vendors are asked to propose their own network designs. Figure 10–5 provides a summary of the key parts of an RFP.

Once the vendors have submitted their proposals, the organization evaluates them against specified criteria and selects the winner(s). Depending on the scope

Information in a Typical RFP

* Background Information
  * Organizational profile
  * Overview of current network
  * Overview of new network
  * Goals of new network
* Network Requirements
  * Choice sets of possible network designs (hardware, software, circuits)
  * Mandatory, desirable, and wish list items
  * Security and control requirements
  * Response time requirements
  * Guidelines for proposing new network designs
* Service Requirements
  * Implementation time plan
  * Training courses and materials
  * Support services (e.g., spare parts on site)
  * Reliability and performance guarantees
* Bidding Process
  * Time schedule for the bidding process
  * Ground rules
  * Bid evaluation criteria
  * Availability of additional information
* Information required from vendor
  * Vendor corporate profile
  * Experience with similar networks
  * Hardware and software benchmarks
  * Reference list

Figure 10-5 Request for proposal.

and complexity of the network, it is sometimes necessary to redesign the network based on the information in the vendor's proposals.

One of the key decisions in the RFP process is the scope of the RFP. Will you use one vendor or several vendors for all hardware, software, and services? Multivendor environments tend to provide better performance because it is unlikely that one vendor makes the "best" hardware, software, and services in all categories. Multivendor networks also tend to be less expensive because it is unlikely that one vendor will always have the cheapest hardware, software, and services in all product categories.

Management Focus: *The Get-Tough Guide to Telecom Contracts*

The fourteen commandments of telecom contracts (or how to reduce your network costs):

1. **Beware of MRC.** The minimum revenue commitment (the minimum amount you agree to spend) is the worst threat lying in wait in a phone contract. Make sure your firm can meet it.

2. **Bargain with everybody.** Beyond the three largest long-distance companies, AT&T, MCI, Sprint, are some smaller firms that offer attractive deals.

3. **Know what everyone else is paying.** Contract tariffs can be found in FCC filings or through consultants.

4. **Get the most overall flexibility possible.** Usually, the best deal is the shortest deal possible in terms of years with the minimum MRC and some ability to switch from leased lines to frame relay.

5. **Get the most fine-grained flexibility possible.** Long-term contracts tend to be less flexible in areas such as the speeds of leased lines.

6. **Demand a fixed price.** Virtually all contracts currently charge floating rates for services included, and they have been increasing annually.

7. **Specify every service you can.** Unless they are written in the contract, special features are not included in the contract, even if they are ordinary services.

8. **Insist on free installations.** In addition to discounts, most carriers are willing to waive the installation fee for leased circuits and services.

9. **Demand "most-favored" status.** Larger firms can negotiate aggressively to receive a lower tariff rate if another customer is awarded a lower tariff.

10. **Worry about the divorce when you get hitched.** You typically have to pay a penalty of about one-half of the remaining agreement.

11. **Beware of monitoring conditions.** Beware of conditions like "60 percent of calls have to be made during regular business hours."

12. **Check your bills.** The more complicated the contract, the more mistakes occur.

13. **Aggregate selectively.** With no flexibility in the contract, don't include anything you'll have to change.

14. **Get professional advice.**

Source: "The Get Tough Guide to Telecom Contracts," *Datamation*, March 15, 1995.

Multivendor environments can be more difficult to manage, however. If equipment is not working properly and it is provided by two different vendors, each can blame the other for the problem. In contrast, a single vendor is solely responsible for everything.

Selling the Proposal to Management
One of the main problems in network design is obtaining the support of senior management. In their mind, the network is simply a cost center, something on which the organization is spending a lot of money with little apparent change. The network keeps on running just as it did the year before.

The key to gaining senior management acceptance lies in speaking their language. It is pointless to talk about upgrades from 10 Mbps to 100 Mbps on the backbone, because this terminology is meaningless to them. A more compelling argument is to discuss the growth in network use. For example, a simple graph that shows network usage growing at 25 percent per year, compared to the network budget growing at 10 percent per year, presents a powerful illustration that the network costs are well managed, not out of control.

Likewise, a focus on network reliability is an easily understandable issue. For example, if the network supports a mission-critical system such as order processing or moving point-of-sale data from retail stores to corporate offices, it is clear from a business perspective that the network must be available and performing properly, or the organization will lose revenue.

Deliverables

There are three key deliverables for this step. The first is an RFP that goes to potential vendors. The second deliverable, after the vendor has been selected, is the revised network set of maps from Figure 10–4 with the technology design complete. Exact products and costs are specified at this point (e.g., a 3Com 3500 Layer-3 switch with four 16-port 10Base-T modules). The third deliverable is the business case that provides support for the network design, expressed in business objectives.

✳✳ COMMON WIDE AREA NETWORK DESIGNS

Most organizations do not build their own WANs by laying cable, building microwave towers, or sending up satellites. Instead, most organizations lease circuits from interexchange carriers (e.g., AT&T, Sprint), and use those to transmit their data. Nonetheless, all organizations must design their data networks, or at least hire a network consultant to design them.

Once the major connection points on the WAN have been identified (e.g., cities), the next step is to design the circuits that will connect those locations. The three basic designs used for WANs are ring, star, and mesh. Each refers to a different *topology*, the basic geometric layout of the network. In practice, most WANs are a mix of these three basic designs. A WAN may start as a pure ring design, for example, and then needs change so that a mesh component is added.

Ring-Based WAN Design

A *ring-based WAN design* connects all computers in a closed loop, with each computer linked to the next, usually with a series of point-to-point dedicated circuits (e.g., T1). In a LAN with a ring topology, messages can pass around the ring only in one

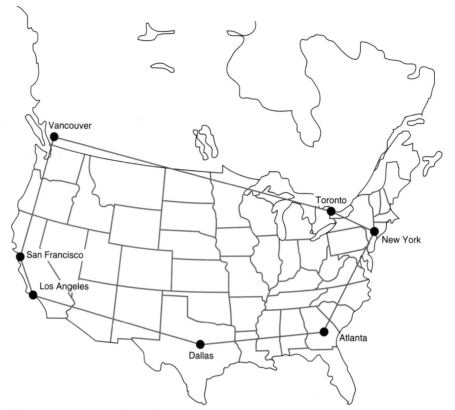

Figure 10–6 Ring-based design.

direction because the circuits are simplex circuits. In a WAN with a ring topology, the circuits are full-duplex circuits, meaning that messages flow in both directions around the ring. Computers in the ring may send data in one direction or the other, depending on which direction is the shortest to the destination. Figure 10–6 shows a basic ring-based WAN.

One disadvantage of the ring topology is that messages can take a long time to travel from the sender to the receiver. Messages usually travel through several computers and circuits before they reach their destination, so traffic delays can build up very quickly if one circuit or computer becomes overloaded. A long delay in any one circuit or computer can significantly affect the entire network.

In general, the failure of any one circuit or computer in the network means that the network can continue to function. Messages are simply routed away from the failed circuit or computer in the opposite direction around the ring. However, if the network is operating close to its capacity, this will dramatically increase transmissions times because the traffic on the remaining part of the network may come close to doubling (because all traffic originally routed in the direction of the failed link will now be routed in the opposite direction through the longest way around the ring).

Star-Based WAN Design

A *star-based WAN design* connects all computers to one central computer that routes messages to the appropriate computer, usually via a series of point-to-point dedicated circuits (see Figure 10–7). Each computer is linked by a separate full-duplex point-to-point circuit through the central computer.

The star topology is easy to manage because the central computer receives and routes all messages in the network. It can also be faster than the ring network because any message needs to travel through at most two circuits to reach its destination (whereas messages may have to travel through far more circuits in the ring network). However, the star topology is the most susceptible to traffic problems because the central computer must process all messages on the network. The central computer must have sufficient capacity to handle traffic peaks or it may become overloaded and network performance will suffer.

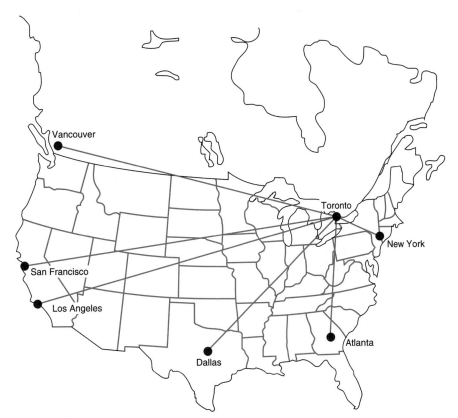

Figure 10–7 Star-based design.

In general, the failure of any one circuit or computer affects only the one computer on that circuit. However, if the central computer fails, the entire network fails because all traffic must flow through it. It is critical that the central computer be extremely reliable.

Mesh-Based WAN Design

Mesh-based WAN designs can be either full mesh or partial mesh. In a *full mesh design,* every computer is connected to every other computer, often by point-to-point dedicated circuits (see Figure 10–8a). Full mesh networks are seldom used because of the extremely high cost. *Partial mesh designs,* in which many, but not all, computers are connected, are far more common (see Figure 10–8b). Most WAN networks use partial mesh topologies.

The effects of the loss of computers or circuits in a mesh network depend entirely on the circuits available in the network. If there are many possible routes through the network, the loss of one or even several circuits or computers may have few effects beyond the specific computers involved. However, if there are only a few circuits in the network, the loss of even one circuit or computer may seriously impair the network.

In general, mesh networks combine the performance benefits of both ring networks and star networks. Mesh networks usually provide relatively short routes through the network (compared to ring networks) and provide many possible routes through the network to prevent any one circuit or computer from becoming overloaded when there is a lot of traffic (compared to star networks in which all traffic goes through one computer).

The drawback is that mesh networks use decentralized routing so that each computer in the network performs its own routing. This requires more processing by each computer in the network than in star or ring networks. Also, the transmission of network status information (e.g., how busy each computer is) "wastes" network capacity.

Cloud-based mesh designs are becoming very popular. With this design, all computers are simply connected into a packet-switched network (e.g., frame relay) provided by a common carrier (e.g., MCI, AT&T, BellSouth); see Figure 10–9. In this case, the common carrier is responsible for switching packets (or circuits) through its network.

Cloud-based designs are simpler for the organization because they move the burden of network design and management from the organization to the common carrier. However, this comes at a price. Cloud-based designs are often more expensive. Cloud-based designs are often used when network managers are uncertain of network demand, particularly in a new or rapidly growing network. They are very flexible because many different data rates are available and because network designers do not need to worry about the traffic sent between each computer, as they would when using dedicated circuits. Instead they just need to specify the amount of traffic entering and leaving each computer and have a great deal of flexibility in

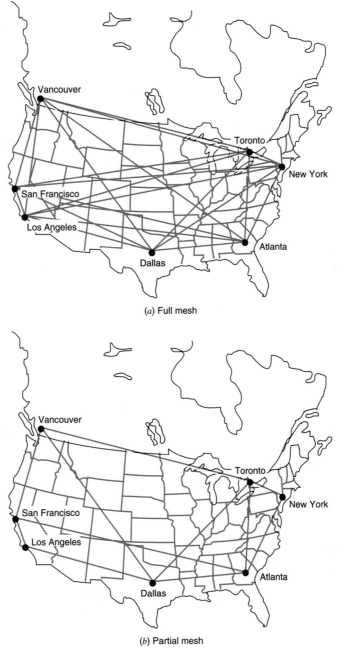

(*a*) Full mesh

(*b*) Partial mesh

Figure 10–8 Mesh design.

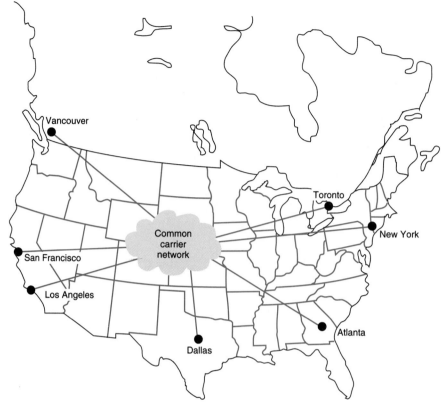

Figure 10–9 Cloud-based mesh design.

specifying that, too; see Chapter 9 for a discussion of the committed information rate versus maximum allowable rate.

✳✳ COMMON BACKBONE NETWORK DESIGNS

With WANs, the most important issues are centered around the geographic layout of the network and basic topology. Topology is also important for backbone networks, but the most important characteristic is the way in which packets are moved from one network segment to another network segment across the backbone. The primary job of the backbone is, after all, to move packets from one network segment to another or to an external WAN such as the Internet.

There are three basic approaches used in backbone networks to move packets from one segment to another: routing (using network layer addresses), bridging

Management Focus: Fish & Richardson's WAN

Fish & Richardson, a technology-savvy law firm with offices across the United States, is pioneering the use of technology in court cases. Most of its cases are conducted by teams of lawyers drawn from two or three of its seven major offices. Communication among the offices is critical.

Fish & Richardson uses a cloud-based design with a frame relay network (see Figure 10–10). Each office is connected into the frame relay cloud using a 3Com router at speeds up to 512 Kbps. The WAN is also connected into the Internet via a T-1 circuit in the Boston office.

Source: "Fast Ethernet and the Law," *PC Week,* June 16, 1997.

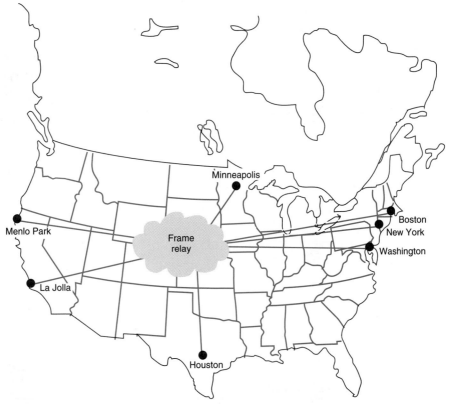

Figure 10–10 Fish & Richardson's WAN.

(using data link layer addresses), and switching (usually using data link layer addresses, but sometimes using network layer addresses). Today, the most common design is a routed backbone, but switched backbones are becoming more common. Some organizations use a combination of these basic designs, a bridged backbone in one place, a routed one in another, and a switched one in another.

We will focus on TCP/IP networks when comparing these three designs. If you have not read Chapters 6 and 8 for a while, you may want to go back and review

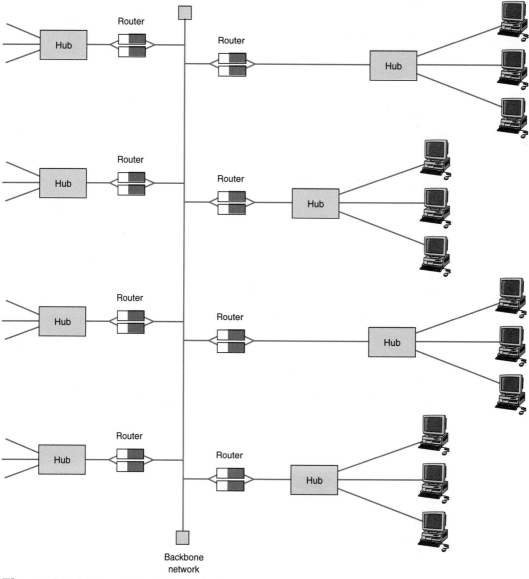

Figure 10–11 Routed backbone design.

the "TCP/IP Example" in Chapter 6 and "Backbone Network Components" in Chapter 8 before you continue.

Routed Backbone Design

Routed backbones move packets along the backbone based on their network layer address (i.e., layer 3 address). The most common form of routed backbone uses a bus topology (e.g., Ethernet 100Base-X). They can also use a ring topology (in which case a technology like FDDI would replace the traditional Ethernet bus), but the essential concepts remain the same. Routed backbones are sometimes called subnetted backbones or hierarchical backbones and are most commonly used to connect different buildings within the same campus area network.

Figure 10–11 illustrates a routed backbone with a bus topology. This figure shows a series of LANs connected by routers to a single shared media backbone network. Each of the LANs are a separate subnet. Message traffic stays within each subnet unless it specifically needs to leave the subnet to travel elsewhere on the network, in which case the network layer address (e.g., TCP/IP) is used to move the packet.

Each LAN is usually a separate entity, relatively isolated from the rest of the network. There is no requirement that all LANs share the same data link layer. One LAN can use Ethernet, while another uses token ring. Each LAN can contain its own server designed to support the users on that LAN, but users can still easily access servers on other LANs as needed.

The primary advantage of the routed backbone is that it clearly segments each part of the network connected to the backbone. Each segment (usually a LAN or another backbone) has its own subnet addresses that can be managed by a different network manager. Each segment off the backbone also can use different data link layer technologies.

There are two primary disadvantages to routed backbones. First, the routers in the network impose time delays. Routing takes more time than bridging or switching, so routed networks can sometimes be slower.

Second, routed networks require a lot of management. Establishing separate subnet addresses for each LAN is time-consuming and requires a large set of TCP/IP addresses. Any time a computer is moved from one LAN to another, it must be reconfigured (unless the network is using dynamic addressing, which imposes costs of its own).

Bridged Backbone Design

Bridged backbones move packets along the backbone based on their data link layer address (i.e., layer 2 address). The most common form uses a bus topology, but ring topologies are also possible. Bridged backbones are sometimes called flat backbones. They are most commonly used as the backbone within one building, but their use is declining.

Figure 10–12 illustrates a bridged backbone with a bus topology. This figure shows a series of LANs connected by bridges to a single shared media backbone

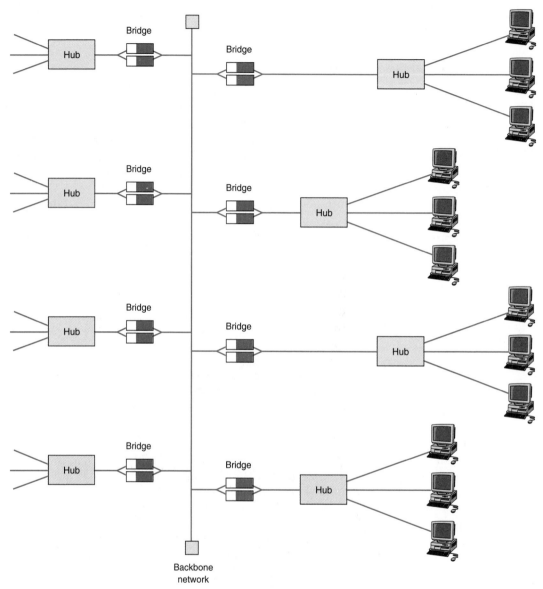

Figure 10–12 Bridged backbone design.

network. As you can see, a bridged backbone looks very similar to a routed backbone. With a bridged backbone, however, the entire network (backbone and all connected network segments) is on the same subnet. All LANs are part of the same overall network and all must have the same data link layer protocol. This is in sharp contrast to the routed backbone, in which the LANs are isolated and may be different.

Bridged backbones have several distinct advantages and disadvantages compared to routed backbones. First, since bridges tend to be less expensive than routers, they are often cheaper. Second, they are usually simpler to install because the network manager does not need to worry about building many different subnets and assigning a whole variety of different subnet masks and addresses in each part of the network. However, since the backbone and all attached networks are considered part of the same subnet, it is more difficult to permit different individuals to manage different parts of the network (e.g., LANs); a change in one part of the network has the potential to significantly affect all other parts. Also, it is possible to run out of IP addresses if the entire network has many computers.

The other major problem is network speed. Bridging is faster than routing, so one might expect the bridged backbones to be faster. For small networks, this is true. For large networks, it is not, bridged backbone are slower than routed backbones. Since bridged backbones and all networks connected to them are part of the same subnet, broadcast messages (e.g., address requests) must be permitted to travel everywhere in the backbone. This means, for example, that a computer in one LAN attempting to find the data link layer address of a server in the same LAN will issue a broadcast message that will travel to every computer on every LAN attached to the backbone. (In contrast, on a routed backbone such messages would never leave the LAN in which they originated.)

There are many different types of broadcast messages other than address requests (e.g., a printer reporting it is out of paper, a server about to be shut down). These broadcast messages quickly use up network capacity in a large bridged network. The result is slower response times for the user. In a small network, the problems are not as great, because there are fewer computers to issue such broadcast messages.

Switched Backbone Design

Most *switched backbones* use the data link layer address to move packets (the same as bridged networks) although newer switches can use the network layer address to move packets in the same manner as routed networks. The most common form of switched backbone uses a star topology and is called a *collapsed backbone*. Full or partial mesh topologies are also possible. Collapsed backbone networks are the dominant type of backbone network used within a building; most new building backbone networks designed today use collapsed backbones. They also are starting to make their way into the campus area backbone, but routed backbones remain more common.

Figure 10–13 shows the collapsed backbone form of switched backbone. Here, the backbone circuit and set of routers or bridges is replaced by one switch and a set of circuits to each LAN. The collapsed backbone has more cable, but fewer devices. There is no backbone cable. The "backbone" exists only in the switch, which is why this is called a collapsed backbone.

There are two major advantages to collapsed backbones. First, performance is improved. With the traditional backbone network, the backbone circuit was shared among many LANs (eight LANs, in the case of Figure 10–13); each had to

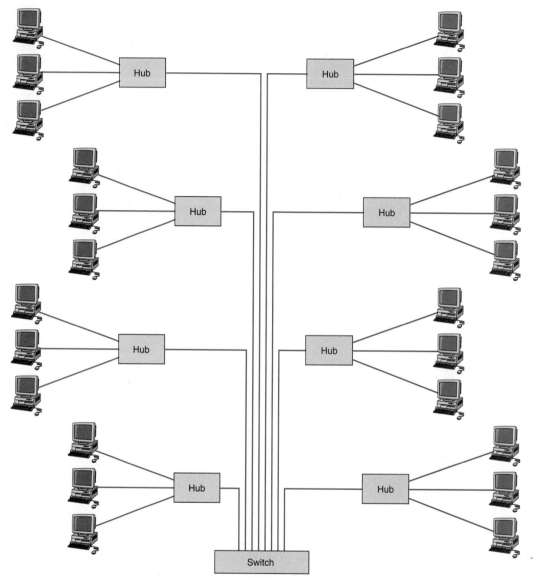

Figure 10–13 Collapsed backbone network design.

take turns sending messages. With the collapsed backbone, each connection into the switch is a separate point-to-point circuit. The switch enables simultaneous access, so that several LANs can send messages to other LANs at the same time. Throughput is increased significantly, often by 200 percent to 600 percent, depending on the number of attached LANs and the traffic pattern.

Second, there are far fewer networking devices in the network. In Figure 10–13, one switch replaces eight routers. This reduces costs and greatly simplifies network management. All the key backbone devices are in the same physical loca-

Each year, the U.S. Department of Education (DOE) processes more than 10 million student loans, such as Pell Grants, Guaranteed Student Loans, and college work-study programs. The DOE has more than 5000 employees that need access to more than 400 gigabytes of student data.

The financial aid network is headquartered in a Washington, D.C., building that has one main collapsed backbone (see Figure 10–14). This main backbone connects two other secondary collapsed backbones that use ATM. Each of the secondary collapsed backbones in turn connects three 10Base-T Ethernet LANs, one switched 10Base-T Ethernet LAN and three high-performance database servers.

This main building-wide backbone is connected into an FDDI backbone that connects the financial aid building to five other DOE buildings in Washington. This FDDI ring is a routed backbone, with each building connected to the ring via a router. Each building has its own TCP/IP subnet and can use different data link layer LANs and backbones. In fact, however, each of the buildings also uses an ATM collapsed backbone with to connect a series of Ethernet LANs.

The main building-wide backbone also provides access to the DOE WAN that uses T1 lines to connect the ten regional DOE offices throughout the U.S. and to other U.S. government agencies. This WAN uses a star design with the Washington financial aid building as the center of the hub.

Source: "The Department of Education's Financial Aid Network," *Network Computing*, May 15, 1996.

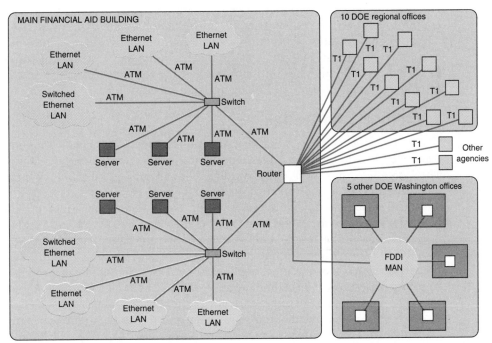

Figure 10–14 The Department of Education's financial aid network.

tion, and all traffic must flow through the switch. If something goes wrong or if new cabling is needed, it can all be done in one place.

Collapsed backbones often, but not always, have two important disadvantages that are the same as those for bridged networks. Because data link layer addresses are used to move packets, there is more broadcast traffic flowing through the network and it is harder to isolate and separately manage the individually attached LANs. Newer switches can use the network layer address, so future collapsed backbones likely will not suffer these problems. Likewise, some newer switches support multiple data link layer protocols permitting both Ethernet and token ring LANs to be attached to them.

Collapsed backbones also have two relatively minor disadvantages. First, they use more cable, and the cable must be run longer distances, which often means that fiber optic cables must be used. Second, if the switch fails, so does the entire backbone network. However, the reliability of the switch has the same reliability as the reliability of the routers in Figure 10–11, then there is less chance of a failure (because there are fewer devices to fail). For most organizations, these disadvantages are outweighed by benefits offered by collapsed backbones.

✳ ✳ COMMON LOCAL AREA NETWORK DESIGNS

For the past ten years, the design of local area networks has remained relatively constant. However, in recent years, the introduction of the high-speed switch has begun to change the way we think about local area networks. Switches offer the opportunity to design radically new approaches to LANs. Most large organizations today have traditional LANs, but most are moving to *virtual LANs*, the new type of LAN design made possible by intelligent, high-speed switches.

Traditional LAN Design

The *traditional LAN design* is that described in Chapter 7. The client computers are connected to a hub that provides the physical connection among the computers. The LAN uses a star topology physically, although the logical topology is either a bus (Ethernet) or a ring (token ring). See Figure 10–15.

This design has dominated LANs for the last decade because it is conceptually simple, and easy to install and manage. The drawback is that the LAN can become overloaded as traffic in the LAN increases. Because every message must travel through the hub to every computer in the LAN, and because the hub can only process one message at a time, significant increases in traffic can produce even larger increases in response time delays.

The introduction of switches (with the ability to transfer messages only to those computers that needed to receive them and the ability to process many messages simultaneously) greatly improved response times in LANs with large traffic flows. In this case, the hub is simply replaced by the switch, so the design of the network remains the same.

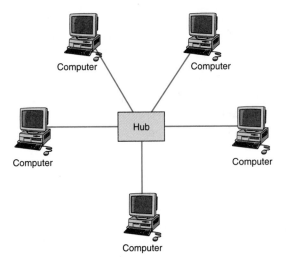

Figure 10–15 Traditional LAN design.

Virtual LAN Design

Switches also have enabled the creation of a new type of LAN design called a virtual LAN (VLAN). In general, VLANs require no changes to the client computers' hardware and software. Virtual LANs are usually faster and provide greater opportunities to manage the flow of traffic on the LAN than the traditional LAN design. However, VLANs are significantly more complex. Therefore, VLANs should only be used for large LANs. In order to understand how VLANs work, we need to first understand how switches operate.

Basic Switches

Figure 10–16 shows a basic approach to switch design. The front of the switch contains a series of *ports* exactly like the ports on the front of a hub. Each of these ports provides one network connection. For example, if the switch in this figure is a 10Base-T switch, one 10Base-T Ethernet cable would connect into each port.

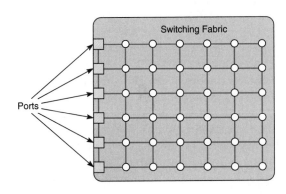

Figure 10–16 Inside a basic switch.

These ports are connected inside the switch by a *switching fabric* (also called the switching matrix or the switching core). In many switches, the switching fabric provides a connection from every port to every other port in the switch. When an incoming packet arrives at one port, the switch examines the address and immediately switches it through the switching fabric to the outgoing destination port. If the destination port is busy (e.g., some other data is being sent or received on that port), then the incoming packet is stored in a buffer (i.e., memory) at the incoming port until the destination port becomes available and the packet can be transmitted. If the buffer is full, then the packet is discarded and the sender must transmit it again.

It is possible to have ports running at different speeds (e.g., 10Base-T on one port and 100-Base-T on another). Since ports connected to servers tend to send and receive the most traffic, it is commonplace to connect servers to faster ports to prevent their port buffer from becoming overloaded. However, this can also cause problems. If a 100 Mbps port from the server is connected to a 10 Mbps port to the client, the destination port can quickly become overwhelmed. Most switches today are designed to handle this situation without causing problems.

Intelligent Switches

Basic switches are designed to support 8- or 16-port LANs. Larger networks need larger switches that are sometimes called *intelligent switches.* These intelligent switches are modular in design. The switch itself has a chassis the size of a large file cabinet with many spaces in which *switch modules* can be connected. Each switch module is designed to support a certain type of network. Some switch modules might provide a set of 16 10Base-T Ethernet ports (i.e., connections), another might provide 16 token ring ports, another four ATM ports, and so on.

As well as being able to support far more computers or network connections than their basic switch counterparts, the key advantage of intelligent switches is their modularity. It becomes simple to add new modules with additional ports as the LAN grows. Likewise, it is simple to upgrade the switch to use new technologies. For example, if you want to add ATM or gigabit Ethernet, you simply lay the cable and insert the appropriate module into the switch.

These switches often can support several hundred ports spread over a dozen or more different modules. With this many ports, each possibly running at different speeds, it becomes extremely expensive to provide a permanent connection from every port to every other port. Instead, most large switches provide a bus or a *backplane* that connects all the ports (see Figure 10–17). This backplane can transfer a very large amount of data but cannot transfer the maximum possible amount that could theoretically enter the switch if all ports were to simultaneously receive data. Since not all ports are likely to be active at one time, this usually works well. Buffers are provided in case the switch is so busy that it cannot transfer all the data it needs.

Since there is not enough capacity in the backplane to support all ports if they become active at one time, the switch must find a way to share the capacity on the backplane among the multitude of network connections (e.g., ports) that might want to transmit. This is done by forming groups of connections and assigning each group some capacity on the backplane using time division multiplexing (TDM).

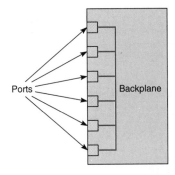

Figure 10–17 Intelligent switch.

In this way, each of the network connections within the same group must share the same capacity on the backplane.

This means that the switch no longer guarantees simultaneous transmission on all ports but will accept simultaneous input on all ports and switch incoming data to outgoing ports as fast as possible. If no other device in the same group is transmitting or receiving data, then the transfer to the outgoing port is immediate. If some other device in the same group is transmitting, then the incoming data will be stored in a buffer until it can be switched. If the buffer becomes full, then the switch stops accepting incoming data (e.g., it would generate a collision if the incoming data is an Ethernet connection).

We should also note that it is possible to have just one computer in a group. In this case, that computer has a dedicated connection and does not need to share the network capacity with any other computer. This is commonly done for servers.

These groups are called virtual LANs (VLANs). There are four ways in which these virtual LANs can be built: using the physical port address on the switch, using the data link layer address, using the network layer address, or using the application type.

Port-Based VLANs

Port-based VLANs (also called *Layer-1 VLANs*) use the physical layer port address to form the groups for the VLAN (see Figure 10–18). The network administrator uses

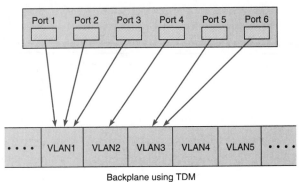

Backplane using TDM

Figure 10–18 Assigning ports to VLANs.

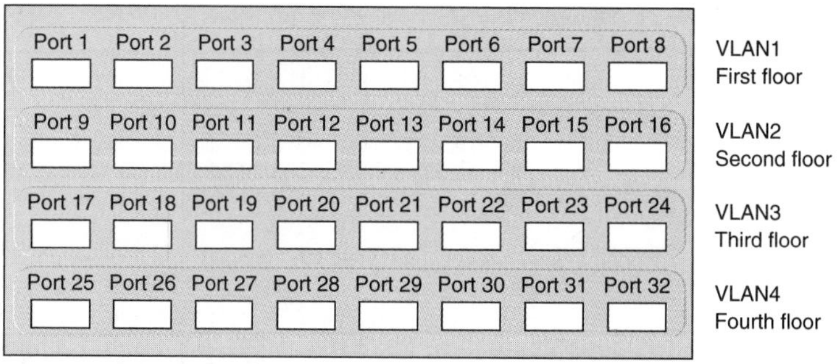

Figure 10–19 Building VLANs.

special software provided by the switch manufacturer to instruct the switch which ports are assigned to which VLAN.

It is logical to connect computers that are physically close together on the LAN into ports that are physically close together on the switch, and it is logical to assign ports that are physically close together into the same VLAN. In this way, users in the same physical location would share the same VLAN. For example, one might build VLANs by assigning each floor in a building into a different VLAN (see Figure 10–19).

This is the approach used in traditional LAN design: physical location determines the LAN into which the user is connected. However, this is not always the most effective approach, because different users may have different needs for network capacity. The users on one floor may generate significantly more network traffic than users on other floors (e.g., floor 2), while other users generate little traffic (e.g., floor 1). VLANs enable network designers to build the VLAN by network traffic needs, not by physical location in a building. Figures 10–20 shows a different VLAN design in which the VLANs are built to balance the traffic flows, rather than to correspond to physical location.

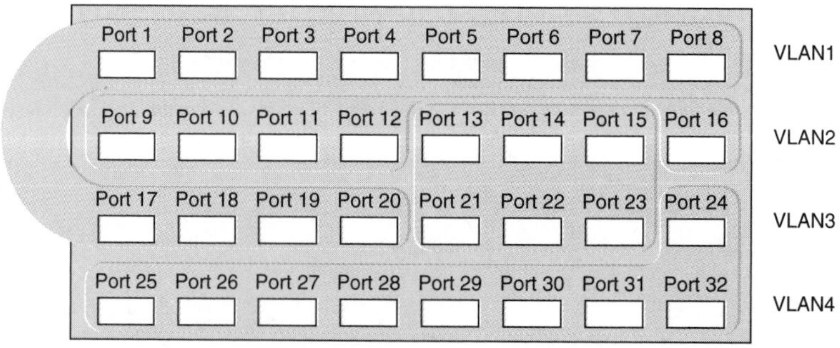

Figure 10–20 VLANs used to balance capacity against network traffic.

MAC-Based VLANs

MAC-based VLANs (also called *Layer-2 VLANs*) use the data link layer address to form the VLAN groups. The network administrator uses special software provided by the switch manufacturer to instruct the switch which incoming data link layer addresses are assigned to which VLAN. This process is a bit more complex, because now the network manager must know the data link layer address for each computer and manually type that into the software (whereas before the manager just had to know the port number and could select that from a list).

The advantage of a layer-2 VLAN is that it is simpler to manage when computers are moved. If a computer is moved in a layer-1 VLAN, then the network manager must reconfigure the switch to keep that computer in the same VLAN because the computer has moved from one port to another. With a layer-2 VLAN, no reconfiguration is needed. Although the computer may have moved from one port to another, it is the permanently assigned data link layer address that is used to determine which VLAN the computer is on.

IP-Based VLANs

IP-based VLANs (also called *Layer 3-VLANs*) use the network layer address (often the TCP/IP address) to form the VLAN groups. As before, the network administrator uses special software to instruct the switch which network layer addresses are assigned to which VLAN. This is also a complex process, because the network manager must know the network layer address for each computer and manually type that into the software.

Layer-3 VLANs reduce the time spent reconfiguring the network when computers move in the same way as layer-2 VLANs. Layer-3 VLANs tend to be a bit slower at processing each message than layer-2 VLANs, because processing layer-3 protocols is slightly slower than processing layer-2 protocols. However, layer-3 VLANs enable a greater reduction in broadcast messages because it is now possible to create virtual TCP/IP subnets inside the switch and limit broadcast messages to computers within those virtual subnets.

Some layer-3 VLANs can also use the network layer protocol to create VLAN groups. For example, many client computers on the LANs today run both TCP/IP (e.g., for Web browsing) and IPX/SPX (e.g., for access to a Novell file server). With a multi-protocol layer-3 VLAN, the network manager could assign all TCP/IP packets issued by a set of client computers into one VLAN and all IPX/SPX transmissions from those same clients into a different VLAN. In fact, there would not need to be any relationship between the membership in the different VLANs, so that one computer could be in a VLAN with one group of computers when it uses TCP/IP packets and in a group with an entirely different set of computers when it uses IPX/SPX packets.

This flexibility enables managers even greater precision in allocation of network capacity. Layer-3 VLANs provide managers some ability to prioritize how network capacity is allocated to applications, something that has never before been possible in the LAN. For example, suppose managers are concerned that some users are "wasting" too much network capacity on Web browsing. A layer-3 switch could allocate all TCP/IP traffic from those users into one 10 Mbps VLAN, while allocating their IPX/SPX packets into many VLANs. This would give good response time for IPX/SPX traffic generated by those users to Novell file servers, but restrict the amount of TCP/IP traffic they could generate and receive. Of course, more than just the Web uses TCP/IP, so this would also restrict FTP and e-mail access.

Application-Based VLANs

Application-based VLANs (also called *rule-based VLANs* or *Layer-4 VLANs*) use the application layer protocol in combination with the data link layer and network layer addresses to form the VLAN groups. As before, the network administrator uses special software to instruct the switch which types of packets from which addresses are assigned to which VLAN. This process is very complex because the network manager must decide on a variety of different factors in forming the VLANs. The advantage is a very precise allocation of network capacity. Now VLANs can be formed to allocate a certain amount of network capacity for Web browsing to certain individuals, so much to Web browsing for others, so much to FTP, and so on.

Summary

Traditional Network Design   The traditional network design approach follows a very structured systems analysis and design process similar to that used to build application systems. It attempts to develop precise estimates of network traffic for each network user and network segment. Although this is expensive and time-consuming, it works well for static or slowly evolving networks. Unfortunately, computer and networking technology is changing very rapidly, the growth in network traffic is immense, and hardware and circuit costs are relatively less expensive than they used to be. Therefore, use of the traditional network design approach is decreasing.

Building Block Approach to Network Design   The building block approach attempts to build the network using a series of simple pre-defined building components resulting in a simpler design process and a more easily managed network built with a smaller range of components. The basic process involves three steps that are performed repeatedly. Needs analysis involves establishing the geographic scope of the network and categorizing current and future network needs of the various network segments, users, and applications as "typical" or "high traffic." During technology design, in which network design and simulation tools can play an important role, "typical" users, applications, and network segments are allocated the "base level" technology, while "high-volume" ones are assigned some "advanced" technology. Cost assessment is the process of gathering cost information for the network, usually through a request for proposal (RFP) that specifies what equipment, software, and services are desired and ask vendors to provide their best prices. One of the keys to gaining senior management acceptance of the network design lies in speaking their language (cost, network growth, and reliability), not the language of the technology (Ethernet, ATM, and DSL).

Common WAN Designs   A ring-based WAN design connects all computers in a closed loop, with each computer linked to the next with dedicated circuits. One disadvantage is that messages can take a long time to travel from the sender to the receiver, but in general, the failure of any one circuit or computer in the network means that the network can continue to function. A star design uses dedicated circuits to connect all computers to one central computer that routes messages to the appropriate computer. The network will suffer major problems if the central computer becomes overloaded or fails, but otherwise operates well. In a mesh design, computers are connected to every other computer (a full mesh design) or to several other computers (a partial mesh) via dedicated circuits. Mesh networks tend to be fast and reliable but are more complex to design. Cloud-based mesh WANs are simpler to build because they use the packet-switched network of a common carrier.

Common Backbone Designs   Routed backbones typically use a bus design to connect a series of LANs that are attached to the backbone via a router. Routed backbones move packets along the backbone based on their network layer address (i.e., layer 3 address), so each LAN can be a separate entity, relatively isolated from the rest of the network. Bridged backbones commonly use a bus design in which LANs are connected to the backbone via bridges. Bridged backbones move packets along the backbone based on their data link layer address (i.e., layer 2 address) so all attached LANs are part of the same overall network and must share the same design and management philosophy. Bridged backbones are often slower than routed backbones because of the amount of broadcast messages that must flow throughout them. Most switched backbones use a star design (called collapsed backbones) and use the data link layer address to move packets (the same as bridged networks), although newer switches can use the network layer in the same manner as routed backbones. Collapsed backbones are significantly faster than routed or bridged backbones and have far fewer networking devices and therefore are becoming common.

Common LAN Designs   The traditional design for a LAN is a physical star provided by a hub as described in Chapter 7. This design has dominated LANs for the last decade because it is conceptually simple and easy to install and manage, but can become overloaded as network traffic increases. Virtual LANs (VLANs) use a star design with an intelligent switch capable of supporting hundreds of computers at their center. VLANs enable the network manager to assign network capacity to groups of users. Port-based VLANs (layer-1 VLANs) use the physical layer port address to form the VLAN groups, MAC-based VLANs (layer-2 VLANs) use the data link layer address, and IP-based VLANs (layer 3-VLANs) use the network layer address. Application-based VLANs (rule-based VLANs or layer-4 VLANs) use the application layer protocol in combination with the data link layer and network layer addresses. Layer-4 VLANs are the most flexible but also most complex, while layer-3 and layer-2 VLANs provide some flexibility with a moderate amount of complexity.

Key Terms

application-based VLAN	IP-based VLAN	rule-based VLAN
backplane	Layer-1 VLAN	simulation
baseline	Layer-2 VLAN	star-based WAN design
baselining	Layer-3 VLAN	switch modules
bridged backbone	Layer-4 VLAN	switched backbone
building block approach	MAC-based VLAN	switching fabric
capacity planning	mandatory requirements	technology design
circuit loading	mesh-based WAN design	topology
cloud-based mesh WAN design	needs analysis	traditional LAN design
collapsed backbones	port	traditional network design
cost assessment	port-based VLAN	approach
desirable requirements	request for proposal (RFP)	turnpike effect
geographic scope	ring-based WAN design	virtual LAN (VLAN)
intelligent switches	routed backbone	wish list requirements

Questions

1. What are the keys to designing a successful data communication network?
2. How does the traditional approach to network design differ from the building block approach?
3. Describe the three major steps in network design.
4. Why is it important to analyze needs in terms of both application systems and users?
5. Describe the key parts of the technology design step.
6. How can a network design tool help in network design?
7. On what should the design plan be based?
8. What is an RFP, and why do companies use them?
9. What are the key parts of an RFP?
10. What are some major problems that can cause network designs to fail?
11. What is a network baseline? When is it established?
12. What issues are important to consider in explaining a network design to senior management?
13. What is the turnpike effect, and why is it important in network design?
14. Compare and contrast four commonly used WAN designs.
15. Under what circumstances would a star design be preferred to a ring design?
16. Compare and contrast three commonly used backbone designs.
17. Under what circumstances would a routed backbone be preferred to a bridged backbone?

18. What are advantages and disadvantages of collapsed backbones compared to routed backbones?

19. Describe the traditional LAN design.

20. How does a basic switch differ from an intelligent switch?

21. What is a virtual LAN?

22. What are the major advantages and disadvantages of a virtual LAN?

23. Compare and contrast the four types of VLAN.

Exercises

A. What factors might cause peak loads in a network? How can a network designer determine if they are important, and how are they taken into account when designing a data communication network?

B. Suppose you arrive at the office on the first day of a new job as a network manager, and the MIS manager asks you whether the company should install a VLAN. Describe how you would investigate whether a VLAN would be appropriate for the company. What information would you gather, and how would that information affect your decision?

C. The market for intelligent switches and VLANs is changing rapidly. Investigate three switches currently on the market and report on their VLAN capabilities.

D. Investigate the network design process at your school or company. Does it differ depending on whether a WAN, backbone or LAN is being designed? Why?

E. Suppose you are designing a 300-computer network for a microcomputer software development company. The goal is to build a new network that will support the company's needs for the next three years with few additional investments. The company is located in three adjacent five-story buildings in an office park, with about 100 computers in each building. The current network is a poorly designed mix of Ethernet and token ring (Ethernet in two buildings and token ring in the other). The networks in all three buildings are heavily overloaded and the company anticipates significant growth in network traffic. There is currently no network connection among the buildings, but this is one objective in building the new network. Describe the network you would recommend and how it would be configured. Be sure to include the devices and type of network circuits you would use. You will need to make some assumptions, so be sure to document your assumptions and explain why you have designed the network in this way.

F. Suppose you are designing a 60-computer network for a small manufacturer. The goal is to build a new network that will support the company's needs for the next three years with few additional investments. The company has one very large manufacturing plant with an adjacent office building. The office building houses 50 computers, with an additional 10 computers in the plant. The current network is an old 4 Mbps token ring that will need to be completely replaced. Describe the network you would recommend and how it would be configured. Be sure to include the devices and type of network circuits you would use. You will need to make some assumptions, so be sure to document your assumptions and explain why you have designed the network in this way.

G. Suppose you are designing a WAN for a consulting firm with offices in Toronto, New York, Los Angeles, Dallas, and Atlanta. They currently use the Internet to transmit data, but the need is growing and they are concerned over the security of the Internet. They want to establish their own private WAN. Consultants in all offices are frustrated at the current 33.6 Kbps modems they use for Internet access, so the firm thinks that they need faster data transmission capabilities. They have no records of data transmission, but believe that the New York and Toronto offices send and receive the most data. The firm is growing by 20 percent per year, and expects to open offices in Vancouver and Chicago within the next year or two. Describe two alternatives for the network and explain what choice you would make under what assumptions.

H. Suppose the firm in Exercise G was located in one region such as California or Ontario. How would this change the options you would propose?

I. Suppose the firm in Exercise G was located internationally, with offices in North America, Europe, Asia, and Australia. How would this change the options you would propose?

NEXT DAY AIR SERVICE CASE STUDY

The holding company that owns NDAS has just purchased a regional trucking company called Sunshine Trucking (ST). They believe that ST offers a way to build revenues in an area in which they have experience (package delivery), even though ST will not operate directly with NDAS. ST focuses on large commercial shipments (e.g., food products for wholesalers, package goods for department stores).

Currently, ST has a very poor data communications network. Since you have done such a good job on the NDAS network, President Coone offers your expertise to ST to help design a new network.

ST operates three regional shipping hubs: Miami, Dallas, and Atlanta. Each of these regional hubs is responsible for taking shipping requests from customers and scheduling pickups and deliveries. Each regional hub has about four dozen computers that will need to be networked to each other and onto a wide area network. The computers access the network server (a Novell file server) and the corporate minicomputer (discussed shortly) almost constantly. The current network is an old 4 Mbps token ring that needs to be completely replaced because it can no longer handle the network traffic. The regional hubs communicate with each other fairly regularly via dial-up modems, usually a dozen times an hour. The staff are irritated at having to constantly dial-up and hang-up for each connection. Sometimes modems are left connected for long periods of time each day.

The Atlanta hub also houses the corporate head office and therefore has an additional 20 computers for use by corporate staff. This office also has the corporate minicomputer that processes all accounting data (a Unix computer). There has been some discussion about establishing a corporate Web site, but no plans have been made.

ST has a series of seven local offices for short-term storage, truck maintenance, and managing the local drivers: Houston, New Orleans, Jackson, Birmingham, Tallahassee, Charlotte, and Memphis. Each regional office has 5 to 10 computers that are not networked, but that need to be networked to each other and to the wide area network. These computers have fairly minimal networking requirements. Each local office sends data to the corporate minicomputer at the end of each day by sending one diskette via overnight courier (NDAS). ST would like to automate this so that they can transmit the data via a network. They also would like to enable the local offices to communicate with all the regional hubs (and perhaps with each other), but do not anticipate needing to send a large amount of data.

Exercises

1. What wide area network would you recommend for ST? Describe each circuit you would recommend in terms of the technology (e.g., dial-up modem) and data rate (e.g., 56K modem).

2. What LANs and/or backbone networks would you recommend for the three regional hubs (including Atlanta, which has the corporate office)? Include the devices you would install.

3. What LANs and/or backbone networks would you recommend for the seven local offices? Include the devices you would install.

CHAPTER 11

Network Management

Network managers perform two key tasks: (1) designing new networks and network upgrades; and (2) managing the day-to-day operation of existing networks. This chapter examines day-to-day network management, discussing the things that must be done to ensure that the network function, properly. We discuss the network management organization and the basic functions that a network manager must perform to operate a successful network.

Objectives

* Understand what is required to manage the day-to-day operation of networks
* Become familiar with the network management organization
* Understand configuration management
* Understand performance and fault management
* Become familiar with end-user support
* Become familiar with cost management
* Understand the role and functions of network management software
* Become familiar with several types of network management hardware tools

Chapter Outline

✴ ✴ INTRODUCTION

Network management is the process of operating, monitoring, and controlling the network to ensure that it works as intended and provides value to its users. The primary objective of the data communication function is to move application layer data from one location to another in a timely fashion, and to provide the resources that allow this transfer to occur. This transfer of information may take place within a single department, between departments in an organization, or with entities outside the organization.

All too often, this objective is sacrificed to the immediacy of day-to-day problem solving caused by factors thought to be outside the control of management. These factors might be problems caused by unexpected circuit failures, pressure from end users to meet critical schedules, unavailability of certain equipment or circuits, or insufficient information (on a day-to-day basis) to ensure that the network provides adequate service to all users. In reality, network managers must gather their own decision-making information in order to measure network performance, identify problem areas, isolate the exact nature of problems, restore the network, and predict future problems.

Without a well-planned and designed network, and a well-organized network management staff, operating the network becomes extremely difficult. Unfortunately, many network managers spend most of their time *firefighting*—dealing with breakdowns and immediate problems. If managers do not spend enough time on planning and organizing the network and networking staff, which are needed to predict and prevent problems, they are destined to be reactive rather than proactive in solving problems.

Management Focus: What Do Network Managers Do?

If you were to become a network manager, some of your responsibilities and tasks would be to:

* Manage the day-to-day operations of the network
* Provide support to network users
* Ensure the network is operating reliably
* Evaluate and acquire network hardware, software, and services
* Manage the network technical staff
* Manage the network budget, with emphasis on controlling costs

* Develop a strategic (long-term) networking and voice communications plan to meet the organization's policies and goals
* Keep abreast of the latest technological developments in computers, data communications devices, network software, and the Internet
* Keep abreast of the latest technological developments in telephone technologies and MAN/WAN services
* Assist senior management in understanding the business implications of network decisions and the role of the network in business operations

In this chapter, we examine the network management function. We begin by examining the job of the network manager and how the network management function can be organized within companies. We then break down the activities that network managers perform into four basic functions: configuration management (knowing what hardware and software is where), performance and fault management (identifying and fixing problems), end-user support (assisting end users), and cost management (minimizing the cost of providing network services). In practice, it is difficult to separate the network manager's job into these four neat categories, but these are useful ways to help understand what a network manager does. The chapter concludes with a discussion of the many different types of network management tools that are available to support the network manager.

✳✳ ORGANIZING THE NETWORK MANAGEMENT FUNCTION

Communication and networking functions present special organizational problems because they are centralized and decentralized at the same time. The developers, gatherers, and users of data are typically decentralized. The need for communications and networking affects every business function. However, the management of voice and data communications on large host mainframes has traditionally been highly centralized. Mainframes were "owned" and operated by centralized information technology (IT) departments that are used to controlling every aspect of the IT and communication environment.

The Shift to LANs and the Web

Since the late 1980s, this picture has changed dramatically. There has been an explosion in the use of microcomputer-based networks. In fact, more than 60 percent of most organizations' total computer processing power (measured in millions of instructions per second) now resides on microcomputer-based LANs. This trend is continuing; since 1992, the number of computers attached to LANs has grown by almost 40 percent *per year* (compared to less than 10 percent per year for mainframe-based terminals and computers), and the number of Web servers has grown even more dramatically. Many experts predict that within five years, most organizations' host mainframe computer will contain less than 20 percent of the organization's total computing power.

Although the management of host-based mainframe networks will always be important, the future of network management lies in the successful management of the LAN, backbone network, and Internet resources. Most LANs and Web servers are owned and operated by different organizational units, not by the central IT department. Most were initially designed and implemented as separate networks and applications, whose goals were to best meet the needs of their individual owners, not to integrate with other networks and applications.

Today, the critical issue is the integration of all organizational networks and applications. This presents two problems. The first problem is technical. Since each LAN was developed by a different department within the organization, not all LANs use the same type of technology. It is not uncommon to find a mixture of Ethernet LANs and token ring LANs in the same organization. Likewise, the protocols on the Web and Internet (TCP/IP) are often different from those traditionally used by the central mainframe (SNA). Having different protocols and technologies means that routers or gateways must be used to connect the different LANs to organizational backbones and mainframe, and that network managers and technicians must be familiar with many types of networks. The more different types of network technology are used, the more complex network management becomes.

The second problem is cultural. Although it is impossible to accurately characterize the personalities and management styles of all network managers, several common traits have been observed across many organizations. WAN managers and managers of mainframe-based host computer networks are typically more comfortable in highly structured and controlled network environments. They are used in standardized processes and gradually changing technologies that need to be studied and evaluated carefully before being implemented. They are used to controling their networks and granting permission for new applications and tools to be installed, and typically have a large support staff. LAN managers often accuse WAN managers of being slow to implement changes and adopt new technologies.

In contrast, LAN managers and Web managers tend to be less interested in corporate standards and more interested in getting the job done. They value quick responses to changing user demands and rapidly changing technology. They often do not like the restrictiveness of corporate standards, preferring a more laissez faire approach to network management. They typically have little control over the applications on their networks, as users can install their own application software. LAN managers are often the ones responsible for all aspects of their networks. Sometimes they also have a few technicians supporting them, but in general, they lack the depth of personnel available to WAN managers. WAN managers often accuse LAN managers of being reactive, short-term thinkers with little concern for long-term planning.

Integrating LANs, WANs, and the Web

The key to integrating LANs, WANs, and the Web into one overall organizational network is for both LAN/Web and WAN managers to recognize that they no longer have the power they once had. No longer can network managers make independent decisions without considering how they affect other parts of the organization's network. There must be a single communications and networking goal that best meets the needs of the entire organization. This will require some network managers to compromise on policies that are not in their own departments' or networks' best interests.

Management Focus: *Key Network Management Skills*

What skills do network managers see as important? A survey of more than 350 network managers identified the following skills:

* Very important skills
  * Network design
  * Project management
  * Knowledge of TCP/IP
  * Knowledge of routing technologies
* Moderately important skills
  * Capacity planning
  * Knowledge of Novell NetWare

* Knowledge of Windows NT
* Knowledge of Unix
* Knowledge of Web technologies
* Less important skills
  * Knowledge of ISDN
  * Knowledge of frame relay
  * Knowledge of ATM
  * Knowledge of Notes/Domino

Source: "Making the Best of a Difficult Situation," *Communications Week*, July 1, 1996.

The central data communication network organization should have a written charter that defines its purpose, operational philosophy, and long-range goals. These goals must conform both to the parent organization's information-processing goals and to its own departmental goals. Along with its long-term policies, the organization must develop individual procedures with which to implement the policies. Individual departments and LAN/Web managers must be free to implement their own policies and procedures within this overall plan. Remember that goals lead to policies, which lead, in turn, to procedures that detail how specific tasks are to be carried out so the organization can meet its goals. These policies and procedures, therefore, provide the structure that guides the day-to-day tasks of data communication workers.

Integrating Voice and Data Communications

Another major organizational challenge is the prospect of combining the voice communication function with the data and image communication functions. Traditionally, voice communications were handled by a manager in the facilities department who supervised the telephone switchboard systems and also coordinated the installation and maintenance of the organization's voice telephone networks. By contrast, data communications traditionally were handled by the IT department because the staff installed their own communication circuits as the need arose, rather than contacting and coordinating with the voice communications management staff.

This separation of voice and data worked well over the years, but now changing communication technologies are causing enormous pressures to combine these functions. These pressures are magnified by the high cost of maintaining separate facilities, the low efficiency and productivity of the organization's employees because there are two separate network functions, and the potential political problems within an organization when neither manager wants to relinquish his or her functional duties or job position. A key factor in voice/data integration might turn out to be the elimination of one key management position and the merging of two staffs.

There is no perfect solution to this problem, because it must be handled in a way unique to each organization. Depending on the business environment and specific communication needs, some organizations might want to combine these functions while others might find it better to keep them separate. An organization that avoids studying this situation might be promoting inefficient communication systems, lower employee productivity, and increased operating costs for its separate voice and data networks.

In communications, we are moving from an era in which the computer system is the dominant IT function to one in which communication networks are the dominant IT function. In some organizations, the total cost of both voice and data communications will equal or exceed the total cost of the computer systems. Sometimes this cost factor is overlooked, ignored, or underestimated.

✳ ✳ CONFIGURATION MANAGEMENT

Configuration management means managing the network's hardware and software configuration and documenting it (and ensuring it is updated as the configuration changes).

Configuring the Network and Client Computers

One of the most common configuration activities is adding and deleting user accounts. When new users are added to the network, they are usually categorized as being a member of some group of users (e.g., faculty, students, accounting department, personnel department). Each user group has its own access privileges, which define what file servers, directories, and files they can access and provide a standard login script. The login script specifies what commands are to be run when the user first logs in (e.g., setting default directories, connecting to public disks, running menu programs).

Another common activity is updating the software on the client computers attached to the network. Every time a new application system is developed or updated (or, for that matter, when a new version of networking software is released), each client computer in the organization must be updated. Traditionally, this has meant that someone from the networking staff has had to go to each client computer and manually install the software, either from diskettes/CDs or by downloading over the network. For a small organization, this is time-consuming, but not a major problem. For a large organization with hundreds or thousands of client computers (possibly with a mixture of Windows and Macintoshes) this can be a nightmare.

Electronic software delivery (ESD), sometimes called automatic software distribution, is one solution to the configuration problem. ESD enables network managers to install software on client computers over the network without needing individual access to each client computer. Most ESD packages provide application layer software for the network server and all client computers. The server software communicates directly with the ESD application software on the clients and can be instructed to download and install certain application packages on each client at some predefined time (e.g., at midnight on Saturday).

ESD software greatly reduces the cost of configuration management over the long term because it eliminates the need to manually update each and every client computer. It also automatically produces and maintains accurate documentation of all software installed on each client computer and enables network managers to produce a variety of useful reports. However, ESD increases costs in the short term because it costs money (typically $50–$100 per client computer) and requires network staff to manually install it on each client computer. The other problem with ESD is that currently there are no standards. Different products from different vendors cannot operate together, and some products work better in one environment than another (e.g., Windows versus Macintosh). Standards are beginning to emerge (e.g., Desktop Management Interface, or DMI), but so far they have not been widely embraced.

Documenting the Configuration

Configuration documentation includes information about network hardware, network software, user and application profiles, and network documentation. The most basic information about network hardware is a set of network configuration maps that document the number, type, and placement of network circuits (whether organization owned or leased from a common carrier), network servers, network devices (e.g., hubs, routers), and client computers. For most organizations, this is a large set of maps: one for each LAN, BN, MAN, and WAN.

These maps must be supplemented by documentation on each individual network component (e.g., circuit, hub, server). Documentation should include the type of device, serial number, vendor, date of purchase, warranty information, repair history, telephone number for repairs, and any additional information or comments the network manager wishes to add. For example, it would be useful to include the dial-in numbers for communication servers, contact names and telephone numbers for the individual network managers responsible for each separate LAN within the network, and common carrier circuit control telephone contact index and log (whenever possible, establish a national account with the common carrier rather than dealing with individual common carriers in separate states and areas).

A similar approach can be used for network software. This includes the network operating system (NOS) and any special-purpose network software. For example, it is important to record which NOS and which version or release date is installed on each network server. The same is true of application software. As discussed in Chapter 7 on LANs, sharing software on networks can greatly reduce costs, although it is important to ensure that the organization is not violating any software license rules.

Software documentation can also help in negotiating site licenses for software. Many users buy software on a copy-by-copy basis, paying full retail price for each copy. It might be cheaper to negotiate the payment of one large fee for an unlimited-use license for widely used software packages instead of paying on a per-copy basis.

The third type of documentation is the user and application profiles, which should be automatically provided by the network operating system or additional vendor or third-party software agreements. These should enable the network manager to easily identify both the files and directories to which each user has access and their access rights (e.g., read-only, edit, delete). Equally important is the ability to access this information in the "opposite" direction; that is, to be able to select a file or directory and obtain a list of all authorized users and their access rights.

In addition, other documentation must be routinely developed and updated pertaining to the network. This includes network hardware and software manuals, application software manuals, standards manuals, operations manuals for network staff, vendor contracts and agreements, and licenses for software. The documentation should include details about performance and fault management (e.g., preventive maintenance guidelines and schedules, disaster recovery plan, and diagnostic techniques), end-user support (e.g., applications software manuals, vendor support telephone numbers), and cost management (e.g., annual budgets, repair costs for each device). The documentation should also include any legal requirements to comply with local or federal laws, control, or regulatory bodies.

Management Focus: *Ten Networking Commandments*

1. Thou shalt back up thy hard disk regularly.
2. Thou shalt schedule downtime before doing major work upon thy server.
3. Thou shalt keep thy network disk clean of old files.
4. Thou shalt keep an adequate supply of spare parts.
5. Thou shalt not covet thy neighbor's software (and upgrade without reason).
6. Thou shalt not steal thy neighbor's software without a license.
7. Thou shalt train thy users.
8. Thou shalt not tinker with thine Autoexec.bat, Config.sys or Startnet.bat unless thou knowest what thou art doing.
9. Thou shalt not drop thy guard against viruses.
10. Thou shalt write down thy network configuration in tablets of stone.

Source: Networking for Dummies, IDG Books, Chicago, 1994.

✳✳ PERFORMANCE AND FAULT MANAGEMENT

Performance management means ensuring the network is operating as efficiently as possible. Improving network performance is its essence. Several strategies for improving performance were discussed in previous chapters.

Fault management means preventing, detecting, and correcting faults in the network circuits, hardware, and software (e.g., a broken hub or improperly installed software). Fault management and performance management are closely related, because any faults in the network reduce performance. Both require network monitoring, which means keeping track of the operation of network circuits and devices to ensure they are functioning properly and to determine how heavily they are used.

Network Monitoring

Most large organizations and many smaller ones use *network management software* to monitor and control their networks. One function provided by these systems is to collect operational statistics from the network devices. For small networks, network monitoring is often done by one person, aided by a few simple tools (discussed later in this chapter). These tools collect information and send messages to the network manager's computer.

In large networks, network monitoring becomes more important. Large networks that support organizations operating 24 hours a day are often mission-critical, which means a network problem can cause serious business consequences. For example, consider the effect of a network failure for an interexchange carrier such as AT&T or for a national air-traffic control system. These networks often have a dedicated *network control center* that is responsible for monitoring and fixing problems. Such centers are staffed by a set of skilled network technicians that use sophisticated network management software. When a problem occurs, the software immediately detects the problems and sends an alarm to the network control center. Staff in the network control center diagnose the problem and can sometimes fix the problem from the control center (e.g., restarting a failed device). Other times when a device or circuit fails they must change routing tables to route traffic away from the device and inform the common carrier or dispatch a technician to fix or replace it.

The parameters monitored by a network management system fall into two distinct categories: physical network statistics and logical network information. Gathering statistics on the *physical network parameters* includes monitoring the operation of the network's modems, multiplexers, circuits linking the various hardware devices, and any other network devices. Monitoring the physical network consists of keeping track of circuits that may be down and tracing malfunctioning devices. *Logical network parameters* include performance measurement systems that keep track of user response times, the volume of traffic on a specific circuit, the destination of data routed across various networks, and any other indicators showing the level of service provided by the network. This type of management software

Management Focus: Long Night on the Net Watch

At an hour when most network personnel are asleep, Walter Snider and Willie Williams are huddled over a network management console trying to determine why a circuit between Jacksonville and Baltimore is down in the railroad giant CSX Corp.'s network. The problem becomes urgent when the dispatcher tells Snider the outage will delay trains if it is not fixed soon.

A quick check of the circuit shows it is fine. The multiplexer ports on both ends pass tests, too. Williams becomes convinced that the dispatcher has reported the wrong circuit number and begins checking other circuits out of Baltimore. He quickly finds one that does not respond, reboots the multiplexer, and the circuit begins working. He calls the dispatcher, who reports that the circuit is working again.

The night shift is the quietest shift at CSX's network control center in Jacksonville, which gives network personnel the chance to learn new skills and identify network improvements. However, staff need the greatest range of skills and have more autonomy to solve problems. Unlike their daytime counterparts, it is harder to reach managers and other network personnel for help. While CSX policy requires the center to contact network managers and support personnel in the event of a major problem, no one likes to wake up their colleagues.

At 4:00 A.M., five hours after beginning the shift, Williams notices an alarm go off, indicating the failure of a major circuit in the Washington area. He begins to zero in on the trouble spot when the circuit comes back up. "Probably just line noise or a power surge," he says, and returns to his donut and coffee.

Source: "Long Night on the Net Watch," *Network World*, February 9, 1998.

Management Focus: Technical Reports

Technical reports that are helpful to network managers are those that provide summary information, as well as details that enable the managers to improve the network. Some technical details include:

* Circuit utilization
* Utilization rate of critical hardware such as host computers, front end processors, and servers
* File activity rates for database systems
* Usage by various categories of client computers

* Response time analysis per circuit or per computer
* Voice versus data usage per circuit
* Queue-length descriptions, whether in the host computer, front end processor, or at remote sites
* Distribution of traffic by time of day, location, and type of application software
* Failure rates for circuits, hardware, and software
* Details of any network faults

operates passively, collecting the information and reporting it back to the network operations control center(s).

Poor network reporting leads to an organization that is overburdened with current problems and lacks time to address future needs. Management requires adequate reports if it is to address future needs. Information for these reports can be gathered from host computers, front end processors, network monitors, the network management group, local area networks, test equipment, and the like.

Failure Control Function

Failure control is handled by the network support group (often starting with a control center or *help desk*) that is called when anything goes wrong in the network. This group has appropriate customer service representatives to record problems, report them to the testing and problem management group, follow up, and generally ensure that the network is back in operation as soon as possible. This group also might be responsible for change scheduling, coordination, and follow-up on any changes, whether they involve hardware, software, or circuits. In other words, this is the user's interface when there is a problem of any kind.

Failure control requires developing a central control philosophy for problem reporting and other user interfaces. This group should maintain a central telephone number for network users to call when any problem occurs in the network. As a central troubleshooting function, only this group or its designee should have the authority to call hardware or software vendors or common carriers.

Many years ago, before the importance (and cost) of network management was widely recognized, most networks ignored the importance of fault management. Network devices were "dumb" in that they did only what they were designed to do (e.g., routing packets), but did not provide any network management information.

For example, suppose a network interface card fails and begins to randomly transmit garbage messages. Network performance immediately begins to deteriorate because these random messages destroy the messages transmitted by other computers, which need to be retransmitted. Users notice a delay in response time, and complain to the network support group, which begins to search for the cause. Even if the network support group suspects a failing network card (which is unlikely, unless such an event has occurred before), locating the faulty card is very difficult and time-consuming.

"Smart" network devices perform their functions and record data on the messages they process. These data can be sent to the network manager's computer when the device receives a special control message requesting the data, or they can send an *alarm* message to the network manager's computer if the device detects a critical situation. In this way, network faults and performance problems can be detected and reported before they become serious. In the case of the failing network card, the network management software could record the increased number of retransmissions required to successfully transmit messages, and then determine the cause of the delayed response time. A "smart" network hub, controller, or switch might even be able to detect the faulty transmissions from the failing network card, disable the incoming port so that the card could not send any more messages, and issue an alarm to the network manager. In either case, finding and fixing the fault is much simpler, requiring minutes, not hours.

Numerous software packages are available for recording fault information. The reports they produce are known as *trouble tickets*. The software packages assist the help desk personnel so they can type the trouble report immediately into a computerized failure analysis program. They also automatically produce various statistical reports to track how many failures have occurred for each piece of hardware, circuit, or software package.

Trouble tickets must be kept if a manager wants to do any type of problem tracking. Automated trouble tickets are better than paper because they allow management to gather problem and vendor statistics. There are four main reasons for trouble tickets: problem tracking, problem statistics, problem-solving methodology, and management reports.

Problem tracking allows the network manager to determine who is responsible for correcting any outstanding problems. This is important because some problems are forgotten in the rush of a hectic day. In addition, anyone might request the status of a problem. The network manager can determine whether the problem-solving mechanism is meeting predetermined schedules. Finally, the manager can be assured that all problems are being addressed. Problem tracking also can assist in problem resolution. Are problems being resolved in a timely manner? Are overdue problems being flagged? Are all resources and information available for problem solving?

Technical Focus: *Elements of a Trouble Report*

When a problem is reported, the trouble log staff should record the following:

* Time and date of the report
* Name and telephone number of the person who reported the problem

* The time and date of the problem (and the time and date of the call)
* Location of the problem
* The nature of the problem
* When the problem was identified
* Why and how the problem happened

Problem statistics are an important control device for the network operators as well as for vendors. With this information, a manager can see how well the network is meeting the needs of end users. The manager can determine whether problem solving by the network operators is excessive. These statistics also can be used to determine whether vendors are meeting their contractual maintenance commitments. Finally, they help to determine whether problem-solving objectives are being met.

Problem prioritizing helps ensure that critical problems get priority over less important ones. For example, a network support staff member should not work on a problem on one client computer if an entire circuit with dozens of computers were waiting for help. Moreover, a manager must know whether problem resolution objectives are being met. For example, how long is it taking to resolve critical problems?

Management reports are required to determine network availability, product and vendor reliability (mean time between failures), and vendor responsiveness. Without them, a manager has nothing more than a "best guess" estimate for the effectiveness of either the network's technicians or the vendor's technicians. Regardless of whether this information is typed immediately into an automated trouble ticket package or recorded manually in a bound notebook-style trouble log, the objectives are the same. If the organization does not have a computerized package, then the notebook format is appropriate. The bound notebook, with two carbon copies for each original trouble report, should have prenumbered pages to ensure that no report is lost. One page always should be kept at the "trouble log" desk. One carbon copy is given to a vendor who is called in to correct the problem and one copy to the internal testing/problem management personnel.

The purpose of the trouble log is to record problems that must be corrected and to keep track of statistics associated with these problems. For example, the log might reveal that there were 37 calls for software problems (3 for one package, 4 for another package, and 30 for a third software package), 26 calls for modems evenly distributed among two vendors, 49 calls for client computers, and 85 calls to the common carrier that provides the network circuits. These data are valuable when the design and analysis group begins redesigning the network to meet future requirements.

Problem Resolution

The purpose of problem resolution is to fix network problems. Network personnel maintain the complex equipment needed to diagnose problems quickly, and most of the time they fix the problem in-house. Their mission is troubleshooting, working with the failure control group that first discovered the problem. The testing and problem management group should report back to the failure control group as soon as they have diagnosed the problem so the time required to diagnose the problem can be recorded. The *mean time to diagnose (MTTD)*, which is an indicator of the efficiency of testing and problem management personnel, is the first of three different *times* that should be kept for future record.

For example, assume a vendor or internal support group is contacted for correction of a problem. Either testing or failure control personnel should keep track of the time it takes to respond. In other words, the *mean time to respond (MTTR)* is identified. This is a valuable statistic because it indicates how quickly vendors and internal groups respond to emergencies. Compilation of these figures over time can lead to a change of vendors or internal management policies, or, at the minimum, can exert severe pressure on vendors who do not respond to problems promptly.

Finally, after the vendor or internal support group arrives on the premises, the last statistic to record is the *mean time to fix (MTTF)*. This figure tells how quickly the staff is able to correct the problem. A very long time to fix in comparison with the time of other vendors may indicate faulty equipment design, inadequately trained customer service technicians, or even the fact that inexperienced personnel are repeatedly sent to fix problems.

So, the *mean time to repair (MTTR)* a failure is:

$$MTTRepair = MTTDiagnose + MTTRespond + MTTFix$$

Another important statistic is the *mean time between failures (MTBF)*, which indicates the reliability of a network component such as a switch or router. As the name suggests, this is the number of hours or days of continuous operation before the component fails.

The MTBF (failure) can be influenced by the original selection of vendor-supplied equipment. The MTTD (diagnose) relates directly to the ability of network personnel to isolate and diagnose failure of hardware, software, or circuits and can often be improved by training. The MTTR (respond) can be influenced by showing vendors or internal groups how good or bad their response times have been in the past. The MTTF (fix) can be affected by the use of redundant interface equipment, alternate circuit paths, adequate recovery or fallback procedures to earlier versions of software, and the technical expertise of internal or vendor staff. Because these mean times affect network availability, their collection is vital if network performance is to be improved.

One important time factor is *availability*, the percentage of time the network is available to users. It is calculated as the number of hours per month the network is available, divided by the total number of hours per month (i.e., 24 hours per day × 30 days/month = 720 hours). The *downtime* includes times when the network is unavailable due to faults and to routine maintenance and network upgrades. Most network managers strive for 99 to 99.5 percent availability, with downtime scheduled after normal working hours.

The network operations group use automated network management software (network monitors and analyzers) to gather a daily record of the normal operation of the network, such as the number of errors (retransmissions) per communication circuit, per terminal, or whatever is appropriate. Network managers should collect these records, along with statistics on the daily volume of transmissions (characters per hour) for each communication link or circuit, each terminal, or whatever is appropriate for the network. It is important to closely monitor utilization rates, the percentage of the theoretical capacity that is being used. These data can identify computers/devices or communication circuits that have higher-than-average error rates, and may be used for predicting future growth patterns and failures. A device or circuit that is approaching maximum utilization obviously needs to be upgraded.

Such predictions can be accomplished by establishing simple *quality control charts* similar to those used in manufacturing. Programs use an upper control limit and a lower control limit with regard to the number of blocks in error per day or per week. Notice how Figure 11–1 identifies when the common carrier moved a

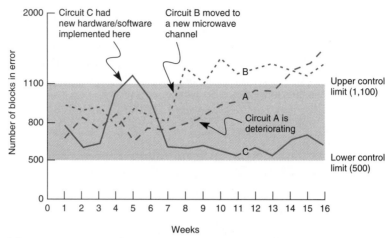

Figure 11–1 Quality control chart for circuits.

circuit from one microwave channel to another (circuit B), how a deteriorating circuit can be located and fixed before it goes through the upper control limit (circuit A) and causes problems for the users, or how a temporary high rate of errors (circuit C) can be encountered when installing new hardware and software.

More organizations are beginning to establish *service level agreements (SLA)* with their common carriers and Internet service providers. An SLA specifies the exact type of performance and fault conditions that the organization will accept. For

---

Management Focus: *Management Reports*

Management-oriented reports that are helpful to network managers and their supervisors provide summary information for overall evaluation and for network planning and design. Some details include:

* Graphs of daily/weekly/monthly usage, number of errors, or whatever is appropriate to the network

* Network availability (uptime) for yesterday, the last five days, the last month, or any other specific period

* Percentage of hours per week the network is unavailable due to network maintenance and repair

* Fault diagnosis

* Whether most response times are less than or equal to 3 seconds for online real-time traffic

* Whether management reports are timely, and contain the most up-to-date statistics

* Peak volume statistics, as well as average volume statistics per circuit

* Comparison of activity between today and a similar previous period

example, the SLA might state that network availability must be 99 percent or higher and that the MTBF for T-1 circuits must be 120 days or more. In many cases, the SLA includes maximum allowable response times. Some organizations are also starting to use an SLA internally to clearly define relationships between the networking group and its organizational "customers."

✳✳ END-USER SUPPORT

Providing end-user support means solving whatever problems users encounter while using the network. There are three main functions within end-user support: resolving network faults, resolving software problems, and training. We have already discussed how to resolve network faults; now we focus on resolving software problems and end-user training.

Resolving Problems

Problems stem from three major sources. The first is a failed hardware device. These are usually the easiest to fix. A network technician simply fixes the device or installs a new part.

The second type of problem is a lack of user knowledge. These problems can usually be solved by discussing the situation with the user and taking that person through the process step by step. This is the next easiest type of problem to solve and can often be done by e-mail or over the telephone.

The third type of problem is a fundamental one with the software or an incompatibility between the software and network software and hardware. In this case, there may be a bug in the software or the software may not function properly on a certain combination of hardware and software. Solving these problems may be difficult, requiring expertise and software upgrades from the vendor.

Resolving either type of software problem begins with a request for assistance from the help desk. Requests for assistance are usually handled in the same manner as network faults. A trouble log (or request log) is maintained to document all incoming requests and the manner in which they are resolved. The staff member receiving the request attempts to resolve the problem in the best manner possible. Staff members should be provided with the set of standard procedures or scripts for soliciting information from the user about problems. In large organizations, this process may be supported by a special software tool.

There are often several levels to the problem resolution process. The first level is the most basic and all staff members working at the help desk should be able to resolve most of these. Most organizations strive to resolve between 75 and 85 percent of these requests in less than an hour. If the request cannot be resolved, it is escalated to the second level of problem resolution. Staff members who handle second level support have specialized skills in certain problem areas or with certain types of software and hardware. In most cases, problems are re-solved at this level. Some large organizations also have a third level of resolution, in which specialists spend many hours developing and testing various solutions to the problem, often in conjunction with staff from vendors of network software and hardware.

Providing End User Training

End-user training is an on-going responsibility of the network manager and is a key part in the implementation of new networks or network components. It is also important to have an on-going training program because employees may change job functions and new employees require training to use the organization's networks.

Training is usually conducted through in-class or one-on-one instruction and through the documentation and training manuals provided. In-class training should focus on the 20 percent of the network functions that the user will use 80 percent of the time, instead of attempting to cover all network functions. By pro-viding in-depth instruction of the fundamentals, users become confident about what they need to do. The training should also explain how to locate additional information from training manuals, documentation, or the help desk.

Management Focus: Reducing Web Goofing

Web goofing, using the corporate network to surf the Web for information unrelated to one's job, is increasing. Little scientific data ex-ist, but observers of goofing estimate that any-where from 5 to 40 percent of Web sites accessed on the job are unrelated to work. Web goofing can cost organizations lots of lost time and greatly increase network traffic. An Atlanta-based Internet company discovered that a 40 percent increase in network traffic from one month to the next was due to employees listen-ing to Web-based radio stations. Web goofing can also cause legal problems if employees download and share adult material.

The first step in reducing Web goofing is to develop and publish a written policy that ex-plains what is and is not permitted. While some organizations take a hard line by prohibiting all non-business use, others regard Internet access in the same light as telephone service (some personal use is permitted, provided that it does not get out of hand).

The second step is to install software that blocks access to tempting targets (e.g., ESPN, adult sites), and monitors all other access. Sim-ply monitoring Web usage often eliminates the problem because employees that know they are being monitored avoid violating corporate policy.

Source: "IS Targeting Web Slackers," *Communications Week,* June 2, 1997.

✳ ✳ COST MANAGEMENT

As the demand for network services grows, so do their costs. Effective and efficient management of data communications networks are important because more and more organizational resources are being spent on network management. In this section, we examine the major sources of costs and several ways to reduce them.

Sources of Costs

The *total cost of ownership (TCO)* is a measure of how much it costs per year to keep one computer operating. TCO includes the cost of support staff to attach it to the network, install software, administer the network (e.g., create userids, backup user data), provide training and technical support, and upgrade hardware and software. It also includes the cost of time "wasted" by the user when problems occur or when the user is attempting to learn new software.

Several studies over the past few years by GartnerGroup Inc. (a leading industry research firm) suggest that the TCO of a computer is astoundingly high. Most studies suggest that the TCO for a typical Windows computer on a network is about $10,000 *per year*. In other words, it costs almost five times as much *each year* to operate a computer as it does to purchase it in the first place. Other studies by firms such as IBM and *Information Week* (an industry magazine) have produced TCO estimates of between $8,000 and $12,000 per year, suggesting that the Gartner-Group's estimates are reasonable.

Although TCO has been accepted by many organizations, other firms argue against the practice of including "wasted" time in the calculation. For example, using the GartnerGroup approach, the TCO of a coffee machine is more than $50,000 per year. Assuming that getting coffee "wastes" 12 minutes per day times five days per week gives one hour per week, or about 50 hours per year of wasted time. If you assume the coffee pot serves 20 employees that have an average cost of $50 per hour (not an unusually high number) you get $50,000 per year. Plus, you have to add in the cost of the coffee and supplies.

Some organizations therefore prefer to focus on costing methods that examine only the direct costs of operating the computers, omitting softer costs such as "wasted" time. Several surveys by Forrester Research have found that network management costs (TCO without "wasted" time) range between $1500 and $3500 *per year* for *each* computer connected to a network. The typical network management group for a 100-user network would therefore have an annual budget of about $150,000 to $350,000. The most expensive item is personnel (network managers and technicians), which typically accounts for 50 to 70 percent of total costs. The second most expensive cost item is WAN circuits, followed by hardware upgrades and replacement parts.

There is one very important message from this pattern of costs. Since the largest cost item is personnel time, the primary focus of cost management lies in designing networks and developing policies to reduce personnel time, not to reduce hardware cost. Over the long term, it makes more sense to buy more expensive equipment if it can reduce the cost of network management.

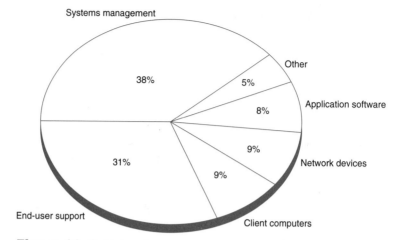

Figure 11–2 Network management personnel costs.

Figure 11–2 shows the average breakdown of personnel costs by function. The largest time cost (where staff spend most of their time) is systems management, which includes configuration, fault, and performance management tasks that focus on the network as a whole. The second largest item is end-user support.

Management Focus: *Always Check the Math*

Phone bills potentially carry mistakes. Fraud is not the issue—complexity is the villain here. The more complex the deal is, the greater the chance that parts of it will not get written up correctly and passed onto the right people at the carrier's office. If it is not handled correctly, you are not going to get the discount.

A case in point is the wording of AT&T Contract Tariff Number 1834: "The average annual duration of each AT&T Megacom service call must be at least 30 seconds but no more than two minutes. If the average call duration is less than 30 seconds, the customer is billed a shortfall charge of $0.00015 for every second that the average call duration falls short of 30 seconds. If the average call duration is more than two minutes, the customer will be billed a shortfall charge of $0.0003 for each second that the average call duration exceeds two minutes."

What AT&T really wanted to do was bill the customer $0.00015 for every second of shortfall for *every call* under 30 seconds and $0.0003 for every second of *every call* over 2 minutes. Instead, it only gets to charge once for a variance for the average call duration of all calls.

In addition to billing errors on contract provisions, other errors are often due to the failure to stop billing for a leased line that has been removed from service. Errors occur in 85 percent of all the bills examined by Telecom Services, Ltd., a telecommunications auditing firm. In money terms, companies are often overcharged between 5 and 15 percent of their monthly telecommunications bills due to errors.

Source: "Always Check the Math," *Datamation*, March 15, 1995.

Network managers often find it difficult to manage their budgets because networks grow so rapidly. They often find themselves having to defend ever-increasing requests for more equipment and staff. To counter these escalating costs, many large organizations have adopted *charge-back policies* for users of WANs and mainframe-based networks. (A charge-back policy attempts to allocate the costs associated with the network to specific users.) These users must "pay" for their network usage by transferring part of their budget allocations to the network group. Such policies are seldom used in LANs, making one more potential cultural difference between network management styles.

Reducing Costs

Given the huge amounts in TCO or even the substantial amounts spent on network management, there is considerable pressure on network managers to reduce costs. Figure 11–3 summarizes five steps to reduce network costs.

The first and most important step is to develop standards for client computers and servers. These standards define one configuration (or a small set of configurations) that are permitted for all client computers and servers. By standardizing hardware and software, it is easier to diagnose and fix problems. Also, there are fewer software packages for the network support staff to learn. The downside, of course, is that rigid adherence to standards reduces innovation.

The second most important step is to automate as much of the network management process as possible. Electronic software delivery (ESD) can significantly reduce the cost to upgrade when new software is released. It also enables faster installation of new computers and faster recovery when software needs to be reinstalled, and helps enforce the standards policies. Dynamic address assignment (e.g., DHCP, see Chapter 6) can reduce time spent on managing TCP/IP addresses. The use of network management software to identify and diagnose problems can significantly reduce time spent in performance and fault management. Likewise, help desk software can cut the cost of the end user support function.

A third step is to do everything possible to reduce the time spent installing new hardware and software. The cost of a network technician spending half a day

Five Steps to Reduce Network Costs

* Develop standard hardware and software configurations for client computers and servers

* Automate as much of the network management function as possible by deploying a solid set of network management tools

* Reduce the costs of installing new hardware and software by working with vendors

* Centralize help desks

* Move to thin client architectures

Figure 11–3 Five steps to reduce network costs.

to install and configure new computers is often $500. ESD is an important step to reducing costs, but careful purchasing can also go a long way. The installation of standard hardware and software by the hardware vendor (e.g., Microsoft Office) can significantly reduce costs. Likewise, careful monitoring of hardware failures can quickly identify vendors of less-reliable equipment that can be avoided in the next purchasing cycle.

Traditionally, help desks have been decentralized into user departments. The result is a proliferation of help desks and support staff, many of whom tend to be generalists rather than specialists in one area. Many organizations have found that centralizing help desks enables them to reduce the number of generalists and provide more specialists in key technology areas. This results in faster resolution of difficult problems. Centralization also makes it easier to identify common problems occurring in different parts of the organization and take actions to reduce them. Some organizations have chosen to use decentralized help desks,

Management Focus: Chevron Cuts Costs

For years, managers have struggled to cut the total cost of ownership. In many cases, organizations attempt to cut costs in a piecemeal fashion by focusing on each network individually. Chevron, which has been at the leading edge of cost management for many years, hopes to cut $50 million from its annual network budget over the next few years by taking an enterprise-wide viewpoint. It appointed two senior executives at the vice-presidential level to develop and implement its cost management plan.

The plan had two major parts. The first, called the "governance model," developed a detailed plan to identify key technologies and decide how much enterprise-wide standardization was needed. This enabled different groups within the organization to identify and negotiate over what software and hardware would comprise the standard enterprise-wide system, and to identify exceptions to the standard.

The second part of the plan was the actual implementation of the resulting "common operating environment" or COE. The COE specifies standard hardware and software for use worldwide at all Chevron locations—more than 40,000 client computers and thousands of servers. The COE includes commercial software (e.g., Microsoft Office) as well as software developed internally, and is installed by hardware vendors before the computers are shipped to Chevron.

Chevron has decided to phase out its Novell servers and IBM mainframes in favor of Windows NT and a few selected Unix sites. The combination of NT servers and Windows clients with standard client software updated through electronic software delivery is expected to provide significant savings.

Chevron is also pilot testing a leasing program in which users automatically receive a new computer every three years. The alternative is a "cascading" or "hand-me-down" plan in which power users get new computers every year, with the older computers transferred to those who can make do with less-powerful computers.

Source: "Chevron Takes Control," *Information Week*, November 4, 1996.

recognizing their increased cost, because they believe that users prefer to interact with the same help desk and support personnel, rather than being assigned a new person for each call.

Finally, many network experts argue that moving to thin client architectures, particularly those using network computers (see Chapter 3), can significantly reduce costs. Although network computers cost slightly less than traditional computers, the real saving lies in the support costs. Since they are restricted to a narrow set of functions and generally do not permit software installations, they become much easier to manage. TCO and network management costs drop by 20 to 40 percent. There is not a lot of software available for network computers today, but this will change. Most organizations anticipate using network computers selectively, in areas when application software is well defined and can easily be restricted (e.g., receptionists, clerks, help desks, order processing).

❋ ❋ NETWORK MANAGEMENT TOOLS

Network managers need a set of tools to help them perform their various functions. Most tools can be classified as being primarily hardware or software, although in practice any software tool needs to be supported by hardware.

Network Management Software

Network management software is designed to provide automated support for some or all of the network management functions. Dozens of network management tools are available (see Figure 11–4). Some software tools support configuration man-

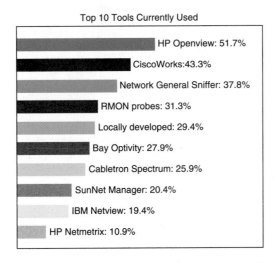

Top 10 Tools Currently Used

- HP Openview: 51.7%
- CiscoWorks:43.3%
- Network General Sniffer: 37.8%
- RMON probes: 31.3%
- Locally developed: 29.4%
- Bay Optivity: 27.9%
- Cabletron Spectrum: 25.9%
- SunNet Manager: 20.4%
- IBM Netview: 19.4%
- HP Netmetrix: 10.9%

Figure 11–4 Top ten network management tools.

Source: "Net Management Tools Fail to Satisfy Users," *Network World, October 13, 1997.*

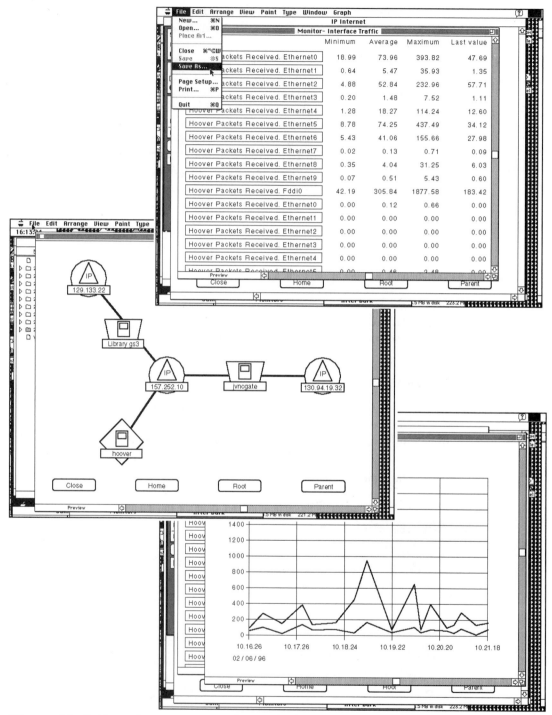

Figure 11-5 Network management software displays.

agement, some support performance and fault management, while some attempt to do both. Some tools have modules to support the help desk, providing end-user support.

A 1997 survey by International Network Services of more than 200 network managers found that more than 40 percent were dissatisfied with current network management software (30 percent were satisfied and 30 percent neither satisfied nor dissatisfied). The most common complaints were problems tracking response time, monitoring network availability, managing critical network applications, and managing server performance.

There are three fundamentally different types of network management software. *Device management software* is designed to provide information about the specific devices on a network. It enables the network manager to monitor important devices such as servers, routers, and gateway, and typically report configuration information, traffic volumes, and error conditions for each device. Figure 11–5 shows some sample displays from a device management package. Device management software requires "smart" or "managed" hardware devices that can collect and report information to the device management software. Such devices contain a processor and memory and run small programs called *agents*. These agents collect information as the devices operate and can issue warning messages in the event of problems.

System management software (sometimes called enterprise management software) adds two additional functions on top of device management. First, system management software provides the same configuration, traffic, and error information as device management systems, but also provides ESD. Second, and most important, system management software can analyze the device information to diagnose patterns, not just display individual device problems. This is important when a critical device fails (e.g., a router into a high-traffic building). With device management software, all of the devices that depend on the failed device will attempt to send warning messages to the network administrator. One failure often generates several dozen problem reports, called an *alarm storm*, making it difficult to quickly pinpoint the true source of the problem. The dozens of error messages are symptoms that mask the root cause. System management software tools correlate the individual error messages into a pattern, and then report the pattern to the network manager. Rather than first seeing pages and pages of error messages, the network manager instead gets a warning that an entire network segment is down, starting with the failed device.

Application management software also builds on the device management software, but instead of monitoring systems, it monitors applications. In many organizations, there are mission-critical applications that should get priority over other network traffic. For example, real-time order-entry systems used by telephone operators need priority over e-mail. Application management systems track delays and problems with application layer packets and inform the network manager if problems occur and these packets for priority applications experience important delays.

Management Focus: *Charles Schwab Masters Tivoli TME*

In 1993, Charles Schwab implemented IBM's Tivoli TME, an enterprise management framework (i.e., system management software). TME was in its infancy and the project was a complete failure.

In 1996, Schwab tried again, this time with the newest version of TME. Although the project was far from simple, it was a success. TME provides the basic building blocks for the network management system—the software equivalents of concrete and lumber. Schwab dedicated two network experts full time to the project. They spent more than a year designing the standard reporting policies and procedures, thresholds for the alarms, and automated responses.

The key to Schwab's success the second time was realizing the importance of network policies that define which problems require immediate action and which ones can wait. For example, for each server and application, what are the acceptable response times and availability percentages, and once a threshold is reached, does the system attempt to remedy the problem, or what human or external system does it notify? Once the organizational issues were thoroughly discussed and organization-wide standards were defined and accepted by users, the technical implementation went more smoothly.

Schwab has more than 1000 servers and 10,000 users at 300 branches across North America. The TME software alone cost several million dollars, but was less than the amount spent on salaries to plan, design, and implement the software and to train network managers. While the costs are enormous, a study by International Data Corp. of 10 global companies similar to Schwab reported an average payback time of a minuscule four months. The IDC study also found that TME reduced the total cost of ownership by an average of $2200 per user per year.

Source: "Management Marathon," *Network World*, January 12, 1998.

Network Management Standards

One important problem is ensuring that hardware devices from different vendors can understand and respond to the messages sent by the network management software of other vendors. By this point, however, the solution should be obvious: standards. A number of formal and de facto standards have been developed for network management. These standards are application layer protocols that define the type of information collected by network devices and the format of control messages that the devices understand. The two most commonly used network management protocols are SNMP and CMIP. Most of the major network management software tools available today (e.g., OpenView) understand SNMP and CMIP and can operate with hardware that uses either standard.

Simple Network Management Protocol (SNMP)

The *simple network management protocol (SNMP)* originally was developed to control and monitor the status of network devices on TCP/IP networks, but now it is available for other network protocols (e.g., IPX/SPX). Each SNMP device (e.g., router, gateway, server) has an *agent* that collects information about itself and the messages it processes, and stores that information in a database called the *management information base (MIB)*. The network manager's management station that runs the network management software has access to these MIBs. Using this software, the network manager can send control messages to individual devices or groups of devices asking them to report the information stored in their MIB.

As the name suggests, SNMP is a simple protocol with a limited number of functions. One problem with SNMP is that many vendors have defined their own extensions to it, so the network devices sold by a vendor may be SNMP compliant, but the MIBs they produce contain additional information that can only be used by network management software produced by the same vendor. Therefore, while SNMP was designed to make it easier to manage devices from different vendors, in practice, this is not always the case.

One important addition to SNMP is the ability for distributed or *remote monitoring (RMON)*. Most first-generation SNMP tools reported all network monitoring information to one central network management database. Each device would transmit updates to its MIB to the server every few minutes, greatly increasing network traffic. RMON SNMP software enables MIB information to be stored on the device itself or on distributed *RMON probes* that store MIB information closer to the devices that generate it. The data is not transmitted to the central server until the network manager requests the data, thus reducing network traffic.

Management Focus: *Discovering OpenView*

The most popular network management system in the world is the OpenView Network Node Manager by Hewlett-Packard. It provides an open-systems standards-compliant tool that can be used with network hardware and software from many different vendors. As might be expected from the market leader, it costs more than $50,000 for a good-sized network.

When we started OpenView, we pointed to a router in the center of our network and let it discover everything in our network. It was exciting to watch it discover more and more subnets, but soon we had so many subnets that the network map required a microscope to read. To make the map more readable, we started the autodiscovery process over again, and this time created one overall network map with dozens of submaps, one for each major part of the network.

OpenView has a powerful set of MIB builders and browsers than can be accessed by the OpenView software or over the Web. We quickly were able to define the statistics to be collected and alarms to be issued for each device. OpenView provides a wide range of alarms that can be defined and can also specify how long an event must exist before the alarm is issued (which prevents transient network overloads from generating unnecessary alarms). OpenView has a good alarm correlation process to prevent alarm storms, but it can be rather complex to define the necessary rules to install it.

Source: "Network Management," *Network Computing,* August 15, 1997; "HP Masters the Enterprise," *PC Week,* September 15, 1997.

The newest versions of SNMP and RMON have added other important capabilities. Network information is recorded based on the data link layer protocols, network layer protocols, and application layer protocols, so that network managers can get a very clear picture of the exact types of network traffic in the network. Statistics are also collected based on network addresses so the network manager can see how much network traffic any particular computer is sending and receiving. A wide variety of alarms can be defined, such as instructing a device to send a warning message if certain items in the MIB exceed certain values (e.g., if circuit utilization exceeds 50 percent).

Common Management Interface Protocol (CMIP)

The *common management interface protocol (CMIP)*, a competitor to SNMP, is a protocol for OSI-type networks developed by the International Standards Organization. It is much newer than SNMP and therefore is not widely used. CMIP monitors and tracks network usage and other parameters for servers, client computers, and other devices in much the same manner as SNMP, except that it is more complete than SNMP, and better in many ways.

The two protocols are incompatible. There are more SNMP devices currently installed and being sold than CMIP-based devices. After seeing CMIP, many SNMP vendors have recognized the limitations of SNMP and are aggressively pushing for improved SNMP standards to ensure that CMIP does not become more popular than SNMP.

Network Management Hardware

Just a decade ago, many data communication facility managers did not have test equipment. They depended on the telephone company when a circuit failed and on other communication vendors when hardware or software failed. Today, everything is changed because of deregulation. For example, you might be using three

---

Management Focus: Selecting Network Management Software

There are a number of important functions to look for when comparing network management software. These include:

* Support for all popular network operating systems (e.g., Novell, Windows NT)
* Support for SNMP/RMON and other protocols such as CMIP
* Automatic discovery and configuration of network hardware and software
* Logical and physical network configuration
* Data import and export in a variety of formats
* Graphical user interface
* User-definable alarms and correlation to pinpoint root causes
* Remote monitoring
* Software license metering
* Virus protection (see Chapter 12)

Source: Insider's Guide to Personal Computing & Networking, Sams Publishing, New York, 1992.

or four telephone companies, five or six hardware vendors, and two or three software vendors. This means that ownership of the proper test equipment is mandatory. Network management *must* be able to diagnose a problem and determine which telephone company, hardware vendor, or software vendor should be contacted for assistance when the problem cannot be fixed in-house.

Testing is divided into analog testing, digital testing, and protocol testing. *Analog testing* involves troubleshooting on the analog side of the modem on the communication circuits supplied by common carriers. *Digital testing* is aimed primarily at testing digital communication circuits. *Protocol testing* focuses on testing the various sign-on/sign-off procedures, checking the content of packets or frames, examining message transmission times, and other items related to software protocols.

Monitors and *analyzers* generally are test sets that allow the operator to simulate specific message streams to test devices, communication circuits, or other workstations. A monitor resembles a portable microcomputer. Protocol analyzers offer both data and protocol analysis for TCP/IP, SNA, X.25, HDLC, T1, frame relay, and the like. Most of today's line monitors and network analyzers use microprocessor chips to perform sophisticated network tests. In other cases, microcomputers with special software handle the required network testing and monitoring.

Analog and digital test sets are found on any network that uses modems in conjunction with telephone company circuits. Most networks require both analog and digital test sets. These devices also resemble portable microcomputers, complete with a video screen and keyboard for data entry.

Patch panels provide electrical connection to all parts of the network. At the minimum, they provide centralized access to each network communication circuit. They are large panels with a number of plugs or connectors that can be cross-connected between different communication circuits. Cross-patching permits the immediate replacement of a failed circuit with a spare.

Data recorders do not always perform tests. They are used to tap into communication circuits and store on disk pertinent activities about various circuits. Basically, they are monitors for collecting and analyzing data and printing out reports. They, too, resemble portable microcomputers.

Handheld test sets are the least expensive and simplest type of network equipment. They can be inserted between two network devices to test voltages or to send and receive various test patterns of bits to isolate errors. They also are used to determine whether there is a problem with the cables.

Breakout Box

The most basic level of data communication monitoring and test equipment is analog test equipment. The *breakout box* is the next level up. It is a handheld device that can be plugged into a modem's digital side to determine the voltage values for the circuit.

Bit-Error Rate Tester (BERT)

The *bit-error rate tester (BERT)* is somewhat more sophisticated than a breakout box because it sends a known pseudo-random pattern over the communication circuit. When this pattern is reflected back, the BERT compares it to the transmitted pattern and calculates the number of bit errors that occurred on the communication circuit. Various test patterns are used, and common pattern lengths are 63, 511, 2047, and 63,511 bit patterns.

Bit-error rate (BER) measurements can be made with this type of equipment. A BER is the number of bits received in error divided by the total number of bits received. Service personnel use BER measurements to tune the communication circuit and to make a subjective evaluation as to the quality of a specific circuit or channel. BER cannot be related directly to throughput because error distribution is not taken into account. Assume that 1000 one-bit errors occur during a time interval of 1000 seconds. If the errors are distributed evenly (one per second), the effect on throughput will be disastrous; however, if all the errors occur in a single second, the effect will be minimal.

Block-Error Rate Tester (BKERT)

The *block-error rate tester (BKERT)* calculates the *block-error rate (BKER)*, which is the number of received blocks that contain at least one bit error divided by the total number of blocks received. A BKER is more closely related to throughput than a BER. Assume a BKER measurement has been made and the BKER value is 10^2 (1/100). This means that out of every 100 blocks received, one contained an error; therefore, you would expect to see one retry for every 100 blocks transmitted (a 1 percent error rate).

Another error-rate parameter used only for digital networks is *error-free seconds (EFS)*. It is similar to BKER except it indicates the probability of success rather than failure, and the block size is the number of bits transmitted in a one-second time period. For example, for a 4800 bps channel, the one-second block would contain 4800 bits.

Fiber Identifier

The *fiber identifier* is to locate a particular nonworking fiber without interrupting service on a fiber optic network. (Remember that a fiber cable may contain a bundle of 72 or 144 glass or plastic fibers.) The fiber identifier consists of a transmitter that injects a light signal, a detector that induces a low stress on the fibers allowing them to be searched without damage, and a receiver that emits an audible and visual signal when the fiber in question has been identified. The detector is a wandlike device that detects the signal at splice locations as it is passed near the splice. Because splices leak light, these are the points at which illegal taps would be inserted.

Cable Analyzer

The *cable analyzer* checks LAN cabling for signal continuity, pulse distortion, parity, conductivity, connectivity, polarity reversals, and excessive noise in the data stream. It also can test to ensure that the cable meets the standards for that type of cable.

Protocol Analyzer/Data Line Monitor

Today, protocol analyzers and data line monitors tend to do the same things. Recognizing this overlap, however, we can distinguish between them by their original purpose. A *data line monitor* traces network activity and response time analysis on a specific circuit. It also checks the actual data. *Protocol analyzers* decode messages on the circuit to allow you to see the content (bits) of a frame or packet during its transmission. Users can capture data in an external tape storage or internal memory, print it, or freeze the most current data on the video screen. A protocol analyzer shows when a carriage return or a line feed occurs, as well as when a communication control code is transmitted. The technician can count the bits within a packet or frame and identify each field and its contents.

Protocol analyzers also measure the responses of all hardware in the network and determine whether the network equipment is meeting specifications. In addition, they can print the captured information or trap information when certain character sequences appear on the send or receive communication circuits. Some analyzers offer performance monitoring operations to help evaluate specific areas of network performance, such as response time and circuit utilization.

These devices may be active or passive. Active analyzers/monitors can generate data, are interactive on the circuit, and can emulate various terminals because they are programmable. Passive analyzers/monitors merely monitor and collect data to be examined later. It should be noted that this test equipment, especially active analyzers, can be a security risk because of its ability to generate data, interactively place it on a communication circuit, and do this while emulating another terminal.

Management Focus: *Time to Outsource Network Management?*

The fastest-growing segment of the computer outsourcing market is network management. As networks and network management becomes more and more complex, more organizations are turning to professional firms to run their networks.

Aspen Medial Group provides health care services to 10 medical centers in the Minneapolis/St. Paul area. Runaway growth of Aspen's LAN and backbone networks had outstripped its network staff's ability to manage them. The IT director was hesitant to invest a lot of time and money in hiring and training an expert network manager, who might then move to a competitor.

The solution was to hand over the management of Aspen's networks to Memorex-Telex Corp., Aspen's major networking equipment vendor. Memorex is one of a growing number of firms that provide complete network management services. Most of these firms are vendors of networking equipment such as Memorex, or vendors of network services who have long experience managing their own networks, such as AT&T and RBOCs.

The management services offered by different companies depend on their expertise, but many offer traffic monitoring and fault management, configuration management of network devices, applications software support, network design and implementation, and help desk operations for end-user support.

The push to outsource network management to specialized firms is growing. International Data Corp. estimates that by 2001, organizations will spend $11 billion on network management services.

Source: "Time to Handoff Your LAN?" *Network World,* March 20, 1995; "Outsourcing Network Management," *Enterprise Systems Journal,* June 1997.

A typical analyzer can monitor data, trap and count data for gathering communication circuit statistics, offer a video screen and printer, poll various stations, offer BERT capabilities, work with both asynchronous and synchronous systems, analyze various protocols, and possess breakout box capabilities. Several vendors sell the hardware and software needed to turn a microcomputer into a limited version of a protocol analyzer, data line monitor, and BERT tester.

Automated Test Equipment

Automated test equipment consists of hardware and specialized software packages. All have built-in microprocessor chips and programmable testing features. You should note that the programs able to do this testing also can be housed within the host mainframe computer or a remote computer somewhere out in the network. Furthermore, the telephone companies offer centralized automated testing equipment for monitoring your network.

Automated testing equipment performs diagnostic testing, polling, statistics gathering, protocol emulation, measurement of bandwidth efficiency, self-diagnosis of its own circuits, analog and digital circuit testing, testing of centralized and remote switches, and automatic restart and recovery in case of disaster.

Summary

Integrating LANs, WANs, and the Web   Today, the critical issue is the integration of all organizational networks, which presents two problems. The first problem is technical; since each LAN was designed separately, not all LANs use the same type of hardware and software. The second problem is cultural. WAN managers and managers of mainframe-based host computer networks are typically more comfortable in highly structured and slow-to-change network environments. In contrast, LAN and Web managers tend to be less interested in standards and more interested in getting the job done. The key to integrating LANs, WANs, and the Web into one overall organization network is for WAN managers to recognize that LAN/Web managers can make independent decisions, and LAN/Web managers to realize that they need to work within organizational standards.

Integrating Voice and Data Communications   Another major challenge is combining voice communications with data and image communications. This separation of voice and data worked well over the years, but changing communication technologies are generating enormous pressures to combine them. A key factor in voice/data integration might turn out to be the elimination of one key management position and the merging of two staffs into one.

Configuration Management   Configuration management means managing the network's hardware and software configuration and documenting it (and ensuring the documentation is updated as the configuration changes). The most common configuration management activity is adding and deleting user accounts. The most basic documentation about network hardware is a set of network configuration maps, supplemented by documentation on each individual network component. A similar approach can be used for network software. Electronic software delivery (ESD) plays a key role in simplifying configuration management by automating and documenting the network configurations. User and application profiles should be automatically provided by the network and ESD software. There is a variety of other documentation that must be routinely developed and updated, including users' manuals and organizational policies.

Performance and Fault Management   Performance management means ensuring the network is operating as efficiently as possible. Fault management means preventing, detecting, and correcting any faults in the network circuits, hardware, and software. The two are closely related because any faults in the network reduce performance, and because both require network monitoring. Today, most networks use a combination of smart devices to monitor the network and issue alarms and a help desk to respond to user problems. Problem tracking allows the network manager to determine problem ownership or who is responsible for correcting any outstanding problems. Problem statistics are important because they are a control device for the network operators as well as for vendors.

Providing End-User Support   Providing end-user support means solving whatever network problems users encounter. Support consists of resolving network faults, resolving software problems, and training. Software problems often stem from lack of user knowledge and fundamental problems with the software or an incompatibility between the software and network's software and hardware. There are often several levels to problem resolution. End-user training is an on-going responsibility of the network manager. Training usually has two parts: in-class instruction, and the documentation and training manuals that the user keeps for reference.

Cost Management   As the demand for network services grows, so does its cost. The total cost of ownership (TCO) for a typical networked PC is about $10,000 per year, far more than the initial purchase price. The direct cost (omitting "wasted" time) is around $2500 per year. The largest single cost item is staff salaries. The best way to control rapidly increasing network costs is to reduce the amount of time taken to perform network management functions, often by automating as many routine ones as possible.

Network Management Software   Network management software is designed to provide automated support for any or all of the network management functions. Device management software provides information about devices. Systems management software provides ESD and analyzes the device-level information providing more useful network-level information. Application management software tracks information about mission-critical applications that run on the network. "Smart" network devices perform their functions and also record data on the messages they process. These data can be sent to the network manager's computer when the device receives a special control message. If the device detects a critical situation, it can send a special control message (called an alarm) to the network manager's computer. The two most commonly used network management protocol standards are SNMP and CMIP.

Network Management Hardware Tools There are five basic categories of test equipment. Monitors and analyzers allow the operator to simulate specific message streams to test devices, communication circuits, or other workstations. Analog and digital test sets are found on any network that uses modems in conjunction with telephone company circuits. Patch panels provide electrical connection to all parts of the network. Data recorders tap into communication circuits and store on disk pertinent activities about various circuits. Handheld test sets can be inserted between two network devices to test voltages or to send and receive various test patterns of bits to isolate errors.

Key Terms

agent

alarms

alarm storm

analog testing

analyzer

application management
  software

automated test equipment

availability

bit-error rate (BER)

bit-error rate tester (BERT)

block-error rate (BKER)

block-error rate tester (BKERT)

breakout box

cable analyzer

charge-back policy

common management
  interface protocol (CMIP)

configuration management

data line monitor

data recorders

device management software

digital testing

downtime

electronic software delivery
  (ESD)

error-free seconds (EFS)

fault management

fiber identifier

firefighting

handheld test set

help desk

logical network parameters

management information base
  (MIB)

mean time between failures
  (MTBF)

mean time to diagnose
  (MTTD)

mean time to fix (MTTF)

mean time to repair (MTTR)

mean time to respond (MTTR)

monitors

network control center

network management

network management software

patch panels

performance management

physical network parameters

problem statistics

problem tracking

protocol analyzer

protocol testing

quality control chart

remote monitoring (RMON)

RMON probe

service level agreement
  (SLA)

simple network management
  protocol (SNMP)

system management software

total cost of ownership (TCO)

trouble ticket

Questions

1. What are some cultural differences between LAN and WAN managers?

2. What is firefighting?

3. Why is combining voice and data a major organizational challenge?

4. Describe what configuration management encompasses.

5. People tend to think of software when documentation is mentioned. What is documentation in a network situation?

6. What is electronic software delivery, and why is it important?
7. What is performance and fault management?
8. What does a help desk do?
9. What do trouble tickets report?
10. Several important statistics related to network uptime and downtime are discussed in this chapter. What are they, and why are they important?
11. What is a service level agreement?
12. How is network availability calculated?
13. What is problem escalation?
14. What are the primary functions of end-user support?
15. What is total cost of ownership?
16. Why is the total cost of ownership so high?

17. How can network costs be reduced?
18. What do network management software systems do, and why are they important?
19. Discuss three types of network management software.
20. What is the simple network management protocol (SNMP)?
21. What is RMON?
22. What is the name of SNMP's OSI competitor? How are they distinguished from one another?
23. What are the five categories of network test equipment?
24. What is the purpose of a fiber identifier?
25. How is a cable analyzer used?
26. What is a protocol analyzer?

Exercises

A. What factors might cause peak loads in a network? How can a network manager determine if they are important and how are they taken into account when designing a data communication network?
B. Today's network managers face a number of demanding problems. Investigate and discuss three major issues.
C. Investigate the latest versions of SMNP and RMON and describe the functions that

have been added in the latest version of the standard.
D. Investigate and report on the purpose, relative advantages and disadvantages of three network management software tools (e.g., OpenView, Tivoli TME, Alert Page).
E. Research the networking budget in your organization and discuss the major cost areas. Discuss several ways of reducing costs over the long term.

NEXT DAY AIR SERVICE CASE STUDY

The NDAS network system is finally in place and operating. President Coone has assigned operational control of the network to the Information Services Department. He believes this is reasonable and justified because of the Information Services Department's data processing responsibilities and experience in operating data communications equipment. In addition, his nephew, Les Coone, is running that department and has expressed considerable interest in data communications.

The Human Resources Department originally set up the telephone system, because—at the time—no one else was interested in doing it. As a result, Human

Resources, headed by Karen Lott, controls the voice and facsimile communication system for the company.

One recurring problem is that two department heads disagree on which department should be responsible for dealing with the common carriers. Each department believes it should be the contact for dealing with the common carriers, and each thinks the other is stopping it from assuming its rightful place within the organization.

Because of your excellent past performance, President Coone has asked you to study certain organizational issues pertaining to the control and operation of both voice and data communications. He wants you to analyze the operations of both departments and propose a method for streamlining the organization and fixing the problem. This analysis should address the possibility of combining the voice and data communication responsibilities under a single manager. You may propose any reorganization that seems appropriate. Be sure to consider economies of scale when submitting any recommendations. President Coone reminds you that you were a staunch advocate of video conferencing. He wants you to include video and image transmission considerations in your analysis.

You should also consider the type of individual that should manage this reorganization. Some of the factors to evaluate are the traits and characteristics needed for successful leadership, the ability to understand current systems, the ability to handle both data and voice networks, and the ability to analyze and manage future growth. The results of this evaluation will help determine whether such an individual exists within Next Day Air Service or whether the firm needs to hire someone from outside the organization.

Another little problem occurred last week when NDAS experienced its first network line failure. President Coone had to ask Karen Lott to determine what failed on the circuit. After fiddling with the problem for an hour and a half, she finally called the modem vendor, who then took three hours to get to the Tampa headquarters building. The good news is that the vendor's maintenance employee swapped a new circuit card into the failed modem and had it fixed in 15 minutes. Needless to say, President Coone was not happy!

Exercises

1. If the responsibilities for managing communications were to be consolidated into one department, which one would you choose, and why? Base your answer on your knowledge of the communication management responsibilities exercised by both the Human Resources and Information Services Departments.

2. Review the organization chart for NDAS, as shown in Figure 1–8, and then develop an organization chart that reflects a realignment of the responsibilities for communications. Show separate organizational entities for both data processing and communications. Consider the pros and cons of creating a new communication manager position. Discuss the reasons why Next Day Air

Service should promote someone from within the company to fill this new position. Now discuss the contrary reasons why NDAS should hire someone from outside the organization for this position. Which position will you take? Why?

3. Sketch out a simple network management system for NDAS. What software and hardware support would you recommend? Be sure you can justify the information items collected and reported for this system, as well as your software and hardware recommendations.

CHAPTER 12

Network Security

This chapter describes why networks need security, and how to provide it. It begins with risk assessment and then describes a series of controls to prevent, detect, and correct disruptions, destruction, disaster, and unauthorized access.

Objectives

* Become familiar the major threats to network security
* Become familiar with how to conduct a risk assessment

* Understand how to prevent, detect, and correct disruptions, destruction, and disaster
* Understand how to prevent, detect, and correct unauthorized access

Chapter Outline

✳ ✳ INTRODUCTION

Both business and government were concerned with security long before they recognized a need for computer-related security. They always have been interested in the physical protection of assets through means such as locks, barriers, and guards. The introduction of computer processing, large databases, and communication networks has increased the need for security. Our concerns about security are focused directly on the computer-related areas of business. Almost 85 percent of 1000 organizations surveyed in 1997 reported experiencing a security problem that resulted in a meaningful dollar loss.

For many people, security means preventing unauthorized access, such as preventing a hacker from breaking into your computer. Security is more than that, however. It also includes being able to recover from temporary service problems (e.g., a broken circuit) or from natural disasters (e.g., fire, earthquake). Figure 12–1 shows some threats to a computer center, the data communication circuits, and the attached computers.

Why Networks Need Security

In recent years, organizations have become increasingly dependent on data communication networks for their daily business communications, database information retrieval, distributed data processing, and the internetworking of LANs. The rise of the Internet with opportunities to connect computers anywhere in the world has significantly increased the potential vulnerability of the organization's assets. Emphasis on network security has also increased, as a result of well-publicized security break-ins and as government regulatory agencies have issued security-related pronouncements.

The losses associated with the security failures can be huge. The most obvious threat is fraud and theft. FBI data show that over the past five years, the average loss from bank robbery (i.e., when someone robs a bank at gunpoint) was about $3000. A 1997 FBI report showed the average loss in a case of computer fraud was $950,000. The average loss in a case of data theft was about $200,000. However, this is just the tip of the iceberg. The potential loss of consumer confidence from a well-publicized security break-in can cost more in lost business.

More important than these, however, are the potential losses from the disruption of application systems that run on computer networks. As organizations have come to depend on computer systems, computer networks have become "mission-critical." NationsBank, one of the largest banks in the United States, estimates that it would cost the bank $50 million if its computer networks were unavailable for 24 hours. Other large organizations have produced similar estimates. The value of the data stored on most organizations' networks and the value provided by the application systems in use far exceeds the cost of the networks themselves. For this reason, the primary goal of network security is to protect the organization's data and application software.

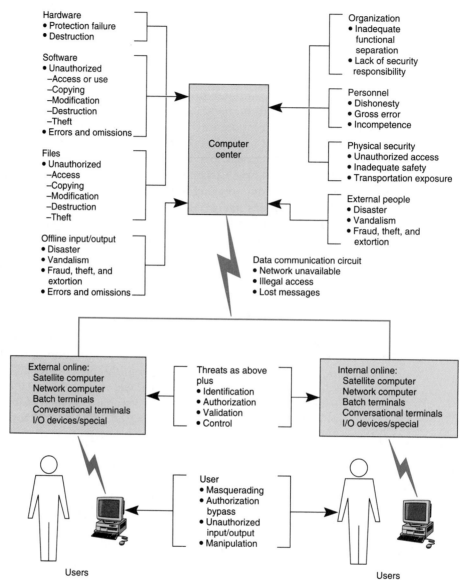

Figure 12-1 Some threats to a computer center, the data communication circuits, and the client computers.

Types of Security Threats

In general, network security threats can be classified into one of two categories: disruption, destruction, and disaster; and unauthorized access.

Disruptions are the loss of or reduction in network service. Disruptions may be minor and temporary. For example, a network switch might fail or a circuit might be cut, causing part of the network to cease functioning until the failed component can be replaced. Some users may be affected, but others can continue. Some disruptions may also be caused by or result in the *destruction* of data. For example, a virus may destroy files, or the "crash" of a hard disk may cause files to be destroyed. Other disruptions may be catastrophic. Natural (or manmade) *disasters* may occur that destroy host computers or large sections of the network. For example, fires, floods, earthquakes, mudslides, tornadoes, or terrorist attacks can destroy large parts of the buildings and networks in their path.

Unauthorized access is often viewed as hackers gaining access to organizational data files and resources. However, most unauthorized access incidents involve employees. Unauthorized access may have only minor effects. A curious intruder may simply explore the system, gaining knowledge that has little value. A more serious intruder may be a competitor bent on industrial espionage who could attempt to gain access to information on products under development, or the details and price of a bid on a large contract. Worse still, the intruder could change files to commit fraud or theft, or destroy information to injure the organization.

Before discussing network security, we summarize past computer security problems involving some aspect of communications to give you some idea of the types of security problems that have been encountered. As you read them, try to identify some security controls that might have prevented, detected, or corrected the problem if they had been in place when it occurred.

The massive fire that destroyed the central office switch of an Illinois Bell Telephone Company demonstrates the need for security and backup. The fire cut voice and data communications to thousands of businesses in the western Chicago area. Many businesses, such as branch banks, cannot continue to operate as viable businesses if their voice and data communications are cut off for even a few days, much less two weeks. The Walgreens drugstore chain in Illinois reported that in the aftermath of the fire, 180 of its 255 drugstores lost access to their central communication network.

In another case, a gunman armed with a shotgun and a pistol entered a telephone company central office and took several hostages. He then blasted away at the central office switch with the shotgun, causing an estimated $10 million in damages. Approximately 15,000 customers lost their telephone service but, to the credit of the telephone company, all service was restored within 22 hours.

A massive virus infection of the Internet (called the Internet worm) started one evening in 1988. Among the first targets were two science and research centers at Berkeley, California, and Cambridge, Massachusetts. The virus then targeted NASA's Ames Research Center in California, the University of Pittsburgh in Pennsylvania, and Los Alamos National Laboratory in New Mexico. By the next morning it also had penetrated computers at Johns Hopkins University (Baltimore) and the University of Michigan (Ann Arbor). This invading virus replicated itself so many times and so often that it overloaded the network, forcing the network operators to shut down for lack of computer cycles. It then moved on to Bellcore in Livingston, New Jersey, SRI International in Menlo Park, California, and New York University. It is noteworthy that the computers of AT&T's Bell Laboratories in Murray Hill, New Jersey, of the University of Maryland, and of Chicago's Argonne National Laboratory were able to repel the virus. The point of this is to demonstrate how quickly a computer virus can infect a nationwide network. In this example, it took less than one day.

In 1996, a group of Russian *hackers* in St. Petersburg stole $12 million from a Citibank computer in New York City. They were later caught and the money was recovered.

In July 1996, the Web site for the Department of Justice was penetrated by outsiders. They relabeled the site the "Department of Injustice" and posted swastikas and pornographic pictures. Although no important or confidential information was stored on these sites, the public humiliation was immense. Similar break-ins have occurred at other government Web sites such as those for the Air Force and the CIA.

Network Controls

Developing a secure network means developing *controls*. Controls are mechanisms that reduce or eliminate the threats to network security. There are three types of controls that *prevent*, *detect*, and *correct* whatever might happen to the organization through the threats faced by its computer-based systems.

Preventive controls mitigate or stop a person from acting or an event from occurring. For example, a password can prevent illegal entry into the system, or backup circuits can prevent network downtime. Preventive controls also act as a deterrent by discouraging or restraining someone from acting or proceeding because of fear or doubt. They also restrain or hinder an event. For example, a guard or a security lock on a door may deter an attempt to gain illegal entry.

Detective controls reveal or discover unwanted events. For example, software that looks for illegal network entry or a virus can detect these problems. They also document an event, a situation, or a trespass, providing evidence for subsequent action against the individuals or organizations involved or to enable corrective action to be taken. For example, the same software that detects the problem must report it immediately so that someone or some automated process can take remedial action.

Corrective controls rectify an unwanted event or a trespass. Either computer programs or humans verify and check data to correct errors or fix a security breach so it will not recur in the future. They also can recover from network errors or disasters. For example, software can recover and restart the communication circuits automatically when there is a data communication failure.

The remainder of this chapter will discuss the various controls that might be used to prevent, detect, and correct threats. We also present a control spreadsheet and risk analysis methodology for identifying the threats and their associated controls. The control spreadsheet provides a data communication network manager with a good view of the current threats and any controls that are in place to mitigate the occurrence of threats.

Nonetheless, it is important to remember that it is not enough to just establish a series of controls; someone or some department must be accountable for the control and security of the network. This includes being responsible for the developing controls, ensuring they are operating effectively, and determining when they need to be updated or replaced.

Controls must reviewed periodically to be sure that they are still useful. They also should be verified and tested. *Verifying* ensures that the control is present, and *testing* determines whether the control is working as originally specified.

It is also important to recognize that there may be occasions in which a person must override a control. This may be a situation in which the network or one of its software or hardware subsystems is not operating properly and controls must be suspended temporarily. Such overrides should be tightly controlled, and there should be a formal procedure to document this occurrence should it happen.

✳✳ RISK ASSESSMENT

One key step in developing a secure network is to conduct a *risk assessment*. This assigns levels of risk to various threats to the network security by comparing the nature of the threats to the controls designed to reduce them. It is done by developing a control spreadsheet and then rating the importance of each risk. This section provides a brief summary of this process. Another good source of information is available on our Web page.

Develop a Control Spreadsheet

To be sure that the data communication network and microcomputer workstations have the necessary controls and that these controls offer adequate protection, it is best to build a *control spreadsheet* (see Figure 12–2). Threats to the network are listed across the top and the network components down the side. The center of the spreadsheet incorporates all the controls that *currently* are in the network. This will become the benchmark on which to base future security reviews.

Threats / Components	Disruption, Destruction, Disaster					Unauthorized Access		
	Fire	Flood	Power Loss	Circuit Failure	Virus	External Intruder	Internal Intruder	Eavesdrop
Host Computers								
Client Computers								
Communication Circuits								
Network Devices								
Network Software								
People								

Figure 12–2 Example control spreadsheet with some threats and components.

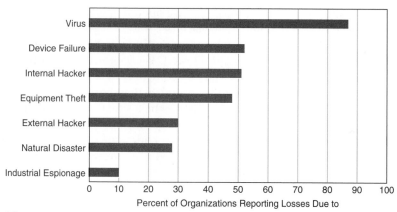

Figure 12-3 Seven most common threats.

Threats

A *threat* to the data communication network is any potential adverse occurrence that can do harm, interrupt the systems using the network, or cause a monetary loss to the organization. While threats may be listed in generic terms, it is better to be specific and use actual data from the organization being assessed—for example, fraud, theft of data, destruction of data, and so on.

Once the threats are identified they must be ranked on their importance. Importance can be based on criteria such as which would have the greatest dollar loss, be the most embarrassing, be the most prone to liability judgments, and have the highest probability of occurrence. A 1998 survey of more than 500 organizations found the single most common security problem that resulted in a meaningful dollar loss was viruses, occurring at an astonishing rate of 87 percent (i.e., 87 percent of organizations are infected at least once per year). Figure 12-3 summarizes the other commonly experienced problems. The relative importance of a threat to your organization depends on your business. A bank, for example, is more likely to be a target of fraud than a restaurant with an electronic marketing site on the Web.

Network Components

The next step is to identify the network components. A *network component* is one of the individual pieces that compose the data communication network. Components include:

* Servers, such as mainframes and LAN servers
* Client computers, such as microcomputers
* Communication circuits, such as circuits provided by common carriers and those installed and owned by the organization
* Network devices, such as hubs, bridges, switches, routers, gateways, front end processors, modems, and multiplexers
* Network software, such as client and host operating systems, network operating systems, communications processing systems, and applications software on the network

＊ Application software, such as transaction processing systems, Web-based systems, databases, and decision support systems

Identify and Document the Controls

Once the specific network threats and components have been identified, you can begin working on the network controls. A control is something that mitigates or stops a threat. A control also restricts, safeguards, or protects a component. During this step, you identify the current in-place controls and put them into each cell for each threat and component.

Begin by considering the network component and the specific threat, and then describe each control that prevents, detects, or corrects that threat. The description of the control (and its role) is placed in a numerical list, and the control's number is placed in the cell. For example, assume 24 controls have been identified as being in use. Each one is described, named, and numbered consecutively. The numbered list of controls has no ranking attached to it: the first control is number 1 just because it is the first control identified. Figure 12–4 shows a partially completed control spreadsheet with a list of in-place controls.

Threats / Components	Disruption, Destruction, Disaster					Unauthorized Access		
	Fire	Flood	Power Loss	Circuit Failure	Virus	External Intruder	Internal Intruder	Eavesdrop
Host Computers	1, 2	1, 3	4	1, 5, 6	7, 8	9, 10, 11, 12	9, 10	
Client Computers								
Communication Circuits								
Network Devices								
Network Software								
People								

Controls
1. Disaster recovery plan
2. Halon fire system in host computer room; sprinklers in rest of building
3. Host computer room on the 5th floor
4. Uninterruptable Power Supply (UPS) on all major network servers
5. Contract guarantees from interexchange carriers
6. Extra backbone fiber cable laid in different conduits between major servers
7. Virus checking software present on the network
8. Extensive user training on virurses and reminders in monthly newsletter
9. Strong password software
10. Extensive user training on password security and reminders in monthly newsletter
11. Call-back modem system
12. Application layer firewall

Figure 12-4 Example control spreadsheet with some threats, components, and controls.

Evaluate the Network's Security

The last step in designing a control spreadsheet is to evaluate the adequacy of the existing controls, and the resulting degree of risk associated with each threat. Based on this assessment, priorities can be established to determine which threats must be addressed immediately. Assessment is done by reviewing each set of controls as it relates to each threat and network component. The objective of this step is to answer the specific question, "Are the controls adequate to effectively prevent, detect, and correct this specific threat?"

The assessment can be done by the network manager, but it is better done by a team of experts chosen for their in-depth knowledge about the network and environment being reviewed. This team, known as the *Delphi team*, is composed of three to nine key people. Key managers should be team members because they deal with both the long-term and day-to-day operational aspects of the network. More importantly, their participation means the final results can be implemented quickly, without further justification, because they make the final decisions affecting the network.

✳✳ CONTROLLING DISRUPTION, DESTRUCTION, AND DISASTER

Disruption, destruction, and disaster are interruptions in network service or loss of data due to network failure. In this section, we discuss controls that attempt to prevent, detect, and correct for these threats.

Preventing Disruption, Destruction, and Disaster

The key principle in preventing disruption, destruction, and disaster—or at least reducing their impact—is *redundancy*. Redundant hardware that automatically recognizes failures and intervenes to replace the failed components can mask a failure that would otherwise result in a service disruption. Redundancy can be built into any network component. The most common example is an *uninterruptable power supply* (UPS). A UPS is installed on the network host so that in the event of a power failure, the host continues to operate for several hours.

You can also buy a special purpose *fault-tolerant server* that contains many redundant components to prevent failure. One common strategy, *disk mirroring*, utilizes a second redundant disk for every disk on the host computer or server. Every data item written to the primary disk is automatically duplicated on the mirrored disk. If the primary disk fails, the mirrored disk automatically takes over, with no observable effects on any network applications. This concept can be extended to include disk controllers (called *disk duplexing*), so that even if the disk controller fails, the server continues to operate.

Management Focus: Another Lesson from the School of Hard Knocks

The American Bible Society had just finished upgrading their LAN infrastructure, including the replacement of four 386-based file servers by two fault-tolerant servers. One of the goals was to eliminate downtime with the super redundancy they built into the system—triple-redundant power supplies, mirrored hard drives with a hot spare, a duplexed fiber NIC, and a four-hour standby battery system.

If computer parts are going to fail, they usually do so within the first 30 days of installation—and fail they did. Fortunately, the component that failed was one of the mirrored disk drives. Because the drive was mirrored, no data were lost. One of the vendor's best technicians was already scheduled to be in the office the next morning. He was the ideal person to replace the disk drive.

Early the following morning, they backed up the server, shut it down, removed the defective drive and installed the new drive. While running the software to configure the newly in-stalled drive, the technician softly said, "oops." Not only was the fix deleted, the technician trashed the original drive that they were mirroring. This meant the system volume containing all the network operating system files was destroyed.

It was 8:30 A.M., and users were about to start work, so they scrambled to begin the new installation. Soon, the CEO visited them, saying, "With all the money we spent on the infrastructure upgrades, I thought you said this wasn't supposed to happen."

Their advice from this experience: Never perform a hardware upgrade or repair before business hours. Always place network operating system files and drivers on the C:\ partition and back them up so you don't have to scramble for disks when you do need an emergency restore. And don't trust the smart guys when it comes to your hardware.

Source: "Another Lesson from the School of Hard Knocks," *LAN Times*, February 13, 1995.

Redundancy can be applied to other network components as well. For example, additional client computers, circuits, or devices (e.g., routers, bridges, multiplexers) can be installed to ensure that the network remains operational should any of these components fail. The last control point is the network personnel and equipment in the network control center, which oversees network management and operation, the test equipment, reports, documentation, and the like.

Disasters are different. In this case, an entire site can be destroyed. Even if redundant components are present, often the scope of the loss is such that returning the network to operation is extremely difficult. The best solution is to have a completely redundant network that duplicates every network component, but is in a separate location.

Generally speaking, preventing disasters is difficult. How do you prevent an earthquake? There are, however, some practical, commonsense steps that can be taken to prevent the full the impact of disasters. The most fundamental principle is to decentralize the network resources. Don't store all critical data on the same server or even multiple servers in the same building (or even in the same part of the country). By decentralizing critical data, you can eliminate the chance that a huge natural disaster can destroy all your data resources.

Other steps depend on the type of disaster to be prevented. For example, to reduce the risks due to flood, key network components should not be located near rivers or oceans, or in the basement or ground floor of buildings. To reduce the risks from fire, halon fire suppression systems should be installed in rooms containing important network equipment. To reduce the risks from terrorist attacks, the location of key network components should be kept secret and protected by security guards.

In some cases, the disruption is intentional. One often-overlooked security risk is theft. Computers and network devices are commonplace items that are relatively expensive. There is a good second-hand market for such equipment, making them valuable to steal. Several industry sources estimate that about $1 billion is lost each year to theft of computers and related equipment. Any security plan should include an evaluation of ways to prevent someone from stealing equipment.

Another special case is the *denial-of-service attack*. With a denial-of-service attack, a hacker attempts to disrupt the network by sending messages to the network that prevent other messages from being processed. In other words, the hacker interrupts the normal service provided by the network. The simplest approach is to flood a Web server or mail server with incoming messages. The server attempts to respond to these, but there are so many messages that it cannot.

Technical Focus: *Denial of Service Attack Hits Minnesota*

At 11:00 A.M. on March 17, 1998, computer networks at the University of Minnesota suffered a denial of service attack that caused data loss and disrupted networks throughout the state. The attack lasted about an hour, although some targets felt the effects for several hours.

Aimed at the university, the attack set off a chain reaction throughout the state, slowing networks and shutting down some computers completely. The University of Minnesota security response team shut down the circuit to the university's Crookston campus, which was the target of the attack. The attack also affected MRNet, the state's largest Internet service provider, which had a cooperative agreement with the university to share communications circuits leased from MCI and Sprint. Because MRNet was affected, so were dozens of Fortune 500 companies, small businesses, and private colleges that are MRNet customers.

The university was one in a long line of targets (including NASA, the U.S. Navy, and several other universities) that were the target of a "smurf" attack. In a "smurf" attack the attacker sends a flood of ping packets to the target computer. Ping packets ask the receiver to respond with an acknowledgement and are used to see if a computer is still operational. In a "smurf" attack, the attacker sends bogus ping packets to the target that list the target as the sender. The target attempts to respond by sending an acknowledgement to itself, which generates an endless cycle.

The "smurf" attack was first reported by the Computer Emergency Response Team (CERT) in January. While many Internet sites have upgraded their software to defeat it, not all sites have completed modifications—as was clearly shown by the Minnesota attack.

Source: " 'Smurf' Attack Hits Minnesota," *News.Com*, March 17, 1998.

Special attention also must be paid to preventing computer *viruses*. Viruses cause unwanted events—some are harmless (such as nuisance messages), others are serious (such as the destruction of data). In most cases, disruptions or the destruction of data are local, and affect only a small number of components (although the failure of one WAN or BN circuit may affect many computers). Such disruptions are usually fairly easy to deal with; the failed component is replaced or the virus is removed and the network continues to operate.

Most viruses attach themselves to other programs or to special parts on disks. As those files execute or are accessed, the virus spreads. Macro viruses, viruses that are contained in documents or spreadsheet files, can spread when an infected file simply is opened. Macro viruses are the fastest growing type of virus, accounting for more than 75 percent of all virus problems. Some viruses change their appearance as they spread, making detection more difficult.

The best way to prevent the spread of viruses is to not copy files or disks of unknown origin. A 1997 survey of 300 organizations found that 37 percent of virus incidents were due to sharing diskettes. Another 36 percent was from reading virus-infected documents attached to e-mail messages. Downloading files from Web sites was the cause in another 12 percent of virus infections.

Many anti-virus software packages are available to check disks and files to ensure that they are virus-free. Always check all diskettes and files for viruses before using them (even those from friends!). Researchers estimate that six new viruses are developed every day, so it is important to frequently update the virus information files that are provided by the anti-virus software.

Detecting Disruption, Destruction, and Disaster

Major problems need to be quickly recognized. As discussed in Chapter 11, one function of network monitoring software is to alert network managers to problems so these can be corrected. Some intelligent network servers can be programmed to send an alarm to a pager if necessary. The organization's disaster procedures should include notifying the network managers as soon as possible.

Detecting minor disruptions and destruction can be more difficult. A network drive may develop bad spots that remain unnoticed unless the drive is routinely checked. Likewise, a network cable may be partially damaged by hungry squirrels, resulting in intermittent problems. These types of problems require on-going monitoring. The network should routinely log fault information to enable network managers to recognize minor service problems before they become major ones. In addition, there should be a clear procedure by which network users can report problems.

Correcting Disruption, Destruction, and Disaster

A critical control is the *disaster recovery plan*, which should address various levels of response to a number of possible disasters and should provide for partial or complete recovery of all data, application software, network components, and physical

Elements of a Disaster Recovery Plan

A good disaster recovery plan should include:

* The name of the decision-making manager who is in charge of the disaster recovery operation. A second manager should be indicated in case the first manager is unavailable.

* Staff assignments and responsibilities during the disaster.

* A pre-established list of priorities that states what is to be fixed first.

* Location of alternative facilities operated by the company or a professional disaster recovery firm and procedures for switching operations to those facilities using backups of data and software.

* Recovery procedures for the data communication facilities (WAN, MAN, BN, and LAN), servers and application systems. This includes information on the location of circuits and devices, whom to contact for information, and the support that can be expected from vendors, along with the name and telephone number of the person to contact.

* Action to be taken in case of partial damage, threats such as a bomb threat, fire, water or electrical damage, sabotage, civil disorders, or vendor failures.

* Manual processes to be used until the network is functional.

* Procedures to ensure adequate updating and testing of the disaster recovery plan.

* Storage of the data, software, and the disaster recovery plan itself in a safe area where they cannot be destroyed by a catastrophe. This area must be accessible, however, to those who need to use the plan.

Figure 12–5 Elements of a disaster recovery plan.

facilities. A complete disaster recovery plan covering all these areas is beyond the scope of this text. Figure 12–5 provides a summary of many key issues.

The most important element of the disaster recovery plan are *backup and recovery controls* that enable the organization to recover its data and restart its application software should some portion of the network fail. The simplest approach to this issue is to routinely make backup copies of all organizational data and software and to store these backup copies offsite at a different location. Most organizations make daily backups of all critical information, with less important information (e.g., e-mail files) backed up weekly.

Backups ensure that important data is safe. However, it does not guarantee the data can be used. The disaster recovery plan should include a documented and tested approach to recovery, going from the backups to an operating application software system. The recovery plan has specific goals for different types of disasters. For example, if the main database server was destroyed, how long should it take the organization to have the software and data back in operation by using the

Management Focus: *Firm on Alert with Disaster Recovery SWAT Team*

Northrop Grumman Corp., an aerospace company, has devised a disaster recovery plan as rigorous as those followed by banking institutions. Daily backup of all mainframe and LAN data is the norm at Northrop. Should computer or network facilities face critical failure, the company's 34-step disaster recovery plan outlines an organized sequence of action. Northrop has compiled an inventory of all its manufacturing and business applications, assigning a priority to each.

Some elements of Northrop's disaster recovery checklist include:

* Take inventory of all hardware and software, and prioritize applications in terms of how quickly they must be recovered

* Establish company-owned, off-site, data processing, backup site, or establish a contract with disaster recovery service

* Develop network configuration documentation as well as document recover guidelines and procedures

* Implement a simulation and testing program

Storage of backup tapes off-site is a daily ritual at Northrop, with the company using several different vendors. If Northrop's data center were disabled, the storage site would be instructed to transfer tapes to the firm's disaster recovery firm, SunGard Recovery Services, Inc. Northrop employees can start data processing and transfer data over a T-1 line to any site selected as the company's remote operations center, where employees can continue working.

When problems hit a Northrop facility, the first calls to action go out to the vice president of information systems and the disaster recovery director. Then, team leaders are called upon to tally the damage, providing an assessment checklist that helps the security director decide whether to attempt to recover on-site or from one of Northrop's remote facilities, or to declare a disaster and go to SunGard, or some combination.

Source: "Firm on Alert with Disaster Recovery SWAT Team," *Network World*, December 5, 1994.

---

backups? Conversely, if the main data center was completely destroyed, how long should it take? As well as having a plan, it is important to regularly test the plan to ensure it is effective.

The answers to these questions have very different implications for costs. Having a spare network server or a server with extra capacity that can be used in the event of the loss of the primary server is one thing. Having a spare data center ready to operate with 12 hours (for example) is an entirely different proposition.

Most large organizations have a two-level disaster recovery plan. When they build networks they build enough capacity and have enough spare equipment to recover from a minor disaster, such as loss of a major server or portion of the network (if any such disaster can truly be called minor). This is the first level. Building a network that has sufficient capacity to quickly recover from a major disaster such as the loss of an entire data center is beyond the resources of most firms. Therefore, most large organizations rely on professional disaster recovery firms to provide second-level support for major disasters.

Disaster recovery firms provide a full range of services. At the simplest, they provide secure storage for backups. Full services include a complete networked data center that clients can use when they experience a disaster. Once a company declares a disaster, the disaster recovery firm immediately begins recovery operations using the backups stored on site and can have the organization's entire data network back in operation on the disaster recovery firm's computer systems within hours. Full services are not cheap, but compared to the potentially millions of dollars that can be lost per day from the inability to access critical data and application systems, these systems quickly pay for themselves in time of disaster.

Management Focus: *Disaster Puts Insurance Company on Ice*

A five-day ice storm in 1998 left millions of homes and businesses in Quebec without power, and caused Canada to declare a state of emergency. Five customers of Montreal-based Comdisco Inc. (a major disaster recovery firm) declared emergencies. One of those customers was International Netherlands Group (ING), one of Canada's largest insurance companies.

Besides losing power at its primary Canada-wide data center, ING found itself processing five times its normal workload and operated seven days a week to process storm-related claims from its insurance customers. When the data center power failed, ING immediately switched to its diesel generators and ran on those until power was restored two weeks later. However, the entire Canada-wide network depended on those generators, so ING declared an emergency.

Comdisco immediately activated its "hot site," creating an identical computing environment to the ING data center that operated in parallel to the main ING center. The ING center worked flawlessly, but if it had failed, ING would have been able to move to the hot site and be back in operation in less than six hours.

Source: "Disaster Puts Insurance Company on Ice," *PC Week,* February 9, 1998.

✳✳ CONTROLLING UNAUTHORIZED ACCESS

A 1997 survey by the Computer Security Institute found that 75 percent of the 568 responding organizations had experienced sabotage or theft of proprietary data due to unauthorized access. A 1997 study by the Defense Information Agency found that its experts were able to penetrate 88 percent of Defense Department computers and were only detected on 5 percent of those penetrations. Unauthorized access is an important problem that is on the increase with the rise of the Web.

Four types of intruders attempt to gain unauthorized access to computer networks. The first are casual computer users who have only limited knowledge of computer security. They simply cruise along the Internet trying to access any computer they come across. Their unsophisticated techniques are the equivalent of trying doorknobs, and only those networks that leave their front doors unlocked are at risk.

The second type of intruders are experts in security, but whose motivation is the thrill of the hunt. They break into computer networks because they enjoy the challenge. Sometimes they also enjoy showing off for friends or embarrassing the network owners. Fortunately, they usually cause little damage and make little attempt to profit from their exploits.

The third type of intruder is the most dangerous. They are professional hackers who break into corporate or government computers for specific purposes, such as espionage or fraud. Less than 5 percent of intrusions by these professionals are detected—unless, of course, they have been hired to destroy data or disrupt the network.

The fourth type of intruder is also very dangerous. These are organization employees who have legitimate access to the network, but who gain access to information they are not authorized to use. This information could be used for their own personal gain, sold to competitors, or fraudulently changed to give the employee extra income. Most security break-ins are caused by this type of intruder.

Preventing Unauthorized Access

The key principle in preventing unauthorized access is to be *proactive*. This means routinely testing your security systems before an intruder does. Many steps can be taken to prevent unauthorized access to organizational data and networks, but no network is completely safe. The best rule for high security is to do what the military does: do not keep extremely sensitive data online. Data that need special security are stored in computers isolated from other networks.

There are six general approaches to preventing unauthorized access: developing a security policy, developing user profiles, plugging known security holes, securing network access points, preventing eavesdropping, and using encryption. A combination of all techniques is best to ensure strong security.

Developing a Security Policy

In the same way that a disaster recovery plan is critical to controlling risks due to disruption, destruction and disaster, a *security policy* is critical to controlling unauthorized access. The security policy should clearly define the important network components to be safeguarded and the important controls needed to do that. It should devote a section to what employees should and should not do. It should contain a clear plan for routinely training employees—particularly end users with little computer expertise—on key security rules and should provide a clear plan for routinely testing and improving the security controls in place. (See Figure 12–6.)

The most common way for hackers to break into a system, even master hackers like Kevin Mitnick (see the Management Focus Box), is through *social engineering*, breaking security simply by asking. For example, hackers routinely phone unsus-

Elements of a Security Policy

A good security policy should include:

* The name of the decision-making manager who is in charge of security.
* An incident reporting system and a rapid response team to respond to security breaches in progress.
* A risk assessment with priorities as to which components are most important.
* Effective controls placed at all major access points into the network to prevent or deter access by external agents.
* Effective controls placed within the network to ensure internal users cannot exceed their authorized access.
* An acceptable use policy that explains to users what they can and cannot do.
* A plan to routinely train users on security policies and build awareness of security risks.
* A plan to routinely test and update all security controls that includes monitoring of popular press and vendor reports of security holes.

Figure 12-6 Elements of a security policy.

pecting users and imitate someone else (e.g., a technician, a boss, a network expert) and ask for a password. Most security experts no longer test for social engineering attacks; they know from past experience that social engineering will eventually succeed in any organization and therefore assume that hackers can gain access at will to "normal" user accounts. Training end users not to divulge passwords may not eliminate social engineering attacks, but it may reduce its effectiveness so that hackers give up and move on to easier targets.

Developing User Profiles

The basis of network access is the *user profile* for each user's *account* that is assigned by the network manager. Each user's profile specifies what data and network resources he or she can access, and the type of access (read only, write, create, delete, etc.). Gaining access to an account can be based on what you know, what you have, or what you are. The most common approach is what you know, usually a password. Before users can login, they need to enter a password. Unfortunately, passwords are often poorly chosen, enabling intruders to guess them and gain access.

More and more systems are requiring users to enter a password in conjunction with something they have, such as a *smart card*. A smart card is a card about the size of a credit card that contains a small processing chip and a memory chip that can be read by a smart device. To gain access to the network, the user must present both the card and the password, intruders must have access to both before they can break in. The best example of this is the Automated Teller Machine (ATM) network

Management Focus: Computer Terrorist Captured

Kevin Mitnick, America's most wanted computer hacker, was captured in February 1995. Mitnick, code-named Condor, was apprehended by government officials after they acquired the assistance of an expert from a firm that Mitnick is suspected of penetrating.

Mitnick was arraigned on charges of violating the terms of his probation for a 1988 California computer hacking conviction, as well as new charges of computer fraud originating in North Carolina. He served a year in prison and was placed on probation after a one-time friend turned him in during 1988 saying, "He's an electronic terrorist." He fled in late 1992, after the FBI showed up at the private investigation firm where he worked. The agents were investigating break-ins to Pacific Bell computers.

This was just a portion of his computer escapades, which began in high school when he broke into the Los Angeles Unified School District's main computers. Eventually, he was able to access a North American Air Defense Command computer in Colorado Springs. Also, the California Department of Motor Vehicles issued a $1 million warrant for him, accusing him of posing as a law enforcement officer to obtain sensitive DMV information.

Authorities are unable to estimate how much damage he wreaked during his years on the run. The cellular telecommunications industry alleges that Mitnick, who used cellular phones to illegally access computers, cost it $1 million a day.

Mitnick even manipulated the telephone system to pull pranks on friends and enemies, and disconnected service to Hollywood stars and to his probation officer.

Source: "Computer Terrorist Captured," *The Atlanta Journal-Constitution*, February 16, 1995.

---

operated by your bank. Before you can gain access to your account, you must have both your ATM card and the access number.

In high-security applications, users may be required to present something they *are*, such as a finger, hand, or the retina of their eye for scanning by the system. These *biometric systems* scan the user to ensure that user is the sole individual authorized to access the network account. Although most biometric systems are developed for high-security users, several low-cost biometric systems to recognize fingerprints are now on the market.

User profiles can limit the allowable log-in days, time of day, physical locations, and the allowable number of incorrect log-in attempts. Some will also automatically log a user out if that person has not performed any network activity for a certain length of time (e.g., the user has gone to lunch and has forgotten to logoff the network). Regular security checks throughout the day when the user is logged in can determine whether a user is still permitted access to the network. For example, the network manager might have disabled the user's profile while the user is logged in, or the user's account may have run out of funds.

Creating accounts and profiles is simple. When a new staff member joins an organization, that person is assigned a user account and profile. One security problem is the removal of user accounts when someone leaves an organization. Often, network managers are not informed of the departure and accounts remain in the system. For example, a 1995 examination of user accounts at The University of Georgia found 30 percent belonged to staff members no longer employed by the university. If the staff member's departure was not friendly, there is a risk that he or she might attempt to access data and resources and use them for personal gain, or destroy them to "get back at" the organization. Many systems permit the network manager to assign expiration dates to user accounts to ensure that unused profiles are automatically deleted or deactivated, but these actions do not replace the need to notify network managers about an employee's departure.

It is important to screen and classify both users and data. Some organizations, especially in government, assign different security clearance levels to users as well as to data, thus permitting users to see only what they "need to know."

Management Focus: Selecting Passwords

The keys to users' accounts are the passwords; each account has a unique password chosen by the user. The problem is that passwords are often chosen poorly and not changed regularly. Many network managers require users to change passwords periodically (e.g., every 90 days), but this does not ensure that users choose "good" passwords.

A good password is one that the user finds easy to remember, but is difficult for potential intruders to guess. Several studies have found that about two-thirds of passwords fall into one of three categories:

* names of family members or pets

* important numbers in the user's life (e.g., SSN, or birthday)
* keyboard patterns (e.g., QWERTY, ASDF)

The best advice is to avoid these categories because such passwords can be guessed easily. Better choices are passwords that:

* are meaningful to the user but no one else
* are made of two or more words that have several letters omitted (e.g., NWYOR (New York), or PPLEPI (apple pie))
* are spelled backwards
* include characters such as numbers or punctuation marks

The effect of any security software packages that restrict or control access to files, records, or data items should be reviewed. Independent of the data communication software, these packages may offer unique password and identification of each user and allow access only to the specific functions assigned to that user. Some packages also offer additional features, such as file security and layers of passwords to the record or field level, terminal security, transaction security, batch reports on all activity, automatic sign-off of unattended terminals, and immediate online notification of security violations.

Adequate user training on network security should be provided through self-teaching manuals, newsletters, policy statements, and short courses. A well-publicized security campaign may deter potential intruders.

Plugging Known Security Holes

Many commonly used operating systems have major security problems (called *security holes*) well known to potential intruders; Unix systems are among the worst. Many security holes have been documented and "patches" are available from vendors to fix them, but network managers may be unaware of all the holes or simply forget to regularly update their systems with new patches.

A complete discussion of security holes is beyond the scope of the book. Many security holes are highly technical; for example, sending a message designed to overflow a network buffer, thereby placing a short command into a very specific memory area that unlocks a user profile. Others are rather simple, but not obvious. For example, in some versions of Unix, a semicolon places the system into command mode, making it process incoming text as commands. In this case, one could attach a semicolon and a Unix command in response to a request for a file name. In another case, the hacker sends a message that lists the server's address as both the sender and the destination, so the server attempts to send messages to itself. The server then crashes as it repeatedly attempts to send a message to itself. A final example is more complex. In this case, the hacker sends a message to a router (using RIP for example) informing it that part of the network is down and to reroute all traffic destined to another subnet via a different router external to the organization. This external router records all incoming messages before sending them back to the correct final destination.

Other security holes are not really holes, but simply policies adopted by computer vendors that open the door for security problems, such as computer systems that come with a variety of preinstalled user accounts. These accounts and their initial passwords are well documented and known to all potential intruders. A 1988 study of Unix computer sites found that 5 to 10 percent of computers still retained their preinstalled accounts with the initial passwords. Network managers had simply forgotten to delete them.

The U.S. government requires certain levels of security in the operating systems and network operating systems it uses for certain applications. The minimum level of security is C2. Most major mainframe operating systems provide at least C2. Several LAN operating systems (e.g., Novell, Windows NT, and IBM's LAN server) are currently under review for C2 certification. Most widely used NOS are also striving to meet the requirements of much higher security levels, such as B2. Very few systems meet the highest levels of security (A1 and A2).

Securing Network Access Points

In general, there are three major ways of gaining access: using a terminal or computer located in the organization's offices, dialing into the network via a modem, or accessing the network from another network to which it is connected (e.g., Internet). We consider each access point in turn.

The physical security of the building or buildings that house any of the hardware, software, or communication circuits must be evaluated. Both local and remote physical facilities should be secured adequately and have the proper controls. Good security requires implementing the proper access controls so that only authorized personnel can access the network or enter closed areas where network equipment is located. Proper security education, background checks, and the implementation of error and fraud controls are important. In many cases, the simplest means to gain access is to become employed as a janitor and access the network at night.

Management Focus: Basic Control Principles of a Secure Network

* The less complex a control, the better.
* A control's cost should be equivalent to the identified risk. It often is not possible to ascertain the expected loss, so this is a subjective judgment in many cases.
* Preventing a security incident is always preferable to detecting and correcting it after it occurs.
* An adequate system of internal controls is one that provides "just enough" control to protect the network, taking into account both the risks and costs of the controls.
* Automated controls (computer-driven) always are more reliable than manual controls that depend on human interaction.
* Controls should apply to everyone, not just a few select individuals.
* When a control has an override mechanism, make sure that it is documented and that the override procedure has its own controls to avoid misuse.
* Institute the various security levels in an organization on the basis of "need to know." If you do not need to know, you do not need to access the network.
* The control documentation should be confidential.
* Names, uses, and locations of network components should not be publicly available.
* Controls must be sufficient to ensure that the network can be audited. This means there should be transaction trails and historical records.

* When designing controls, assume that you are operating in a hostile environment.
* Always convey an image of high security by providing education and training.
* Make sure the controls provide the proper separation of duties. This applies especially to those who design and install the controls and those who are responsible for everyday use and monitoring.
* It is desirable to implement entrapment controls in networks to identify hackers who gain illegal access.
* When a control fails, the network should default to a condition in which everyone is denied access. A period of failure is when the network is most vulnerable.
* Controls should still work, even when only one part of a network fails. For example, if a backbone network fails, all local area networks connected to it should still be operational, with their own independent controls providing protection.
* Don't forget the LAN. Security and disaster recovery planning has traditionally focused on host mainframe computers and WANs. However, LANs now play an increasingly important role in most organizations but are often overlooked by central site network managers.
* Always have insurance as the last resort, should all controls fail.
* Always assume your opponent (a hacker) is smarter than you.

The network components themselves also have a level of physical security. Terminals and computers can have locks on their power switches or locks that disable the screen and keyboard. Network circuits can be locked by having the network manager disable them after hours.

Any organization that permits staff members to access its network via dial-in modems opens itself to a broader range of intruders. Some dial-up modem controls include changing the modem telephone numbers periodically, keeping telephone numbers confidential, and requiring the use of computers that have an electronic identification chip for all dial-up ports.

Another common strategy is to use a *call-back modem*. In this case, the user dials the organization's modem's telephone number and logs into his or her account. Once the user enters the correct password, the modem automatically hangs ups and dials the user's modem's telephone number. In this way, unauthorized intruders cannot access others' accounts because the host computer or communications server will only permit access via modems calling from prespecified numbers. The drawback to this is that only one remote telephone number can be defined for each account. If users have several locations from which they wish to have access (e.g., the users' home and remote office), call-back modems won't work. In recent years, this technique has been extended to use automatic number identification (ANI). The network manager can specify several telephone numbers authorized to access each account. When a user successfully logs onto an account, the source of incoming phone call is identified using ANI. If it is one of the authorized numbers, the login is accepted; otherwise, the host computer or communications server disconnects the call.

Neither call-back modems nor the use of ANI permits users who frequently travel (e.g., sales representatives) to have secure dial-in access. Such users often call from hotel rooms and have no knowledge of telephone numbers in advance. One solution is to use *one-time passwords*. The user connects into the network as usual, and after the user's password is accepted, the system generates a one-time password. The user must enter this password to gain access, otherwise the connection is terminated. The user can receive this one-time password in a number of ways. Some systems send the password to the user's pager. Other systems provide the user with a unique number that must be entered into a separate handheld device (called a *token* system), which, in turn, displays the password for the user to enter. To gain access, an intruder must know the user's account name and password, and must have access to the user's pager or password device.

With the increasing use of the Internet and information superhighway, it becomes important to prevent unauthorized access to your network from intruders on other networks. The obvious solution is to disconnect any computer or network containing confidential information from the Internet. This is often not a practical solution. In many cases, organizations are disconnecting unneeded applications to improve security. For example, a Web server often does not need e-mail, so network managers often remove the e-mail system to reduce the number of entry points that a hacker has into the network. A firewall is another solution.

A *firewall* is a router, gateway, or special-purpose computer that examines packets flowing into and out of a network and restricts access to the organization's

Figure 12–7 Using a firewall to protect networks.

network. The network is designed so that a firewall is placed on every network connection between the organization and the Internet (see Figure 12–7). No access is permitted except through the firewall. Some firewalls have the ability to detect and prevent denial-of-service attacks, as well as unauthorized access attempts. Two commonly used types of firewalls are packet level, and application level.

A *packet-level firewall* examines the source and destination address of every network packet that passes through it. It only allows packets into or out of the organization's networks that have acceptable source and destination addresses. In general, the addresses are examined only to the network level (e.g., TCP/IP). Some packet-level firewalls also examine the type of packet (e.g., FTP, telnet) and allow or deny certain types of packets to or from certain addresses. Each packet is examined individually, so the firewall has no knowledge of what the user is attempting to do. It simply chooses to permit entry or exit based on the contents of the packet itself. This type of firewall is the simplest and least secure because it does not monitor the contents of the packets or why they are being transmitted, and typically does not log the packets for later analysis.

Some packet-level firewalls are vulnerable to *IP spoofing*. The goal of an intruder using IP spoofing is to send packets to a target computer requesting certain privileges be granted to some user (e.g., setting up a new account for the intruder or changing access permission or password for an existing account). Such a message would not be accepted by the target computer unless it can be fooled into believing that the request is genuine.

Spoofing is done by changing the source address on incoming packets from their real address to an address inside the organization's network. Seeing a valid internal address, the firewall lets the packets through to their destination. The destination computer believes the packets are from a valid internal user and processes them. Typically, IP spoofing is more complex than this, because such changes often require a dialogue between the computers. Since the target computer believes it is talking to an internal computer, it directs its messages to it, not to the intruder's computer. Intruders therefore have to guess at the nature and timing of these messages, so that they can generate more spoofed messages that appear to be responses to the target computer's messages. In practice, expert intruders have enough knowledge to have a reasonable chance of getting this right.

Many firewalls have had their security strengthened since the first documented case of IP spoofing occurred in December 1994. For example, some firewalls automatically delete any packets arriving from the Internet that have internal source addresses. However, IP spoofing still remains a problem, because not all packet-level firewalls prevent it.

Technical Focus: How Packet-Level Firewalls Work

Remember from Chapter 6 that TCP/IP networks such as the Internet use two types of packets at the network layer. IP packets provide the source and destination IP addresses. TCP packets provide application-layer port numbers that indicate the application layer software to which the packet should be sent. For example, the Web uses port 80, telnet uses port 23, and FTP uses port 21.

Packet-level firewalls enable the network administrator to establish a series of rules that define what packets should be allowed to pass through and what packets should be deleted. Suppose, for example, that the organization had a Web server with an IP address of 128.192.55.55 that was for internal use only. The administrator could define a rule on the firewall that instructed the firewall to delete

any packet from the Internet that listed 128.192.55.55 as a destination. In this case, the firewall simply needs to examine the destination address.

Suppose, however, the organization had a Web server (128.192.44.44) that was intended to be available to Internet users. However, to prevent anyone on the Internet from making changes to the server, the organization wants to prevent any telnet, FTP, or other similar packets from reaching the server. In this case, the administrator could define a rule that instructed the firewall to permit TCP packets with a destination port address of 80 and a destination IP address of 128.192.44.44 to pass through. A second rule would instruct the firewall to delete any packets with any other port number and that destination IP address.

An *application-level firewall* acts as an intermediate host computer or gateway between the Internet and the rest of the organization's networks. These firewalls are generally more complicated to install and manage than packet-level ones. Users wishing to access the organization's networks from the Internet must login to this firewall, and can only access the information for which they are authorized based on the firewall account profile they access. This places an additional burden on users, who must now remember an additional set of passwords. With application-level firewalls, any access that has not been explicitly authorized is prohibited. In contrast, with a packet-level firewall, any access that has not been disabled is permitted.

In many cases, special programming code must be written to permit the use of application software unique to the organization (as opposed to commercial off-the-shelf software, such as e-mail, which is built into the firewall). Many application-level firewalls prohibit external users from uploading executable files. In this way, intruders (or authorized users) cannot modify any software unless they have physical access to the firewall. Some refuse changes to their software unless it is done by the vendor. Others also actively monitor their own software and automatically disable outside connections if they detect any changes.

A *proxy server* is a new type of application-level firewall that addresses some of the compatibility problems with traditional application level firewalls. The proxy server is transparent, in that no other computer notices that it is on the network.

The proxy server uses an address table to translate network addresses (i.e., IP addresses) inside the organization into fake addresses for use on the Internet. When a computer inside the organization accesses a computer on the Internet, the proxy server changes the source address in the outgoing IP packet to its own address. It also sets the source port number in the TCP packet to a unique number that it uses as an index into its address table to find the IP address of the actual sending computer in the organization's internal network. When the external computer responds to the request, it addresses the message to the proxy server. The proxy server receives the incoming message, and after ensuring the packet should be permitted inside, changes the destination to the actual address of the internal computer before transmitting it on the internal network. This process is sometimes called *network address translation* or address mapping.

This way systems outside the organization never see the actual internal IP addresses. They think there is only one computer on the internal network, the proxy server. Some organizations also increase security by using illegal internal addresses. For example, if the organization has been assigned the 128.192.55.X subnet, the proxy server would be assigned an address such as 128.192.55.1. Internal computers, however, would *not* be assigned addresses in the 128.192.55.X subnet. Instead, they would be assigned unauthorized Internet addresses (e.g., 3.3.3.55). Since these internal addresses are never used on the Internet, but are always converted by the proxy server, this poses no problems for the users. However, even if intruders discovered the actual internal IP address, it would be impossible for them to reach the internal address from the Internet because the address would be assigned to a different company.

Proxy servers work very well and are becoming the application-level firewall of choice. They do, however, slow message transfer between internal networks and the Internet. They also require a separate DNS server for use by external users on the Internet and a separate internal DNS server for use on the internal networks. Since an organization's own employees are the greatest risk for unauthorized access, many organizations use internal firewalls to prevent employees in one part of an organization from accessing resources in a different part.

Many organizations use a combination of packet-level and application-level firewalls (see Figure 12–8). Packet-level firewalls are used as an initial screen from the Internet into a network devoted solely to servers intended to provide public access (e.g., Web servers, public DNS servers). This network is sometimes called the DMZ (demilitarized zone) because it contains the organization's servers but does not provide complete security for them. This packet-level firewall will permit Web requests and similar access to the DMZ network servers, but will deny FTP access to these servers from the Internet, because no one except internal users should have the right to modify the servers. This DMZ network contains a proxy server that provides access to the organization's internal networks. Each major portion of the organization's internal networks has its own proxy server to grant (or deny) access based on rules established by that part of the organization.

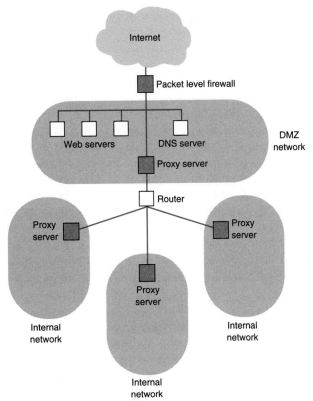

Figure 12–8 A typical network design using firewalls.

Preventing Eavesdropping

Another way to gain unauthorized access is to *eavesdrop* on network traffic. In some ways this is easier than the previous methods because the intruder only has to insert a listening device or computer into the organization's network to record messages. Two areas are vulnerable to this type of unauthorized access: network cabling and network devices.

Network cables are the easiest target for eavesdropping because they often run long distances and usually are not regularly checked for tampering. The cables owned by the organization and installed within its facility are usually the first choice for eavesdropping. It is much easier to tap a local cable than it is to tap an interexchange circuit, because it is extremely difficult to identify the specific circuits belonging to any one organization in a highly multiplexed switched interexchange circuit operated by a common carrier. Local cables should be secured behind walls and above ceilings, and telephone equipment and switching rooms (wiring closets) should be locked and their doors equipped with alarms. The primary goal is to control physical access by employees or vendors to the connector cables and

Management Focus: Teenagers Break into the Pentagon

In late February 1998, hackers broke into computers at the Pentagon, a culmination of a series of break-ins at a variety of government and military computers across the United States. Within days, the FBI had identified the attackers as two high school students in Northern California. The FBI confiscated their computer equipment and software, but because the two were minors they were not arrested or charged, although the investigation continues.

The pair were apparently part of a larger ring of teenage hackers who held a competition to see how many government sites they could enter. They did no damage and did not steal critical information. The goal was apparently thrill-seeking and an attempt to gain power over the government systems. The FBI and the Department of Defense stated that no classified

computers were entered, but there is some evidence that the hackers acquired the systems administrator password for a computer at Lawrence Livermore National Laboratory with access to classified information.

The hackers used simple hacking tools available on the Internet that attacked known security holes in NT and Unix computers. They attempted to conceal their tracks by breaking into a research park in Spain and a technical school in Japan and using stolen accounts from there to attack computers in the United States. But in the end, FBI and DoD experts traced the pair to their homes in California.

Source: Stories in *Yahoo News* and *ZDNet News*, February-March 1998.

modems. This includes restricting their access to the wiring closets in which all the communication wires and cables are connected.

Certain types of cable can impair or increase security by making eavesdropping easier or more difficult. Obviously, any wireless network is at extreme risk for eavesdropping because anyone in the area of the transmission can easily install devices to monitor the radio or infrared signals. Conversely, fiber optic cables are harder to tap, thus increasing security. Some companies offer armored cable that is virtually impossible to cut without special tools. Other cables have built-in alarm systems. The U.S. Air Force, for example, uses pressurized cables that are filled with gas. If the cable is cut, the gas escapes, pressure drops, and an alarm is sounded.

Physical security of the network's local loop and interexchange telephone circuits is the responsibility of the common carrier. You cannot do much about it, except to audit the telephone company's physical security procedures and possibly encrypt the data before it leaves your building to go out onto the public network. All local loops leaving the building should be physically secured and out of harm's way to prevent physical damage or an easy telephone tap. Formal procedures should exist to help identify breaches of security or illegal entries to the network.

Network devices such as controllers, hubs, and bridges should be secured in a locked wiring closet. As discussed in Chapter 7, all messages within a given local area network are actually received by all computers on the LAN, although they only process those messages addressed to them. It is rather simple to install a *sniffer program* that records all messages received for later (unauthorized) analysis. A computer with a sniffer program could then be plugged into an unattended hub or bridge to eavesdrop on all message traffic.

A *secure hub* for Ethernet networks makes this type of eavesdropping more difficult. This hub requires a special authorization code to be entered before new computers can be added, thus making it difficult to add unauthorized devices. More interesting, though, is the way it handles messages. When new devices are added to the hub, their network addresses are defined to the hub so that it knows which device is connected to which port. When the hub receives a message, it checks the address and forwards the message only to the port connected to the device with that address. All other ports receive a message of exactly the same length that contains only a random set of characters.

A review of software controls that can be programmed into remote network devices is also needed. For example, daily downloading of network programs can help ensure that only authorized programs are in these devices. Another control is the periodic counting of bits in the memory space of the remote device. This identifies a program change so that a new one can be downloaded immediately. Each controller should have its unique address on a memory chip (instead of software) to thwart anyone who wants to change controller addresses in order to receive copies of messages.

Encryption

One of the best ways to prevent unauthorized access is *encryption*, which is a means of disguising information by the use of mathematical rules known as *algorithms*. Actually, *cryption* is the more general and proper term. *Encryption* is the process of disguising information, whereas *decryption* is the process of restoring it to readable form. Of course, it makes no sense to have one process without the other. When information is in readable form, it is called *plaintext;* when in encrypted form, it is called *ciphertext.*

An encryption system has two parts: the algorithm itself and the *key,* which personalizes the algorithm by making the transformation of data unique. Two pieces of identical information encrypted with the same algorithm but with different keys produce completely different ciphertexts. When using most encryption systems, communicating parties must share this key. If the algorithm is adequate and the key is kept secret, acquisition of the ciphertext by unauthorized personnel is of no consequence to the communicating parties.

Good encryption systems do not depend on keeping the algorithm secret. Only the keys need to be kept secret. The key is a relatively small numeric value (in terms of the number of bits). The larger the key, the more secure the encryption because large "key space" protects the ciphertext against those who try to break it by trying every possible key. There should be a large enough number of possible keys that an exhaustive computer search would take an inordinately long time or would cost more than the value of the encrypted information.

Today, the U.S. government considers encryption to be weapon and regulates its export in the same way it regulates the export of machine guns or bombs. Current rules prohibit the export of encryption techniques with keys longer than 56 bits, although this policy is under review and may change (U.S. banks and Fortune 100 companies are now permitted to use more powerful encryption techniques in their foreign offices). This policy made sense when only U.S. companies had the expertise to develop powerful encryption software. Today, however, many non-U.S. companies are developing encryption software that is more powerful than the 56-bit versions of U.S. software. Therefore, the U.S. software industry is lobbying the government to change the rules so that they can successfully compete overseas.

The U.S. government is also trying to develop a policy to require *key escrow* (also called key recovery). With key escrow, any organization using encryption must register its keys with the government which enables the government, after receiving a legally authorized search warrant, to decrypt and read any messages sent by that organization. Without key escrow, the government is worried that criminal organizations will use encryption to prevent police agencies from performing legally authorized wiretaps. Free-speech advocates are concerned that key encryption will be abused by police agencies who will illegally monitor transactions by otherwise innocent citizens.

One commonly used encryption algorithm is the *data encryption standard* (DES), which was developed in the mid-1970s by the U.S. government in conjunction with IBM. DES is maintained by the National Institute of Standards and Technology.

DES is a *symmetric algorithm,* which means that the key used to decrypt a particular bit stream is the *same* as the one used to encrypt it. Using any other key produces plaintext that appears as random as the ciphertext.

Symmetric algorithms can cause problems with *key management;* keys must be dispersed and stored carefully. Before two computers in a network can communicate using encryption, both must have the same key. This means that both computers can then send and read any messages that use that key. Companies often do not want other companies to be able to read messages they send to a specific recipient, so this means that there must be a separate key used for communication with each company. These keys must be recorded but kept secure so that they cannot be stolen. Because the DES algorithm is known publicly, disclosure of the key can mean total compromise of encrypted messages. Managing this system of keys can be challenging.

A 56-bit version of DES is the most commonly used encryption technique today. DES is classified as a *block cipher* because it encrypts data in independent 56-bit blocks under the control of a 56-bit key. However, encryption experts have shown that it is possible to break 56-bit DES and read messages without having the key in less than one week. This testing is enhanced further by the use of very specialized mathematical algorithms that are designed to quickly invalidate large groups of these combinations. In addition, specially designed computers may be able to test hundreds of thousands of combinations each second. A 64-bit and a 128-bit key version of DES are also available, which are much more secure (requiring 1 year and 10^{19} years to break with current technology, respectively), but cannot be exported outside of the United States under current laws.

A second popular technique is *public key encryption,* the most popular of which is *RSA*. RSA was invented at MIT in 1977 by Rivest, Shamir, and Adleman. The inventors of the initial algorithm founded RSA Data Security in 1982, and many companies have licensed the RSA technique.

Public key encryption is inherently different from secret key systems like DES, because it is an *asymmetric algorithm*; there are two keys. One key (called the *public key*) is used to encrypt the message and a second, very different *private key* is used to decrypt the message. Public key systems are based on one-way functions. Even though you originally know both the contents of your message and the public encryption key, once it is encrypted by the one-way function, the message cannot be decrypted without the private key. One-way functions, which are relatively easy to calculate in one direction, are impossible to "uncalculate" in the reverse direction. Public key encryption is one of the most secure encryption techniques available, excluding special encryption techniques developed by national security agencies.

Public key encryption greatly reduces the key management problem. Each user has a public key that it uses to encrypt messages sent to it. These public keys are widely publicized (e.g., listed in a telephone book-style directory)—that's why they're called "public" keys. In addition, each user has a private key that decrypts only the messages that were encrypted by its public key. This private key is kept secret (that's why it's called "private" key). The net result is that if two parties wish to communicate with one another, there is no need to exchange keys beforehand. Each knows the other's public key from the listing in a public directory and can communicate encrypted information immediately. The key management problem is reduced to the on-site protection of the private key.

Figure 12–9 illustrates how this process works. All public keys are published in a directory. When Organization A wants to send an encrypted message to Organization B, it looks through the directory to find its public key. It then encrypts the message using B's public key. This encrypted message is sent through the network to Organization B, which decrypts the message using its private key.

Public key encryption also permits *authentication* (or digital signatures). When one user sends a message to another, it is difficult to legally prove who actually sent the message. Legal proof is important in many communications, such as bank transfers and buy/sell orders in currency and stock trading, which normally require legal signatures. Public key encryption algorithms are *invertable*, meaning that text encrypted with either key can be decrypted by the other. Normally, we encrypt with the public key and decrypt with the private key, but it is possible to do the inverse: encrypt with the private key and decrypt with the public key. Since the private key is secret, only the real user could use it to encrypt a message. Thus, a digital signature or authentication sequence is used as a legal signature on many financial transactions. This signature is usually the name of the signing party plus other *key-contents* such as unique information from the message (e.g., date, time, or dollar amount). This signature and the other key-contents are encrypted by the sender using the private key. The receiver uses the sender's public key to decrypt the signature block and compares the result to the name and other key contents in the rest of the message to ensure a match.

Figure 12–10 illustrates how authentication can be combined with public encryption to provide a secure and authenticated transmission. The plaintext message is first encrypted using Organization A's private key and then encrypted using Or-

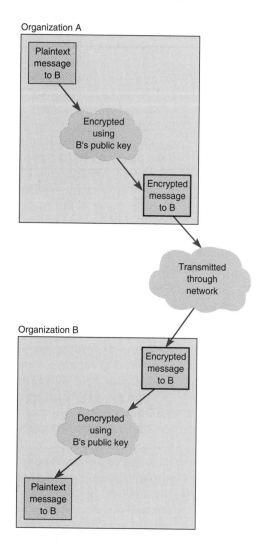

Figure 12–9 Secure transmission with public key encryption.

ganization's B public key. It is then transmitted to B. Organization B first decrypts the message using its private key. It sees that part of the message (the key-contents) is still in cyphertext, indicating it is an authenticated message. B then decrypts the key-contents part of the message using A's public key to produce the plaintext message. Since only A has the private key that matches A's public key, B can safely assume that A sent the message.

The only problem with this approach lies in ensuring that the person or organization who sent the document with the correct private key is actually the person or organization they claim to be. Anyone can post a public key on the Internet, so there is no way of knowing for sure who the person or organization actually is. For example, it would be possible for someone other than "Organization A" in this example to claim to be Organization A, when in fact the sender is an imposter.

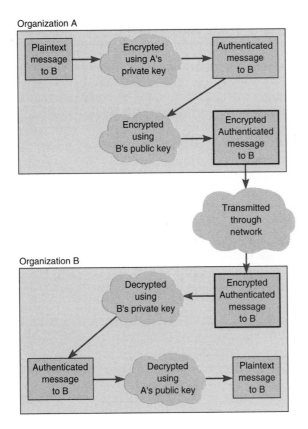

Figure 12–10
Authenticated and secure transmission with public key encryption.

A *certificate authority (CA)* is a trusted organization that can vouch for the authenticity of the person or organization using authentication (e.g., VeriSign). A person wanting to use a CA registers with the CA and must provide some proof of identity. There are several levels of certification, ranging from a simple confirmation from valid e-mail address to a complete police-style background check with an in-person interview. The CA issues a digital *certificate* that is the requestor's public key encrypted using the CA's private key as proof of identity. This certificate is then attached to the user's e-mail or Web transactions in addition to the authentication information. The receiver then verifies the certificate by decrypting it with the CA's public key—and must also contact the CA to ensure that the user's certificate has not been revoked by the CA.

For higher-security certifications, the CA requires that a unique "fingerprint" be issued by the CA for each message sent by the user. The user submits the message to the CA, who creates the unique fingerprint by combining the CA's private key with the message's authentication key contents. Because the user must obtain a unique fingerprint for each message, this ensures that the CA has not revoked the certificate between the time it was issued and the time the message was sent by the user.

Management Focus: Anatomy of a Friendly Hack

If you've seen the movie *Sneakers*, you know that there are professional security firms that organizations can hire to break in to their own networks to test security. BABank was about to launch a new online banking service, so it hired such a firm to test its security before the launch. The bank's system failed the security test.

The security team began by mapping the bank's network. It used DNS searches, sniffer software, network security analysis software (e.g., SATAN), and dialing software to test for dial-in ports. The mapping process found a computer running an old mail program with a known security hole and a bunch of maintenance accounts with unchanged passwords.

The team then used social engineering to gain passwords to several high-privilege accounts. Once into these computers, the team used password-cracking software to find passwords on these computers and ultimately gain the administrator passwords on several servers and routers.

At this point, the team transferred $1000 into their test account. They could have transferred more, but the security point was made. Finally, the team launched a successful denial-of-service attack that crashed the online banking system.

Source: "Anatomy of a Friendly Hack," *Network World*, February 2, 1998.

Several encryption standards are widely used today. *Secure HTTP* (S-HTTP) was one of the first protocols to include encryption for the Web. *Secure sockets layer* (SSL) is another protocol designed for use of the Web.

Detecting Unauthorized Access

Detecting unauthorized access means looking for anything out of the ordinary. It means logging all messages sent and received by the network, all software used, and all logins (or attempted logins) to the network. These logs should be monitored both by network security personnel and by software programmed to issue alarms or take action if certain parameters are exceeded or if something unusual occurs. For example, if the number of accesses to a file server or an account suddenly escalates, it may indicate that an intruder has gained access and is doing things that authorized users do not do (or it may simply mean a change in user behavior). In any event, the cause of the unusual activity should be identified. This technique identified the unauthorized use of a file server at the University of Florida in 1994. Intruders gained access and posted a series of pirated software programs (including a pre-release version of Windows 95), which were then copied by thousands of users around the world.

Another example is if there are an unusual number of unsuccessful login attempts to a user's account or to several users' accounts. This suggests that an intruder is attempting to gain access. The best solution in this case is to program the network to disconnect after several failed attempts, forcing the potential user (or intruder) to reconnect. After more failed login attempts, the account should be disabled until the network manager has discussed the events with the account owner.

Regular monitoring should also extend to network hardware. All cables and network devices should be regularly inspected for tampering. All service calls by vendor employees should be logged and periodically spot checked with their offices to ensure that they are actually vendor employees on a legitimate call. Otherwise, the installation of eavesdropping devices may go unnoticed.

While monitoring is important, it has little value unless there is a clear plan for responding once a security breach is discovered. Every organization should have a clear response planned if a break-in is discovered. Many large organizations have special "SWAT" teams ready to be called into action if a problem is discovered.

Management Focus: *A SWAT Team in Cyberspace*

The Computer Emergency Response Team center at Carnegie Mellon University in Pittsburgh is the SWAT team of the electronic frontier. CERT was created by the Defense Department in 1989 after a widespread Internet break-in. They have no legal power to arrest or prosecute; instead, the team of about 156 programmers pokes through violated systems using their only weapons: dozens of computers. Like hackers they track, CERT team members often work around the clock.

Ten years ago, hackers were usually youthful pranksters, mostly interested in demonstrating technical ingenuity. Now there's a growing feeling that more sinister forces may be loose.

A panicky New York computer bulletin board operator called CERT at 3:00 A.M. one day to report the discovery of an unauthorized program that could surreptitiously record users' secret passwords. This New York bulletin board is hooked up to the Internet. If one system is compromised, many more are vulnerable.

As a result of the investigation, the team concluded there was an organized effort to infiltrate the Internet. CERT's detective work has won respect for the team and brought them new attention on the Net. However, finding holes is often easier than fixing them. The reality of this situation is that there will be many more attempted and actual break-ins in the future.

Source: "A SWAT Team in Cyberspace," *Newsweek*, February 21, 1994.

Correcting Unauthorized Access

Once an unauthorized access has been detected, the next step is to identify how the security breach occurred and fix it so that it will not reoccur. Then the intruder is disciplined by civil or criminal action. Law enforcement agencies have traditionally been reluctant to take action, given the difficulty in proving losses in this sort of crime and the inadequacy of many laws.

Many organizations have taken their own steps to detect intruders by using *entrapment* techniques. The objective is to divert the hacker's attention from the real network to an attractive server that contains only fake information. This server often called a *honey pot*, contains highly interesting fake information available only through illegal intrusion to "bait" the intruder. The honey pot server has sophisticated tracking software to monitor access to this information, which allows the organization and law enforcement officials to trace and legally document the intruder's actions. Possession of this information then becomes final legal proof of the intrusion.

In recent years, there has been a stiffening of computer security laws and in the legal interpretations of other laws that pertain to computer networks. As the information superhighway expands, laws and their enforcement should also continue to increase.

Summary

Types of Security Threats In general, network security threats can be classified into one of two categories: disruption, destruction, and disaster; and unauthorized access. Disruptions are usually minor and temporary. Some disruptions may also be caused by or result in the destruction of data. Natural (or manmade) disasters may occur that destroy host computers or large sections of the network. Unauthorized access refers to intruders (external hackers or organizational employees) gaining unauthorized access to files. The intruder may gain knowledge, change files to commit fraud or theft, or destroy information to injure the organization.

Risk Assessment Developing a secure network means developing controls that reduce or eliminate threats to the network. Controls prevent, detect, and correct whatever might happen to the organization when its computer-based systems are threatened. The first step in developing a secure network is to conduct a risk assessment. This is done by comparing the nature of the threats to the controls designed to reduce them, thus deriving levels of risk. A control spreadsheet lists the threats, the network components, and the controls, which a network manager uses to assess the level of risk.

Controlling Disruption, Destruction, and Disaster The key principle in controlling these threats—or at least reducing their impact—is redundancy. Redundant hardware that automatically recognizes failure and intervenes to replace the failed component can mask a failure that would otherwise result in a service disruption. Special attention needs to be given to preventing computer viruses and denial-of-service attacks. Generally speaking, preventing disasters is difficult, so the best option is a well-designed disaster recovery plan that includes backups and sometimes a professional disaster recovery firm.

Controlling Unauthorized Access The key principle in controlling unauthorized access is to be proactive in routinely testing and upgrading security controls. Contrary to popular belief, unauthorized intruders are usually organization employees, not external hackers. There are six general approaches to preventing unauthorized access: developing a security policy, developing user profiles, plugging known security holes, securing network access points (e.g., physical security, call-back modems, and firewalls), preventing eavesdropping (by restricting access to network cables and devices), and using encryption. The basic principle in detecting unauthorized access is looking for anything out of the ordinary. This means logging all messages sent and received by the network, all software used, and all logins (or attempted logins) to the network. These logs should be monitored both by network security personnel and by software programmed to issue alarms or take action if certain parameters are exceeded or if there is an abnormal occurrence.

Key Terms

account
algorithm
application-level firewall
asymmetric algorithm
authentication
backup controls
biometric system
block cipher
call-back modem
certificate
certificate authority (CA)
ciphertext
control spreadsheet
controls
data encryption standard (DES)
decryption
Delphi team
denial-of-service attack
destruction
disaster
disaster recovery firm
disaster recovery plan

disk duplexing
disk mirroring
disruption
eavesdropping
encryption
entrapment
fault-tolerant server
firewall
hacker
honey pot
IP spoofing
key
key-contents
key escrow
key management
network address translation
network component
one-time password
packet-level firewall
password
physical security
plaintext
private key

proxy server
public key
public key encryption
recovery controls
redundancy
risk assessment
RSA
secure hub
security hole
security policy
smart card
sniffer program
social engineering
symmetric algorithm
unauthorized access
uninterruptable power supply (UPS)
user profile
testing
threat
token
virus

Questions

1. What factors have brought increased emphasis on network security?
2. What is the first thing you must do when conducting a network security review?
3. Briefly outline the steps required to complete a control spreadsheet.
4. Name at least six areas that should have controls in a data communication network.
5. As the manager of a major data communication network, how many types of disaster plans might you consider?

6. What is a Delphi team?
7. What are some of the criteria that can be used to rank risk in a data communication network?
8. Briefly outline the steps required to rank threats to a network.
9. What is the fundamental principle in reducing threats from disruption, destruction, and disaster?
10. What is the purpose of a disaster recovery plan? What are five major elements of a typical disaster recovery plan?
11. What are the most common security threats? What are the most critical?
12. What is a computer virus? A macro virus?
13. Explain how a denial-of-service attack works.
14. What is a disaster recovery firm? When and why would you establish a contract with them?
15. What is the fundamental principle in reducing threats from unauthorized access?
16. People who attempt unauthorized access can be classified into four different categories. Describe them.
17. What are five major elements of a security policy?
18. What is social engineering?
19. What is a token (in the security meaning of the word, not the medium access control meaning of the word)? A smart card?
20. Explain how a biometric system can improve security.
21. What is a security hole and how do you fix it?
22. What is a sniffer?
23. Describe the purpose of a call-back modem.
24. Describe the three general ways of restricting access to a network.
25. What do you think are the three most important security controls that can be placed on a network? Why?
26. What is a firewall?
27. What are the differences between the different types of firewalls?
28. What is IP spoofing?
29. Is it possible first to encrypt with a public key and then to decrypt with a private (secret) key, as well as first to encrypt with the private key and then to decrypt that message with the public key?
30. Describe how encryption and decryption works.
31. What does it mean when an algorithm is classified as a symmetric algorithm?
32. What is key management?
33. Compare and contrast DES and public key encryption.
34. What is key escrow? Do you think it is a good idea? Explain.
35. Explain how authentication works.
36. What is a certificate authority?
37. What encryption techniques are used for commercial purposes?

Exercises

A. Conduct a risk assessment of your organization's networks. Some information may be confidential, so report what you can.
B. Investigate and report on the activities of CERT (the Computer Emergency Response Team), NCSA (National Computer Security Association) and FIRST (the Forum of Incident Response and Security Teams).

C. Break the class into several teams, each of which conducts a small risk assessment of threats to the network at your school or office. Identify four or five threats. Make some assumptions regarding the type of network. Finally, identify the judgment criteria that will be used to rank the various threats, rank the threats, and then identify network-oriented controls that would mitigate or stop each threat.

D. Conduct a risk assessment (i.e., control spreadsheet) for the following mini-case study.

The Belmont State Bank uses an online data communication network for several of its business functions. This network is used for online inquiries of the passbook savings system and of the demand deposit checking accounts system.

This is a large bank with hundreds of branches that are connected to a central computer system. Each branch has a variety of terminals and terminal controllers connected to the central system via the public telephone network. Some of these terminals are on dedicated leased lines, and others use the dial-up telephone network.

The security team visited six branch offices to conduct threat scenario sessions with the operations staffs. The sessions provided a good perspective of branch management, operations personnel, security, and prevailing attitudes toward embezzlement and other threats.

The bank's network uses video terminals, transaction terminals, local intelligent controllers, a decentralized database, and a variety of other hardware devices and software programs. When possible, the bank purchases outside packages rather than developing application systems "from scratch."

Terminals at all sites and the central headquarters are physically secure. Vendors who perform maintenance are responsible for ensuring that the remote intelligent controllers, modems, and other devices operate effectively. Terminal operators use a four-digit numeric password, and each terminal is transaction-coded to accept only its authorized transactions. The nine largest branches are allowed direct entry of their wire transfer business, which constitutes 92 percent of the wire transfers sent or received by the bank. There are written procedures at the local branches. Employees at several branches have started using their own or locally purchased microcomputers to increase the efficiency and throughput of the system.

Training instructions for operators are provided in an extensive looseleaf manual that is updated monthly. It is maintained centrally, and the updates are distributed to the various branches.

During transmission, the front end processor performs error detection and correction and orders the retransmission of any erroneous message. One of the system's good features is its message switching with store-and-forward capability. This gives everyone in the bank access to e-mail. Wire transfer messages are switched from this computer to the more secure and separate wire transfer control system computer. When a user calls in, the central system calls that user back in order to control which telephone numbers are connected to its dial-up modems. Encryption currently is under consideration.

The application programs are maintained by local bank employees, although a few of the packages still use some outside consultants for maintenance. An effective program change control procedure is operational.

The communication network control group has line monitors and other devices that are required to maintain an effective uptime ratio for this network. The network has been operating at a 98.95 percent uptime. Some of the terminal operators, however, have begun to complain about slow response time, which has been measured at an average of three seconds.

The Open Systems Interconnection (OSI) Model

One of the oldest models for defining network layers is the OSI model. During the late 1970s, the International Standards Organization (ISO) created the Open System Interconnection (OSI) subcommittee whose task was to develop a framework of standards for computer-to-computer communications. In 1984, this effort produced the *Open Systems Interconnection Reference Model,* which is commonly referred to as the OSI Model.

Today, the OSI model is being overtaken in the marketplace by the TCP/IP model. TCP/IP is the standard approach used by the Internet and is discussed in Chapter 6. The four-layer model used throughout this book is based on the TCP/IP model.

The OSI model has seven layers (see Figure A–1). It was originally developed for mainframe-oriented networks, so some of the layers do not apply to local area networks. The three layers of the OSI model (physical, data link, application) correspond to some extent to the same layers used in this book. The middle four layers in the OSI model (network, transport, session, presentation) have been condensed into one (the network layer) in this book.

Layer 1: Physical Layer

The *physical layer* is concerned primarily with transmitting data bits (zeros or ones) over a communication circuit. This layer defines the rules by which zeros and ones are transmitted, such as voltages of electricity, timing factors, full duplex or half duplex transmission, and connector cable standards, such as RS232 and RS449.

Layer 2: Data Link Layer

The *data link layer* manages the basic transmission circuit established in layer 1 and transforms it into a circuit that is free of transmission errors as far as layers above are concerned. A major task of layer 2 is to solve the problems caused by damaged, lost, or duplicate messages so the succeeding layers are shielded from transmission errors and can therefore presume that no errors occur.

Because layer 1 accepts and transmits only a serial stream of bits without understanding their meaning or structure, the data link layer must create and recognize message boundaries and check for errors. Layer 2 performs error detection, correction, and retransmission, definition of the beginning and end of the message, resolution of competing requests for the same communication link, and flow control, which keeps a rapidly transmitting device from drowning a slower receiver.

The data link layer is sometimes further divided into two sublayers: the *media access control* (MAC) sublayer and the *logical link control* (LLC) sublayer. The MAC sublayer performs most of the data link layer functions. The LLC sublayer is just an interface between the MAC sublayer and software in layer 3 (the network layer) that enables the software and hardware in the MAC sublayer to be separated from the logical functions in the LLC sublayer. In this way, the LLC sublayer performs a similar role to that performed by middleware in client-server networks (see Chapter 3). By separating the LLC sublayer from the MAC sublayer, it is simpler to change the MAC hardware and software without affecting the software in layer 3.

Layer 3: Network Layer

The *network layer* performs addressing and routing. It actually controls the operation of the combined layers, 1, 2, and 3, which are sometimes called the *subnetwork.* Software at this layer accepts messages from layer 4, and ensures that the packets are directed to

Application layer

7 Workers here identify the receiving terminal or application program and display the message on the screen of the network user's microcomputer or pass it to the application program.

Presentation layer

6 On the sixth floor employees convert code (ASCII to EBDIC) and, if required, decompress and decrypt the message.

Session layer

5 Fifth-floor workers hold all message blocks until they have received the entire message, which they pass to those on the sixth floor.

Transport layer

4 Those on the fourth floor recalculate checksums to confirm receipt of all message blocks and request retransmission of a block that appears damaged or is missing.

Network layer

3 The third-floor workers recount incoming packets for error, security, and billing purposes, and reconvert the packets to message blocks.

Data link layer

2 On the second-floor they recalculate the checksum, request frame retransmission if there is an error, confirm arrival, and log-in the frame.

Physical layer

1 First-floor employees reconvert the bits into frames.

Notice that the people on the fourth floor confirm the receipt of all packets that belong to the same message block, whereas the second floor only confirms the correct receipt of a single frame (containing one packet).

Packet/Frame
.......1001010........

Application layer

7 Employees on the seventh floor convert input from a terminal or application program into a "message block," which includes the data (message contents) along with the sender's and receiver's addresses. When the block is complete, they pass it to the sixth floor. Application programs or terminals access the network only at this floor.

Presentation layer

6 Workers on the sixth floor convert code (EBCDIC to ASCII or vice versa), define the format of the data, and (when requested) encrypt the data and compress it before passing the message block to the fifth floor.

Session layer

5 Those on the fifth floor mark the beginning and ending of message blocks, set up a session connecting two terminals (log-in, passwords, user ID, etc.), end sessions, and determine whether the transmission will be half duplex or full duplex before passing the message blocks to the fourth floor.

Transport layer

4 Fourth-floor employees divide very long message blocks into shorter message blocks for transmission, add a sequence number to each block, add a checksum for error detection, check for duplicate blocks, retransmit the blocks after an error or a timeout, add security to message blocks, and pass the message blocks to the third floor.

Network layer

3 Third-floor employees resize the message blocks into packets (usually 128 characters) to meet specific network requirements, attach the addresses and sequence numbers to each packet, identify routes for packets through the network, and then pass the packets to the second floor.

Data link layer

2 Workers here supervise the transmission. They insert the packet into a frame that becomes the envelope for carrying the packet during transmission, add a frame sequence number, confirm checksums for error detection, keep a copy of the frame to use for retransmission in case of error, and then pass the completed frame to the first floor for transmission.

Physical layer

1 The first floor is concerned with hardware, whereas the upper floors are concerned with software. The hardware on the first floor includes the RS-232 connector cables, network interface aids, modems, and circuits. What began on the seventh floor as a long message block is now sent over the circuits as a frame containing a packet in the form of a serial stream of bits.

Figure A-1 This figure depicts the OSI model as a seven-floor office building in which people handle messages instead of software programs doing the work. A message to be sent across the network enters the OSI software at the seventh floor, travels down to the first floor, goes out the front door, travels across the network, and reaches the other building, where it travels through the front door and up to the receiving terminal on the seventh floor of that building.

their proper destination. After its routing has been established, the packet is passed down to the data link layer.

Layer 4: Transport Layer

The *transport layer* often is called the *host-to-host layer* or *end-to-end layer* because it establishes, maintains, and terminates logical connections for the transfer of data between end users. It is responsible for generating the address of the end user, breaking a large data transmission into smaller packets if needed, ensuring that all the packets have been received, and eliminating duplicate packets. The transport layer deals with end-to-end issues, such as procedures for entering and departing from the network.

The transport layer can multiplex several streams of messages onto one physical circuit, or use inverse multiplexing to create one fast circuit from several slower ones. It also performs flow control by controlling the movement of messages, whereas layers 1 and 2 control the physical flow of packets or frames.

Layer 5: Session Layer

The *session layer* is responsible for initiating, maintaining, and terminating each logical session between end users. To understand the session layer, think of your telephone. When you lift the receiver, listen for a dial tone, and dial a number, you begin to create a physical connection that goes through layer 1 as a person-to-network protocol. When you start speaking with the person at the other end of the telephone circuit, you are engaged in a person-to-person session; the session is the dialogue between the two.

This layer is responsible for managing and structuring all sessions. Session initiation must arrange for all the desired and required services between session participants, such as logging onto circuit equipment, transferring files, using various terminal types, and performing security checks. Session termination provides an orderly way to end the session, as well as a means to abort a session prematurely. It may have some redundancy built in to recover from a broken transport (layer 4) connection in case of failure. The session layer also handles session accounting so the correct party receives the bill. In many networks, the functions defined at this layer are actually performed by the data link layer (layer 2) or the transport layer (layer 4), so no software is actually present at layer 5.

Layer 6: Presentation Layer

The *presentation layer* formats the data for presentation to the user. Its job is to accommodate the totally different interfaces on different terminals or computers so the application program need not worry about them. It is concerned with displaying, formatting, and editing user inputs and outputs. For example, layer 6 might perform data compression, translation between different data formats, and screen formatting. Any function (except those in layers 1 to 5) that is requested sufficiently often to warrant finding a general solution is placed in the presentation layer, although some of these functions can be performed by separate hardware and software (e.g., encryption).

Layer 7: Application Layer

The *application layer* is the end user's access to the network. The primary purpose is to provide a set of utilities for application programs. Each user program determines the set of messages and any action it might take upon receipt of a message. Other considerations at this layer include network management statistics, remote system initiation and termination, network monitoring, application diagnostics, making the network transparent to users, simple processor sharing between host computers, use of distributed databases, and industry-specific protocols (such as those in banking).

Private Branch Exchange (PBX)

A *private branch exchange* (PBX) is a switch (more commonly called a *switchboard*) operated for one organization into which all telephone lines connect. The term *PABX* (private automatic branch exchange) was popular for many years, but today the term PBX is more common. Usually, several circuits go from this switchboard to the telephone company's end office. These circuits generally are referred to as trunk lines when they are devoted primarily to voice transmissions from a switchboard. In data transmission, we refer to these same circuits as leased circuits, private circuits, or dedicated circuits.

Without a PBX, all telephones must be connected directly to the telephone company's trunk line. Each telephone has a separate telephone number, and forwarding a call from one telephone to another is difficult. For each of these telephone connections, the company must pay a monthly connection fee.

With a PBX, all telephones are connected to the one PBX, which is connected to the trunk line. This PBX performs much the same functions as a switch. All calls made to any of the company's telephones are connected to the PBX, which switches them to the correct telephone. It is also simple to have one central telephone number, from which an internal company operator or computerized system can forward (i.e., switch) calls to specific telephones. Each telephone has its own telephone number, the last four or five digits of which are an internal organization telephone extension number. In this way, incoming telephone calls can go directly to the telephone being called. People within the organization can dial inside extensions (four or five digits) or outside telephone calls to other organizations, also bypassing the telephone company and the switchboard operator. Any central telephone numbers still can be routed to a switchboard operator if the organization wishes.

PBX Benefits

PBXs provide many other benefits, the most important of which is cost saving. All telephones in a company are seldom in use simultaneously. Most companies do not need one trunk line connection for every telephone they have. With a PBX, you can connect as many telephones as you like to the PBX, and have a different number of connections from the PBX to the telephone company's trunk line. For example, a company with 100 telephones that expected no more than 25 percent of its telephones to be in use at one time might pay for only 25 trunk line connections. This results in considerable savings, although if more than 25 users attempted to make or receive a call, they would get a busy signal.

To control voice calls, business organizations install *call management systems*. These systems monitor telephone call traffic, point out peak periods, identify the number of operators needed to handle different call volumes, and keep track of telephone operator efficiency and other factors relevant to voice telephone communications. Call accounting software is a specialized database application that records every call that is completed or other specific actions. This output usually is called the *station message detail recording* (SMDR), but some vendors use their own terminology.

Recording the SMDR records is the first task in call accounting, followed by processing the records, assessing the cost of calls made, and reporting and administration. Before widespread use of microcomputers, many companies connected a serial printer to the PBX's serial port to record the information on each call.

Today's systems send this output to a call recorder, which holds the SMDR data until it is transferred to a microcomputer for analysis. The software, called a *call accounting package*, can "price" the calls and prepare a bill for each telephone extension. Most call accounting packages come with a standard

Management Focus: PBX Fraud

Estimates of telephone fraud losses in the United States range from $500 million to $4 billion per year. One type of fraud involves thieves obtaining access codes to the user's PBX account. Once they have this access, the hackers break the password required for access to long-distance services. Upon obtaining access to the system, hackers can make personal use of the services to further other criminal enterprises, or to sell the access code for a profit.

Although the sale and use of remote access dialing codes appears less frequently, this particular crime is on the rise. The loss to one corporation exceeded $220,000 within the first 13 hours after the fraudulent activation of a remote-access dialing code.

Instead of fighting over losses and who is responsible for paying the bill, carriers are working aggressively to eliminate the fraud. They now use software that quickly spots unusual calling patterns much like stock trading software searches for a trend. They can then alert the owner of the PBX to verify the unusual charges.

AT&T Global Business Communications Systems formed an investigative team that will "track the theft of business long distance service to the hacker's hideout." The sole purpose of the GBCS is to monitor, track, and catch phone-system bandits in the act of committing toll fraud.

Sources: Datamation, September 15, 1994; *Business Week,* July 13, 1992; *The FBI Law Enforcement Bulletin,* July 1994.

repertoire of call accounting reports. At the minimum, you can expect a report detailing the calls made from each extension, including the time, length, total cost, cost per minute, average call length, the number called, and so forth. Some packages can group the telephone extensions according to an organization's departments and divisions. The best programs produce ad hoc reports on demand.

Call monitoring systems monitor the levels of call activity by showing the current status of various trunk lines, the number of calls in progress, the number of calls waiting in queues, the wait time before incoming calls are answered, the length of calls, the number of calls lost because the caller hangs up, and the status of different operators. Such information helps manage telephone operator performance by measuring the number of calls handled, the length of each call, the percentage of time spent on the telephone, the average time on hold, and the time spent waiting to be connected.

Some of these systems actively control outgoing telephone circuits by not allowing certain area codes or the first three digits of certain telephone exchanges to be dialed, thereby restricting outgoing

calls. *Least cost routing* means that the PBX can decide the least expensive route to place a long-distance call. For example, the PBX could choose between a telephone trunk line the organization already leases, different common carriers, or dial-up. In this case, the lease line would have the lowest cost, with varying common carriers next, and dial-up the highest cost. But, these functions need to be programmed into the PBX by specifying the area codes and the carriers. As a result, the addition of new area codes sometimes causes problems; every PBX needs to be reprogrammed to add the new area code and the interexchange carrier's charges into the list of valid area codes.

Other features include the ability to make outgoing long-distance calls from outside the office served by the PBX. With this feature, the user calls into the PBX (from home for example), dials an authorization code and gets a dial tone that can be used to make long-distance calls. In this way, the call is paid for by the company (using whatever volume discounts apply), rather than by the individual caller.

Most local telephone companies now offer extra cost services that provide many of the same benefits of a PBX. The CENTREX service, for example, offers call forwarding, call holding, automatic call backs, conference calling, paging, and more. For those companies that do not want to pay the initial purchase cost for a PBX, these services can be valuable.

Digital PBX

The newest PBXs, called fourth generation, are all-digital and therefore are sometimes referred to as a *digital PBX*. Digital PBXs are popular because the switching is so fast and so error-free that it allows high-speed data transmissions to go through the same switchboard as the one used for voice communications. In fact, if you are using a digital switchboard, your voice transmissions must be digitized prior to going through the switchboard. With digital switchboards, therefore, everything is transmitted in a digital format. These PBXs have three main characteristics: distributed architecture, nonblocking operation, and integrated voice and data.

Digital PBXs use a *distributed architecture* that is either hierarchical or fully distributed. *Hierarchical systems* distribute routine functions to the switching module, but real control resides in the central processor. In *fully distributed systems*, the switch module processes its calls independent of any other system component. Fully distributed systems are said to be inherently more reliable because failure of a single control module, no matter how catastrophic, cannot produce overall system outages. Proponents of the hierarchical system counter that fully distributed PBXs cannot perform under high load conditions because of internode control and synchronization problems.

In a *nonblocking operation*, intraoffice calls *always* can be placed between any two telephones within an organization. For example, if the switchboard carries lines for 2000 telephones within the organization, then 1000 people always can be talking with people at the other 1000 extensions. *Integrated voice and data* means both voice and data can be transmitted over the same communication circuit and through the same PBX.

These newer digital PBXs can use digital transmission and switching techniques because they are designed with 32-bit microprocessor chips that act as the central controller/central intelligence. A typical

---

Management Focus: Buying a PBX

Here are some features to look for when buying a PBX:

* Call forwarding
* Call holding/transfer
* Conference calling
* Voice mail
* Ability to connect to dictation equipment
* Least-cost routing to ensure that long-distance calls are routed over the least-cost communication service
* Paging people throughout a facility
* Speed calling in which often-used numbers are stored in the system
* Station message detail recording (SMDR) to provide cost accounting information
* Nonblocking switching

* Ability to change a telephone number through software rather than rewiring to a new telephone instrument
* Automatic call-back where a calling party encountering a busy station can be called back automatically when the called station becomes available
* Simultaneous transmission of voice and data
* Format and protocol conversion that allows the interconnection of different vendors' word processors, host mainframes, microcomputers, and terminals.
* Authorization codes to restrict access for security purposes
* Connection to high-speed outgoing circuits, such as T-1

digital PBX permits individual telephones or micro-computers to be connected directly to the central digital switchboard. A local area network can be controlled from within the switchboard. Micro-computer workstations on the local area network connect to the switchboard in a star configuration, and the PBX digital switch redirects messages among microcomputers connected to the local area network.

Now there are even wireless PBXs. One wireless PBX is capable of supporting 2000 lines and 400 simultaneous telephone calls. This system does not have a nonblocking switch. A *wireless PBX* uses spread spectrum radio technology in frequencies just above 900 megahertz. The obvious major benefit of a wireless PBX is that twisted-pair telephone wires do not have to be installed throughout the building for connecting the telephones to the PBX. Once a telephone message leaves the PBX, it is on regular telephone cabling for the trunk lines to the local loop between the business and the telephone company. The wireless part of the PBX is within the building, not between the building and the telephone company's central office.

Cellular Technology

Cellular technology is becoming increasingly popular. Its most common use is to provide *cellular telephone* services, but the cellular network is also being used more and more by data communication devices such as pagers and personal digital assistants (PDAs).

Cellular technology is a form of high-frequency radio in which antennas are spaced strategically throughout a metropolitan area. A service area or city is divided into many cells, each with its own antenna. This arrangement generally provides subscribers with reliable mobile telephone service of a quality almost that of a hardwired telephone system. Users (voice or data transmission) dial or log into the system, and their voices or data are transmitted directly from their automobile, home, or place of business to one of these antennas. In this way, the cellular system replaces the hardwired local loop.

This system is intelligent. For example, as you drive your automobile across the service area or city, you move away from one antenna and closer to another. As the signal weakens at the first antenna, the system automatically begins picking up your signal at the second antenna. Transmission is switched automatically to the closest antenna without communication being lost.

When you speak on a cellular telephone, anyone might be listening to your conversation. Cellular telephone calls are transmitted over the 870 to 890 megahertz frequency bands, which are easily accessible by today's scanners. These devices can scan the

---

Management Focus: *Airwaves Auction*

The federal government set out to sell the sky and the enormous sale brought in a total collection of $833 million for the U.S. Treasury. The FCC raised $617 million from the sale of ten licenses for nationwide advanced paging networks. In addition to this, it took in $216 million from the sale of some 300 licenses that may be used by interactive television services in the future.

The biggest winners of the licenses were already prominent in wireless communications. Paging Network Inc. and McCaw Cellular Communications were the front runners. Another company backed by the Microsoft Corporation and its billionaire founders, William H. Gates and Paul Allen, also purchased a license.

Most companies that won paging licenses plan to offer a new service called *acknowledgment paging* in which a pager automatically responds to a message with a signal indicating that the message got through. Holders of the most valuable licenses plan more elaborate networks that would allow users to enter messages on their computers or personal ditigial assistants (PDAs) and transmit them anywhere in the country.

The results of the auction vividly demonstrate how precious the nation's airwaves are at a time when wireless communications business is seeing explosive growth.

Source: "Airwaves Auction," *The New York Times*, July 30, 1994.

frequencies and stop and listen in at the specific frequency your call is using. Even though federal law says it is illegal to manufacture scanners for this frequency range or to use them to listen in on a cellular telephone call, it is virtually impossible to enforce this law because thousands of people own scanners.

Cellular telephone fraud is also becoming a problem. Unscrupulous people purchase a cellular telephone and replace its security EPROM (erasable programmable read only memory) with "thumbwheel" EPROM substitutes. They do this by turning the wheels at random until they discover some other person's cellular telephone security code, at which point they can begin making calls on that code—at least until that person receives the next telephone bill. Some of the more sophisticated fraud perpetrators use scanners and laptop microcomputers to find large numbers of cellular telephone codes automatically. As yet, this type of fraud is not very common, but owners of cellular telephones should check their bills immediately. Also, remember that you pay for both incoming and outgoing cellular airtime. Thus, you pay not only for calls you make, but also for those other people make to you.

A pager may be better for incoming calls than a cellular telephone if you want to save money and also have more security. For security reasons, you should not provide cellular telephone numbers to strangers. Instead, you should provide a beeper number for others to call you. Then you call them back on the cellular telephone. This procedure is more secure and eliminates the cost of incoming cellular calls.

The real future of cellular technology is based on the philosophy of dividing the entire United States, or even the world, into cells so a person can call from anywhere to anywhere. It would be easy to interconnect the cells of the entire United States with the cells of, say, France by using either satellite communications or fiber optic undersea cables. Most of us today think of a telephone as a fixed-location device (located in our home, school, business, or pay telephone booth), but cellular pay telephones will appear in taxicabs, buses, and trains. (They already are in airplanes and as emergency phones on interstate highways.) Burglar alarm systems will use cellular radio, because when burglars defeat alarm systems, 90 percent of the time they do it by cutting the telephone wires. Paramedic rescue units already use cellular radio.

The telephone is also rapidly becoming a personal item. You will carry it with you, just as you might carry a calculator or a microcomputer. Thirty years ago, no one anticipated that we all would have electronic calculators small enough to carry with us. In the future, you will have small portable cellular telephones, with the number assigned to you, and the telephone unit will be carried rather than connected to the wall of your home. AT&T already is offering personal telephone numbers with the 700 area code that a person can use for life.

Connector Cables

When a message leaves the microcomputer or terminal and begins to move onto the network, the first component it encounters is the *connector cable* between the microcomputer (or terminal) and the circuit. When people discuss connector cables, the focus is on the standards (such as RS232 or RS449).

RS232 (DB-25)/RS449 (DB-9)

When people talk about connector cables, they frequently refer to them as a RS232, DB-25, RS449, or DB-9. This is because each connector cable is based on a specified standard. Calling the connector by its standard designation allows everyone to know precisely which connector is being discussed.

The RS232 standard is the most frequently mentioned. It was first issued in 1962, and its third revision, RS232C, was issued in 1969. The RS232D standard was issued in 1987 to expand on RS232C. The RS232D standard also is known as the EIA-232-D.

The RS232 connector cable is the standard interface for connecting data terminal equipment (DTE) to data circuit terminating equipment (DCE). The newer RS232D is specified as having 25 wires and using the DB-25 connector plug like the one used on microcomputers. If this connector cable is attached to a microcomputer, people may refer to it simply as DB-25; if it is not attached to a microcomputer, they may refer to it as the RS232 interface.

Data terminal equipment (DTE) comprises the data source, the data sink, or both. In reality, it is any piece of equipment at which a data communication path begins or ends, such as a terminal. *Data circuit terminating equipment (DCE)* provides all the functions required to establish, maintain, and terminate a connection. This includes signal conversion and coding between the DTE and the common carrier's circuit, including the modem. A modem is DCE.

Figure A–2 shows a picture of the RS232D interface plug and describes each of its 25 protruding pins. It is the standard connector cable (25 wires/pins) that passes control signals and data between the terminal (DTE) and the modem (DCE). This standard has been supplied by the Electronic Industries Association (EIA). Outside the United States, this RS232D connector cable is known as the V.24 and V.28. The V.24 and V.28 standards have been accepted by the international standards group known as the ITU-T. These standards provide a common description of what the signal coming out of, and going into, the serial port of a computer or terminal looks like electrically. Specifically, RS232 provides for a signal changing from a nominal +12 volts to a nominal −12 volts. The standard also defines the cables and connectors used to link data communication devices. This is the cable that connects the modem to your microcomputer.

The RS232 has a maximum 50-foot cable length, but it can be increased to 100 feet or more by means of a special low capacitance, extended distance cable. This is not advised, however, because some vendors may not honor maintenance agreements if the cable is lengthened beyond the 50-foot standard.

As an illustration, let us present the cable distances for Texas Instruments' products. The cable length of the RS232 varies according to the speed at which you transmit. For Texas Instruments, the connector cable length can be up to 914 meters (1 meter 1.1 yards) when transmitting at 1200 bits per second, 549 meters when transmitting at 2400 bits per second, 244 meters when transmitting at 4800 bits per second, and 122 meters when transmitting at 9600 bits per second. When end users operate at maximum distances, it is important to remember that they must meet the restrictions on all types of equipment used, including the electrical environment, cable construction, and cable wiring. This means that when you want to operate at a maximum cable distance, you must contact the terminal and/or modem

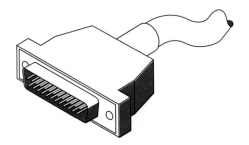

Pin	Circuit Name
1	Shield
2	Transmitted Data
3	Received Data
4	Request to Send
5	Clear to Send
6	DCE Ready
7	Signal Ground
8	Received Line Signal Detector
9	(Reserved for testing)
10	(Reserved for testing)
11	(Unassigned)
12	Secondary Received Line Signal Detector/Data Signal Rate Select (DCE source)
13	Secondary Clear to Send
14	Secondary Transmitted Data
15	Transmitter Signal Element Timing (DCE source)
16	Secondary Received Data
17	Receiver Signal Element Timing (DCE source)
18	Local Loopback
19	Secondary Request to Send
20	DTE Ready
21	Remote Loopback/Signal Quality Detector
22	Ring Indicator
23	Data Signal Rate Select (DTE/DCE source)
24	Transmitter Signal Element Timing (DTE source)
25	Text Mode

Figure A–2 RS232 cable specifications.

vendors to obtain their maximum cable distance before you proceed.

The RS449 standard has been adopted as U.S. Federal Standard 1031. The RS449 is shown in Figure A–3. A 4000-foot cable length can be used, there are 37 pins instead of 25 (useful for digital transmission), and various other circuit functions have been added, such as diagnostic circuits and digital circuits.

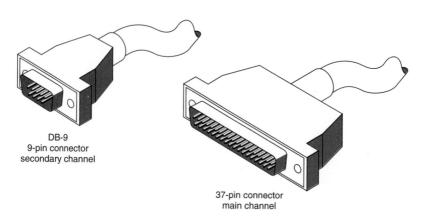

DB-9
9-pin connector
secondary channel

37-pin connector
main channel

37-Pin Connector				9-Pin Connector	
Pin	**First Segment Assignment Function**	**Pin**	**Second Segment Assignment Function**	**Pin**	**Function**
1	Shield	20	Receive Common	1	Shield
2	Signaling Rate Indicator	21	Unassigned	2	Sec. Receiver Ready
		22	Send Data	3	Sec. Send Data
3	Unassigned	23	Send Timing	4	Sec. Receive Data
4	Send Data	24	Receive Data	5	Signal Ground
5	Send Timing	25	Request to Send	6	Receive Common
6	Receive Data	26	Receive Timing	7	Sec. Request to Send
7	Request to Send	27	Clear to Send		
8	Receive Timing	28	Terminal in Service	8	Sec. Clear to Send
9	Clear to Send	29	Data Mode	9	Send Common
10	Local Loopback	30	Terminal Ready		
11	Data Mode	31	Receiver Ready		
12	Terminal Ready	32	Select Standby		
13	Receiver Ready	33	Signal Quality		
14	Remote Loopback	34	New Signal		
15	Incoming Call	35	Terminal Timing		
16	Select Frequency/ Signaling Rate Selector	36	Standby Indicator		
17	Terminal Timing	37	Send Common		
18	Test Mode				
19	Signal Ground				

Figure A–3 RS449 cable specifications.

In addition, secondary channel circuits (reverse channel) have been put into a separate 9-pin connector known as a DB-9. The serial port on your microcomputer may be either a DB-9 or a DB-25.

For some of the new features, look at pin 32 (SELECT STANDBY). With this pin, the terminal can instruct the modem to use an alternate standby network such as changing from a private leased line to a public packet network, either for backup or simply to access another database not normally used. In other words, a terminal can be connected to two different networks, and the operator can enter a keyboard command to switch the connection from one network to another. With regard to LOOPBACK (pins 10 and 14), the terminal can allow basic tests without special test equipment or the manual exchanging of equipment or cables.

With microcomputers, the RS232 and RS449 also are referred to as D-type connectors. The RS232 may be called a DB-25, and the 9-pin RS449 may be called a DB-9. Look at Figure A–4 to see the microcomputer pin configurations for these two connectors.

There are also X.20 and X.21 interface cables. The X.20 interface is for asynchronous communications, and the X.21 is for synchronous communi-

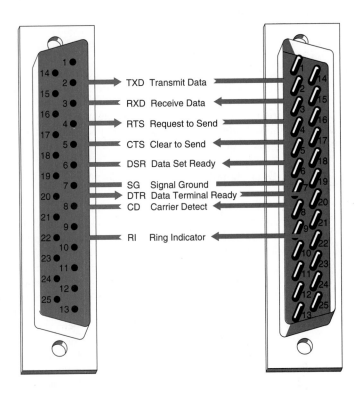

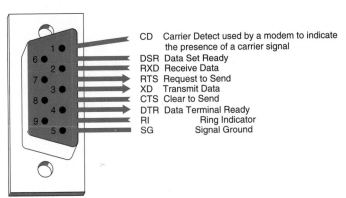

Figure A–4 Pin configurations.

cations. Each is based on only 15 pins (wires) connecting the DTE and the DCE, and fewer pins require an increased intelligence in both the DTE and the DCE. X.20 and X.21 are international standards intended to provide an interface with the X.25 packet switching networks discussed later in this book.

Another option that may become available in the near future is a fiber optic cable in place of the standard RS232 electrical cables. Currently, by using fiber optic cable, we can locate a terminal 1000 meters (3280 feet) from a host mainframe computer. With a 1000-meter fiber optic cable, these products can communicate at speeds ranging from 19,200 bits per second up to twice that speed. Therefore, you get not only greater distance (1000 meters) but also greater speed. This may be another example in which fiber optics eventually will replace electronics.

The *high-speed serial interface (HSSI)* is beginning to appear in new products. HSSI defines the physical and electrical interface between the DTE and the DCE equipment. It was developed by Cisco Systems of Menlo Park, California, and T3plus of Santa Clara, California. They have submitted it to the American National Standards Institute, which also formalized the EIA-232 and V.35 standards. HSSI allows data transfers over the connector cable at 52 million bits per second, whereas RS-449 cannot handle more than 10 million bits per second. HSSI is a 50-pin connector using shielded twisted-pair cabling.

Null Modem Cable Connections

Null modem cables allow transmission between two microcomputers that are next to each other (six to eight feet apart) without using a modem. If you discover that the diskette from your microcomputer will not fit into another one, that transmitting over telephone lines is impossible, or that you cannot transmit data easily from one microcomputer to another for any reason, then it is time to get a null modem cable.

First, bring the two microcomputers close together. Next, obtain a null modem cable (more on the pin connections shortly). The cable runs from the serial communication port on the first microcomputer to the serial communication port on the second one. The cable is called a "null" modem cable because it eliminates the need for a modem. You can either build a null modem cable or buy one from any microcomputer store. Null modem connector

blocks are available to connect between two cables you already own.

To transfer data between two microcomputers, just hook the null modem cable between them and call up one of the computers by using the communication software you normally use. To do so, put one microcomputer in answer mode and use the other one to call it, but skip the step of dialing the telephone number. After the receiving computer has answered that it is ready, the data can be sent, just as you would on a normal long-distance dial-up connection.

With null modem cables, a higher bits per second rate is accomplished easily; transmission can be 9600 bits per second, for example. This may be a great advantage for high-volume data transfers from microcomputer to microcomputer, because your modem might limit transmission to 1200 bits per second or less. Basically, a null modem cable switches pins 2 and 3 (TRANSMIT and RECEIVE) of the RS232 connector plug.

Data Signaling/Synchronization

Let us look at *data signaling* or *synchronization* as it occurs on a RS232 connector cable. Figure A–5 shows the 13 most frequently used pins of the 25-pin RS232 connector cable. A microcomputer is on the left side of the figure and a modem is on the right.

Do you ever wonder what happens when you press the "send" key to transmit synchronous data? When a synchronous block of data is sent, the microcomputer and the modem raise and lower electrical signals (plus and minus voltages of electricity) between themselves over the RS232 connector. This usually is a nominal +12 or −12 volts. For example, a modem with a RS232 interface might indicate that it is on and ready to operate by raising the signal on pin 6, DATA SET READY. (Data set is an older term for a modem.) When a call comes in, the modem shows the microcomputer that the telephone line is ringing by raising a signal on pin 22, the RING INDICATOR. Raising a signal means putting +12 volts on the wire or pin. The microcomputer may then tell the modem to answer the call by raising a signal on pin 20, DATA TERMINAL READY. After the modems connect, the modem may indicate the connection status to the microcomputer by raising a signal on pin 8, CARRIER DETECT. At the end of the session, the microcomputer may tell the modem to drop the telephone call (release the circuit) by lowering the signal on pin 20, DATA TERMINAL

Computer DTE side   Name and pin number   Modem DCE side

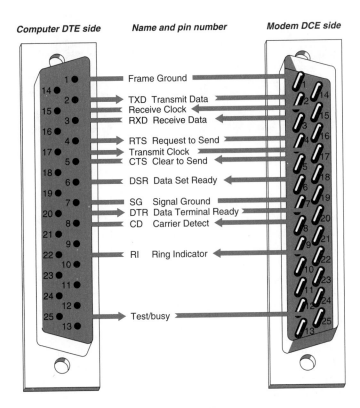

Figure A–5 Data signaling with RS232 cables.

READY. The REQUEST TO SEND and CLEAR TO SEND signals go over pins 4 and 5, which are used in half duplex modems to manage control of the communication channel. Incidentally, some of these basic procedures may vary slightly from one manufacturer to another.

Follow the pins and signal direction arrows in Figure A–5 as we discuss an example that handles the flow of a block of synchronous data. When the microcomputer operator presses the "send" key to transmit a block of data, pin 4, REQUEST TO SEND, transmits the signal from the microcomputer to the modem. This informs the modem that a block of data is ready to be sent. The modem then sends a CLEAR TO SEND signal back to the microcomputer by using pin 5, thus telling the microcomputer that it can send a synchronous block of data.

The microcomputer now out-pulses a serial stream of bits that contain two 8-bit SYN (synchronization) characters in front of the message block. A SYN character is 0110100 (decimal 22 in ASCII code). This bit stream passes over the connector ca-

ble to the modem using pin 2, TRANSMIT DATA. The modem then modulates this data block to convert it from the digital signal (plus and minus voltages of electricity) to an analog signal (discussed in the next section). From the modem, the data go out onto the local loop circuit between your business premises and the telephone company central office. From there, it goes to the long-distance interexchange channels (IXC) and the receiving end's telephone company central office. Then it moves to the local loop, into the modem, across the connector cable, and into the host mainframe computer at the other end of the circuit.

This process is repeated for each synchronous message block in half duplex transmission. The data signaling that takes place between the microcomputer and the modem involves the REQUEST TO SEND, CLEAR TO SEND, and TRANSMIT DATA pins. Accurate timing between blocks of data is critical in data signaling and synchronization. If this timing is lost, the entire block of data is destroyed and must be retransmitted.

Systems Network Architecture (SNA)

IBM developed its own architecture and protocols for networking, called *Systems Network Architecture (SNA)*. SNA describes an integrated structure that provides for all modes of data communications and upon which new data communication networks can be planned and implemented. SNA is similar to the OSI model in concept, but is different in implementation; SNA is not OSI compliant.

The major problem with SNA is that it uses proprietary nonstandard protocols at the network layer and above. This means that it is difficult to integrate SNA networks with other networks that use industry standard network layer protocols. Routing messages between SNA networks and other networks, and even between IBM SNA networks and IBM LANs (which use industry standard protocols) requires special equipment. In many cases, network managers using both IBM SNA and IBM LANs have built two separate networks into the same offices, laying two sets of cable to each location, one for SNA, one for the LAN. For this reason, use of SNA is prohibited under GOSIP, although some exempt agencies have been permitted to purchase SNA-based networks for their IBM mainframes. IBM has announced a new form of SNA (APPN) that uses industry standard protocols, as discussed next. In a 1995 survey of mainframe network managers, 68 percent said that SNA and APPN was not important to their future plans (9 percent said it was critical and 23 percent said it was important).

SNA is built around four basic principles. First, SNA encompasses distributed functions in which many network responsibilities can be moved from the central computer to other network components, such as remote concentrators. Second, it describes paths between the end users (programs, devices, or operators) of the data communication network separately from the users themselves, thus allowing network configuration modifications or extensions without affecting the end users. Third, it uses the principle of device independence, which permits an application program to communicate with an input/output device without regard to any unique device requirements. This also allows application programs and communication equipment to be added or changed without affecting other elements of the communication network. Fourth, SNA uses both logical and physical standardized functions and protocols for the communication of information between any two points. This means there can be *one* architecture for general purpose and industry terminals of many varieties, and *one* network protocol.

The appropriate place to begin understanding the SNA concept is to look at it from the viewpoint of the end user. The end user (terminal operator) talks to the network through what is called a *logical unit (LU)*. These logical units are implemented as program code or microcode (firmware), and they provide the end user with a point of access to the network. The program code or microcode can be built into the terminal or implemented into an intelligent terminal controller, concentrator, or remote front end.

Before one end user of a SNA network can communicate with any other end user, each of their respective logical units must be connected in a mutual relationship called a *session*. Because a session joins two logical units, it is called a *LU-LU session*. The terminal user enters the request to talk to another terminal, and the network's software connects the two LUs.

The exchange of data by end users is subject to a number of procedural rules that the logical units specify before beginning the exchange of information. These procedural rules specify how the session is to be conducted, the frame size, the amount of data to be sent by one end user before the other end user replies, actions to be taken if errors occur, the transmission speed, sequencing, what route the frame will take, what to do if the circuit fails, and the like.

Each logical unit (LU) in a network is assigned a network name. Before a session begins, the SNA network determines the network address that corresponds to each LU network name. This scheme allows one end user (for example, a terminal operator) to establish communication with another end user (for example, an application program) without having to specify where that end user is located in the network. These network names and addresses are used for addressing messages.

The flow of data between users moves between two logical units in a session. This flow moves as a bit sequence carried in an Synchronous Data Link Control (SDLC) frame and generally is referred to as a *message unit*. The message unit also contains the network addresses of the logical unit that originated the message and the logical unit that is to receive the message. These are the basic protocols at work.

A session between a pair of logical units is initiated when one of them (the end user) issues a REQUEST TO SEND message. Once a session has been activated between a pair of logical units, the LUs can begin to exchange data. This is where the SDLC protocol handles the movement of data to have an orderly data flow. A session between a pair of logical units is deactivated when one of them sends a deactivation request or when some other outside event—intervention by a network operator or failure at some other part of the network—interrupts the session.

The logical organization of a SNA network, regardless of its physical configuration, is divided into two broad categories of components: network addressable units and path control network.

Network Addressable Units

Network addressable units (NAUs) are sets of SNA components that provide services enabling end users to send data through the network and helping network operators perform network control and management functions. Physically, network addressable units are hardware and programming components within terminals, intelligent controllers, and front end processors. Network addressable units communicate with one another through the path control network (discussed in the next section).

There are three kinds of network addressable units in SNA. The first one, the logical unit (LU), has already been introduced. The second is the *physical unit (PU)*, which is a set of SNA components that provides services to control communication links, terminals, intelligent controllers, front end processors, and host computers. Each terminal, intelligent controller, front end processor, and the like contains a physical unit that represents that particular device to the SNA network. The third kind of network addressable unit is the *system services control point (SSCP)*. This also is a set of SNA components, but its duties are broader than those of the physical units and logical units. Physical units and logical units represent machine resources and end users, whereas the SSCP manages the entire SNA network or a significant part of it called a *domain*. A SSCP controls many other devices.

Just as sessions exist between logical units, sessions can exist between other kinds of network addressable units, such as a *SSCP-LU, SSCP-PU,* or *SSCP-SSCP session*. In a family, the mother, father, and children are all PUs. You conduct a LU session when speaking with your father, mother, sister, or brother, but your mother or father is the SSCP controlling the children's LUs.

Systems Network Architecture defines a *node* as a point within the SNA network that contains SNA components. For example, each terminal, intelligent controller, and front end processor that is designed into the SNA specifications can be a node.

An expanded definition of a node is any microcomputer, minicomputer, mainframe computer, or database that constitutes a point on the network at which data might be stored, forwarded, input into the network, or removed from the network as output. Depending on which vendor's literature you read, they might refer to a node as a station, an intelligent microprocessor-based device, a terminal, or a workstation.

Each SNA node contains a physical unit that represents that node and its resources to the system services control point. When the SSCP activates a session with a physical unit (SSCP-PU session), it makes the node (terminal, intelligent controller, or front end processor) containing that physical unit an active part of the SNA network. It is convenient to think of an SNA node as being a terminal, intelligent controller, or front end processor within the network. Certain more powerful nodes also can be a SSCP.

Path Control Network

Remember that the logical organization of SNA is divided into two broad categories of components: network addressable units and the path control network. The *path control network* provides for routing and flow control. Logical units must establish a path before a LU-LU session can begin. Each SSCP, PU, and LU has a different network address, which identifies it to other network addressable units as well as to the path control network. Path control provides for the following:

* Virtual routing so all sessions can send their messages by different routes

* Transmission priorities

* Multiple links to maximize throughput

* Message pacing (flow control) to keep a fast transmitter from drowning a slow receiver

* Ability to detect and recover from errors as they occur

* Facilities to handle disruption because of a circuit failure

* Facilities to inform network operators when there is a disruption in the network

The path control network has two layers: the *path control layer* and the *data link control layer* (similar to layers 2 and 3 in the OSI model). Routing and flow control are provided by the path control layer, whereas transmitting data over individual links is provided by the data link control layer, which uses SDLC.

Telecommunication Access Programs

Access to SNA networks is controlled by a series of telecommunications access programs, including TCAM, VTAM, NCP, and CICS. Each provides certain functions, although there is some overlap among the four. All are not used at the same time.

Telecommunications Access Method (TCAM). The *telecommunications access method (TCAM)* provides the basic functions needed for controlling data communication circuits. It provides facilities for polling terminals, transmitting and receiving messages, detecting errors, automatically retransmitting erro-

neous messages, translating code, dialing and answering calls, logging transmission errors, allocating blocks of buffer storage, and performing online diagnostics to facilitate the testing of terminal equipment. It supports asynchronous terminals, synchronous communications, and audio response units. Residing in the host computer, TCAM's most significant features are those for network control and system recovery. An operator control facility also provides network supervision and modification.

TCAM handles the data communications in a network that uses a high degree of multiprogramming. Unlike the prior basic data communication software, TCAM has its own control program that commands and schedules traffic-handling operations. In some cases, it can handle an incoming message by itself without passing it to an application program—for example, routing a message to another terminal in a message switching system. TCAM also provides status reporting on terminals, lines, and queues. It has significant recovery and serviceability features to increase the security and availability of the data communication network. The checkpoint and restart facilities are very good. TCAM has prewritten routines for checkpointing, logging, date and time stamping, sequence numbering and checking, message interception and rerouting, and error message transmission, and it supports a separate master terminal for the data communication network operator.

Virtual Telecommunications Access Method (VTAM). The *virtual telecommunications access method (VTAM)* is the data communication software package that complements IBM's advanced hardware and software. It resides in the host computer. VTAM manages a network structured on SNA principles. It directs the transmission of data between the application programs in the host computer and the components of the data communication network. It operates with front end processors. The basic services performed by VTAM include establishing, controlling, and terminating access between the application programs and the terminals. It moves data between application programs and terminals and permits application programs to share communication circuits, communication controllers, and terminals. In addition, VTAM controls the configuration of the entire network, creates virtual connections, and permits the network to be monitored and altered.

When VTAM establishes sessions, one end of the session is understood to be the host and the other the terminal. VTAM makes the mainframe the primary end of the session and the remote terminal the secondary end. In technical terms, the host program is said to be the *primary logical unit (PLU)*, and the terminal or microcomputer is considered to be the *secondary logical unit (SLU)*. Only the primary logical unit can start a session, end the session, and perform key aspects of error recovery. When personal computers are linked to SNA hosts, they are considered to be secondary logical units just like terminals.

VTAM can be the sole telecommunication access method in the host, or it can operate in conjunction with the Network Control Program (described next), which allows some of the network control functions to be offloaded to the front end processor.

Network Control Program (NCP). The *network control program (NCP)* is a telecommunication access method located in the front end processors that control IBM's Synchronous Data Link Control (SDLC) communications between host computers and remote terminals. (SDLC is the protocol developed for SNA by IBM.) It also works with host resident VTAM software to route information through networks. NCP routes data and controls its flow between the front end processor and any other network resources. These other network resources can be the host mainframe computer or an intelligent control unit located either locally or at the remote end of the communication link. IBM's primary network control program is the Advanced Communication Function/Network Control Program (ACF/NCP). Network control programs reside in the front end processor, primarily in IBM's 3704, 3705, 3725, and 3745. NCP is *not* a replacement for TCAM or VTAM; it provides an interface with TCAM and VTAM by taking over some of their functions and moving them to the front end.

NCP can handle polling, error detection, error recovery, and intermediate routing. It provides some flow control (such as various types of message pacing), prevents network congestion, provides Internetwork communication, and insulates VTAM from being overburdened by having to speak to an excessive number of other protocols. NCP version 5 supports dial-up lines and improves support for multipoint lines. It also supports SDLC's PU 2.1 functionality, enabling the front end processor to initiate sessions with remote terminals. With NCP version 5, one front end processor can communicate with other front end processors via an IBM token-ring network. It includes load balancing across network bridges and backbone rings, port swapping, backup capabilities, and remote controller support. NCP is IBM's effort to move the telecommunication access method software out from the host mainframe to the front end processor. NCP is the only one of these five telecommunication access programs that actually resides in a front end processor; all the others reside in the host mainframe.

Customer Information Control System (CICS). Some functions overlap between the telecommunication access programs—such as TCAM and Customer Information Control System (CICS) (a teleprocessing monitor), both of which reside in the host computer. IBM's front end has its own program called the Network Control Program or NCP (this also is a telecommunication access program). TCAM and NCP overlap; therefore, functions such as polling/selecting can be performed from either the host computer or the front end processor.

Teleprocessing monitors such as CICS are software programs that directly relieve the host computer's operating system of many tasks involved in handling message traffic between the host and the front end or the host and other internal central processing unit (CPU) software packages (such as the host database management system). Generally speaking, teleprocessing monitors perform such functions as message handling, access methods, task scheduling, and system recovery. The teleprocessing monitor acts as the interface with the telecommunication access programs on one side and with all of the host computer's software on the other side. Teleprocessing monitors must be the interface with various operating systems, computer architectures, database management systems, security software packages, and application programs.

Customer Information Control System (CICS) is the world's most widely used mainframe teleprocessing monitor. It may not be perfect, but even IBM's direct competitors implicitly acknowledge that CICS has few alternatives. Whatever comes along to supplant it will be an evolving CICS rather than a totally new replacement. CICS is a table-driven teleprocessing program that offers 64 layers or systems it can service.

Like any other teleprocessing monitor, CICS runs in conjunction with the host computer's operating system. CICS takes over the communication-related tasks that previously were handled by the operating system, thus allowing the operating system to concentrate on other control tasks or application programs.

CICS also offers an additional level of security. It can accommodate a unique password and identification for each terminal operator and allow access only to the specific functions assigned to that operator password and/or terminal identifier. It can assign highly sensitive functions to a specific terminal or a group of terminals. Some security features might be security sign-on fields, darkened password fields, and a complete log of terminal sign-ons, including any security violations.

Other tasks conducted by teleprocessing monitors such as CICS are logging of all messages (both input and output), accounting procedures for cost control, restart and recovery procedures in case of failure, utility features that perform special maintenance tasks, and queue management of both inbound and outbound message queues, as well as the ability to place priorities on messages and/or queues. A teleprocessing monitor should be able to interact with multiple front end processors, terminals, microcomputers, and various data communication transmission speeds. The monitor provides input/output job task queue management, various methods of instituting priorities for certain transactions or jobs, file and database management, application program management, task and resource control, restart and recovery procedures in case of failure, and special utilities that carry out tasks often

enough to warrant establishing them as a utility feature (OSI model layer 6). It keeps track of accounting features and operating statistics and isolates various programs or parts of the system from other programs or parts of the system. In other words, a teleprocessing monitor can be considered a "mini" operating system with data communication interfaces.

Advanced Peer-to-Peer Networking and the "New" SNA

A newer part of IBM's systems network architecture is *Advanced Peer-to-Peer Networking (APPN)*. This approach supports peer-to-peer communication between two or more network devices in which either side can initiate sessions. No primary–secondary relationship exists, and either side is able to poll or answer to polls. Before the introduction of peer-to-peer communications, a primary–secondary relationship always existed where only one of the two nodes could initiate or start a communication session.

IBM has a new form of SNA that provides two important advantages over the traditional SNA. First, the "new" SNA supports a variety of industry standard network and data link protocols,. This will solve many of the problems that now exist in integrating SNA networks with other networks. Second, the host computer does not have to mediate the connection between the two end-user terminals or computers. This allows microcomputers to speak as equals to the host mainframe computer, and eliminates the bonds of IBM micro-to-mainframe emulation that confine the microcomputer to terminal status in its communications with host mainframes.

Network Game

Introduction

The purpose of this game is to help you better understand how messages are transmitted in computer networks. Players are organized into four-person teams. Each person in the team assumes the role of one layer in a communication network (e.g., data link layer) and works with the others to send messages through the network.

General Rules

1. This is a team game. The class will be broken into a set of four-member groups, with each group being one computer in the communications network. Each person in the group will role-play one layer in the computer, either the application layer, the network layer, the data link layer, or the physical layer.

2. Messages will be created by the application layer and passed to the network layer. The network layer will address and route the message, and pass the message to the data link layer. The data link layer will format the message, perform error control (which will involve sending ACKs and

NAKs), and pass the message to the physical layer for transmission. The physical layer will transmit the message to the physical layer of the destination computer. Messages are sent using the two types of forms in Figure A–6. Be sure to make lots of copies of both forms before the game starts.

3. Each layer will have a set of instructions to follow to ensure the messages are sent and received properly. Follow them carefully. These instructions explain what you are to write on the message forms. Never write anything on the message form in an area used by some other layer.

4. At some point, someone will make a mistake. If you receive a message that contains an error, hand it back to the person who gave it to you and explain the error to them.

5. And remember, the game is meant to be fun, too!

Application Layer

Activities

1. Send messages to other computers
2. Respond to messages from other computers

Data Link Layer				Network Layer		Application Layer			
Source	Destination	Control	Message Number	Final Destination	Next Node	From	To	Message	BCC

Transmission Form For Physical Layer

Figure A–6 Forms for network game.

Tools Needed

* Message forms
* List of messages
* Network map (Figure A–7 shows an example; you will need to draw your own on the blackboard.)
* A blank piece of paper

Sending Messages. To send a message, you must:

1. Find a blank message form.

2. Write the *application layer address* (not numeric address) of your computer in the **From** box.

3. Use the network map to select a computer to which to send a message. Write the *application layer address* of this computer (not numeric address) in the **To** box. Don't send all your messages to one computer; we want to even out the messages. Try to send a few messages to computers close to you and a few to computers far away.

4. Write the message you wish to send in the **Message** box. To make the message simple to understand, please use a hyphen (-) to indicate spaces between words. Select a message from the list of messages.

5. Write the message and the name of the computer to which you send the message on the blank piece of paper. This will help you understand the responses you get to your messages.

6. Pass the message to the network layer.

Responding to Messages. Eventually, you will receive a message from some other computer asking you a

question. To respond to the message you will send a message that answers the question. Follow the same steps above to send a message, but in step 4, write your answer in the message box. For example, if the message you received asked what your favorite color was, you might write *red* or *blue* in the message box.

List of Messages. Here is are a list of messages you can send. Remember to use a hyphen instead of a space to separate the words. Rather than writing the entire message, you can omit the words "what is your":

* What is your favorite color?
* What is your birthday?
* What is your phone number?
* What is your major?
* What is your favorite holiday?
* What is your favorite car?

Network Layer

Activities

1. Accept messages from the application layer, address them, route them, and pass them to the data link layer.

2. Accept messages from the data link layer. If they are addressed to you, pass them to the application layer; if they are not addressed to you, route them, and pass them back to the data link layer.

Tools Needed

* Network map

Accepting Messages from the Application Layer. Every few minutes, the application layer will hand you a message to transmit. To transmit a message, you must:

1. Address the message by translating the application layer address of the destination computer into its network layer (IP) address. Find the application layer address of the computer in the **To** box in the network map, and write its IP address in the **Final Destination** box.

2. Route the message by finding the next computer to which the message should be sent in the network map, and writing its *data link layer (DL) address* in the **Next Node** box. If your computer is directly connected to the final destination com-

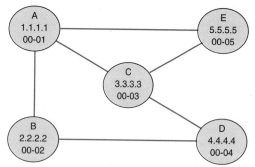

Figure A–7 Sample network map.

puter, the next node is the same as the final destination. If your computer is not directly connected to the destination, you must select the best route that the message should follow and specify one of the computers to which you are connected.

3. Pass the message to the data link layer.

Accepting Messages from the Data Link Layer. Every few minutes, the data link layer will hand you a message to process. You must:

A. If the message is addressed to you (that is, if the **Final Destination** box lists your network address):

   1. Pass the message to the application layer.

B. If the message is *not* addressed to you (that is, if the **Final Destination** box lists someone else's IP address):

   1. Route the message by finding the next computer to which the message should be sent in the network map, and writing its DL address in the **Next Node** box. If your computer is directly connected to the destination computer, the next node is the same as the destination. If your computer is not directly connected to the destination, you must select the best route that the message should follow and specify one of the computers to which you are connected.

   2. Pass the message to the data link layer.

Data Link Layer

Activities

1. Accept messages from the network layer, format them, add error control information, and pass them to the physical layer.

2. Accept messages from the physical layer. If they are data messages and contain no errors, send an ACK and pass them to the network layer. If they are data messages with an error, send a NAK. If they are an ACK, destroy the message they acknowledge. If they are a NAK, retransmit the original message.

Tools Needed

* Message forms
* Network map

* Some blank pieces of paper. You will discover that you will be receiving and storing many different types of messages. To help you organize those messages, we suggest that before you begin, you use three blank pieces of paper to create three message storage piles with these labels:
  * Messages from the Network Layer
  * Messages from the Physical Layer
  * Messages Transmitted

Accepting Messages from the Network Layer. Every few minutes, the Network Layer will hand you a message to transmit. If you receive more messages from the network layer than you can process right away, put them in the **Messages from the Network Layer** pile until you can process them. For each message, you must:

1. Format the message for the physical layer. Write your data link layer (DL) address in the **Source** box. Write the DL address contained in the **Next Node** box in the **Destination** box. Write an asterisk (*) in the **Control** box.

2. Number the message. Write a two-digit number in the **Message Number** box. This should be 01 for the first message you send, 02 for the second, and so on. Use the blank piece of paper to help you remember what numbers you have used.

3. Add error control information. Count the number of letters (including hyphens and punctuation such as question marks) in the **Message** box (count only the letters in the message box, not all the letters in the entire message), and write it in the **BCC** box. Obviously, this is a very simple error control protocol.

4. Pass the message to the physical layer. In a few moments, the physical layer will return the form to you. *Save it* in the Messages Transmitted pile!

Accepting Messages from the Physical Layer. Every few minutes, the physical layer will hand you a message to process. If you receive more messages than you can process right away, put them in the **Messages from the Physical Layer** pile. These messages will either be data messages, ACKs, or NAKs. Each is different.

1. Copy the contents of the Transmission Form on to a Message Form, making sure you put all the information in the correct boxes. Destroy the transmission form.

2. If the **Control** box contains an asterisk (*), this is a data message. Do the following:

1. Perform error checking. Count the letters (including hyphens and punctuation) in the **Message** box (not all the letters in the entire message). If this number is the same as the number in the **BCC** box, no errors have occurred. If they are different, an error has occurred.

2. If no errors have occurred, you must send an ACK to the sender:

   1. Take a new message form to send the ACK. Write your DL address in **Source** box. Write the DL address contained in the **Source** box of the incoming message in the **Destination** box (this ACK message is going to the sender of the original message). Write the word ACK in the **Control** box. Write the two-digit number contained in the **Message Number** box in the incoming message in the **Message Number** box.

   2. Pass the ACK message to the physical layer.

   3. Pass the incoming message to the network layer.

3. If an error has occurred, you must send a NAK to the sender:

   1. Take a new Message Form to send the NAK. Write your DL address in **Source** box. Write the DL address contained in the **Source** box of the incoming message in the **Destination** box (this NAK message is going to the sender of the original message). Write the word NAK in the **Control** box. Write the two-digit number contained in the **Message Number** box in the incoming message in the **Message Number** box.

   2. Pass the NAK message to the physical layer.

   3. Destroy the incoming message containing the error.

3. If the **Control** box contains an ACK, this is an ACK message. Do the following:

   1. Find the original message you sent in the **Messages Transmitted** pile that has the same message number as the ACK.

   2. Destroy the original message and the ACK.

4. If the **Control** box contains a NAK, this is a NAK message. Do the following.

   1. Find the original message you sent in the **Messages Transmitted** pile that has the same message number as the NAK.

   2. Give the original message to the physical layer to transmit. In a few moments, the physical layer will return the form to you. *Save it* in the **Messages Transmitted** pile!

   3. Destroy the NAK.

Physical Layer

Activities

1. Accept messages from the data link layer, and pass them to the physical layer of the computer to which they are to go, possibly introducing a transmission error.

2. Accept messages from the physical layer of other computers and pass them to the data link layer.

Tools Needed

* Network map
* Transmission forms
* Two coins

Accepting Messages from the Data Link Layer. Every few minutes, the data link layer will hand you a message to transmit. To transmit them, you must:

1. Determine if there will be an error in transmission. If the **Control** box contains an asterisk (*), then toss two coins; if they are both heads, you will introduce an error. If the **Control** box is something other than an asterisk, do not introduce an error; things are complicated enough without ACKs and NAKs getting destroyed.

2. Copy the entire contents of the message form onto a transmission form. If you are to introduce an error, omit the last letter in the **Message** box.

3. Pass the transmission form to the physical layer of the computer whose address is listed in the **Destination** box.

4. If the **Control** box contains an asterisk (*), pass the message form back to the data link layer and make sure that that person understands that you are giving back the message form that he/she just gave you to transmit. Otherwise, if the **Con-**

trol box contains an ACK or a NAK, destroy the message form.

Accepting Messages from the Physical Layer. Every few minutes, the physical layer of another computer will hand you a message. Simply hand the message to the data link layer.

Note to Instructors

Background. This games helps students *really* understand what the various layers actually do and how they must work together in order to send a message. Reading about it is one thing; having to perform a simple version of the function is something else altogether. Experiential learning can be an extremely powerful tool. I have noticed a distinct improvement in students' understanding of this material since I have begun using the game.

The game is an extremely simplified version of what happens in a real network. Nonetheless, it can be complicated. Students have to work together and sometimes make mistakes. Ideally, mistakes will be recognized by the students themselves and they will help each other learn. Participation is key to the learning objectives. It's also key to making a somewhat dry, conceptual set of issues more "real"—and more fun.

When I teach the course, I usually use this game after I complete Chapter 6, "The Network Layer." At this point students will have learned everything they need to know to run the game, and it will reinforce the material. The other option is to use the game immediately after Chapter 1 as a way to introduce the roles of the different layers in the network. I have never done this, but several of my students have suggested it.

Preparing to Teach the Game. This game contains all the materials you will need to run the game, except a set of coins and paper (which you can rely on students to have) and a network map (which you draw on the board just before the game starts). You will also have to make copies of the message form and transmission form. It takes an average of about four message forms and two transmission forms for each message, so you will need a lot of them. I usually plan on the class sending about 10 to 15 messages per four-person group; for a 40-person class, this means

you will need 200 to 300 message forms and 150 to 200 transmission slips.

I have found from experience that it takes the students a little while to catch onto the game. Be sure to tell the students to read the game before they come to class.

Teaching the Game. It usually takes 15 minutes before the game gets going. The first step is to organize the class into four-person groups. Each group represents one computer in the network. If you have extra people, you may choose to build three-person groups (combine the application and network layers) or five-person groups (have two people play the data link layer).

Draw the network map on the board. The map will have a circle to represent each group (i.e., computer). Try to draw the circles to represent the actual physical placement of the groups within the classroom. Inside each circle write:

* the application layer address (e.g.,xyz.com). Ask each group for a catchy name, but keep it short!
* the numeric network layer (IP) address (e.g., 1.1.1.1). Arbitrarily choose a number for each group but keep it short and easy to remember.
* the numeric data link layer (DL) address (e.g., 11-11). Arbitrarily choose a number for each group but keep it short and easy to remember. It helps if it matches the IP address in some way.

Next connect the computers (i.e., groups) by drawing lines (i.e., circuits) between the circles. Don't draw in all possible circuits because you want some groups to have to route messages through other groups to reach their final destination. Likewise, don't draw too few circuits, or else all messages will take a long time to send.

Do a simple example. Walk through the sending of one message on the board and have the students follow by replicating each step you do for one of their own messages. Once the message has reached the physical layer on the next computer, I turn the class loose and let them play. I usually walk around the class answering questions and listening in on discussions as the class progresses.

Because each layer performs a unique function, it is useful to have each student play each layer if time permits. I try to have students rotate layers after 15 to 20 minutes. I keep the game going so that the students playing one layer need to explain to the person taking over their layer what is going on and how to play. The easiest way to rotate is "downward;" that is, the person playing the application layer moves to the network layer, and so on.

Discussion Questions

After each person has had the opportunity to play each layer, it is useful to ask what the students have learned. This gives you the opportunity to reinforce the concepts the game was designed to teach. Some possible discussion questions include:

1. Why are standards important?
2. How could you improve network performance by changing topology?
3. What layer is the busiest?
   a. How could a front end processor help?
   b. How could you improve network performance by changing the protocol?

Glossary

A

ACK An ASCII or EBCDIC code character indicating a positive acknowledgment that a message has been received correctly.

ACM Association for Computing Machinery. The ACM is an association of computer professionals.

address A coded representation of the destination or source of a transmission. Most computers have a data link layer address (e.g., Ethernet) and a network layer address (e.g., TCP/IP). Servers usually also have an application layer address (e.g., Internet address).

ADSL See **DSL**.

AFIPS American Federation of Information Processing Societies.

agent Intelligent agents are relatively simple software programs that perform management functions without human involvement. They use a knowledge base and/or learn from experience to make simple decisions.

ALOHA A system using a "transmit at will" access method similar to CSMA/CD. The name comes from a method of telecommunications whereby signals are beamed at satellites when transmission is ready to go. If it gets through, fine; if it does not, then the sender tries again. The ALOHA method of transmission was used first by Hawaiians who had satellite dishes beaming at communication satellites over the equator. It also was used for communicating with dishes in other Pacific Basin countries.

alternating current (AC) The electrical current used to power computers.

American National Standards Institute (ANSI) The principal standards-setting body in the United States. ANSI is a nonprofit, nongovernmental organization supported by more than 1000 trade organizations, professional societies, and companies. It belongs to the Consultative Committee

on International Telegraph and Telephone (CCITT) and the International Organization for Standardization (ISO).

American Standard Code for Information Interchange See **ASCII**.

amplifier A device used to boost the strength of a signal. Amplifiers are spaced at intervals throughout the length of a communication circuit to increase the distance a signal can travel. See also **repeater**.

amplitude modulation See **modulation, amplitude**.

analog Pertaining to representation by means of continuously variable quantity, such as varying frequencies. Physical quantities such as temperature are continuous variable and, therefore, are "analog."

analog signal A signal in the form of a continuously varying quantity such as amplitude, which reflects variations in the loudness of the human voice.

analog transmission Transmission of a continuously variable signal as opposed to a discrete on/off signal. The traditional way of transmitting a telephone or voice signal is analog.

ANI See **automatic number identification**.

anonymous FTP See **FTP**.

ANSI See **American National Standards Institute**.

API Application program interface. API is the way IBM links incompatible equipment for micro-to-mainframe links. API allows applications on microcomputers and mainframes to speak directly to each other at the application software level, even though the equipment is from different vendors.

APPC Advanced program-to-program communications. APPC is a part of IBM's systems network architecture that provides peer-to-peer communications. It is a high-level program interface that allows two application programs to communicate. Also called **LU 6.2** after its most important component.

AppleTalk A set of communication protocols that defines networking for Apple computers. Rarely used today.

Arcnet Attached resource computing network. A proprietary token-bus local area network developed by the Datapoint Corporation.

area code A number assigned to the geographical subdivision or operating area to facilitate message and circuit switching. Called city code outside of the United States. See also **numbering plan area**.

ARPANET One of the early packet switching networks. ARPANET was developed by the U.S. Department of Defense Advanced Research Projects Agency. It was the predecessor of the Internet.

ARQ Automatic repeat request. A system employing an error detecting code so conceived that any error initiates a repetition of the transmission of the incorrectly received message.

ASCII American Standard Code for Information Interchange. Pronounced "ask'-ee." An eight-level code for data transfer adopted by the American National Standards Institute to achieve compatibility among data devices.

asynchronous transfer mode (ATM) A communication switch that handles interface speeds ranging from 25 million bits per second to 622 million bits per second. It multiplexes data streams onto the same backbone network by using cell relay techniques. ATM switches can handle multimedia traffic, such as data, graphics, voice, and video.

asynchronous transmission Transmission in which each information character is individually synchronized, usually by start and stop bits. The gap between each character is not a fixed length. Compare with **synchronous transmission**.

AT&T Communications The name of American Telephone and Telegraph (AT&T), reflecting its current emphasis on providing long-distance communication services. AT&T is one of the oldest providers of communication equipment and circuits. It is commonly known as "Ma Bell" and was the parent organization of the various Bell Telephone companies before deregulation.

ATM
1. See **asynchronous transfer mode**.
2. In banking, an automated teller machine.

attenuation As a signal travels through a circuit, it gradually attenuates, or loses power. Expressed in decibels, attenuation is the difference between the transmitted and received power caused by loss of signal strength through the equipment, communication circuits, or other devices.

authentication A security method of guaranteeing that a message is genuine, that it has arrived unaltered, and that it comes from the source indicated. Authentication is often done using public key encryption.

automatic number identification (ANI) The process whereby a long distance common carrier provides its customers with a visual display of an incoming caller's telephone number.

automatic repeat request See **ARQ**.

B

backbone network (BN) A large network to which many networks within an organization are connected. It usually is a network that interconnects most or all networks on a single site.

BALUN BALanced/UNbalanced. An impedance-matching device to connect balanced twisted pair cabling with unbalanced coaxial cable.

bandwidth The difference between the highest and lowest frequencies in a band. For example, a voice-grade circuit has a 4000 hertz bandwidth. In common usage, bandwidth refers to circuit capacity; when people say they need more bandwidth, they need a higher transmission speed.

bandwidth-on-demand The ability to add more circuit capacity automatically and as needed. Instead of having several fractional T-1 circuits, an organization can have one T-1 circuit and use inverse multiplexers to dedicate some of the circuits to switched 56,000 bits per second usage. As one 56 Kbps circuit fills to capacity, a second one is brought into service automatically for the next message transmission. See also **digital cross-connect switch**.

baseband signaling Transmission of a signal in its original form, not changed by modulation. It is a digital signal and is usually in direct electrical voltage.

basic rate interface In ISDN, two 64,000 bits per second B circuits for data transmission and one 16,000 bits per second D circuit for signaling (2 B+D). Also called basic rate access. See also **primary Rate Interface**.

baud Unit of signaling speed. The speed in baud is the number of signal elements per second. If each signal represents only one bit, *baud* is the same as *bits per second.* When each signal contains more than one bit, baud does not equal bits per second. Baud is often misused in common language, so several organizations are replacing it with the term *signaling rate.*

BCC See **block check character.**

Bell Operating Company See **RBOC.**

BER Bit-error rate. The number of bits received in error divided by the total number of bits received. An indicator of circuit quality.

BERT Bit-error rate testing. Testing a data line with a pattern of bits that are compared before and after the transmission to detect errors.

binary A number system using only the two symbols zero and one, which is especially well adapted to computer usage because 0 and 1 can be represented as "on" and "off," or as negative charges and positive charges. The binary digits appear in strings of 0s and 1s.

binary synchronous communications (BSC or bisync) A half duplex, character-oriented synchronous data communication protocol devised by IBM in the early 1960s. Not used very often today.

biometric system A security system that checks some physical aspect of the user (e.g., fingerprint) before granting access to the network.

bipolar transmission A method of digital transmission in which binary zero is sent as a negative pulse and binary one is sent as a positive pulse.

BISYNC See **binary synchronous communications.**

bit
1. An abbreviation of the term *binary digit.*
2. A single pulse in a group of pulses.
3. A unit of information capacity.

bit-error rate (BER) See **BER.**

bit-error rate testing See **BERT.**

bit rate The rate at which bits are transmitted over a communication path. Normally expressed in bits per second (bps). The bit rate should not be confused with the data signaling rate (*baud*), which measures the rate of signal changes being transmitted. See also **bps.**

bit stream A continuous series of bits being transmitted on a transmission line.

BKER Block-error rate. The number of blocks received in error divided by the total number of blocks received.

BKERT Block-error rate testing. Testing a data link with groups of information arranged into transmission blocks for error checking.

block Sets of contiguous bits or bytes that make up a message, frame, or packet.

block check character (BCC) The character(s) at the end of a binary synchronous communications (BSC) message used to check for errors.

block-error rate See **BKER.**

block-error rate testing See **BKERT.**

BN See **backbone network.**

BOC See **RBOC.**

bonding Bonding (Bandwidth ON Demand Interoperability Networking Group) is an inverse multiplexing proposal for combining several 56 Kbps or 64 Kbps circuits into one higher-speed circuit.

bootp A protocol that enables computers using TCP/IP to receive configuration information (e.g., their IP addresses) from a server when they are first turned on, rather than requiring that information to be stored on their hard disks. Being replaced by **DHCP.**

BPS Bits per second. The basic unit of data communication rate measurement. Usually refers to rate of information bits transmitted. Contrast with **baud** and **bit rate.**

bridge A device that connects two similar networks using the same data link layer and network protocols. It operates on the data link layer, using data link layer addresses to decide where to transmit packets. Compare with **gateway**, **router**, and **brouter.**

broadband circuit An analog communication circuit.

broadband Ethernet The 10Broad36 version of Ethernet IEEE 802.3, meaning that it transmits at 10 million bits per second in broadband with a maximum distance of 3600 meters.

broadcast routing See **decentralized routing.**

brouter A piece of hardware that combines the functions of a bridge and a router. See also **bridge** and **router.**

BSC See **binary synchronous communications.**

buffer A device used for the temporary storage of data, primarily to compensate for differences in data flow rates (for example, between a terminal and its transmission circuit), but also as a security measure to allow retransmission of data if an error is detected during transmission.

burst error A series of consecutive errors in data transmission. Refers to the phenomenon on communication circuits in which errors are highly prone to occurring in groups or clusters.

bus   A transmission path or circuit. Typically an electrical connection with one or more conductors in which all attached devices receive all transmissions at the same time.

byte   A small group of data bits that is handled as a unit. In most cases, it is an 8-bit byte and is known as a *character*.

C

C band   The frequency range from 4 to 6 GHz that is used for commercial satellite communications.

C type conditioning   A North American term for a type of conditioning that controls attenuation, distortion, and delay distortion so they fall within specified limits.

cable modem   A high-speed data modem that enables signals to be sent over cable TV networks. Data rates can be as high as 10 Mbps.

call-back modem   When a user calls a host computer, the modem disconnects the call after receiving the password and calls back to the caller's predefined telephone number to establish a connection.

call detail recording (CDR)   A private branch exchange (PBX) feature to keep track of telephone call costs so they can be charged to the proper department. Also called *station message detail recording (SMDR)*.

call management system   A system that monitors voice calls in organizations to keep track of call traffic and other factors relevant to voice communications.

carrier   An analog signal at some fixed amplitude and frequency which then is combined with an information-bearing signal to produce an intelligent output signal suitable for transmission of meaningful information. Also called *carrier wave* or **carrier frequency**.

carrier frequency   The basic frequency or pulse repetition rate of a signal bearing no intelligence until it is modulated by another signal that does impart intelligence.

carrier sense multiple access   See **CSMA/CA** and **CSMA/CD**.

CCITT   Consultative Committee on International Telegraph and Telephone. Now known as the **International Telecommunications Union–Telecommunications**.

CD
1. Collision detection in the CSMA (carrier sense multiple access) protocol for local area networks.
2. Carrier detection occurs when a modem detects a carrier signal to be received.

CDR   See **call detail recording**.

central office   The switching and control facility set up by the local telephone company (common carrier) where the subscriber's local loop terminates. Central offices handle calls within a specified geographic area, which is identified by the first three digits of the telephone number. Also called an **end office** or **exchange office**.

CENTREX   A widespread telephone company switching service that uses dedicated central office switching equipment. CENTREX CPE is where the user site also has **customer premises equipment (CPE)**.

channel
1. A path for transmission of electromagnetic signals. Synonym for *line* or *link*. Compare with **circuit**.
2. A data communication path. Circuits may be divided into subcircuits.

channel extender   A scaled-down front end that links remote host computers with the central host computer. It is used in place of a front end processor at the host end.

character   A member of a set of elements used for the organization, control, or representation of data. Characters may be letters, digits, punctuation marks, or other symbols. Also called a **byte**.

cheapnet   See **Thin Ethernet**.

checking, echo   A method of checking the accuracy of transmitted data in which the received data are returned to the sending end for comparison with the original data.

checking, parity   See **parity**.

checking, polynomial   See **polynomial checking**.

CICS   Customer Information Control System. CICS is the most widely used teleprocessing monitor program on IBM host computers.

circuit   The path over which the voice, data, or image transmission travels. Circuits can be twisted-pair cables, coaxial cables, fiber optic cables, microwave transmissions, and so forth. Compare with **channel**, **line**, and **link**.

circuit switching   A method of communications whereby an electrical connection between calling and called stations is established on demand for exclusive use of the circuit until the connection is terminated.

cladding A layer of material (usually glass) that surrounds the glass core of an optical fiber. Prevents loss of signal by reflecting light back into the core.

client The input/output hardware device at the user's end of a communication circuit. There are three major categories of clients: terminals, microcomputers/workstations, and special-purpose terminals.

clipper chip The clipper chip is an encryption chip that can be installed in telephones, fax machines, modems, and network interface cards. Transparent to the user, it automatically encrypts all messages sent, and decrypts all messages received. The most controversial part of the clipper proposals is that the government has access to the key of all chips manufactured.

cluster controller A device that controls the input/output operations of the cluster of devices (microcomputers, terminals, printers, and so forth) attached to it. Also called a **terminal controller**. For example, the 3274 Control Unit is a cluster controller that directs all communications between the host computer and remote devices attached to it.

CMIP CMIP is a network management system that monitors and tracks network usage and other parameters for user workstations and other nodes. It is similar to SNMP, but it is more complete, and better in many ways.

coaxial cable An insulated wire that runs through the middle of a cable. A second braided wire surrounds the insulation of the inner wire like a sheath. Used on local area networks for transmitting messages between devices.

code A transformation or representation of information in a different form according to some set of pre-established conventions. See also **ASCII** and **EBCDIC**.

codec A codec translates analog voice data into digital data for transmission over computer networks. Two codecs are needed; one at the sender's end and one at the receiver's end.

code conversion A hardware box or software that converts from one code to another, such as from ASCII to EBCDIC.

collapsed backbone network In a collapsed backbone network, the set of bridges in a typical backbone network is replaced by one switch and a set of circuits to each LAN. The collapsed backbone has more cable, but fewer devices. There is no backbone cable. The "backbone" exists only in the switch.

committed information rate (CIR) In packet switched networks, this is the data rate guaranteed by the common carrier. It is usually possible to transmit data faster than this rate, but if the network becomes busy, any packets above this rate are not transmitted.

common carrier An organization in the business of providing regulated telephone, telegraph, telex, and data communication services, such as AT&T, MCI, BellSouth, and NYNEX. This term is applied most often to U.S. and Canadian commercial organizations, but sometimes it is used to refer to telecommunication entities, such as government-operated suppliers of communication services in other countries. See also **PTT**.

common management interface protocol See **CMIP**.

communication services A group of transmission facilities that is available for lease or purchase.

comparison risk ranking The process by which the members of a Delphi team reach a consensus on which network threats have the highest risk. It produces a ranked list from high risk to low risk.

component One of the specific pieces of a network, system, or application. When these components are assembled, they become the network, system, or application. Components are the individual parts of the network that we want to safeguard or restrict by using controls.

compression See **data compression**.

concentrator A device that multiplexes several low-speed communication circuits onto a single high-speed trunk. A remote data concentrator (RDC) is similar in function to a multiplexer, but differs because the host computer software usually must be rewritten to accommodate the RDC. RDCs differ from statistical multiplexers because the total capacity of the high-speed outgoing circuit, in characters per second, is equal to the total capacity of the incoming low-speed circuits. On the other hand, output capacity of a statistical multiplexer (stat mux) is less than the total capacity of the incoming circuits.

conditioning A technique of applying electronic filtering elements to a communication line to improve the capability of that line so it can support higher data transmission rates. See also **equalization**.

configuration The actual or practical layout of a network that takes into account its software, hardware, and cabling. Configurations may be multi-point, point-to-point, local area networks, and the like. By contrast, a topology is the geometric layout (ring, bus, star) of the configuration. Topologies are the building blocks of configurations. Compare with **topology**.

connectionless routing Connectionless routing means each packet is treated separately and makes its own way through the network. It is possible that different packets will take different routes through the network depending upon the type of routing used and the amount of traffic.

connection-oriented routing Connection-oriented routing sets up a virtual circuit (one that appears to use point-to-point circuit-switching) between the sender and receiver. The network layer makes one routing decision when the connection is established, and all packets follow the same route. All packets in the same message arrive at the destination in the same order in which they were sent.

Consultative Committee on International Telegraph and Telephone (CCITT) An international organization that sets worldwide communication standards. Its new name is International Telecommunications Union–Telecommunications (ITU-T).

contention A "dispute" between two or more devices that attempt to use the same shared common circuit at the same time.

control A mechanism to ensure that the threats to a network are mitigated. There are two levels of controls: system level controls and application level controls.

control character A character whose occurrence in a particular context specifies some network operation or function.

control spreadsheet A two-dimensional matrix showing the relationship between the controls in a network, the threats that are being mitigated, and the components that are being protected. The controls listed in each cell represent the spe-

cific control enacted to reduce or eliminate the exposure.

COS Corporation for Open Systems. An organization of computer and communication equipment vendors and users formed to accelerate the introduction of products based on the seven-layer OSI model. Its primary interest is the application layer (layer 7) of the OSI model and the X.400 electronic mail standard.

CPU Central processing unit.

CRC Cyclical redundancy check. An error-checking control technique using a specific binary prime divisor that results in a unique remainder. It usually is a 16- to 32-bit character.

CSMA/CA Carrier sense multiple access (CSMA) with collision avoidance (CA). This protocol is similar to the carrier sense multiple access (CSMA) with collision detection (CD) protocol. Whereas CSMA/CD sends a data packet and then reports back if it collides with another packet, CSMA/CA sends a small preliminary packet to determine whether the network is busy. If there is a collision, it is with the small packet rather than with the entire message. CA is thought to be more efficient because it reduces the time required to recover from collisions.

CSMA/CD Carrier sense multiple access (CSMA) with collision detection (CD). A system used in contention networks. The network interface unit listens for the presence of a carrier before attempting to send and detects the presence of a collision by monitoring for a distorted pulse.

customer premises equipment (CPE) Equipment that provides the interface between the customer's CENTREX system and the telephone network. It physically resides at the customer's site rather than the telephone company's end office. CPE generally refers to voice telephone equipment instead of data transmission equipment.

cyclical redundancy check See **CRC**.

D

data
1. Specific individual facts or a list of such items.
2. Facts from which conclusions can be drawn.

data circuit terminating equipment See **DCE**.

data compression The technique that provides for the transmission of fewer data bits without the loss of information. The receiving location expands the received data bits into the original bit sequence. See also **compression**.

data encryption standard See **DES**.

data-over-voice (DOV) When data and voice share the same transmission medium. Data transmissions are superimposed over the voice transmission.

data terminal equipment See **DTE**.

datagram A datagram is a connectionless service in packet switched networks. Each packet has a destination and sequence number, and may follow a different route through the network. Different routes may deliver packets at different speeds, so data packets often arrive out of sequence. The sequence number tells the network how to reassemble the packets into a continuous message.

dB See **decibel**.

DCE Data circuit terminating equipment. The equipment (usually the modem) installed at the user's site that provides all the functions required to establish, maintain, and terminate a connection, including the signal conversion and coding between the data terminal equipment (DTE) and the common carrier's line.

decentralized routing With decentralized routing, all computers in the network make their own routing decisions. There are three major types of decentralized routing. With static routing, the routing table is developed by the network manager, and remains unchanged until the network manager updates it. With dynamic routing, the goal is to improve network performance by routing messages over the fastest possible route; an initial routing table is developed by the network manager, but is continuously updated to reflect changing network conditions, such as message traffic. With broadcast routing, the message is sent to all computers, but it is only processed by the computer to which it is addressed.

decibel (dB) A tenth of a bel. A unit for measuring relative strength of a signal parameter such as power and voltage. The number of decibels is ten times the logarithm (base 10) of the ratio of the power of two signals, or ratio of the power of one signal to a reference level. The reference level always must be indicated, such as 1 milliwatt for power ratio.

dedicated circuit A leased communication circuit that goes from your site to some other location. It is a clear unbroken communication path that is yours to use 24 hours per day, seven days per week. Also called a **private circuit** or **leased circuit**.

delay distortion A distortion on communication lines that is caused because some frequencies travel more slowly than others in a given transmission medium and, therefore, arrive at the destination at slightly different times. Delay distortion is measured in microseconds of delay relative to the delay at 1700 Hz. This type of distortion does not affect voice, but it can have a serious effect on data transmissions.

delay equalizer A corrective device for making the phase delay or envelope delay of a circuit substantially constant over a desired frequency range. See also **equalizer**.

Delphi group A small group of experts (three to nine people) who meet to develop a consensus when it may be impossible or too expensive to collect more accurate data. For example, a Delphi group of communication experts might assemble to reach a consensus on the various threats to a communication network, the potential dollar losses for each occurrence of each threat, and the estimated frequency of occurrence for each threat.

demand priority access method (DPAM) DPAM is the media access control techniques used by 100Base-VG. It is a form of roll call polling managed by the hub.

DES Data encryption standard. A widely used single-key encryption system that often uses a 56- or 64-bit key.

desktop video conferencing With desktop video conferencing, small cameras are installed on top of each user's computer so that participants can hold meetings from their offices.

DHCP Dynamic host control protocol. It enables computers using TCP/IP to receive configuration information (e.g., their IP addresses) from a server when they are first turned on, rather than requiring that information to be stored on their hard disks.

digital cross-connect switch Used by long-distance common carriers to establish 56,000 bits per second circuit connections for organizations on an as-needed basis. May be called a *digital access and cross-connect system* (DACS). See also **bandwidth-on-demand**.

Digital PBX   A PBX (switchboard) designed to switch digital signals. Telephones used in a digital PBX must digitize the voice signals. Computers and terminals can communicate directly through the digital PBX that functions as a point-to-point local area network.

digital signal   A discrete or discontinuous signal whose various states are discrete intervals apart, such as +15 volts and −15 volts.

digital termination system   See **DTS**.

digital subscriber line   See **DSL**.

direct-sequence spread spectrum (DSSS)   A wireless data transmission approach in which the signal is transmitted along a range of frequencies simultaneously. See also **frequency-hopping spread spectrum**.

discussion groups   Discussion groups are Internet users who have joined together to discuss some topic, such as cooking, skydiving, or politics. Usenet newsgroups are the most formally organized; they are a set of huge bulletin boards on which anyone on the Internet can read and post messages. A listserver (or listserv) is simply a mailing list.

distance learning   Distance learning allows a student to attend classes at another location through teleconferencing. When a distance-learning class is in session, the instructor stands in front of a set of cameras that he or she manages from the control panel. One of the monitors in the studio displays the image that is being broadcast, and the other shows the students in the classroom located elsewhere.

distortion   The unwanted modification or change of signals from their true form by some characteristic of the communication line or equipment being used for transmission; for example, delay distortion and amplitude distortion.

distortion types

1. *Bias:* a type of distortion resulting when the intervals of modulation do not all have exactly their normal durations.
2. *Characteristic:* distortion caused by transient disturbances that are present in the transmission circuit because of modulation.
3. *Delay:* distortion occurring when the envelope delay of a circuit is not consistent over the frequency range required for transmission.
4. *End:* distortion of start–stop signals. The shifting of the end of all marking pulses from their proper positions in relation to the beginning of the start pulse.
5. *Jitter:* a type of distortion that results in the intermittent shortening or lengthening of the signals. This distortion is entirely random in nature and can be caused by hits on the line.
6. *Harmonic:* the resultant process of harmonic frequencies (due to nonlinear characteristics of a transmission circuit) in the response when a sinusoidal stimulus is applied.

download   The process of loading software and data into the nodes of a network from the central node. Downloading usually refers to the movement of data from a host mainframe computer to a remote terminal or microcomputer.

DNS   Domain name server. A server that provides directory services on the Internet. It can provide the IP address for an application layer address (e.g., it can translate *www.uga.edu* into its numeric IP address).

DPAM   See **demand priority access method**.

DPSK   Differential phase shift keying; see **modulation**, **phase**.

DSL   Digital subscriber line. This is a relatively new form of dedicated circuit that connects residences and offices to the telephone company network over traditional telephone lines. DSL provides both traditional voice transmission and high-speed full duplex digital data transmission. There are many different types of DSL. Symmetric DSL (SDSL) provides the same data transmission rate to and from the telephone network, often 1 Mbps in both directions. Asymmetric DSL (ADSL) provides lower upstream data rates (i.e., to the telephone network), usually only 64 Kbps, combined with faster downstream rates (i.e., from the network), usually 1.544 Mbps. Very high-speed DSL (VDSL) provides much faster asymmetric rates, usually over very short distances (often 1.6 Mbps upstream and 51 Mbps downstream).

DTE   Data terminal equipment. Any piece of equipment at which a communication path begins or ends, such as a terminal.

DTS   Digital termination system. A form of local loop. It connects private homes or business locations to the common carrier switching facility.

duplexing   An alternative to the process of mirroring, which occurs when a database server mirrors or backs up the database with each transaction. In mirroring, the server writes on two different hard disks through two different disk controllers. Duplexing is more redundant, and therefore even safer than mirroring, because the database is written to two different hard disks on two different disk circuits. Compare with **mirroring**.

dynamic host control protocol (DHCP) See **DHCP**.

dynamic routing See **decentralized routing**.

E

e-mail A networking application that allows users to send and receive mail electronically.

EBCDIC Extended binary coded decimal interchange code. A standard code consisting of a set of 8-bit characters used for information representation and interchange among data processing and communication systems. Very common in IBM equipment.

echo cancellation Used in higher-speed modems to isolate and filter out (cancel) echoes when half-duplex transmissions use stop and wait ARQ (Automatic Repeat reQuest) protocols. Needed especially for satellite links.

echo checking See **checking, echo**.

echo suppressor A device for use in a two-way telephone circuit (especially circuits over 900 miles long) to attenuate echo currents in one direction caused by telephone currents in the other direction. This is done by sending an appropriate disabling tone to the circuit.

EDI See **electronic data interchange**.

EIA See **Electronic Industries Association**.

electronic commerce Doing business over the Internet, often through an electronic store.

Electronic Data Interchange (EDI) Electronic Data Interchange for Administration, Commerce, and Transport. Standardizes the electronic interchange of business documents for both ASCII and graphics. Endorsed by ISO. Defines major components of the ANSI X.12 EDI standard.

Electronic Industries Association (EIA) Composed of electronic manufacturers in the United States. Recommends standards for electrical and functional characteristics of interface equipment. Belongs to the ANSI. Known for the RS232 interface connector cable standard.

electronic mail (e-mail) A networking application that allows users to send and receive mail electronically.

electronic software delivery (ESD) Electronic software delivery enables software on client computers to be automatically updated by the server. Special application layer software must be installed on the client and on the server, but once this software is installed, the network manager never again needs to visit the user's office to install software; it can all be done over the network.

Emulate Computer vendors provide software and hardware emulators that accept hardware and software from other vendors and enable them to run on their hardware or software.

encapsulation A technique in which a packet from one network is placed within the message field of a packet in another network for transmission on the second network. For example, it enables a message initiated on an Ethernet LAN to be transmitted over an ATM backbone and then placed onto another Ethernet LAN at the other end.

encryption The technique of modifying a known bit stream on a transmission circuit so that, to an unauthorized observer, it appears to be a random sequence of bits.

end office The telephone company switching office for the interconnection of calls. See also **central office**.

enterprise-wide network The network that results when all the networks in a single organization are connected together.

envelope delay distortion A derivative of the circuit phase shift with respect to the frequency. This distortion affects the time it takes for different frequencies to propagate the length of a communication circuit so that two signals arrive at different times.

equalization The process of reducing frequency and phase distortion of a circuit by introducing time differences to compensate for the difference in attenuation or time delay at the various frequencies in the transmission band.

equalizer Any combination (usually adjustable) of coils, capacitors, or resistors inserted in the transmission circuit or amplifier to improve its frequency response.

error control An arrangement that detects the presence of errors. In some networks, refinements are added that correct the detected errors, either by operations on the received data or by retransmission from the source.

Ethernet A local area network developed by the Xerox Corporation. It uses coaxial cable or twisted pair wires to connect the stations.

ETX A control character used in ASCII and EBCDIC data communications to indicate end of text.

European Computer Manufacturers Association (ECMA) Recommends standards for computer components manufactured or used in Europe. Belongs to the International Organization for Standardization (ISO).

exchange office See **central office**.

exposure The calculated or estimated loss resulting from the occurrence of a threat, as in "The loss from theft could be $42,000 this year." It can be either tangible and therefore measurable in dollars, or intangible and therefore not directly measurable in dollars. See also **comparison risk ranking**.

Extended Binary Coded Decimal Interchange Code See **EBCDIC**.

F

FCC A board of seven commissioners appointed by the U.S. president under the Communication Act of 1934, having the power to regulate all interstate and foreign electrical communication systems originating in the United States.

FCS See **frame check sequence**.

FDDI A token-ring local area network technology that permits transmission speeds of 100 million bits per second using fiber optic cables (ANSI standard X3T9.5).

FDM Frequency division multiplexing. See **multiplexer**.

feasibility study A study undertaken to determine the possibility or probability of improving the existing system within a reasonable cost. Determines what the problem is and what its causes are, and makes recommendations for solving the problem.

FEC See **forward error correction**.

Federal Communications Commission (FCC) See **FCC**.

FEP See **front end processor**.

Fiber Distributed Data Interface (FDDI) See **FDDI**.

fiber optic cable A transmission medium that uses glass or plastic cable instead of copper wires.

fiber optics A transmission technology in which modulated visible lightwave signals containing information are sent down hair-thin plastic or glass fibers and demodulated back into electrical signals at the other end by a special light-sensitive receiver.

fibre channel A type of high-speed switched networking technology that is not yet very common. It uses the French spelling of the word *fiber*.

file transfer protocol See **FTP**.

firewall A firewall is a router, gateway, or special-purpose computer that filters packets flowing into and out of a network. No access to the organization's networks is permitted, except through the firewall. Three commonly used types of firewalls are packet-level firewall, application-level firewall and proxy server.

firmware A set of software instructions set permanently or semipermanently into a read-only memory (ROM).

flow control The capability of the network nodes to manage buffering schemes that allow devices of different data transmission speeds to communicate with each other.

forward error correction (FEC) A technique that identifies errors at the received station and automatically corrects those errors without retransmitting the message.

fractional T-1 A portion of a T-1 circuit. A full T-1 allows transmission at 1,544,000 bits per second. A fractional T-1 circuit allows transmission at lower speeds of 384,000, 512,000, or 768,000 bits per second. See also **T-1 circuit**.

frame Generally, a group of data bits having bits at each end to indicate the beginning and end of the frame. Frames also contain source addresses, destination addresses, frame type identifiers, and a data message. Also called a packet.

frame check sequence (FCS) Used for error checking. FCS uses a 16-bit field with cyclical redundancy checking for error detection with retransmission.

frame relay Frame relay is a type of packet switching technology that transmits data faster than the X.25 standard. The key difference is that unlike X.25 networks, frame relay does not perform error correction at each computer in the network. Instead, it simply discards any messages with errors. It is up to the application software at the source and destination to perform error correction and to control for lost messages.

frequency The rate at which a current alternates, measured in hertz, kilohertz, megahertz, and so forth. Other units of measure are cycles, kilocycles, or megacycles; hertz and cycles per second are synonymous.

frequency division multiplexing See **multiplexer**.

frequency-hopping spread spectrum A wireless data transmission approach in which the signal is transmitted along a range of frequencies. The frequency is "randomly" changed several times per second to prevent eavesdropping and limit the effects of interference. See also **direct sequence spread spectrum**.

frequency modulation See **modulation, frequency**.

front end processor (FEP) An auxiliary processor that is placed between a computer's central processing unit and the transmission facilities. This device normally handles housekeeping functions like circuit management and code translation, which otherwise would interfere with efficient operation of the central processing unit.

FSK Frequency shift keying. A modulation technique whereby zero and one are represented by a different frequency and the amplitude does not vary.

FTP File transfer protocol (FTP) enables you to send and receive files over the Internet. There are two types of FTP sites: closed (which require users to have an account and a password) and anonymous (which permit anyone to use them).

full duplex (FDX) The capability of transmission in both directions at one time. Contrast with **half duplex** and **simplex**.

G

gateway A device that connects two dissimilar networks. Allows networks of different vendors to communicate by translating one vendor's protocol into another. See also **bridge**, **router**, and **brouter**.

Gaussian noise See **noise, Gaussian**.

GHz Gigahertz. One gigahertz is equal to one billion cycles per second in a frequency.

gigabyte One billion bytes.

gopher Gopher is a menu-based tool that enables you to search for publicly available information posted on the Internet.

Government Open Systems Interconnection Protocol (GOSIP) A subset of the protocols that vendors must satisfy when bidding on U.S. government networking Requests for Proposals (RFPs).

group support systems (GSS) Group support systems (GSS), also called electronic meeting systems, are software tools designed to improve group decision making. Most GSS are used in special-purpose meeting rooms that provide each group member with a networked computer, plus large-screen video projection systems that act as electronic blackboards.

groupware Groupware is software that helps groups of people to work together more productively. Groupware permits people in different places to communicate either at the same time (like a telephone) or at different times. Groupware also can be used to improve communication and decision making among those who work together in the same room, either at the same time or at different times.

guardband A small bandwidth of frequency that separates two voice-grade circuits. Also the frequencies between subcircuits in FDM systems that guard against subcircuit interference.

H

hacker A person who sleuths for passwords or security holes to gain illegal access to computer files. Hackers may rummage through corporate trash cans looking for carelessly discarded printouts or trick users into revealing their passwords.

half duplex (HDX) A circuit that permits transmission of a signal in two directions but not at the same time. Contrast with **full duplex** and **simplex**.

Hamming Code A forward error correction (FEC) technique named for its inventor.

handshaking Exchange of predetermined signals when a connection is established between two data set devices. This is used to establish the circuit and message path.

HDLC A bit-oriented protocol in which control of data links is specified by series of bits rather than by control characters (bytes).

Hertz (Hz) Same as cycles per second; for example, 3000 hertz is 3000 cycles per second.

high-level data link control (HDLC) See **HDLC**.

home page A home page is the main starting point or page for a World Wide Web entry.

host computer The computer that lies at the center of the network. It generally performs the basic centralized data processing functions for which the network was designed. The host used to be where the network communication control functions took place, but today these functions tend to take place in the front end processor or further out in the network. Also called a *central computer*. In a local area network, the server may be the host.

HTML Web text files or pages use a structured language called HTML (Hypertext Markup Language) to store their information. HTML enables the author to define different type styles and sizes for the text, titles, and headings, and a variety of other formatting information.

HTTP Hypertext Transfer Protocol. The application layer protocol used to communicate between Web servers and Web browsers.

hub Network hubs act as junction boxes, permitting new computers to be connected to the network as easily as plugging a power cord into an electrical socket. They provide an easy way to connect network cables. Hubs also act as repeaters or amplifiers. Hubs are sometimes called concentrators, multistation access units, or transceivers.

hybrid network A local area network or wide area network with a mixture of topologies and access methods.

hypertext markup language See **HTML**.

Hz Hertz. The number of cycles per second in a frequency. One hertz is equal to one cycle per second.

I

idle character A transmitted character indicating ''no information'' that does not manifest itself as part of a message at the destination point.

IEEE See **Institute of Electrical and Electronics Engineers.** IEEE has defined numerous standards for LANs and BNs; see Chapters 8 and 10.

IMAP Internet Mail Access Protocol. An application layer protocol used to communicate between mail servers and mail software on client computers.

impulse noise See **noise, impulse**.

in-band signaling The transmission signaling information at some frequency or frequencies that lie within a carrier circuit, normally used for information transmission.

Institute of Electrical and Electronics Engineers (IEEE) A professional organization for engineers in the United States. Issues standards and belongs to the ANSI and the ISO.

integrated services digital network See **ISDN**.

intelligent terminal controller A microprocessor-based intelligent device that controls a group of terminals.

interactive voice response (IVR) A telephone call receiving unit that permits callers to select the information they want by pressing the appropriate number on their telephone keypad. It enables an organization to offer various options for callers so they can receive specific information automatically.

interexchange circuit (IXC) A circuit or circuit between end offices (central offices).

interLATA Circuits that cross from one LATA (local access and transport area) into another.

intermodulation distortion An analog line impairment whereby two frequencies create a third erroneous frequency, which in turn distorts the data signal representation.

International Telecommunications Union–Telecommunications (ITU–T) An international organization that sets worldwide communication standards. Its old name was CCITT.

Internet The information superhighway. The network of networks that spans the world linking more than 40 million users.

Internet access providers Access providers offer connections to the Internet via a modem. Some access providers charge a flat monthly fee for unlimited access (much like the telephone company), while others charge per hour of use (much like a long-distance telephone call).

internetworking Connecting several networks together so workstations can address messages to the workstations on each of the other networks.

interoperability The interconnection of dissimilar networks in a manner that allows them to operate as though they were similar.

intraLATA Circuits that are totally within one LATA (local access transport area).

inverse multiplexer Hardware that takes one high-speed transmission and divides it among several transmission circuits. See also **bandwidth-on-demand**.

IPX/SPX Internetwork packet exchange/sequenced packet exchange (IPX/SPX), based on a routing protocol developed by Xerox in the 1970s, is the primary network protocol used by Novell Netware. About 40 percent of all installed local area networks use it.

ISDN Integrated services digital network. A hierarchy of digital switching and transmission systems. The ISDN provides voice, data, and image in a unified manner. It is synchronized so all digital elements speak the same "language" at the same speed. See also **basic rate interface** and **primary rate interface**.

ISO International Organization for Standardization, Geneva, Switzerland. The initials ISO stand for its French name. This international standards-making body is best known in data communications for developing the internationally recognized seven-layer network model called the Open Systems Interconnection (OSI) Reference Model. See also **OSI model**.

ISP Internet service provider (ISP). A company providing access to the Internet.

isochronous transmission Isochronous transmission combines the elements of both synchronous and asynchronous data transmission. Each character is required to have both a start bit and a stop bit; however, as in synchronous data transmission, the sender and receiver are synchronized.

ITU–T See **International Telecommunications Union–Telecommunications**.

IVR See **interactive voice response**.

IXC See **interexchange circuit**.

J

jack The physical connecting device at the interface that mates with a compatible receptacle—a plug. (e.g., **RJ-11** and **RJ-45**.)

jitter Type of analog communication line distortion caused by the variation of a signal from its reference timing positions, which can cause data transmission errors, particularly at high speeds. This variation can be amplitude, time, frequency, or phase.

K

K A standard quantity measurement of computer storage. A K is defined loosely as 1000 bytes. In fact, it is 1024 bytes, which is the equivalent of two raised to the tenth power (2^{10}).

Kbps Kilobits per second. A data rate equal to 10^3 bps (1000 bps).

KERMIT KERMIT is a very popular asynchronous file transfer protocol named after Kermit the Frog. KERMIT protocol was developed by Columbia University, which released it as a free software communication package. Various versions of KERMIT can be found on public bulletin board systems and downloaded to your microcomputer.

key management The process of controlling the secret keys used in encryption.

KHz Kilohertz. One kilohertz is equal to 1000 cycles per second in a frequency.

kilobits per second See **Kbps**.

kilometer A metric measurement equal to 0.621 mile or 3280.8 feet.

ku band The frequency range between 12 and 14 GHz used for satellite communications.

L

LAN A network that is located in a small geographic area, such as an office, a building, a complex of buildings, or a campus, and whose communication technology provides a high bandwidth, low-cost medium to which many nodes can be connected. These networks typically do not use common carrier circuits, and their circuits do not cross public thoroughfares or property owned by others. LANs are not regulated by the FCC or state PUCs.

LANE LAN Emulation is a protocol used to transfer LAN packets over an ATM backbone. LANE operates at the data link layer and uses the data link layer addresses to forward messages. A newer protocol (MPOA) performs the same function using the network layer addresses.

laser Light Amplification by Stimulated Emission of Radiation. A device that transmits an extremely narrow and coherent beam of electromagnetic energy in the visible light spectrum. (Coherent means that the separate waves are in phase with one another, rather than jumbled as in normal light.)

LATA Local access transport area. One of approximately 200 local telephone service areas in the United States, roughly paralleling major metropolitan areas. The LATA subdivisions were established as a result of the AT&T/Bell divestiture to distinguish local from long-distance service. Circuits with both end points within the LATA (intraLATA) generally are the sole responsibility of the local telephone company. Circuits that cross outside the LATA (interLATA) are passed on to an interexchange carrier like AT&T, MCI, or U.S. Sprint.

LDAP Lightweight directory access protocol. An application layer protocol used to communicate between clients and computers providing directory services.

leased circuit A leased communication circuit that goes from your site to some other location. It is a clear, unbroken communication path that is yours to use 24 hours per day, seven days per week. Also called **private circuit** or **dedicated circuit**.

line A circuit, channel, or link. It carries the data communication signals. An early telephone technology term that may imply a physical connection, such as with a copper wire. Compare with **channel**, **circuit**, and **link**.

link An unbroken circuit path between two points. Sometimes called a **line**, **channel**, or **circuit**.

listserv A listserver (or listserv) is a mailing list. One part, the listserv processor, processes commands such as requests to subscribe, unsubscribe, or to provide more information about the listserv. The second part is the listserv mailer. Any message sent to the listserv mailer is re-sent to everyone on the mailing list.

LLC The logical link control sublayer is just an interface between the MAC sublayer and software in layer 3 (the network layer) that enables the software and hardware in the MAC sublayer to be separated from the logical functions in the LLC sublayer. By separating the LLC sublayer from the MAC sublayer, it is simpler to change the MAC hardware and software without affecting the software in layer 3. The most commonly used LLC protocol is IEEE 802.2.

local area network (LAN) See **LAN**.

local exchange carrier (LEC) The local telephone company, such as one of the seven Bell Operating Companies (BOCs).

local loop The part of a communication circuit between the subscriber's equipment and the equipment in the local central office.

log

1. A record of everything pertinent to a system function.
2. A collection of messages that provides a history of message traffic.

logical unit (LU) In systems network architecture (SNA), a port through which an end user accesses the SNA network to communicate with another end user and through which the end user accesses the functions provided by system services control points (SSCPs).

logical unit (LU) services In systems network architecture (SNA), capabilities in a logical unit to

1. Receive requests from an end user and issue requests to the system services control point (SSCP)

to perform the requested functions, typically for session initiation.

2. Receive requests from the SSCP, for example, to activate LU-LU sessions via bind session requests.
3. Provide session presentation and other services for LU-LU sessions.

long haul network A network most frequently used to transfer data over distances from several thousand feet to several thousand miles. These networks can use the international telephone network to transport messages over most or part of these distances. Compare with **wide area network**.

longitudinal redundancy check (LRC) See **LRC**.

loopback Type of diagnostic test in which the transmitted signal is returned to the sending device after passing through a data communication link or network. This test allows a technician or hardware circuit board to compare the returned signal with the transmitted signal to get some sense of what is wrong. Loopbacks often are done by excluding one piece of equipment after another. This allows you to figure out logically what is wrong.

LRC A system of error control based on the formation of a block check following pre-set rules. The check formation rule is applied in the same manner to each character. In a simple case, the LRC is created by forming a parity check on each bit position of all characters in the block. (That is, the first bit of the LRC character creates odd parity among the 1-bit positions of the characters in the block.)

LU 6.2 In systems network architecture, the set of protocols that makes it possible for applications to communicate directly. It enables **peer-to-peer communications**.

M

M Mega. The designation for one million, as in 3 megabits per second (3 Mbit/s).

MAC See **media access control**.

MAN A network that usually covers a city-wide area. Because MANs use local area network and fiber optic technologies, transmission speeds can vary from 2 million to 100 million bits per second.

management information base (MIB) See **MIB**.

MAP Manufacturing Automation Protocol. A six-layer protocol model that endorses the IEEE 802.4 token-passing broadband bus local area network designed to transmit at 1, 5, or 10 million bits per second. When MAP is combined with

TOP (Technical and Office Protocol), office functions can be integrated. When MAP is combined with CIM (Computer Integrated Manufacturing), manufacturing, design, and business functions can be integrated.

MAU A hub. See also **medium access unit** and **multistation access unit**.

Mbps A data rate equal to 10^6 bps. Sometimes called megabits per second (1,000,000 bps).

mean times See **MTBF, MTTD, MTTF,** and **MTTR.**

media access control (MAC) A data link layer protocol that defines how packets are transmitted on a local area network. See also **CSMA/CD, token bus,** and **token ring.**

medium The matter or substance that carries the voice or data transmission. For example, the medium can be copper (wires), glass (fiber optic cables), or air (microwave or satellite).

medium access unit (MAU) A device that connects a microcomputer station to a network. Sometimes called a hub.

megabit One million bits.

megabyte One million bytes.

mesh network A network topology in which there are direct point-to-point connections among the computers.

message A communication of information from a source to one or more destinations. A message usually is composed of three parts.

1. A heading, containing a suitable indicator of the beginning of the message, together with some of the following information: source, destination, date, time, routing.

2. A body containing the information to be communicated.

3. An ending containing a suitable indicator of the end of the message.

message switching An operation in which the entire message being transmitted is switched to the other location without regard to whether the circuits actually are interconnected at the time of your call. This usually involves a message store and forward facility.

meter A metric measurement equal to 39.37 inches.

metropolitan area network (MAN) See **MAN.**

MHz Megahertz. One megahertz is equal to one million cycles per second in a frequency.

MIB The extent of information that can be retrieved from a user microcomputer when using the Simple Network Management Protocol (SNMP) for network management. MIBs are sets of attributes and definitions that pertain to specific network devices.

MIME Multipurpose Internet Mail Extension. Enables graphics and binary files to be attached to e-mail messages using SMTP.

MIPS One million instructions per second. Used to describe a computer's processing power.

mirroring A process in which the database server automatically backs up the disk during each database transaction. During this process, the computer writes on two different hard disks on the same disk circuit every time the hard disk is updated. This creates two mirror images of the database data. Disk mirroring can be accomplished only when the database server contains two physical disk drives because the records or data structures are written to both disks simultaneously. Should a problem develop with one disk, the second disk is available instantly with identical information on it. Compare with **duplexing.**

mnemonic A group of characters used to assist the human memory. The mnemonic frequently is an acronym.

MNP Microcom networking protocol. A proprietary error correcting protocol for modems.

modem A contraction of the words MOdulator–DEModulator. A modem is a device for performing necessary signal transformation between terminal devices and communication circuits. Modems are used in pairs, one at either end of the communication circuit.

modem eliminator A tiny short-haul modem used to connect two microcomputers. It can transmit up to 3000 feet at 9600 bits per second or up to six miles at 1200 bits per second. Modem emulators get their power through the serial ports. Compare with **null modem cable.**

modulation, amplitude The form of modulation in which the amplitude of the carrier is varied in accordance with the instantaneous value of the modulating signal.

modulation, frequency A form of modulation in which the frequency of the carrier is varied in accordance with the instantaneous value of the modulating signal.

modulation, phase A form of modulation in which the phase of the carrier is varied in accordance with the instantaneous value of the modulating signal. Phase modulation has two related techniques. Phase shift keying (PSK) uses a 180 A7 change in phase to indicate a change in the binary value (0 or 1). Differential phase shift keying (DPSK) uses a 180 A7 change in phase every time a 1 bit is transmitted; otherwise the phase remains the same.

modulation, pulse code   See **pulse code modulation**.

MPOA   Multiprotocol over ATM is a protocol used to transfer LAN packets over an ATM backbone. MPOA operates at the network layer and uses the network layer addresses to forward messages. Another protocol (LANE) performs the same function using the data link layer addresses.

MTBF   Mean Time between failures. The statistic developed by vendors to show the reliability of their equipment. It can be an actual calculated figure that generally is more accurate, or it can be a practical (theoretical) figure.

MTTD   Mean time to diagnose. The time it takes the network testing and problem management staff to diagnose a network problem.

MTTF   Mean time to fix. The time it takes vendors to remedy a network problem once they arrive on the premises.

MTTR

1. Mean time to repair: the combination of mean time to diagnose, mean time to respond, and mean time to fix, indicating the entire length of time it takes to fix a fault in equipment.

2. Mean time to respond: the time it takes the vendor to respond when a network problem is reported.

multicast   The transmission of one message to a series of computers at the same time, commonly used in videoconferencing. Computers wishing to participate in a multicast send a message to the sending computer or some other computer performing routing to subscribe to a specific multicast "channel."

multiplexer   A device that combines data traffic from several low-speed communication circuits onto a single high-speed circuit. The two popular types of multiplexing are FDM (frequency division multiplexing) and TDM (time division multiplexing). In FDM, the voice-grade link is divided into subcircuits, each covering a different frequency range in such a manner that each subcircuit can be employed as though it were an individual circuit. In TDM, separate time segments are assigned to each terminal. During these time segments, data may be sent without conflicting with data sent from another terminal.

multiplexing   The subdivision of a transmission circuit into two or more separate circuits. This can be achieved by splitting the frequency range of the circuit into narrow frequency bands (*frequency division multiplexing*) or by assigning a given circuit successively to several different users at different times (*time division multiplexing*).

multipoint   A line or circuit interconnecting several stations/nodes in a sequential fashion.

multistation access unit (MAU)   A hub that connects microcomputers to an IBM Token-Ring Network.

multithreading   Concurrent processing of more than one message (or similar service requested) by an application program.

MUX   Shorthand for multiplexer or multiplexing.

N

NAK   The return signal that reports an error in the message received. The opposite of *ACK*, or acknowledgment.

nanosecond   One billionth (1/1,000,000,000) of a second or 10^{-9}.

National Institute of Standards and Technology   Formerly the National Bureau of Standards. The agency of the U.S. government responsible for developing information-processing standards for the federal government.

NAU   See **network addressable unit**.

NCP   See **network control program**.

NetView   IBM's network management program to manage multivendor voice and data networks from the host computer in a systems network architecture environment.

netware loadable module (NLM)   NLMs are Novell Netware programs that handle network communication, printing, and monitoring. They can either be stand-alone application programs used entirely on the server or the server portion of a client–server application. Four types of NLMs exist in the Netware system. Disk controller NLMs are the interface between the NCP and the disk subsystems on the server. NIC NLMs contain the instructions on how the NCP controls and passes information to the network interface card. NLMs associated with management utilities allow the network manager to configure and monitor the network and file server. Name space NLMs enable non-DOS files to be stored and accessed on Netware servers.

NetWare management system (NMS)   Novell's NetWare management system allows local area network managers to manage NetWare LANs and attached devices that are spread throughout an enterprise-wide network.

network

1. A series of points connected by communication circuits.
2. The switched telephone network is the network of telephone lines normally used for dialed telephone calls.
3. A private network is a network of communication circuits confined to the use of one customer.

network addressable unit (NAU)   Components in the path control portion of a Systems Network Architecture network. They are the origin or destination points of information. There are three kinds of host-based network addressable units: logical unit (LU), physical unit (PU), and system services control point (SSCP). Each NAU has a unique network address containing a subarea and an element identifier.

network architecture   A framework of principles to facilitate the operation, maintenance, and growth of a communication network by isolating the user and the application programs from the details of the network. Protocols and software are packaged together into a usable network architecture system that organizes functions, data formats, and procedures.

network control center (NCC)   Any centralized network diagnostic and management control site.

network control program (NCP)   The telecommunication access program for front end processors. The NCP controls IBM's Synchronous Data Link Control (SDLC) communications between host computers and remote terminals as part of the systems network architecture (SNA).

network interface card (NIC)   A network interface card (NIC) allows the computer to be physically connected to the network cable; the NIC provides the physical layer connection from the computer to the network.

network interface controller   A communication device that allows interconnection of information processing devices to a network.

network operating system (NOS)   The network operating system (NOS) is the software that controls the network. The NOS provides the data link and the network layers, and must interact with the application software and the computer's own operating system. Every NOS provides two sets of

software: one that runs on the network server(s) and one that runs on the network client(s).

network profile   Every local area network microcomputer has a profile that outlines what resources it has available to other microcomputers in the network and what resources it can use elsewhere in the network.

network service   An application available on a network, for example, file storage.

NIC   A network interface card (NIC) allows the computer to be physically connected to the network cable; the NIC provides the physical layer connection from the computer to the network.

NIST   See **National Institute of Standards and Technology**.

NLM   See **Netware loadable module**.

node   In a description of a network, the point at which the links join input/output devices. The word *node* also has come to mean a computer or switching center in the context of data networks, particularly in the context of packet switching. Also called a *station*.

noise   The unwanted change in waveform that occurs between two points in a transmission circuit.

noise, amplitude   A sudden change in the level of power with differing effects, depending on the type of modulation used by the modem.

noise, cross-talk   Noise resulting from the interchange of signals on two adjacent circuits; manifests itself when you hear other people's telephone conversations.

noise, echo   The "hollow" or echoing characteristic that is heard on voice-grade lines with improper echo suppression.

noise, Gaussian   Noise that is characterized statistically by a Gaussian, or random, distribution.

noise, impulse   Noise caused by individual impulses on the circuit.

noise, intermodulation   Noise that occurs when signals from two independent lines intermodulate. A new signal forms and falls into a frequency band differing from those of both inputs. The new signal may fall into a frequency band reserved for another signal.

nonprinting character   A control character that is transmitted as part of the information, but not reproduced on the hard copy.

North American signal hierarchy   The signaling format used on T-1 circuits.

Notes Notes was the first document database designed to store and manage large collections of text and graphics, and was the first product to provide a solution. Documents can have different sections, and can be organized into a hierarchical structure of sections, documents, and folders.

NRZ Nonreturn to zero. A binary encoding and transmission scheme in which 1s and 0s are represented by opposite and alternating high and low voltages, and in which there is no return to a reference (zero) voltage between encoded bits.

NRZI Nonreturn to zero inverted. A binary encoding scheme that inverts the signal on a 1 and leaves the signal unchanged for a 0, and in which a change in the voltage state signals a 1 bit and the absence of a change denotes a 0-bit value.

null modem cable A 6- to 8-foot RS232 cable that makes the two microcomputers connected at each end of the cable think they are talking through modems.

O

office, central or end The common carrier's switching office closest to the subscriber.

office, toll A switching office that terminates a toll trunk circuit.

open systems interconnection (OSI) reference model See **OSI model**.

open shortest path first (OSPF) A dynamic routing protocol.

optical fibers Hair-thin strands of very pure glass (sometimes plastic) over which light waves travel. They are used as a medium over which information is transmitted.

OSI model The seven-layer open systems interconnection (OSI) reference model developed by the ISO subcommittee. The OSI model serves as a logical framework of protocols for computer-to-computer communications. Its purpose is to facilitate the interconnection of networks.

OSPF See **open shortest path first**.

out-of-band signaling A method of signaling that uses a frequency that is within the passband of the transmission facility but outside of a carrier circuit normally used for data transmission.

P

packet A group of binary digits, including data and control signals, that is switched as a composite whole. The data, control signals, and error control information are arranged in a specific format.

packet assembler/disassembler See **PAD**.

packet switching Process whereby messages are broken into finite-size packets that always are accepted by the network. The message packets are forwarded to the other party over a multitude of different circuit paths. At the other end of the circuit, the packets are reassembled into the message, which is then passed on to the receiving terminal.

packet switching network (PSN) A network designed to carry data in the form of packets. The packet and its format are internal to that network. The external interfaces may handle data in different formats, and format conversion may be done by the user's computer.

PAD Packet assembler/disassembler. Equipment providing packet assembly and disassembly facilities between asynchronous transmission and the packet switching network.

PAM See **pulse amplitude modulation**.

parallel Describes the way the internal transfer of binary data takes place within a computer. It may be transmitted as a parallel word, but it is converted to a serial or bit-by-bit data stream for transmission.

parity bit A binary bit appended to an array of bits to make the number of 1 bits always be odd or even for an individual character. For example, odd parity may require three 1 bits and even parity may require four 1 bits.

parity check Addition of noninformation bits to a message in order to detect any changes in the original bit structure from the time it leaves the sending device to the time it is received.

parity checking See **checking, parity**.

path control (PC) network In systems network architecture (SNA), the part that includes the data link control and path control layers.

PBX Private branch exchange. Telephone switch located at a customer's site that primarily establishes voice communications over tie lines or circuits as well as between individual users and the switched telephone network. Typically, also provides switching within a customer site and usually offers numerous other enhanced features, such as least-cost routing and call detail recording.

PCM See **pulse code modulation**.

PDN See **public data network**.

peer A dictionary definition of peer is "a person who is equal to another in abilities." A peer-to-peer network, therefore, is one in which each microcomputer node has equal abilities. In communications, a peer is a node or station that is on the same protocol layer as another.

peer-to-peer communications

1. Communication between two or more processes or programs by which both ends of the session exchange data with equal privilege.

2. Communication between two or more network nodes in which either side can initiate sessions because no primary-secondary relationship exists.

peer-to-peer local area network A network in which a microcomputer can serve as both a server and a user. Every microcomputer has access to all the network's resources on an equal basis.

permanent virtual circuit A virtual circuit that resembles a leased line because it can be dedicated to a single user. Its connections are controlled by software.

phase modulation See **modulation, phase**.

physical unit (PU) In systems network architecture (SNA), the component that manages and monitors the resources (such as attached links and adjacent link stations) of a node, as requested by a system services control point (SSCP) via an SSCP-PU session. Each node of a SNA network contains a physical unit.

physical unit control point (PUCP) In systems network architecture (SNA), a component that provides a subset of system services control point (SSCP) functions for activating the physical unit (PU) within its node and its local link resources. Each peripheral node and each subarea node without an SSCP contains a PUCP.

pirate A person who obtains the latest software programs without paying for them. A skilled software pirate is able to break the protection scheme that is designed to prevent copying.

PLP Packet layer protocol (PLP) is the routing protocol that performs the network layer functions (e.g., routing and addressing) in X.25 networks.

point of presence (POP) Since divestiture, refers to the physical access location within a local access transport area (LATA) of a long distance or interLATA common carrier. The point to which the local telephone company terminates subscribers' circuits for long distance dial-up or leased line communications.

point-to-point Denoting a circuit, channel, or line that has only two terminals. A link. An example is a single microcomputer connected to a mainframe.

polling Any procedure that sequentially queries several terminals in a network.

polling, hub A type of sequential polling in which the polling device contacts a terminal, that terminal contacts the next terminal, and so on until all the terminals have been contacted.

polling, roll call Polling accomplished from a prespecified list in a fixed sequence, with polling restarted when the list is completed.

polynomial checking A checking method using polynomial functions to test for errors in data in transmission. Also called **cyclical redundancy check**, or **CRC**.

POP

1. Post office protocol. An application layer protocol used to communicate between mail servers and mail software on client computers.

2. See **point of presence**.

port One of the circuit connection points on a front end processor or local intelligent controller.

Postal Telephone and Telegraph See **PTT**.

PPP Multilink point-to-point protocol (PPP) is a data link layer protocol commonly used on the Internet. It can also be used for inverse multiplexing to combining circuits of different speeds (e.g., a 64,000 bps circuit with a 28,800 bps circuit), with data allocated to each circuit based on speed and need. PPP is the successor to SLIP.

preamble A sequence of encoded bits that is transmitted before each frame to allow synchronization of clocks and other circuitry at other sites on the circuit. In the Ethernet specification, the preamble is 64 bits.

primary access service See **primary rate interface**.

primary rate interface In ISDN, twenty-three 64,000 bits per second D circuits for data and one 64,000 bits per second B circuit for signaling (23 B+D). See also **basic rate interface**.

private branch exchange See **PBX**.

private circuit A leased communication circuit that goes from your premises to some other location. It is a clear unbroken communication path that is yours to use 24 hours per day, seven days per week.

propagation delay The time necessary for a signal to travel from one point on the circuit to another, such as from a satellite dish up to a satellite or from Los Angeles to New York.

protocol A formal set of conventions governing the format and control of inputs and outputs between two communicating devices. This includes the rules by which these two devices communicate, as well as handshaking and line discipline.

protocol converter A hardware device that changes the protocol of one vendor to the protocol of another. For example, if you want to connect an IBM data communication network to a Honeywell data communication network, the protocol converter converts the message formats so they are compatible. It is similar to a person who translates between French and English for two people who do not speak each other's language.

proxy server A type of application level firewall that changes the IP addresses of messages leaving (and entering) the private section of an organization's network. Since the IP addresses are not known to those outside the network, it is more difficult for hackers to gain unauthorized access.

PSK Phase shift keying; see **modulation, phase**.

PSN See **packet switching network**.

PTT Postal Telephone and Telegraph. These are the common carriers owned by governments; the government is the sole or monopoly supplier of communication facilities.

PU See **physical unit**.

public data network (PDN) A network established and operated for the specific purpose of providing data transmission services to the public. It can be a public packet switched network or a circuit switched network. Public data networks normally offer value-added services for resource sharing at reduced costs and with high reliability. These timesharing networks are available to anyone with a modem.

public key encryption Public key encryption uses two keys. The public key is used to encrypt the message and a second, very different, private key is used to decrypt the message. Even though you know both the contents of your message and the public encryption key, once it is encrypted, the message cannot be decrypted without the private key. Public key encryption is one of the most secure encryption techniques available.

PUC Public Utility Commission. The state regulatory agency responsible for overseeing intrastate communications. There is one PUC in each of the 50 states.

PUCP See **physical unit control point**.

pulse A brief change of current or voltage produced in a circuit to operate a switch or relay or which can be detected by a logic circuit.

pulse amplitude modulation (PAM) Amplitude modulation of a pulse carrier. PAM is used to translate analog voice data into a series of binary digits before they are transmitted.

pulse code modulation (PCM) Representation of a speech signal by sampling at a regular rate and converting each sample to a binary number. In PCM, the information signals are sampled at regular intervals and a series of pulses in coded form are transmitted, representing the amplitude of the information signal at that time.

Q

QAM Quadrature amplitude modulation. A sophisticated modulation technique that uses variations in signal amplitude, which allows data-encoded symbols to be represented as any of 16 states to send four bits on each signal.

quality of service (QoS) The ability to prioritize packets based on their contents. For example, QoS enables the user to specify that packets containing voice transmissions get priority over packets contain e-mail messages.

quantizing error The difference between the PAM signal and the original voice signal. The original signal has a smooth flow, but the PAM signal has jagged "steps."

R

RBOC Regional Bell Operating Company. One of the seven companies created after divestiture of the old Bell system to provide local communications. Includes Ameritech, Bell Atlantic, BellSouth, NYNEX, Pacific Telesis, Southwestern Bell, and US West.

reclocking time See **turnaround time**.

redundancy The portion of the total information contained in a message that can be eliminated without loss of essential information.

reliability A characteristic of the equipment, software, or network that relates to the integrity of the system against failure. Reliability usually is measured in terms of mean time between failures

(MTBF), the statistical measure of the interval between successive failures of the hardware or software under consideration.

remote data concentrator See **concentrator**.

Request for Proposal (RFP) A request for proposal is used to solicit bids from vendors for new network hardware, software, and services. They specify what equipment, software, and services are desired and ask vendors to provide their best prices.

repeater A device used to boost the strength of a signal. Repeaters are spaced at intervals throughout the length of a communication circuit.

response time The time the system takes to react to a given input; the time interval from when the user presses the last key to the terminal's typing the first letter of the reply. Response time includes (1) transmission time to the computer; (2) processing time at the computer, including access time to obtain any file records needed to answer the inquiry; and (3) transmission time back to the terminal.

retrain time See **turnaround time**.

ring A local area network topology having a logical geometric arrangement in the shape of a ring.

RIP Routing information protocol. A dynamic routing protocol.

risk The level or amount of exposure to an item when compared with other items. It is a hazard or chance of loss. Risk is the degree of difference, as in, ''What level of risk does one threat have when compared to the other threats?''

risk assessment The process by which one identifies threats, uses a methodology to determine the tangible or intangible exposures, and develops a sequenced list of the threats from the one having the highest risk to the one having the lowest risk. The list may be in a sequence based on tangible dollar losses or on intangible criteria such as public embarrassment, likelihood of occurrence, most dangerous, most critical to the organization, and greatest delay. Also called *risk ranking* or *risk analysis*.

RMON The definitions of what is stored and, therefore, retrievable from a remote user microcomputer when using the simple network management protocol (SNMP). It is referred to as the RMON MIB (management information base). See also **MIB** and **SNMP**.

router A device that connects two similar networks having the same network protocol. It operates at the network layer and forwards packets based on their network layer address. It also chooses the best route between two networks when there are multiple paths between them. Compare with **bridge**, **brouter**, and **gateway**.

RS232 A technical specification published by the Electronic Industries Association that specifies the mechanical and electrical characteristics of the interface for connecting data terminal equipment (DTE) and data circuit terminating equipment (DCE). It defines interface circuit functions and their corresponding connector pin assignments.

RS449 An Electronic Industries Association standard for data terminal equipment (DTE) and data circuit terminating equipment (DCE) connection that specifies interface requirements for expanded transmission speeds (up to 2 million bits per second), longer cable lengths, and ten additional functions.

S

SC See **session control**.

SDLC Synchronous data link control, a data link layer protocol developed by IBM. Transmission exchanges may be full duplex or half duplex and over switched or nonswitched links. The configurations of the link connection may be point to point, multipoint, or loop. SDLC is the protocol used in IBM's Systems Network Architecture.

SDSL See **DSL**.

security hole A bug in an operating system, network software, or application program that enables a hacker to gain unauthorized access or disrupt the network. For example, a security hole in some servers and routers enables them to be crashed by sending them a message with their own address as the source; they attempt to repeatedly contact themselves and eventually overload.

serial
1. Transmitting bits one at a time and in sequence.
2. The sequential or consecutive occurrence of two or more related activities in a single device or circuit.

server A computer that provides a particular service to the client computers on the network. In larger LANs, the server is dedicated to being a server. In a peer-to-peer LAN, the server may be both a server and a client computer. There are file, database, network, access, modem, facsimile, printer, and gateway servers.

session A logical connection between two terminals. This is the part of the message transmission when the two parties are exchanging messages. It takes place after the communication circuit has been set up and is functioning.

session control (SC) In systems network architecture (SNA), one of the components of transmission control. Session control is used to purge data flowing in a session after an unrecoverable error occurs, to resynchronize the data flow after such an error, and to perform cryptographic verification.

signal A signal is something that is sent over a communication circuit. It might be a control signal used by the network to control itself.

signal-to-noise ratio The ratio, expressed in decibels, of the usable signal to the noise signal present.

simple mail transfer protocol (SMTP) See **SMTP**.

simple network management protocol (SNMP) See **SNMP**.

simplex A circuit capable of transmission in one direction only. Contrast with **full duplex** and **half duplex**.

sine wave A continuous analog waveform of a single frequency having a constant amplitude and phase.

single cable A one-cable system in broadband local area networks in which a portion of the bandwidth is allocated for "send" signals and a portion for "receive" signals, with a guardband in between to provide isolation from interference.

SLIP Serial line internet protocol (SLIP) is a data link layer protocol used on the Internet. It has been surpassed by **PPP**.

SMDS Switched multimegabit data service. A packet switched service offered by several common carriers. A competitor to ATM and frame relay.

SMTP Simple mail transfer protocol. An application layer protocol used to move messages from mail server to mail server on the Internet. It requires messages to be text only. Binary files can be sent using **MIME**.

SNA See **systems network architecture**.

SNMP Simple network management protocol is the most commonly used network management protocol for monitoring and configuring network devices. See also **MIB** and **RMON**.

social engineering The act of obtaining unauthorized access to a network by manipulating authorized users into revealing their passwords and access information.

software defined network (SDN) Built on public packet switched networks using virtual circuits instead of the normal physical voice-grade circuit. Customer routing information is stored in switch memories so SDNs can operate like leased circuits.

SOH A control character used in ASCII and EBCDIC data communications to indicate start of header or the beginning of the control characters in a data block.

SONET The National Exchange Carriers Association standard for point-to-point dedicated optical transmission for high-speed transmission. The slowest synchronous optical network (SONET) OC-1 optical transmission rate of 51,840,000 bits per second is slightly faster than the T-3 rate.

spike A sudden increase of electrical power on a communication circuit. Spike is a term used in the communication industry. Contrast with **surge**.

spread spectrum The U.S. military developed spread spectrum through-the-air radio transmission technology primarily to overcome the problem of intentional interference by hostile jamming and secondarily for security. A spread spectrum signal is created by modulating the original transmitted radio frequency (RF) signal with a spreading code that causes "hopping" of the frequency from one frequency to another. By contrast, conventional AM and FM radio uses only one frequency to transmit its signal.

SSCP Part of the systems network architecture (SNA). See **system services control point**.

start bit A bit that precedes the group of bits representing a character. Used to signal the arrival of the character in asynchronous transmission.

static routing See **decentralized routing**.

station One of the input or output points on a network. Also called a **node**.

statistical multiplexer Stat mux or STDM. A time division multiplexer (TDM) that dynamically allocates communication circuit time to each of the various attached terminals, according to whether a terminal is active or inactive at a particular moment. Buffering and queuing functions also are included. See also **concentrator**.

stop bit A bit that follows the group of bits representing a character. Used to signal the end of a character in asynchronous transmission.

store and forward A data communication technique that accepts messages or transactions, stores them, and then forwards them to the next location or person as addressed in the message header.

STX A control character used in ASCII and EBCDIC data communications to mean start of text.

subnet A network segment in a TCP/IP network that contains one set of network layer addresses. A TCP/IP subnet often matches a LAN segment. Subnets are defined by the subnet mask and often are the first three byes of the IP address (e.g., a computer with an IP address of 128.192.56.4 would be in the 128.192.56 subnet).

subnet mask The means by which a computer can determine whether a computer is in the same subnet (network segment) or not.

switch Switches connect more than two LAN segments that use the same data link and network protocol. They may connect the same or different types of cable. Switches typically provide ports for 4, 8, 16, or 32 separate LAN segments, and most enable all ports to be in use simultaneously, so they are faster than bridges.

switched circuit A dial-up circuit in which the communication path is established by dialing. If the entire circuit path is unavailable, you get a busy signal, which prevents completion of the circuit connection.

switched multimegabit data service See **SMDS**.

SYN An 8-bit control character that is sent at the beginning of a message block to establish synchronization (timing) between the sender and the receiver.

synchronous data link control (SDLC) See **SDLC**.

synchronous optical network (SONET) See **SONET**.

synchronous transmission Form of transmission in which data is sent as a block using frames or packets.

system services control point (SSCP) Within systems network architecture (SNA), a focal point for managing the configuration, coordinating network operator and problem determination requests, and providing directory support and other session services for end users of the network. Mul-

tiple SSCPs, cooperating with one another as peers, can divide the network into domains of control, with each SSCP having a hierarchical control relationship to the physical units and logical units within its own domain.

systems network architecture (SNA) The name of IBM's conceptual framework that defines the data communication interaction between computer systems or terminals.

T

T carrier A hierarchy of digital circuits designed to carry speech and other signals in digital form. Designated T-1 (1.544 Mbps), T-2 (6.313 Mbps), T-3 (44.736 Mbps), and T-4 (274.176 Mbps).

tap
1. In baseband, the component or connector that attaches a transceiver to a cable.
2. In broadband, a passive device used to remove a portion of the signal power from the distribution line and deliver it onto the drop line. Also called a *directional tap* or a *multipoint.*
3. In security, unauthorized and illegal access to a network circuit. It involves placing a "tap" or an illegal connection on a communication circuit.

tariff The formal schedule of rates and regulations pertaining to the communication services, equipment, and facilities that constitute the contract between the user and the common carrier. Tariffs are filed with the appropriate regulatory agency (FCC or state PUC) for approval and published when approved.

TASI Time assisted speech interpolation. The process of interleaving two or more voice calls on the same telephone circuit simultaneously.

TCAM Telecommunications Access Method. One of IBM's telecommunication access software packages.

TCM Trellis coded modulation (TCM) is a modulation technique related to QAM that combines phase modulation and amplitude modulation. There are several different forms of TCM that transmit five, six, seven, eight, or more bits per signal.

TCP/IP Transmission control protocol/Internet protocol is probably the oldest networking standard, developed for ARPANET, and now used on the Internet. The most commonly used network layer protocol.

TDM See **multiplexer**.

telecommunication access programs The software programs (usually located in the front end processor) that handle all tasks associated with the routing, scheduling, and movement of messages between remote terminal sites and the central host computer.

telecommunications A term encompassing voice, data, and image transmissions that are sent over some medium in the form of coded signals.

telecommuting Telecommuting employees perform some or all of their work at home instead of going to the office each day.

teleconferencing With teleconferencing, people from diverse geographic locations can "attend" a business meeting in both voice and picture format. In fact, even documents can be shown and copied at any of the remote locations.

telephony A generic term to describe voice communications. Pronounced tel'-ef-on-é.

telnet Telnet enables users on one computer to log into other computers on the Internet.

terminal controller See **cluster controller**.

thick Ethernet Refers to the original Ethernet specification that uses thick coaxial cable (10Base5).

thin Ethernet Refers to 10Base2 Ethernet. Also called *cheapnet*.

threat A potentially adverse occurrence or unwanted event that could be injurious to the network, the EDP environment, the organization, or a business application. Threats are acts or events the organization wants to prevent from taking place, such as lost data, theft, disasters, virus infections, errors, illegal access, and unauthorized disclosure. In other words, threats are events we do not want to occur.

throughput The total amount of useful information that is processed or communicated during a specific time period.

time assisted speech interpolation See **TASI**.

time division multiplexing (TDM) See **multiplexer**.

token The special sequence of characters used to gain access to a token-ring or token-bus network in order to transmit a packet.

token bus A local area network with a bus topology that uses a token-passing approach to network access. In a token-bus LAN, the next logical node or station is not necessarily the next physical node because it uses preassigned priority algorithms. Message requests are not handled in consecutive order by stations. Contrast with **token ring**.

token passing A method of allocating network access wherein a terminal can send a message only after it has acquired the network's electronic token.

token ring A local area network with a ring topology that uses a token-passing approach to network access. In a token ring LAN, the next logical station also is the next physical station because the token passes from node to node. Contrast with **token bus**.

topology The basic physical or geometric arrangement of the network, for example, a ring, star, or bus layout. The topology is the network's logical arrangement, but it is influenced by the physical connections of its links and nodes. This is in contrast to its configuration, which is the actual or practical layout, including software and hardware constraints. Topologies are the building blocks of a network configuration. Compare with **configuration**.

total cost of ownership (TCO) A method of calculating the full cost of a computer. TCO has been criticized because it includes "wasted" time, the time users lose because their computer is unavailable due to problems or time they spend fixing problems caused by the computer. The TCO for a typical is about $10,000 per year.

transceiver A device that transmits and/or receives data to or from computers on an Ethernet local area network. Also called a **hub**. See also **medium access unit**, **multistation access unit**, or **communication interface unit**.

transmission rate of information bits See **TRIB**.

tree A network arrangement in which the stations hang off a common "branch," or data bus, like leaves on the branch of a tree.

TRIB Transmission rate of information bits. A TRIB is the network's throughput. It is the effective rate of data transfer over a communication circuit per unit of time. Usually expressed in bits per second.

trunk A voice communication circuit between switching devices or end offices.

turnaround time The time required to reverse the direction of transmission from send to receive or vice versa on a half duplex circuit.

twisted pair A pair of wires used in standard telephone wiring. They are twisted to reduce interference caused by the other twisted pairs in the same cable bundle. Twisted-pair wires go from homes and offices to the telephone company end office.

U

UART See **universal asynchronous receiver and transmitter**.

uninterruptible power supply (UPS) Provides backup electrical power if the normal electrical power fails or if the voltage drops to unacceptably low levels.

unipolar transmission A form of digital transmission in which the voltage changes between zero volts to represent a binary 0 and some positive value (e.g., +15v) to represent a binary 1. Also see **bipolar transmission**.

universal asynchronous receiver and transmitter (UART) A circuit chip that serializes the stream of data bits for the COM1 and COM2 serial ports so they can transmit data. The UART chip handles asynchronous communications. Compare with **universal synchronous asynchronous receiver and transmitter (USART)**.

universal resource locator See **URL**.

universal synchronous asynchronous receiver and transmitter (USART) A circuit chip that handles both synchronous and asynchronous communications. It may be incorporated on a serial interface card, which may be an optional accessory for a microcomputer, or it may be built into the microcomputer. Compare with **universal asynchronous receiver and transmitter**.

unshielded twisted-pair wires (UTP) See **UTP**.

upload The process of loading software and data from the nodes of a network (terminals or microcomputers), over the network media, and to the host mainframe computer.

UPS See **uninterruptible power supply**.

URL To use a browser to access a Web server, you must enter the server's addresses or URL (universal resource locator). All Web addresses begin with seven characters: http://.

USART See **universal synchronous asynchronous receiver and transmitter**.

USASCII See **ASCII**.

usenet newsgroups Usenet newsgroups are the most formally organized of the Internet discussion groups. They are a set of huge bulletin boards on which anyone who wishes can read and post messages. The usenet "newsfeed" of the discussions within each of these groups is available

to all computers on the Internet (about 50 megabytes of new messages each *day*).

user profile The user profile specifies what data and network resources a user can access, and the type of access (read only, write, create, delete, etc.).

UTP The type of wiring used in 10Base-T Ethernet networks. Same as **twisted pair**.

V

V.nn The V.*nn* series of Consultative Committee on International Telegraph and Telephone standards relating to the connection of digital equipment to the analog telephone network. Primarily concerned with the modem interface. See Chapter 4 for definitions.

value-added network (VAN) A corporation that sells services of a value-added network. Such a network is built using the communication offerings of traditional common carriers, connected to computers that permit new types of telecommunication tariffs to be offered. The network may be a packet switching or message switching network.

VDSL See **DSL**.

vertical redundancy checking See **parity check**.

video teleconferencing Video teleconferencing provides real-time transmission of video and audio signals to enable people in two or more locations to have a meeting.

virtual Conceptual or appearing to be, rather than actually being.

virtual circuit A temporary transmission circuit in which sequential data packets are routed between two points. It is created by the software in such a way that users think they have a dedicated point-to-point leased circuit.

virtual LAN See **VLAN**.

virtual private network (VPN) A hybrid network that includes both public and private facilities. The user leases a bundle of circuits and configures the VPN on an as-needed basis so that some traffic travels on the private leased network and some travels on the common carrier's public network.

virus Viruses are executable programs that copy themselves onto other computers. Most viruses attach themselves to other programs or to special parts on disks, and as those files execute or are accessed, the virus spreads. Viruses cause unwanted events—some are harmless (such as nuisance messages), others are serious (such as the destruction of data). Some viruses change their appearances as they spread, making detection more difficult.

VLAN A virtual LAN replaces the hub with an intelligent switch. The switch creates a number of network segments, each with some dedicated network capacity. The network segments can be easily changed, enabling the attached computers to be moved from one network segment to another by software—no change in the network cabling is required. VLANs can be defined using the switch's port numbers (port-based VLANs), the computers' data link layer addresses (MAC-based VLANs), the computers' network layer addresses (IP-based VLANs), or the application data contained within the transmitted packets (application-based VLANs).

voice grade circuit A term that applies to circuits suitable for transmission of speech, digital, or analog data, or facsimile, generally with a frequency range of about 300 to 3300 hertz contained within a 4000-hertz circuit.

VPN See **virtual private network**.

VRC Vertical redundancy check. Same as **parity check**.

VTAM Virtual telecommunications access method. One of IBM's more advanced telecommunication access software programs.

W

walk time The time required for the message to travel completely around a ring local area network.

WAN A network spanning a large geographical area. Its nodes can span city, state, or national boundaries. They typically use circuits provided by common carriers. Contrast with **backbone network, LAN, MAN.**

WATS Wide area telephone service. A special bulk-rate service that allows direct-dial inbound and outbound station-to-station calls. These are the area code numbers that start with 800 and 888 and are associated with toll-free dialing. Costs are based on hourly usage per WATS circuit and on distance-based bands, to and from which calls are placed.

Web See **World Wide Web**.

Web browser A Web browser is a software package on the client computer that enables a user to access a Web server.

Web crawler A Web crawler searches through all the Web servers it knows to find information about a particular topic.

Web server A Web server stores information in a series of text files called pages. These text files or pages use a structured language called HTML (Hypertext Markup Language) to store their information.

wide area network (WAN) See **WAN**.

wiring closet A central point at which all the circuits in a system begin or end, to allow cross-connection.

work group A group of two or more individuals who need to share files and databases. Local area networks sometimes are designed around work groups to provide the sharing of files, programs, databases, or printers, and to promote interaction among the members of a particular work group.

World Wide Web One of the fastest-growing information resources on the Internet is the World Wide Web. The Web provides a graphical user interface and enables the display of rich graphical images, pictures, full-motion video, and sound clips (provided you have a sound board and speakers in your computer).

X

X.nn The X.*nn* series of Consultative Committee on International Telegraph and Telephone standards relating to transmission over public data networks. See Chapters 7 and 8.

X.400 An OSI standard that defines how messages are to be encoded for the transmission of e-mail and graphics between dissimilar computers and terminals. X.400 defines what is in an electronic address and what the electronic envelope should look like. Approved by the CCITT.

X.500 An OSI standard that defines where to find the address to put on the electronic envelope of an X.400 transmission. X.500 is the directory of names and addresses similar to the yellow pages of a telephone directory.

XMODEM XMODEM is an asynchronous file transmission protocol that takes the data being transmitted and divides it into blocks. Each block has a start of header character (SOH), a 1-byte block number, 128 bytes of data, and a 1-byte checksum for error checking.

Y

YMODEM YMODEM is an asynchronous file transmission protocol. The primary benefit of the YMODEM protocol is CRC-16 error checking.

Z

ZMODEM ZMODEM is a newer asynchronous file transmission protocol written to overcome some of the problems in packet-switching networks like SprintNet or Tymnet. It uses CRC-32 with continuous ARQ, and dynamically adjusts its packet size according to communication circuit conditions to increase efficiency. It usually is the preferred protocol of most bulletin board systems.

10

10Base-T An Ethernet local area network standard (IEEE 802.3) that runs at 10 million bits per second and uses unshielded twisted-pair wires.

10Base2 An Ethernet local area network standard that runs at 10 million bits per second, uses baseband transmission techniques, and allows 200 meters maximum cable length.

10Base5 An Ethernet local area network standard that runs at 10 million bits per second, uses baseband transmission techniques, and allows 500 meters maximum cable length. The many layers of shielding are of polyvinyl and aluminum, which make the cable wider in diameter than other Ethernet cables. The heavy shielding also makes the cable more expensive and less flexible; therefore, it is impractical for many installations.

10Broad36 An Ethernet local area network that runs at 10 million bits per second, uses broadband transmission techniques, and allows 3600 meters maximum cable length.

100Base-F An Ethernet local area network standard that runs at 100 million bits per second and uses fiber optic cables.

100Base-T An Ethernet local area network standard that runs at 100 million bits per second and uses unshielded twisted-pair wires.

100Base-VG An Ethernet local area network standard that runs at 100 million bits per second and uses DPAM.

1000Base-T An Ethernet local area network standard ("gigabit Ethernet") that runs at 1000 million bits per second on twisted-pair wires.

Index